# Jefferson: Political Writings

Thomas Jefferson (1743–1826) is among the most important and controversial of American political thinkers: his influence (libertarian, democratic, participatory, and agrarian–republican) is still felt today. A prolific writer, Jefferson left 18,000 letters, *Notes on the State of Virginia*, an unfinished *Autobiography*, and numerous other papers. Joyce Appleby and Terence Ball have selected the most important of these for presentation in the *Cambridge Texts* series: Jefferson's views on topics such as revolution, self-government, the role of women, and African-Americans and Native Americans emerge to give a fascinating insight into a man who owned slaves, yet advocated the abolition of slavery. The texts are supported by a concise introduction, suggestions for further reading and short biographies of key figures, all providing invaluable assistance to the student encountering the breadth and richness of Jefferson's thought for the first time.

JOYCE APPLEBY is Professor of History at UCLA, and a former President of the American Historical Association.

TERENCE BALL was formerly Professor of Political Science at the University of Minnesota, and now teaches political theory at Arizona State University. He has previously edited the works of James Mill for the *Cambridge Texts* series.

D0706097

# CAMBRIDGE TEXTS IN THE HISTORY OF POLITICAL THOUGHT

*Series editors*

RAYMOND GEUSS

*Lecturer in Social and Political Sciences, University of Cambridge*

QUENTIN SKINNER

*Regius Professor of Modern History in the University of Cambridge*

Cambridge Texts in the History of Political Thought is now firmly established as the major student textbook series in political theory. It aims to make available to students all the most important texts in the history of Western political thought, from ancient Greece to the early twentieth century. All the familiar classic texts will be included but the series seeks at the same time to enlarge the conventional canon by incorporating an extensive range of less well-known works, many of them never before available in a modern English edition. Wherever possible, texts are published in complete and unabridged form, and translations are specially commissioned for the series. Each volume contains a critical introduction together with chronologies, biographical sketches, a guide to further reading and any necessary glossaries and textual apparatus. When completed, the series will aim to offer an outline of the entire evolution of Western political thought.

*For a list of titles published in the series, please see end of book.*

# THOMAS JEFFERSON

# *Political Writings*

### EDITED BY
### JOYCE APPLEBY
*University of California Los Angeles*

### AND

### TERENCE BALL
*Arizona State University*

### CAMBRIDGE
### UNIVERSITY PRESS

CAMBRIDGE UNIVERSITY PRESS
Cambridge, New York, Melbourne, Madrid, Cape Town, Singapore, São Paulo

Cambridge University Press
The Edinburgh Building, Cambridge CB2 2RU, UK

Published in the United States of America by Cambridge University Press, New York

www.cambridge.org
Information on this title: www.cambridge.org/9780521640510

First published 1999
Third printing 2005

A catalogue record for this publication is available from the British Library

Library of Congress Cataloguing in Publication data

Jefferson, Thomas, 1743–1826.
[Selections 1999]
Thomas Jefferson, political writings/edited by Joyce Appleby and Terence Ball.
p. cm. – (Cambridge texts in the history of political thought)
ISBN 0 521 64051 2 (hb). – ISBN 0 521 64841 6 (pb)
1. Political science. 2. State, The. 3. United States – Politics and government – Sources.
I. Appleby, Joyce Oldham. II. Ball, Terence. III. Title. IV. Series.
JC176.J4    1999
973.4′6′092–dc21    98–40304 CIP

ISBN-13  978-0-521-64051-0 hardback
ISBN-10  0-521-64051-2 hardback

ISBN-13  978-0-521-64841-7 paperback
ISBN-10  0-521-64841-6 paperback

Transferred to digital printing 2007

# Contents

# Preface

Thomas Jefferson is surely among the most original, complex, and important of American political thinkers. He wrote the Declaration of Independence, served two terms as President, founded the Library of Congress and the University of Virginia, and was also an architect, inventor, scientist, and – amongst his many other complexities – a slave-owner who advocated the abolition of slavery. There is in American political thought a distinctly "Jeffersonian" strain – "small-l" libertarian, democratic, participatory, and agrarian–republican – that has long locked horns with an alternative "Hamiltonian" vision (nationalist, commercial and credit-based, and relying on a strong central government). This tension, sometimes described as "Main Street *vs.* Wall Street," has been a staple of American political thought for more than two centuries. The purpose of the present volume is to give the former a full and fair hearing by letting its main proponent speak at length for himself.

To edit Jefferson's political writings is no easy task. Indeed it is doubly difficult. First, Jefferson was a prolific writer. His complete *Papers*, edited by Julian P. Boyd *et al.* (Princeton, 1950–  ), have so far taken up twenty-seven fat volumes, bringing that series up to 1793 with no end in sight – he was to live another thirty-three years, during eight of which he was President of the United States. Second, Jefferson wrote no systematic treatise on politics. While he did have a political philosophy, he did not present it whole, as a more systematic thinker might, but expressed his views in a scattered, unsystematic and piecemeal way in his massive and meandering *Notes on the State of Virginia*, a posthumously published

*Autobiography*, several of his state papers, some 18,000 letters, and elsewhere.

The selection of Jefferson's political writings presented here includes excerpts from his *Notes on the State of Virginia* as well as a generous sampling of his letters, arranged chronologically and by topic (natural rights, revolution, self-government, civic education, the Constitution and Bill of Rights, slavery, religious liberty and toleration, etc.). The present edition also reprints several of Jefferson's most important public papers, including of course his draft of the Declaration of Independence – a more radical document which differed in several significant respects from the version approved by the Congress.

In our Introduction we have tried – not always successfully, we fear – to deal forthrightly with some of the more troubling aspects of Jefferson's life and thinking, including his views about women, race and slavery. This is not a ritualistic bow to the false god of "political correctness"; it stems instead from a recognition that we do in fact, and perhaps inevitably, view and pass judgment on the past from the perspective of the present – including our own understandings of liberty, justice, and equality. In many respects Jefferson was well ahead of his time; in other ways he was very much a man of his time, with all the partialities and prejudices of his age. To recognize and acknowledge this is not to exonerate Thomas Jefferson, and still less ourselves. Quite the contrary. It is also to recognize that we, too, will be judged by our descendants for faults that we fail to see in ourselves. As Vershinin, in Chekhov's *The Three Sisters*, says:

> The things that seem great, significant, and very important to us now will no more seem to be important with time. It's certainly an interesting fact that we cannot possibly know today what in the future will be considered great and important or just pitiful and ridiculous . . . It is quite likely that our present life, to which we are so reconciled, will in time appear to be odd, uncomfortable, stupid, not particularly clean and perhaps even immoral.

Happily, no white Americans of the present generation own slaves; most abhor the evils of racial and sexual discrimination; but we are not without faults of our own, about which we are at best only dimly aware. One of these, about which future generations could conceivably and justly complain, concerns our excessive present-mindedness and our corresponding failure to take their well-being into adequate (or any) account. And on this and other scores, perhaps, Jefferson still has something to teach us.

We are much indebted to a number of people, and none more than the editors of the Cambridge Texts series. Quentin Skinner and Raymond Geuss have been characteristically generous with their time and their suggestions for improving the present volume. Richard Fisher, our editor at Cambridge University Press, has been himself, which is to say, unfailingly supportive, enthusiastic, and endlessly patient with our delays. James Farr read an early draft of our Introduction and made many helpful suggestions for improving it. We are differently but no less deeply indebted to our extraordinarily able research assistant, Robert W. T. Martin, for his help in identifying and tracking down sometimes elusive sources, and to Barbara Dagger, Michael Mitchell and John Zumbrunnen for further research assistance. We are also grateful to the librarians at the Library of Congress, the Massachusetts Historical Society, the University of Virginia, and to Lucia C. Stanton and her staff at Monticello for supplying several references and items of information.

Finally, though not least, each of the editors wishes to thank the other for the pleasure of the collaboration.

J.A.<br>T.B.

# Introduction

Thomas Jefferson (1743–1826) wrote no systematic treatise on political theory. And yet there is order and system in his unsystematic observations and reflections as found in his only book, in parliamentary manuals, legislative reports, public addresses, executive orders and a voluminous correspondence consisting of some 18,000 letters. It is from these disparate sources that we must glean his political philosophy. He, like the fox, knew a great many things; but, like the hedgehog, he knew and was guided by one big thing – his unswerving belief that people are by nature, and ought to be by law, free to govern themselves. Everything else is either a means or an obstacle to this single overriding end. Tyrannies deny and virtuous republics promote it; ignorance undermines and education encourages it; censorship obscures and a free press reveals it; invasive government negates and self-rule affirms it – but when all is said and done the truth and value of this end is so obvious as to be "self-evident." Jefferson changed his mind about many things; but on this single point his conviction never wavered.

## Life and times

Jefferson was born at Shadwell, in Albemarle County, Virginia, in 1743. His father, Peter, a self-educated man of many talents and interests, made his living as a surveyor, map-maker, and farmer. He was also an amateur scientist and musician who passed his love of these and other interests to his son Tom. His mother, Jane Randolph, was of a higher social station than her husband. Several

xiii

members of her family feared that she had married beneath her, but by the time of his death in 1757 Peter Jefferson had allayed all doubts about his prospects for worldly success. He bequeathed to his widow and children a sizeable estate, which included more than sixty slaves. It was, as inheritances go, a decidedly mixed blessing.

Three years after his father's death, Jefferson, at age seventeen, enrolled in the College of William and Mary. There he came under the gentle but demanding tutelage of Dr. William Small, a Scotsman who carried his considerable learning lightly and left a deep impression on his pupil. The young Jefferson, already an able classical scholar, was exposed to new discoveries and developments in physics, chemistry, astronomy and botany. He retained throughout his life a keen interest in the natural sciences. No less interesting were the "moral sciences" of ethics, politics, and jurisprudence. Jefferson was schooled in Scottish "moral sense" theory which held that the sense of right and wrong, of just and unjust, is no less real than the physical senses of sight, touch, smell, taste, and hearing. This view, as we shall see, played an important part in forming Jefferson's democratic political sympathies.

After three years at William and Mary, Jefferson turned to the study of law. To the works of Coke, Blackstone, and other legal scholars were added those of Grotius, Pufendorf and Locke, amongst other political theorists. By the time he was admitted to the bar in 1767 Jefferson's learning in the law and allied areas was both wide and deep. Throughout his life he remained a voracious reader and avid bibliophile.

Jefferson's small but growing legal practice was curtailed by his election to the Virginia House of Burgesses, the colonial state legislature, in 1769. Five years later, in 1774, that body was dissolved by the British authorities for its outspoken protests against the "Coercive Acts" passed by Parliament. The Burgesses reconstituted themselves as a revolutionary convention, transforming Jefferson the politician into Jefferson the revolutionary author and activist. *A Summary View of the Rights of British America*, written to give guidance to members of the convention and later published as a pamphlet, consists of a characteristically Jeffersonian mixture of themes and arguments drawn from the tradition of English constitutionalism and from the theory of natural law and natural right.[1] Although

---

[1] See *infra*, selection II.1.

*A Summary View* ended on a conciliatory note, the convention believed the language too strong, the tone too strident, and accordingly declined to adopt it. They did, however, elect Jefferson a delegate to the Second Continental Congress in 1774, then meeting in Philadelphia.

When in the following year Jefferson took his seat in the Continental Congress, the first shots had already been fired at Lexington. Revolution was in the air. Ideas and arguments deemed too radical only a year earlier now seemed more acceptable. The young author of *A Summary View* arrived in Philadelphia with, as John Adams later put it, "a reputation for literature, science, and a happy talent of composition."[2] Recognizing this talent, the Congress gave to Jefferson the delicate and dangerous task of drafting a reply to Lord North's last-ditch efforts to damp down the fires of revolution. His second assignment was to write (with John Dickinson of New Jersey) the *Declaration of the Causes and Necessity of Taking Up Arms*.[3] Neither has any of the conciliatory tone of the *Summary View*. The measured militancy of Jefferson's prose prefigures the language of the Declaration of Independence.

On June 7, 1776 Richard Henry Lee of Virginia introduced a resolution in Congress stating "That these United Colonies are, and of right ought to be, free and independent States, that they are absolved from all allegiance to the British Crown, and that all political connection between them and the State of Great Britain is, and ought to be, totally dissolved." Three days later Congress appointed Jefferson to a committee of five of its most eminent members to draft a declaration of independence. The other four – Benjamin Franklin, John Adams, Roger Sherman, and Robert Livingston – deferred to Jefferson, who set to work immediately and soon produced a first draft modeled in part on the English Declaration of Rights of 1689 and on George Mason's early draft of the Virginia Declaration of Rights. Adams and Franklin suggested several small changes, which Jefferson incorporated along with his own revisions before presenting it to the five-man committee. It was approved without amendment and sent at once to the Congress which, after two days of debate, made various changes – several of them quite substantial – to Jefferson's draft. On July 4, 1776 the duly revised Declaration of Independence was adopted by the Congress.

[2] John Adams to Timothy Pickering, Aug. 22, 1822, repr. in Appendix B *infra*.
[3] See *infra*, II.2.

Jefferson's draft Declaration does not coincide at all points with the Declaration as we now know it.[4] To be sure, the famous phrases are the same, as are the overall design and structure – a statement of general principles followed by a bill of particulars detailing the acts of atrocity and tyranny perpetrated by the Crown, and concluding with a pledge of mutual allegiance and solidarity. But Jefferson's draft Declaration is a more strident and radical document than is the one revised and adopted by Congress. Most radical of all, perhaps, is his denunciation of the slave trade, which was struck out of the version edited and approved by the Congress. Thus the document that begins with a ringing affirmation of liberty and equality remains silent on the subject of slavery – a deafening silence noted with particular relish by British critics. "Why is it that we hear the loudest *yelps* for liberty from the drivers of negroes?" asked Samuel Johnson.[5]

Jefferson's Declaration had to do several things at once. He had first and most obviously to declare America's independence to the world. He also had to state the reasons for America's resorting to revolution, and to ground these reasons in principle and in fact. The principles come first, and the facts follow. These are tied together with a Lockean thread.[6] And, not least, Jefferson's task was the rhetorical one of calling upon his countrymen to come together in the common cause of revolution – to risk life, limb and estate for the sake of liberty. To accomplish this, his prose had to persuade and inspire his audience, many of whom could not read. Many Americans would hear the Declaration read aloud at a coffee-house or tavern, or on a street-corner, or sometimes even from a pulpit. Its striking beginning, its measured cadences, its memorable phrases – all are meant to stir republican passions, to instill civic pride, and to kindle revolutionary ardor. The ideas and principles articulated in the Declaration therefore could not be, and were not,

[4] See the alterations highlighted by TJ in his *Autobiography*; *infra*, II.5.

[5] Samuel Johnson, *Taxation No Tyranny: An Answer to the Resolutions and Addresses of the American Congress* (London, 1775); quoted in James Boswell, *Life of Johnson* (1791; Oxford, 1960), p. 876.

[6] Richard Henry Lee stretched the truth only slightly when he said that the Declaration had been "copied from Locke's treatise on government": TJ to Madison, Aug. 30, 1823; *infra*, II.16. For a systematic comparison of the Declaration and Locke's *Second Treatise of Government*, see Garrett Ward Sheldon, *The Political Philosophy of Thomas Jefferson* (Baltimore, 1991), pp. 46–9.

novel. They formed a distillation and articulation of ideas already widely shared.[7] As Jefferson later wrote,

> the object of the Declaration of Independence [was] not to find out new principles, or new arguments, never before thought of, not merely to say things which had never been said before; but to place before mankind the common sense of the subject, in terms so plain and firm as to command their assent . . . Neither aiming at originality of principle or sentiment, nor yet copied from any particular and previous writing, it was intended to be an expression of the American mind . . . All its authority rests then on the harmonizing sentiments of the day, whether expressed in conversation, in letters, printed essays, or in the elementary books of public right, as Aristotle, Cicero, Locke, Sidney, &c.[8]

But if the ideas were well known and widely shared, it was Jefferson's unique way of shaping and articulating them that gave the Declaration its great rhetorical power and lasting fame. Jefferson's Declaration, along with Paine's *Common Sense* and other rousing pro-revolutionary pamphlets, had the desired effect. Independence was declared. The American Revolution had begun.

During the Revolution, Jefferson served as governor of Virginia and as a delegate to the Continental Congress where his draft of a Northwest Ordinance first suggested banning slavery from the American territories to the west.[9] He also undertook a revision of the state's laws and drafted the Virginia Statute for Religious Freedom.[10] On the whole, however, these were calamitous years for him. A British raid on Richmond forced him to flee on horseback carrying the state's most critical records and stirred up charges of cowardice, not quieted until after a formal inquiry. His beloved wife died in 1782, leaving him a widower with three daughters to raise. Monticello, the estate he had designed and built on one of the rolling hills of the Virginia Piedmont, then became his domestic retreat, and rebuilding and adorning it his solace and most consistent passion.

---

[7] See Pauline Maier, *American Scripture: The Making of the Declaration of Independence* (New York, 1997), esp. ch. 2.
[8] TJ to Henry Lee, May 8, 1825; *infra*, II.17.
[9] "Report of Government for the Western Territory," March 22, 1784; *infra*, IX.1.
[10] Jefferson ranked this statute (*infra*, VII.1) as one of his three greatest achievements.

In 1784 Congress appointed Jefferson minister to the court of Louis XVI. For the next four years he fully indulged his tastes for travel, music, literature, architecture, science, and high politics. Naturally gregarious and charming, and a talented violinist and good dancer as well, Jefferson throve in the salons of a Paris teetering on the brink of revolution. Succeeding Benjamin Franklin, he also inherited his friends: Lavoisier, Condorcet, DuPont de Nemours, the Ducs de La Rochefoucauld, and the alluring (and married) Maria Cosway, who prompted Jefferson to pen a poignant colloquy between his head and his heart.[11]

During Jefferson's absence from the United States, his friend and closest political ally, James Madison, spearheaded a movement to replace the wartime Articles of Confederation with a constitution that would rein in the powers of the virtually sovereign thirteen states. Sharing Madison's vision of America's destiny as a continental nation, Jefferson disagreed with those who feared the political awakening of ordinary men which the states' autonomy had fostered. When he heard that an armed band of indebted farmers in western Massachusetts had closed the county courts, Jefferson penned some of his most memorable lines: "The tree of liberty must be refreshed from time to time with the blood of patriots and tyrants. It is it's natural manure."[12] Shays's Rebellion, which fearful conservatives and creditors viewed as part of a larger plot being hatched by democrats and debtors, was seen by Jefferson as a useful purgative of the body politic.

Despite his political foes' attempts to portray him as a lawless radical, Jefferson was in fact deeply committed to the rule of law – at least insofar as it served as a bulwark of the weak against the strong. After receiving the draft Constitution reported out of Philadelphia in 1787, Jefferson noted with dismay its failure to ensure civil liberties. To Madison he confessed his belief "that a bill of rights is what the people are entitled to against every government on earth, general or particular, & what no just government should refuse, or rest on inferences." He then went on to express his reservations about the extended powers created by the Constitution. "I

---

[11] TJ to Maria Cosway, Oct. 12 1786; *infra*, I.4.
[12] TJ to William Stephens Smith, Nov. 13, 1787; *infra*, II.9. We reproduce TJ's idiosyncratic spelling here and throughout.

own I am not a friend to a very energetic government. It is always oppressive."[13]

During his last days in Paris, Jefferson witnessed the revolutionary actions of 1789 when France's ancient Estates General transformed itself into a modern legislative body. Memories of the Tennis Court Oath, the storming of the Bastille, the abolition of feudal privileges, and the adoption of the Declaration of the Rights of Man and Citizen were still fresh in his mind when he arrived in New York City to take up his new duties as George Washington's Secretary of State. The great desideratum of the Federalists, who had recently shepherded the Constitution through the ratification process, was to preserve the fragile coalition of recently united states, to restore the dignity of government, and to attach the rich and well born firmly to the fledgling nation. Fearful that energetic government meant social oppression, Jefferson responded to this program with dismay. After dining with members of President George Washington's cabinet he wrote, "I cannot describe the wonder and mortification with which the table conversations filled me," going on to note that "Politics were the chief topic, and a preference of kingly over republican government was evidently the favorite sentiment. An apostate I could not be, nor yet a hypocrite; and I found myself, for the most part, the only advocate on the republican side . . ."[14] The chief champion of monarchy, and in Jefferson's view the most contemptible of his fellow cabinet members, was his arch-foe Alexander Hamilton, Washington's Secretary of the Treasury.

Despite the odium attached to political factions, Jefferson in the 1790s began to organize an opposition to the Federalists, which he believed to be "an Anglican monarchical, and aristocratical party."[15] His eye on the presidency, he set out, in league with Madison, to reach the voters directly and convince them that they should exert themselves as a sovereign people. At this crucial juncture news reached the United States that the French had executed the king and established a republic. Jefferson and his followers found in the fury of the French Revolution a confirmation that they were living in a revolutionary age and that the time for change had just begun,

[13] TJ to James Madison, Dec. 20, 1787; *infra*, VI.4.
[14] *Autobiography*; *infra*, VIII.13.
[15] TJ to Philip Mazzei, April 24, 1796; *infra*, VIII.4.

and not ended, as the Federalists so fervently wished. Jefferson's warm and early support of the French Revolution was roundly condemned by his Federalist foes who wished to paint him as a wild-eyed radical who, if elected president, would bring the country to anarchy and ruin.

The presidential election campaign of 1800 was among the most vicious in American history. Jefferson was reviled as a radical, a Jacobin, and an atheist. Undeterred by Federalist vilification, Jefferson and his followers engaged the Federalists in a sustained discussion of the most fundamental questions about democratic government. Public debates swirled around specific measures of the Washington and Adams administrations but the Jeffersonians turned the polemics to the larger theme of social distinctions and their political implications. They mocked the aristocratic pretensions of the Federalists and railed at their elitist contempt for ordinary people. They drew attention to the way that the gentry imposed its values, using tacit understandings among gentlemen to thwart literal readings of such terms as popular sovereignty, public servant, natural rights, and free association. They ridiculed the aristocratic norm of not discussing affairs of state "out of doors" by opening and then dismantling the doors that divided office-holders from electors. And, most decisively of all, they won the hard-fought and hotly contested election of 1800.

As President, Jefferson turned himself into an agent of profound and transformative change in the political forms of the new nation. There were many possible futures for the United States. Jefferson seized on one of them, imposing his will upon the federal government and his spirit upon the American electorate. This self-described enemy of "energetic government" proved to be a most energetic President. An extraordinarily attentive administrator, he eliminated domestic taxes, substantially reduced the national debt, let Federalist programs lapse, and shrank the size of the bureaucracy despite the growth in population and territory. Wishing to exorcise all taint of aristocracy, he removed an entire cohort of young Federalists from civil and military offices. Jefferson hastened the conveyance of national land to ordinary farmers and replaced Federalist formality with a degree of informality in matters of protocol that quite amazed foreign dignitaries.[16] He interpreted the Constitution narrowly and

---

[16] "Rules of Etiquette [for President Jefferson's White House]"; *infra*, 1.10.

strictly, although his 1803 purchase of the Louisiana Territory from France stretched presidential prerogative up to, if not past, the constitutional breaking-point. Not a symbol, civil servant, or presidential initiative escaped his consideration as a tool for dismantling the "energetic" government of his Federalist predecessors.

Fearful that the popular President would win a second term, angry Federalists found a useful instrument in James Callender, a former ally turned enemy when Jefferson refused to appoint him to public office. Callender accused Jefferson of keeping a mulatto mistress named Sally Hemings, one of his slaves at Monticello. "Dusky Sally" was said to have had several children sired by Jefferson. The President, for his part, never responded to stories about this alleged affair.[17] Despite the scandal, fanned by the Federalist press, President Jefferson easily won re-election in 1804. And after his two terms, he had the exceptional good fortune to see the presidency pass successively to two close political allies – James Madison (1809–17) and James Monroe (1817–25).

Leaving the presidency in 1809, Jefferson returned permanently to Monticello where his sole surviving daughter and a houseful of grandchildren awaited him. His long life of public service took a different form as he counseled young admirers, maintained his worldwide correspondence, and completed plans for the University of Virginia visible from his hilltop. It was during this period that he resumed his friendship with John Adams, which resulted in one of the most moving and remarkable correspondences in the history of American letters.[18]

Thomas Jefferson died on July 4, 1826 – exactly fifty years to the day after his Declaration proclaimed America's independence. His old friend John Adams died on the same day. Jefferson was buried on the hillside just below his beloved Monticello. Inscribed on his tombstone are the deeds for which he wished to be remembered, in the order of their importance: "Author of the Declaration of American Independence, of the statute of Virginia for religious freedom, and father of the University of Virginia." There is no mention of his having served two terms as President of the United States.

[17] DNA tests suggest very strongly that TJ fathered at least one son (Eston, b. 1808) by Sally Hemings: see *Nature*, 396 (Nov. 5, 1998), pp. 13–14, 27–8. See also Annette Gordon-Reid, *Thomas Jefferson and Sally Hemings: An American Controversy* (Charlottesville, 1997).

[18] Their correspondence is collected in Lester J. Cappon, ed., *The Adams–Jefferson Letters* (Chapel Hill, 1988).

## Jefferson as theorist

A number of themes recur throughout Jefferson's writings. Of these, three are particularly prominent. The first is his faith in the common man or, more precisely, the common farmer. Endowed by their Creator with reason and an innate moral sense, ordinary mortals – rightly educated and freed from sophistry, superstition and meddlesome government – are capable of achieving quite extraordinary things. The second is his optimism. Jefferson looked to the future, not to the past, and believed progress possible if perhaps not inevitable. A third theme is his recurring reliance on "nature." A life lived rightly is one lived according to nature's norms and dictates. A government governs rightly only insofar as its laws accord with natural law. Let us look a little more closely at each of these themes.

Jefferson's willingness to trust the common people to govern themselves set him apart from many of his contemporaries, and most especially from his Federalist critics. Writing to John Adams's wife Abigail about the bitterly contested election of 1800, he focused upon the contrasting concerns that continued to animate the two parties. "One fears most the ignorance of the people: the other the selfishness of rulers independant of them."[19] Although Jefferson tactfully conceded that time alone would tell which was right, he could not resist noting that the conservatives' fear of the people had prevailed a long time without promoting the good of the people. Later, in a letter to John Adams, Jefferson contrasted "the enemies of reform" with those who believed with him that no limits could be placed on the progress possible in both social institutions and scientific knowledge. Still eager to define their differences thirteen years after his victory, Jefferson summed them up in opposing pairs: the belief in "the improvability of the human mind" *vs.* the denial that such improvement is possible; "the progress of science" *vs.* the veneration of custom and tradition; the "reformation of institutions" *vs.* "steady adherence to the principles, practices and institutions of our fathers."[20]

Jefferson's trust in the common man follows from his conviction that the Creator had endowed all men with reason and a moral

[19] TJ to Abigail Adams, Sept. 11, 1804; *infra*, VIII.8.
[20] TJ to Adams, June 15, 1813; *infra*, XIII.2.

sense. "The moral sense, or conscience, is as much a part of man as his leg or arm. It is given to all human beings in a stronger or weaker degree ... It may be strengthened by exercise."[21] For republican government to survive and freedom flourish, the moral sense and civic capacities of ordinary men must be strengthened by education, in the broadest sense of that term. Theoretical and historical knowledge gleaned from books must be supplemented by practical knowledge derived from experience. The citizens of a free republic can best sharpen their civic sensibilities by participating in politics at the local level. To this end Jefferson envisaged a system of decentralized and self-governing "ward republics." "I consider the continuance of republican government as absolutely hanging on these two hooks," he wrote, "the public education and the subdivision of counties into wards."[22] "These will be pure and elementary republics, the sum of all which, taken together, composes the State, and will make the whole a true democracy as to the business of the wards, which is that of nearest and daily concern."[23]

Without local control and eternal vigilance, the liberty of the people is in constant danger from the predations of the powerful. The best, indeed the only, antidote to concentrated power is power diffused among the people themselves. This indeed is what Jefferson means by "the term *republic*":

> [W]e may say with truth and meaning, that governments are more or less republican, as they have more or less of the element of popular election and control in their composition; and believing, as I do, that the mass of the citizens is the safest depository of their own rights and especially, that the evils flowing from the duperies of the people, are less injurious than those from the egoism of their agents, I am a friend to that composition of government which has in it the most of this ingredient.[24]

Another noteworthy feature of Jefferson's character and his political philosophy is his love of the new and heretofore untrodden path. He was by temperament and conviction an optimist with an

---

[21] TJ to Peter Carr, Aug. 10, 1787; *infra*, IV.6.
[22] TJ to Joseph Cabell, Jan. 31, 1814; *infra*, III.19.
[23] TJ to Samuel Kercheval, Sept. 5, 1816; *infra*, III.26.
[24] TJ to John Taylor, May 28, 1816; *infra*, III.22.

almost unbounded faith in the future and a radical with a distaste for the old and the orthodox. One of the most damning things Jefferson could say about his Federalist opponents was that they had looked "backwards not forwards, for improvement." And although they favored education, "it was to be the education of our ancestors." President Adams had actually told audiences that "we were never to expect to go beyond them in real science." But the political triumph of the Jeffersonian movement means that "we can no longer say there is nothing new under the sun. For this whole chapter in the history of man is new. The great extent of our Republic is new. Its sparse habitation is new. The mighty wave of public opinion which has rolled over it is new."[25]

The greatest danger to the new American Republic was that it would grow old and feeble and infirm. Its citizens and leaders could lose their nerve and their love of the new, and settle comfortably into their dotage. To postpone such civic sclerosis, Jefferson advocated a number of strategies. The most radical of these was to have a revolution every generation. Such a revolution need not be violent; it can be brought about by ballots instead of bullets. Indeed, Jefferson saw his own election to the presidency as a second American Revolution "as real a revolution in the principles of our government as that of 1776 was in its form."[26]

Among other less precipitous ways of keeping the citizenry virtuous and vigilant was the education of the public. One of the chief aims of civic education was the inculcation of attitudes of skepticism toward tradition and the past, and even toward the Constitution itself. Inasmuch as the veneration of historical documents could be used to inhibit change, Jefferson chided those who looked upon constitutions with "sanctimonious reverence, and deem them like the ark of the covenant, too sacred to be touched," adding that

> I am certainly not an advocate for frequent and untried changes in laws and constitutions. I think moderate imperfections had better be borne with . . . But I know also, that laws and institutions must go hand in hand with the progress of the human mind. As that becomes more developed, more enlightened, as new discoveries are made, new truths disclosed . . . institutions

[25] TJ to Joseph Priestley, March 21, 1801; *infra*, XIII.1.
[26] TJ to Spencer Roane, Sept. 6, 1819; *infra*, VI.12.

must advance also, and keep pace with the times. We might as well require a man to wear still the coat which fitted him when a boy, as civilized society to remain ever under the regimen of their barbarous ancestors.[27]

John Adams was surely right when he remarked that Jefferson "like[d] better the dreams of the Future, than the History of the Past."[28]

The future social and civic order of which Jefferson dreamed required a significant reworking of traditional ideas about time and history. In classical republican thought, time brought cycles of degeneration against which mere mortals labored largely in vain. Corruption could be slowed but not stopped. Jeffersonian discourse, by contrast, embedded the idea of time in the dynamic concepts of process, development and progress. The future would be fundamentally different because underlying processes were slowly but surely transforming society. As strictly as any French *philosophe*, Jefferson marked his own age as a great divide. In the past lay superstition, sophistry, and priestcraft; in the future, science, progress and the growth of knowledge. A salutary "change has sensibly taken place in the mind of man. Science has liberated the ideas of those who read and reflect ... An insurrection has consequently begun, of science, talents, and courage, against rank and birth, which have fallen into contempt ... Science is progressive ..."[29] The burden of old ways of thinking, of prescientific prejudices and antediluvian conceits, of controlling institutions, had to be shed once and for all. Only liberation from archaic authorities of all kinds would lift the dead hand of the past off the shoulders of present and future generations.

Logically, this expectation of almost inexorable improvement undercut the importance of past knowledge, an attitude that Jefferson nicely epitomized when extolling modern forms of representation. "The introduction of this new principle of representative democracy," he said, "has rendered useless almost everything written before on the structure of government." He then adds the startling suggestion that this fact "in a great measure, relieves our regret,

---

[27] TJ to Samuel Kercheval, July 12, 1816; *infra*, III.23.
[28] John Adams to TJ, Aug. 9, 1816, in Cappon, ed., *Adams–Jefferson Letters*, p. 487.
[29] TJ to John Adams, Oct. 28, 1813; *infra*, III.16.

if the political writings of Aristotle, or of any other ancient, have been lost."[30] This, however, is Jefferson at his most hyperbolic. For, far from delivering the *coup de grâce* to classical learning, he emphasized repeatedly its continuing relevance and importance. "For classical learning I have ever been a zealous advocate," he wrote, and that zeal was amply evident in his design of the curriculum of the University of Virginia.[31]

A third noteworthy feature of Jefferson's political thought is the myriad ways in which it relies upon appeals to "nature." His writings abound with references to nature, to natural right, to natural law and the laws of nature. In the Declaration he famously invokes "the laws of nature and of nature's God." An ardent enthusiast for the natural sciences, Jefferson declared Newton, Locke and Bacon the greatest of all great men.[32] His amateur scientific curiosity never flagged, nor did his belief that the orderly and predictable processes of nature offered a better model for society than any that could be devised by legislatures. Not man-made laws, but nature, secured human needs. He spoke of "the natural right of trading with our neighbors" and grounded property in "the natural wants" of men.[33] The claim that there is a universal and uniform "human nature" carried considerable political import. The assertion of an underlying uniformity in the face of conspicuous human differences enabled the Jeffersonians to enlist nature in the war against hierarchical society. Claiming to interpret the laws of nature, Jefferson described a complex intellectual trajectory that linked the American nation to a grand human destiny. Where traditional society recognized a variety of statuses, ethnic groups, and regional identities, Jeffersonians obliterated that variety in the celebration of all free men, except where, as Jefferson wrote, "the difference is fixed in nature."[34]

It is just here that the darker side of Jefferson's Enlightenment faith in nature and the natural emerges in ways that shock modern sensibilities. The "nature" to which Jefferson so frequently

[30] TJ to Isaac H. Tiffany, Aug. 26, 1816; *infra*, III.24.
[31] TJ to Dr. Thomas Cooper, Oct. 7, 1814 (*infra*, IV.20) and his *Report of the Commissioners for the University of Virginia*, 1818 (*infra*, IV.23).
[32] TJ to Dr. Benjamin Rush, Jan. 16, 1811; *infra*, VIII.10.
[33] Quoted in John Dewey, ed., *The Living Thoughts of Thomas Jefferson* (New York, 1940), p. 75; TJ to Pierre-Samuel DuPont de Nemours, April 24, 1816 (*infra*, II.14).
[34] Jefferson, *Notes on Virginia*, Query XIV; *infra*, IX.6.

appealed endowed ordinary white men with the capacity for self-government even as it denied that capacity to women and people of color. He expected nature to ratify the conventional exclusion of women, African-Americans, and Native Americans from the ranks of autonomous people. Forming far too large and important a presence in Jefferson's world to be ignored, their exclusion demarcates the boundary of Jefferson's reforming zeal. His prejudices and preconceptions about black Africans, Native Americans, and women were widely if not universally shared in his day. In Jefferson's case these attitudes are reinforced by his repeated recourse to nature and natural law. A mighty liberator in the face of historic privilege, natural law doctrine raised its own form of exclusion. Indeed, nature, when viewed as forever fixed and universal, could discriminate just as effectively as society.

Jefferson assumed without argument that women were by their very nature excluded from the public realm. They think naturally of home and hearth, of husband and children, and rarely (if at all) of wider public concerns. They are therefore rightly excluded from voting and holding public office. To have believed otherwise was conceivable, for others far less bold than Jefferson had recognized women's capacity for citizenship and public office. When his Secretary of the Treasury Albert Gallatin, concerned about the shortage of talented applicants for government office, suggested naming women to certain posts, Jefferson's reply was curt: "The appointment of a woman to office is an innovation for which the public is not prepared, nor am I."[35] Women, as he explained to several correspondents, were formed by nature for men's need and pleasure, and suited by nature for domestic, not political, life. "The tender breasts of ladies were not formed for political convulsion," Jefferson wrote, and women "miscalculate much their own happiness when they wander from the true field of their influence into that of politicks."[36] Indeed, a good part of the pleasure of women's company comes from their having little or no interest in politics. Men need respite from the demands of public life, and the company of women supplies that relief. The "good ladies" of America, unlike the busybodies of Paris, "have been too wise to wrinkle their

[35] TJ to Albert Gallatin, Jan. 13, 1807; *infra*, XI.4.
[36] TJ to Angelica Schuyler Church, Sept. 21, 1788; in J. P. Boyd *et al.*, eds., *Papers of Thomas Jefferson*, XIII, p. 623.

foreheads with politics. They are contented to soothe and calm the minds of their husbands returning ruffled from political debate. They have the good sense to value domestic happiness above all other, and the art to cultivate it beyond all other."[37] Men's inferiors in politics, women are men's valued companions at home.

For Native Americans, it was not so much innate inferiority as cultural obstinacy that accounted for their disqualifying differences. Jefferson was enough of an Enlightenment *philosophe* to have a certain regard and respect for "noble savages" living in harmony with nature. But living in harmony with nature was one thing, and living harmoniously with an ever-increasing number of European settlers was quite another. It was up to the American Indians to accommodate the newcomers, not the other way around. Those who refused to accept the newly arrived and land-hungry inhabitants were to be driven westward or even exterminated. In 1780, Governor Jefferson wrote to the revolutionary frontier leader, George Rogers Clark, about how best to deal with "those tribes of Indians between the Ohio and Illinois rivers who have harassed us with eternal hostilities, and whom experience has shewn to be incapable of reconciliation . . . If we are to wage a campaign against these Indians the end proposed should be their extermination, or their removal beyond the lakes of the Illinois river. The same world will scarcely do for them and us."[38] For the less warlike and more accommodating tribes Jefferson proposed profound changes in their way of life. If they are to survive, they must exchange the nomadic life of the hunter for the settled life of the farmer.[39]

Jefferson's views on black Africans are, to modern eyes, no less benighted and backward than his views regarding women and Native Americans. Several remarks in his *Notes on the State of Virginia* suggest that he held views that we would today term racist. African-Americans, Jefferson wrote, were "inferior to the whites in the endowments both of body and mind." These views he advances "as a suspicion only," and not as a settled conviction.[40] His suspicion appears to have been undermined as he grew older. In a letter to Benjamin Banneker – a black astronomer and mathema-

---

[37] TJ to Anne Willing Bingham, May 11, 1788; *infra*, XI.2.
[38] TJ to George Rogers Clark, Jan. 1, 1780, in Boyd, *et al.*, eds., *Papers*, III, p. 259.
[39] Second Inaugural Address, March 4, 1805; *infra*, X.9.
[40] *Notes on Virginia*; *infra*, IX.6.

tician much admired by Jefferson, who as President had appointed him official surveyor of the District of Columbia – Jefferson wrote: "No body wishes more than I do to see such proofs as you exhibit, that nature has given to our black brethren, talents equal to those of the other colors of men, and that the appearance of a want of them is owing merely to the degraded condition of their existence, both in Africa and America."[41] Jefferson later expressed further doubts about his earlier views on race: "no person living wishes more sincerely than I do, to see a complete refutation of the doubts I have myself entertained and expressed on the grade of understanding allotted to them by nature ... My doubts [in the *Notes on Virginia*] were the result of personal observation on the limited sphere of my own State [i.e., Virginia] where the opportunities for the development of their genius were not favorable." Jefferson then adds that *even if* one individual or race were more intelligent or talented than another, that fact carries no moral or political weight: "their degree of talent ... is no measure of their rights. Because Sir Isaac Newton was superior to others in understanding, he was not therefore lord of the person or property of others."[42]

And yet Jefferson was himself lord and master of some two hundred black slaves whom he bought and sold. He knew that slavery was an evil institution; but he remained immersed in and indebted to the very institution whose evils he so eloquently condemned. The ardent champion of republican liberty denied that liberty to his human "property." What to modern eyes looks like a rank contradiction between Jefferson's political theory and his personal practice was not universally so regarded in Jefferson's day. Many an *ante bellum* Southern writer noted that just as the republics of antiquity – Athens, Sparta, Rome – had relied on the labor of slaves, so would and should the American Republic. The right to liberty belongs to citizens only; to deny that liberty to non-citizens – women, resident aliens, and slaves – is therefore quite consistent with republican principles and no violation of anyone's rights.[43]

But Jefferson never subscribed to such a view. The right to liberty is a human, not a civil, right; and slavery is quite clearly and

---

[41] TJ to Benjamin Banneker, Aug. 30, 1791; *infra*, IX.9.
[42] TJ to Henri Grégoire, Feb. 25, 1809; *infra*, IX.15.
[43] See Rogers M. Smith, *Civic Ideals: Conflicting Views of Citizenship in US History* (New Haven, 1997), p. 86.

unequivocally a violation of that right. Jefferson never ceased to decry "those violations of human rights which have been so long continued on the unoffending inhabitants of Africa."[44] But neither in life nor in death did he practice what he preached. In his will Jefferson freed only five of his approximately two hundred slaves, most of whom were sold to pay his enormous debts. Where slavery was concerned, Jefferson's deeds did not match his magnificent words.

Yet in the end it was Jefferson's words – his power as author – that outstripped and transcended his prejudices as a man. Like some Sorcerer's Apprentice, he had got hold of and articulated a vision whose power he felt but whose full implications he barely comprehended. His words and phrases – most especially those of the Declaration of Independence – would later be borrowed, repeated, and refashioned for purposes that Jefferson did not intend, could not foresee, and almost certainly could not have imagined.[45] When in 1848 the delegates at the Seneca Falls conference sought a model for their own declaration of feminist principles, they turned almost immediately to Jefferson's Declaration.[46] The ex-slave and ardent Abolitionist Frederick Douglass looked back to the Declaration's color-blind and universal principles for inspiration and legitimation. And Abraham Lincoln saw in Jefferson's Declaration the real charter of American liberty for all, black and white alike. A product of political compromise, the Constitution had recognized, and thus legitimized, slavery; the Declaration in its magnificent abstractness had not. Thus the "four score and seven years" before Lincoln's 1863 Gettysburg Address locates 1776 as America's better origin and the real birth-date of the republic. If America had originated in an "idea," then Jefferson was father to the thought.

Skeptics rightly regard Lincoln's view of Jefferson and the Declaration as wishful thinking, as political propaganda, as balm for the wounds of civil war, and subsequently as a mainstay of an American civil religion. One has gone so far as to claim that Lincoln's Gettys-

[44] Sixth Annual Message to Congress, Dec. 2, 1806; in P. L. Ford, ed., *Writings of Thomas Jefferson* (New York, 1892–9), VIII, p. 492.

[45] For a sampling of the uses to which Jefferson's Declaration was later put, see Philip S. Foner, ed., *We the Other People: Alternative Declarations of Independence by Labor Groups, Farmers, Women's Rights Advocates, Socialists, and Blacks, 1829–1975* (Urbana, 1976).

[46] Seneca Falls Declaration (1848); *infra*, Appendix C.

burg Address was a "giant (if benign) swindle" and "one of the most daring acts of open-air sleight-of-hand ever witnessed by the unsuspecting." So successful was Lincoln that he single-handedly gave the Americans "a new past . . . that would change their future indefinitely."[47]

Yet it is through this and allied channels that Jefferson's ideas have entered and become part of mainstream political thought in America and beyond. The American civil rights movement of the 1960s more readily invoked the ideas of the slave-owning Sage of Monticello than of any others. The Reverend Martin Luther King, Jr., quoted Jefferson almost as readily as he quoted scripture; indeed, one might almost say that he, like Lincoln a century earlier, quoted Jefferson's words *as* scripture – uniquely and readily recognizable "American scripture," as one critic has complained.[48] For better or worse, Jefferson the man has been supplanted by Jefferson the legend.

Perhaps a little less attention to the legend, and more careful attention to Thomas Jefferson's own words, and the highly charged political contexts in which he wrote them, will supply a more balanced and nuanced picture of this remarkably complex and sometimes contradictory American political thinker.

---

[47] See Garry Wills, *Lincoln at Gettysburg: Words that Made American History* (New York, 1992), p. 38.
[48] See Maier, *American Scripture*, ch. 4.

# Chronology

|       | reconstitute as a revolutionary convention; Jefferson elected delegate to First Continental Congress; retires from legal practice; birth of daughter Jane Randolph |
|-------|---|
| 1775  | Publishes *A Summary View of the Rights of British America*; elected to Second Continental Congress; daughter Jane Randolph dies; (April 19) battles of Lexington and Concord; (June 17) battle of Bunker Hill |
| 1776  | (July 4) Declaration of Independence adopted by Congress; mother Jane Randolph Jefferson dies |
| 1777  | Drafts Virginia Statute for Religious Freedom; Articles of Confederation drafted by Congress; son is born but dies shortly thereafter |
| 1778  | Drafts Bill for the More General Diffusion of Knowledge; daughter Mary (Maria) born |
| 1779–81 | Governor of Virginia |
| 1780  | Begins writing *Notes on the State of Virginia*; daughter Lucy Elizabeth born |
| 1782  | His wife, Martha Jefferson, dies; deeply despondent, Jefferson retreats to Monticello |
| 1783  | Elected delegate to Congress; (Sept. 3) peace treaty with Great Britain signed |
| 1784  | Daughter Lucy Elizabeth dies |
| 1784–9 | Serves as Commissioner and U.S. Minister to France; observes outbreak of French Revolution |
| 1786  | Shays's Rebellion in Massachusetts |
| 1787  | *Notes on the State of Virginia* published in London; (May 25–Sept. 17) Constitutional Convention meets in Philadelphia; Ratification Debate begins |
| 1789  | Named Secretary of State by President Washington |
| 1794  | Retires to private life; returns to Monticello |
| 1796  | Elected Vice-President of the United States; serves in Administration of John Adams, second President of U.S. |
| 1800  | Elected President of the United States |
| 1801  | (March 4) First Inaugural Address articulates key principles of what has come to be known as "Jeffersonian" democracy |
| 1802  | Accused by disappointed office-seeker of having an |

|        | affair with, and fathering children by, Sally Hemings, one of his slaves at Monticello |
|--------|---|
| 1803   | *Marbury* v. *Madison* establishes precedent that the Supreme Court can declare acts of Congress unconstitutional; Louisiana Territory purchased from France, more than doubling the size of the American Republic |
| 1804   | Lewis and Clark Expedition launched to explore and map newly acquired Louisiana Territory; Jefferson re-elected President; daughter Maria dies |
| 1805   | Lewis and Clark reach Pacific coast |
| 1807   | Rejects pleas that he run for a third term as President; announces impending retirement from political life; Great Britain outlaws slave trade in all its colonies |
| 1808   | James Madison elected President; U.S. law prohibits importation of African slaves |
| 1809   | Second term as President ends; retires to Monticello |
| 1812   | Responds favorably to John Adams's overtures that the two resume their correspondence |
| 1812–14| War of 1812 |
| 1814   | British burn U.S. Capitol; President Madison and Congress forced to flee to avoid capture |
| 1815   | Deepening debts force Jefferson to sell his 6,700-volume library to Congress; becomes basis of the Library of Congress |
| 1819   | Founds the University of Virginia |
| 1821   | Writes *Autobiography* for his own and family's use |
| 1825   | University of Virginia opens |
| 1826   | (July 4) Jefferson dies at Monticello; John Adams dies on same day |

# Biographical synopses

**Adams, Abigail** (1744–1818) was the wife of John Adams to whom Jefferson drew very close during the years that he and Adams served in France and England as America's foreign ministers. A woman of great learning and wit, Abigail Adams broke with Jefferson after the election of 1800 because of what she saw as his unfair treatment of her husband and subsequently their son. The breach was healed with time and no little effort on John Adams's part.

**Adams, John** (1735–1826) and Thomas Jefferson served together on the committee to draft the Declaration of Independence and as fellow diplomats before returning to join George Washington's administration, Adams as Vice-President, Jefferson as Secretary of State. Bitter rivals for the presidency in 1800, they resumed their friendship in retirement, both dying on the 50th anniversary of July 4, 1776.

**Banister, John, Jr.** (d. 1788) was a political leader in colonial Virginia, serving in the House of Burgesses. During the Revolution when Jefferson was Governor of Virginia, Colonel Banister was the County Lieutenant of Dinwiddie County.

**Banneker, Benjamin** (1731–1806) was a free black clockmaker, mathematician, and astronomer. In 1791, when Jefferson was Secretary of State, Banneker wrote him asking him to accept the manuscript of his almanac as proof that men were endowed by their Creator with qualities and capacities that had no bearing on racial differences. Jefferson later had Banneker appointed surveyor in the

District of Columbia, failing to take umbrage at Banneker's charge that by holding slaves he was violating his own principles.

**Barlow, Joel** (1754–1812) was a poet, lawyer, and diplomat. He lived in Europe for a decade while promoting land sales for the Scioto Company. An enthusiastic democrat, Barlow is remembered for his epic poem, "The Columbiad," and his political essay, "Advice to the Privileged Orders."

**Bingham, Anne Willing** (1764–1801) was a leading figure in Philadelphia society during the years (1791–9) that the city was the capital of the United States. Known for her beauty and wit, she and Jefferson exchanged several letters.

**Cabell, Joseph** (1778–1856) worked closely with Jefferson in the founding of the University of Virginia. A Virginia civic leader, he also pioneered various canal projects in the state.

**Carr, Peter** (1770–1815) was Jefferson's nephew, one of several young men in whose education and well-being Jefferson took an active interest.

**Carrington, Edward** (1749–1810) was a Virginia political leader and longtime friend of Jefferson's whose conservative views seemed to provoke Jefferson to a warm and enthusiastic defense of democracy. He served as U.S. Marshal for Virginia when Jefferson was President.

**Cartwright, John** (1740–1824) was an Englishman and parliamentary reformer who had warmly supported the American colonists in their protests over taxation.

**Coles, Edward** (1786–1868) was a young neighbor of Jefferson's who left Virginia for Illinois, in part out of dislike for slavery. Later chosen Governor of Illinois, Coles led the campaign to keep Illinois from sanctioning slavery after it became a state and the Northwest Ordinance ban no longer applied.

**Cooper, Thomas** (1759–1839) was an English radical who emigrated to the United States with his good friend, Joseph Priestley. Identifying himself closely with the Jeffersonian party, he was prosecuted and imprisoned for his pamphleteering under the Federalists' Sedition Law. Becoming considerably more conservative in later life, Cooper moved to South Carolina where, as president of the South Carolina College, he became an outspoken defender of slavery and states' rights.

**Cosway, Maria** (1760–1838) was an Italian woman whom Jefferson met in Paris. The wife of an English painter, she and Jefferson were constant companions in the fall of 1786. It was for her that he composed his delightful discourse between the heart and the head.

**Dickinson, John** (1732–1808) achieved fame as the writer of the "Letters from a Farmer in Pennsylvania to the Inhabitants of the British Colonies" in 1769. A conservative in the end, he refused to sign the Declaration of Independence, but remained in Delaware which he later represented at the Constitutional Convention.

**DuPont de Nemours, Pierre-Samuel** (1739–1817) was one of the thinkers, denominated *Economistes*, surrounding the great French reform minister, Turgot. Jefferson and DuPont de Nemours carried on an extended correspondence until DuPont's death. His son, Eleuthère-Irénée, founded the DuPont chemical firm in the United States.

**Fabbroni, Giovanni** (1752–1822) belonged to a peripatetic group of enlightened Europeans with a reformist bent to whom Jefferson's friend, Philip Mazzei, introduced him.

**Franklin, Benjamin** (1706–90) was a Philadelphia printer, self-taught scientist, sage, inventor, author, revolutionary, and diplomat. He was, by age and experience, the senior member of the committee that charged Jefferson with the task of drafting the Declaration of independence. Eleven years later the elderly Franklin helped draft the new United States Constitution. In the interim he served as American ambassador to France, where he was lionized as the epitome of American openness and candor. His contributions to American letters include his *Autobiography* and *Poor Richard's Almanac*.

**Gallatin, Albert** (1761–1849) emigrated from his native Switzerland and invested his patrimony in land in western Pennsylvania from which he was elected to both the House and the Senate. An ardent Jeffersonian, he served as Secretary of the Treasury from 1801 to 1814 and later as U.S. minister to France and to Great

Britain. He shared Jefferson's keen interest in American Indian tribes and founded the Ethnological Society of America.

**Gerry, Elbridge** (1744–1814) was a member of the Continental Congress, a delegate to the Constitutional Convention of 1787, Governor of Massachusetts, and Vice-President under James Madison. As Governor he oversaw the redistricting of Massachusetts so as to minimize Federalist electoral victories. One district was so oddly shaped that someone suggested it looked like a salamander, to which a local wit replied that it looked more like a Gerrymander. The name stuck and has become a byword for the unfair division of electoral districts.

**Gilmer, Francis Walker** (1790–1826) was a young neighbor of Jefferson's in Albemarle County. He was the grandson of Dr. Thomas Walker, Jefferson's guardian and the first white man to visit Kentucky. An author and lawyer, Gilmer traveled to Europe in 1824 to seek professors and to buy books and equipment, at Jefferson's request, for the University of Virginia.

**Grégoire, Henri** (1750–1831) was a political figure Jefferson met in Paris. He was a member of the Convention and was named the Bishop of Blois by the Constitution. An ardent champion of racial equality, he compiled a book *De la littérature des Nègres* (Paris, 1808) to exhibit the literary talents of writers of African ancestry.

**Hamilton, Alexander** (1755–1804) served as *aide-de-camp* to General Washington during the Revolution, co-authored *The Federalist Papers*, and served as first Secretary of the Treasury. A leading proponent of a strong central government, he proposed a plan for a National Bank and had the federal government assume and pay the Revolutionary War debts of the several states. He and Jefferson despised one another, albeit more for principled than personal reasons. He was killed in a duel with Aaron Burr, Jefferson's Vice-President.

**Henry, Patrick** (1736–99) was a prominent Virginia lawyer, politician and orator whose ringing periods still reverberate ("I know not what course others may take, but as for me, give me liberty or give me death"). He served as Governor of Virginia and helped draft that state's Constitution. He refused to be a delegate to the constitutional convention in Philadelphia in 1787, and later justified his refusal by saying "I smell a rat" – the rat being that the new Constitution granted too much power to the federal government and contained no Bill of Rights. After the Bill of Rights was ratified in 1791, however, he accepted the new Constitution and became an ardent advocate of American unity.

**Hopkinson, Francis** (1737–91) was a prominent leader of the revolutionary movement in Pennsylvania. Later a Judge of Admiralty, he continued to write satirical essays, poetry and songs throughout his long public career.

**Humboldt, Baron Friedrich von** (1769–1859), German geographer, oceanographer, diplomat, and author. A tireless traveler, he conducted serious scientific researches in many parts of the globe. Returning as *raconteur* to the *salons* of Paris and other European capitals, he met and was greatly admired by Jefferson and other leading thinkers of the day.

**Humphreys, David** (1752–1818) was a poet and diplomat in revolutionary America. His interests extended to promoting the raising of merino sheep and textile manufacturing.

**Jay, John** (1745–1829) played a prominent role in the political life of the new nation, serving New York as a delegate to the Second Continental Congress, signing the Declaration of Independence and presiding over Congress before he was sent to Spain as American minister. He also wrote five of the *Federalist Papers* in collaboration with Alexander Hamilton and James Madison and served as the first Chief Justice of the Supreme Court under the new Constitution.

**Jefferson, Martha** (1748–82) was Jefferson's beloved wife. They were married but ten years before she died, survived by three of their daughters.

**Johnson, William** (1771–1834) was Jefferson's first appointee to the Supreme Court. The judge, a native of Charleston, South Carolina, was named to the court in April, 1804.

**Kercheval, Samuel** (?–?) lived in western Virginia. Resentful of the malapportionment of state legislative representatives, he began a campaign for a state constitutional convention which Jefferson supported.

**Lafayette, Marie Joseph Paul, Marquis de** (1757–1834) came to the United States at the beginning of the Revolutionary War where he served on Washington's staff as major-general at the age of twenty. Identifying himself closely with the American cause, Lafayette maintained close ties with America, returning to the country for a triumphal and nostalgic tour in 1824–5. His grave in Paris's Picpus Cemetery is covered with earth from Bunker Hill, the first major battle of the Revolutionary War.

**Lee, Richard Henry** (1732–94) was an important figure in Virginia politics and the American move toward independence. A member of the first Continental Congress, he helped organize the pre-revolutionary Committees of Correspondence. In the Second Continental Congress he introduced the resolution for declaring American independence, stating "That these United Colonies are, and of Right ought to be Free and Independent States; that they are Absolved from all Allegiance to the British Crown." Lee also introduced the resolution to draft the Articles of Confederation. Like his fellow Virginian Patrick Henry, he initially opposed the new Constitution of 1787, fearing its consolidation of power in the central government and the absence of a Bill of Rights. He later demurred, and as Senator from Virginia he supplied James Madison with propositions that the latter incorporated into the Bill of Rights.

**Madison, Rev. James** (1749–1812) served as president of Jefferson's *alma mater*, William and Mary College, from 1777 until his death. An Episcopal clergyman, he was a first cousin of the statesman, James Madison.

**Madison, James** (1751–1836) became Jefferson's closest friend, working closely with him for fifty years. Fourth President of the United States, Madison is more enduringly known as the father of the United States Constitution, a tribute to the central role he played in the Constitutional Convention of 1787.

**Mason, George** (1725–92) was an influential figure in revolutionary Virginia. He wrote the Virginia Constitution of 1776, best remembered for its declaration of rights. He was also a delegate to the Constitutional Convention in 1787. Although initially a supporter of the new Constitution, he became increasingly suspicious of its tendency to concentrate power in the central government at the several states' expense. He became an Antifederalist opponent of the Constitution, his opposition later mollified only in part by the adoption of the Bill of Rights a year before his death.

**Melish, John** (1771–1822) was a native of Scotland who traveled extensively in America in connection with his mercantile interests and geographic curiosity. His *Travels in the United States of America* (1812) was remarkable for its descriptive accuracy. He also wrote numerous statistical accounts of the United States, where he finally settled in 1811.

**Monroe, James** (1758–1831) became Jefferson's close friend and political ally, after studying law with him between 1780 and 1783. Monroe began his public service in the Continental Army, moving on to a successful career as a legislator, diplomat and Governor of Virginia, before becoming the fifth President of the United States.

**Morris, Gouverneur** (1752–1816), American stateman, diplomat, and champion of religious toleration and the abolition of slavery. His plan for a decimalized monetary system, as adapted by Jefferson, became the basis of U.S. coinage. As an active member of the 1787 Constitutional Convention he favored a strong central government. In 1792 he was appointed by President Washington to be U.S. Minister to France. His hostility to the French Revolution led to his recall in 1794. Elected to the Senate in 1800, he became a high Federalist and opponent of Jeffersonian republicanism.

**Morris, Robert** (1734–1806), was an English-born American banker and signer of the Declaration of Independence. He helped arrange domestic and foreign financing for the American Revolution. Elected to the Senate in 1789, he allied himself with Treasury Secretary Hamilton and his Federalist policies, much to Jefferson's dismay. Leaving the Senate, he speculated heavily – and unsuccessfully – in western lands, went bankrupt, and spent three years (1798–1801) in debtors' prison, leaving him broken in health and spirit.

**Nicholas, Wilson C.** (1761–1820) was an influential Jeffersonian leader in Virginia politics, going on to serve the state as U.S. Senator and Congressman. As Governor of Virginia, he collaborated with Jefferson on the founding of the University of Virginia. Jefferson cosigned one of Nicholas's notes, seeing his own finances collapse when Nicholas's failed in 1819.

**Norvell, John** (1789–1850) was studying law at the time he wrote Jefferson for advice. A newspaper editor in Baltimore, he later moved to Michigan territory and served the state as one of its first U.S. Senators.

**Paine, Thomas** (1737–1809), English-born American author, inventor, and revolutionary. He emigrated to America in 1774, on the eve of the American Revolution. Early in 1776 Paine published *Common Sense*, a rousing patriotic pamphlet, and an equally spirited series, *The Crisis*. A later work, *The Rights of Man* (1791–2), directed against Edmund Burke's *Reflections on the Revolution in France* (1790), led to his indictment for treason in England. He fled to France, where he wrote *The Age of Reason*, which (fairly or not) sealed his reputation as an atheist and a Jacobin. Jefferson, who never ceased to defend his friend and ally, was similarly tarred by Federalist foes.

**Pendleton, Edmund** (1721–1803) was one of Virginia's most distinguished political leaders, having served in almost every legislative and constituent body during his public career. He presided over the Virginia Convention of 1776 which recommended independence. While president of the Virginia Supreme Court of Appeals, he threw himself behind the U.S. Constitution.

**Price, Richard** (1723–91), the distinguished English Unitarian minister and political philosopher, corresponded with many Americans whose revolutionary cause he openly embraced.

**Priestley, Joseph** (1733–1804), the English natural philosopher, came to the United States after being the target of mob violence because of his sympathy for the French Revolution. Moving to rural Pennsylvania, Priestley exchanged many letters with Jefferson.

**Randolph, Thomas Mann** (1768–1828) was married to Jefferson's daughter, Martha. An amateur botanist, Randolph also represented Virginia in the House of Representatives (as did Jefferson's other son-in-law, John Wayles Eppes) and served as Governor of Virginia.

**Roane, Spencer** (1762–1822) served on the Virginia Supreme Court of Appeals for twenty-seven years, distinguishing himself in politics as a vigorous Jeffersonian. With his cousin, Thomas Richie, he founded the *Richmond Enquirer* to which he contributed a series of articles, many of them critical of his fellow Virginian, Supreme Court Chief Justice John Marshall.

**Rush, Benjamin** (1745–1813), a Philadelphia physician, enjoyed the close friendship of most of the revolutionary leadership. Surgeon-general in the Continental Army, he was also a signer of the Declaration of Independence. An indefatigable pamphleteer, Rush wrote on disease, insanity, alcoholism and women's intelligence. It was he who persuaded Jefferson to resume his correspondence with John Adams after both men had retired from public life.

**Short, William** (1759–1849) became Jefferson's private secretary when he went to Paris in 1784, serving as Chargé d'Affaires after Jefferson's departure until 1792 when he was appointed U.S. Minister at The Hague.

**Skipwith, Robert** (?–?) was the brother-in-law of Jefferson's wife, Martha Wayles Jefferson, having married her half-sister, Tabitha.

**Smith, William Stephens** (1755–1816) served as an aide to George Washington during the Revolutionary War. He married Abigail, the daughter of John Adams, and later served as a Federalist Congressman from New York.

**Sullivan, James** (1744–1808) became an early supporter of Jefferson in that stronghold of Federalism, New England. A successful lawyer, he served as Governor of Massachusetts from 1807 to 1808 during which time he was embroiled in a public controversy with Timothy Pickering over Jefferson's Embargo. He wrote a number of legal and historical treatises.

**Taylor, John** (1753–1824) exercised considerable influence in his day as a political thinker and agricultural promoter. A thoroughgoing Jeffersonian, he wrote a number of important treatises on constitutional issues and political economy. He was an active state legislator, and also represented Virginia in the U.S. Senate.

**Tiffany, Isaac** (?–?) was a resident of Schoharie, New York, who corresponded with Jefferson in 1816–17 about his plan for a chart of state governments and other sundry schemes.

**Wythe, George** (1726–1806) took the lead in Virginia's resistance to the Crown, serving in the Second Continental Congress and later with Jefferson revising the Virginia laws after Independence. Jefferson studied law with Wythe before the Revolution.

# A note on sources

In 1783 Jefferson advised his young daughter Martha ("Patsy"), "Take care that you never spell a word wrong. Always before you write a word consider how it is spelt, and if you do not remember it, turn to a dictionary. It produces great praise to a lady to spell well." Jefferson, alas, did not follow his own advice. His spelling is often unusual, not to say idiosyncratic, even by eighteenth-century standards. For example, he writes "it's" when we would write "its" – as in "the tree of liberty must be refreshed from time to time with the blood of patriots and tyrants. It is it's [*sic*] natural manure." He sometimes drops letters that we expect to see, as when he writes "knoledge" instead of knowledge, and substitutes one for another, as in "scull" for skull. And he often abbreviates words, e.g. "govt" for government, "consn" for constitution, and the like. Our practice has been to leave Jefferson's spelling as it is (or as it has been altered, alas, by his later well-meaning editors), unless it seems likely to mislead or confuse modern readers. We have also left Greek and Latin terms, phrases, and quotations untranslated, since Jefferson – good didactic democrat that he was – almost always goes on to translate or paraphrase so as to give some sense of their meaning. (His inscription of Greek, Anglo-Saxon, Latin and French characters is sometimes peculiar, however.)

Most of Jefferson's writings reproduced here are drawn from the following sources, abbreviated thus:

Ford  Paul Leicester Ford, ed., *The Writings of Thomas Jefferson* (New York, 1892–9), 10 vols.

L & B      Andrew A. Lipscomb and Albert Ellery Bergh, eds.
           *The Writings of Thomas Jefferson* (Washington, D.C.,
           1903–4), 20 vols.
Randolph   Thomas Jefferson Randolph, ed., *The Memoirs, Cor-
           respondence and Private Papers of Thomas Jefferson*
           (Charlottesville, 1829), 4 vols.
Washington Henry A. Washington, ed., *The Writings of Thomas
           Jefferson* (Washington, D.C., 1853–4), 8 vols.

Of these, Ford is the most reliable, Lipscomb and Bergh the most
complete. Their (and Washington's) editorial practices do not
always pass muster by modern scholarly standards. And so wherever
possible we have compared these earlier editions with the later and
more authoritative ones to be found in J. P. Boyd *et al.*, eds., *The
Papers of Thomas Jefferson* (Princeton, 1950–   ), 27 vols. to date
(through 1793); Lester J. Cappon, ed., *The Adams–Jefferson Letters*
(Chapel Hill, 1988); and James Morton Smith, ed., *The Republic
of Letters: The Correspondence between Thomas Jefferson and James
Madison, 1776–1826* (New York, 1995), 3 vols. We have in several
instances consulted the original sources at the Library of Congress,
the Department of State in Washington, D.C., the Massachusetts
Historical Society, and the University of Virginia. Jefferson's letter
to Isaac Tiffany (April 4, 1819; III. 28) is transcribed from a micro-
film copy of the original in the Library of Congress.

Limitations on space have precluded the reprinting of Jefferson's
*Autobiography*. We have, however, reprinted the relevant parts as
prefaces to his letters and state papers, including the Declaration of
Independence.

The Cambridge Texts series follows the altogether admirable
policy of reproducing texts in their entirety. We have adhered to
this policy wherever possible and deviated from it where necessary.
Our deviations are due to Jefferson's having written no systematic
treatise on politics. Most of his political ideas he put into letters
dealing with various subjects in addition to politics – weather, the
price of tobacco and other crops, news of neighbors, friends, and
family, and the like. Jefferson's letters are wherever possible reproduced in their entirety; those that are not have the missing portions
clearly indicated with ellipses. Jefferson's only book – *Notes on the
State of Virginia* – was written in response to a series of questions

or "queries" posed to then-Governor Jefferson by François de Marbois and deals much more with flora, fauna, soil conditions, climate, etc., than with moral and political matters. We have accordingly extracted and reprinted only those sections of the *Notes on Virginia* dealing with race and slavery, white–Indian relations, constitutional questions, and other broadly political topics. In order to clarify references or allusions that might confuse the modern reader, we sometimes place a name or term in brackets in the text. So as not to encumber the text unduly, we have kept our own explanatory footnotes to a minimum and indicated these with "– *Eds.*" Other footnotes are Jefferson's unless indicated otherwise. We have numbered footnotes consecutively through each selection. We have silently made dates complete in letter headings and have omitted the signatures at the end of letters.

# Bibliographical note

There is as yet no complete and definitive edition of Jefferson's voluminous writings. His only book is *Notes on the State of Virginia* (1787; ed. William Peden, Chapel Hill, 1955). As its title suggests, the *Notes* is not a systematic treatise but a series of observations on the agriculture, geography, laws and many other features of his native state. Most of his political thought is to be found in his voluminous correspondence. The herculean labors begun by Julian P. Boyd and continued by Charles T. Cullen and John Catanzariti have so far produced twenty-seven volumes of *The Papers of Thomas Jefferson* (Princeton, 1950– ), bringing that series up through 1793 – seven years short of his presidency and thirty-three years before his death. When completed, this will be the definitive edition of Jefferson's writings on subjects ranging from architecture to zoology. Earlier editions include P. L. Ford, ed., *The Writings of Thomas Jefferson* (New York, 1892–9), 10 vols., and A. L. Lipscomb and A. E. Bergh, eds., *The Writings of Thomas Jefferson* (Washington, D.C., 1903–4), 20 vols. Selections from Jefferson's state papers and correspondence can be found in Saul K. Padover's somewhat misleadingly titled *The Complete Jefferson* (New York, 1943; repr. 1991); and in Merrill D. Peterson, ed., *The Portable Thomas Jefferson* (New York, 1975). For Jefferson's correspondence with his best friend and closest political ally, see James Morton Smith, ed., *The Republic of Letters: The Correspondence between Thomas Jefferson and James Madison, 1776–1826* (New York, 1995), 3 vols. His correspondence with his personal friend and sometime political foe John Adams is collected in Lester J. Cappon, ed., *The*

*Adams–Jefferson Letters* (Chapel Hill, 1988). Jefferson's familial correspondence is conveniently collected in Edwin M. Betts and James A. Bear, eds., *The Family Letters of Thomas Jefferson* (Charlottesville, 1986). Not to be missed is the handsomely produced single-volume selection edited by Merrill D. Peterson and published by the Library of America: *Thomas Jefferson: Writings* (New York, 1984). For a fascinating look inside Jefferson's mind, see *Thomas Jefferson's Library: A Catalog with the Entries in His Own Order*, eds. James Gilreath and Douglas L. Wilson (Washington, D.C., 1989).

Jefferson's posthumously published *Autobiography* (written in 1821; publ. New York, n.d.) is an interesting if not always entirely reliable *apologia pro vita sua*; unfortunately it stops at 1790, a decade before Jefferson's election as President. It should be supplemented with the *Anas*, a collection of notes taken by Jefferson from 1791 to 1806. Biographies of Jefferson range from the relatively brief *Thomas Jefferson* by Norman K. Risjord (Madison House, 1994), Page Smith's *Jefferson: A Revealing Biography* (American Heritage, 1976), and Merrill D. Peterson's *Thomas Jefferson and the New Nation* (Oxford, 1970) to Noble Cunningham's *In Pursuit of Reason: The Life of Thomas Jefferson* (Baton Rouge, 1987), 3 vols., and Dumas Malone's magisterial *Jefferson in his Time* (Boston, 1948–81), 6 vols. On Jefferson's larger-than-life reputation, see Merrill D. Peterson, *The Jefferson Image in the American Mind* (New York, 1960) and Bernard Mayo, *Myths and Men* (Athens, Ga. 1959). For an unsentimental and still-unsurpassed history of Jefferson's presidency, see Henry Adams, *History of the United States of America during the Administration of Thomas Jefferson* (vol. I, New York, 1889; vol. II, New York, 1909; repr. by the Library of America, New York, 1986). Adams's study should be supplemented by Norman K. Risjord, *Jefferson's America, 1760–1815* (Madison, 1991); Stanley Elkins and Eric McKitrick, *The Age of Federalism* (New York, 1993); and Noble E. Cunningham, Jr., *The Jeffersonian Republicans in Power: Party Operatives, 1801–1809* (Chapel Hill, 1963) and the same author's *The Process of Government under Jefferson* (Princeton, 1978). Accounts of Jefferson's close personal and political alliance with James Madison include Adrienne Koch, *Jefferson and Madison: The Great Collaboration* (New York, 1964) and Lance Banning, *Jefferson and Madison* (Madison, 1995).

During his first term as President, Jefferson was dogged by rumors that he had had an affair with, and one or more children by, his slave Sally Hemings. That the alleged affair was a partisan political scandal exploited (and perhaps invented) by Jefferson's enemies is claimed by Douglass Adair in *Fame and the Founding Fathers*, ed. Trevor Colbourne (New York, 1974) and by Virginius Dabney, *The Jefferson Scandals: A Rebuttal* (New York, 1981). More recently, Annette Gordon-Reid in *Thomas Jefferson and Sally Hemings: An American Controversy* (Charlottesville, 1997) has re-opened the case. DNA tests performed in 1998 show that Jefferson almost certainly sired at least one of Sally Hemings's sons (Eston Hemings Jefferson, b. 1808). For the genetic evidence, see the reports in *Nature*, 396 (Nov. 5, 1998), pp. 13–14, 27–8. The complexities and contradictions of Jefferson's character are explored in Joseph Ellis, *American Sphinx: The Character of Thomas Jefferson* (New York, 1997) and Andrew Burstein, *The Inner Jefferson: Portrait of a Grieving Optimist* (Charlottesville, 1995).

The economic context in (and sometimes against) which Jefferson did his political thinking is brilliantly sketched in Rhys Isaac's *The Transformation of Virginia, 1740–1790* (Chapel Hill, 1982) and Drew McCoy's *The Elusive Republic: Political Economy in Jeffersonian America* (Chapel Hill, 1980). For an interpretation of Jefferson's own economic views, see Joyce Appleby, *Capitalism and a New Social Order: The Republican Vision of the 1790s* (New York, 1984). An astute account of Jefferson's social and familial *milieu* is sketched by Jan Lewis, *The Pursuit of Happiness: Family and Values in Jefferson's Virginia* (New York, 1983). On Jefferson's intellectual *milieu*, see Daniel J. Boorstin, *The Lost World of Thomas Jefferson* (New York, 1948; repr. Chicago, 1993) and H. Trevor Colbourn, *The Lamp of Experience: Whig History and the Intellectual Origins of the American Revolution* (Chapel Hill, 1965). A good discussion of Jefferson's legal and constitutional views can be found in David N. Mayer, *The Constitutional Thought of Thomas Jefferson* (Charlottesville, 1994).

Studies of Jefferson's political thought can be conveniently classified according to whether they deal with the Declaration of Independence only (or mainly), or take a more synoptic view. The former include Carl L. Becker's *The Declaration of Independence: A Study in the History of Political Ideas* (New York, 1958), which views the Declaration as a largely Lockean–liberal document. By contrast, Garry Wills, *Inventing America: Jefferson's Declaration of Independence* (New York, 1978) sees the Declaration as a distillation of Scottish moral-sense philosophy. For a fascinating account of the rhetorical background see Jay Fliegelman, *Declaring Independence: Jefferson, Natural Language, and the Culture of Performance* (Stanford, 1993). On the drafting of the Declaration, see J. P. Boyd, *The Declaration of Independence: The Evolution of the Text* (Washington, D.C., 1943); on its reception and subsequent elevation to "scriptural" status, see Pauline Maier, *American Scripture: Making The Declaration of Independence* (New York, 1997); and, for further insight into its ritualistic uses, Len Travers, *Celebrating the Fourth: Independence Day and the Rites of Nationalism in the Early Republic* (Amherst, 1997). On the Declaration as a model manifesto for later liberation movements, see Philip S. Foner, ed., *We the Other People: Alternative Declarations of Independence by Labor Groups, Farmers, Women's Rights Advocates, Socialists, and Blacks, 1829–1975* (Urbana, 1976).

More synoptic studies of Jefferson as a political thinker include Gilbert Chinard, *Thomas Jefferson: The Apostle of Americanism* (Boston, 1929); Daniel Boorstin, *The Lost World of Thomas Jefferson*; Adrienne Koch, *The Philosophy of Thomas Jefferson* (Chicago, 1964), all of which emphasize the Lockean–liberal and Enlightenment aspects of Jefferson's political thought. Richard K. Matthews, *The Radical Politics of Thomas Jefferson* (Lawrence, Kan., 1984), resurrects the Hamiltonian–Federalist view of Jefferson as a wild-eyed radical – rather a good thing to be, too, Matthews (unlike Hamilton) holds. Lance Banning, *The Jeffersonian Persuasion* (Ithaca, 1978), views Jefferson as a resuscitator and defender of republican ideals, an interpretation modified in part in his subsequent "Jeffersonian Ideology Revisited: Liberal and Classical Ideals in the New American Republic," *William and Mary Quarterly*, n.s., 43 (1986), 3–19. The thesis of a "republican" (or even classical republican) Jefferson is challenged by, *inter alios*, Isaac Kramnick, "Republican Revisionism Revisited," *American Historical Review*, 87 (1982), 629–64, and Joyce Appleby, "What is Still American in Jefferson's Political Philosophy?," *William and Mary Quarterly*, n.s., 39 (1982), 287–309, and "Republicanism in Old and New Contexts," *William and Mary Quarterly*, n.s., 43 (1986), 20–34; both are reprinted, with several other studies, in her *Liberalism and Republicanism in the Historical Imagination* (Cambridge, Mass., 1992). Garrett Ward Sheldon, *The Political Philosophy of Thomas Jefferson* (Baltimore, 1991), rather sensibly sees Jefferson as an eclectic borrower from different discourses and traditions – Lockean liberalism, republicanism, Scottish moral-sense theory, Christianity, and English common law – depending on time, circumstance, situation, and the audience he was addressing. On Jefferson's debts to, and differences with, ancient authors, see Karl Lehmann, *Thomas Jefferson: American Humanist* (Charlottesville, 1985).

For a sensitive and critical discussion of Jefferson's ideas regarding race and slavery, see John Chester Miller, *The Wolf by the Ears: Thomas Jefferson and Slavery* (New York, 1977) and, more broadly, Winthrop D. Jordan, *White over Black: American Attitudes toward the Negro, 1550–1812* (Chapel Hill, 1968). For a modern self-styled Burkean's splenetic attack on Jefferson as a racist and apostle of anarchic "absolute liberty" for whites and abject slavery for blacks, see Conor Cruise O'Brien, *The Long Affair: Thomas Jefferson and the French Revolution, 1785–1800* (Chicago, 1996). Jefferson's views regarding native Americans are probed by Bernard W. Sheehan, *Seeds of Extinction: Jeffersonian Philanthropy and the American Indian* (Chapel Hill, 1973).

Numerous attempts have been made to modernize or update Jefferson. Many of these quite uncritically appropriate a few tags from the Sage of Monticello for partisan purposes. An exception is Leonard W. Levy's *Jefferson and Civil Liberties: The Darker Side* (Cambridge, Mass., 1963) which excoriates Jefferson for not being a twentieth-century civil libertarian. The contributors to Peter S. Onuf, ed., *Jeffersonian Legacies* (Charlottesville, 1993) attempt, always suggestively and often successfully, to exhibit the relevance of Jeffersonian political thinking to contemporary concerns such as the national debt, civil rights, and foreign policy.

There is a sizeable and still-growing literature on Jefferson's interests in nature and the natural sciences. See Charles A. Miller's *Jefferson and Nature: An Interpretation* (Baltimore, 1988). Jefferson's conception of the United States as a continental nation stretching from the Atlantic to the Pacific led to the Louisiana Purchase and thence the Lewis and Clark expedition in which Jefferson's continental vision was combined with his scientific curiosity. The former has been analyzed by, *inter alios*, Henry Nash Smith, *Virgin Land: The American Frontier as Myth and Symbol* (Cambridge, Mass., 1950) and John Logan Allen, *Passage through the Garden: Lewis and Clark and the Image of the American Northwest* (Urbana, 1975), and the latter by Raymond D. Burroughs, *The Natural History of the Lewis and Clark Expedition* (East Lansing, 1961) and Daniel Botkin, *Our Natural History: The Lessons of Lewis and Clark* (New York, 1995). For a riveting account of the Lewis and Clark Expedition, see Stephen E. Ambrose, *Undaunted Courage: Meriwether Lewis, Thomas Jefferson, and the Opening of the American West* (New York, 1996).

On Jefferson's changing attitude toward political parties, see Richard Hofstadter, *The Idea of a Party System* (Berkeley and Los Angeles, 1970) and Terence Ball, *Transforming Political Discourse* (Oxford, 1988), ch. 2. President Jefferson's reform of the American military is discussed in detail by Theodore J. Crackel, *Mr. Jefferson's Army: Political and Social Reform of the Military Establishment, 1801–1809* (New York, 1987).

Last, and certainly least, are the fictionalized accounts of Jefferson's life and loves. Jefferson is unusual in attracting the attention of novelists and filmmakers. Their efforts range from the mildly interesting to the truly awful. Max Byrd's *Jefferson: A Novel* (New York, 1993) is a fine work of fiction. Barbara Chase-Riboud's *Sally Hemings: A Novel* offers a fictionalized account of the alleged affair between Jefferson and Sally Hemings. Hardly less fictional, but claiming not to be, is Fawn M. Brodie's potted psychobiography, *Thomas Jefferson: An Intimate History* (New York, 1974). The film "Jefferson in Paris" (Merchant Ivory films, 1995) is colorful and entertaining, but by no means always reliable as an account of Jefferson's love-life or anything else. Much more reliable is Ken Burns's television documentary, "Jefferson" (PBS-TV, 1997), now available on video cassette.

# I  A Private Man in Public Life

## 1.1 To Giovanni Fabbroni

Williamsburg in Virginia, June 8, 1778

Dear Sir, – Your letter of Sep. 15. 1777 from Paris comes safe to hand. We have not however had the pleasure of seeing Mr. De Cenis, the bearer of it in this country, as he joined the army in Pennsylvania as soon as he arrived. I should have taken particular pleasure in serving him on your recommendation. From the kind anxiety expressed in your letter as well as from other sources of information we discover that our enemies have filled Europe with Thrasonic accounts of victories they had never won and conquests they were fated never to make. While these accounts alarmed our friends in Europe they afforded us diversion. We have long been out of all fear for the event of the war. I enclose you a list of the killed, wounded, and captives of the enemy from the commencement of hostilities at Lexington in April, 1775, until November, 1777, since which there has been no event of any consequence. This is the best history of the war which can be brought within the compass of a letter. I believe the account to be near the truth, tho' it is difficult to get at the numbers lost by an enemy with absolute precision. Many of the articles have been communicated to us from England as taken from the official returns made by their General. I wish it were in my power to send you as just an account of our loss. But this cannot be done without an application to the war office which being in another county is at this time out of my reach. I think that upon the whole it has been about one half the number lost by them, in some instances more, but in others less. This difference is ascribed to our superiority in taking aim when we fire; every soldier in our army having been intimate with his gun from his infancy. If there could have been a doubt before as to the event of the war it is now totally removed by the interposition of France, & the generous alliance she has entered into with us. Tho' much of my time is employed in the councils of America I have yet a little leisure to indulge my fondness for philosophical studies. I could wish to correspond with you on subjects of that kind. It might not be unacceptable to you to be informed for instance of the true power of our climate as discoverable from the thermometer, from the force & direction of the winds, the quantity of rain, the plants which grow without shelter in winter &c. On the other hand we should be much pleased with co-temporary observations on the same particulars in your country, which will give us a comparative view of the two climates. Farenheit's thermometer is the only one in use with us, I make my daily observations as early as possible in the morning & again about 4 o'clock in the afternoon, these generally showing the maxima of cold & heat in the course of 24 hours. I wish I could gratify your Botanical taste; but I am acquainted with nothing more than the first principles of that science; yet myself & my friends may furnish you with any Botanical subjects which this country affords, and are not to be had with you; and I shall take pleasure in procuring them when pointed out by you. The greatest difficulty will be the means of conveyance during the continuance of the war.

If there is a gratification which I envy any people in this world, it is to your country its music. This is the favorite passion of my soul, & fortune has cast my lot in a country where it is in a state of deplorable barbarism. From the line of life in which we conjecture you to be, I have for some time lost the hope of seeing you here. Should the event prove so, I shall ask your assistance in procuring a substitute, who may be a proficient in singing, & on the Harpsichord. I should be contented to receive such an one two or three years hence, when it is hoped he may come more safely and find here a greater plenty of those useful things which commerce alone can furnish. The bounds of an American fortune will not admit the indulgence of a domestic band of musicians, yet I have thought that a passion for music might be reconciled with that economy which we are obliged to observe. I retain for instance among my domestic servants a gardener (*Ortolans*), a weaver (*Tessitore di lino e lin*), a cabinet maker (*Stipeltaio*) and a stone cutter (*Scalpellino laborante in piano*) to which I would add a *vigneron*. In a country where like yours music is cultivated and practised by every class of men I suppose there might be found persons of those trades who could perform on the French horn, clarinet or hautboy & bassoon, so that one might have a band of two French horns, two clarinets, & hautboys & a bassoon, without enlarging their domestic expenses. A certainty of employment for a half dozen years, and at the end of that time to find them if they choose a conveyance to their own country might induce them to come here on reasonable wages.

Without meaning to give you trouble, perhaps it might be practicable for you in [your] ordinary intercourse with your people, to find out such men disposed to come to America. Sobriety and good nature would be desirable parts of their characters. If you think such a plan practicable, and will be so kind as to inform me what will be necessary to be done on my part I will take care that it shall be done. The necessary expenses, when informed of them, I can remit before they are wanting, to any port in France, with which country alone we have safe correspondence. I am Sir with much esteem your humble servant.

Ford II: 156–60

## 1.2 To James Monroe

Monticello, May 20, 1782

Dear Sir, – I have been gratified with the receipt of your two favours of the 6th. and 11th. inst. It gives me pleasure that your county has been wise enough to enlist your talents into their service. I am much obliged by the kind wishes you express of seeing me also in Richmond, and am always mortified when any thing is expected from me which I cannot fulfill, and more especially if it relate to the public service. Before I ventured to declare to my countrymen my determination to retire from public employment I examined well my heart to know whether it were thoroughly cured of every principle of political ambition, whether no lurking particle remained which might leave me uneasy when reduced within the limits of mere private life. I became satisfied that every fibre of that passion was thoroughly eradicated. I examined also in other views my right to withdraw. I considered that I had been thirteen years engaged in public service, that during that time I had so totally abandoned all attention to my private affairs as to permit them to run into great disorder and ruin, that I had now a family advanced to years which require my attention and instruction, that to this was added the hopeful offspring of a deceased friend whose memory must be for ever dear to me who have no other reliance for being rendered useful to themselves and their country, that by a constant sacrifice of time, labour, loss, parental and friendly duties, I had been so far from gaining the affection of my countrymen which was the only reward I ever asked or could have felt, that I had even lost the small estimation I before possessed: that however I might have comforted myself under the disapprobation of the well-meaning but uninformed people yet that of their representatives was a shock on which I had not calculated: that this indeed had been followed by an exculpatory declaration, but in the mean time I had been suspected and suspended in the eyes of the world without the least hint then or afterwards made public which might restrain them from supposing I stood arraigned for treasons of the heart and not mere weaknesses of the head. And I felt that these injuries, for such they have been since acknowleged, had inflicted a wound on my spirit which will only be cured by the all-healing grave. If reason and inclination unite in justifying my retirement, the laws of my country are equally in favor of it. Whether the state may command the political services of all it's members to an indefinite extent, or if these be among the rights never wholly ceded to the public power, is a question which I do not find expressly decided in England. Obiter dictums on the subject I have indeed met with, but the complection of the times in which these have dropped would generally answer them, and besides that, this species of authority is not acknowleged in our profession. In this country however since the present government has been established the point has been settled by uniform, pointed, and multiplied precedents. Offices of every kind, and given by every power, have been daily and hourly declined and resigned from the declaration of independance to this moment. The General assembly has accepted these without discrimination of office, and without ever questioning them in point of right. If a difference between the office of a delegate and any other could ever have been supposed, yet in the case of Mr. Thompson Mason who declined the office of delegate and was permitted by the house so to do that supposition has been proved to be groundless. But indeed no such distinction of offices can be admitted; reason and the opinions of the lawyers putting all on a footing as to this question and giving to the delegate the aid of all the precedents of the refusal of other offices, the law then does not warrant the assumption of such a power by the state over it's members. For if it does where is that law? Nor yet does reason, for tho' I will admit that this does subject every individual if called on to an equal tour of political duty yet it can never go so far as to submit to it his whole existence. If we are made in some degree for others, yet in a greater are we made for ourselves. It were contrary to feeling and indeed ridiculous to suppose a man had less right in himself than one of his neighbors or all of them put together. This would be slavery and not that liberty which the bill of rights has made inviolable and for the preservation of which our government has been changed. Nothing could so completely divest us of that liberty as the establishment of the opinion that the state has a *perpetual* right to the services of all it's members. This to men of certain ways of thinking would be to annihilate the blessing of existence; to contradict the giver of life who gave it for happiness and not for wretchedness, and certainly to such it were better that they had never been born. However with these I may think public service and private misery inseparably linked together, I have not the vanity to count myself among those whom the state would think worth oppressing with perpetual service. I have received a sufficient memento to the contrary. I am persuaded that having hitherto dedicated to them the whole of the active and useful part of my life I shall be permitted to pass the rest in mental quiet. I hope too that I did not mistake the mode any more than the matter of right when I preferred a simple act of renunciation to the taking sanctuary under those many disqualifications (provided by the law for other purposes indeed but) which afford asylum also for rest to the wearied. I dare say you did not expect by the few words you dropped on the right of renunciation to expose yourself to the fatigue of so long a letter, but I wished you to see that if I had done wrong I had been betrayed by a semblance of right at least.

I take the liberty of inclosing to you a letter for Genl. Chattlux for which you will readily find means of conveyance. But I meant to give you more trouble with the one to Pelham who lives in the neighborhood of Manchester and to ask the favor of you to send it by your servant express which I am in hopes may be done without absenting him from your person but during those hours in which you will be engaged in the house. I am anxious that it should be received immediately. Mrs. Jefferson has added another daughter to our family. She has been ever since and still continues very dangerously ill. It will give me great pleasure to see you here whenever you can favor us with your company. You will find me still busy but in lighter occupations. But in these and all others you will find me to retain a due sense of your friendship & to be with sincere esteem Dr. Sir Your mo. ob. & mo. hble servt.

Ford III: 56–60

## 1.3 To Archibald Stuart

Paris, January 25, 1786

Dear Sir, – I have received your favor of the 17th of October, which, though you have mentioned it as the third you have written me, is the first that has come to hand. I sincerely thank you for the communication it contains. Nothing is so grateful to me, at this distance, as details, both great and small, of what is passing in my own country. Of the latter, we receive little here, because they either escape my correspondents, or are thought unworthy of notice. This, however, is a very mistaken opinion, as every one may observe, by recollecting, that when he has been long absent from his neighborhood, the small news of that is the most pleasing, and occupies his first attention, either when he meets with a person from thence, or returns thither himself. I still hope, therefore, that the letter, in which you have been so good as to give me the minute occurrences in the neighborhood of Monticello, may yet come to hand, and I venture to rely on the many proofs of friendship I have received from you, for a continuance of your favors. This will be the more meritorious, as I have nothing to give you in exchange.

The quiet of Europe, at this moment, furnishes little which can attract your notice. Nor will that quiet be soon disturbed, at least for the current year. Perhaps it hangs on the life of the King of Prussia, and that hangs by a very slender thread. American reputation in Europe is not such as to be flattering to its citizens. Two circumstances are particularly objected to us: the non-payment of our debts, and the want of energy in our government. These discourage a connection with us. I own it to be my opinion, that good will arise from the destruction of our credit. I see nothing else which can restrain our disposition to luxury, and to the change of those manners which alone can preserve republican government. As it is impossible to prevent credit, the best way would be to cure its ill effects, by giving an instantaneous recovery to the creditor. This would be reducing purchases on credit to purchases for ready money. A man would then see a prison painted on everything he wished, but had not ready money to pay for.

I fear from an expression in your letter, that the people of Kentucky think of separating, not only from Virginia (in which they are right), but also from the confederacy. I own, I should think this a most calamitous event, and such a one as every good citizen should set himself against. Our present federal limits are not too large for good government, nor will the increase of votes in Congress produce any ill effect. On the contrary, it will drown the little divisions at present existing there. Our confederacy must be viewed as the nest, from which all America, North and South, is to be peopled. We should take care, too, not to think it for the interest of that great Continent to press too soon on the Spaniards. Those countries cannot be in better hands. My fear is, that they are too feeble to hold them till our population can be sufficiently advanced to gain it from them, piece by piece. The navigation of the Mississippi we must have. This is all we are, as yet, ready to receive. I have made acquaintance with a very sensible, candid gentleman here, who was in South America during the revolt which took place there,[1] while our Revolution was going on. He says, that those disturbances (of which we scarcely heard anything) cost, on both sides, an hundred thousand lives.

I have made a particular acquaintance here, with Monsieur de Buffon,[2] and have a great desire to give him the best idea I can of our elk. Perhaps your situation may enable you to aid me in this. You could not oblige me more than by sending me the horns, skeleton, and skin of an elk, were it possible to procure them. The most desirable form of receiving them would be, to have the skin slit from the under jaw along the belly to the tail, and down the thighs to the knee, to take the animal out, leaving the legs and hoofs, the bones of the head, and the horns attached to the skin. By sewing up the belly, &c., and stuffing the skin, it would present the form

---

[1] TJ refers to the revolt in Peru led by Tupac Amaru (José Gabriel Condorcanqui, 1742?–81). In 1776 he petitioned the Spanish government, asking that Indians be exempted from forced labor in local mines; the petition was rejected; the conflict escalated into armed resistance and full-scale revolt in which many thousands of Indians were killed. Tupac was captured and executed in 1781. – *Eds.*

[2] Georges Louis Leclerc, Comte de Buffon (1707–88), French naturalist and author of *Histoire Naturelle* (Paris, 1770–99), 44 vols. – *Eds.*

of the animal. However, as an opportunity of doing this is scarcely to be expected, I shall be glad to receive them detached, packed in a box, and sent to Richmond, to the care of Dr. Currie. Everything of this kind is precious here. And to prevent my adding to your trouble, I must close my letter, with assurances of the esteem and attachment with which I am, dear Sir, your friend and servant.

Ford iv: 187–90

## 1.4 To Maria Cosway

Paris, October 12, 1786

My Dear Madam, – Having performed the last sad office of handing you into your carriage at the pavillon de St. Denis, and seen the wheels get actually into motion, I turned on my heel & walked, more dead than alive, to the opposite door, where my own was awaiting me. Mr. Danquerville was missing. He was sought for, found, & dragged down stairs. We were crammed into the carriage, like recruits for the Bastille, & not having soul enough to give orders to the coachman, he presumed Paris our destination, & drove off. After a considerable interval, silence was broke with a "*Je suis vraiment affligé du départ de ces bons gens.*" This was a signal for a mutual confession of distress. We began immediately to talk of Mr. & Mrs. Cosway, of their goodness, their talents, their amiability; & tho we spoke of nothing else, we seemed hardly to have entered into matter when the coachman announced the rue St. Denis, & that we were opposite Mr. Danquerville's. He insisted on descending there & traversing a short passage to his lodgings. I was carried home. Seated by my fireside, solitary & sad, the following dialogue took place between my Head & my Heart:

> *Head.* Well, friend, you seem to be in a pretty trim.
> *Heart.* I am indeed the most wretched of all earthly beings. Overwhelmed with grief, every fibre of my frame distended beyond its natural powers to bear, I would willingly meet whatever catastrophe should leave me no more to feel or to fear.
> *Head.* These are the eternal consequences of your warmth & precipitation. This is one of the scrapes into which you

are ever leading us. You confess your follies indeed; but still you hug & cherish them; & no reformation can be hoped, where there is no repentance.

*Heart.* Oh, my friend! this is no moment to upbraid my foibles. I am rent into fragments by the force of my grief! If you have any balm, pour it into my wounds; if none, do not harrow them by new torments. Spare me in this awful moment! At any other I will attend with patience to your admonitions.

*Head.* On the contrary I never found that the moment of triumph with you was the moment of attention to my admonitions. While suffering under your follies, you may perhaps be made sensible of them, but, the paroxysm over, you fancy it can never return. Harsh therefore as the medicine may be, it is my office to administer it. You will be pleased to remember that when our friend Trumbull used to be telling us of the merits & talents of these good people, I never ceased whispering to you that we had no occasion for new acquaintance; that the greater their merits & talents, the more dangerous their friendship to our tranquillity, because the regret at parting would be greater.

*Heart.* Accordingly, Sir, this acquaintance was not the consequence of my doings. It was one of your projects which threw us in the way of it. It was you, remember, & not I, who desired the meeting at Legrand & Molinos. I never trouble myself with domes nor arches. The Halle aux bleds might have rotted down before I should have gone to see it. But you, forsooth, who are eternally getting us to sleep with your diagrams & crotchets, must go & examine this wonderful piece of architecture. And when you had seen it, oh! it was the most superb thing on earth! What you had seen there was worth all you had yet seen in Paris! I thought so too. But I meant it of the lady & gentleman to whom we had been presented; & not of a parcel of sticks & chips put together in pens. You then, Sir, & not I, have been the cause of the present distress.

*Head.* It would have been happy for you if my diagrams & crotchets had gotten you to sleep on that day, as you are pleased to say they eternally do. My visit to Legrand & Molinos had public utility for it's object. A market is to be built in Richmond. What a commodious plan is that of Legrand & Molinos; especially if we put on it the noble dome of the Halle aux bleds. If such a bridge as they shewed us can be thrown across the Schuylkill at Philadelphia, the floating bridges taken up & the navigation of that river opened, what a copious resource will be added, of wood & provisions, to warm & feed the poor of that city? While I was occupied with these objects, you were dilating with your new acquaintances, & contriving how to prevent a separation from them. Every soul of you had an engagement for the day. Yet all these were to be sacrificed, that you might dine together. Lying messengers were to be despatched into every quarter of the city, with apologies for your breach of engagement. You particularly had the effrontery to send word to the Dutchess Danville that, on the moment we were setting out to dine with her, despatches came to hand which required immediate attention. You wanted me to invent a more ingenious excuse; but I knew you were getting into a scrape, & I would have nothing to do with it. Well, after dinner to St. Cloud, from St. Cloud to Ruggieri's, from Ruggieri to Krumfoltz, & if the day had been as long as a Lapland summer day, you would still have contrived means among you to have filled it.

*Heart.*    Oh! my dear friend, how you have revived me by recalling to my mind the transactions of that day! How well I remember them all, & that when I came home at night & looked back to the morning, it seemed to have been a month agone. Go on then, like a kind comforter & paint to me the day we went to St. Germains. How beautiful was every object! the Port de Reuilly, the hills along the Seine, the rainbows of the machine of Marly, the terrace of St. Germains, the *châteaux*, the gardens, the statues of Marly, the pavillon of Lucienne. Recollect too Madrid, Bagatelle, the King's garden, the Dessert. How grand the idea excited by the remains of such a column! The spiral staircase too was beautiful. Every moment was filled with something agreeable. The wheels of time moved on with a rapidity of which those of our carriage gave but a faint idea. And yet in the evening when one took a retrospect of the day, what a mass of happiness had we travelled over! Retrace all those scenes to me, my good companion, & I will forgive the unkindness with which you were chiding me. The day we went to St. Germains was a little too warm, I think; was it not?

*Head.*   Thou art the most incorrigible of all the beings that ever sinned! I reminded you of the follies of the first day, intending to deduce from thence some useful lessons for you, but instead of listening to these, you kindle at the recollection, you retrace the whole series with a fondness which shews you want nothing but the opportunity to act it over again. I often told you during its course that you were imprudently engaging your affections under circumstances that must have cost you a great deal of pain: that the persons indeed were of the greatest merit, possessing good sense, good humour, honest hearts, honest manners, & eminence in a lovely art; that the lady had moreover qualities & accomplishments, belonging to her sex, which might form a chapter apart for her: such as music, modesty, beauty, & that softness of disposition which is the ornament of her sex & charm of ours, but that all these considerations would increase the pang of separation: that their stay here was to be short: that you rack our whole system when you are parted from those you love, complaining that such a separation is worse than death, inasmuch as this ends our sufferings, whereas that only begins them: & that the separation would in this instance be the more severe as you would probably never see them again.

*Heart.*   But they told me they would come back again the next year.

*Head.*   But in the meantime see what you suffer: & their return too depends on so many circumstances that if you had a grain of prudence you would not count upon it. Upon the whole it is improbable & therefore you should abandon the idea of ever seeing them again.

*Heart.*   May heaven abandon me if I do!

*Head.*   Very well. Suppose then they come back. They are to stay two months, & when these are expired, what is to follow? Perhaps you flatter yourself they may come to America?

*Heart.*   God only knows what is to happen. I see nothing impossible in that supposition. And I see things wonderfully contrived sometimes to make us happy. Where could they find such objects as in America for the exercise of their enchanting art? especially the lady, who paints landscapes so inimitably. She wants only subjects worthy of immortality to render her pencil immortal. The Falling Spring, the Cascade of Niagara, the Passage of the Potowmac through the Blue Mountains, the Natural bridge. It is worth a voyage across the Atlantic to see these objects; much more to paint, and make them, & thereby ourselves, known to all ages. And our own dear Monticello, where has nature spread so rich a mantle under the eye? mountains, forests, rocks, rivers. With what majesty do we there ride above the storms! How sublime to look down into the workhouse of nature, to see her clouds, hail, snow, rain, thunder, all fabricated at our feet! and the glorious sun when rising as if out of a distant water, just gilding the tops of the mountains, & giving life to all nature! I hope in God no circumstance may ever make either seek an asylum from grief! With what sincere sympathy I would open every cell of my composition to receive the effusion of their woes! I would pour my tears into their wounds: & if a drop of balm could be found on the top of the Cordilleras, or at the remotest sources of the Missouri, I would go thither myself to seek & to bring it. Deeply practised in the school of affliction, the human heart knows no joy which I have not lost, no sorrow of which I have not drunk! Fortune can present no grief of unknown form to me! Who then can so softly bind up the wound of another as he who has felt the same wound himself? But Heaven forbid they should ever know a sorrow! Let us turn over another leaf, for this has distracted me.

*Head.*   Well. Let us put this possibility to trial then on another point. When you consider the character which is given of our country by the lying newspapers of London, & their credulous copyers in other countries; when you reflect that all Europe is made to believe we are a lawless *banditti,* in a state of absolute anarchy, cutting one another's throats, & plundering without distinction, how can you expect that any reasonable creature would venture among us?

*Heart.*   But you & I know that all this is false: that there is not a country on earth where there is greater tranquillity, where the laws are milder, or better obeyed: where every one is more attentive to his own business, or meddles less with that of others: where strangers are better received, more hospitably treated, & with a more sacred respect.

*Head.* True, you & I know this, but your friends do not know it.

*Heart.* But they are sensible people who think for themselves. They will ask of impartial foreigners who have been among us, whether they saw or heard on the spot any instances of anarchy. They will judge too that a people occupied as we are in opening rivers, digging navigable canals, making roads, building public schools, establishing academies, erecting busts & statues to our great men, protecting religious freedom, abolishing sanguinary punishments, reforming & improving our laws in general, they will judge I say for themselves whether these are not the occupations of a people at their ease, whether this is not better evidence of our true state than a London newspaper, hired to lie, & from which no truth can ever be extracted but by reversing everything it says.

*Head.* I did not begin this lecture my friend with a view to learn from you what America is doing. Let us return then to our point. I wished to make you sensible how imprudent it is to place your affections, without reserve, on objects you must so soon lose, & whose loss when it comes must cost you such severe pangs. Remember the last night. You knew your friends were to leave Paris to-day. This was enough to throw you into agonies. All night you tossed us from one side of the bed to the other. No sleep, no rest. The poor crippled wrist too, never left one moment in the same position, now up, now down, now here, now there; was it to be wondered at if it's pains returned? The Surgeon then was to be called, & to be rated as an ignoramus because he could not divine the cause of this extraordinary change. *In fine,* my friend, you must mend your manners. This is not a world to live at random in as you do. To avoid those eternal distresses, to which you are forever exposing us, you must learn to look forward before you take a step which may interest our peace. Everything in this world is a matter of calculation. Advance then with caution, the balance in your hand. Put into one scale the pleasures which any object may offer; but put fairly into the other the pains which are to follow, & see which preponderates. The making an acquaintance is not a matter of indifference. When a new one is proposed to you, view it all round. Consider what advantages it presents, & to what inconveniences it may expose you. Do not bite at the bait of pleasure till you know there is no hook beneath it. The art of life is the art of avoiding pain: & he is the best pilot who steers clearest of the rocks & shoals with which he is beset. Pleasure is always before us; but misfortune is at our side: while running after that, this arrests us. The most effectual means of being secure against pain is to retire within ourselves, & to suffice for our own happiness. Those, which depend on ourselves, are the only pleasures a wise man will count on: for nothing is ours which another may deprive us of. Hence the inestimable value of intellectual pleasures. Even in our power, always leading us to something new, never cloying, we ride serene & sublime above the concerns of this mortal world, contemplating truth & nature, matter & motion, the laws which bind up their existence, & that eternal being who made & bound them up by those laws. Let this be our employ. Leave the bustle & tumult of society to those who have not talents to occupy themselves without them. Friendship is but another name for an alliance with the follies & the misfortunes of others. Our own share of miseries is sufficient: why enter then as volunteers into those of another? Is there so little gall poured into our cup that we must needs help to drink that of our neighbor? A friend dies or leaves us: we feel as if a limb was cut off. He is sick: we must watch over him, & participate of his pains. His fortune is shipwrecked; ours must be laid under contribution. He loses a child, a parent, or a partner: we must mourn the loss as if it were our own.

*Heart.*   And what more sublime delight than to mingle tears with one whom the hand of heaven hath smitten! to watch over the bed of sickness, & to beguile it's tedious & it's painful moments! to share our bread with one to whom misfortune has left none! This world abounds indeed with misery: to lighten it's burthen we must divide it with one another. But let us now try the virtues of your mathematical balance, & as you have put into one scale the burthen of friendship, let me put it's comforts into the other. When languishing then under disease, how grateful is the solace of our friends! how are we penetrated with their assiduities & attentions! how much are we supported by their encouragements & kind offices! When heaven has taken from us some object of our love, how sweet is it to have a bosom whereon to recline our heads, & into which we may pour the torrent of our tears! Grief, with such a comfort, is almost a luxury! In a life where we are perpetually exposed to want & accident, yours is a wonderful proposition, to insulate ourselves, to retire from all aid, & to wrap ourselves in the mantle of self-sufficiency! For assuredly nobody will care for him who cares for nobody. But friendship is precious, not only in the shade but in the sunshine of life; & thanks to a benevolent arrangement of things, the greater part of life is sunshine. I will recur for proof to the days we have lately passed. On these indeed the sun shone brightly. How gay did the face of nature appear! Hills, valleys, *châteaux*, gardens, rivers, every object wore it's liveliest hue! Whence did they borrow it? From the presence of our charming companion. They were pleasing, because she seemed pleased. Alone, the scene would have been dull & insipid: the participation of it with her gave it relish. Let the gloomy monk, sequestered from the world, seek unsocial pleasures in the bottom of his cell! Let the sublimated philosopher grasp visionary happiness while pursuing phantoms dressed in the garb of truth! Their supreme wisdom is supreme folly; & they mistake for happiness the mere absence of pain. Had they ever felt the solid pleasure of one generous spasm of the heart, they would exchange for it all the frigid speculations of their lives, which you have been vaunting in such elevated terms. Believe me then my friend, that that is a miserable arithmetic which could estimate friendship at nothing, or at less than nothing. Respect for you has induced me to enter into this discussion, & to hear principles uttered which I detest & abjure. Respect for myself now obliges me to recall you into the proper limits of your office. When nature assigned us the same habitation, she gave us over it a divided empire. To you she allotted the field of science; to me that of morals. When the circle is to be squared, or the orbit of a comet to be traced; when the arch of greatest strength, or the solid of least resistance is to be investigated, take up the problem; it is yours; nature has given me no cognizance of it. In like manner, in denying to you the feelings of sympathy, of benevolence, of gratitude, of justice, of love, of friendship, she has excluded you from their controul. To these she has adapted the mechanism of the heart. Morals were too essential to the happiness of man to be risked on the incertain combinations of the head. She laid their foundation therefore in sentiment, not in science. That she gave to all, as necessary to all: this to a few only, as sufficing with a few. I know indeed that you pretend authority to the sovereign controul of our conduct in all its parts: & a respect for your grave saws & maxims, a desire to do what is right, has sometimes induced me to conform to your counsels. A few facts however which I can readily recall to your memory, will suffice to prove to you that nature has not organized you for our moral direction. When the poor wearied souldier whom we overtook at Chickahomony with his pack on his back, begged us to let him get up behind our chariot, you began to calculate that the road was full of souldiers, & that if all should be taken up our horses would fail in their journey. We drove on therefore. But soon becoming sensible you had made me do wrong, that tho we cannot relieve all the distressed we should relieve as many as we can, I turned about to take up the souldier; but he had entered a bye path, & was no more to be found; & from that moment to this I could never find him out to ask his forgiveness. Again, when the poor woman came to ask a charity in Philadelphia, you whispered that she looked like a drunkard, & that half a dollar was enough to give her for the ale-house. Those who want the dispositions to give, easily find reasons why they ought not to give. When I sought her out afterwards, & did what I should have done at first, you know that she employed the money immediately towards placing her child at school. If our country, when pressed with wrongs at the point of the bayonet, had been governed by it's heads instead of it's hearts, where should we have been now? Hanging on

a gallows as high as Haman's. You began to calculate &
to compare wealth and numbers: we threw up a few pul-
sations of our warmest blood; we supplied enthusiasm
against wealth and numbers; we put our existence to the
hazard when the hazard seemed against us, and we saved
our country; justifying at the same time the ways of
Providence, whose precept is to do always what is right,
and leave the issue to him. In short, my friend, as far as
my recollection serves me, I do not know that I ever did
a good thing on your suggestion, or a dirty one without
it. I do forever then disclaim your interference in my
province. Fill papers as you please with triangles &
squares: try how many ways you can hang & combine
them together. I shall never envy nor controul your sublime delights. But leave me to decide when & where
friendships are to be contracted. You say I contract them
at random. So you said the woman at Philadelphia was a
drunkard. I receive no one into my esteem till I know
they are worthy of it. Wealth, title, office, are no recommendations to my friendship. On the contrary great
good qualities are requisite to make amends for their
having wealth, title, & office. You confess that in the
present case I could not have made a worthier choice.
You only object that I was so soon to lose them. We are
not immortal ourselves, my friend; how can we expect
our enjoyments to be so? We have no rose without it's
thorn; no pleasure without alloy. It is the law of our
existence; & we must acquiesce. It is the condition
annexed to all our pleasures, not by us who receive, but
by him who gives them. True, this condition is pressing
cruelly on me at this moment. I feel more fit for death
than life. But when I look back on the pleasures of which
it is the consequence, I am conscious they were worth
the price I am paying. Notwithstanding your endeavours
too to damp my hopes, I comfort myself with expectations of their promised return. Hope is sweeter than
despair, & they were too good to mean to deceive me. In
the summer, said the gentleman; but in the spring, said
the lady: & I should love her forever, were it only for
that! Know then, my friend, that I have taken these good
people into my bosom; that I have lodged them in the
warmest cell I could find: that I love them, & will

continue to love them through life: that if fortune should
dispose them on one side the globe, & me on the other,
my affections shall pervade it's whole mass to reach
them. Knowing then my determination, attempt not to
disturb it. If you can at any time furnish matter for their
amusement, it will be the office of a good neighbor to do
it. I will in like manner seize any occasion which may
offer to do the like good turn for you with Condorcet,
Rittenhouse, Madison, La Cretelle, or any other of those
worthy sons of science whom you so justly prize.

I thought this a favorable proposition whereon to rest the issue
of the dialogue. So I put an end to it by calling for my night-cap.
Methinks I hear you wish to heaven I had called a little sooner, &
so spared you the *ennui* of such a sermon. I did not interrupt them
sooner because I was in a mood for hearing sermons. You too were
the subject; & on such a thesis I never think the theme long; not
even if I am to write it, and that slowly & awkwardly, as now,
with the left hand. But that you may not be discouraged from a
correspondence which begins so formidably, I will promise you on
my honour that my future letters shall be of a reasonable length. I
will even agree to express but half my esteem for you, for fear of
cloying you with too full a dose. But, on your part, no curtailing.
If your letters are as long as the bible, they will appear short to me.
Only let them be brimful of affection. I shall read them with the
dispositions with which Arlequin, in *Les deux billets* spelt the words
"*je t'aime*," and wished that the whole alphabet had entered into
their composition.

We have had incessant rains since your departure. These make
me fear for your health, as well as that you had an uncomfortable
journey. The same cause has prevented me from being able to give
you any account of your friends here. This voyage to Fontainebleau
will probably send the Count de Moustier & the Marquise de
Brehan to America. Danquerville promised to visit me, but has not
done it as yet, De la Tude comes sometimes to take family soup
with me, & entertains me with anecdotes of his five & thirty years
imprisonment. How fertile is the mind of man which can make the
Bastile & Dungeon of Vincennes yield interesting anecdotes! You
know this was for making four verses on Mme de Pompadour. But
I think you told me you did not know the verses. They were these:

*"Sans esprit, sans sentiment, Sans être belle, ni neuve, En France on peut avoir le premier amant: Pompadour en est l'épreuve."* I have read the memoir of his three escapes. As to myself my health is good, except my wrist which mends slowly, & my mind which mends not at all, but broods constantly over your departure. The lateness of the season obliges me to decline my journey into the south of France. Present me in the most friendly terms to Mr. Cosway, & receive me into your own recollection with a partiality & a warmth, proportioned, not to my own poor merit, but to the sentiments of sincere affection & esteem with which I have the honour to be, my dear Madam, your most obedient humble servant.

Ford IV: 311–23

## 1.5 To Angelica Schuyler Church

Germantown, November 27, 1793

I have received, my very good friend, your kind letter of Aug. 19 with the extract from that of La Fayette, for whom my heart has been constantly bleeding. The influence of the United States has been put into action, as far as it could be either with decency or effect. But I fear that distance and difference of principle give little hold to Genl. Washington on the jailors of La Fayette. However his friends may be assured that our zeal has not been inactive. Your letter gives me the first information that our dear friend Madame de Corny has been, as to her fortune, among the victims of the times. Sad times indeed! and much lamented victim! I know no country where the remains of a fortune could place her so much at her ease as this, and where public esteem is so attached to worth, regardless of wealth. But our manners, and the state of society here are so different from those to which her habits have been formed, that she would lose more perhaps in that scale. – And Madame Cosway in a convent! I knew that, to much goodness of heart, she joined enthusiasm and religion: but I thought that very enthusiasm would have prevented her from shutting up her adoration of the god of the Universe within the walls of a cloyster; that she would rather have sought the *mountain-top.* How happy should I be that it were *mine* that you, she and Mde. de Corny would seek. You say indeed that you are coming to America. But I know that means New York. In the mean time I am going to Virginia. I have at length been able to fix that to the beginning of the new year. I am then to be liberated from the hated occupations of politics, and to sink into the bosom of my family, my farm and my books. I have my house to build, my feilds to form, and to watch for the happiness of those who labor for mine. I have one daughter married to a man of science, sense, virtue, and competence; in whom indeed I have nothing more to wish. They live with me. If the other shall be as fortunate in due process of time, I shall imagine myself as blessed as the most blessed of the patriarchs. Nothing could then withdraw my thoughts a moment from home, but the recollection of my friends abroad. I often put the question Whether yourself and Kitty will ever come to see your friends at Monticello? But it is my affection, and not my experience of things, which has leave to answer. And I am determined to believe the answer; because, in that belief, I find I sleep sounder and wake more chearful. *En attendant*, god bless you; accept the homage of my sincere & constant affection.

Ford VI: 454–6

## 1.6 To Dr. Benjamin Rush

Monticello, January 22, 1797

Dear Sir, – I received yesterday your kind favor of the 4th instant, and the eulogium it covered on the subject of our late invaluable friend Rittenhouse, and perused it with the avidity and approbation and the matter and manner of everything from your pen have long taught me to feel. I thank you too for your congratulations on the public call on me to undertake the second office in the United States, but still more for the justice you do me in viewing as I do the *escape* from the first. I have no wish to meddle again in public affairs, being happier at home than I can be anywhere else. Still less do I wish to engage in an office where it would be impossible to satisfy either friends or foes, and least of all at a moment when the storm is about to burst, which has been conjuring up for four years past. If I am to act however, a more tranquil and unoffending station could not have been found for me, nor one so analogous to the dispositions of my mind. It will give me philosophical evenings in the winter, and rural days in summer. I am indebted to the Philosophical Society a communication of some bones of an animal of the lion kind, but of most exaggerated size. What are we to think of a creature whose claws were eight inches long, when those of the lion are not $1\frac{1}{2}$ inches; whose thigh-bone was $6\frac{1}{4}$ diameter; when that of the lion is not $1\frac{1}{2}$ inches? Were not the things within the jurisdiction of the rule and compass, and of ocular inspection, credit to them could not be obtained. I have been disappointed in getting the femur as yet, but shall bring on the bones I have, if I can, for the Society, and have the pleasure of seeing you for a few days in the first week of March. I wish the usual delays of the publications of the Society may admit the addition to our new volume, of this interesting article, which it would be best to have first announced under the sanction of their authority. I am, with sincere esteem, dear Sir, your friend and servant.

L & B XI: 373–5

## 1.7 To Samuel Smith

Monticello, August 22, 1798

Dear Sir, – Your favor of Aug 4 came to hand by our last post, together with the "extract of a letter from a gentleman of Philadelphia, dated July 10," cut from a newspaper stating some facts which respect me. I shall notice these facts. The writer says that "the day after the last despatches were communicated to Congress, Bache, Leib, &c., and a Dr. Reynolds were *closeted* with me." If the receipt of visits in my public room, the door continuing free to every one who should call at the same time, may be called *closeting*, then it is true that I was *closeted* with every person who visited me; in no other sense is it true as to any person. I sometimes received visits from Mr. Bache & Dr. Leib. I received them always with pleasure, because they are men of abilities, and of principles the most friendly to liberty & our present form of government. Mr. Bache has another claim on my respect, as being the grandson of Dr. Franklin, the greatest man & ornament of the age and country in which he lived. Whether I was visited by Mr. Bache or Dr. Leib the day after the communication referred to, I do not remember. I know that all my motions at Philadelphia, here, and everywhere, are watched & recorded. Some of these spies, therefore, may remember better than I do, the dates of these visits. If they say these two gentlemen visited me on the day after the communications, as their trade proves their accuracy, I shall not contradict them, tho' I affirm that I do not recollect it. However, as to Dr. Reynolds I can be more particular, because I never saw him but once, which was on an introductory visit he was so kind as to pay me. This, I well remember, was before the communication alluded to, & that during the short conversation I had with him, not one word was said on the subject of any of the communications. Not that I should not have spoken freely on their subject to Dr. Reynolds, as I should also have done to the letter writer, or to any other person who should have introduced the subject. I know my own principles to be pure, & therefore am not ashamed of them. On the contrary, I wish them known, & therefore willingly express them to every one. They are the same I have acted on from the year 1775 to this day, and are the same, I am sure, with those of the great body of the American people. I only wish the real principles of those who censure mine were also known. But warring against those of the people, the delusion of the people is necessary to the dominant party. I see the extent to which that delusion has been already carried, and I see there is no length to which it may not be pushed by a party in possession of the revenues & the legal authorities of the U.S., for a short time indeed, but yet long enough to admit much particular mischief. There is no event, therefore, however atrocious, which may not be expected. I have contemplated every event which the Maratists of the day can perpetrate, and am prepared to meet every one in such a way, as shall not be derogatory either to the public liberty or my own personal honor. The letter writer says, I am "for peace; but it is only with France." He has told half the truth. He would have told the whole, if he had added England. I am for peace with both countries. I know that both of them have given, & are daily giving, sufficient cause of war; that in defiance of the laws of nations, they are every day trampling on the rights of all the neutral powers, whenever they can thereby do the least injury, either to the other. But, as I view a peace between France & England the ensuing winter to be certain, I have thought it would have been better for us to continue to bear from France through the present summer, what we have been bearing both from her & England these four years, and still continue to bear from England, and to have required indemnification in the hour of peace, when I verily believe it would have been yielded by both. This seems to be the plan of the other neutral nations; and whether this, or the commencing war on one of them, as we have done, would have been wisest, time & events must decide. But I am quite at a loss on what ground the letter writer can question the opinion, that France had no intention of making war on us, & was willing to treat with Mr. Gerry, when we have this from Taleyrand's letter, and from the written and verbal information of our envoys. It is true then, that, as with England, we might of right have chosen either peace or war, & have chosen peace, and prudently in my opinion, so with France, we might also of right have chosen either peace or war, & we have chosen war. Whether the choice may be a popular one in the other States, I know not. Here it certainly is not; & I have no doubt the whole American people will rally ere long to the same sentiment, & rejudge those who, at present, think they have all judgment in their own hands.

These observations will show you, how far the imputations in the paragraph sent me approach the truth. Yet they are not intended for a newspaper. At a very early period of my life, I determined never to put a sentence into any newspaper. I have religiously adhered to the resolution through my life, and have great reason to be contented with it. Were I to undertake to answer the calumnies of the newspapers, it would be more than all my own time, & that of 20 aids could effect. For while I should be answering one, twenty new ones would be invented. I have thought it better to trust to the justice of my countrymen, that they would judge me by what they *see* of my conduct on the stage where they have placed me, & what they knew of me *before* the epoch since which a particular party has supposed it might answer some view of theirs to vilify me in the public eye. Some, I know, will not reflect how apocryphal is the testimony of enemies so palpably betraying the views with which they give it. But this is an injury to which duty requires every one to submit whom the public think proper to call into it's councils. I thank you, my dear Sir, for the interest you have taken for me on this occasion. Though I have made up my mind not to suffer calumny to disturb my tranquillity, yet I retain all my sensibilities for

the approbation of the good & just. That is, indeed, the chief consolation for the hatred of so many, who, without the least personal
knowledge, & on the sacred evidence of Porcupine[1] & Fenno[2] alone,
cover me with their implacable hatred. The only return I will ever
make them, will be to do them all the good I can, in spite of their
teeth.

I have the pleasure to inform you that all your friends in this
quarter are well, and to assure you of the sentiments of sincere
esteem & respect with which I am, dear Sir, your friend and servant.

Ford VII: 275–80

## I.8 Services to My Country

[1800?]

I have sometimes asked myself whether my country is the better
for my having lived at all? I do not know that it is. I have been the
instrument of doing the following things; but they would have been
done by others; some of them, perhaps, a little better.

The Rivanna had never been used for navigation; scarcely an
empty canoe had ever passed down it. Soon after I came of age, I
examined its obstructions, set on foot a subscription for removing
them, got an Act of Assembly passed, and the thing effected, so as
to be used completely and fully for carrying down all our produce.

The Declaration of Independence.

I proposed the demolition of the church establishment, and the
freedom of religion. It could only be done by degrees; to wit, the
Act of 1776, c. 2, exempted dissenters from contributions to the
church, and left the church clergy to be supported by voluntary
contributions of their own sect; was continued from year to year,
and made perpetual 1779, c. 36. I prepared the act for religious
freedom in 1777, as part of the revisal, which was not reported to
the Assembly till 1779, and that particular law not passed till 1785,
and then by the efforts of Mr. Madison.

---

[1] "Peter Porcupine" was the pen-name of the prickly and ardently anti-Jeffersonian
Federalist spokesman, William Cobbett (1763–1835). – *Eds.*
[2] John Fenno was the publisher of the *Gazette of the United States* which represented Hamiltonian–Federalist, pro-British and anti-French Revolutionary
views, much to TJ's chagrin. – *Eds.*

The act putting an end to entails.

The act prohibiting the importation of slaves.

The act concerning citizens, and establishing the natural right of man to expatriate himself, at will.

The act changing the course of descents, and giving the inheritance to all the children, &c., equally, I drew as part of the revisal.

The act for apportioning crimes and punishments, part of the same work, I drew. When proposed to the legislature, by Mr. Madison, in 1785, it failed by a single vote. G. K. Taylor afterwards, in 1796, proposed the same subject; avoiding the adoption of any part of the diction of mine, the text of which had been studiously drawn in the technical terms of the law, so as to give no occasion for new questions by new expressions. When I drew mine, public labor was thought the best punishment to be substituted for death. But, while I was in France, I heard of a society in England, who had successfully introduced solitary confinement, and saw the drawing of a prison at Lyons, in France, formed on the idea of solitary confinement. And, being applied to by the Governor of Virginia for the plan of a Capitol and Prison, I sent him the Lyons plan, accompanying it with a drawing on a smaller scale, better adapted to our use. This was in June, 1786. Mr. Taylor very judiciously adopted this idea (which had now been acted on in Philadelphia, probably from the English model), and substituted labor in confinement, to the public labor proposed by the Committee of revisal; which themselves would have done, had they been to act on the subject again. The public mind was ripe for this in 1796, when Mr. Taylor proposed it, and ripened chiefly by the experiment in Philadelphia; whereas, in 1785, when it had been proposed to our assembly, they were not quite ripe for it.

In 1789 and 1790, I had a great number of olive plants, of the best kind, sent from Marseilles to Charleston, for South Carolina and Georgia. They were planted, and are flourishing; and, though not yet multiplied, they will be the germ of that cultivation in those States.

In 1790, I got a cask of heavy upland rice, from the river Denbigh, in Africa, about lat. 9° 30′ North, which I sent to Charleston, in hopes it might supersede the culture of the wet rice, which renders south Carolina and Georgia so pestilential through the summer. It was divided, and a part sent to Georgia. I know not whether it has been attended to in South Carolina; but it has spread in the upper parts of Georgia, so as to have become almost general, and is highly prized. Perhaps it may answer in Tennessee and Kentucky. The greatest service which can be rendered any country is, to add an useful plant to its culture; especially, a bread grain; next in value to bread is oil.

Whether the act for the more general diffusion of knowledge will ever be carried into complete effect, I know not. It was received by the legislature with great enthusiasm at first; and a small effort was made in 1796, by the act to establish public schools, to carry a part of it into effect, viz., that for the establishment of free English schools; but the option given to the courts has defeated the intention of the act.

Ford VII: 475–7

## 1.9 To Dr. Benjamin Rush

Monticello, September 23, 1800

Dear Sir, – I have to acknolege the receipt of your favor of Aug. 22, and to congratulate you on the healthiness of your city. Still Baltimore, Norfolk & Providence admonish us that we are not clear of our new scourge. When great evils happen, I am in the habit of looking out for what good may arise from them as consolations to us, and Providence has in fact so established the order of things, as that most evils are the means of producing some good. The yellow fever will discourage the growth of great cities in our nation, & I view great cities as pestilential to the morals, the health and the liberties of man. True, they nourish some of the elegant arts, but the useful ones can thrive elsewhere, and less perfection in the others, with more health, virtue & freedom, would be my choice.

I agree with you entirely, in condemning the mania of giving names to objects of any kind after persons still living. Death alone can seal the title of any man to this honor, by putting it out of his power to forfeit it. There is one other mode of recording merit, which I have often thought might be introduced, so as to gratify the living by praising the dead. In giving, for instance, a commission of chief justice to Bushrod Washington, it should be in consideration of his integrity, and science in the laws, and of the services

28

rendered to our country by his illustrious relation, &c. A commission to a descendant of Dr. Franklin, besides being in consideration of the proper qualifications of the person, should add that of the great services rendered by his illustrious ancestor, Benjamin Franklin, by the advancement of science, by inventions useful to man, &c. I am not sure that we ought to change all our names. And during the regal government, sometimes, indeed, they were given through adulation; but often also as the reward of the merit of the times, sometimes for services rendered the colony. Perhaps, too, a name when given, should be deemed a sacred property.

I promised you a letter on Christianity, which I have not forgotten. On the contrary, it is because I have reflected on it, that I find much more time necessary for it than I can at present dispose of. I have a view of the subject which ought to displease neither the rational Christian nor Deists, and would reconcile many to a character they have too hastily rejected. I do not know that it would reconcile the *genus irritable vatum* who are all in arms against me. Their hostility is on too interesting ground to be softened. The delusion into which the X.Y.Z. plot[1] shewed it possible to push the people; the successful experiment made under the prevalence of that delusion on the clause of the constitution, which, while it secured the freedom of the press, covered also the freedom of religion, had given to the clergy a very favorite hope of obtaining an establishment of a particular form of Christianity thro' the U.S.; and as every sect believes its own form the true one, every one perhaps hoped for his own, but especially the Episcopalians & Congregationalists. The returning good sense of our country threatens abortion to their hopes, & they believe that any portion of power confided to me, will be exerted in opposition to their schemes. And they believe rightly; for I have sworn upon the altar of god, eternal hostility against every form of tyranny over the mind of man. But this is all they have to fear from me: & enough too in their opinion, & this is the cause of their printing lying pamphlets against me, forging conversations for me with Mazzei, Bishop Madison, & c., which are absolute falsehoods without a circumstance of truth to

[1] Three Frenchmen – referred to in diplomatic dispatches as X, Y and Z – attempted to bribe members of an American delegation to France in 1797. The publication of these dispatches in 1798 created a furore in the U.S. – *Eds.*

rest on; falsehoods, too, of which I acquit Mazzei & Bishop Madison, for they are men of truth.

But enough of this: it is more than I have before committed to paper on the subject of all the lies that has been preached and printed against me. I have not seen the work of Sonnoni which you mention, but I have seen another work on Africa (Parke's), which I fear will throw cold water on the hopes of the friends of freedom. You will hear an account of an attempt at insurrection in this state. I am looking with anxiety to see what will be it's effect on our state. We are truly to be pitied. I fear we have little chance to see you at the Federal city or in Virginia, and as little at Philadelphia. It would be a great treat to receive you here. But nothing but sickness could effect that; so I do not wish it. For I wish you health and happiness, and think of you with affection. Adieu.

Ford VII: 458–61

## I.10 Rules of Etiquette [for President Jefferson's White House]

[1803]

I. In order to bring the members of society together in the first instance, the custom of the country has established that residents shall pay the first visit to strangers, and, among strangers, first comers to later comers, foreign and domestic; the character of stranger ceasing after the first visits. To this rule there is a single exception. Foreign ministers, from the necessity of making themselves known, pay the first visit to the ministers of the nation, which is returned.

II. When brought together in society, all are perfectly equal, whether foreign or domestic, titled or untitled, in or out of office.

All other observances are but exemplifications of these two principles.

I. 1st. The families of foreign ministers, arriving at the seat of government, receive the first visit from those of the national ministers, as from all other residents.

2d. Members of the Legislature and of the Judiciary, independent of their offices, have a right as strangers to receive the first visit.

II. 1st. No title being admitted here, those of foreigners give no precedence.

2d. Differences of grade among diplomatic members, gives no precedence.

3d. At public ceremonies, to which the government invites the presence of foreign ministers and their families, a convenient seat or station will be provided for them, with any other strangers invited and the families of the national ministers, each taking place as they arrive, and without any precedence.

4th. To maintain the principle of equality, or of *pêle mêle*, and prevent the growth of precedence out of courtesy, the members of the Executive will practice at their own houses, and recommend an adherence to the ancient usage of the country, of gentlemen in mass giving precedence to the ladies in mass, in passing from one apartment where they are assembled into another.

Ford VIII: 276–7

## I.II To P.-S. DuPont de Nemours

Washington, March 2, 1809

Dear Sir, – My last to you was of May the 2nd; since which I have received yours of May the 25th, June the 1st, July the 23rd, 24th, and September the 5th, and distributed the two pamphlets according to your desire. They are read with the delight which every thing from your pen gives.

After using every effort which could prevent or delay our being entangled in the war of Europe, that seems now our only resource. The edicts of the two belligerents, forbidding us to be seen on the ocean, we met by an embargo. This gave us time to call home our seamen, ships and property, to levy men and put our sea ports into a certain state of defence. We have now taken off the embargo, except as to France and England and their territories, because fifty millions of exports, annually sacrificed, are the treble of what war would cost us; besides that, by war we should take something, and lose less than at present. But to give you a true description of the state of things here, I must refer you to Mr. Coles, the bearer of this, my secretary, a most worthy, intelligent and well informed young man, whom I recommend to your notice, and conversation on our affairs. His discretion and fidelity may be relied on. I expect he will find you with Spain at your feet, but England still afloat, and a barrier to the Spanish colonies. But all these concerns I am now leaving to be settled by my friend Mr. Madison. Within a few days I retire to my family, my books and farms; and having gained the harbor myself, I shall look on my friends still buffeting the storm, with anxiety indeed, but not with envy. Never did a prisoner, released from his chains, feel such relief as I shall on shaking off the shackles of power. Nature intended me for the tranquil pursuits of science, by rendering them my supreme delight. But the enormities of the times in which I have lived, have forced me to take a part in resisting them, and to commit myself on the boisterous ocean of political passions. I thank God for the opportunity of retiring from them without censure, and carrying with me the most consoling proofs of public approbation. I leave every thing in the hands of men so able to take care of them, that if we are destined to meet misfortunes, it will be because no human wisdom could avert them. Should you return to the United States, perhaps your curiosity may lead you to visit the hermit of Monticello. He will receive you with affection and delight; hailing you in the mean time with his affectionate salutations, and assurances of constant esteem and respect.

P.S. If you return to us, bring a couple of pair of true-bred shepherd's dogs. You will add a valuable possession to a country now beginning to pay great attention to the raising sheep.

Randolph IV: 125–6

## I.12 To the Inhabitants of Albemarle County, in Virginia

April 3, 1809

Returning to the scenes of my birth and early life to the society of those with whom I was raised, and who have been ever dear to me, I receive, fellow citizens and neighbors, with inexpressible pleasure, the cordial welcome you are so good as to give me. Long absent on duties which the history of a wonderful era made incumbent on those called to them, the pomp, the turmoil, the bustle and splendor of office, have drawn but deeper sighs for the tranquil and irresponsible

occupations of private life, for the enjoyment of an affectionate intercourse with you, my neighbors and friends, and the endearments of
family love, which nature has given us all, as the sweetener of every
hour. For these I gladly lay down the distressing burthen of power,
and seek, with my fellow citizens, repose and safety under the watchful cares, the labors, and perplexities of younger and abler minds. The
anxieties you express to administer to my happiness, do, of themselves, confer that happiness; and the measure will be complete, if my
endeavors to fulfil my duties in the several public stations to which I
have been called, have obtained for me the approbation of my
country. The part which I have acted on the theatre of public life, has
been before them; and to their sentence I submit it; but the testimony
of my native country, of the individuals who have known me in private life, to my conduct in its various duties and relations, is the more
grateful, as proceeding from eye witnesses and observers, from triers
of the vicinage.[1] Of you, then, my neighbors, I may ask, in the face of
the world, "whose ox have I taken, or whom have I defrauded? Whom
have I oppressed, or of whose hand have I received a bribe to blind
mine eyes therewith?" On your verdict I rest with conscious security.
Your wishes for my happiness are received with just sensibility, and I
offer sincere prayers for your own welfare and prosperity.

Ford IX: 250

## I.13 To Charles Willson Peale

Poplar Forest, August 20, 1811

It is long, my dear Sir, since we have exchanged a letter. Our former
correspondence had always some little matter of business inter-
spersed; but this being at an end, I shall still be anxious to hear
from you sometimes, and to know that you are well and happy. I
know indeed that your system is that of contentment under any
situation. I have heard that you have retired from the city to a farm,
and that you give your whole time to that. Does not the museum
suffer? And is the farm as interesting? Here, as you know, we are
all farmers, but not in a pleasing style. We have so little labor in

---

[1] A "trier" is a juror – i.e. one who "tries" someone in a court – and a "vicinage"
is a vicinity, locale or neighborhood. – *Eds.*

33

proportion to our land that, although perhaps we make more profit from the same labor, we cannot give to our grounds that style of beauty which satisfies the eye of the amateur. Our rotations are corn, wheat, and clover, or corn, wheat, clover and clover, or wheat, corn, wheat, clover and clover; preceding the clover by a plastering. But some, instead of clover substitute mere rest, and all are slovenly enough. We are adding the care of Merino sheep. I have often thought that if heaven had given me choice of my position and calling, it should have been on a rich spot of earth, well watered, and near a good market for the productions of the garden. No occupation is so delightful to me as the culture of the earth, and no culture comparable to that of the garden. Such a variety of subjects, some one always coming to perfection, the failure of one thing repaired by the success of another, and instead of one harvest a continued one through the year. Under a total want of demand except for our family table, I am still devoted to the garden. But though an old man, I am but a young gardener.

Your application to whatever you are engaged in I know to be incessant. But Sundays and rainy days are always days of writing for the farmer. Think of me sometimes when you have your pen in hand, and give me information of your health and occupations; and be always assured of my great esteem and respect.

Washington VI: 6

## 1.14 To Dr. Benjamin Rush

Poplar Forest, December 5, 1811

Dear Sir, – While at Monticello I am so much engrossed by business or society, that I can only write on matters of strong urgency. Here I have leisure, as I have everywhere the disposition to think of my friends. I recur, therefore, to the subject of your kind letters relating to Mr. John Adams and myself, which a late occurrence has again presented to me. I communicated to you the correspondence which had parted Mrs. Adams and myself, in proof that I could not give friendship in exchange for such sentiments as she had recently taken up towards myself, and avowed and maintained in her letters to me. Nothing but a total renunciation of these could admit a reconciliation, and that could be cordial only in proportion as the return to ancient opinions was believed sincere. In these jaundiced sentiments of hers I had associated Mr. Adams, knowing the weight which her opinions had with him, and notwithstanding she declared in her letters that they were not communicated to him. A late incident has satisfied me that I wronged him as well as her, in not yielding entire confidence to this assurance on her part. Two of the Mr.—, my neighbors and friends, took a tour to the northward during the last summer. In Boston they fell into company with Mr. Adams, and by his invitation passed a day with him at Braintree. He spoke out to them everything which came uppermost, and as it occurred to his mind, without any reserve; and seemed most disposed to dwell on those things which happened during his own administration. He spoke of his *masters*, as he called his Heads of departments, as acting above his control, and often against his opinions. Among many other topics, he adverted to the unprincipled licentiousness of the press against myself, adding, "I always loved Jefferson, and still love him."

This is enough for me. I only needed this knowledge to revive towards him all the affections of the most cordial moments of our lives. Changing a single word only in Dr. Benjamin Franklin's character of him I knew him to be always an honest man, often a great one, but sometimes incorrect and precipitate in his judgments; and it is known to those who have ever heard me speak of Mr. Adams, that I have ever done him justice myself, and defended him when assailed by others, with the single exception as to political opinions. But with a man possessing so many other estimable qualities, why should we be dissocialized by mere differences of opinion in politics, in religion, in philosophy, or anything else? His opinions are as honestly formed as my own. Our different views of the same subject are the result of a difference in our organization and experience. I never withdrew from the society of any man on this account, although many have done it from me; much less should I do it from one with whom I had gone through, with hand and heart, so many trying scenes. I wish, therefore, but for an apposite occasion to express to Mr. Adams my unchanged affections for him. There is an awkwardness which hangs over the resuming a correspondence so long discontinued, unless something could arise which should call for a letter. Time and chance may perhaps generate such an occasion, of which I shall not be wanting in promptitude to avail myself. From this fusion of mutual affections, Mrs. Adams is of course separated. It will only be necessary that I never name her. In your letters to Mr. Adams, you can, perhaps, suggest my continued cordiality towards him, and knowing this, should an occasion of writing first present itself to him, he will perhaps avail himself of it, as I certainly will, should it first occur to me. No ground for jealousy now existing, he will certainly give fair play to the natural warmth of his heart. Perhaps I may open the way in some letter to my old friend Gerry, who I know is in habits of the greatest intimacy with him.

I have thus, my friend, laid open my heart to you, because you were so kind as to take an interest in healing again revolutionary affections, which have ceased in expression only, but not in their existence. God ever bless you, and preserve you in life and health.

L & B XIII: 114–17

## 1.15 To John Adams

Monticello, January 21, 1812

Dear Sir, – I thank you before hand (for they are not yet arrived) for the specimens of homespun you have been so kind as to forward me by post. I doubt not their excellence, knowing how far you are advanced in these things in your quarter. Here we do little in the fine way, but in coarser and middling goods a great deal. Every family in the country is a manufactory within itself, and is very generally able to make within itself all the stouter and middling stuffs for its own clothing and household use. We consider a sheep for every person in the family as sufficient to clothe it, in addition to the cotton, hemp and flax which we raise ourselves. For fine stuff we shall depend on your northern manufactories. Of these, that is to say, of company establishments, we have none. We use little machinery. The spinning jenny, and loom with the flying shuttle, can be managed in a family; but nothing more complicated. The economy and thriftiness resulting from our household manufactures are such that they will never again be laid aside; and nothing more salutary for us has ever happened than the British obstructions to our demands for their manufactures. Restore free intercourse when they will, their commerce with us will have totally changed its form, and the articles we shall in future want from them will not exceed their own consumption of our produce.

A letter from you calls up recollections very dear to my mind. It carries me back to the times when, beset with difficulties and dangers, we were fellow-laborers in the same cause, struggling for what is most valuable to man, his right of self-government. Laboring always at the same oar, with some wave ever ahead, threatening to overwhelm us, and yet passing harmless under our bark, we knew not how we rode through the storm with heart and hand, and made a happy port. Still we did not expect to be without rubs and difficulties; and we have had them. First, the detention of the western posts, then the coalition of Pilnitz, outlawing our commerce with France, and the British enforcement of the outlawry. In your day, French depredations; in mine, English, and the Berlin and Milan decrees; now the English orders of council, and the piracies they authorize. When these shall be over, it will be the impressment of our seamen or something else; and so we have gone on, and so we shall go on puzzled and prospering beyond example in the history of man. And I do believe we shall continue to grow, to multiply and prosper until we exhibit an association, powerful, wise and happy beyond what has yet been seen by men. As for France and England, with all their preëminence in science, the one is a den of robbers, and the other of pirates. And if science produces no better fruits than tyranny, murder, rapine and destitution of national morality, I would rather wish our country to be ignorant, honest and estimable, as our neighboring savages are. But whither is senile garrulity leading me? Into politics, of which I have taken final leave. I think little of them and say less. I have given up newspapers in exchange for Tacitus and Thucydides, for Newton and Euclid, and I find myself much the happier. Sometimes, indeed, I look back to former occurrences, in remembrance of our old friends and fellow-laborers, who have fallen before us. Of the signers of the Declaration of Independence, I see now living not more than half a dozen on your side of the Potomac, and on this side, myself alone. You and I have been wonderfully spared, and myself with remarkable health, and a considerable activity of body and mind. I am on horseback three or four hours of every day; visit three or four times a year a possession I have ninety miles distant, performing the winter journey on horseback. I walk little, however, a single mile being too much for me, and I live in the midst of my grandchildren, one of whom has lately promoted me to be a great grandfather. I have heard with pleasure that you also retain good health, and a greater power of exercise in walking than I do. But I would rather have heard this from yourself, and that, writing a letter like mine, full of egotisms, and of details of your health, your habits, occupations and enjoyments, I should have the pleasure of knowing that in the race of life, you do not keep, in its physical decline, the same distance ahead of me which you have done in political honors and achievements. No circumstances have lessened the interest I feel in these particulars respecting yourself; none have suspended for one moment my sincere esteem for you, and I now salute you with unchanged affection and respect.

Ford IX: 332–4

## 1.16 To Dr. Walter Jones

Monticello, January 2, 1814

Dear Sir, – Your favor of November the 25th reached this place December the 21st, having been near a month on the way. How this could happen I know not, as we have two mails a week both from Fredericksburg and Richmond. It found me just returned from a long journey and absence, during which so much business had accumulated, commanding the first attentions, that another week has been added to the delay.

I deplore, with you, the putrid state into which our newspapers have passed, and the malignity, the vulgarity, and mendacious spirit of those who write for them; and I enclose you a recent sample, the production of a New England judge, as a proof of the abyss of degradation into which we are fallen. These ordures are rapidly depraving the public taste, and lessening its relish for sound food. As vehicles of information, and a curb on our functionaries, they have rendered themselves useless, by forfeiting all title to belief. That this has, in a great degree, been produced by the violence and malignity of party spirit, I agree with you; and I have read with great pleasure the paper you enclosed me on that subject, which I now return. It is at the same time a perfect model of the style of discussion which candor and decency should observe, of the tone which renders difference of opinion even amiable, and a succinct, correct, and dispassionate history of the origin and progress of party among us. It might be incorporated as it stands, and without changing a word, into the history of the present epoch, and would give to posterity a fairer view of the times than they will probably derive from other sources. In reading it with great satisfaction, there was but a single passage where I wished a little more development of a very sound and catholic idea; a single intercalation to rest it solidly on true bottom. It is near the end of the first page, where you make a statement of genuine republican maxims; saying, "that the people ought to possess as much political power as can possibly exist with the order and security of society." Instead of this, I would say, "that the people, being the only safe depository of power, should exercise in person every function which their qualifications enable them to exercise, consistently with the order and security of society; that we now find them equal to the election of those who shall be invested with their executive and legislative powers, and to act themselves in the judiciary, as judges in questions of fact; that the range of their powers ought to be enlarged," &c. This gives both the reason and exemplification of the maxim you express, "that they ought to possess as much political power," &c. I see nothing to correct either in your facts or principles.

You say that in taking General Washington on your shoulders, to bear him harmless through the federal coalition, you encounter a perilous topic. I do not think so. You have given the genuine history of the course of his mind through the trying scenes in which it was engaged, and of the seductions by which it was deceived, but not depraved. I think I knew General Washington intimately and thoroughly; and were I called on to delineate his character, it should be in terms like these.

His mind was great and powerful, without being of the very first order; his penetration strong, though not so acute as that of a Newton, Bacon, or Locke; and as far as he saw, no judgment was ever sounder. It was slow in operation, being little aided by invention or imagination, but sure in conclusion. Hence the common remark of his officers, of the advantage he derived from councils of war, where hearing all suggestions, he selected whatever was best; and certainly no General ever planned his battles more judiciously. But if deranged during the course of the action, if any member of his plan was dislocated by sudden circumstances, he was slow in re-adjustment. The consequence was, that he often failed in the field, and rarely against an enemy in station, as at Boston and York. He was incapable of fear, meeting personal dangers with the calmest unconcern. Perhaps the strongest feature in his character was prudence, never acting until every circumstance, every consideration, was maturely weighed; refraining if he saw a doubt, but, when once decided, going through with his purpose, whatever obstacles opposed. His integrity was most pure, his justice the most inflexible I have ever known, no motives of interest or consanguinity, of friendship or hatred, being able to bias his decision. He was, indeed, in every sense of the words, a wise, a good, and a great man. His temper was naturally high toned; but reflection and resolution had obtained a firm and habitual ascendency over it. If ever, however, it broke its bonds, he was most tremendous in his wrath. In his expenses he was honorable, but exact; liberal in contributions to whatever promised utility; but frowning and unyielding on all visionary projects and all unworthy calls on his charity. His heart was not warm in its affections; but he exactly calculated every man's value, and gave him a solid esteem proportioned to it. His person, you know, was fine, his stature exactly what one would wish, his deportment easy, erect and noble; the best horseman of his age, and the most graceful figure that could be seen on horseback. Although in the circle of his friends, where he might be unreserved with safety, he took a free share in conversation, his colloquial talents were not above mediocrity, possessing neither copiousness of ideas, nor fluency of words. In public, when called on for a sudden opinion, he was unready, short and embarrassed. Yet he wrote readily, rather diffusely, in an easy and correct style. This he had acquired by conversation with the world, for his education was merely reading, writing and common arithmetic, to which he added surveying at a later day. His time was employed in action chiefly, reading little, and that only in agriculture and English history. His correspondence became necessarily extensive, and, with journalizing his agricultural proceedings, occupied most of his leisure hours within doors. On the whole, his character was, in its mass, perfect, in nothing bad, in few points indifferent; and it may truly be said, that never did nature and fortune combine more perfectly to make a man great, and to place him in the same constellation with whatever worthies have merited from man an everlasting remembrance. For his was the singular destiny and merit, of leading the armies of his country successfully through an arduous war, for the establishment of its independence; of conducting its councils through the birth of a government, new in its forms and principles, until it had settled down into a quiet and orderly train; and of scrupulously obeying the laws through the whole of his career, civil and military, of which the history of the world furnishes no other example.

How, then, can it be perilous for you to take such a man on your shoulders? I am satisfied the great body of republicans think of him as I do. We were, indeed, dissatisfied with him on his ratification of the British treaty. But this was short lived. We knew his honesty, the wiles with which he was encompassed, and that age had already begun to relax the firmness of his purposes; and I am convinced he is more deeply seated in the love and gratitude of the republicans, than in the Pharisaical homage of the federal monarchists. For he was no monarchist from preference of his judgment. The soundness of that gave him correct views of the rights of man, and his severe justice devoted him to them. He has often declared to me that he considered our new constitution as an experiment on the practicability of republican government, and with what dose of liberty man could be trusted for his own good; that he was determined the experiment should have a fair trial, and would lose the last drop of his blood in support of it. And these declarations he repeated to me the oftener and more pointedly, because he knew my suspicions of Colonel Hamilton's views, and probably had heard from him the same declarations which I had, to wit, "that the British constitution, with its unequal representation, corruption and other existing abuses, was the most perfect government which had ever been established on earth, and that a reformation of those abuses would make it an impracticable government." I do believe that General Washington had not a firm confidence in the durability of our government. He was naturally distrustful of men, and inclined to gloomy apprehensions; and I was ever persuaded that a belief that we must at length end in something like a British constitution, had some weight in his adoption of the ceremonies of levees, birth-days, pompous meetings with Congress, and other forms of the same character, calculated to prepare us gradually for a change which he believed possible, and to let it come on with as little shock as might be to the public mind.

These are my opinions of General Washington, which I would vouch at the judgment seat of God, having been formed on an acquaintance of thirty years. I served with him in the Virginia legislature from 1769 to the Revolutionary war, and again, a short time in Congress, until he left us to take command of the army. During the war and after it we corresponded occasionally, and in the four years of my continuance in the office of Secretary of State, our intercourse was daily, confidential and cordial. After I retired from that office, great and malignant pains were taken by our federal monarchists, and not entirely without effect, to make him view me as a theorist, holding French principles of government, which would lead infallibly to licentiousness and anarchy. And to this he listened the more easily, from my known disapprobation of the British treaty. I never saw him afterwards, or these malignant insinuations should have been dissipated before his just judgment, as mists before the sun. I felt on his death, with my countrymen, that "verily a great man hath fallen this day in Israel."

More time and recollection would enable me to add many other traits of his character; but why add them to you who knew him well? And I cannot justify to myself a longer detention of your paper.

*Vale, proprieque tuum, me esse tibi persuadeas.*

Ford IX: 446–51

## 1.17 To John Adams

Monticello, July 5, 1814

Dear Sir, –
   . . . I am just returned from one of my long absences, having been at my other home for five weeks past. Having more leisure there than here for reading, I amused myself with reading seriously Plato's Republic. I am wrong, however, in calling it amusement, for it was the heaviest task-work I ever went through. I had occasionally before taken up some of his other works, but scarcely ever had patience to go through a whole dialogue. While wading through the whimsies, the puerilities, and unintelligible jargon of this work, I laid it down often to ask myself how it could have been, that the world should have so long consented to give reputation to such nonsense as this? How the *soi-disant* Christian world, indeed, should have done it, is a piece of historical curiosity. But how could the Roman good sense do it? And

particularly, how could Cicero bestow such eulogies on Plato! Although Cicero did not wield the dense logic of Demosthenes, yet he was able, learned, laborious, practised in the business of the world, and honest. He could not be the dupe of mere style, of which he was himself the first master in the world. With the moderns, I think, it is rather a matter of fashion and authority. Education is chiefly in the hands of persons who, from their profession, have an interest in the reputation and the dreams of Plato. They give the tone while at school, and few in their after years have occasion to revise their college opinions. But fashion and authority apart, and bringing Plato to the test of reason, take from him his sophisms, futilities and incomprehensibilities, and what remains? In truth, he is one of the race of genuine sophists, who has escaped the oblivion of his brethren, first, by the elegance of his diction, but chiefly, by the adoption and incorporation of his whimsies into the body of artificial Christianity. His foggy mind is forever presenting the semblances of objects which, half seen through a mist, can be defined neither in form nor dimensions. Yet this, which should have consigned him to early oblivion, really procured him immortality of fame and reverence. The Christian priesthood, finding the doctrines of Christ levelled to every understanding, and too plain to need explanation, saw in the mysticism of Plato materials with which they might build up an artificial system, which might, from its indistinctness, admit everlasting controversy, give employment for their order, and introduce it to profit, power and preeminence. The doctrines which flowed from the lips of Jesus himself are within the comprehension of a child; but thousands of volumes have not yet explained the Platonisms engrafted on them; and for this obvious reason, that nonsense can never be explained. Their purposes, however, are answered. Plato is canonized; and it is now deemed as impious to question his merits as those of an Apostle of Jesus. He is peculiarly appealed to as an advocate of the immortality of the soul; and yet I will venture to say, that were there no better arguments than his in proof of it, not a man in the world would believe it. It is fortunate for us, that Platonic republicanism has not obtained the same favor as Platonic Christianity; or we should now have been all living, men, women and children, pell mell together, like beasts of the field or forest. Yet "Plato is a great philosopher," said La Fontaine. But, says Fontenelle, "Do you find his ideas very clear?" "Oh no! he is of an obscurity impenetrable." "Do you not find him full of contradictions?" "Certainly," replied La Fontaine, "he is but a sophist." Yet immediately after he exclaims again, "Oh, Plato was a great philosopher." Socrates had reason, indeed, to complain of the misrepresentations of Plato; for in truth, his dialogues are libels on Socrates.

But why am I dosing you with these antediluvian topics? Because I am glad to have some one to whom they are familiar, and who will not receive them as if dropped from the moon. Our post-revolutionary youth are born under happier stars than you and I were. They acquire all learning in their mother's womb, and bring it into the world ready made. The information of books is no longer necessary; and all knowledge which is not innate, is in contempt, or neglect at least. Every folly must run its round; and so, I suppose, must that of self-learning and self-sufficiency; of rejecting the knowledge acquired in past ages, and starting on the new ground of intuition. When sobered by experience, I hope our successors will turn their attention to the advantages of education. I mean of education on the broad scale, and not that of the petty *academies*, as they call themselves, which are starting up in every neighborhood, and where one or two men, possessing Latin and sometimes Greek, a knowledge of the globes, and the first six books of Euclid, imagine and communicate this as the sum of science. They commit their pupils to the theatre of the world, with just taste enough of learning to be alienated from industrious pursuits, and not enough to do service in the ranks of science. We have some exceptions, indeed. I presented one to you lately, and we have some others. But the terms I use are general truths. I hope the necessity will, at length, be seen of establishing institutions here, as in Europe, where every branch of science, useful at this day, may be taught in its highest degree. Have you ever turned your thoughts to the plan of such an institution? I mean to a specification of the particular sciences of real use in human affairs, and how they might be so grouped as to require so many professors only as might bring them within the views of a just but enlightened economy? I should be happy in a communication of your ideas on this problem, either loose or digested. But to avoid my being run away with by another subject, and adding to the length and *ennui* of the present letter, I will here present to Mrs. Adams and yourself, the assurance of my constant and sincere friendship and respect.

Ford XI: 460–5

# I.18 [Classification of Books in Jefferson's Library, 1815]

BOOKS may be classed according to the faculties of the mind employed on them: these are

I. MEMORY  II. REASON  III. IMAGINATION

Which are applied respectively to

I. HISTORY  II. PHILOSOPHY  III. FINE ARTS

| | | | | Subject | Chapt. |
|---|---|---|---|---|---|
| **I. History** — Civil | Civil Proper | Ancient | | Ancient History | 1 |
| | | Modern | | Foreign | 2 |
| | | | | British | 3 |
| | | | | American | 4 |
| | Ecclesiastical | | | Ecclesiastical | 5 |
| Natural | Physics | | | Natural Philosophy | 6 |
| | | | | Agriculture | 7 |
| | | | | Chemistry | 8 |
| | | | | Surgery | 9 |
| | | | | Medicine | 10 |
| | Nat. Hist. Proper | Animals | | Anatomy | 11 |
| | | | | Zoology | 12 |
| | | Vegetables | | Botany | 13 |
| | | Minerals | | Mineralogy | 14 |
| | Occupations of Man | | | Technical Arts | 15 |
| **II. Philosophy** — Moral | Ethics | | | Moral Philosophy } L. of Nations | 16 |
| | Religious | | | Religion | 17 |
| | Jurisprudence | Municipal | Domestic | Equity | 18 |
| | | | | Common Law | 19 |
| | | | | Law Merchant | 20 |
| | | | | Law Maritime | 21 |
| | | | | Law Ecclesiastical | 22 |
| | | | Foreign | Foreign Law | 23 |
| | | Occonomical | | Politics } Commerce | 24 |
| Mathematical | Pure | | | Arithmetic | 25 |
| | | | | Geometry | 26 |
| | Physico-Mathematical | | | Mechanics } Statics } Dynamics } Pneumatics } Phonics } Optics | 27 |
| | | | | Astronomy | 28 |
| | | | | Geography | 29 |
| **III. Fine Arts** | Architecture | | | Architecture | 30 |
| | Gardening | | | Gardening } Painting } Sculpture | 31 |
| | Painting | | | | |
| | Sculpture | | | | |
| | Music | | | Music | 32 |
| | Poetry | | | Epic | 33 |
| | | | | Romance | 34 |
| | | | | Pastorals } Odes } Elegies | 35 |
| | | | | Didactic | 36 |
| | | | | Tragedy | 37 |
| | | | | Comedy | 38 |
| | | | | Dialogue } Epistles | 39 |
| | Oratory | | | Logic } Rhetoric } Orations | 40 |
| | Criticism | | | Theory | 41 |
| | | | | Bibliography | 42 |
| | | | | Language | 43 |
| Authors who have written on various branches | | | | Polygraphical | 44 |

Adapting Bacon's scheme for classifying all knowledge (*Advancement of Learning*, Bk. II), Jefferson devised this classification of the 6,700 books in his library. His classificatory scheme and his books became the basis for the Library of Congress  *Eds.*

## 1.19 To John Adams

Monticello, August 10, 1815

Dear Sir, – The simultaneous movements in our correspondence have been remarkable on several occasions. It would seem as if the state of the air, or state of the times, or some other unknown cause, produced a sympathetic effect on our mutual recollections. I had sat down to answer your letters of June the 19th, 20th and 22d, with pen, ink and paper before me, when I received from our mail that of July the 30th. You ask information on the subject of Camus. All I recollect of him is, that he was one of the deputies sent to arrest Dumourier at the head of his army, who were, however, themselves arrested by Dumourier, and long detained as prisoners. I presume, therefore, he was a Jacobin. You will find his character in the most excellent revolutionary history of Toulongeon. I believe, also, he may be the same person who has given us a translation of Aristotle's Natural History, from the Greek into French. Of his report to the National Institute on the subject of the Bollandists, your letter gives me the first information. I had supposed them defunct with the society of Jesuits, of which they were; and that their works, although above ground, were, from their bulk and insignificance, as effectually entombed on their shelves, as if in the graves of their authors. Fifty-two volumes in folio, of the *acta sanctorum*, in dog-Latin, would be a formidable enterprise to the most laborious German. I expect, with you, they are the most enormous mass of lies, frauds, hypocrisy and imposture, that was ever heaped together on this globe. By what chemical process M. Camus supposed that an extract of truth could be obtained from such a farrago of falsehood, I must leave to the chemists and moralists of the age to divine.

On the subject of the history of the American Revolution, you ask who shall write it? Who can write it? And who will ever be able to write it? Nobody; except merely its external facts; all its councils, designs and discussions having been conducted by Congress with closed doors, and no members, as far as I know, having even made notes of them. These, which are the life and soul of history, must forever be unknown. Botta, as you observe, has put his own speculations and reasonings into the mouths of persons whom he names, but who, you and I know, never made such speeches. In this he has followed the example of the ancients, who made their great men deliver long

speeches, all of them in the same style, and in that of the author himself. The work is nevertheless a good one, more judicious, more
chaste, more classical, and more true than the party diatribe of Marshall. Its greatest fault is in having taken too much from him. I possessed the work, and often recurred to considerable portions of it,
although I never read it through. But a very judicious and well-
informed neighbor of mine went through it with great attention, and
spoke very highly of it. I have said that no member of the old Congress, as far as I knew, made notes of the discussion. I did not know of
the speeches you mention of Dickinson and Witherspoon. But on the
questions of Independence, and on the two articles of Confederation
respecting taxes and votings, I took minutes of the heads of the arguments. On the first, I threw all into one mass, without ascribing to the
speakers their respective arguments; pretty much in the manner of
Hume's summary digests of the reasonings in parliament for and
against a measure. On the last, I stated the heads of the arguments
used by each speaker. But the whole of my notes on the question of
Independence does not occupy more than five pages, such as of this
letter; and on the other questions, two such sheets. They have never
been communicated to any one. Do you know that there exists in
manuscript the ablest work of this kind ever yet executed, of the
debates of the constitutional convention of Philadelphia in 1788? The
whole of everything said and done there was taken down by Mr.
Madison, with a labor and exactness beyond comprehension.

I presume that our correspondence has been observed at the post
offices, and thus has attracted notice. Would you believe, that a
printer has had the effrontery to propose to me the letting him
publish it? These people think they have a right to everything, however secret or sacred. I had not before heard of the Boston pamphlet
with Priestley's letters and mine.

At length Bonaparte has got on the right side of a question. From
the time of his entering the legislative hall to his retreat to Elba, no
man has execrated him more than myself. I will not except even the
members of the Essex Junto;[1] although for very different reasons; I,

---

[1] The Essex Junto was an influential group of Hamiltonian high Federalist politicians in Massachusetts in the late 1700s–early 1800s. They were especially hostile
to Jefferson and the French Revolution and strongly pro-British during the War
of 1812. The group included Senator George Cabot, the jurist Theophilus Par-
sons, and Timothy Pickering. Their strong support of and participation in the

because he was warring against the liberty of his own country, and independence of others; they, because he was the enemy of England, the Pope, and the Inquisition. But at length, and as far as we can judge, he seems to have become the choice of his nation. At least, he is defending the cause of his nation, and that of all mankind, the rights of every people to independence and self-government. He and the allies have now changed sides. They are parcelling out among themselves Poland, Belgium, Saxony, Italy, dictating a ruler and government to France, and looking askance at our republic, the splendid libel on their governments, and he is fighting for the principles of national independence, of which his whole life hitherto has been a continued violation. He has promised a free government to his own country, and to respect the rights of others; and although his former conduct inspires little confidence in his promises, yet we had better take the chance of his word for doing right, than the certainty of the wrong which his adversaries are doing and avowing. If they succeed, ours is only the boon of the Cyclops to Ulysses, of being the last devoured.

Present me affectionately and respectfully to Mrs. Adams, and Heaven give you both as much more of life as you wish, and bless it with health and happiness.

P.S. August the 11th. – I had finished my letter yesterday, and this morning receive the news of Bonaparte's second abdication. Very well. For him personally, I have no feeling but reprobation. The representatives of the nation have deposed him. They have taken the allies at their word, that they had no object in the war but his removal. The nation is now free to give itself a good government, either with or without a Bourbon; and France unsubdued, will still be a bridle on the enterprises of the combined powers, and a bulwark to others.

Ford IX: 526–31

## 1.20 To John Adams

Monticello, April 8, 1816

Dear Sir, – I have to acknolege your two favors of Feb. 16. and Mar. 2. and to join sincerely in the sentiment of Mrs. Adams, and

infamous Hartford Convention of 1814 signaled the end of their dominance in Massachusetts politics. – *Eds.*

regret that distance separates us so widely. An hour of conversation would be worth a volume of letters. But we must take things as they come.

You ask if I would agree to live my 70. or rather 73. years over again? To which I say Yea. I think with you that it is a good world on the whole, that it has been framed on a principle of benevolence, and more pleasure than pain dealt out to us. There are indeed (who might say Nay) gloomy and hypocondriac minds, inhabitants of diseased bodies, disgusted with the present, and despairing of the future; always counting that the worst will happen, because it may happen. To these I say How much pain have cost us the evils which have never happened? My temperament is sanguine. I steer my bark with Hope in the head, leaving Fear astern. My hopes indeed sometimes fail; but not oftener than the forebodings of the gloomy. There are, I acknolege, even in the happiest life, some terrible convulsions, heavy set-offs against the opposite page of the account. I have often wondered for what good end the sensations of Grief could be intended. All our other passions, within proper bounds, have an useful object. And the perfection of the moral character is, not in a Stoical apathy, so hypocritically vaunted, and so untruly too, because impossible, but in a just equilibrium of all the passions. I wish the pathologists then would tell us what is the use of grief in the economy, and of what good it is the cause, proximate or remote.

Did I know Baron Grimm while at Paris? Yes, most intimately. He was the pleasantest, and most conversible member of the diplomatic corps while I was there: a man of good fancy, acuteness, irony, cunning, and egoism: no heart, not much of any science, yet enough of every one to speak it's language. His forte was *Belles-lettres*, painting and sculpture. In these he was the oracle of the society, and as such was the empress Catharine's private correspondent and factor in all things not diplomatic. It was thro' him I got her permission for poor Ledyard[1] to go to Kamschatka, and cross over thence to the Western coast of

---

[1] John Ledyard (1751–89) was an American adventurer and explorer who accompanied Captain Cook on his last voyage. In 1785 he approached Jefferson in Paris and told him of his plan to travel from Russia to Alaska and down the Pacific coast to what is now Washington state. From there he hoped to traverse the continent to the American east coast. Before he could cross to Alaska Ledyard was arrested by the Russian authorities in Siberia and deported to the U.S. via Poland. – *Eds.*

America, in order to penetrate across our continent in the opposite direction to that afterwards adopted for Lewis and Clarke: which permission she withdrew after he had got within 200. miles of Kamschatska, had him siesed, brought back and set down in Poland. Altho' I never heard Grimm express the opinion, directly, yet I always supposed him to be of the school of Diderot, D'Alembert, D'Holbach, the first of whom committed their system of atheism to writing in "Le bon sens," and the last in his "Système de la Nature." It was a numerous school in the Catholic countries, while the infidelity of the Protestant took generally the form of Theism. The former always insisted that it was a mere question of definition between them, the hypostasis of which on both sides was "Nature" or "the Universe": that both agreed in the order of the existing system, but the one supposed it from eternity, the other as having begun in time. And when the atheist descanted on the unceasing motion and circulation of matter thro' the animal, vegetable and mineral kingdoms, never resting, never annihilated, always changing form, and under all forms gifted with the power of reproduction; the Theist pointing "to the heavens above, and to the earth beneath, and to the waters under the earth," asked if these did not proclaim a first cause, possessing intelligence and power; power in the production, and intelligence in the design and constant preservation of the system; urged the palpable existence of final causes, that the eye was made to see, and the ear to hear, and not that we see because we have eyes, and hear because we have ears; an answer obvious to the senses, as that of walking across the room was to the philosopher demonstrating the non-existence of motion. It was in D'Holbach's conventicles that Rousseau imagined all the machinations against him were contrived; and he left, in his Confessions, the most biting anecdotes of Grimm. These appeared after I left France; but I have heard that poor Grimm was so much afflicted by them, that he kept his bed several weeks. I have never seen these Memoirs of Grimm. Their volume has kept them out of our market.

I have been lately amusing myself with Levi's book in answer to Dr. Priestley. It is a curious and tough work. His style is inelegant and incorrect, harsh and petulent to his adversary, and his reasoning flimsey enough. Some of his doctrines were new to me, particularly that of his two resurrections: the first a particular one of all the dead, in body as well as soul, who are to live over again, the Jews in a state of perfect obedience to god, the other nations in a state of corporeal punishment for the sufferings they have inflicted on the Jews. And he explains this resurrection of bodies to be only of the original stamen of Leibnitz, or the *homunculus in semine masculino*, considering that as a mathematical point, insusceptible of separation, or division. The second resurrection a general one of souls and bodies, eternally to enjoy divine glory in the presence of the supreme being. He alledges that the Jews alone preserve the doctrine of the unity of god. Yet their god would be deemed a very indifferent man with us: and it was to correct their Anamorphosis of the deity that Jesus preached, as well as to establish the doctrine of a future state. However Levi insists that that was taught in the old testament, and even by Moses himself and the prophets. He agrees that an anointed prince was prophecied and promised: but denies that the character and history of Jesus has any analogy with that of the person promised. He must be fearfully embarrassing to the Hierophants of fabricated Christianity; because it is their own armour in which he clothes himself for the attack. For example, he takes passages of Scripture from their context (which would give them a very different meaning), strings them together, and makes them point towards what object he pleases; he interprets them figuratively, typically, analogically, hyperbolically; he calls in the aid of emendation, transposition, ellipsis, metonymy, and every other figure of rhetoric; the name of one man is taken for another, one place for another, days and weeks for months and years; and finally avails himself of all his advantage over his adversaries by his superior knolege of the Hebrew, speaking in the very language of the divine communication, while they can only fumble on with conflicting and disputed translations. Such is this war of giants. And how can such pigmies as you and I decide between them? For myself I confess that my head is not formed *tantas componere lites.* And as you began your Mar. 2. with a declaration that you were about to write me the most frivolous letter I had ever read, so I will close mine by saying I have written you a full match for it, and by adding my affectionate respects to Mrs. Adams, and the assurance of my constant attachment and consideration for yourself.

L & B XIV: 466–71

# 1.21 To John Adams

Monticello, August 1, 1816

Dear Sir, – Your two philosophical letters of May 4 and 6 have been too long in my carton of "Letters to be answered." To the question indeed on the utility of Grief, no answer remains to be given. You have exhausted the subject. I see that, with the other evils of life, it is destined to temper the cup we are to drink.

> Two urns by Jove's high throne have ever stood,
> The source of evil one, and one of good;
> From thence the cup of mortal man he fills,
> Blessings to these, to those distributes ills;
> To most he mingles both.[1]

Putting to myself your question, Would I agree to live my 73 years over again for ever? I hesitate to say. With Chew's limitations from 25 to 60, I would say Yes; and might go further back, but not come lower down. For, at the latter period, with most of us, the powers of life are sensibly on the wane, sight becomes dim, hearing dull, memory constantly enlarging it's frightful blank and parting with all we have ever seen or known, spirits evaporate, bodily debility creeps on palsying every limb, and so faculty after faculty quits us, and where then is life? If, in it's full vigor, of good as well as evil, your friend Vassall could doubt it's value, it must be purely a negative quantity when it's evils alone remain. Yet I do not go into his opinion entirely. I do not agree that an age of pleasure is no compensation for a moment of pain. I think, with you, that life is a fair matter of account, and the balance often, nay generally, in it's favor. It is not indeed easy, by calculation of intensity and time, to apply a common measure, or to fix the par between pleasure and pain: yet it exists, and is measurable. On the question, for example, whether to be cut for the stone? the young, with a longer prospect of years, think these overbalance the pain of the operation. Dr. Franklin, at the age of 80, thought his residuum of life, not worth that price. I should have thought with him, even taking the stone out of the scale. There is a ripeness of time for death, regarding others as well as ourselves, when it is reasonable we should drop off, and make room for another growth. When we have lived our generation out, we should not wish to encroach on another. I enjoy good

[1] Homer's *Iliad*, XXIV, 663–7 (Pope transl.) – *Eds.*

health; I am happy in what is around me. Yet I assure you I am ripe for leaving all, this year, this day, this hour. If it could be doubted whether we would go back to 25 how can it be, whether we would go forward from 73? Bodily decay is gloomy in prospect; but of all human contemplations the most abhorrent is body without mind. Perhaps however I might accept of time to read Grimm before I go. 15 volumes of anecdotes and incidents, within the compass of my own time and cognisance, written by a man of genius, of taste, of point, an acquaintance, the measure and traverses of whose mind I knew, could not fail to turn the scale in favor of life during their perusal. I must write to Ticknor to add it to my catalogue, and hold on till it comes.

There is a Mr. Vanderkemp of N.Y., a correspondent I believe of yours, with whom I have exchanged some letters, without knowing who he is. Will you tell me?

I know nothing of the history of the Jesuits you mention in 4 vols. Is it a good one? I dislike, with you, their restoration; because it marks a retrograde step from light towards darkness. We shall have our follies without doubt. Some one or more of them will always be afloat. But ours will be the follies of enthusiasm, not of bigotry, not of Jesuitism. Bigotry is the disease of ignorance, of morbid minds; enthusiasm of the free and buoyant. Education and free discussion are the antidotes of both. We are destined to be a barrier against the returns of ignorance and barbarism. Old Europe will have to lean on our shoulders, and to hobble along by our side, under the monkish trammels of priests and kings, as she can. What a Colossus shall we be when the Southern continent comes up to our mark! What a stand will it secure as a ralliance for the reason and freedom of the globe. I like the dreams of the future better than the history of the past. So good night. I will dream on, always fancying that Mrs. Adams and yourself are by my side marking the progress and the obliquities of ages and countries.

L & B xv: 56-8

## I.22 To John Adams

Monticello, October 12, 1823

Dear Sir, – I do not write with the ease which your letter of Sep. 18 supposes. Crippled wrists and fingers make writing slow and laborious. But, while writing to you, I lose the sense of these things, in the recollection of antient times, when youth and health made happiness out of every thing. I forget for a while the hoary winter of age, when we can think of nothing but how to keep ourselves warm, and how to get rid of our heavy hours until the friendly hand of death shall rid us of all at once. Against this *tedium vitae* however I am fortunately mounted on a Hobby, which indeed I should have better managed some 30 or 40 years ago, but whose easy amble is still sufficient to give exercise and amusement to an Octogenary rider. This is the establishment of an University, on a scale more comprehensive, and in a country more healthy and central than our old William and Mary, which these obstacles have long kept in a state of languor and inefficiency. But the tardiness with which such works proceed may render it doubtful whether I shall live to see it go into action.

Putting aside these things however for the present, I write this letter as due to a friendship co-eval with our government, and now attempted to be poisoned, when too late in life to be replaced by new affections. I had for some time observed, in the public papers, dark hints and mysterious innuendoes of a correspondence of yours with a friend [Wm. Cunningham], to whom you had opened your bosom without reserve, and which was to be made public by that friend, or his representative. And now it is said to be actually published. It has not yet reached us, but extracts have been given, and such as seemed most likely to draw a curtain of separation between you and myself. Were there no other motive than that of indignation against the author of this outrage on private confidence, whose shaft seems to have been aimed at yourself more particularly, this would make it the duty of every honorable mind to disappoint that aim, by opposing to it's impression a seven-fold shield of apathy and insensibility. With me however no such armour is needed. The circumstances of the times, in which we have happened to live, and the partiality of our friends, at a particular period, placed us in a state of apparent opposition, which some might suppose to be personal also; and there might not be wanting those who wish'd to make it so, by filling our ears with malignant falsehoods, by dressing up hideous phantoms of their own creation, presenting them to you under my name, to me under your's, and endeavoring to instill into our minds things concerning each other the most destitute of truth.

And if there had been, at any time, a moment when we were off our guard, and in a temper to let the whispers of these people make us forget what we had known of each other for so many years, and years of so much trial, yet all men who have attended to the workings of the human mind, who have seen the false colours under which passion sometimes dresses the actions and motives of others, have seen also these passions subsiding with time and reflection, dissipating, like mists before the rising sun, and restoring to us the sight of all things in their true shape and colours. It would be strange indeed if, at our years, we were to go an age back to hunt up imaginary, or forgotten facts, to disturb the repose of affections so sweetening to the evening of our lives. Be assured, my dear Sir, that I am incapable of recieving the slightest impression from the effort now made to plant thorns on the pillow of age, worth, and wisdom, and to sow tares between friends who have been such for near half a century. Beseeching you then not to suffer your mind to be disquieted by this wicked attempt to poison it's peace, and praying you to throw it by, among the things which have never happened, I add sincere assurances of my unabated, and constant attachment, friendship and respect.

L & B xv: 471–3

## 1.23 To Thomas Jefferson Smith

Monticello, February 21, 1825

This letter will, to you, be as one from the dead. The writer will be in the grave before you can weigh its counsels. Your affectionate and excellent father has requested that I would address to you something which might possibly have a favorable influence on the course of life you have to run, and I too, as a namesake, feel an interest in that course. Few words will be necessary, with good dispositions on your part. Adore God. Reverence and cherish your parents. Love your neighbor as yourself, and your country more than yourself. Be just. Be true. Murmur not at the ways of Providence. So shall the life into which you have entered, be the portal to one of eternal and ineffable bliss. And if to the dead it is permitted to care for the things of this world, every action of your life will be under my regard. Farewell.

*The portrait of a good man by the most sublime of poets, for your imitation*

Lord, who's the happy man that may to Thy blest courts repair,
Not stranger-like to visit them, but to inhabit there?
'Tis he whose every thought and deed by rules of virtue moves,
Whose generous tongue disdains to speak the thing his heart
disproves.
Who never did a slander forge, his neighbor's fame to wound,
Nor hearken to a false report, by malice whispered round.
Who vice, in all its pomp and power, can treat with just neglect;
And piety, though clothed in rags, religiously respect.
Who to his plighted vows and trust has ever firmly stood,
And though he promise to his loss, he makes his promise good.
Whose soul in usury disdains his treasure to employ,
Whom no rewards can ever bribe the guiltless to destroy.
The man who, by this steady course, has happiness insur'd,
When earth's foundations shake, shall stand, by Providence
secur'd.

*A Decalogue of Canons for observation in practical life*

1.  Never put off till to-morrow what you can do to-day.
2.  Never trouble another for what you can do yourself.
3.  Never spend your money before you have it.
4.  Never buy what you do not want, because it is cheap; it will be dear to you.
5.  Pride costs us more than hunger, thirst, and cold.
6.  We never repent of having eaten too little.
7.  Nothing is troublesome that we do willingly.
8.  How much pain have cost us the evils which have never happened.
9.  Take things always by their smooth handle.
10. When angry, count ten, before you speak; if very angry, an hundred.

Ford x: 340–1

# 1.24 To John Adams

Monticello, December 18, 1825

Dear Sir, – Your letters are always welcome, the last more than all others, it's subject being one of the dearest to my heart. To my grand-daughter your commendations cannot fail to be an object of high ambition, as a certain passport to the good opinion of the world. If she does not cultivate them with assiduity and affection, she will illy fulfill my parting injunctions. I trust she will merit a continuance of your favor, and find in her new situation the general esteem she so happily possessed in the society she left.

You tell me she repeated to you an expression of mine that I should be willing to go again over the scenes of past life. I should not be unwilling, without however wishing it. And why not? I have enjoyed a greater share of health than falls to the lot of most men; my spirits have never failed me except under those paroxysms of grief which you, as well as myself, have experienced in every form: and with good health and good spirits the pleasures surely outweigh the pains of life. Why not then taste them again, fat and lean together. Were I indeed permitted to cut off from the train the last 7 years, the balance would be much in favor of treading the ground over again. Being at that period in the neighborhood of our Warm springs, and well in health, I wished to be better, and tried them. They destroyed, in a great degree, my internal organism, and I have never since had a moment of perfect health. I have now been 8 months confined almost constantly to the house, with now and then intervals of a few days on which I could get on horseback.

I presume you have recieved a copy of the life of Richd. H. Lee, from his grandson of the same name, author of the work. You and I know that he merited much during the revolution. Eloquent, bold, and ever watchful at his post, of which his biographer omits no proof. I am not certain whether the friends of George Mason, of Patrick Henry, yourself, and even of Genl. Washington may not reclaim some feathers of the plumage given him, notable as was his proper and original coat. But on this subject I will not anticipate your own judgment.

I learn with sincere pleasure that you have experienced lately a great renovation of your health. That it may continue to the ultimate period of your wishes is the sincere prayer of *usque ad aras amicissimi tui.*

Ford x: 350-1

## 1.25 To James Madison

Monticello, February 17, 1826

Dear Sir, – My Circular was answered by General Breckinridge, approving, as we had done, of the immediate appointment of Terril to the chair of Law, but our 4. colleagues who were together in Richmond concluded not to appoint until our meeting in April. In the meantime the term of the present lamented incumbent draws near to a close. About 150 students have already entered, many of those who engaged for a 2nd year are yet to come. What I think we may count [on is] that our dormitories will be filled. Whether there will be any overflowing for the accommodations provided in the vicinage, which are quite considerable, is not yet known. None will enter there while a dormitory remains vacant. Were the law chair filled, it would add 50 at least to the number.

Immediately on seeing the overwhelming vote of the House of Representatives against giving us another Dollar, I rode to the University and desired Mr. Brockenbrough to engage in nothing new, to stop everything on hand which could be done without, and to employ all his force and funds in finishing the Circular room for the books, and the Anatomical theatre. These cannot be done without; and for these and all our debts we have funds enough. But I think it prudent then to clear the decks thoroughly, to see how we shall stand, and what we may accomplish further. In the meanwhile, there are arrived for us, in different ports of the United States, 10 boxes of books from Paris, 7 from London, and from Germany I know not how many; in all, perhaps, about 25 boxes. Not one of these can be opened until the bookroom is completely finished, and all the shelves ready to receive their charge directly from the boxes as they shall be opened. This cannot be till May. I hear nothing definitive of the 2000 dollars duty of which we are asking the remission from Congress.

In the selection of our Law Professor, we must be rigorously attentive to his political principles. You will recollect that before the revolution, Coke Littleton was the Universal elementary book of Law students, and a sounder whig never wrote, nor of profounder learning in the orthodox doctrines of the British constitution, or in what were called English liberties. You remember also that our lawyers were then all Whigs. But when his black-letter text, and uncouth but cunning learning got out of fashion, and the honied Mansfieldism of Blackstone became the Student's Hornbook, from that moment, that profession (the nursery of our Congress) began to slide into toryism, and nearly all the young brood of lawyers now are of that hue. They suppose themselves, indeed, to be whigs, because they no longer know what whigism or republicanism means. It is in our Seminary that that Vestal flame is to be kept alive; it is thence it is to spread anew over our own and the sister states. If we are true and vigilant in our trust, within a dozen or 20. years a majority of our own legislature will be from our school, and many disciples will have carried it's doctrines home with them to their several States, and will have leavened thus the whole mass. New York has taken strong ground in vindication of the constitution; South Carolina had already done the same. Although I was against our leading, I am equally against omitting to follow in the same line, and backing them firmly; and I hope that yourself or some other will mark out the track to be pursued by us.

You will have seen in the newspapers some proceedings in the legislature, which have cost me much mortification. My own debts had become considerable, but not beyond the effect of some lopping of property, which would been little felt, when our friend W.C.N.[1] gave me the *coup de grâce*. Ever since that I have been paying 1200 dollars a year interest on his debt, which, with my own, was absorbing so much of my annual income, as that the Maintenance of my family was making deep and rapid inroads on my capital. Still, sales at a fair price would leave me competently provided. Had crops and prices for several years been such as to maintain a steady competition of substantial bidders at market, all would have been safe. But the long succession of years of stunted crops, of reduced prices, the general prostration of the farming business, under levies for supporting manufactures, etc., with the calamitous fluctuations of value in our paper medium, have kept agriculture in a state of abject depression, which has peopled the Western States, by silently breaking up those on the Atlantic, and glutted the land market, while it drew off its bidders. In such a state of things, property has lost its character of being a resource for debts. Highland in Bedford, which, in the days of our plethory, sold readily for from 50 to 100 dollars the acre (and such sales were many there), would not now sell for more than from 10 to 20 dollars, or $\frac{1}{4}$ or $\frac{1}{5}$ of their former price. Reflecting on these things, the practice occurred to me, of selling, on fair valuation, and by way of lottery, often resorted to

---

[1] Wilson Cary Nicholas, who had defaulted on debts for which TJ had cosigned notes. – *Eds.*

before the Revolution, to effect large sales, and still in constant usage in every State for individual as well as corporation purposes. If it is permitted in my case, my lands here alone, with the mills, etc., will pay every thing, and leave me Monticello and a farm free. If refused, I must sell everything here, perhaps considerably in Bedford, move thither with my family, where I have not even a log hut to put my head into, and whether ground for burial, will depend on the depredations which, under the form of sales, shall have been committed on my property. The question then with me was *utrum horum?* But why afflict you with these details? I cannot tell, indeed, unless pains are lessened by communication with a friend. The friendship which has subsisted between us, now half a century, and the harmony of our political principles and pursuits, have been sources of constant happiness to me through that long period. And if I remove beyond the reach of attentions to the University, or beyond the bourne of life itself, as I soon must, it is a comfort to leave that institution under your care, and an assurance that they will neither be spared, nor ineffectual. It has also been a great solace to me, to believe that you are engaged in vindicating to posterity the course we have pursued for preserving to them, *in all their purity*, the blessings of self-government, which we had assisted too in acquiring for them. If ever the earth has beheld a system of administration conducted with a single and steadfast eye to the general interest and happiness of those committed to it, one which, protected by truth, can never know reproach, it is that to which our lives have been devoted. To myself you have been a pillar of support through life. Take care of me when dead, and be assured that I shall leave with you my last affections.

Ford x: 375–8

## II  Natural Law, Natural Right, and Revolution

61

A

SUMMARY VIEW

OF THE

RIGHTS

OF

BRITISH AMERICA.

SET FORTH IN SOME

RESOLUTIONS

INTENDED FOR THE

INSPECTION

OF THE PRESENT

DELEGATES

OF THE

PEOPLE OF VIRGINIA.

NOW IN

CONVENTION.

BY A NATIVE, AND MEMBER OF THE
HOUSE OF BURGESSES.
*by Thomas Jefferson*

WILLIAMSBURG:
PRINTED BY CLEMENTINA RIND.

## II.1 *A Summary View of the Rights of British America*

[July 1774]

Est proprium munus magistratus intelligere, se gerere personam civitatis, debereque; ejus dignitatem & decus sustinere, servare leges, jura discribere, ea fidei suæ commissa meminisse.
CICERO, *De Of.*, l. I. c. 34.

It is the indispensible duty of the supreme magistrate to consider himself as acting for the whole community, and obliged to support its dignity, and assign to the people, with justice their various rights, as he would be faithful to the great trust reposed in him.

Resolved, that it be an instruction to the said deputies, when assembled in general congress with the deputies from the other states of British America, to propose to the said congress that an humble and dutiful address be presented to his Majesty, begging leave to lay before him, as Chief Magistrate of the British empire, the united complaints of his Majesty's subjects in America; complaints which are excited by many unwarrantable encroachments and usurpations, attempted to be made by the Legislature of one part of the empire, upon those rights which God and the laws have given equally and independently to all. To represent to his Majesty that these his states have often individually made humble application to his imperial throne to obtain, through its intervention, some redress of their injured rights, to none of which was ever even an answer condescended; humbly to hope that this their joint address, penned in the language of truth, and divested of those expressions of servility which would persuade his Majesty that we were asking favours, and not rights, shall obtain from his Majesty a more respectful acceptance. And this his Majesty will think we have reason to expect when he reflects that he is no more than the chief officer of the people, appointed by the laws, and circumscribed with definite powers, to assist in working the great machine of government, erected for their use and consequently subject to their superintendance. And in order that these our rights, as well as the invasions of them, may be laid more fully before his Majesty, to take a view of them from the origin and first settlement of these countries.

To remind him that our ancestors, before their emigration to America, were the free inhabitants of the British dominions in Europe, and possessed a right which nature has given to all men, of departing from the country in which chance, not choice, has placed them, of going in quest of new habitations, and of there establishing new societies, under such laws and regulations as to them shall seem most likely to promote public happiness. That their Saxon ancestors had, under this universal law, in like manner left their native wilds and woods in the north of Europe, had possessed themselves of the island of Britain, then less charged with inhabitants, and had established there that system of laws which has so long been the glory and protection of that country. Nor was ever any claim of superiority or dependence asserted over them by that mother country from which they had migrated; and were such a claim made, it is believed that his Majesty's subjects in Great Britain have too firm a feeling of the rights derived to them from their ancestors, to bow down the sovereignty of their state before such visionary pretensions. And it is thought that no circumstance has occurred to distinguish materially the British from the Saxon emigration. America was conquered, and her settlement made, and firmly established, at the expense of individuals, and not of the British public. Their own blood was spilt in acquiring lands for their settlements, their own fortunes expended in making that settlement effectual; for themselves they fought, for themselves they conquered, and for themselves alone they have right to hold. Not a shilling was ever issued from the public treasures of his Majesty, or his ancestors, for their assistance, till, of very late times, after the colonies had become established on a firm and permanent footing. That then, indeed, having become valuable to Great Britain for her commercial purposes, his Parliament was pleased to lend them assistance against the enemy, who would fain have drawn to herself the benefits of their commerce, to the great aggrandizement of herself, and danger of Great Britain. Such assistance, and in such circumstances, they had often before given to Portugal, and other allied states, with whom they carry on a commercial intercourse; yet these states never supposed, that by calling in her aid, they thereby submitted themselves to her sovereignty. Had such terms been proposed, they would have rejected them with disdain, and trusted for better to the moderation of their enemies, or to a vigorous exertion of their own force. We do not, however, mean to under-rate those aids, which to us were doubtless valuable, on whatever principles granted; but we would shew that they cannot give a title to that authority which the British Parliament would arrogate over us, and that they may amply be repaid by our giving to the inhabitants of Great Britain such exclusive privileges in trade as may be advantageous to them, and at the same time not too restrictive to ourselves. That settlements having been thus effected in the wilds of America, the emigrants thought proper to adopt that system of laws under which they had hitherto lived in the mother country, and to continue their union with her by submitting themselves to the same common Sovereign, who was thereby made the central link connecting the several parts of the empire thus newly multiplied.

But that not long were they permitted, however far they thought themselves removed from the hand of oppression, to hold undisturbed the rights thus acquired, at the hazard of their lives, and loss of their fortunes. A family of princes was then on the British throne, whose treasonable crimes against their people brought on them afterwards the exertion of those sacred and sovereign rights of punishment reserved in the hands of the people for cases of extreme necessity, and judged by the constitution unsafe to be delegated to any other judicature. While every day brought forth some new and unjustifiable exertion of power over their subjects on that side of the water, it was not to be expected that those here, much less able at that time to oppose the designs of despotism, should be exempted from injury.

Accordingly that country, which had been acquired by the lives, the labours, and the fortunes of individual adventurers, was by these princes, several times, parcelled out and distributed among the favourites and[1] followers of their fortunes, and, by an assumed right

---

[1] 1632 Maryland was granted to Lord Baltimore, 14, c. 2. Pennsylvania to Penn, and the province of Carolina was in the year 1663 granted by letters patent of majesty, king Charles II. in the 15th year of his reign, in propriety, unto the right honourable Edward earl of Clarendon, George duke of Albermarle, William earl of Craven, John lord Berkeley, Anthony lord Ashley, sir George Carteret, sir John Coleton, knight and barronet, and sir William Berkeley, knight; by which letters patent the laws of England were to be in force in Carolina: But the lords proprietors had power, with the consent of the inhabitants, to make by-laws for the better government of the said province; so that no money could be received or law made, without the consent of the inhabitants or their representatives.

to the crown alone, were erected into distinct and independent governments; a measure which it is believed his Majesty's prudence and understanding would prevent him from imitating at this day, as no exercise of such power, of dividing and dismembering a country, has ever occurred in his Majesty's realm of England, though now of very ancient standing; nor could it be justified or acquiesced under there, or in any other part of his Majesty's empire. That the exercise of a free trade with all parts of the world, possessed by the American colonists, as of natural right, and which no law of their own had taken away or abridged, was next the object of unjust encroachment. Some of the colonies having thought proper to continue the administration of their government in the name and under the authority of his Majesty King Charles the First, whom, notwithstanding his late deposition by the commonwealth of England, they continued in the sovereignty of their state; the Parliament for the commonwealth took the same in high offence, and assumed upon themselves the power of prohibiting their trade with all other parts of the world, except the island of Great Britain. This arbitrary act, however, they soon recalled, and by solemn treaty, entered into on the 12th day of March, 1651, between the said commonwealth by their commissioners, and the colony of Virginia by their house of burgesses, it was expressly stipulated, by the 8th article of the said treaty, that they should have "free trade as the people of England do enjoy to all places and with all nations, according to the laws of that commonwealth." But that, upon the restoration of his majesty king Charles the second, their rights of free commerce fell once more a victim to arbitrary power; and by several acts[2] of his reign, as well as of some of his successors, the trade of the colonies was laid under such restrictions as shew what hopes they might form from the justice of a British Parliament, were its uncontrouled power admitted over these states. History has informed us that bodies of men, as well as individuals, are susceptible of the spirit of tyranny. A view of these acts of parliament for regulation, as it has been affectedly called, of the American trade, if all other evidence were removed out of the case, would undeniably evince the truth of this observation. Besides the duties they

[2] 12. C. 2. c. 18. 15. C. 2. c. 11. 25. C. 2. c. 7. 7. 8. W. M. c. 22. 11. W. 3. 4. Anne. 6. G. 2. c. 13. [TJ's citations are often incomplete and sometimes mistaken. – *Eds.*]

impose on our articles of export and import, they prohibit our going to any markets northward of Cape Finisterre, in the kingdom of Spain, for the sale of commodities which Great Britain will not take from us, and for the purchase of others, with which she cannot supply us, and that for no other than the arbitrary purposes of purchasing for themselves, by a sacrifice of our rights and interests, certain privileges in their commerce with an allied state, who in confidence that their exclusive trade with America will be continued, while the principles and power of the British parliament be the same, have indulged themselves in every exorbitance which their avarice could dictate, or our necessities extort; have raised their commodities called for in America, to the double and treble of what they sold for before such exclusive privileges were given them, and of what better commodities of the same kind would cost us elsewhere, and at the same time give us much less for what we could carry thither than might be had at more convenient ports. That these acts prohibit us from carrying in quest of other purchasers the surplus of our tobaccoes remaining after the consumption of Great Britain is supplied; so that we must leave them with the British merchant for whatever he will please to allow us, to be by him reshipped to foreign markets, where he will reap the benefits of making sale of them for full value. That to heighten still the idea of parliamentary justice, and to shew with what moderation they are like to exercise power, where themselves are to feel no part of its weight, we take leave to mention to his majesty certain other acts of British parliament, by which they would prohibit us from manufacturing for our own use the articles we raise on our own lands with our own labour. By an act[3] passed in the 5th year of the reign of his late majesty king George the second, an American subject is forbidden to make a hat for himself of the fur which he has taken perhaps on his own soil; an instance of despotism to which no parallel can be produced in the most arbitrary ages of British history. By one other act[4] passed in the 23d year of the same reign, the iron which we make we are forbidden to manufacture, and heavy as that article is, and necessary in every branch of husbandry,

[3] 5. G. 2.
[4] 23. G. 2. c. 29

besides commission and insurance, we are to pay freight for it to
Great Britain, and freight for it back again, for the purpose of supporting not men, but machines, in the island of Great Britain. In
the same spirit of equal and impartial legislation is to be viewed the
act of parliament[5] passed in the 5th year of the same reign, by
which American lands are made subject to the demands of British
creditors, while their own lands were still continued unanswerable
for their debts; from which one of these conclusions must necessarily follow, either that justice is not the same in America as in Britain,
or else that the British parliament pay less regard to it here than
there. But that we do not point out to his majesty the injustice of
these acts, with intent to rest on that principle the cause of their
nullity; but to shew that experience confirms the propriety of those
political principles which exempt us from the jurisdiction of the
British parliament. The true ground on which we declare these acts
void is, that the British parliament has no right to exercise its authority over us.

That these exercises of usurped power have not been confined to
instances alone, in which themselves were interested, but they have
also intermeddled with the regulation of the internal affairs of the
colonies. The act of the 9th of Anne for establishing a post office
in America seems to have had little connection with British convenience, except that of accommodating his majesty's ministers and
favourites with the sale of a lucrative and easy office.

That thus we have hastened through the reigns which preceded
his majesty's during which the violations of our rights were less
alarming, because repeated at more distant intervals than that rapid
and bold succession of injuries which is likely to distinguish the
present from all other periods of American story. Scarcely have our
minds been able to emerge from the astonishment into which one
stroke of parliamentary thunder had involved us, before another
more heavy, and more alarming, is fallen on us. Single acts of tyranny may be ascribed to the accidental opinion of a day; but a
series of oppressions begun at a distinguished period, and pursued,
unalterably through every change of ministers, too plainly prove a
deliberate and systematical plan of reducing us to slavery.

[5] 5. G. 270.

69

That the act,[6] passed in the 4th year of his majesty's reign, entitled "An act for granting certain duties in the British colonies and plantations in America, &c."

One other act,[7] passed in the 5th year of his reign, entitled. "An act for granting and applying certain stamp duties and other duties in the British colonies and plantations in America, &c."

One other act,[8] passed in the 6th year of his reign, entitled "An act for the better securing the dependency of his majesty's dominions in America upon the crown and parliament of Great Britain;" and one other act,[9] passed in the 7th year of his reign, entitled "An act for granting duties on paper, tea, &c." form that connected chain of parliamentary usurpation, which has already been the subject of frequent applications to his majesty, and the houses of lords and commons of Great Britain; and no answers having yet been condescended to any of these, we shall not trouble his majesty with a repetition of the matters they contained.

But that one other act,[10] passed in the same 7th year of his reign, having been a peculiar attempt, must ever require peculiar mention; it is entitled "An act for suspending the legislature of New York." One free and independent legislature hereby takes upon itself to suspend the powers of another, free and independent as itself; this exhibiting a phœnomenon unknown in nature, the creator and creature of his own power. Not only the principles of common-sense, but the common feelings of human nature, must be surrendered up before his majesty's subjects here can be persuaded to believe that they hold their political existence at the will of a British parliament. Shall these governments be dissolved, their property annihilated, and their people reduced to a state of nature, at the imperious breath of a body of men, whom they never saw, in whom they never confided, and over whom they have no powers of punishment or removal, let their crimes against the American public be ever so great? Can any one reason be assigned why 160,000 electors in the island of Great Britain should give law to four millions in the states of America, every individual of whom is equal to every individual

[6] 4. G. 3. c. 15.
[7] 5. G. 3. c. 12.
[8] 6. G. 3. c. 12.
[9] 7. G. 3.
[10] 7. G. 3. c. 59.

of them, in virtue, in understanding, and in bodily strength? Were this to be admitted, instead of being a free people, as we have hitherto supposed, and mean to continue ourselves, we should suddenly be found the slaves not of one but of 160,000 tyrants, distinguished too from all others by this singular circumstance, that they are removed from the reach of fear, the only restraining motive which may hold the hand of a tyrant.

That by "an act[11] to discontinue in such manner and for such time as they are therein mentioned, the landing and discharging, lading or shipping, of goods, wares, and merchandize, at the town and within the harbour of Boston, in the province of Massachusetts Bay, in North America" which was passed at the last session of British parliament; a large and populous town, whose trade was their sole subsistence, was deprived of that trade, and involved in utter ruin. Let us for a while suppose the question of right suspended, in order to examine this act on principles of justice: An act of parliament had been passed imposing duties on teas, to be paid in America, against which act the Americans had protested as inauthoritative. The East India Company, who till that time had never sent a pound of tea to America on their own account, step forth on that occasion the assertors of parliamentary right, and send hither many ship loads of that obnoxious commodity. The masters of their several vessels, however, on their arrival to America, wisely attended to admonition, and returned with their cargoes. In the province of New England alone the remonstrances of the people were disregarded, and a compliance, after being many days waited for, was flatly refused. Whether in this the master of the vessel was governed by his obstinacy, or his instructions, let those who know say. There are extraordinary situations which require extraordinary interposition. An exasperated people, who feel that they possess power, are not easily restrained within limits strictly regular. A number of them assembled in the town of Boston, threw the tea into the ocean, and dispersed without doing any other act of violence. If in this they did wrong, they were known and were amenable to the laws of the land, against which it could not be objected that they had ever, in any instance, been obstructed or diverted from their regular course in favour of popular offenders. They should

[11] 7. G. 3. c. 59.

therefore not have been distrusted on this occasion. But that ill fated colony had formerly been bold in their enmities against the house of Stuart, and were now devoted to ruin by that unseen hand which governs the momentous affairs of this great empire. On the partial representations of a few worthless ministerial dependants, whose constant office it has been to keep that government embroiled, and who, by their treacheries, hope to obtain the dignity of the British knighthood, without calling for the party accused, without asking a proof, without attempting a distinction between the guilty and the innocent, the whole of that ancient and wealthy town is in a moment reduced from opulence to beggary. Men who had spent their lives in extending the British commerce, who had invested in that place the wealth their honest endeavors had merited, found themselves and their families thrown at once on the world for subsistence by its charities. Not the hundredth part of the inhabitants of that town had been concerned in the act complained of, many of them were in Great Britain and in other parts beyond sea, yet all were involved in one indiscriminate ruin, by a new executive power unheard of till then, that of a British Parliament. A property, of the value of many millions of money, was sacrificed to revenge, not repay, the loss of a few thousands. This is administering justice with a heavy hand indeed! and when is this tempest to be arrested in its course? Two wharfs are to be opened again when his Majesty shall think proper. The residue, which lined the extensive shores of the bay of Boston, are forever interdicted the exercise of commerce. This little exception seems to have been thrown in for no other purpose than that of setting a precedent for investing his majesty with legislative powers. If the pulse of his people shall beat calmly under this experiment, another and another shall be tried, till the measure of despotism be filled up. It would be an insult on common sense to pretend that this exception was made in order to restore its commerce to that great town. The trade which cannot be received at two wharfs alone must of necessity be transferred to some other place; to which it will soon be followed by that of the two wharfs. Considered in this light, it would be insolent and cruel mockery at the annihilation of the town of Boston.

By the act[12] for the suppression of riots and tumults in the town of Boston, passed also in the last session of parliament, a murder com-

---

[12] 14.G.3.

mitted there is, if the governor pleases, to be tried in a court of King's
Bench, in the island of Great Britain, by a jury of Middlesex. The
witnesses, too, on receipt of such a sum as the governor shall think it
reasonable for them to expend, are to enter into recognizance to
appear at the trial. This is, in other words, taxing them to the moment
of their recognizance, and that amount may be whatever a governor
pleases; for who does his majesty think can be prevailed on to cross
the Atlantic for the sole purpose of bearing evidence to a fact? His
expences are to be borne, indeed, as they shall be estimated by a governor; but who are to feed the wife and children whom he leaves
behind and who have had no other subsistence but his daily labour?
Those epidemical disorders too, so terrible in a foreign climate, is the
cure of them to be estimated among the articles of expence, and their
danger to be warded off by the almighty power of parliament? And
the wretched criminal, if he happen to have offended on the American
side, stripped of his privilege of trial by peers of his vicinage, removed
from the place where alone full evidence could be obtained, without
money, without council, without friends, without exculpatory proof,
is tried before judges predetermined to condemn. The cowards who
would suffer a countryman to be torn from the bowels of their society,
in order to be thus offered a sacrifice to parliamentary tyranny, would
merit that everlasting infamy now fixed on the authors of the act! A
clause[13] for a similar purpose had been introduced into an act passed
in the twelfth year of his majesty's reign, entitled "An act for the
better securing and preserving his majesty's dockyards, magazines,
ships, ammunition and stores," against which, as meriting the same
censures, the several colonies have already protested.

That these are acts of power, assumed by a body of men, foreign
to our constitutions, and unacknowledged by our laws, against
which we do, on behalf of the inhabitants of British America, enter
this our solemn and determined protest; and we do earnestly entreat
his majesty, as yet the only mediatory power between the several
states of the British empire, to recommend to his parliament of
Great Britain the total revocation of these acts, which, however
nugatory they be, may yet prove the cause of further discontents
and jealousies among us.

That we next proceed to consider the conduct of his majesty, as
holding the executive powers of the laws of these states, and mark

[13] 12.G.3.c.23.

73

out his deviations from the line of duty. By the constitution of Great Britain, as well of the several American states, his majesty professes the power of refusing to pass into a law any bill which has already passed the other two branches of legislature. His majesty, however, and his ancestors, conscious of the impropriety of opposing their single opinion to the united wisdom of two houses of parliament, while their proceedings were unbiassed by interested principles, for several ages past have modestly declined the exercise of this power in that part of his empire called Great Britain. But by change of circumstances, other principles than those of justice simply obtained an influence on their determinations; the addition of new states to the British empire has produced an addition of new, and sometimes opposite interests. It is now, therefore, the great office of his majesty, to resume exercise of his negative power, and to prevent the passage of laws by any one legislature of the empire, which might bear injuriously on the rights and interests of another. Yet this will not excuse the wanton exercise of this power which we have seen his Majesty practise on the laws of the American legislatures. For the most trifling reasons, and sometimes for no conceivable reason at all, his majesty has rejected laws of the most salutary tendency. The abolition of domestic slavery is the great object of desire in those colonies, where it was unhappily introduced in their infant state. But previous to the enfranchisement of the slaves we have, it is necessary to exclude all further importations from Africa; yet our repeated attempts to effect this by prohibitions, and by imposing duties which might amount to a prohibition, have been hitherto defeated by his majesty's negative: Thus preferring the immediate advantages of a few British corsairs to the lasting interests of the American states, and to the rights of human nature deeply wounded by this infamous practice. Nay, the single interposition of an interested individual against a law was scarcely ever known to fail of success, though in the opposite scale were placed the interests of a whole country. That this is so shameful an abuse of a power trusted with his majesty for other purposes, as if not reformed, would call for some legal restrictions.

With equal inattention to the necessities of his people here has his Majesty permitted our laws to lie neglected in England for years, neither confirming them by his assent, nor annulling them by his negative; so that such of them as have no suspending clause we hold on the most precarious of all tenures, his majesty's will, and such of them as suspend themselves till his majesty's assent be obtained, we have feared, might be called into existence at some future and distant period, when the time and change of circumstances shall have rendered them destructive to his people here. And to render this aggrievance still more oppressive, his majesty by his instructions has laid his governors under such restrictions that they can pass no law of any moment unless it have such suspending clause; so that, however immediate may be the call for legislative interposition, the law cannot be executed till it has twice crossed the Atlantic, by which time the evil may have spent its whole force.

But in what terms, reconcileable to majesty, and at the same time to truth, shall we speak of a late instruction to his majesty's governor of the colony of Virginia, by which he is forbidden to assent to any law for the division of a county, unless the new county will consent to have no representative in assembly? That colony has as yet fixed no boundary to the westward. Their westward counties, therefore, are of indefinite extent; some of them are actually seated many hundred miles from their eastward limits. Is it possible, then, that his majesty can have bestowed a single thought on the situation of those people, who, in order to obtain justice for injuries, however great or small, must, by the laws of that colony, attend their county court, at such a distance, with all their witnesses, monthly, till their litigation be determined? Or does his majesty seriously wish, and publish it to the world, that his subjects should give up the glorious right of representation, with all the benefits derived from that, and submit themselves the absolute slaves of his sovereign will? Or is it rather meant to confine the legislative body to their present numbers, that they may be the cheaper bargain whenever they shall become worth a purchase.

One of the articles of impeachment against Trestlain, and the other judges of Westminster-Hall, in the reign of Richard the second, for which they suffered death, as traitors to their country, was, that they had advised the king that he might dissolve his parliament at any time; and succeeding kings have adopted the opinion of these unjust judges. Since the establishment, however, of the British constitution, at the glorious revolution, on its free and antient principles, neither his majesty, nor his ancestors, have exercised such a power of dissolution in the island of Great Britain; and when his majesty was petitioned, by the united voice of his people there, to dissolve the present parliament, who had become obnoxious to them, his ministers were heard to declare, in open parliament, that his majesty possessed no such power by the constitution.[14] But how different their language and his practice here! To declare, as their duty required, the known rights of their country, to oppose the usurpations of every foreign judicature, to disregard the imperious mandates of a minister or governor, have been the avowed causes of dissolving houses of representatives in America. But if such powers be really vested in his majesty, can he suppose they are there placed to awe the members from such purposes as these? When the representative body have lost their confidence of their constituents, when they have notoriously made sale of their most valuable rights, when they have assumed to themselves powers which the people never put into their hands, then indeed their continuing in office becomes dangerous to the state, and calls for an exercise of the power of dissolution. Such being the causes for which the representative body should, and should not be dissolved, will it not appear strange to an unbiased observer, that that of Great Britain was not dissolved, while those of the colonies have repeatedly incurred that sentence?

But your majesty, or your governors, have carried this power beyond every limit known, or provided for, by the laws: After dissolving one house of representatives, they have refused to call another, so that for a great length of time, the legislature provided by the laws has been out of existence. From the nature of things, every society must at all times possess within itself the sovereign powers of legislation. The feelings of human nature revolt against the supposition of a state so situated as that it may not in any emergency provide against dangers which perhaps threatened immediate ruin. While those bodies are in existence to whom the people have delegated the powers of legislation, they alone possess

---

[14] "Since this period the king has several times dissolved the parliament a few weeks before its expiration, merely as an assertion of right." [*MS note in TJ's copy. – Eds.*] "On further inquiry I find two instances of dissolutions before the Parliament would, of itself, have been at an end: viz., the Parliament called to meet August 24, 1698, was dissolved by King William, December 19, 1700, and a new one called, to meet February 6, 1701, which was also dissolved November 11, 1701, and a new one met December 30, 1701." [*Additional note by TJ, in MS copy, Department of State Archives. – Eds.*]

and may exercise those powers; but when they are dissolved by the lopping off one or more of their branches, the power reverts to the people, who may exercise it to unlimited extent, either assembling together in person, sending deputies, or in any other way they may think proper.[15] We forbear to trace consequences further; the dangers are conspicuous with which this practice is replete.

That we shall at this time take notice of an error in the nature of our land holdings, which crept in at a very early period of our settlement. The introduction of the feudal tenures into the kingdom of England, though ancient, is well enough understood to set this matter in a proper light. In the earlier ages of the Saxon settlement feudal holdings were certainly altogether unknown; and very few, if any, had been introduced at the time of the Norman conquest. Our Saxon ancestors held their lands, as they did their personal property, in absolute dominion, disencumbered with any superior, answering nearly to the nature of those possessions which the feudalists term allodial. William, the Norman, first introduced that system generally. The land which had belonged to those who fell in the battle of Hastings, and in the subsequent insurrections of his reign, formed a considerable proportion of the lands of the whole kingdom. These he granted out, subject to feudal duties, as did he also those of a great number of his new subjects, who, by persuasions or threats, were induced to surrender them for that purpose. But still much was left in the hands of his Saxon subjects; held of no superior and not subject to feudal conditions. These, therefore, by express laws, enacted to render uniform the system of military defence, were made liable to the same military duties as if they had been feuds; and the Norman lawyers soon found means to saddle them also with all the other feudal burthens. But still they had not been surrendered to the king, they were not derived from his grant, and therefore they were not holden of him. A general principle indeed, was introduced, that "all lands in England were held either mediately or immediately of the crown," but this was borrowed from those holdings, which were truly feudal, and only applied to others for the purposes of illustration. Feudal holdings

*[feudalism versus 18th C. realities]*

[15] "insert 'and the frame of government thus dissolved, should the people take upon them to lay the throne of your majesty prostrate, or to discontinue their connection with the British empire, none will be so bold as to decide against the right or the efficacy of such avulsion.'" [*MS note in TJ's copy. – Eds.*]

were therefore but exceptions out of the Saxon laws of possession, under which all lands were held in absolute right. These, therefore, still form the basis, or groundwork, of the common law, to prevail wheresoever the exceptions have taken place. America was not conquered by William the Norman, nor its lands surrendered to him, or any of his successors. Possessions there are undoubtedly of the allodial nature. Our ancestors, however, who emigrated hither, were farmers, not lawyers. The fictitious principle that all lands belong originally to the king, they were early persuaded to believe real; and accordingly took grants of their own lands from the crown. And while the crown continued to grant for small sums, and on reasonable rents, there was no inducement to arrest the error, and lay it open to the public view. But his majesty has lately taken on him to advance the terms of purchase, and of holding to the double of what they were, by which means the acquisition of lands being rendered difficult, the population of our country is likely to be checked. It is time, therefore, for us to lay this matter before his majesty, and to declare that he has no right to grant lands of himself. From the nature and purpose of civil institutions, all the lands within the limits which any particular society has circumscribed around itself are assumed by that society, and subject to their allotment only. This may be done by themselves assembled collectively, or by their legislature, to whom they may have delegated sovereign authority; and if they are alloted in either of these ways, each individual of the society may appropriate to himself such lands as he finds vacant, and occupancy will give him title.

That in order to force the arbitrary measures before complained of, his majesty has from time to time sent among us large bodies of armed forces, not made up of the people here, nor raised by the authority of our laws. Did his majesty possess such a right as this, it might swallow up all our other rights whenever he should think proper. But his majesty has no right to land a single armed man on our shores, and those whom he sends here are liable to our laws made for the suppression and punishment of riots, and unlawful assemblies; or are hostile bodies, invading us in defiance of the law. When in the course of the late war it became expedient that a body of Hanoverian troops should be brought over for the defence of Great Britian, his majesty's grandfather, our late sovereign, did not pretend to introduce them under any authority he possessed. Such a measure would have given just alarm to his subjects in Great Britain, whose liberties would not be safe if armed men of another country, and of another spirit, might be brought into the realm at any time without the consent of their legislature. He therefore applied to parliament, who passed an act for that purpose, limiting the number to be brought in, and the time they were to continue. In like manner is his majesty restrained in every part of the empire. He possesses, indeed, the executive power of the laws in every state, but they are the laws of the particular state which he is to administer within that state, and not those of any one within the limits of another. Every state must judge for itself the number of armed men which they may safely trust among them, of whom they are to consist, and under what restrictions they shall be laid.

To render these proceedings still more criminal against our laws, instead of subjecting the military to the civil powers, his majesty has expressly made the civil subordinate to the military. But can his majesty thus put down all law under his feet? Can he erect a power superior to that which erected himself? He has done it indeed by force, but let him remember that force cannot give right.

That these are our grievances which we have thus laid before his majesty, with that freedom of language and sentiment which becomes a free people claiming their rights, as derived from the laws of nature, and not as the gift of their chief magistrate: Let those flatter who fear, it is not an American art. To give praise which is not due might be well from the venal, but would ill beseem those who are asserting the rights of human nature. They know, and will therefore say, that kings are the servants, not the proprietors of the people. Open your breast, sire, to liberal and expanded thought. Let not the name of George the third be a blot in the page of history. You are surrounded by English counsellors, but remember that they are parties. You have no minister for American affairs, because you have none taken up from among us, nor amenable to the laws on which they are to give you advice. It behooves you, therefore, to think and to act for yourself and your people. The great principles of right and wrong are legible to every reader; to pursue them requires not the aid of many counsellors. The whole art of government consists in the art of being honest. Only aim to do your duty, and mankind will give you credit where you fail. No longer persevere in sacrificing the rights of one part of the empire to the inordinate desires of another; but deal out to all equal and impartial right. Let no act be passed by any one legislature which may infringe on the rights and liberties of another. This is the important post in which fortune has placed you, holding the balance of a great, if a well poised empire. This, sire, is the advice of your great American council, on the observance of which may perhaps depend your felicity and future fame, and the preservation of that harmony which alone can continue both in Great Britain and America the reciprocal advantages of their connection. It is neither our wish nor our interest to separate from her. We are willing, on our part, to sacrifice everything which reason can ask to the restoration of that tranquillity for which all must wish. On their part, let them be ready to establish union on a generous plan. Let them name their terms, but let them be just. Accept of every commercial preference it is in our power to give for such things as we can raise for their use, or they make for ours. But let them not think to exclude us from going to other markets to dispose of those commodities which they cannot use, or to supply those wants which they cannot supply. Still less let it be proposed that our properties within our own territories shall be taxed or regulated by any power on earth but our own. The God who gave us life gave us liberty at the same time; the hand of force may destroy, but cannot disjoin them. This, sire, is our last, our determined resolution; and that you will be pleased to interpose with that efficacy which your earnest endeavors may ensure to procure redress of these our great grievances to quiet the minds of your subjects in British America, against any apprehensions of future encroachment, to establish fraternal love and harmony through the whole empire, and that these may continue to the latest ages of time, is the fervent prayer of all British America.

Ford I: 428–47

## II.2 Declaration of the Causes and Necessity of Taking Up Arms

[adopted by Congress July 6, 1775]

A DECLARATION by the REPRESENTATIVES of the United Colonies of North-America, now met in Congress at Philadelphia, setting forth the Causes and Necessity of their taking up Arms.

*the predication of this argument is one Lockean social contract & humanism (right of the people (man)).*

If it was possible for Men, who exercise their Reason to believe, that the Divine Author of our Existence intended a Part of the human Race to hold an absolute Property in, and an unbounded Power over others, marked out by his infinite Goodness and Wisdom, as the Objects of a legal Domination never rightfully resistible, however severe and oppressive, the Inhabitants of these Colonies might at least require from the Parliament of Great-Britain some Evidence, that this dreadful Authority over them has been granted to that Body. But a Reverence for our great Creator, Principles of Humanity, and the Dictates of Common Sense, must convince all those who reflect upon the Subject, that Government was instituted to promote the Welfare of Mankind, and ought to be administered for the Attainment of that End. The Legislature of Great-Britain, however, stimulated by an inordinate Passion for a Power not only unjustifiable, but which they know to be peculiarly reprobated by the very Constitution of that Kingdom, and desperate of Success in any Mode of Contest, where Regard should be had to Truth, Law, or Right, have at Length, deserting those, attempted to effect their cruel and impolitic Purpose of enslaving these Colonies by Violence, and have thereby rendered it necessary for us to close with their last Appeal from Reason to Arms. Yet, however blinded that Assembly may be, by their intemperate Rage for unlimited Domination, so to Slight Justice and the Opinion of Mankind, we esteem ourselves bound by Obligations of Respect to the Rest of the World, to make known the Justice of our Cause.

Our Forefathers, Inhabitants of the Island of Great-Britain, left their Native Land, to seek on these Shores a Residence for civil and religious Freedom. At the Expence of their Blood, at the Hazard of their Fortunes, without the least Charge to the Country from which they removed, by unceasing Labour and an unconquerable Spirit, they effected Settlements in the distant and inhospitable Wilds of America, then filled with numerous and warlike Nations of Barbarians. Societies or Governments, vested with perfect Legislatures, were formed under Charters from the Crown, and an harmonious Intercourse was established between the Colonies and the Kingdom from which they derived their Origin. The mutual Benefits of this Union became in a short Time so extraordinary, as to excite Astonishment. It is universally confessed, that the amazing Increase of the Wealth, Strength, and Navigation of the Realm, arose from this

Source; and the Minister, who so wisely and successfully directed the Measures of Great-Britain in the late War, publicly declared, that these Colonies enabled her to triumph over her Enemies. Towards the Conclusion of that War, it pleased our Sovereign to make a Change in his Counsels. From that fatal Moment, the Affairs of the British Empire began to fall into Confusion, and gradually sliding from the Summit of glorious Prosperity to which they had been advanced by the Virtues and Abilities of one Man, are at length distracted by the Convulsions, that now shake it to its deepest Foundations. The new Ministry finding the brave Foes of Britain, though frequently defeated, yet still contending, took up the unfortunate Idea of granting them a hasty Peace, and of then subduing her faithful Friends.

These devoted Colonies were judged to be in such a State, as to present Victories without Bloodshed, and all the easy Emoluments of statuteable Plunder. The uninterrupted Tenor of their peaceable and respectful Behaviour from the Beginning of Colonization, their dutiful, zealous, and useful Services during the War, though so recently and amply acknowledged in the most honourable Manner by his Majesty, by the late King, and by Parliament, could not save them from the meditated Innovations. Parliament was influenced to adopt the pernicious Project, and assuming a new Power over them, have in the Course of eleven Years given such decisive Specimens of the Spirit and Consequences attending this Power, as to leave no Doubt concerning the Effects of Acquiescence under it. They have undertaken to give and grant our Money without our Consent, though we have ever exercised an exclusive Right to dispose of our own Property; Statutes have been passed for extending the Jurisdiction of Courts of Admiralty and Vice-Admiralty beyond their ancient Limits; for depriving us of the accustomed and inestimable Privilege of Trial by Jury in Cases affecting both Life and Property; for suspending the Legislature of one of the Colonies; for interdicting all Commerce to the Capital of another; and for altering fundamentally the Form of Government established by Charter, and secured by Acts of its own Legislature solemnly confirmed by the Crown; for exempting the "Murderers" of Colonists from legal Trial, and in Effect, from Punishment; for erecting in a neighbouring Province, acquired by the joint Arms of Great-Britain and America, a Despotism dangerous to our very Existence; and for quartering Soldiers upon the Colonists in Time of profound Peace. It has also been resolved in Parliament, that Colonists charged with committing certain Offences, shall be transported to England to be tried.

But why should we enumerate our Injuries in detail? By one Statute it is declared, that Parliament can "of right make Laws to bind us in all Cases whatsoever." What is to defend us against so enormous, so unlimited a Power? Not a single Man of those who assume it, is chosen by us; or is subject to our Controul or Influence; but on the Contrary, they are all of them exempt from the Operation of such Laws, and an American Revenue, if not diverted from the ostensible Purposes for which it is raised, would actually lighten their own Burdens in Proportion, as they increase ours. We saw the Misery to which such Despotism would reduce us. We for ten Years incessantly and ineffectually besieged the Throne as Supplicants; we reasoned, we remonstrated with Parliament in the most mild and decent Language.

Administration sensible that we should regard these oppressive Measures as Freemen ought to do, sent over Fleets and Armies to enforce them. The Indignation of the Americans was roused, it is true; but it was the Indignation of a virtuous, loyal, and affectionate People. A Congress of Delegates from the United Colonies was assembled at Philadelphia, on the fifth Day of last September. We resolved again to offer an humble and dutiful Petition to the King, and also addressed our Fellow Subjects of Great-Britain. We have pursued every temperate, every respectful Measure; we have even proceeded to break off our commercial Intercourse with our Fellow Subjects, as the last peaceable Admonition, that our Attachment to no Nation upon Earth should supplant our Attachment to Liberty. This, we flattered ourselves, was the ultimate Step of the Controversy: But subsequent Events have shewn, how vain was this Hope of finding Moderation in our Enemies.

Several threatening Expressions against the Colonies were inserted in His Majesty's Speech; our Petition, tho' we were told it was a Decent one, and that his Majesty had been pleased to receive it graciously, and to promise laying it before his Parliament, was huddled into both Houses among a Bundle of American Papers, and there neglected. The Lords and Commons in their Address, in the Month of February, said, that "a Rebellion at that Time actually existed within the Province of Massachusetts-Bay; and that those concerned in it, had been countenanced and encouraged by unlawful Combinations and Engagements, entered into by his Majesty's Subjects in several of the other Colonies; and therefore they besought his Majesty, that he would take the most effectual Measures to inforce due Obedience to the Laws and Authority of the Supreme Legislature." Soon after, the commercial Intercourse of whole Colonies, with foreign Countries, and with each other, was cut off by an Act of Parliament; by another, several of them were intirely prohibited from the Fisheries in the Seas near their Coasts, on which they always depended for their Sustenance; and large Reinforcements of Ships and Troops were immediately sent over to General Gage.

Fruitless were all the entreaties, arguments, and eloquence of an Illustrious Band of the most distinguished Peers, and Commoners, who nobly and strenuously asserted the Justice of our Cause, to stay, or even to mitigate the heedless fury with which these accumulated and unexampled Outrages were hurried on. Equally fruitless was the interference of the City of London, of Bristol, and many other respectable Towns in our Favour. Parliament adopted an insidious Manoeuvre calculated to divide us, to establish a perpetual Auction of Taxations where Colony should bid against Colony, all of them uninformed what Ransom would redeem their Lives; and thus to extort from us, at the Point of the Bayonet, the unknown sums that should be sufficient to gratify, if possible to gratify, ministerial Rapacity, with the miserable indulgence left to us of raising, in our own Mode, the prescribed Tribute. What Terms more rigid and humiliating could have been dictated by remorseless Victors to conquered Enemies? In our circumstances to accept them, would be to deserve them.

Soon after the Intelligence of these proceedings arrived on this Continent, General Gage, who in the course of the last Year had taken Possession of the Town of Boston, in the Province of Massachusetts-Bay, and still occupied it as a Garrison, on the 19th day of April, sent out from that Place a large detachment of his Army, who made an unprovoked Assault on the Inhabitants of the said Province, at the Town of Lexington, as appears by the Affidavits of a great Number of Persons, some of whom were Officers and Soldiers of that detachment, murdered eight of the Inhabitants, and wounded many others. From thence the Troops proceeded in war-like Array to the Town of Concord, where they set upon another Party of the Inhabitants of the same Province, killing several and wounding more, until compelled to retreat by the country People suddenly assembled to repel this cruel Aggression. Hostilities, thus commenced by the British Troops, have been since prosecuted by them without regard to Faith or Reputation. The Inhabitants of Boston being confined within that Town by the General their Governor, and having, in order to procure their dismission, entered into a Treaty with him, it was stipulated that the said Inhabitants having deposited their Arms with their own Magistrates, should have liberty to depart, taking with them their other Effects. They accordingly delivered up their Arms, but in open violation of Honour, in defiance of the obligation of Treaties, which even savage Nations esteemed sacred, the Governor ordered the Arms deposited as aforesaid, that they might be preserved for their owners, to be seized by a Body of Soldiers; detained the greatest part of the Inhabitants in the Town, and compelled the few who were permitted to retire, to leave their most valuable Effects behind.

By this perfidy Wives are separated from their Husbands, Children from their Parents, the aged and the sick from their Relations and Friends, who wish to attend and comfort them; and those who have been used to live in Plenty and even Elegance, are reduced to deplorable Distress.

The General, further emulating his ministerial Masters, by a Proclamation bearing date on the 12th day of June, after venting the grossest Falsehoods and Calumnies against the good People of these Colonies, proceeds to "declare them all, either by Name or Description, to be Rebels and Traitors, to supersede the course of the Common Law, and instead thereof to publish and order the use and exercise of the Law Martial." His Troops have butchered our Countrymen, have wantonly burnt Charlestown, besides a considerable number of Houses in other Places; our Ships and Vessels are seized; the necessary supplies of Provisions are intercepted, and he is exerting his utmost Power to spread destruction and devastation around him.

We have received certain Intelligence, that General Carleton, the Governor of Canada, is instigating the People of that Province and the Indians to fall upon us; and we have but too much reason to apprehend, that Schemes have been formed to excite domestic Enemies against us. In brief, a part of these Colonies now feel, and all of them are sure of feeling, as far as the Vengeance of Administration can inflict them, the complicated Calamities of Fire, Sword, and Famine. We are reduced to the alternative of chusing an unconditional Submission to the tyranny of irritated Ministers, or resistance by Force. The latter is our choice. We have counted the cost of this contest, and find nothing so dreadful as voluntary Slavery. Honour, Justice, and Humanity, forbid us tamely to surrender that Freedom which we received from our gallant Ancestors, and which our innocent Posterity have a right to receive from us. We cannot endure the infamy and guilt of resigning succeeding Generations to that wretchedness which inevitably awaits them, if we basely entail hereditary Bondage upon them.

Our cause is just. Our union is perfect. Our internal Resources are great, and, if necessary, foreign Assistance is undoubtedly attainable. We gratefully acknowledge, as signal Instances of the Divine Favour towards us, that his Providence would not permit us to be called into this severe Controversy, until we were grown up to our present strength, had been previously exercised in warlike Operation, and possessed of the means of defending ourselves. With hearts fortified with these animating Reflections, we most solemnly, before God and the World, declare, that, exerting the utmost Energy of those Powers, which our beneficent Creator hath graciously bestowed upon us, the Arms we have been compelled by our Enemies to assume, we will, in defiance of every Hazard, with unabating Firmness and Perseverence, employ for the preservation of our Liberties; being with one Mind resolved to die Freemen rather than to live Slaves.

Lest this Declaration should disquiet the Minds of our Friends and Fellow-Subjects in any part of the Empire, we assure them that we mean not to dissolve that Union which has so long and so happily subsisted between us, and which we sincerely wish to see restored. Necessity has not yet driven us into that desperate Measure, or induced us to excite any other Nation to War against them. We have not raised Armies with ambitious Designs of separating from Great-Britain, and establishing Independent States. We fight not for Glory or for Conquest. We exhibit to Mankind the remarkable Spectacle of a People attacked by unprovoked Enemies, without any imputation or even suspicion of Offence. They boast of their Privileges and Civilization, and yet proffer no milder Conditions than Servitude or Death.

In our own native Land, in defence of the Freedom that is our Birthright, and which we ever enjoyed till the late Violation of it – for the protection of our Property, acquired solely by the honest Industry of our fore-fathers and ourselves, against Violence actually offered, we have taken up Arms. We shall lay them down when Hostilities shall cease on the part of the Aggressors, and all danger of their being renewed shall be removed, and not before.

With an humble Confidence in the Mercies of the supreme and impartial Judge and Ruler of the Universe, we most devoutly implore his Divine Goodness to protect us happily through this great Conflict, to dispose our Adversaries to reconciliation on reasonable Terms, and thereby to relieve the Empire from the Calamities of civil War.

> Worthington Chauncy Ford (ed.), *Journals of the Continental Congress* (Washington, DC, 1834), II: 140–6.

## II.3 To John Randolph

Monticello, August 25, 1775

Dear Sir, – I received your message by Mr. Braxton and immediately gave him an order on the Treasurer for the money, which the Treasurer assured me should be answered on his return. I now send the bearer for the violin and such musick appurtaining to her as may be of no use to the young ladies. I beleive you had no case to her. If so, be so good as to direct Watt Lenox to get from Prentis's some bays or other coarse woollen to wrap her in, and then to pack her securely in a wooden box.

I am sorry the situation of our country should render it not eligible to you to remain longer in it. I hope the returning wisdom of Great Britain will e'er long put an end to this unnatural contest. There may be people to whose tempers and dispositions Contention may be pleasing, and who may therefore wish a continuance of confusion. But to me it is of all states, but one, the most horrid. My first wish is a restoration of our just rights; my second a return of the happy period when, consistently with duty, I may withdraw myself totally from the public stage and pass the rest of my days in domestic ease and tranquillity, banishing every desire of afterwards even hearing what passes in the world. Perhaps ardour for the latter may add considerably to the warmth of the former wish. Looking with fondness towards a reconciliation with Great Britain, I cannot help hoping you may be able to contribute towards expediting this good work. I think it must be evident to yourself that the ministry have been deceived by their officers on this side the water, who (for what purposes I cannot tell) have constantly represented the American opposition as that of a small faction, in which the body of the people took little part. This you can inform them of your own knolege to be untrue. They have taken it into their heads too that we are cowards and shall surrender at discretion to an armed force. The past and future operations of the war must confirm or undeceive them on that head. I wish they were thoroughly and minutely acquainted with every circumstance relative to America as it exists in truth. I am persuaded this would go far towards disposing them to reconciliation. Even those in parliament who are called friends to America seem to know nothing of our real determinations. I observe they pronounced in the last parliament that the Congress of 1774 did not mean to insist rigorously on the terms they held out, but kept something in reserve to give up; and in fact that they would give up everything but the article of taxation. Now the truth is far from this, as I can affirm, and put my honor to the assertion; and their continuance in this error may perhaps have very ill consequences. The Congress stated the lowest terms they thought possible to be accepted in order to convince the world they were not unreasonable. They gave up the monopoly and regulation of trade, and all the acts of parliament prior to 1764, leaving to British generosity to render these at some future time as easy to America as the interest of Britain would admit. But this was before blood was spilt. I cannot affirm, but have reason to think, these terms would not now be accepted. I wish no false sense of honor, no ignorance of our real intentions, no vain hope that partial concessions of right will be accepted may induce the ministry to trifle with accomodation till it shall be put even out of our own power ever to accomodate. If indeed Great Britain, disjoined from her colonies, be a match for the most potent nations of Europe with the colonies thrown into their scale, they may go on securely. But if they are not assured of this, it would be certainly unwise, by trying the event of another campaign, to risque our accepting a foreign aid which perhaps may not be obtainable but on a condition of ever-lasting avulsion from Great Britain. This would be thought a hard condition to those who still wish for reunion with their parent country. I am sincerely one of those, and would rather be in dependance on Great Britain, properly limited, than on any nation upon earth, or than on no nation. But I am one of those too who rather than submit to the right of legislating for us assumed by the British parliament, and which late experience has shewn they will so cruelly exercise, would lend my hand to sink the whole island in the ocean.

If undeceiving the minister as to matters of fact may change his dispositions, it will perhaps be in your power by assisting to do this, to render service to the whole empire, at the most critical time certainly that it has ever seen. Whether Britain shall continue the head of the greatest empire on earth, or shall return to her original station in the political scale of Europe depends perhaps on the resolutions of the succeeding winter. God send they may be wise and salutary for us all!

I shall be glad to hear from you as often as you may be disposed to think of things here. You may be at liberty I expect to communicate some things consistently with your honor and the duties you will owe to a protecting nation. Such a communication among individuals may be mutually beneficial to the contending parties. On this or any future occasion if I affirm to you any facts, your knolege of me will enable you to decide on their credibility; if I hazard opinions on the dispositions of men, or other speculative points, you can only know they are my opinions. My best wishes for your felicity attend you wherever you go, and beleive me to be assuredly Your friend & servt.,

P.S. My collection of classics and of books of parliamentary learning particularly is not so complete as I could wish. As you are going to the land of literature and of books you may be willing to dispose of some of yours here and replace them there in better editions. I should be willing to treat on this head with any body you may think proper to empower for that purpose.

Ford I: 482

## II.4 From the *Autobiography*

On the 15th of May, 1776, the convention of Virginia instructed their delegates in Congress to propose to that body to declare the colonies independent of G. Britain, and appointed a committee to prepare a declaration of rights and plan of government.

In Congress, Friday June 7. 1776. The delegates from Virginia moved in obedience to instructions from their constituents that the Congress should declare that these United colonies are & of right ought to be free & independent states, that they are absolved from all allegiance to the British crown, and that all political connection between them & the state of Great Britain is & ought to be, totally dissolved; that measures should be immediately taken for procuring the assistance of foreign powers, and a Confederation be formed to bind the colonies more closely together.[1]

The house being obliged to attend at that time to some other business, the proposition was referred to the next day, when the members were ordered to attend punctually at ten o'clock.

Saturday June 8. They proceeded to take it into consideration and referred it to a committee of the whole, into which they immediately resolved themselves, and passed that day & Monday the 10th in debating on the subject.

It was argued by Wilson, Robert R. Livingston, E. Rutledge, Dickinson and others

That tho' they were friends to the measures themselves, and saw the impossibility that we should ever again be united with Gr. Britain, yet they were against adopting them at this time:

That the conduct we had formerly observed was wise & proper now, of deferring to take any capital step till the voice of the people drove us into it:

That they were our power, & without them our declarations could not be carried into effect;

That the people of the middle colonies (Maryland, Delaware, Pennsylv[ani]a, the Jerseys & N. York) were not yet ripe for bidding adieu to British connection, but that they were fast ripening & in a short time would join in the general voice of America:

[1] The resolution was introduced by Richard Henry Lee of Virginia. – *Eds.*

That the resolution entered into by this house on the 15th of May for suppressing the exercise of all powers derived from the crown, had shown, by the ferment into which it had thrown these middle colonies, that they had not yet accommodated their minds to a separation from the mother country:

That some of them had expressly forbidden their delegates to consent to such a declaration, and others had given no instructions, & consequently no powers to give such consent:

That if the delegates of any particular colony had no power to declare such colony independant, certain they were the others could not declare it for them; the colonies being as yet perfectly independant of each other:

That the assembly of Pennsylvania was now sitting above stairs, their convention would sit within a few days, the convention of New York was now sitting, & those of the Jerseys & Delaware counties would meet on the Monday following, & it was probable these bodies would take up the question of Independance & would declare to their delegates the voice of their state:

That if such a declaration should now be agreed to, these delegates must retire & possibly their colonies might secede from the Union:

That such a secession would weaken us more than could be compensated by any foreign alliance:

That in the event of such a division, foreign powers would either refuse to join themselves to our fortunes, or, having us so much in their power as that desperate declaration would place us, they would insist on terms proportionably more hard and prejudicial:

That we had little reason to expect an alliance with those to whom alone as yet we had cast our eyes:

That France & Spain had reason to be jealous of that rising power which would one day certainly strip them of all their American possessions:

That it was more likely they should form a connection with the British court, who, if they should find themselves unable otherwise to extricate themselves from their difficulties, would agree to a partition of our territories, restoring Canada to France, & the Floridas to Spain, to accomplish for themselves a recovery of these colonies:

That it would not be long before we should receive certain information of the disposition of the French court, from the agent whom we had sent to Paris for that purpose:

That if this disposition should be favorable, by waiting the event of the present campaign, which we all hoped would be successful, we should have reason to expect an alliance on better terms:

That this would in fact work no delay of any effectual aid from such ally, as, from the advance of the season & distance of our situation, it was impossible we could receive any assistance during this campaign:

That it was prudent to fix among ourselves the terms on which we should form alliance, before we declared we would form one at all events:

And that if these were agreed on, & our Declaration of Independance ready by the time our Ambassador should be prepared to sail, it would be as well as to go into that Declaration at this day.

On the other side it was urged by J. Adams, Lee, Wythe, and others

That no gentleman had argued against the policy or the right of separation from Britain, nor had supposed it possible we should ever renew our connection; that they had only opposed its being now declared:

That the question was not whether, by a declaration of independance, we should make ourselves what we are not; but whether we should declare a fact which already exists:

That as to the people or parliament of England, we had alwais been independent of them, their restraints on our trade deriving efficacy from our acquiescence only, & not from any rights they possessed of imposing them, & that so far our connection had been federal only & was now dissolved by the commencement of hostilities:

That as to the King, we had been bound to him by allegiance, but that this bond was now dissolved by his assent to the late act of parliament, by which he declares us out of his protection, and by his levying war on us, a fact which had long ago proved us out of his protection; it being a certain position in law that allegiance & protection are reciprocal, the one ceasing when the other is withdrawn:

That James the IId. never declared the people of England out of his protection yet his actions proved it & the parliament declared it:

No delegates then can be denied, or ever want, a power of declaring an existing truth:

That the delegates from the Delaware counties having declared their constituents ready to join, there are only two colonies Pennsylvania & Maryland whose delegates are absolutely tied up, and that these had by their instructions only reserved a right of confirming or rejecting the measure:

That the instructions from Pennsylvania might be accounted for from the times in which they were drawn, near a twelvemonth ago, since which the face of affairs has totally changed:

That within that time it had become apparent that Britain was determined to accept nothing less than a carte-blanche, and that the King's answer to the Lord Mayor Aldermen & common council of London, which had come to hand four days ago, must have satisfied every one of this point:

That the people wait for us to lead the way:

That *they* are in favour of the measure, tho' the instructions given by some of their *representatives* are not:

That the voice of the representatives is not always consonant with the voice of the people, and that this is remarkably the case in these middle colonies:

That the effect of the resolution of the 15th of May has proved this, which, raising the murmurs of some in the colonies of Pennsylvania & Maryland, called forth the opposing voice of the freer part of the people, & proved them to be the majority, even in these colonies:

That the backwardness of these two colonies might be ascribed partly to the influence of proprietary power & connections, & partly to their having not yet been attacked by the enemy:

That these causes were not likely to be soon removed, as there seemed no probability that the enemy would make either of these the seat of this summer's war:

That it would be vain to wait either weeks or months for perfect unanimity, since it was impossible that all men should ever become of one sentiment on any question:

That the conduct of some colonies from the beginning of this contest, had given reason to suspect it was their settled policy to keep in the rear of the confederacy, that their particular prospect might be better, even in the worst event:

That therefore it was necessary for those colonies who had thrown themselves forward & hazarded all from the beginning, to come forward now also, and put all again to their own hazard:

That the history of the Dutch revolution, of whom three states only confederated at first proved that a secession of some colonies would not be so dangerous as some apprehended:

That a declaration of Independence alone could render it consistent with European delicacy for European powers to treat with us, or even to receive an Ambassador from us:

That till this they would not receive our vessels into their ports, nor acknowledge the adjudications of our courts of admiralty to be legitimate, in cases of capture of British vessels:

That though France & Spain may be jealous of our rising power, they must think it will be much more formidable with the addition of Great Britain; and will therefore see it their interest to prevent a coalition; but should they refuse, we shall be but where we are; whereas without trying we shall never know whether they will aid us or not:

That the present campaign may be unsuccessful, & therefore we had better propose an alliance while our affairs wear a hopeful aspect:

That to await the event of this campaign will certainly work delay, because during this summer France may assist us effectually by cutting off those supplies of provisions from England & Ireland on which the enemy's armies here are to depend; or by setting in motion the great power they have collected in the West Indies, & calling our enemy to the defence of the possessions they have there:

That it would be idle to lose time in settling the terms of alliance, till we had first determined we would enter into alliance:

That it is necessary to lose no time in opening a trade for our people, who will want clothes, and will want money too for the paiment of taxes:

And that the only misfortune is that we did not enter into alliance with France six months sooner, as besides opening their ports for the vent of our last year's produce, they might have marched an army into Germany and prevented the petty princes there from selling their unhappy subjects to subdue us.

It appearing in the course of these debates that the colonies York, New Jersey, Pennsylvania, Delaware, Maryland, and Carolina were not yet matured for falling from the parent stem, but that they were fast advancing to that state, it was thought most prudent to wait a while for them, and to postpone the final decision to July 1. but that this might occasion as little delay as possible a committee was appointed to prepare a declaration of independence. The committee were J. Adams, Dr. Franklin, Roger Sherman, Robert R. Livingston & myself. Committees were also appointed at the same time to prepare a plan of confederation for the colonies, and to state the terms proper to be proposed for foreign alliance. The committee for drawing the declaration of Independence desired me to do it. It was accordingly done, and being approved by them, I reported it to the house on Friday the 28th of June when it was read and ordered to lie on the table. On Monday, the 1st of July the house resolved itself into a committee of the whole & resumed the consideration of the original motion made by the delegates of Virginia, which being again debated through the day, was carried in the affirmative by the votes of N. Hampshire, Connecticut, Massachusetts, Rhode Island, N. Jersey, Maryland, Virginia, N. Carolina, & Georgia. S. Carolina and Pennsylvania voted against it. Delaware having but two members present, they were divided. The delegates for New York declared they were for it themselves & were assured their constituents were for it, but that their instructions having been drawn near a twelvemonth before, when reconciliation was still the general object, they were enjoined by them to do nothing which should impede that object. They therefore thought themselves not justifiable in voting on either side, and asked leave to withdraw from the question, which was given them. The committee rose & reported their resolution to the house. Mr. Edward Rutledge of S. Carolina then requested the determination might be put off to the next day, as he believed his colleagues, tho' they disapproved of the resolution, would then join in it for the sake of unanimity. The ultimate question whether the house would agree to the resolution of the committee was accordingly postponed to the next day, when it was again moved and S. Carolina concurred in voting for it. In the meantime a third member had come post from the Delaware counties and turned the vote of that colony in favour of the resolution. Members of a different sentiment attending that morning from Pennsylvania also, their vote was changed, so that the whole 12 colonies who were authorized to vote at all, gave their voices for it; and within a few days, the convention of N. York approved of it and thus supplied the void occasioned by the withdrawing of her delegates from the vote.

Congress proceeded the same day to consider the declaration of Independance which had been reported & lain on the table the Friday preceding, and on Monday referred to a committee of the whole. The pusillanimous idea that we had friends in England worth keeping terms with, still haunted the minds of many. For this reason those passages which conveyed censures on the people of England were struck out, lest they should give them offence. The clause too, reprobating the enslaving the inhabitants of Africa, was struck out in complaisance to South Carolina and Georgia, who had never attempted to restrain the importation of slaves, and who on the contrary still wished to continue it. Our northern brethren also I believe felt a little tender under those censures; for tho' their people have very few slaves themselves yet they had been pretty considerable carriers of them to others. The debates having taken up the greater parts of the 2d, 3d & 4th days of July were, in the evening of the last, closed, the declaration was reported by the committee, agreed to by the house and signed by every member present except Mr. Dickinson. As the sentiments of men are known not only by what they receive, but what they reject also, I will state the form of the declaration as originally reported. The parts struck out by Congress shall be distinguished by a black line drawn under them; & those inserted by them shall be placed in the margin or in a concurrent column.[2]

## II.5 A Declaration by the Representatives of the United States of America, in General Congress Assembled [Jefferson's draft]

When in the course of human events it becomes necessary for one people to dissolve the political bands which have connected them with another, and to assume among the powers of the earth the separate & equal station to which the laws of nature and of nature's God entitle

---

[2] TJ notes only major changes of wording, omitting to note minor editorial changes in spelling, punctuation, etc., made by the Congress. – *Eds.*

them, a decent respect to the opinions of mankind requires that they should declare the causes which impel them to the separation.

We hold these truths to be self-evident: that all men are created <sup>certain</sup> equal; that they are endowed by their creator with <u>inherent and</u> inalienable rights; that among these are life, liberty, & the pursuit of happiness: that to secure these rights, governments are instituted among men, deriving their just powers from the consent of the governed; that whenever any form of government becomes destructive of these ends, it is the right of the people to alter or abolish it, & to institute new government, laying it's foundation on such principles, & organizing it's powers in such form, as to them shall seem most likely to effect their safety & happiness. Prudence indeed will dictate that governments long established should not be changed for light & transient causes; and accordingly all experience hath shown that mankind are more disposed to suffer while evils are sufferable, than to right themselves by abolishing the forms to which they are accustomed. But when a long train of abuses & usurpations <u>begun at a distinguished period and</u> pursuing invariably the same object, evinces a design to reduce them under absolute despotism, it is their right, it is their duty to throw off such government, & to provide new guards for their future security. Such has been the patient sufferance of these colonies; & such is now the <sup>alter</sup> necessity which constrains them to <u>expunge</u> their former systems of government. The history of the present king of Great Britain is <sup>repeated</sup> a history of <u>unremitting</u> injuries & usurpations, <u>among which appears no solitary fact to contradict the uniform tenor of the rest but all have</u> in direct object the establishment of an absolute <sup>all having</sup> tyranny over these states. To prove this let facts be submitted to a candid world <u>for the truth of which we pledge a faith yet unsullied by falsehood.</u>

He has refused his assent to laws the most wholesome & necessary for the public good.

He has forbidden his governors to pass laws of immediate & pressing importance, unless suspended in their operation till his assent should be obtained; & when so suspended, he has utterly neglected to attend to them.

He has refused to pass other laws for the accommodation of large districts of people, unless those people would relinquish the right of representation in the legislature, a right inestimable to them, & formidable to tyrants only.

He has called together legislative bodies at places unusual, uncomfortable, and distant from the depository of their public records, for the sole purpose of fatiguing them into compliance with his measures.

He has dissolved representative houses repeatedly & continually for opposing with manly firmness his invasions on the rights of the people.

He has refused for a long time after such dissolutions to cause others to be elected, whereby the legislative powers, incapable of annihilation, have returned to the people at large for their exercise, the state remaining in the meantime exposed to all the dangers of invasion from without & convulsions within.

He has endeavored to prevent the population of these states; for that purpose obstructing the laws for naturalization of foreigners, refusing to pass others to encourage their migrations hither, & raising the conditions of new appropriations of lands.

<sup>obstructed</sup> He has suffered the administration of justice totally to cease in some of these states refusing his assent to laws for <sup>by</sup> establishing judiciary powers.

He has made our judges dependant on his will alone, for the tenure of their offices, & the amount & paiment of their salaries.

He has erected a multitude of new offices by a self assumed power and sent hither swarms of new officers to harass our people and eat out their substance.

He has kept among us in times of peace standing armies and ships of war without the consent of our legislatures.

He has affected to render the military independant of, & superior to the civil power.

He has combined with others to subject us to a jurisdiction foreign to our constitutions & unacknowledged by our laws, giving his assent to their acts of pretended legislation for quartering large bodies of armed troops among us; for protecting them by a mock-trial from punishment for any murders which they should commit on the inhabitants of these states; for cutting off our trade with all parts of the world; for imposing taxes on us without our consent; for depriving us [ ] of the benefits of trial by jury; for trans- <sup>in many cases</sup> porting us beyond seas to be tried for pretended offences; for abolishing the free system of English laws in a neighboring province, establishing therein an arbitrary government, and enlarging it's boundaries, so as to render it at once an example and fit instrument for introducing the same absolute rule into these states; for <sub>colonies</sub> taking away our charters, abolishing our most valuable laws, and altering fundamentally the forms of our governments; for suspending our own legislatures, & declaring themselves invested with power to legislate for us in all cases whatsoever.

He has abdicated government here withdrawing <sup>by declaring us out of</sup> his governors, and declaring us out of his <sup>his protection, and</sup> allegiance & protection. <sup>waging war against us.</sup>

He has plundered our seas, ravaged our coasts, burnt our towns, & destroyed the lives of our people.

He is at this time transporting large armies of foreign mercenaries to compleat the works of death, desolation & tyranny already begun <sup>scarcely paralleled</sup> with circumstances of cruelty and perfidy [ ] unworthy <sup>in the most barbar-</sup> the head of a civilized nation. <sup>ous ages, & totally</sup>

He has constrained our fellow citizens taken captive on the high seas to bear arms against their country, to become the executioners of their friends & brethren, or to fall themselves by their hands. <sup>excited domestic</sup> He has [ ] endeavored to bring on the inhabitants <sup>insurrection among</sup> of our frontiers the merciless Indian savages, whose <sup>us, & has</sup> known rule of warfare is an undistinguished destruction of all ages, sexes, & conditions of existence.

He has incited treasonable insurrections of our fellow-citizens, with the allurements of forfeiture & confiscation of our property.

He has waged cruel war against human nature itself, violating it's most sacred rights of life and liberty in the persons of a distant people who never offended him, captivating & carrying them into slavery in another hemisphere, or to incur miserable death in their transportation thither. This piratical warfare, the opprobium of INFIDEL powers, is the warfare of the CHRISTIAN king of Great Britain. Determined to keep open a market where MEN should be bought & sold, he has prostituted his negative for suppressing every legislative attempt to prohibit or to restrain this execrable commerce. And that this assemblage of horrors might want no fact of distinguished die, he is now exciting those very people to rise in arms among us, and to purchase that liberty of which he has deprived them, by murdering the people on whom he also obtruded them: thus paying off former crimes committed against the

LIBERTIES of one people, with crimes which he urges them to commit against the LIVES of another.

In every stage of these oppressions we have petitioned for redress in the most humble terms: our repeated petitions have been answered only by repeated injuries.

A prince whose character is thus marked by every act which may define a tyrant is unfit to be the ruler of a [ ] people who mean to <sup>free</sup> be free. Future ages will scarcely believe that the hardiness of one man adventured, within the short compass of twelve years only, to lay a foundation so broad & so undisguised for tyranny over a people fostered & fixed in principles of freedom.

Nor have we been wanting in attentions to our British brethren. We have warned them from time to time of attempts by their legislature to extend a jurisdiction over these our states. <sup>an unwarrantable</sup> <sup>us</sup>

We have reminded them of the circumstances of our emigration & settlement here, no one of which could warrant so strange a pretension: that these were effected at the expense of our own blood & treasure, unassisted by the wealth or the strength of Great Britain: that in constituting indeed our several forms of government, we had adopted one common king, thereby laying a foundation for perpetual league & amity with them: but that submission to their parliament was no part of our constitution, nor ever in idea, if history

have | may be credited: and, we [ ] appealed to their
and we have | native justice and magnanimity as well as to the ties
conjured them by | of our common kindred to disavow these usurpations
would inevitably | which were likely to interrupt our connection and

correspondence. They too have been deaf to the voice of justice & of consanguinity, and when occasions have been given them, by the regular course of their laws, of removing from their councils the disturbers of our harmony, they have, by their free election, reestablished them in power. At this very time too they are permitting their chief magistrate to send over not only soldiers of our common blood, but Scotch & foreign mercenaries to invade & destroy us. These facts have given the last stab to agonizing affection, and manly spirit bids us to renounce forever these unfeeling brethren. We must endeavor to forget our former love for them, and hold them as we hold the rest of mankind, enemies in war, in peace friends. We might have been a free and a great people together; but a communication of grandeur & of freedom it seems is below their dignity. Be it so, since they will have it. The road of happiness & to glory is open to us too.

We will tread it apart from them, and acquiesce in <small>We must therefore</small> the necessity which denounces our eternal separation <small>and hold them as we hold the rest of mankind, enemies in war, in peace friends.</small>
[  ]!

We therefore the representatives of the United States of America in General Congress assembled do in the name & by authority of the good people of these states reject & renounce all allegiance & subjection to the kings of Great Britain & all others who may hereafter claim by, through or under them: we utterly dissolve all political connection which may heretofore have subsisted between us & the people or parliament of Great Britain: & finally we do assert & declare these colonies to be free & independent states, & that as free & independent states, they have full power to levy war, conclude peace, contract alliances, establish commerce, & to do all other acts & things which independent states may of right do.

And for the support of this declaration we mutually pledge to each other our lives, our fortunes, & our sacred honor.

We therefore the representatives of the United States of America in General Congress assembled, appealing to the supreme judge of the world for the rectitude of our intentions, do in the name, & by the authority of the good people of these colonies, solemnly publish & declare that these united colonies are & of right ought to be free & independent states; that they are absolved from all allegiance to the British crown, and that all political connection between them & the state of Great Britain is, & ought to be, totally dissolved; & that as free & independent states they have full power to levy war, conclude peace, contract alliances, establish commerce & to do all other acts & things which independant states may of right do.

And for the support of this declaration, with a firm reliance on the protection of divine providence we mutually pledge to each other our lives, our fortunes, & our sacred honor.

The Declaration thus signed on the 4th, on paper was engrossed on parchment, & signed again on the 2d. of August.

*Ford* I: 18–38

## II.6 The Declaration of Independence [as amended and adopted in Congress], July 4, 1776

**The unanimous declaration of the thirteen United States of America**

When, in the course of human events, it becomes necessary for one people to dissolve the political bands which have connected them with another, and to assume, among the powers of the earth, the separate and equal station to which the laws of nature and of nature's God entitle them, a decent respect to the opinions of mankind requires that they should declare the causes which impel them to the separation.

We hold these truths to be self-evident: That all men are created equal; that they are endowed by their creator with certain unalienable rights; that among these are life, liberty, and the pursuit of happiness; that, to secure these rights, governments are instituted among men, deriving their just powers from the consent of the governed; that whenever any form of government becomes destructive of these ends, it is the right of the people to alter or to abolish it, and to institute new government, laying its foundation on such principles, and organizing its power in such form, as to them shall seem most likely to effect their safety and happiness. Prudence, indeed, will dictate that governments long established should not be changed for light and transient causes; and accordingly all experience hath shown that mankind are more disposed to suffer, while evils are sufferable, than to right themselves by abolishing the forms to which they are accustomed. But when a long train of abuses and usurpations, pursuing invariably the same object, evinces a design to reduce them under absolute despotism, it is their right, it is their duty, to throw off such government, and to provide new guards for their future security. Such has been the patient sufferance of these colonies; and such is now the necessity which constrains them to alter their former systems of government. The history of the present King of Great Britain is a history of repeated injuries and usurpations, all having in direct object the establishment of an absolute tyranny over these states. To prove this, let facts be submitted to a candid world.

He has refused his assent to laws, the most wholesome and necessary for the public good.

He has forbidden his governors to pass laws of immediate and pressing importance, unless suspended in their operation till his assent should be obtained; and, when so suspended, he has utterly neglected to attend to them.

He has refused to pass other laws for the accommodation of large districts of people, unless those people would relinquish the right of representation in the legislature, a right inestimable to them, and formidable to tyrants only.

He has called together legislative bodies at places unusual, uncomfortable, and distant from the depository of their public records, for the sole purpose of fatiguing them into compliance with his measures.

He has dissolved representative houses repeatedly, for opposing, with manly firmness, his invasions on the rights of the people.

He has refused for a long time, after such dissolutions, to cause others to be elected; whereby the legislative powers, incapable of annihilation, have returned to the people at large for their exercise; the state remaining, in the mean time, exposed to all the dangers of invasions from without and convulsions within.

He has endeavored to prevent the population of these states; for that purpose obstructing the laws for naturalization of foreigners; refusing to pass others to encourage their migration hither, and raising the conditions of new appropriations of lands.

He has obstructed the administration of justice, by refusing his assent to laws for establishing judiciary powers.

He has made judges dependent on his will alone, for the tenure of their offices, and the amount and payment of their salaries.

He has erected a multitude of new offices, and sent hither swarms of officers to harass our people and eat out their substance.

He has kept among us, in times of peace, standing armies, without the consent of our legislatures.

He has affected to render the military independent of, and superior to, the civil power.

He has combined with others to subject us to a jurisdiction

foreign to our constitution, and unacknowledged by our laws, giving his assent to their acts of pretended legislation:

For quartering large bodies of armed troops among us;

For protecting them, by a mock trial, from punishment for any murders which they should commit on the inhabitants of these states;

For cutting off our trade with all parts of the world;

For imposing taxes on us without our consent;

For depriving us, in many cases, of the benefits of trial by jury;

For transporting us beyond seas, to be tried for pretended offenses;

For abolishing the free system of English laws in a neighboring province, establishing therein an arbitrary government, and enlarging its boundaries, so as to render it at once an example and fit instrument for introducing the same absolute rule into these colonies;

For taking away our charters, abolishing our most valuable laws, and altering fundamentally the forms of our governments;

For suspending our own legislatures, and declaring themselves invested with power to legislate for us in all cases whatsoever.

He has abdicated government here, by declaring us out of his protection and waging war against us.

He has plundered our seas, ravaged our coasts, burned our towns, and destroyed the lives of our people.

He is at this time transporting large armies of foreign mercenaries to complete the works of death, desolation, and tyranny already begun with circumstances of cruelty and perfidy scarcely paralleled in the most barbarous ages, and totally unworthy the head of a civilized nation.

He has constrained our fellow-citizens, taken captive on the high seas, to bear arms against their country, to become the executioners of their friends and brethren, or to fall themselves by their hands.

He has excited domestic insurrection among us, and has endeavoured to bring on the inhabitants of our frontiers the merciless Indian savages, whose known rule of warfare is an undistinguished destruction of all ages, sexes, and conditions.

In every stage of these oppressions we have petitioned for redress in the most humble terms; our repeated petitions have been answered only by repeated injury. A prince, whose character is thus marked by every act which may define a tyrant, is unfit to be the ruler of a free people.

Nor have we been wanting in our attentions to our British brethren. We have warned them, from time to time, of attempts by their legislature to extend an unwarrantable jurisdiction over us. We have reminded them of the circumstances of our emigration and settlement here. We have appealed to their native justice and magnanimity; and we have conjured them, by the ties of our common kindred, to disavow these usurpations, which would inevitably interrupt our connections and correspondence. They, too, have been deaf to the voice of justice and of consanguinity. We must, therefore, acquiesce in the necessity which denounces our separation, and hold them, as we hold the rest of mankind, enemies in war, in peace friends.

We, therefore, the representatives of the United States of America, in General Congress assembled, appealing to the Supreme Judge of the world for the rectitude of our intentions, do, in the name and by the authority of the good people of these colonies, solemnly publish and declare, that these United Colonies are, and of right ought to be, FREE AND INDEPENDENT STATES, that they are absolved from all allegiance to the British crown, and that all political connection between them and the state of Great Britain is, and ought to be, totally dissolved; and that, as free and independent states, they have full power to levy war, conclude peace, contract alliances, establish commerce, and do all other acts and things which independent states may of right do. And for the support of this declaration, with a firm reliance on the protection of Divine Providence, we mutually pledge to each other our lives, our fortunes, and our sacred honor.

[signatures omitted – *Eds.*]

## II.7 To Rev. James Madison[1]

Fontainebleau, October 28, 1795[2]

Dear Sir, – Seven o'clock, and retired to my fireside, I have determined to enter into conversation with you. This is a village of about 5,000 inhabitants when the court is not here & 20,000 when they

---

[1] President of William and Mary College. – *Eds.*
[2] Misdated: the actual date of this letter is ten years earlier, Jefferson having written 1795 instead of 1785. – *Eds.*

are, occupying a valley thro' which runs a brook and on each side
of it a ridge of small mountains most of which are naked rock. The
King comes here, in the fall always, to hunt. His court attend him,
as do also the foreign diplomatic corps. But as this is not indispensably required & my finances do not admit the expense of a continued residence here, I propose to come occasionally to attend the
King's levees, returning again to Paris, distant 40 miles. This being
the first trip I set out yesterday morning to take a view of the place.
For this purpose I shaped my course towards the highest of the
mountains in sight, to the top of which was about a league. As soon
as I had got clear of the town I fell in with a poor woman walking
at the same rate with myself & going the same course. Wishing to
know the condition of the laboring poor I entered into conversation
with her, which I began by enquiries for the path which would lead
me into the mountain: & thence proceeded to enquiries into her
vocation, condition & circumstances. She told me she was a day
labourer, at 8 *sous* or 4*d* sterling the day; that she had two children
to maintain, & to pay a rent of 30 *livres* for her house, (which would
consume the hire of 75 days) that often she could get no emploi-
ment, and of course was without bread. As we had walked together
near a mile & she had so far served me as a guide, I gave her, on
parting, 24 *sous*. She burst into tears of a gratitude which I could
perceive was unfeigned because she was unable to utter a word.
She had probably never before received so great an aid. This little
*attendrissement*, with the solitude of my walk led me into a train of
reflections on that unequal division of property which occasions the
numberless instances of wretchedness which I had observed in this
country & is to be observed all over Europe. The property of this
country is absolutely concentrated in a very few hands, having revenues of from half a million of guineas a year downwards. These
employ the flower of the country as servants, some of them having
as many as 200 domestics, not labouring. They employ also a great
number of manufacturers, & tradesmen, & lastly the class of labouring husbandmen. But after all there comes the most numerous of
all the classes, that is, the poor who cannot find work. I asked myself
what could be the reason that so many should be permitted to beg
who are willing to work, in a country where there is a very considerable proportion of uncultivated lands? These lands are undisturbed
only for the sake of game. It should seem then that it must be

because of the enormous wealth of the proprietors which places them above attention to the encrease of their revenues by permitting these lands to be laboured. I am conscious that an equal division of property is impracticable. But the consequences of this enormous inequality producing so much misery to the bulk of mankind, legislators cannot invent too many devices for subdividing property, only taking care to let their subdivisions go hand in hand with the natural affections of the human mind. The descent of property of every kind therefore to all the children, or to all the brothers & sisters, or other relations in equal degree is a politic measure, and a practicable one. Another means of silently lessening the inequality of property is to exempt all from taxation below a certain point, & to tax the higher portions of property in geometrical progression as they rise. Whenever there is in any country, uncultivated lands and unemployed poor, it is clear that the laws of property have been so far extended as to violate natural right. The earth is given as a common stock for man to labour & live on. If for the encouragement of industry we allow it to be appropriated, we must take care that other employment be provided to those excluded from the appropriation. If we do not the fundamental right to labour the earth returns to the unemployed. It is too soon yet in our country to say that every man who cannot find employment but who can find uncultivated land shall be at liberty to cultivate it, paying a moderate rent. But it is not too soon to provide by every possible means that as few as possible shall be without a little portion of land. The small land holders are the most precious part of a state.

Ford VII: 33–5

## II.8 To James Madison

Paris, January 30, 1787

Dear sir, – My last to you was of the 16th of Dec, since which I have received yours of Nov 25, & Dec 4, which afforded me, as your letters always do, a treat on matters public, individual & œconomical. I am impatient to learn your sentiments on the late troubles in the Eastern states. So far as I have yet seen, they do not appear to threaten serious consequences. Those states have suffered by the stoppage of the channels of their commerce, which have not yet found other issues. This must render money scarce, and make the people uneasy. This uneasiness has produced acts absolutely unjustifiable; but I hope they will provoke no severities from their governments. A consciousness of those in power that their administration of the public affairs has been honest, may perhaps produce too great a degree of indignation: and those characters wherein fear predominates over hope may apprehend too much from these instances of irregularity. They may conclude too hastily that nature has formed man insusceptible of any other government but that of force, a conclusion not founded in truth, nor experience. Societies exist under three forms sufficiently distinguishable. 1. Without government, as among our Indians. 2. Under governments wherein the will of every one has a just influence, as is the case in England in a slight degree, and in our states, in a great one. 3. Under governments of force: as is the case in all other monarchies and in most of the other republics. To have an idea of the curse of existence under these last, they must be seen. It is a government of wolves over sheep. It is a problem, not clear in my mind, that the 1st condition is not the best. But I believe it to be inconsistent with any great degree of population. The second state has a great deal of good in it. The mass of mankind under that enjoys a precious degree of liberty & happiness. It has it's evils too: the principal of which is the turbulence to which it is subject. But weigh this against the oppressions of monarchy, and it becomes nothing. *Malo periculosam libertatem quam quietam servitutem.* Even this evil is productive of good. It prevents the degeneracy of government, and nourishes a general attention to the public affairs. I hold it that a little rebellion now and then is a good thing, & as necessary in the political world as storms in the physical. Unsuccessful rebellions indeed generally establish the encroachments on the rights of the people which have produced them. An observation of this truth should render honest republican governors so mild in their punishment of rebellions, as not to discourage them too much. It is a medicine necessary for the sound health of government . . .

I send you by Colo. Franks, your pocket telescope, walking stick & chemical box. The two former could not be combined together. The latter could not be had in the form you referred to. Having a great desire to have a portable copying machine, & being satisfied from some experiments that the principle of the large machine might be applied in a small one, I planned one when in England & had it made.[1] It answers perfectly. I have since set a workman to making them here, & they are in such demand that he has his hands full. Being assured that you will be pleased to have one, when you shall have tried it's convenience, I send you one by Colo. Franks. The machine costs 96 *livres*, the appendages 24 *livres*, and I send you paper & ink for 12 *livres*; in all 132 *livres*. There is a printed paper of directions; but you must expect to make many essays before you succeed perfectly. A soft brush, like a shaving brush, is more convenient than the sponge. You can get as much ink & paper as you please from London. The paper costs a guinea a ream.

Ford IV: 361–9

## II.9 To William Stephens Smith

Paris, November 13, 1787

Dear Sir, – I am now to acknoledge the receipt of your favours of October the 4th, 8th, & 26th. In the last you apologise for your letters of introduction to Americans coming here. It is so far from needing apology on your part, that it calls for thanks on mine. I endeavor to shew civilities to all the Americans who come here, & will give me opportunities of doing it: and it is a matter of comfort to know from a good quarter what they are, & how far I may go in my attentions to them. Can you send me Woodmason's bills for the two copying presses for the M. de la Fayette, & the M. de Chastel-lux? The latter makes one article in a considerable account, of old standing, and which I cannot present for want of this article. – I do not know whether it is to yourself or Mr. Adams I am to give my thanks for the copy of the new constitution. I beg leave through you to place them where due. It will be yet three weeks before I shall receive them from America. There are very good articles in it: & very bad. I do not know which preponderate. What we have lately read in the history of Holland, in the chapter on the

---

[1] TJ refers to his "polygraph," an ingenious device that allowed its user to make simultaneous and exact copies of any piece of writing – *Eds*.

*Stadtholder*, would have sufficed to set me against a chief magistrate eligible for a long duration, if I had ever been disposed towards one: & what we have always read of the elections of Polish kings should have forever excluded the idea of one continuable for life. Wonderful is the effect of impudent & persevering lying. The British ministry have so long hired their gazetteers to repeat and model into every form lies about our being in anarchy, that the world has at length believed them, the English nation has believed them, the ministers themselves have come to believe them, & what is more wonderful, we have believed them ourselves. Yet where does this anarchy exist? Where did it ever exist, except in the single instance of Massachusetts?[1] And can history produce an instance of rebellion so honourably conducted? I say nothing of its motives. They were founded in ignorance, not wickedness. God forbid we should ever be 20 years without such a rebellion. The people cannot be all, & always, well informed. The part which is wrong will be discontented in proportion to the importance of the facts they misconceive. If they remain quiet under such misconceptions it is a lethargy, the forerunner of death to the public liberty. We have had 13. states independent 11. years. There has been one rebellion. That comes to one rebellion in a century & a half for each state. What country before ever existed a century & half without a rebellion? & what country can preserve it's liberties if their rulers are not warned from time to time that their people preserve the spirit of resistance? Let them take arms. The remedy is to set them right as to facts, pardon & pacify them. What signify a few lives lost in a century or two? The tree of liberty must be refreshed from time to time with the blood of patriots & tyrants. It is it's natural manure. Our Convention has been too much impressed by the insurrection of Massachusetts: and in the spur of the moment they are setting up a kite to keep the henyard in order. I hope in God this article will be rectified before the new constitution is accepted. – You ask me if any thing transpires here on the subject of S. America?[2] Not a word. I know that there are combustible materials there, and that they wait the torch only. But this country probably will join the extinguishers. – The want of facts worth communicating to you has

[1] Shays's Rebellion in Western Massachusetts. – *Eds.*
[2] See *supra*, I.3, note 1. – *Eds.*

occasioned me to give a little loose to dissertation. We must be contented to amuse, when we cannot inform.

Ford IV: 465–8

## II.10 To David Humphreys

Paris, March 18, 1789

Dear Sir, – Your favor of Nov. 29, 1788, came to hand the last month. How it happened that mine of Aug. 1787, was fourteen months on it's way is inconceivable. I do not recollect by what conveyance I sent it. I had concluded however either that it had miscarried or that you had become indolent as most of our countrymen are in matters of correspondence.

The change in this country since you left it is such as you can form no idea of. The frivolities of conversation have given way entirely to politics. Men, women & children talk nothing else: and all you know talk a great deal. The press groans with daily productions, which in point of boldness make an Englishman stare, who hitherto has thought himself the boldest of men. A complete revolution in this government has, within the space of two years (for it began with the Notables of 1787) been effected merely by the force of public opinion, aided indeed by the want of money which the dissipations of the court had brought on. And this revolution has not cost a single life, unless we charge to it a little riot lately in Bretagne which began about the price of bread, became afterwards political and ended in the loss of 4. or 5. lives. The assembly of the states general begins the 27th of April. The representation of the people will be perfect. But they will be alloyed by an equal number of nobility & clergy. The first great question they will have to decide will be whether they shall vote by orders or persons, & I have hopes that the majority of the nobles are already disposed to join the *tiers état* in deciding that the vote shall be by persons. This is the opinion *à la mode* at present, and mode has acted a wonderful part in the present instance. All the handsome young women, for example, are for the *tiers état*, and this is an army more powerful in France than the 200,000 men of the king. Add to this that the court itself is for the *tiers état*, as the only agent which

111

can relieve their wants; not by giving money themselves (they are squeezed to the last drop) but by pressing it from the non-contributing orders. The king stands engaged to pretend no more to the power of laying, continuing or appropriating taxes, to call the States general periodically, to submit *lettres de cachet* to legal restrictions, to consent to freedom of the press, and that all this shall be fixed by a fundamental constitution which shall bind his successors. He has not offered a participation in the legislature, but it will surely be insisted on. The public mind is so ripened on all these subjects, that there seems to be now but one opinion. The clergy indeed think separately, & the old men among the Nobles. But their voice is suppressed by the general one of the nation. The writings published on this occasion are some of them very valuable: because, unfettered by the prejudices under which the English labour, they give a full scope to reason, and strike out truths as yet unperceived & unacknoleged on the other side the channel. An Englishman, dosing under a kind of half reformation, is not excited to think by such gross absurdities as stare a Frenchman in the face wherever he looks, whether it be towards the throne or the altar. *In fine* I believe this nation will in the course of the present year have as full a portion of liberty dealt out to them as the nation can bear at present, considering how uninformed the mass of their people is. This circumstance will prevent their immediate establishment of the trial by jury. The palsied state of the executive in England is a fortunate circumstance for France, as it will give them time to arrange their affairs internally. The consolidation & funding their debts will give them a credit which will enable them to do what they please. For the present year the war will be confined to the two empires & Denmark, against Turkey & Sweden. It is not yet evident whether Prussia will be engaged. If the disturbances of Poland break out into overt acts, it will be a power divided in itself, & so of no weight. Perhaps by the next year England & France may be ready to take the field. It will depend on the former principally, for the latter, tho she may be then able, must wish still a little time to see her new arrangements well under way. The English papers & English ministry say the king is well. He is better, but not well: no malady requires a longer time to ensure against its return, than insanity. Time alone can distinguish accidental insanity from habitual lunacy.

The operations which have taken place in America lately, fill me with pleasure. In the first place they realize the confidence I had that whenever our affairs go obviously wrong the good sense of the people will interpose and set them to rights. The example of changing a constitution by assembling the wise men of the State, instead of assembling armies, will be worth as much to the world as the former examples we had given them. The constitution too which was the result of our deliberations, is unquestionably the wisest ever yet presented to men, and some of the accommodations of interest which it has adopted are greatly pleasing to me who have before had occasions of seeing how difficult those interests were to accommodate. A general concurrence of opinion seems to authorize us to say it has some defects. I am one of those who think it a defect that the important rights, not placed in security by the frame of the constitution itself, were not explicitly secured by a supplementary declaration. There are rights which it is useless to surrender to the government, and which governments have yet always been fond to invade. These are the rights of thinking, and publishing our thoughts by speaking or writing; the right of free commerce; the right of personal freedom. There are instruments for administering the government, so peculiarly trust-worthy, that we should never leave the legislature at liberty to change them. The new constitution has secured these in the executive & legislative departments; but not in the judiciary. It should have established trials by the people themselves, that is to say by jury. There are instruments so dangerous to the rights of the nation, and which place them so totally at the mercy of their governors, that those governors, whether legislative or executive, should be restrained from keeping such instruments on foot, but in well-defined cases. Such an instrument is a standing army. We are now allowed to say such a declaration of rights, as a supplement to the constitution where that is silent, is wanting to secure us in these points. The general voice has legitimated this objection. It has not however authorized me to consider as a real defect what I thought and still think one, the perpetual re-eligibility of the president. But three states out of 11 having declared against this, we must suppose we are wrong according to the fundamental law of every society, the *lex majoris partis*, to which we are bound to submit. And should the majority change their opinion, & become sensible that this trait in their constitution is wrong,

I would wish it to remain uncorrected, as long as we can avail ourselves of the services of our great leader [George Washington], whose talents and whose weight of character I consider as peculiarly necessary to get the government so under way as that it may afterwards be carried on by subordinate characters.

I must give you sincere thanks for the details of small news contained in your letter. You know how precious that kind of information is to a person absent from his country, and how difficult it is to be procured. I hope to receive soon permission to visit America this summer, and to possess myself anew, by conversation with my countrymen, of their spirit & their ideas. I know only the Americans of the year 1784. They tell me this is to be much a stranger to those of 1789. This renewal of acquaintance is no indifferent matter to one acting at such a distance as that instructions cannot be received hot and hot. One of my pleasures too will be that of talking over the old & new with you.

Ford v: 86–91

## II.11 From the *Autobiography*

On my return from Holland, I had found Paris still in high fermentation as I had left it. Had the Archbishop, on the close of the assembly of Notables, immediately carried into operation the measures contemplated, it was believed they would all have been registered by the parliament, but he was slow, presented his edicts, one after another, & at considerable intervals of time, which gave time for the feelings excited by the proceedings of the Notables to cool off, new claims to be advanced, and a pressure to arise for a fixed constitution, not subject to changes at the will of the King. Nor should we wonder at this pressure when we consider the monstrous abuses of power under which this people were ground to powder, when we pass in review the weight of their taxes, and inequality of their distribution; the oppressions of the tythes, of the *tailles*, the *corvées*, the *gabelles*, the farms & barriers; the shackles on Commerce by monopolies; on Industry by gilds & corporations; on the freedom of conscience, of thought, and of speech; on the Press by the Censure; and of person by *lettres de Cachet*. The cruelty of the criminal code generally, the atrocities of the Rack, the venality of judges, and their partialities to the rich; the Monopoly of Military honors by the *Noblesse*; the enormous expenses of the Queen, the princes & the Court; the prodigalities of pensions; & the riches, luxury, indolence & immorality of the clergy. Surely under such a mass of misrule and oppression, a people might justly press for a thoro' reformation, and might even dismount their rough-shod riders, & leave them to walk on their own legs. The edicts relative to the *corvées* & free circulation of grain, were first presented to the parliament and registered. But those for the *impôt territorial*, & stamp tax, offered some time after, were refused by the parliament, which proposed a call of the States General as alone competent to their authorization. Their refusal produced a Bed of justice, and their exile to Troyes. The advocates however refusing to attend them, a suspension in the administration of justice took place. The Parliament held out for awhile, but the *ennui* of their exile and absence from Paris begun at length to be felt, and some dispositions for compromise to appear. On their consent therefore to prolong some of the former taxes, they were recalled from exile, the King met them in session Nov. 19. 87. promised to call the States General in the year 92. and a majority expressed their assent to register an edict for successive and annual loans from 1788. to 92. But a protest being entered by the Duke of Orleans and this encouraging others in a disposition to retract, the King ordered peremptorily the registry of the edict, and left the assembly abruptly. The parliament immediately protested that the votes for the enregistry had not been legally taken, and that they gave no sanction to the loans proposed. This was enough to discredit and defeat them. Hereupon issued another edict for the establishment of a *cour plenière*, and the suspension of all the parliaments in the kingdom. This being opposed as might be expected by reclamations from all the parliaments & provinces, the King gave way and by an edict of July 5. 88 renounced his *cour plenière*, & promised the States General for the 1st. of May of the ensuing year: and the Archbishop finding the times beyond his faculties, accepted the promise of a Cardinal's hat, was removed [Sept. 88] from the ministry, and Mr. Necker was called to the department of finance. The innocent rejoicings of the people of Paris on this change provoked the interference of an officer of the city guards, whose order for their dispersion not being obeyed, he charged them with fixed bayonets, killed two or three, and wounded many. This dispersed them for the moment; but they collected the next day in great numbers, burnt 10 or 12 guard houses, killed two or three of the guards, & lost 6 or 8 more of their own number. The city was hereupon put under martial law, and after awhile the tumult subsided. The effect of this change of ministers, and the promise of the States General at an early day, tranquillized the nation. But two great questions now occurred. 1. What proportion shall the number of deputies of the *tiers état* bear to those of the Nobles and Clergy? And 2. shall they sit in the same, or in distinct apartments? Mr. Necker, desirous of avoiding himself these knotty questions, proposed a second call of the same Notables, and that their advice should be asked on the subject. They met Nov. 9. 88 and, by five *bureaux* against one, they recommended the forms of the States General of 1614 wherein the houses were separate, and voted by orders, not by persons. But the whole nation declaring at once against this, and that the *tiers état* should be, in numbers, equal to both the other orders, and the Parliament deciding for the same proportion, it was determined so to be, by a declaration of Dec. 27. 88. A Report of Mr. Necker to the King, of about the same date, contained other very important concessions. 1. That the King could neither lay a new tax, nor prolong an old one. 2. It expressed a readiness to agree on the periodical meeting of the States. 3. To consult on the necessary restriction on *lettres de Cachet*. And 4. how far the Press might be made free 5. It admits that the States are to appropriate the public money; and 6. that Ministers shall be responsible for public expenditures. And these concessions came from the very heart of the King. He had not a wish but for the good of the nation, and for that object no personal sacrifice would ever have cost him a moment's regret. But his mind was weakness itself, his constitution timid, his judgment null, and without sufficient firmness even to stand by the faith of his word. His Queen too, haughty and bearing no contradiction, had an absolute ascendency over him; and around her were rallied the King's brother d'Artois, the court generally, and the aristocratic part of his ministers, particularly Breteuil, Broglie, Vauguyon, Foulon, Luzerne, men whose principles of government were those of the age of Louis XIV. Against this host the good counsels of Necker, Montmorin, St. Priest, altho' in unison with the wishes of the King himself, were of little avail. The resolutions of the morning formed under their advice, would be reversed in the evening by the influence of the Queen & court. But the hand of heaven weighed heavily indeed on the machinations of this junto; producing collateral incidents, not arising out of the case, yet powerfully co-exciting the nation to force a regeneration of it's government, and overwhelming with accumulated difficulties this liberticide resistance. For, while laboring under the want of money for even ordinary purposes, in a government which required a million of *livres* a day, and driven to the last ditch by the universal call for liberty, there came on a winter of such severe cold, as was without example in the memory of man, or in the written records of history. The Mercury was at times 50° below the freezing point of Fahrenheit and 22° below that of Reaumur. All out-door labor was suspended, and the poor, without the wages of labor, were of course without either bread or fuel. The government found it's necessities aggravated by that of procuring immense quantities of fire-wood, and of keeping great fires at all the cross-streets, around which the people gathered in crowds to avoid perishing with cold. Bread too was to be bought, and distributed daily gratis, until a relaxation of the season should enable the people to work: and the slender stock of bread-stuff had for some time threatened famine, and had raised that article to an enormous price. So great indeed was the scarcity of bread that from the highest to the lowest citizen, the bakers were permitted to deal but a scanty allowance per head, even to those who paid for it; and in cards of invitation to dine in the richest houses, the guest was notified to bring his own bread. To eke out the existence of the people, every person who had the means, was called on for a weekly subscription, which the *Curés* collected and employed in providing messes for the nourishment of the poor, and vied with each other in devising such economical compositions of food as would subsist the greatest number with the smallest means. This want of bread had been foreseen for some time past and M. de Montmorin had desired me to notify it in America, and that, in addition to the market price, a premium should be given on what should be brought from the U.S. Notice was accordingly given and produced considerable supplies. Subsequent information made the importations from America, during the months of March, April & May, into the Atlantic ports of France, amount to about 21,000 barrels of flour, besides what went to other ports, and in other months, while our supplies to their West-Indian islands relieved them also from that drain. This distress for bread continued till July.

Hitherto no acts of popular violence had been produced by the struggle for political reformation. Little riots, on ordinary incidents, had taken place, as at other times, in different parts of the kingdom, in which some lives, perhaps a dozen or twenty, had been lost, but in the month of April a more serious one occurred in Paris, unconnected indeed with the revolutionary principle, but making part of the history of the day. The Fauxbourg St. Antoine is a quarter of the city inhabited entirely by the class of day-laborers and journeymen in every line. A rumor was spread among them that a great paper manufacturer, of the name of Reveillon, had proposed, on some occasion, that their wages should be lowered to 15 *sous* a day. Inflamed at once into rage, & without inquiring into it's truth, they flew to his house in vast numbers, destroyed everything in it, and in his magazines & work shops, without secreting however a pin's worth to themselves, and were continuing this work of devastation when the regular troops were called in. Admonitions being disregarded, they were of necessity fired on, and a regular action ensued, in which about 100. of them were killed, before the rest would disperse. There had rarely passed a year without such a riot in some part or other of the Kingdom; and this is distinguished only as cotemporary with the revolution, altho' not produced by it.

The States General were opened on the 5th. of May 89 by speeches from the King, the *Garde des Sceaux* Lamoignon, and Mr. Necker. The last was thought to trip too lightly over the constitutional reformations which were expected. His notices of them in this speech were not as full as in his previous "*Rapport au Roi.*" This was observed to his disadvantage. But much allowance should have been made for the situation in which he was placed between his own counsels, and those of the ministers and party of the court. Overruled in his own opinions, compelled to deliver, and to gloss over those of his opponents, and even to keep their secrets, he could not come forward in his own attitude.

The composition of the assembly, altho' equivalent on the whole to what had been expected, was something different in it's elements. It had been supposed that a superior education would carry into the scale of the Commons a respectable portion of the *Noblesse*. It did so as to those of Paris, of it's vicinity and of the other considerable cities, whose greater intercourse with enlightened society had liberalized their minds, and prepared them to advance up to the measure of the times. But the *Noblesse* of the country, which constituted two thirds of that body, were far in their rear. Residing constantly on their patrimonial feuds, and familiarized by daily habit with Seigneurial powers and practices, they had not yet learned to suspect their inconsistence with reason and right. They were willing to submit to equality of taxation, but not to descend from their rank and prerogatives to be incorporated in session with the *tiers état*. Among the clergy, on the other hand, it had been apprehended that the higher orders of the hierarchy, by their wealth and connections, would have carried the elections generally. But it proved that in most cases the lower clergy had obtained the popular majorities. These consisted of the *Curés*, sons of the peasantry who had been employed to do all the drudgery of parochial services for 10, 20, or 30 *Louis* a year; while their superiors were consuming their princely revenues in palaces of luxury & indolence.

The objects for which this body was convened being of the first order of importance, I felt it very interesting to understand the views of the parties of which it was composed, and especially the ideas prevalent as to the organization contemplated for their government. I went therefore daily from Paris to Versailles, and attended their debates, generally till the hour of adjournment. Those of the *Noblesse* were impassioned and tempestuous. They had some able men on both sides, and actuated by equal zeal. The debates of the Commons were temperate, rational and inflexibly firm. As preliminary to all other business, the awful questions came on, Shall the States sit in one, or in distinct apartments? And shall they vote by heads or houses? The opposition was soon found to consist of the Episcopal order among the clergy, and two thirds of the *Noblesse*; while the *tiers état* were, to a man, united and determined. After various propositions of compromise had failed, the Commons undertook to cut the Gordian knot. The Abbé Sieyès, the most logical head of the nation (author of the pamphlet *Qu'est-ce que le tiers état?* which had electrified that country, as Paine's *Common Sense* did us), after an impressive speech on the 10th of June, moved that a last invitation should be sent to the Nobles and Clergy, to attend in the Hall of the States, collectively or individually for the verification of powers, to which the commons would proceed immediately, either in their presence or absence. This verification being finished, a motion was made, on the 15th. that they should constitute themselves a National assembly; which was decided on the 17th. by a majority of four fifths. During the debates on this question, about twenty of the *Curés* had joined them, and a proposition was made in the chamber of the clergy that their whole body should join them. This was rejected at first by a small majority only; but, being afterwards somewhat modified, it was decided affirmatively, by a majority of eleven. While this was under debate and unknown to the court, to wit, on the 19th. a council was held in the afternoon at Marly, wherein it was proposed that the King should interpose by a declaration of his sentiments, in a *séance royale*. A form of declaration was proposed by Necker, which, while it censured in general the proceedings both of the Nobles and Commons, announced the King's views, such as substantially to coincide with the Commons. It was agreed to in council, the *séance* was fixed for the 22d, the meetings of the States were till then to be suspended, and everything, in the meantime, kept secret. The members the next morning (20th.) repairing to their house as usual, found the doors shut and guarded, a proclamation posted up for a *séance royale* on the 22d. and a suspension of their meetings in the meantime. Concluding that their dissolution was now to take place, they repaired to a building called the "*Jeu de paume*" (or Tennis court) and there bound themselves by oath to each other, never to separate of their own accord, till they had settled a constitution for the nation, on a solid basis, and if separated by force, that they would reassemble in some other place. The next day they met in the church of St. Louis, and were joined by a majority of the clergy. The heads of the Aristocracy saw that all was lost without some bold exertion. The King was still at Marly. Nobody was permitted to approach him but their friends. He was assailed by falsehoods in all shapes. He was made to believe that the Commons were about to absolve the army from their oath of fidelity to him, and to raise their pay. The court party were now all rage and desperate. They procured a committee to be held consisting of the King and his ministers, to which Monsieur & the Count d'Artois should be admitted. At this committee the latter attacked Mr. Necker personally, arraigned his declaration, and proposed one which some of his prompters had put into his hands. Mr. Necker was brow-beaten and intimidated, and the King shaken. He determined that the two plans should be deliberated on the next day and the *séance royale* put off a day longer. This encouraged a fiercer attack on Mr. Necker the next day. His draught of a declaration was entirely broken up, & that of the Count d'Artois inserted into it. Himself and Montmorin offered their resignation, which was refused, the Count d'Artois saying to Mr. Necker "No sir, you must be kept as the hostage; we hold you responsible for all the ill which shall happen." This change of plan was immediately whispered without doors. The *Noblesse* were in triumph; the people in consternation. I was quite alarmed at this state of things. The soldiery had not yet indicated which side they should take, and that which they should support would be sure to prevail. I considered a successful reformation of government in France, as ensuring a general reformation thro Europe, and the resurrection, to a new life, of their people, now ground to dust by the abuses of the governing powers. I was much acquainted with the leading patriots of the assembly. Being from a country which had successfully passed thro' a similar reformation, they were disposed to my acquaintance, and had some confidence in me. I urged most strenuously an immediate compromise; to secure what the government was now ready to yield, and trust to future occasions for what might still be wanting. It was well understood that the King would grant at this time 1. Freedom of the person by *habeas corpus*. 2. Freedom of conscience. 3. Freedom of the press. 4. Trial by jury. 5. A representative legislature. 6. Annual meetings. 7. The origination of laws. 8. The exclusive right of taxation and appropriation. And 9. The responsibility of ministers; and with the exercise of these powers they would obtain in future whatever might be further necessary to improve and preserve their constitution. They thought otherwise however, and events have proved their lamentable error. For after 30 years of war, foreign and domestic, the loss of millions of lives, the prostration of private happiness, and foreign subjugation of their own country for a time, they have obtained no more, nor even that securely. They were unconscious of (for who could foresee?) the melancholy sequel of their well-meant perseverance; that their physical force would be usurped by a first tyrant to trample on the independance, and even the existence, of other nations: that this would afford fatal example for the atrocious conspiracy of Kings against their people; would generate their unholy and homicide alliance to make common cause among themselves, and to crush, by the power of the whole, the efforts of any part, to moderate their abuses and oppressions.

When the King passed, the next day, thro' the lane formed from the Château to the Hôtel des états, there was a dead silence. He was about an hour in the House delivering his speech & declaration. On his coming out a feeble cry of "*Vive le Roy*" was raised by some children, but the people remained silent & sullen. In the close of his speech he had ordered that the members should follow him, & resume their deliberations the next day. The *Noblesse* followed him, and so did the clergy, except about thirty, who, with the *tiers*, remained in the room, and entered into deliberation. They protested against what the King had done, adhered to all their former proceedings, and resolved the inviolability of their own persons. An officer came to order them out of the room in the King's name. "Tell those who sent you," said Mirabeau, "that we shall not move hence but at our own will, or the point of the bayonet." In the afternoon the people, uneasy, began to assemble in great numbers in the courts, and vicinities of the palace. This produced alarm. The Queen sent for Mr. Necker. He was conducted amidst the shouts and acclamations of the multitude who filled all the apartments of the palace. He was a few minutes only with the queen, and what passed between them did not transpire. The King went out to ride. He passed thro' the crowd to his carriage and into it, without being in the least noticed. As Mr. Neckar followed him universal acclamations were raised of "*vive Monsr. Neckar, vive le sauveur de la France opprimée.*" He was conducted back to his house with the same demonstrations of affection and anxiety. About 200. deputies of the *Tiers*, catching the enthusiasm of the moment, went to his house, and extorted from him a promise that he would not resign. On the 25th. 48 of the Nobles joined the *tiers*, & among them the D. of Orleans. There were then with them 164 members of the Clergy, altho' the minority of that body still sat apart & called themselves the chamber of the clergy. On the 26th. the Archbp. of Paris joined the *tiers*, as did some others of the clergy and of the *Noblesse*.

These proceedings had thrown the people into violent ferment. It gained the souldiery, first of the French guards, extended to those of every other denomination, except the Swiss, and even to the body guards of the King. They began to quit their barracks, to assemble in squads, to declare they would defend the life of the King, but would not be the murderers of their fellow-citizens. They called themselves the souldiers *of the nation*, and left now no doubt on which side they would be, in case of rupture. Similar accounts came in from the troops in other parts of the kingdom, giving good reason to believe they would side with their fathers and brothers rather than with their officers. The operation of this medicine at Versailles was as sudden as it was powerful. The alarm there was so compleat that in the afternoon of the 27th. the King wrote with his own hand letters to the Presidents of the clergy and Nobles, engaging them immediately to join the *Tiers*. These two bodies were debating & hesitating when notes from the Ct. d'Artois decided their compliance. They went in a body and took their seats with the *tiers*, and thus rendered the union of the orders in one chamber compleat.

The Assembly now entered on the business of their mission, and first proceeded to arrange the order in which they would take up the heads of their constitution, as follows:

First, and as Preliminary to the whole a general Declaration of the Rights of Man. Then specifically the Principles of the Monarchy; rights of the Nation; rights of the King; rights of the citizens; organization & rights of the national assembly; forms necessary for the enactment of laws; organization & functions of the provincial & municipal assemblies; duties and limits of the Judiciary power; functions & duties of the military power.

A declaration of the rights of man, as the preliminary of their work, was accordingly prepared and proposed by the Marquis de la Fayette.

But the quiet of their march was soon disturbed by information that troops, and particularly the foreign troops, were advancing on Paris from various quarters. The King had been probably advised to this on the pretext of preserving peace in Paris. But his advisers were believed to have other things in contemplation. The Marshal de Broglio was appointed to their command, a high flying aristocrat, cool and capable of everything. Some of the French guards were soon arrested, under other pretexts, but really on account of their dispositions in favor of the National cause. The people of Paris forced their prison, liberated them, and sent a deputation to the Assembly to solicit a pardon. The Assembly recommended peace and order to the people of Paris, the prisoners to the king, and asked from him the removal of the troops. His answer was negative and dry, saying they might remove themselves, if they pleased, to Noyons or Soissons. In the meantime these troops, to the number of twenty or thirty thousand, had arrived and were posted in, and between Paris and Versailles. The bridges and passes were guarded. At three o'clock in the afternoon of the 11th July the Count de la Luzerne was sent to notify Mr. Neckar of his dismission, and to enjoin him to retire instantly without saying a word of it to anybody. He went home, dined, and proposed to his wife a visit to a friend, but went in fact to his country house at St. Ouen, and at midnight set out for Brussels. This was not known till the next day, 12th when the whole ministry was changed, except Villedeuil, of the Domestic department, and Barenton, *Garde des sceaux*. The changes were as follows.

The Baron de Breteuil, president of the council of finance; de la Galaisiere, Comptroller general in the room of Mr. Neckar; the Marshal de Broglio, minister of War, & Foulon under him in the room of Puy-Segur; the Duke de la Vauguyon, minister of foreign affairs instead of the Ct. de Montmorin; de La Porte, minister of Marine, in place of the Ct. de la Luzerne; St. Priest was also removed from the council. Luzerne and Puy-Segur had been strongly of the Aristocratic party in the Council, but they were not considered as equal to the work now to be done. The King was now compleatly in the hands of men, the principal among whom had been noted thro' their lives for the Turkish despotism of their characters, and who were associated around the King as proper instruments for what was to be executed. The news of this change began to be known at Paris about 1. or 2. o'clock. In the afternoon a body of about 100 German cavalry were advanced and drawn up in the Place Louis XV. and about 200 Swiss posted at a little distance in their rear. This drew people to the spot, who thus accidentally found themselves in front of the troops, merely at first as spectators; but as their numbers increased, their indignation rose. They retired a few steps, and posted themselves on and behind large piles of stones, large and small, collected in that Place for a bridge which was to be built adjacent to it. In this position, happening to be in my carriage on a visit, I passed thro' the lane they had formed, without interruption. But the moment after I had passed, the people attacked the cavalry with stones. They charged, but the advantageous position of the people, and the showers of stones obliged the horse to retire, and quit the field altogether, leaving one of their number on the ground, & the Swiss in their rear not moving to their aid. This was the signal for universal insurrection, and this body of cavalry, to avoid being massacred, retired towards Versailles. The people now armed themselves with such weapons as they could find in armorer's shops and private houses, and with bludgeons, and were roaming all night thro' all parts of the city, without any decided object. The next day (13th.) the assembly pressed on the king to send away the troops, to permit the *Bourgeoisie* of Paris to arm for the preservation of order in the city, and offer[ed] to send a deputation from their body to tranquillize them; but their propositions were refused. A committee of magistrates and electors of the city are appointed by those bodies to take upon them it's government. The people, now openly joined by the French guards, force the prison of St. Lazare, release all the prisoners, and take a great store of corn, which they carry to the Corn-market. Here they get some arms, and the French guards begin to form & train them. The City-committee determined to raise 48.000. *Bourgeoise*, or rather to restrain their numbers to 48.000. On the 14th. they send one of their members (Mons. de Corny) to the *Hôtel des Invalides*, to ask arms for their *Garde-Bourgeoise*. He was followed by, and he found there a great collection of people. The Governor of the Invalids came out and represented the impossibility of his delivering arms without the orders of those from whom he received them. De Corny advised the people then to retire, and retired himself; but the people took possession of the arms. It was remarkable that not only the Invalids themselves made no opposition, but that a body of 5000 foreign troops, within 400 yards, never stirred. M. de Corny and five others were then sent to ask arms of M. de Launay, governor of the Bastile. They found a great collection of people already before the place, and they immediately planted a flag of truce, which was answered by a like flag hoisted on the Parapet. The deputation prevailed on the people to fall back a little, advanced themselves to make their demand of the Governor, and in that instant a discharge from the Bastile killed four persons, of those nearest to the deputies. The deputies retired. I happened to be at the house of M. de Corny when he returned to it, and received from him a narrative of these transactions. On the retirement of the deputies, the people rushed forward & almost in an instant were in possession of a fortification defended by 100 men, of infinite strength, which in other times had stood several regular sieges, and had never been taken. How they forced their entrance has never been explained. They took all the arms, discharged the prisoners, and such of the garrison as were not killed in the first moment of fury, carried the Governor and Lt. Governor to the Place de Grève (the place of public execution), cut off their heads, and sent them thro' the city in triumph to the Palais royal. About the same instant a treacherous correspondence having been discovered in M. de Flesselles, *prévot des marchands*, they seized him in the Hotel de Ville where he was in the execution of his office, and cut off his head. These events carried imperfectly to Versailles were the subject of two successive deputations from the assembly to the king, to both of which he gave dry and hard answers for nobody had as yet been permitted to inform him truly and fully of what had passed at Paris. But at night the Duke de Liancourt forced his way into the king's bed chamber, and obliged him to hear a full and animated detail of the disasters of the day in Paris. He went to bed fearfully impressed. The decapitation of de Launai worked powerfully thro' the night on the whole aristocratic party, insomuch that, in the morning, those of the greatest influence on the Count d'Artois represented to him the absolute necessity that the king should give up everything to the Assembly. This according with the dispositions of the king, he went about 11. o'clock, accompanied only by his brothers, to the Assembly, & there read to them a speech, in which he asked their interposition to re-establish order. Altho' couched in terms of some caution, yet the manner in which it was delivered made it evident that it was meant as a surrender at discretion. He returned to the Château afoot, accompanied by the assembly. They sent off a deputation to quiet Paris, at the head of which was the Marquis de la Fayette who had, the same morning, been named *Commandant en chef* of the *Milice Bourgeoise* and Mons Bailly, former President of the States General, was called for as *Prévôt des marchands*. The demolition of the Bastile was now ordered and begun. A body of the Swiss guards of the regiment of Ventimille, and the city horse guards joined the people. The alarm at Versailles increased. The foreign troops were ordered off instantly. Every minister resigned. The king confirmed Bailly as *Prévôt des Marchands*, wrote to Mr. Neckar to recall him, sent his letter open to the assembly, to be forwarded by them, and invited them to go with him to Paris the next day, to satisfy the city of his dispositions; and that night, and the next morning the Count d'Artois and M. de Montesson a deputy connected with him, Madame de Polignac, Madame de Guiche, and the Count de Vaudreuil, favorites of the queen, the Abbé de Vermont her confessor, the Prince of Condé and Duke of Bourbon fled. The king came to Paris, leaving the queen in consternation for his return. Omitting the less important figures of the procession, the king's carriage was in the center, on each side of it the assembly, in two ranks afoot, at their head the M. de la Fayette, as Commander-in-chief, on horseback, and *Bourgeois* guards before and behind. About 60,000 citizens of all forms and conditions, armed with the muskets of the Bastile and Invalids, as far as they would go, the rest with pistols, swords, pikes, pruning hooks, scythes &c. lined all the streets thro' which the procession passed, and with the crowds of people in the streets, doors & windows, saluted them everywhere with cries of "*vive la nation,*" but not a single "*vive le roy*" was heard. The King landed at the Hôtel de Ville. There M. Bailly presented and put into his hat the popular cockade, and addressed him. The King being unprepared, and unable to answer, Bailly went to him, gathered from him some scraps of sentences, and made out an answer, which he delivered to the audience as from the king. On their return the popular cries were "*vive le roy et la nation.*" He was conducted by a *garde bourgeoise* to his palace at Versailles, & thus concluded an *amende honorable* as no sovereign ever made, and no people ever received.

And here again was lost another precious occasion of sparing to France the crimes and cruelties thro' which she has since passed, and to Europe, & finally America the evils which flowed on them also from this mortal source. The king was now become a passive machine in the hands of the National assembly, and had he been left to himself, he would have willingly acquiesced in whatever they should devise as best for the nation. A wise constitution would have been formed, hereditary in his line, himself placed at it's head, with powers so large as to enable him to do all the good of his station, and so limited as to restrain him from it's abuse. This he would have faithfully administered, and more than this I do not believe he ever wished. But he had a Queen of absolute sway over his weak mind, and timid virtue; and of a character the reverse of his in all points. This angel, as gaudily painted in the rhapsodies of the Rhetor [Edmund] Burke, with some smartness of fancy, but no sound sense was proud, disdainful of restraint, indignant at all obstacles to her will, eager in the pursuit of pleasure, and firm enough to hold to her desires, or perish in their wreck. Her inordinate gambling and dissipations, with those of the Count d'Artois and others of her clique, had been a sensible item in the exhaustion of the treasury, which called into action the reforming hand of the nation; and her opposition to it, her inflexible perverseness, and dauntless spirit, led herself to the Guillotine, & drew the king on with her, and plunged the world into crimes & calamities which will forever stain the pages of modern history. I have ever believed that had there been no queen, there would have been no revolution. No force would have been provoked nor exercised. The king would have gone hand in hand with the wisdom of his sounder counsellors, who, guided by the increased lights of the age, wished only, with the same pace, to advance the principles of their social institution. The deed which closed the mortal course of these sovereigns, I shall neither approve nor condemn. I am not prepared to say that the first magistrate of a nation cannot commit treason against his country, or is unamenable to it's punishment: nor yet that where there is no written law, no regulated tribunal, there is not a law in our hearts, and a power in our hands, given for righteous employment in maintaining right, and redressing wrong. Of those who judged the king, many thought him wilfully criminal, many that his existence would keep the nation in perpetual conflict with the horde of kings, who would war against a regeneration which might come home to themselves, and that it were better that one should die than all. I should not have voted with this portion of the legislature. I should have shut up the Queen in a Convent, putting harm out of her power, and placed the king in his station, investing him with limited powers, which I verily believe he would have honestly exercised, according to the measure of his understanding. In this way no void would have been created, courting the usurpation of a military adventurer, nor occasion given for those enormities which demoralized the nations of the world, and destroyed, and is yet to destroy millions and millions of it's inhabitants. There are three epochs in history signalized by the total extinction of national morality. The first was of the successors of Alexander, not omitting himself. The next the successors of the first Cæsar, the third our own age. This was begun by the partition of Poland, followed by that of the treaty of Pilnitz[1] next the conflagration of Copenhagen; then the enormities of Bonaparte partitioning the earth at his will, and devastating it with fire and sword; now the conspiracy of kings, the successors of Bonaparte, blasphemously calling themselves the Holy Alliance, and treading in the footsteps of their incarcerated leader, not yet indeed usurping the government of other nations avowedly and in detail, but controuling by their armies the forms in which they will permit them to be governed; and reserving *in petto* the order and extent of the usurpations further meditated. But I will return from a digression, anticipated too in time, into which I have been led by reflection on the criminal passions which refused to the world a favorable occasion of saving it from the afflictions it has since suffered.

M. Necker had reached Basle before he was overtaken by the letter of the king, inviting him back to resume the office he had recently left. He returned immediately, and all the other ministers having resigned, a new administration was named, to wit St. Priest & Montmorin were restored; the Archbishop of Bordeaux was appointed *Garde des sceaux*; La Tour du Pin Minister of War; La Luzerne Minister of Marine. This last was believed to have been effected by the friendship of Montmorin; for altho' differing in politics, they continued firm in friendship, & Luzerne, altho' not an able man was thought an honest one. And the Prince of Bauvau was taken into the Council.

Seven princes of the blood royal, six ex-ministers, and many of the high *Noblesse* having fled, and the present ministers, except Luzerne, being all of the popular party, all the functionaries of government moved for the present in perfect harmony.

In the evening of Aug. 4. and on the motion of the Viscount de Noailles, brother in law of La Fayette, the assembly abolished all titles of rank, all the abusive privileges of feudalism, the tythes and casuals of the clergy, all provincial privileges, and, *in fine*, the

---

[1] The 1791 agreement between Prussia and Austria threatening to declare war on France if the king were harmed. – *Eds.*

Feudal regimen generally. To the suppression of tythes the Abbé Sieyès was vehemently opposed; but his learned and logical arguments were unheeded, and his estimation lessened by a contrast of his egoism (for he was beneficed on them) with the generous abandonment of rights by the other members of the assembly. Many days were employed in putting into the form of laws the numerous demolitions of ancient abuses; which done, they proceeded to the preliminary work of a Declaration of rights. There being much concord of sentiment on the elements of this instrument, it was liberally framed, and passed with a very general approbation. They then appointed a Committee for the reduction of a projet of a Constitution, at the head of which was the Archbishop of Bordeaux. I received from him, as Chairman of the Committee, a letter of July 20. requesting me to attend and assist at their deliberations; but I excused myself on the obvious considerations that my mission was to the king as Chief Magistrate of the nation, that my duties were limited to the concerns of my own country, and forbade me to intermeddle with the internal transactions of that in which I had been received under a specific character only. Their plan of a constitution was discussed in sections, and so reported from time to time, as agreed to by the Committee. The first respected the general frame of the government; and that this should be formed into three departments, Executive, Legislative and Judiciary was generally agreed. But when they proceeded to subordinate developments, many and various shades of opinion came into conflict, and schism, strongly marked, broke the Patriots into fragments of very discordant principles. The first question Whether there should be a king, met with no open opposition, and it was readily agreed that the government of France should be monarchical & hereditary. Shall the king have a negative on the laws? shall that negative be absolute, or suspensive only? Shall there be two chambers of legislation? or one only? If two, shall one of them be hereditary? or for life? or for a fixed term? and named by the king? or elected by the people? These questions found strong differences of opinion, and produced repulsive combinations among the Patriots. The Aristocracy was cemented by a common principle of preserving the ancient regime, or whatever should be nearest to it. Making this their Polar star, they moved in phalanx, gave preponderance on every question to the minorities of the Patriots, and always to those who advocated the least change. The features of the new constitution were thus assuming a fearful aspect, and great alarm was produced among the honest patriots by these dissensions in their ranks. In this uneasy state of things, I received one day a note from the Marquis de la Fayette, informing me that he should bring a party of six or eight friends to ask a dinner of me the next day. I assured him of their welcome. When they arrived, they were La Fayette himself, Duport, Barnave, Alexander La Meth, Blacon, Mounier, Maubourg, and Dagout. These were leading patriots, of honest but differing opinions, sensible of the necessity of effecting a coalition by mutual sacrifices, knowing each other, and not afraid therefore to unbosom themselves mutually. This last was a material principle in the selection. With this view the Marquis had invited the conference and had fixed the time & place inadvertently as to the embarrassment under which it might place me. The cloth being removed and wine set on the table, after the American manner, the Marquis introduced the objects of the conference by summarily reminding them of the state of things in the Assembly, the course which the principles of the constitution were taking, and the inevitable result, unless checked by more concord among the Patriots themselves. He observed that altho' he also had his opinion, he was ready to sacrifice it to that of his brethren of the same cause: but that a common opinion must now be formed, or the Aristocracy would carry everything, and that whatever they should now agree on, he, at the head of the National force, would maintain. The discussions began at the hour of four, and were continued till ten o'clock in the evening; during which time I was a silent witness to a coolness and candor of argument unusual in the conflicts of political opinion; to a logical reasoning, and chaste eloquence, disfigured by no gaudy tinsel of rhetoric or declamation, and truly worthy of being placed in parallel with the finest dialogues of antiquity, as handed to us by Xenophon, by Plato and Cicero. The result was an agreement that the king should have a suspensive veto on the laws, that the legislature should be composed of a single body only, & that to be chosen by the people. This Concordate decided the fate of the constitution. The Patriots all rallied to the principles thus settled, carried every question agreeably to them, and reduced the Aristocracy to insignificance and impotence. But duties of exculpation were now incumbent on me. I waited on Count Montmorin the next morning, and explained to him with truth and candor how it had happened that my house had been made the scene of conferences of such a character. He told me he already knew everything which had passed, that, so far from taking umbrage at the use made of my house on that occasion, he earnestly wished I would habitually assist at such conferences, being sure I should be useful in moderating the warmer spirits, and promoting a wholesome and practicable reformation only. I told him I knew too well the duties I owed to the king, to the nation, and to my own country to take any part in councils concerning their internal government, and that I should persevere with care in the character of a neutral and passive spectator, with wishes only and very sincere ones, that those measures might prevail which would be for the greatest good of the nation. I have no doubt indeed that this conference was previously known and approved by this honest minister, who was in confidence and communication with the patriots, and wished for a reasonable reform of the Constitution.

Here I discontinue my relation of the French revolution. The minuteness with which I have so far given it's details is disproportioned to the general scale of my narrative. But I have thought it justified by the interest which the whole world must take in this revolution. As yet we are but in the first chapter of it's history. The appeal to the rights of man, which had been made in the U.S., was taken up by France, first of the European nations. From her the spirit has spread over those of the South. The tyrants of the North have allied indeed against it, but it is irresistible. Their opposition will only multiply it's millions of human victims; their own satellites will catch it, and the condition of man thro' the civilized world will be finally and greatly ameliorated. This is a wonderful instance of great events from small causes. So inscrutable is the arrangement of causes & consequences in this world that a two-penny duty on tea, unjustly imposed in a sequestered part of it, changes the condition of all it's inhabitants. I have been more minute in relating the early transactions of this regeneration because I was in circumstances peculiarly favorable for a knowledge of the truth. Possessing the confidence and intimacy of the leading patriots, & more than all of the Marquis Fayette, their head and Atlas, who had no secrets from me, I learnt with correctness the views & proceedings of that party; while my intercourse with the diplomatic missionaries of

Europe at Paris, all of them with the court, and eager in prying into it's councils and proceedings, gave me a knolege of these also. My information was always and immediately committed to writing, in letters to Mr. Jay, and often to my friends, and a recurrence to these letters now insures me against errors of memory.

These opportunities of information ceased at this period, with my retirement from this interesting scene of action. I had been more than a year soliciting leave to go home with a view to place my daughters in the society & care of their friends, and to return for a short time to my station at Paris. But the metamorphosis thro' which our government was then passing from it's Chrysalid to it's Organic form suspended it's action in a great degree; and it was not till the last of August that I received the permission I had asked. – And here I cannot leave this great and good country without expressing my sense of it's preeminence of character among the nations of the earth. A more benevolent people, I have never known, nor greater warmth & devotedness in their select friendships. Their kindness and accommodation to strangers is unparalleled, and the hospitality of Paris is beyond anything I had conceived to be practicable in a large city. Their eminence too in science, the communicative dispositions of their scientific men, the politeness of the general manners, the ease and vivacity of their conversation, give a charm to their society to be found nowhere else. In a comparison of this with other countries we have the proof of primacy, which was given to Themistocles after the battle of Salamis. Every general voted to himself the first reward of valor, and the second to Themistocles. So ask the travelled inhabitant of any nation. In what country on earth would you rather live? – Certainly in my own, where are all my friends, my relations, and the earliest & sweetest affections and recollections of my life. Which would be your second choice? France.

Ford I: 118–48

## II.12 To William Short

Philadelphia, January 3, 1793

Dear Sir, – My last private letter to you was of Oct. 16. since which I have recieved your private one of Sep. 15. The tone of your letters had for some time given me pain, on account of the extreme warmth with which they censured the proceedings of the Jacobins of France. I considered that sect as the same with the Republican patriots, and the *Feuillants* as the Monarchical patriots, well known in the early part of the revolution, and but little distant in their views, both having in object the establishment of a free constitution, and differing only on the question whether their chief Executive should be hereditary or not. The Jacobins (as since called) yeilded to the *Feuillants* and tried the experiment of retaining their hereditary Executive. The experiment failed completely, and would have brought on the reestablishment of despotism had it been pursued. The Jacobins saw this, and that the expunging that officer was of absolute necessity, and the Nation was with them in opinion, for however they might have been formerly for the constitution framed by the first assembly, they were come over from their hope in it, and were now generally Jacobins. In the struggle which was necessary, many guilty persons fell without the forms of trial, and with them some innocent. These I deplore as much as any body, and shall deplore some of them to the day of my death. But I deplore them as I should have done had they fallen in battle. It was necessary to use the arm of the people, a machine not quite so blind as balls and bombs, but blind to a certain degree. A few of their cordial friends met at their hands the fate of enemies. But time and truth will rescue and embalm their memories, while their posterity will be enjoying that very liberty for which they would never have hesitated to offer up their lives. The liberty of the whole earth was depending on the issue of the contest, and was ever such a prize won with so little innocent blood? My own affections have been deeply wounded by some of the martyrs to this cause, but rather than it should have failed, I would have seen half the earth desolated. Were there but an Adam and an Eve left in every country, and left free, it would be better than as it now is. I have expressed to you my sentiments, because they are really those of 99 in an hundred of our citizens. The universal feasts, and rejoicings which have lately been had on account of the successes of the French shewed the genuine effusions of their hearts. You have been wounded by the sufferings of your friends, and have by this circumstance been hurried into a temper of mind which would be extremely disrelished if known to your countrymen. The reserve of the Prest. of the U.S. had never permitted me to discover the light in which he viewed it, and as I was more anxious that you should satisfy him than me, I had still avoided explanations with you on the subject. But [you] induced him to break silence and to notice the extreme acrimony of your expressions. He added that he had been informed the sentiments you expressed in your conversations were equally offensive to our allies, and that you should consider yourself as the representative of your country and that what you say might be imputed to your constituents. He desired me therefore to write to you on this subject. He added that he considered France as the sheet anchor of this country and its friendship as a first object. There are in the U.S. some characters of opposite principles; some of them are high in office, others possessing great wealth, and all of them hostile to France and fondly looking to England as the staff of their hope. These I named to you on a former occasion. Their prospects have certainly not brightened. Excepting them, this country is entirely republican, friends to the constitution, anxious to preserve it and to have it administered according to it's own republican principles. The little party above mentioned have espoused it only as a stepping stone to monarchy, and have endeavored to approximate it to that in it's administration, in order to render it's final transition more easy. The successes of republicanism in France have given the *coup de grâce* to their prospects, and I hope to their projects – I have developed to you faithfully the sentiments of your country, that you may govern yourself accordingly. I know your republicanism to be pure, and that it is no decay of that which has embittered you against it's votaries in France, but too great a sensibility at the partial evil by which it's object has been accomplished there. I have written to you in the stile to which I have been always accustomed with you, and which perhaps it is time I should lay aside. But while old men feel sensibly enough their own advance in years, they do not sufficiently recollect it in those whom they have seen young. In writing too the last private letter which will probably be written under present circumstances, in contemplating that your correspondence will shortly be turned over to I know not whom, but certainly to some one not in the habit of considering your interests with the same fostering anxieties I do, I have presented things without reserve, satisfied you will ascribe what I have said to it's true motive, use it for your own best interest, and in that fulfill completely what I had in view.

With respect to the subject of your letter of Sep. 15. you will be sensible that many considerations would prevent my undertaking the reformation of a system of which I am so soon to take leave. It is but common decency to leave to my successor the moulding of his own business. – Not knowing how otherwise to convey this letter to you with certainty, I shall appeal to the friendship and honour of the Spanish commissioners here, to give it the protection of their cover, as a letter of private nature altogether. We have no remarkable event here lately, but the death of Dr. Lee: nor have I any thing new to communicate to you of your friends or affairs. I am with unalterable affection & wishes for your prosperity, my dear Sir, your sincere friend and servant.

Ford VI: 153–7

## II.13 To Dr. Thomas Cooper

Monticello, September 10, 1814

Dear Sir, – I regret much that I was so late in consulting you on the subject of the academy we wish to establish here.[1] The progress of that business has obliged me to prepare an address to the President of the Board of Trustees, – a plan for its organization. I send you a copy of it with a broad margin, that, if your answer to mine of August 25th be not on the way, you may be so good as to write your suggestions either in the margin or on a separate paper. We shall still be able to avail ourselves of them by way of amendments.

Your letter of August 17th is received. Mr. Ogilvie left us four days ago, on a tour of health, which is to terminate at New York, from whence he will take his passage to Britain to receive livery and seisin of his new dignities and fortunes. I am in the daily hope of seeing M. Corrica, and the more anxious as I must in two or three weeks commence a journey of long absence from home.

A comparison of the conditions of Great Britain and the United States, which is the subject of your letter of August 17th, would be

---

[1] The University of Virginia – *Eds.*

II.13 To Dr. Thomas Cooper, Sept. 10, 1814

an interesting theme indeed. To discuss it minutely and demonstratively would be far beyond the limits of a letter. I will give you, therefore, in brief only, the result of my reflections on the subject. I agree with you in your facts, and in many of your reflections. My conclusion is without doubt, as I am sure yours will be, when the appeal to your sound judgment is seriously made. The population of England is composed of three descriptions of persons (for those of minor note are too inconsiderable to affect a general estimate). These are, 1. The aristocracy, comprehending the nobility, the wealthy commoners, the high grades of priesthood, and the officers of government. 2. The laboring class. 3. The eleemosynary class, or paupers, who are about one-fifth of the whole. The aristocracy, which have the laws and government in their hands, have so managed them as to reduce the third description below the means of supporting life, even by labor; and to force the second, whether employed in agriculture or the arts, to the maximum of labor which the construction of the human body can endure, and to the minimum of food, and of the meanest kind, which will preserve it in life, and in strength sufficient to perform its functions. To obtain food enough, and clothing, not only their whole strength must be unremittingly exerted, but the utmost dexterity also which they can acquire; and those of great dexterity only can keep their ground, while those of less must sink into the class of paupers. Nor is it manual dexterity alone, but the acutest resources of the mind also which are impressed into this struggle for life; and such as have means a little above the rest, as the master-workmen, for instance, must strengthen themselves by acquiring as much of the philosophy of their trade as will enable them to compete with their rivals, and keep themselves above ground. Hence the industry and manual dexterity of their journeymen and day-laborers, and the science of their master-workmen, keep them in the foremost ranks of competition with those of other nations; and the less dexterous individuals, falling into the eleemosynary ranks, furnish materials for armies and navies to defend their country, exercise piracy on the ocean, and carry conflagration, plunder and devastation, on the shores of all those who endeavor to withstand their aggressions. A society thus constituted possesses certainly the means of defence. But what does it defend? The pauperism of the lowest class, the abject oppression of the laboring, and the luxury, the riot, the domination and the vicious happiness of the aristocracy. In their hands, the paupers are used as tools to maintain their own wretchedness, and to keep down the laboring portion by shooting them whenever the desperation produced by the cravings of their stomachs drives them into riots. Such is the happiness of scientific England; now let us see the American side of the medal.

And, first, we have no paupers, the old and crippled among us, who possess nothing and have no families to take care of them, being too few to merit notice as a separate section of society, or to affect a general estimate. The great mass of our population is of laborers; our rich, who can live without labor, either manual or professional, being few, and of moderate wealth. Most of the laboring class possess property, cultivate their own lands, have families, and from the demand for their labor are enabled to exact from the rich and the competent such prices as enable them to be fed abundantly, clothed above mere decency, to labor moderately and raise their families. They are not driven to the ultimate resources of dexterity and skill, because their wares will sell although not quite so nice as those of England. The wealthy, on the other hand, and those at their ease, know nothing of what the Europeans call luxury. They have only somewhat more of the comforts and decencies of life than those who furnish them. Can any condition of society be more desirable than this? Nor in the class of laborers do I mean to withhold from the comparison that portion whose color has condemned them, in certain parts of our Union, to a subjection to the will of others. Even these are better fed in these States, warmer clothed, and labor less than the journeymen or day-laborers of England. They have the comfort, too, of numerous families, in the midst of whom they live without want, or fear of it; a solace which few of the laborers of England possess. They are subject, it is true, to bodily coercion; but are not the hundreds of thousands of British soldiers and seamen subject to the same, without seeing, at the end of their career, when age and accident shall have rendered them unequal to labor, the certainty, which the other has, that he will never want? And has not the British seaman, as much as the African, been reduced to this bondage by force, in flagrant violation of his own consent, and of his natural right in his own person? and with the laborers of England generally, does not the moral coercion of want subject their will as despotically to that of their employer, as the physical constraint does the soldier, the seaman, or the slave? But do not mistake me. I am not advocating slavery. I am not justifying the wrongs we have committed on a foreign people, by the example of another nation committing equal wrongs on their own subjects. On the contrary, there is nothing I would not sacrifice to a practicable plan of abolishing every vestige of this moral and political depravity. But I am at present comparing the condition and degree of suffering to which oppression has reduced the man of one color, with the condition and degree of suffering to which oppression has reduced the man of another color; equally condemning both. Now let us compute by numbers the sum of happiness of the two countries. In England, happiness is the lot of the aristocracy only; and the proportion they bear to the laborers and paupers, you know better than I do. Were I to guess that they are four in every hundred, then the happiness of the nation would be to its misery as one in twenty-five. In the United States it is as eight millions to zero, or as all to none. But it is said they possess the means of defence, and that we do not. How so? Are we not men? Yes; but our men are so happy at home that they will not hire themselves to be shot at for a shilling a day. Hence we can have no standing armies for defence, because we have no paupers to furnish the materials. The Greeks and Romans had no standing armies, yet they defended themselves. The Greeks by their laws, and the Romans by the spirit of their people, took care to put into the hands of their rulers no such engine of oppression as a standing army. Their system was to make every man a soldier, and oblige him to repair to the standard of his country whenever that was reared. This made them invincible; and the same remedy will make us so. In the beginning of our government we were willing to introduce the least coercion possible on the will of the citizen. Hence a system of military duty was established too indulgent to his indolence. This is the first opportunity we have had of trying it, and it has completely failed; an issue foreseen by many, and for which remedies have been proposed. That of classing the militia according to age, and allotting each age to the particular kind of service to which it was competent, was proposed to Congress in 1805, and subsequently; and, on the last trial was lost, I believe, by a single vote only. Had it prevailed, what has now happened would not have happened. Instead of burning our Capitol, we should have possessed theirs in Montreal and

Quebec. We must now adopt it, and all will be safe. We had in the United States in 1805, in round numbers of free, able-bodied men,

| | | | | |
|---|---|---|---|---|
| 120,000 of | the | ages of | 18 to 21 | inclusive |
| 200,000 of | the | ages | 22 to 26 | inclusive |
| 200,000 of | the | ages | 27 to 35 | inclusive |
| 200,000 of | the | ages | 35 to 45 | inclusive |
| In all, 720,000 of | the | ages of | 18 to 45 | inclusive |

With this force properly classed, organized, trained, armed and subject to tours of a year of military duty, we have no more to fear for the defence of our country than those who have the resources of despotism and pauperism.

But, you will say, we have been devastated in the meantime. True, some of our public buildings have been burnt, and some scores of individuals on the tide-water have lost their movable property and their houses. I pity them, and execrate the barbarians who delight in unavailing mischief. But these individuals have their lands and their hands left. They are not paupers, they have still better means of subsistence than $\frac{24}{25}$ of the people of England. Again, the English have burnt our Capitol and President's house by means of their force. We can burn their St. James' and St. Paul's by means of our money, offered to their own incendiaries, of whom there are thousands in London who would do it rather than starve. But it is against the laws of civilized warfare to employ secret incendiaries. Is it not equally so to destroy the works of art by armed incendiaries? Bonaparte, possessed at times of almost every capital of Europe, with all his despotism and power, injured no monument of art. If a nation, breaking through all the restraints of civilized character, uses its means of destruction (power, for example) without distinction of objects, may we not use our means (*our* money and *their* pauperism) to retaliate their barbarous ravages? Are we obliged to use for resistance exactly the weapons chosen by them for aggression? When they destroyed Copenhagen by superior force, against all the laws of God and man, would it have been unjustifiable for the Danes to have destroyed their ships by torpedoes? Clearly not; and they and we should now be justifiable in the conflagration of St. James' and St. Paul's. And if we do not carry it into execution, it is because we think it more moral and more honorable to set a good example, than follow a bad one.

So much for the happiness of the people of England, and the morality of their government, in comparison with the happiness and the morality of America. Let us pass to another subject.

The crisis, then, of the abuses of banking is arrived. The banks have pronounced their own sentence of death. Between two and three hundred millions of dollars of their promissory notes are in the hands of the people, for solid produce and property sold, and they formally declare they will not pay them. This is an act of bankruptcy of course, and will be so pronounced by any court before which it shall be brought. But *cui bono?* The law can only uncover their insolvency, by opening to its suitors their empty vaults. Thus by the dupery of our citizens, and tame acquiescence of our legislators, the nation is plundered of two or three hundred millions of dollars, treble the amount of debt contracted in the Revolutionary war, and which, instead of redeeming our liberty, has been expended on sumptuous houses, carriages, and dinners. A fearful tax! if equalized on all; but overwhelming and convulsive by its partial fall. The crush will be tremendous; very different from that brought on by our paper money. That rose and fell so gradually that it kept all on their guard, and affected severely only early or long-winded contracts. Here the contract of yesterday crushes in an instant the one or the other party. The banks stopping payment suddenly, all their mercantile and city debtors do the same; and all, in short, except those in the country, who, possessing property, will be good in the end. But this resource will not enable them to pay a cent on the dollar. From the establishment of the United States Bank, to this day, I have preached against this system, but have been sensible no cure could be hoped but in the catastrophe now happening. The remedy was to let banks drop gradation at the expiration of their charters, and for the State governments to relinquish the power of establishing others. This would not, as it should not, have given the power of establishing them to Congress. But Congress could then have issued treasury notes payable within a fixed period, and founded on a specific tax, the proceeds of which, as they came in, should be exchangeable for the notes of that particular emission only. This depended, it is true, on the will of the State legislatures, and would have brought on us the phalanx of paper interest. But that interest is now defunct. Their gossamer castles are dissolved, and they can no longer impede and overawe the salutary measures of the government. Their paper was received on a belief that it was cash on demand. Themselves have declared it was nothing, and such scenes are now to take place as will open the eyes of credulity and of insanity itself, to the dangers of a paper medium abandoned to the discretion of avarice and of swindlers. It is impossible not to deplore our past follies, and their present consequences, but let them at least be warnings against like follies in future. The banks have discontinued themselves. We are now without any medium; and necessity, as well as patriotism and confidence, will make us all eager to receive treasury notes, if founded on specific taxes. Congress may now borrow of the public, and without interest, all the money they may want, to the amount of a competent circulation, by merely issuing their own promissory notes, of proper denominations for the larger purposes of circulation, but not for the small. Leave that door open for the entrance of metallic money. And, to give readier credit to their bills, without obliging themselves to give cash for them on demand, let their collectors be instructed to do so, when they have cash; thus, in some measure, performing the functions of a bank, as to their own notes. Providence seems, indeed, by a special dispensation, to have put down for us, without a struggle, that very paper enemy which the interest of our citizens long since required ourselves to put down, at whatever risk. The work is done. The moment is pregnant with futurity, and if not seized at once by Congress, I know not on what shoal our bark is next to be stranded. The State legislatures should be immediately urged to relinquish the right of establishing banks of discount. Most of them will comply, on patriotic principles, under the convictions of the moment; and the non-complying may be crowded into concurrence by legitimate devices. *Vale, et me, ut amaris, ama.*

L & B xiv: 179–90

## II.14  To Francis W. Gilmer

Monticello, June 7, 1816

Dear Sir, – I received a few days ago from Mr. Dupont the enclosed manuscript, with permission to read it, and a request, when read, to forward it to you, in expectation that you would translate it. It is well worthy of publication for the instruction of our citizens, being profound, sound, and short. Our legislators are not sufficiently apprised of the rightful limits of their power; that their true office is to declare and enforce only our natural rights and duties, and to take none of them from us. No man has a natural right to commit aggression on the equal rights of another: and this is all from which the laws ought to restrain him; every man is under the natural duty of contributing to the necessities of the society; and this is all the laws should enforce on him; and, no man having a natural right to be the judge between himself and another, it is his natural duty to submit to the umpirage of an impartial third. When the laws have declared and enforced all this, they have fulfilled their functions; and the idea is quite unfounded, that on entering into society we give up any natural right. The trial of every law by one of these texts, would lessen much the labors of our legislators, and lighten equally our municipal codes. There is a work of the first order of merit now in the press at Washington, by Destutt Tracy, on the subject of political economy,[1] which he brings into the compass of three hundred pages, octavo. In a preliminary discourse on the origin of the right of property, he coincides much with the principles of the present manuscript; but is more developed, more demonstrative. He promises a future work on morals, in which I lament to see that he will adopt the principles of Hobbes, or humiliation to human nature; that the sense of justice and injustice is not derived from our natural organization, but founded on convention only. I lament this the more, as he is unquestionably the ablest writer living, on abstract subjects. Assuming the fact, that the earth has been created in time, and consequently the dogma of final causes, we yield, of course, to this short syllogism. Man was created for social intercourse; but social intercourse cannot be maintained without a sense of justice; then man must have been created with a sense of justice. There is an error into which most of the speculators on government have fallen, and which the well-known state of society of our Indians ought, before now, to have corrected. In their hypothesis of the origin of government, they suppose it to have

[1] I.e. TJ's revised translation of Destutt de Tracy's *A Treatise on Political Economy* (Georgetown, D.C., 1817). – *Eds.*

commenced in the patriarchal or monarchical form. Our Indians are evidently in that state of nature which has passed the association of a single family; and not yet submitted to the authority of positive laws, or of any acknowledged magistrate. Every man, with them, is perfectly free to follow his own inclinations. But if, in doing this, he violates the rights of another, if the case be slight, he is punished by the disesteem of his society, or, as we say, by public opinion; if serious, he is tomahawked as a dangerous enemy. Their leaders conduct them by the influence of their character only; and they follow, or not, as they please, him of whose character for wisdom or war they have the highest opinion. Hence the origin of the parties among them adhering to different leaders, and governed by their advice, not by their command. The Cherokees, the only tribe I know to be contemplating the establishment of regular laws, magistrates, and government, propose a government of representatives, elected from every town. But of all things, they least think of subjecting themselves to the will of one man. This, the only instance of actual fact within our knowledge, will be then a beginning by republican, and not by patriarchal or monarchical government, as speculative writers have generally conjectured.

We have to join in mutual congratulations on the appointment of our friend Corrèa [da Serra], to be minister or envoy of Portugal, here. This, I hope, will give him to us for life. Nor will it at all interfere with his botanical rambles or journeys. The government of Portugal is so peaceable and inoffensive, that it has never any altercations with its friends. If their minister abroad writes them once a quarter that all is well, they desire no more. I learn, (though not from Corrèa himself,) that he thinks of paying us a visit as soon as he is through his course of lectures. Not to lose this happiness again by my absence, I have informed him I shall set out for Poplar Forest the 20th instant, and be back the first week of July. I wish you and he could concert your movements so as to meet here, and that you would make this your headquarters. It is a good central point from which to visit your connections; and you know our practice of placing our guests at their ease, by showing them we are so ourselves and that we follow our necessary vocations, instead of fatiguing them by hanging unremittingly on their shoulders. I salute you with affectionate esteem and respect.

L & B XV: 23–7

## II.15  To James Madison

Monticello, August 30, 1823

Dear Sir, – I received the enclosed letters from the President, with a request, that after perusal I would forward them to you, for perusal by yourself also and to be returned then to him.

You have doubtless seen Timothy Pickering's 4th. of July observations on the Declaration of Independence.[1] If his principles and prejudices personal and political, gave us no reason to doubt whether he had truly quoted the information he alledges to have recieved from Mr. Adams,[2] I should then say that, in some of the particulars, Mr. Adams' memory has led him into unquestionable error. At the age of 88, and 47 years after the transactions of Independence, this is not wonderful. Nor should I, at the age of 80, on the small advantage of that difference only, venture to oppose my memory to his, were it not supported by written notes, taken by myself at the moment and on the spot. He says, "the committee (of 5 to wit, Dr. Franklin, Sherman, Livingston, and ourselves) met, discussed the subject, and then appointed him and myself to make the draught; that we, as a subcommittee met, and after the urgencies of each on the other, I consented to undertake the task; that the draught being made, we, the subcommittee, met, and conned the paper over, and he does not remember that he made or suggested a single alteration." Now these details are quite incorrect. The committee of 5 met, no such thing as as a subcommittee was proposed, but they unanimously pressed on myself alone to undertake the draught. I consented; I drew it; but before I reported it to the committee, I communicated it *separately* to Dr. Franklin and Mr. Adams, requesting their corrections, because they were the two members of whose judgments and amendments I wished most to have the benefit, before presenting it to the Committee; and you have seen the original paper now in my hands, with the corrections of Doctor Franklin and Mr. Adams interlined in their own handwritings. Their alterations were two or three only, and merely

---

[1] "Colonel Pickering's Observations Introductory to Reading the Declaration of Independence at Salem, July 4, 1823"; repr. as Appendix D in Charles W. Upham, *The Life of Timothy Pickering* (Boston, 1873), IV, pp. 463–9. – *Eds.*

[2] John Adams to Timothy Pickering, Aug. 22, 1822; repr. *infra*, Appendix B. – *Eds.*

verbal. I then wrote a fair copy, reported it to the Committee, and from them, unaltered to Congress. This personal communication and consultation with Mr. Adams, he has misremembered into the actings of a sub-committee. Pickering's observations, and Mr. Adams' in addition, "that it contained no new ideas, that it is a commonplace compilation, it's sentiments hackneyed in Congress for two years before, and its essence contained in Otis's pamphlet," may all be true. Of that I am not to be the judge. Richard Henry Lee charged it as copied from Locke's treatise on government. Otis's pamphlet I never saw, and whether I had gathered my ideas from reading or reflection I do not know. I know only that I turned to neither book or pamphlet while writing it. I did not consider it as any part of my charge to invent new ideas altogether and to offer no sentiment which had ever been expressed before. Had Mr. Adams been so restrained, Congress would have lost the benefit of his bold and impressive advocations of the rights of revolution. For no man's confident and fervid addresses, more than Mr. Adams's, encouraged and supported us thro' the difficulties surrounding us, which, like the ceaseless action of gravity, weighed on us by night and by day. Yet, on the same ground, we may ask what of these elevated thoughts was new, or can be affirmed never before to have entered the conceptions of man?

Whether also the sentiments of independence, and the reasons for declaring it which make so great a portion of the instrument, had been hackneyed in Congress for two years before the 4th. of July '76, or this dictum also of Mr. Adams be another slip of memory, let history say. This however I will say for Mr. Adams, that he supported the Declaration with zeal and ability, fighting fearlessly for every word of it. As to myself, I thought it a duty to be, on that occasion, a passive auditor of the opinions of others, more impartial judges than I could be, of its merits or demerits. During the debate I was sitting by Dr. Franklin, and he observed that I was writhing a little under the acrimonious criticisms on some of its parts; and it was on that occasion that, by way of comfort, he told me the story of John Thompson, the Hatter, and his new sign.

Timothy [Pickering] thinks the instrument the better for having a fourth of it expunged. He would have thought it still better had the other three-fourths gone out also, all but the single sentiment (the only one he approves), which recommends friendship to his dear England, whenever she is willing to be at peace with us. His insinuations are that altho' "the high tone of the instrument was in unison with the warm feelings of the times, this sentiment of habitual friendship to England should never be forgotten, and that the duties it enjoins should *especially* be borne in mind on every celebration of this anniversary." In other words, that the Declaration, as being a libel on the government of England, composed in times of passion, should now be buried in utter oblivion to spare the feelings of our English friends and Angloman fellow citizens. But it is not to wound them that we wish to keep it in mind; but to cherish the principles of the instrument in the bosoms of our own citizens: and it is a heavenly comfort to see that these principles are yet so strongly felt, as to render a circumstance so trifling as this little lapse of memory of Mr. Adams worthy of being solemnly announced and supported at an anniversary assemblage of the nation on its birthday. In opposition however to Mr. Pickering, I pray God that these principles may be eternal and close the prayer with my affectionate wishes for yourself of long life, health and happiness.

L & B xv: 460–4

## II.16 To Henry Lee

Monticello, May 8, 1825

Dear Sir, – That George Mason was author of the [Virginia] bill of rights, and of the constitution founded on it, the evidence of the day established fully in my mind. Of the paper you mention, purporting to be instructions of the Virginia delegation in Congress, I have no recollection. If it were anything more than a project of some private hand, that is to say, had any such instructions been ever given by the convention, they would appear in the journals, which we possess entire. But with respect to our rights, and the acts of the British government contravening those rights, there was but one opinion on this side of the water. All American whigs thought alike on these subjects. When forced, therefore, to resort to arms for redress, an appeal to the tribunal of the world was deemed proper for our justification. This was the object of the

Declaration of Independence. Not to find out new principles, or new arguments, never before thought of, not merely to say things which had never been said before; but to place before mankind the common sense of the subject, in terms so plain and firm as to command their assent, and to justify ourselves in the independent stand we are compelled to take. Neither aiming at originality of principle or sentiment, nor yet copied from any particular and previous writing, it was intended to be an expression of the American mind, and to give to that expression the proper tone and spirit called for by the occasion. All its authority rests then on the harmonizing sentiments of the day, whether expressed in conversation, in letters, printed essays, or in the elementary books of public right, as Aristotle, Cicero, Locke, Sidney, &c. The historical documents which you mention as in your possession, ought all to be found, and I am persuaded you will find, to be corroborative of the facts and principles advanced in that Declaration. Be pleased to accept assurances of my great esteem and respect.

Ford x: 342–3

## II.17 To Roger C. Weightman

Monticello, June 24, 1826

Respected Sir, – The kind invitation I receive from you, on the part of the citizens of the city of Washington, to be present with them at their celebration on the fiftieth anniversary of American Independence, as one of the surviving signers of an instrument pregnant with our own, and the fate of the world, is most flattering to myself, and heightened by the honorable accompaniment proposed for the comfort of such a journey. It adds sensibly to the sufferings of sickness, to be deprived by it of a personal participation in the rejoicings of that day. But acquiescence is a duty, under circumstances not placed among those we are permitted to control. I should, indeed, with peculiar delight, have met and exchanged there congratulations personally with the small band, the remnant of that host of worthies, who joined with us on that day, in the bold and doubtful election we were to make for our country, between submission or the sword; and to have enjoyed with them the consolatory fact, that our fellow citizens, after half a century of experience and prosperity, continue to approve the choice we made. May it be to the world, what I believe it will be, (to some parts sooner, to others later, but finally to all,) the signal of arousing men to burst the chains under which monkish ignorance and superstition had persuaded them to bind themselves, and to assume the blessings and security of self-government. That form which we have substituted, restores the free right to the unbounded exercise of reason and freedom of opinion. All eyes are opened, or opening, to the rights of man. The general spread of the light of science has already laid open to every view the palpable truth, that the mass of mankind has not been born with saddles on their backs, nor a favored few booted and spurred, ready to ride them legitimately, by the grace of God. These are grounds of hope for others. For ourselves, let the annual return of this day forever refresh our recollections of these rights, and an undiminished devotion to them.

I will ask permission here to express the pleasure with which I should have met my ancient neighbors of the city of Washington and its vicinities, with whom I passed so many years of a pleasing social intercourse; an intercourse which so much relieved the anxieties of the public cares, and left impressions so deeply engraved in my affections, as never to be forgotten. With my regret that ill health forbids me the gratification of an acceptance, be pleased to receive for yourself, and those for whom you write, the assurance of my highest respect and friendly attachments.

Ford x: 390–2

# III  Self-government

# III.1 To Edward Carrington

Paris, January 16, 1787

Dear Sir, – Uncertain whether you might be at New York at the moment of Colo. Franks's arrival, I have inclosed my private letters for Virginia under cover to our delegation in general, which otherwise I would have taken the liberty to inclose particularly to you, as best acquainted with the situation of the persons to whom they are addressed. Should this find you at New York, I will still ask your attention to them. The two large packages addressed to Colo. N. Lewis contain seeds, not valuable enough to pay passage, but which I would wish to be sent by the stage, or any similar quick conveyance. The letters to Colo. Lewis & Mr. Eppes (who take care of my affairs) are particularly interesting to me. The package for Colo. Richd. Cary our judge of Admiralty near Hampton, contains seeds & roots, not to be sent by Post. Whether they had better go by the stage, or by water, you will be the best judge. I beg your pardon for giving you this trouble. But my situation & your goodness will I hope excuse it. In my letter to Mr. Jay, I have mentioned the meeting of the Notables appointed for the 29th inst. It is now put off to the 7th or 8th of next month. This event, which will hardly excite any attention in America, is deemed here the most important one which has taken place in their civil line during the present century. Some promise their country great things from it, some nothing. Our friend de La Fayette was placed on the list originally. Afterwards his name disappeared; but finally was reinstated. This shews that his character here is not considered as an indifferent one; and that it excites agitation. His education in our school has drawn on him a very jealous eye from a court whose principles are the most absolute despotism. But I hope he has nearly passed his crisis. The King, who is a good man, is favorably disposed towards him: & he is supported by powerful family connections, & by the public good will. He is the youngest man of the Notables except one whose office placed him on the list.

The Count de Vergennes has within these ten days had a very severe attack of what is deemed an unfixed gout. He has been well enough however to do business to-day. But anxieties for him are not yet quieted. He is a great & good minister, and an accident to him might endanger the peace of Europe.

The tumults in America,[1] I expected would have produced in Europe an unfavorable opinion of our political state. But it has not. On the contrary, the small effect of these tumults seems to have given more confidence in the firmness of our governments. The interposition of the people themselves on the side of government has had a great effect on the opinion here. I am persuaded myself that the good sense of the people will always be found to be the best army. They may be led astray for a moment, but will soon correct themselves. The people are the only censors of their governors: and even their errors will tend to keep these to the true principles of their institution. To punish these errors too severely would be to suppress the only safeguard of the public liberty. The way to prevent these irregular interpositions of the people is to give them full information of their affairs thro' the channel of the public papers, & to contrive that those papers should penetrate the whole mass of the people. The basis of our governments being the opinion of the people, the very first object should be to keep that right; and were it left to me to decide whether we should have a government without newspapers or newspapers without a government, I should not hesitate a moment to prefer the latter. But I should mean that every man should receive those papers & be capable of reading them. I am convinced that those societies (as the Indians) which live without government enjoy in their general mass an infinitely greater degree of happiness than those who live under the European governments. Among the former, public opinion is in the place of law, & restrains morals as powerfully as laws ever did anywhere. Among the latter, under pretence of governing they have divided their nations into two classes, wolves & sheep. I do not exaggerate. This is a true picture of Europe. Cherish therefore the spirit of our people, and keep alive their attention. Do not be too severe upon their errors, but reclaim them by enlightening them. If once they become inattentive to the public affairs, you & I, & Congress & Assemblies, judges & governors shall all become wolves. It seems to be the law of our general nature, in spite of individual exceptions;

---

[1] Shays's Rebellion in western Massachusetts. – *Eds.*

and experience declares that man is the only animal which devours his own kind, for I can apply no milder term to the governments of Europe, and to the general prey of the rich on the poor. The want of news has led me into disquisition instead of narration, forgetting you have every day enough of that. I shall be happy to hear from you sometimes, only observing that whatever passes thro' the post is read, & that when you write what should be read by myself only, you must be so good as to confide your letter to some passenger or officer of the packet. I will ask your permission to write to you sometimes, and to assure you of the esteem & respect with which I have honour to be Dear Sir your most obedient & most humble serv[an]t.

Ford IV: 357–61

## III.2 To Thomas Paine

Paris, July 11, 1789

Dear Sir, – Since my last, which was of May the 19th, I have received yours of June the 17th and 18th. I am struck with the idea of the geometrical wheelbarrow, and will beg of you a farther account, if it can be obtained. I have no news yet of my *congé*.[1]

Though you have doubtless heard most of the proceedings of the [French] States General since my last, I will take up the narration where that left it, that you may be able to separate the true from the false accounts you have heard. A good part of what was conjectured in that letter, is now become true history.

The *National Assembly* then (for that is the name they take), having shown through every stage of these transactions a coolness, wisdom, and resolution to set fire to the four corners of the kingdom and to perish with it themselves, rather than to relinquish an iota from their plan of a total change of government, are now in complete and undisputed possession of the sovereignty. The executive and aristocracy are at their feet; the mass of the nation, the mass of

---

[1] TJ had requested a leave of absence (*congé*) to return to Virginia to put his personal and financial affairs in order. On his return at the end of November he learned that he was to be President Washington's first Secretary of State. – *Eds.*

the clergy, and the army are with them; they have prostrated the old government, and are now beginning to build one from the foundation. A committee, charged with the arrangement of their business, gave in, two days ago, the order of proceedings.

1. Every government should have for its only end, the preservation of the rights of man; whence it follows, that to recall constantly the government to the end proposed, the constitution should begin by a declaration of the natural and imprescriptible rights of man.

2. Monarchical government being proper to maintain those rights, it has been chosen by the French nation. It suits especially a great society; it is necessary for the happiness of France. The declaration of the principles of this government, then, should follow immediately the declaration of the rights of man.

3. It results from the principles of monarchy, that the nation, to assure its own rights, has yielded particular rights to the monarch; the constitution, then, should declare, in a precise manner, the rights of both. It should begin by declaring the rights of the French nation, and then it should declare the rights of the King.

4. The rights of the King and nation not existing but for the happiness of the individuals who compose it, they lead to an examination of the rights of citizens.

5. The French nation not being capable of assembling individually, to exercise all its rights, it ought to be represented. It is necessary, then, to declare the form of its representation and the rights of its representatives.

6. From the union of the powers of the nation and King, should result the enacting and execution of the laws; thus, then, it should first be determined how the laws shall be established, afterwards should be considered, how they shall be executed.

7. Laws have for their object the general administration of the kingdom, the property and the actions of the citizens. The execution of the laws which concern the general administration, requires Provincial and Municipal Assemblies. It is necessary to examine, therefore, what should be the organization of the Provincial Assemblies, and what of the Municipal.

8. The execution of the laws which concern the property and actions of the citizens, call for the judiciary power. It should be

determined how that should be confided, and then its duties and limits.

9. For the execution of the laws and the defence of the kingdom, there exists a public force. It is necessary, then, to determine the principles which should direct it, and how it should be employed.

### Recapitulation

Declaration of the rights of man. Principles of the monarchy. Rights of the nation. Rights of the King. Rights of the citizens.

Organization and rights of the National Assembly. Forms necessary for the enaction of laws. Organization and functions of the Provincial and Municipal Assemblies. Duties and limits of the judiciary power. Functions and duties of the military power.

You see that these are the materials of a superb edifice, and the hands which have prepared them, are perfectly capable of putting them together, and of filling up the work of which these are only the outlines. While there are some men among them of very superior abilities, the mass possess such a degree of good sense, as enables them to decide well. I have always been afraid their numbers might lead to confusion. Twelve hundred men in one room are too many. I have still that fear. Another apprehension is, that a majority cannot be induced to adopt the trial by jury; and I consider that as the only anchor ever yet imagined by man, by which a government can be held to the principles of its constitution. Mr. Paradise is the bearer of this letter. He can supply those details which it would be too tedious to write.

I am, with great esteem, dear Sir, your friend and servant.

L & B XIX: 404–8

## III.3 To Diodati

à Paris ce 3me. Août, 1789

Je viens de recevoir, mon cher Monsieur, l'honneur de votre lettre du 24. Juillet. La peine avec laquelle je m'exprime en François feroit que ma réponse seroit bien courte s'il ne m'étoit pas permis de répondre que dans cette langue. Mais je sçais qu'avec quelque connoissance de la langue Angloise vous-même, vous aurez une aide très suffisante dans Madame la comtesse que j'ose prier d'ajouter à ses amitiés multipliées devers moi celle de devenir l'interprète de ce que je vais écrire en ma propre langue, et qu'elle embellira en la rendant en François.

I presume that your correspondents here have given you a history of all the events which have happened. The Leyden gazette, tho' it contains several inconsiderable errors, gives on the whole a just enough idea. It is impossible to conceive a greater fermentation than has worked in Paris, nor do I believe that so great a fermentation ever produced so little injury in any other place. I have been thro' it daily, have observed the mobs with my own eyes in order to be satisfied of their objects, and declare to you that I saw so plainly the legitimacy of them, that I have slept in my house as quietly thro' the whole as I ever did in the most peaceable moments. So strongly fortified was the despotism of this government by long posession, by the respect and the fears of the people, by possessing the public force, by the imposing authority of forms and of faste, that had it held itself on the defensive only, the national assembly with all their good sense, could probably have only obtained a considerable improvement of the government, not a total revision of it. But, ill informed of the spirit of their nation, the despots around the throne had recourse to violent measures, the forerunners of force. In this they have been completely overthrown, and the nation has made a total resumption of rights, which they had certainly never before ventured even to think of. The National assembly have now as clean a canvas to work on here as we had in America. Such has been the firmness and wisdom of their proceedings in moments of adversity as well as prosperity, that I have the highest confidence that they will use their power justly. As far as I can collect from conversation with their members, the constitution they will propose will resemble that of England in it's outlines, but not in it's defects. They will certainly leave the king possessed completely of the Executive powers, and particularly of the public force. Their legislature will consist of one order only, and not of two as in England: the representation will be equal and not abominably partial as that of England: it will be guarded against corruption, instead of having a majority sold to the king, and rendering his will absolute: whether it will be in one chamber, or broke into two cannot be foreseen. They will meet at certain epochs and sit as long as they please, instead of meeting only when, and sitting only as long as, the king pleases as in England. There is a difference of opinion whether the king shall have an absolute, or only a qualified Negative on their acts. The parliaments will probably be suppressed; and juries provided in criminal cases perhaps even in civil ones. This is what appears probable at present. The Assembly is this day discussing the question whether they will have a declaration of rights. Paris has been led by events to assume the government of itself. It has hitherto worn too much the appearance of conformity to continue thus independently of the will of the nation. Reflection will probably make them sensible that the security of all depends on the dependance of all on the national legislature. I have so much confidence in the good sense of man, and his qualifications for self-government, that I am never afraid of the issue where reason is left free to exert her force; and I will agree to be stoned as a false prophet if all does not end well in this country. Nor will it end with this country. Here is but the first chapter of the history of European liberty.

The capture of the Baron Besenval is very embarrassing for the States general. They are principled against retrospective laws, and will make it one of the corner stones of their new building. But it is very doubtful whether the antient laws will condemn him, and whether the people will permit him to be acquitted. The Duke de la Vauguyon also and his son are taken at Havre. – In drawing the parallel between what England is, and what France is to be, I forgot to observe that the latter will have a real constitution, which cannot be changed by the ordinary legislature; whereas England has no constitution at all; that is to say there is not one principle of their government which the parliament does not alter at pleasure. The omnipotence of parliament is an established principle with them. – Postponing my departure to America till the end of September I shall hope to have the pleasure of seeing you at Paris before I go, and of renewing in person to yourself and Madame la Comtesse assurances of those sentiments of respect and attachment with which I have the honor to be Dear Sir Your most obedient humble servt.

P.S. It is rumored and believed in Paris that the English have fomented with money the tumults of this place, and that they are arming to attack France. I have never seen any reason to believe either of these rumors.

MS, Massachusetts Historical Society

## III.4 Opinion on Residence Bill

[July 15, 1790]

*Opinion upon the question whether the President should veto the Bill, declaring that the seat of government shall be transferred to the Potomac, in the year 1790.*

A bill having passed both houses of Congress, and being now before the President, declaring that the seat of the federal government shall be transferred to the Potomac in the year 1790, that the session of Congress next ensuing the present shall be held in Philadelphia, to which place the offices shall be transferred before the 1st of December next, a writer in a public paper of July 13, has urged on the consideration of the President, that the constitution has given to the two houses of Congress the exclusive right to adjourn themselves; that the will of the President mixed with theirs in a decision of this kind, would be an inoperative ingredient, repugnant to the constitution, and that he ought not to permit them to part, in a single instance, with their constitutional rights; consequently, that he ought to negative the bill.

That is now to be considered:

Every man, and every body of men on earth, possesses the right of self-government. They receive it with their being from the hand of nature. Individuals exercise it by their single will; collections of men by that of their majority; for the law of the *majority* is the natural law of every society of men. When a certain description of men are to transact together a particular business, the times and places of their meeting and separating, depend on their own will; they make a part of the natural right of self-government. This, like all other natural rights, may be abridged or modified in its exercise by their own consent, or by the law of those who depute them, if they meet in the right of others; but as far as it is not abridged or modified, they retain it as a natural right, and may exercise them in what form they please, either exclusively by themselves, or in association with others, or by others altogether, as they shall agree.

Each house of Congress possesses this natural right of governing itself, and, consequently, of fixing its own times and places of meeting, so far as it has not been abridged by the law of those who employ them, that is to say, by the Constitution. This act manifestly considers them as possessing this right of course, and therefore has nowhere given it to them. In the several different passages where it touches this right, it treats it as an existing thing, not as one called into existence by them. To evince this, every passage of the constitution shall be quoted, where the right of adjournment is touched; and it will be seen that no one of them pretends to give that right; that, on the contrary, every one is evidently introduced either to enlarge the right where it would be too narrow, to restrain it where, in its natural and full exercise, it might be too large, and lead to inconvenience, to defend it from the latitude of its own phrases, where these were not meant to comprehend it, or to provide for its exercise by others, when they cannot exercise it themselves.

"A majority of each house shall constitute a quorum to do business; but a smaller number may adjourn from day to day, and may be authorized to compel the attendance of absent members." Art. I, Sec. 5. A majority of every collection of men being naturally necessary to constitute its will, and it being frequently to happen that a majority is not assembled, it was necessary to enlarge the natural right by giving to "a smaller number than a majority" a right to compel the attendence of the absent members, and, in the meantime, to adjourn from day to day. This clause, then, does not pretend to give to a majority a right which it knew that majority would have of themselves, but to a number *less than a majority*, a right to which it knew that lesser number could not have of themselves.

"Neither house, during the session of Congress, shall, without the consent of the other, adjourn for more than three days, nor to any other place than that in which the two houses shall be sitting." Ibid. Each house exercising separately its natural right to meet when and where it should think best, it might happen that the two houses would separate either in time or place, which would be inconvenient. It was necessary, therefore, to keep them together by restraining their natural right of deciding on separate times and places, and by requiring a concurrence of will.

But, as it might happen that obstinacy, or a difference of object, might prevent this concurrence, it goes on to take from them, in that instance, the right of adjournment altogether, and to transfer it to another, by declaring, Art. II, Sec. 3, that "in case of disagreement between the two houses, with respect to the time of adjournment, the President may adjourn them to such time as he shall think proper."

These clauses, then, do not import a gift, to the two houses, of a general right of adjournment, which it was known they would have without that gift, but to restrain or abrogate the right it was known they would have, in an instance where, exercised in its full extent, it might lead to inconvenience, and to give that right to another who would not naturally have had it. It also gives to the President a right, which he otherwise would not have had, "to convene both houses, or either of them, on extraordinary occasions." Thus substituting the will of another, where they are not in a situation to exercise their own.

"Every order, resolution, or vote, to which the concurrence of the Senate and House of Representatives may be necessary (except on a question of adjournment), shall be presented to the President for his approbation, &c." Art. I, Sec. 7. The latitude of the general words here used would have subjected the natural right of adjournment of the two houses to the will of the President, which was not intended. They therefore expressly "except questions of adjournment" out of their operation. They do not here give a right of adjournment, which it was known would exist without their gift, but they defend the existing right against the latitude of their own phrases, in a case where there was no good reason to abridge it. The exception admits they will have the right of adjournment, without pointing out the source from which they will derive it.

These are all the passages of the constitution (one only excepted, which shall be presently cited) where the right of adjournment is touched; and it is evident that none of these are introduced to give that right; but every one supposes it to be existing, and provides some specific modification for cases where either a defeat in the natural right, or a too full use of it, would occasion inconvenience.

The right of adjournment, then, is not given by the constitution, and consequently it may be modified by law without interfering with that instrument. It is a natural right, and, like all other natural rights, may be abridged or regulated in its exercise by law; and the concurrence of the third branch in any law regulating its exercise is so efficient an ingredient in that law, that the right cannot be otherwise exercised but after a repeal by a new law. The express terms of the constitution itself show that this right may be modified by law, when, in Art. 1, Sec. 4, (the only remaining passage on the subject not yet quoted) it says, "The Congress shall assemble at least once in every year, and such meeting shall be the first Monday in December, unless they shall, *by law*, appoint a different day." Then another day may be appointed *by law*; and the President's assent is an efficient ingredient in that law. Nay, further, they cannot adjourn over the first Monday of December but by *a law*. This is another constitutional abridgment of their natural right of adjournment; and completing our review of all the clauses in the constitution which touch that right, authorizes us to say no part of that instrument gives it; and that the houses hold it, not from the constitution, but from nature.

A consequence of this is, that the houses may, by a joint resolution, remove themselves from place to place, because it is a part of their right of self-government; but that as the right of self-government does not comprehend the government of others, the two houses cannot, by a joint resolution of their majorities only, remove the executive and judiciary from place to place. These branches possessing also the rights of self-government from nature, cannot be controlled in the exercise of them but by a law, passed in the forms of the constitution. The clause of the bill in question, therefore, was necessary to be put into the form of a law, and to be submitted to the President, so far as it proposes to effect the removal of the Executive and Judiciary to Philadelphia. So far as respects the removal of the present houses of legislation thither, it was not necessary to be submitted to the President; but such a submission is not repugnant to the constitution. On the contrary, if he concurs, it will so far fix the next session of Congress at Philadelphia that it cannot be changed but by a regular law.

The sense of Congress itself is always respectable authority. It has been given very remarkably on the present subject. The address to the President in the paper of the 13th is a complete digest of all the arguments urged on the floor of the Representatives against the constitutionality of the bill now before the President; and they were overruled by a majority of that house, comprehending the delegation of all the States south of the Hudson, except South Carolina. At the last cession of Congress, when the bill for remaining a certain term at New York and then removing to Susquehanna or Germantown was objected to on the same ground, the objection was overruled by a majority comprehending the delegations of the northern half of the union with that of South Carolina. So that the sense of every State in the union has been expressed, by its delegation, against this objection South Carolina excepted, and excepting also Rhode Island, which has never yet had a delegation in place to vote on the question. In both these instances the Senate concurred with the majority of the Representatives. The sense of the two houses is stronger authority in this case, as it is given against their own supposed privilege.

It would be as tedious, as it is unnecessary, to take up and discuss one by one, the objections proposed in the paper of July 13. Every one of them is founded on the supposition that the two houses hold their right of adjournment from the constitution. This error being corrected, the objections founded on it fall of themselves.

It would also be work of mere supererogation to show that, granting what this writer takes for granted (that the President's assent would be an inoperative ingredient, because excluded by the constitution, as he says), yet the particular views of the writer would be frustrated, for on every hypothesis of what the President may do, Congress must go to Philadelphia. 1. If he assents to the bill, that assent makes good law of the part relative to the Patomac; and the part for holding the next session at Philadelphia is good, either as an ordinance, or a vote of the two houses, containing a complete declaration of their will in a case where it is competent to the object; so that they must go to Philadelphia in that case. 2. If he dissents from the bill it annuls the part relative to the Patomac; but as to the clause for adjourning to Philadelphia, his dissent being as inefficient as his assent, it remains a good ordinance or vote, of the two houses for going thither, and consequently they must go in this case also. 3. If the President withholds his will out of the bill altogether,

by a ten days' silence, then the part relative to the Potomac becomes
a good law without his will, and that relative to Philadelphia is good
also, either as a law, or an ordinance, or a vote of the two houses;
and consequently in this case also they go to Philadelphia.

Ford v: 205–10

## III.5 Petition on Election of Jurors

[October 1798]

To the General Assembly of the Commonwealth of Virginia

The Petition of Sundry persons inhabitants of the county of
Albermarle and citizens of the said Commonwealth respectfully
sheweth.

That though civil govemt duly framed and administered be one
of the greatest blessings and most powerful instruments for procuring safety and happiness to men collected in large societies, yet such
is the proneness of those to whom its powers are necessarily deputed
to pervert them to the attainment of personal wealth and
dominion & to the utter oppression of their fellowmen, that it has
become questionable whether the condition of our aboriginal neighbors who live without laws or magistracies be not preferable to that
of the great mass of the nations of the earth who feel their laws and
magistrates but in the weight of their burthens. That the citizens
of these U.S. impressed with this mortifying truth when they
deposed the abusive govmt under which they have lived, founded
their new forms, as well particular as general in that fact and principle, that the people themselves are the safest deposit of power,
and that none therefore should be trusted to others which they can
competently exercise themselves, that their own experience having
proved that the people are competent to the appointment or election
of their agents, that of their chief executive magistrates was reserved
to be made by themselves or by others chosen by themselves: as
was also the choice of their legislatures whether composed of one
or more branches: that in the judiciary department, sensible that
they were inadequate to questions of law, these were in ordinary
cases confided to permanent judges, reserving to juries only extraordinary cases where a bias in the permanent judge might be

suspected, and where honest ignorance would be safer than perverted science: and reserving to themselves also the whole department of fact which constitutes indeed the great mass of judiciary litigations: that the wisdom of these reservations will be apparent on a recurrence to the history of that country from which we chiefly emigrated, where the faint glimmerings of liberty and safety now remaining to the nation are kept in feeble life by the reserved powers of the people only. That in the establishment of the trial by jury, however, a great inconsistence, has been overlooked in this and some others of the states, or rather has been copied from their original without due attention: for while the competence of the people to the appointmt even of the highest executive and the legislative agents is admitted & established, and their competence to be themselves the triers of judiciary facts, the appointment of the special individuals from among themselves who shall be such triers of fact has not been left in their hands, but has been placed by law in officers dependent on the executive or judiciary bodies: that triers of fact are therefore habitually taken in this state from among accidental bystanders and too often composed of foreigners attending on matters of business and of idle persons collected for purposes of dissipation, and in cases interesting to the powers of the public functionaries may be specially selected from descriptions of persons to be found in every country, whose ignorance or dependance renders them pliable to the will and designs of power. That in others of these states, and particularly in those to the eastward of the union, this germ of rottedness in the constitution of juries has been carefully excluded, and their laws have provided with laudable foresight for the appointment of jurors by selectmen chosen by the people themselves: and to a like restitution of principle and salutary precaution against the abuse of power by the public functionaries, who never did yet in any country fail to betray and oppress those for the care of whose affairs they were appointed, by force if they possessed it, or by fraud and delusion if they did not, your petitioners pray the timely attention of their legislature, while that legislature (and with a heartfelt satisfaction the petitioners pronounce it) are still honest enough to wish the preservation of the rights of the people, and wise enough to circumscribe in time the spread of that gangrene which sooner than many are aware may reach the vitals of our political existence.

And lest it should be supposed that the popular appointmt of jurors may scarcely be practicable in a state so exclusive and circumstanced as ours, your petitioners will undertake to suggest one mode, not presumg to propose it for the adoption of the legislature, but firmly relying that their wisdom will devise a better: they observe then that by a law already passed for the establishment of schools provision has been made for laying off every county into districts or precincts; that this division which offers so many valuable resources for the purposes of information, of justice, of order and police, may be recurred to for the object now in contemplation, and may be completed for this purpose where it has not been done for the other, and the inhabitants of every precinct may meet at a given time and place in their precinct and in the presence of the constable or other head officer of the precinct, elect from among themselves someone to be a juror, that from among those so chosen in every county some one may be designated by lot, who shall attend the ensuing session of the federal court within the state to act as grand and petty jurors, one of those from every senatorial district being designated by lot for a grand juror, and the residue attending to serve as petty jurors to be in like manner designated by lot in every particular case: that of the others so chosen in every county composing a district for the itinerant courts of this Commonwealth so many may be taken by lot as shall suffice for grand and petty juries for the district court next ensuing their election; and the residue so chosen in each county may attend their own county courts for the same purposes till another election, or if too numerous the supernumeraries may be discharged by lot: and that such compensation may be allowed for these services as without rendering the office an object worth canvassing may yet protect the juror from actual loss. That an institution on this outline, or such better as the wisdom of the Gen. ass. will devise, so modified as to guard it against the intrigue of parties, the influence of power, or irregularities of conduct, and further matured from time to time as experience shall develop its imperfections, may long preserve the trial by jury, in its pure and original spirit, as the true tribunal of the people, for a mitigation in the execution of hard laws when the power of preventing their passage is lost, and may afford some protection to persecuted man, whether alien or citizen, which the aspect of the times warns we may want.

And your petitioners, waiving the expression of many important considerations which will offer themselves readily to the reflection of the general assembly, pray them to take the premises into deep and serious consideration and to do therein for their country what their wisdom shall deem best, and they as in duty bound shall ever pray &c.

Ford VII: 284–7

## III.6 To Elbridge Gerry

Philadelphia, January 26, 1799

My Dear Sir, – . . . I shall make to you a profession of my political faith; in confidence that you will consider every future imputation on me of a contrary complexion, as bearing on its front the mark of falsehood & calumny.

I do then, with sincere zeal, wish an inviolable preservation of our present federal constitution, according to the true sense in which it was adopted by the States, that in which it was advocated by it's friends, & not that which it's enemies apprehended, who therefore became it's enemies; and I am opposed to the monarchising it's features by the forms of it's administration, with a view to conciliate a first transition to a President & Senate for life, & from that to a hereditary tenure of these offices, & thus to worm out the elective principle. I am for preserving to the States the powers not yielded by them to the Union, & to the legislature of the Union it's constitutional share in the division of powers; and I am not for transferring all the powers of the States to the general government, & all those of that government to the Executive branch. I am for a government rigorously frugal & simple, applying all the possible savings of the public revenue to the discharge of the national debt; and not for a multiplication of officers & salaries merely to make partisans, & for increasing, by every device, the public debt, on the principle of it's being a public blessing. I am for relying, for internal defence, on our militia solely, till actual invasion, and for such a naval force only as may protect our coasts and harbors from such depredations as we have experienced; and not for a standing army in time of peace, which may overawe the public sentiment; nor for a navy, which, by it's own expenses and the eternal wars in which it will implicate us, will grind us with public burthens, & sink us under them. I am for free commerce with all nations; political connection with none; & little or no diplomatic establishment. And I am not for linking ourselves by new treaties with the quarrels of Europe; entering that field of slaughter to preserve their balance, or joining in the confederacy of kings to war against the principles of liberty. I am for freedom of religion, & against all maneuvres to bring about a legal ascendancy of one sect over another: for freedom of the press, & against all violations of the constitution to silence by force & not by reason the complaints or criticisms, just or unjust, of our citizens against the conduct of their agents. And I am for encouraging the progress of science in all it's branches; and not for raising a hue and cry against the sacred name of philosophy; for awing the human mind by stories of raw-head & bloody bones to a distrust of its own vision, & to repose implicitly on that of others; to go backwards instead of forwards to look for improvement; to believe that government, religion, morality, & every other science were in the highest perfection in ages of the darkest ignorance, and that nothing can ever be devised more perfect than what was established by our forefathers. To these I will add, that I was a sincere well-wisher to the success of the French-revolution, and still wish it may end in the establishment of a free & well-ordered republic; but I have not been insensible under the atrocious depredations they have committed on our commerce. The first object of my heart is my own country. In that is embarked my family, my fortune, & my own existence. I have not one farthing of interest, nor one fibre of attachment out of it, nor a single motive of preference of any one nation to another, but in proportion as they are more or less friendly to us. But though deeply feeling the injuries of France, I did not think war the surest means of redressing them. I did believe, that a mission sincerely disposed to preserve peace, would obtain for us a peaceable & honorable settlement & retribution; and I appeal to you to say, whether this might not have been obtained, if either of your colleagues had been of the same sentiment with yourself.

These, my friend, are my principles; they are unquestionably the principles of the great body of our fellow citizens, and I know there is not one of them which is not yours also. In truth, we never differed but on one ground, the funding system; and as, from the moment of it's being adopted by the constituted authorities, I became religiously principled in the sacred discharge of it to the uttermost farthing, we are united now even on that single ground of difference . . .

Ford VII: 327–9

## III.7 To Gideon Granger

[Monticello,] August 13, 1800

Dear Sir, – I received with great pleasure your favor of June 4, and am much comforted by the appearance of a change of opinion in your state; for tho' we may obtain, & I believe shall obtain, a majority in the legislature of the United States, attached to the preservation of the Federal constitution according to it's obvious principles, & those on which it was known to be received; attached equally to the preservation to the states of those rights unquestionably remaining with them; friends to the freedom of religion, freedom of the press, trial by jury & to economical government; opposed to standing armies, paper systems, war, & all connection, other than commerce, with any foreign nation; in short, a majority firm in all those principles which we have espoused and the federalists have opposed uniformly; still, should the whole body of New England continue in opposition to these principles of government, either knowingly or through delusion, our government will be a very uneasy one. It can never be harmonious & solid, while so respectable a portion of it's citizens support principles which go directly to a change of the federal constitution, to sink the state governments, consolidate them into one, and to monarchize that. Our country is too large to have all its affairs directed by a single government. Public servants at such a distance, & from under the eye of their constituents, must, from the circumstance of distance, be unable to administer & overlook all the details necessary for the good government of the citizens, and the same circumstance, by rendering detection impossible to their constituents, will invite the public agents to corruption, plunder & waste. And I do verily believe, that if the principle were to prevail, of a common law being in force in the U.S., (which principle possesses the general govern-

169

ment at once of all the powers of the state governments, and reduces us to a single consolidated government), it would become the most corrupt government on the earth. You have seen the practises by which the public servants have been able to cover their conduct, or, where that could not be done, delusions by which they have varnished it for the eye of their constituents. What an augmentation of the field for jobbing, speculating, plundering, office-building & office-hunting would be produced by an assumption of all the state powers into the hands of the general government. The true theory of our constitution is surely the wisest & best, that the states are independent as to everything within themselves, & united as to everything respecting foreign nations. Let the general government be reduced to foreign concerns only, and let our affairs be disentangled from those of all other nations, except as to commerce, which the merchants will manage the better, the more they are left free to manage for themselves, and our general government may be reduced to a very simple organization, & a very unexpensive one; a few plain duties to be performed by a few servants. But I repeat, that this simple & economical mode of government can never be secured, if the New England States continue to support the contrary system. I rejoice, therefore, in every appearance of their returning to those principles which I had always imagined to be almost innate in them. In this State, a few persons were deluded by the X. Y. Z. duperies. You saw the effect of it in our last Congressional representatives, chosen under their influence. This experiment on their credulity is now seen into, and our next representation will be as republican as it has heretofore been. On the whole, we hope, that by a part of the Union having held on to the principles of the constitution, time has been given to the states to recover from the temporary frenzy into which they had been decoyed, to rally round the constitution, & to rescue it from the destruction with which it had been threatened even at their own hands. I see copied from the American Magazine two numbers of a paper signed Don Quixotte, most excellently adapted to introduce the real truth to the minds even of the most prejudiced.

I would, with great pleasure, have written the letter you desired in behalf of your friend, but there are existing circumstances which render a letter from me to that magistrate as improper as it would be unavailing. I shall be happy, on some more fortunate occasion, to prove to you my desire of serving your wishes . . .

I am, with great and sincere esteem, dear Sir, your friend and servant.

Ford VII: 450–3

## III.8 To Jeremiah Moor

Monticello, August 14, 1800

Sir, – I have to acknowl[e]ge the receipt of your favor of July 12. The times are certainly such as to justify anxiety on the subject of political principles, & particularly those of the public servants. I have been so long on the public theatres that I supposed mine to be generally known. I make no secret of them: on the contrary I wish them known to avoid the imputation of those which are not mine. You may remember perhaps that in the year 1783 after the close of the war there was a general idea that a convention would be called in this state to form a constitution. In that expectation I then prepared a scheme of constitution which I meant to have proposed. This is bound up at the end of the Notes on Virginia,[1] which being in many hands, I may venture to refer to it as giving a general view of my principles of government. It particularly shews what I think on the question of the right of electing & being elected, which is principally the subject of your letter. I found it there on a year's residence in the country; or the possession of property in it, or a year's enrollment in it's militia. When the constitution of Virginia was formed I was in attendance at Congress. Had I been here I should probably have proposed a general suffrage: because my opinion has always been in favor of it. Still I find very honest men who, thinking the possession of some property necessary to give due independence of mind, are for restraining the elective franchise to property. I believe we may lessen the danger of buying and selling votes, by making the number of voters too great for any means of purchase: I may further say that I have not observed men's

---

[1] See *infra*, v. 4. – *Eds.*

honesty to increase with their riches. I observe however in the same scheme of a constitution, an abridgment of the right of being elected, which after 17 years more of experience & reflection, I do not approve. It is the incapacitation of a clergyman from being elected. The clergy, by getting themselves established by law, & ingrafted into the machine of government, have been a very formidable engine against the civil and religious rights of man. They are still so in many countries & even in some of these United States. Even in 1783, we doubted the stability of our recent measures for reducing them to the footing of other useful callings. It now appears that our means were effectual. The clergy here seem to have relinquished all pretension to privilege and to stand on a footing with lawyers, physicians &c. They ought therefore to possess the same rights.

I have with you wondered at the change of political principles which has taken place in many in this state however much less than in others. I am still more alarmed to see, in the other states, the general political dispositions of those to whom is confided the education of the rising generation. Nor are all the academies of this state free from grounds of uneasiness. I have great confidence in the common sense of mankind in general: but it requires a great deal to get the better of notions which our tutors have instilled into our minds while incapable of questioning them, & to rise superior to antipathies strongly rooted. However, I suppose when the evil rises to a certain height, a remedy will be found, if the case admits any other than the prudence of parents and guardians. The candour & good sense of your letter made it a duty in me to answer it, & to confide that no uncandid use will be made of the answer: & particularly that it be kept from the newspapers, a bear-garden field into which I do not chuse to enter. I am with esteem sir, your most obedient servant.

Ford VII: 453–6

## III.9 First Inaugural Address, March 4, 1801

Friends and Fellow Citizens

Called upon to undertake the duties of the first executive office of our country, I avail myself of the presence of that portion of my fellow citizens which is here assembled, to express my grateful thanks for the favor with which they have been pleased to look toward me, to declare a sincere consciousness that the task is above my talents, and that I approach it, with those anxious and awful presentiments which the greatness of the charge and the weakness of my powers so justly inspire. A rising nation, spread over a wide and fruitful land, traversing all the seas with the rich productions of their industry, engaged in commerce with nations who feel power and forget right, advancing rapidly to destinies beyond the reach of mortal eye – when I contemplate these transcendent objects, and see the honor, the happiness, and the hopes of this beloved country committed to the issue and the auspices of this day, I shrink from the contemplation, and humble myself before the magnitude of the undertaking. Utterly indeed, should I despair, did not the presence of many whom I here see remind me, that in the other high authorities provided by our constitution, I shall find resources of wisdom, of virtue, and of zeal, on which to rely under all difficulties. To you, then, gentlemen, who are charged with the sovereign functions of legislation, and to those associated with you, I look with encouragement for that guidance and support which may enable us to steer with safety the vessel in which we are all embarked amid the conflicting elements of a troubled world.

During the contest of opinion through which we have passed, the animation of discussion and of exertions has sometimes worn an aspect which might impose on strangers unused to think freely and to speak and to write what they think; but this being now decided by the voice of the nation, announced according to the rules of the constitution, all will, of course, arrange themselves under the will of the law, and unite in common efforts for the common good. All, too, will bear in mind this sacred principle, that though the will of the majority is in all cases to prevail, that will, to be rightful, must be reasonable; that the minority possess their equal rights, which equal laws must protect, and to violate which would be oppression. Let us, then, fellow citizens, unite with one heart and one mind. Let us restore to social intercourse that harmony and affection without which liberty and even life itself are but dreary things. And let us reflect that having banished from our land that religious intolerance under which mankind so long bled and suffered, we have yet gained little if we countenance a political intolerance as despotic, as wicked, and capable of as bitter and bloody persecutions. During the throes and convulsions of the ancient world, during the agonizing spasms of infuriated man, seeking through blood and slaughter his long-lost liberty, it was not wonderful that the agitation of the billows should reach even this distant and peaceful shore; that this should be more felt and feared by some and less by others; that this should divide opinions as to measures of safety. But every difference of opinion is not a difference of principle. We have called by different names brethren of the same principle. We are all republicans – we are federalists. If there be any among us who would wish to dissolve this Union or to change its republican form, let them stand undisturbed as monuments of the safety with which error of opinion may be tolerated where reason is left free to combat it. I know, indeed, that some honest men fear that a republican government cannot be strong; that this government is not strong enough. But would the honest patriot, in the full tide of successful experiment, abandon a government which has so far kept us free and firm, on the theoretic and visionary fear that this government, the world's best hope, may by possibility want energy to preserve itself? I trust not. I believe this, on the contrary, the strongest government on earth. I believe it is the only one where every man, at the call of the laws, would fly to the standard of the law, and would meet invasions of the public order as his own personal concern. Sometimes it is said that man cannot be trusted with the government of himself. Can he, then, be trusted with the government of others? Or have we found angels in the forms of kings to govern him? Let history answer this question.

Let us, then, with courage and confidence pursue our own federal and republican principles, our attachment to our union and representative government. Kindly separated by nature and a wide ocean from the exterminating havoc of one quarter of the globe; too high-minded to endure the degradations of the others; possessing a chosen country, with room enough for our descendants to the hundredth and thousandth generation; entertaining a due sense of our equal right to the use of our own faculties, to the acquisitions of our industry, to honor and confidence from our fellow citizens, resulting not from birth but from our actions and their sense of them; enlightened by a benign religion, professed, indeed, and practiced in various forms, yet all of them including honesty, truth, temperance, gratitude, and the love of man; acknowledging and adoring an overruling Providence, which by all its dispensations proves that it delights in the happiness of man here and his greater happiness hereafter; with all these blessings, what more is necessary to make us a happy and prosperous people? Still one thing more, fellow citizens – a wise and frugal government, which shall restrain men from injuring one another, which shall leave them otherwise free to regulate their own pursuits of industry and improvement, and shall not take from the mouth of labor the bread it has earned. This is the sum of good government, and this is necessary to close the circle of our felicities.

About to enter, fellow citizens, on the exercise of duties which comprehend everything dear and valuable to you, it is proper that you should understand what I deem the essential principles of our government, and consequently those which ought to shape its administration. I will compress them within the narrowest compass they will bear, stating the general principle, but not all its limitations. Equal and exact justice to all men, of whatever state or persuasion, religious or political; peace, commerce, and honest friendship, with all nations – entangling alliances with none; the support of the state governments in all their rights, as the most competent administrations for our domestic concerns and the surest bulwarks against anti-republican tendencies; the preservation of the general government in its whole constitutional vigor, as the sheet anchor of our peace at home and safety abroad; a jealous care of the right of election by the people – a mild and safe corrective of abuses which are lopped by the sword of the revolution where peaceable remedies are unprovided; absolute acquiescence in the decisions of the majority, the vital principle of republics, from which there is no appeal but to force, the vital principle and immediate parent of despotism; a well-disciplined militia – our best reliance in peace and for the first moments of war, till regulars may relieve them; the supremacy of the civil over the military authority; economy in the public expense, that labor may be lightly burdened; the honest payment of our debts and sacred preservation of the public faith; encouragement of agriculture, and of commerce as its handmaid; the diffusion of information and the arraignment of all abuses at the bar of public reason; freedom of religion;

freedom of the press; freedom of person under the protection of the *habeas corpus*; and trial by juries impartially selected – these principles form the bright constellation which has gone before us, and guided our steps through an age of revolution and reformation. The wisdom of our sages and the blood of our heroes have been devoted to their attainment. They should be the creed of our political faith – the text of civil instruction – the touchstone by which to try the services of those we trust; and should we wander from them in moments of error or alarm, let us hasten to retrace our steps and to regain the road which alone leads to peace, liberty, and safety.

I repair, then, fellow citizens, to the post you have assigned me. With experience enough in subordinate offices to have seen the difficulties of this, the greatest of all, I have learned to expect that it will rarely fall to the lot of imperfect man to retire from this station with the reputation and the favor which bring him into it. Without pretensions to that high confidence reposed in our first and great revolutionary character, whose preëminent services had entitled him to the first place in his country's love, and destined for him the fairest page in the volume of faithful history, I ask so much confidence only as may give firmness and effect to the legal administration of your affairs. I shall often go wrong through defect of judgment. When right, I shall often be thought wrong by those whose positions will not command a view of the whole ground. I ask your indulgence for my own errors, which will never be intentional; and your support against the errors of others, who may condemn what they would not if seen in all its parts. The approbation implied by your suffrage is a consolation to me for the past; and my future solicitude will be to retain the good opinion of those who have bestowed it in advance, to conciliate that of others by doing them all the good in my power, and to be instrumental to the happiness and freedom of all.

Relying, then, on the patronage of your good will, I advance with obedience to the work, ready to retire from it whenever you become sensible how much better choice it is in your power to make. And may that Infinite Power which rules the destinies of the universe, lead our councils to what is best, and give them a favorable issue for your peace and prosperity.

L & B III: 317–23

## III.10 To Dr. Thomas Cooper

Washington, November 29, 1802

Dear Sir, – Your favor of October 25th was received in due time, and I thank you for the long extract you took the trouble of making from Mr. Stone's letter. Certainly the information it communicates as to [Czar] Alexander [of Russia] kindles a great deal of interest in his existence, and strong spasms of the heart in his favor. Though his means of doing good are great, yet the materials on which he is to work are refractory. Whether he engages in private correspondences abroad, as the King of Prussia did much, and his grandfather sometimes, I know not; but certainly such a correspondence would be very interesting to those who are sincerely anxious to see mankind raised from their present abject condition. It delights me to find that there are persons who still think that all is not lost in France: that their retrogradation from a limited to an unlimited despotism, is but to give themselves a new impulse. But I see not how or when. The press, the only tocsin of a nation, is completely silenced there, and all means of a general effort taken away. However, I am willing to hope, and as long as anybody will hope with me; and I am entirely persuaded that the agitations of the public mind advance its powers, and that at every vibration between the points of liberty and despotism, something will be gained for the former. As men become better informed, their rulers must respect them the more. I think you will be sensible that our citizens are fast returning, from the panic into which they were artfully thrown, to the dictates of their own reason; and I believe the delusions they have seen themselves hurried into will be useful as a lesson under similar attempts on them in future. The good effects of our late fiscal arrangements will certainly tend to unite them in opinion, and in confidence as to the views of their public functionaries, legislative and executive. The path we have to pursue is so quiet that we have nothing scarcely to propose to our Legislature. A noiseless course, meddling with the affairs of others, unattractive of notice, is a mark that society is going on in happiness. If we can prevent the government from wasting the labors of the people, under the pretence of taking care of them, they must become happy. Their finances are now under such a course of application as nothing could derange but war or federalism. The gripe of the latter has shown itself as deadly as the jaws of the former. Our adversaries say we are indebted to their providence for the means of paying the public debt. We never charged them with the want of foresight in providing money, but with the misapplication of it after they had provided it. We say they raised not only enough, but too much; and that after giving back the surplus we do more with a part than they did with the whole.

Your letter of November 18th is also received. The places of midshipman are so much sought that (being limited) there is never a vacancy. Your son shall be set down for the 2d place, which shall be vacant; the 1st being anticipated. We are not long generally without vacancies happening. As soon as he can be appointed you shall know it. I pray you to accept assurances of my great attachment and respect.

Ford VIII: 176–8

## III.11 To Dr Joseph Priestley

Washington, November 29, 1802

Dear Sir, – Your favour of Oct. 29 was received in due time, and I am very thankful for the extract of Mr. Stone's letter on the subject of [Czar] Alexander [of Russia]. The apparition of such a man on a throne is one of the phænomena which will distinguish the present epoch so remarkable in the history of man. But he must have an herculean task to devise and establish the means of securing freedom and happiness to those who are not capable of taking care of themselves. Some preparation seems necessary to qualify the body of a nation for self-government. Who could have thought the French nation incapable of it? Alexander will doubtless begin at the right end, by taking means for diffusing instruction and a sense of their natural rights through the mass of his people, and for relieving them in the meantime from actual oppression. I should be puzzled to find a person capable of preparing for him the short analytical view of our constitution which you propose. It would be a short work, but a difficult one. Mr. Cooper's Propositions respecting the foundation of civil government; your own piece on the First principles of government; Chipman's Sketches on the principles of government, and the Federalist [Papers] would furnish the principles of our constitution and their practical development in the several parts of that instrument. I question whether such a work can be so well executed for his purpose by any other, as by a Russian presenting exactly that view of it which that people would seize with advantage. It would be easy to name some persons who could give a perfect abstract view, adapted to an English or an American mind: But they would find it difficult to disengage themselves sufficiently from other pursuits. However, if we keep it in view we may perhaps get it done. Your letter to Mr. Stone shall be taken care of.

Our busy scene is now approaching. The quiet tract into which we are endeavoring to get, neither meddling with the affairs of other nations, nor with those of our fellow citizens, but letting them go on in their own way, will show itself in the statement of our affairs to Congress. We have almost nothing to propose to them but "to let things alone." The effects of the fiscal arrangements of the last session will show themselves very satisfactorily. The only speck in our horizon which can threaten anything, is the cession of Louisiana to France. Tho' probable, it is not yet entirely certain how far it will be carried into effect. I am sorry you cannot be absent this winter from the cold of the position in which you are. I have a great opinion of the favorable influence of genial climates in winter, and especially on old persons. Altho' Washington does not offer the best yet it is probably much milder than that in which you are. Otherwise it could offer little but the affectionate reception you should have experienced. The notice of me which you are so good as to prefix to your book, cannot but be consolatory, in as much as it testifies what one great and good man thinks of me. But in truth I have no pretensions but to have wished the good of mankind with very moderate talents for carrying it into effect. My chief object is to let the good sense of the nation have fair play, believing it will best take care of itself. Praying for you many days of life and health, and of leisure still to inform the understandings of man, I tender you the assurances of my sincere esteem and attachment and high respect.

Ford VIII: 179–81

## III.12 To John Breckenridge

Washington, November 24, 1803

Dear Sir, – I thought I perceived in you the other day a dread of the job of preparing a constitution for the new acquisition. With more boldness than wisdom I therefore determined to prepare a canvass, give a few daubs of outline, and send it to you to fill up. I yesterday morning took up the subject and scribbled off the inclosed. In communicating it to you I must do it in confidence that you will never let any person know that I have put pen to paper on the subject and that if you think the inclosed can be of any aid to you will take the trouble to copy it & return me the original. I am this particular, because you know with what bloody teeth & fangs the federalists will attack any sentiment or principle known to come from me, & what blackguardisms & personalities they make it the occasion of vomiting forth. My time does not permit me to go into explanation of the inclosed by letter. I will only observe therefore as to a single feature of the legislature, that the idea of an Assembly of Notables came into my head while writing, as a thing more familiar & pleasing to the French, than a legislation of judges. True it removes their dependence from the judges to the Executive: but this is what they are used to & would prefer. Should Congress reject the nomination of judges for 4 years & make them during good behavior, as is probable, then, should the judges take a kink in their heads in favor of leaving the present laws of Louisiana unaltered, that evil will continue for their lives, unamended by us, and become so inveterate that we may never be able to introduce the uniformity of law so desirable. The making the same persons so directly judges & legislators is more against principle, than to make the same persons Executive, and the elector of the legislative members. The former too are placed above all responsibility, the latter is under a perpetual control if he goes wrong. The judges have to act on 9 out of 10 of the laws which are made; the governor not on one in 10. But strike it out & insert the judges if you think it better, as it was a sudden conceit to which I am not attached; and make what alterations you please, as I had never before [had] time to think on the subject, or form the outlines of any plan, & probably shall not again. Accept my friendly salutations.

Ford VIII: 279–81

## III.13 To DeWitt Clinton

Washington, December 2, 1803

Dear Sir, – Your favor of the 26th ult. has been received. Mr. Van Wyck's appointment as comm[issione]r of bankruptcy only awaits Mr. Sandford's resignation. The papers in the case of Lt. Wolstencroft shall be recommended to the inquiries & attentions of the Secretary at War. I should think it indeed a serious misfortune should a change in the administration of your government be hazarded before its present principles be well established through all its parts. Yet, on reflection, you will be sensible that the delicacy of my situation, considering who may be competitors, forbids my intermeddling, even so far as to write the letter you suggest. I can therefore only brood in silence over my secret wishes.

I am less able to give you the proceedings of Congress than your correspondents who are of that body. More difference of opinion seems to exist as to the manner of disposing of Louisiana, than I had imagined possible: and our leading friends are not yet sufficiently aware of the necessity of accommodation & mutual sacrifice of opinion for conducting a numerous assembly, where the opposition too is drilled to act in phalanx on every question. Altho' it is acknoleged that our new fellow citizens are as yet as incapable of self government as children, yet some cannot bring themselves to suspend its principles for a single moment. The temporary or territorial government of that country therefore will encounter great difficulty. The question too whether the settlement of upper Louisiana shall be prohibited occasions a great division of our friends. Some are for prohibiting it till another amendment of the cons[tituti]on shall permit it; others for prohibiting by authority of the legislature only, a third set for permitting immediate settlement. Those of the first opinion apprehend that if the legislature may open a land office there, it will become the ruling principle of elections, & end in a yazoo scheme:[1] those of the 2d opinion fear they may never get an

---

[1] In 1795 the Georgia state legislature ceded some 35 million acres of its western territory to the Yazoo Companies in which many legislators held stock. The phrase "Yazoo scheme" became a generic name for shady land deals involving similar conflicts of interest. – *Eds.*

amendment of the constitution permitting the settlement. Accept my friendly salutations & assurances of great esteem & respect.

Ford VIII: 282–3

## III.14 To John Tyler

Monticello, May 26, 1810

Dear Sir, – Your friendly letter of the 12th has been duly received. Although I have laid it down as a law to myself, never to embarrass the President with my solicitations, and have not till now broken through it, yet I have made a part of your letter the subject of one to him, and have done it with all my heart, and in the full belief that I serve him and the public in urging that appointment. We have long enough suffered under the base prostitution of law to party passions in one judge, and the imbecility of another. In the hands of one the law is nothing more than an ambiguous text, to be explained by his sophistry into any meaning which may subserve his personal malice. Nor can any milk-and-water associate maintain his own dependence, and by a firm pursuance of what the law really is, extend its protection to the citizens or the public. I believe you will do it, and where you cannot induce your colleague to do what is right, you will be firm enough to hinder him from doing what is wrong, and by opposing sense to sophistry, leave the juries free to follow their own judgment.

I have long lamented with you the depreciation of law science. The opinion seems to be that Blackstone[1] is to us what the Alcoran is to the Mahometans, that everything which is necessary is in him, and what is not in him is not necessary. I still lend my counsel and books to such young students as will fix themselves in the neighborhood. Coke's institutes[2] and reports are their first, and Blackstone their last book, after an intermediate course of two or three years. It is nothing more than an elegant digest of what they will then have acquired from the real fountains of the law. Now men are born scholars, lawyers, doctors;

---

[1] Sir William Blackstone (1723–80), *Commentaries on the Laws of England* (London, 1765–9). – *Eds.*

[2] Sir Edward Coke (1552–1634), *Institutes of the Laws of England* (London, 1628). – *Eds.*

in our day this was confined to poets. You wish to see me again in the legislature, but this is impossible; my mind is now so dissolved in tranquillity, that it can never again encounter a contentious assembly; the habits of thinking and speaking off-hand, after a disuse of five and twenty years, have given place to the slower process of the pen. I have indeed two great measures at heart, without which no republic can maintain itself in strength. 1. That of general education, to enable every man to judge for himself what will secure or endanger his freedom. 2. To divide every county into hundreds, of such size that all the children of each will be within reach of a central school in it. But this division looks to many other fundamental provisions. Every hundred, besides a school, should have a justice of the peace, a constable and a captain of militia. These officers, or some others within the hundred, should be a corporation to manage all its concerns, to take care of its roads, its poor, and its police by patrols, &c. (as the select men of the Eastern townships). Every hundred should elect one or two jurors to serve where requisite, and all other elections should be made in the hundreds separately, and the votes of all the hundreds be brought together. Our present Captaincies might be declared hundreds for the present, with a power to the courts to alter them occasionally. These little republics would be the main strength of the great one. We owe to them the vigor given to our revolution in its commencement in the Eastern States, and by them the Eastern States were enabled to repeal the embargo in opposition to the Middle, Southern and Western States, and their large and lubberly division into counties which can never be assembled. General orders are given out from a centre to the foreman of every hundred, as to the sergeants of an army, and the whole nation is thrown into energetic action, in the same direction in one instant and as one man, and becomes absolutely irresistible. Could I once see this I should consider it as the dawn of the salvation of the republic, and say with old Simeon, "nunc dimittas Domine." But our children will be as wise as we are, and will establish in the fulness of time those things not yet ripe for establishment. So be it, and to yourself health, happiness and long life.

Ford IX: 276–8

## III.15 To Dr. Samuel Brown

Monticello, July 14, 1813

Dear Sir, – Your favors of May 25th and June 13th have been duly received, as also the first supply of Capsicum, and the second of the same article with other seeds. I shall set great store by the Capsicum, if it is hardy enough for our climate, the species we have heretofore tried being too tender. The Galvance too, will be particularly attended to, as it appears very different from what we cultivate by that name. I have so many grand-children and others who might be endangered by the poison plant, that I think the risk overbalances the curiosity of trying it. The most elegant thing of that kind known is a preparation of the Jamestown weed, Datura-Stramonium, invented by the French in the time of Robespierre. Every man of firmness carried it constantly in his pocket to anticipate the guillotine. It brings on the sleep of death as quietly as fatigue does the ordinary sleep, without the least struggle or motion. Condorcet, who had recourse to it, was found lifeless on his bed a few minutes after his landlady had left him there, and even the slipper which she had observed half suspended on his foot, was not shaken off. It seems far preferable to the Venesection of the Romans, the Hemlock of the Greeks, and the Opium of the Turks. I have never been able to learn what the preparation is, other than a strong concentration of its lethiferous principle. Could such a medicament be restrained to self-administration, it ought not to be kept secret. There are ills in life as desperate as intolerable, to which it would be the rational relief, e.g., the inveterate cancer. As a relief from tyranny indeed, for which the Romans recurred to it in the times of the emperors, it has been a wonder to me that they did not consider a poignard [dagger] in the breast of the tyrant as a better remedy.

I am sorry to learn that a *banditti* from our country are taking part in the domestic contests of the country adjoining you; and the more so as from the known laxity of execution in our laws, they cannot be punished, although the law has provided punishment. It will give a wrongful hue to a rightful act of taking possession of Mobile, and will be imputed to the national authority as Meranda's[1] [*sic*] enterprise was, because not punished by it. I fear, too, that the Spaniards are too heavily oppressed by ignorance and superstition for self-government, and whether a change from foreign to domestic despotism will be to their advantage remains to be seen.

We have been unfortunate in our first military essays by land. Our men are good, but our generals unqualified. Every failure we have incurred has been the fault of the general, the men evincing courage in every instance. At sea we have rescued our character; but the chief fruit of our victories there is to prove to those who have fleets, that the English are not invincible at sea, as [Czar] Alexander [of Russia] has proved that Bonaparte is not invincible by land. How much to be lamented that the world cannot unite and destroy these two land and sea monsters! The one drenching the earth with human gore, the other ravaging the ocean with lawless piracies and plunder. Bonaparte will die, and the nations of Europe will recover their independence with, I hope, better governments. But the English government never dies, because their king is no part of it, he is a mere formality, and the real government is the aristocracy of the country, for their House of Commons is of that class. Their aim is to claim the dominion of the ocean by conquest, and to make every vessel navigating it pay a tribute to the support of the fleet necessary to maintain that dominion, to which their own resources are inadequate. I see no means of terminating their maritime dominion and tyranny but in their own bankruptcy, which I hope is approaching. But I turn from these painful contemplations to the more pleasing one of my constant friendship and respect for you.

L & B XIII: 310–12

## III.16 To John Adams

Monticello, October 28, 1813

Dear Sir, – According to the reservation between us, of taking up one of the subjects of our correspondence at a time, I turn to your letters of August the 16th and September the 2d.

[1] General Francisco Miranda (1750–1816) was a Venezuelan adventurer and revolutionary who helped prepare the way for independence from Spain. – *Eds.*

The passage you quote from Theognis, I think has an ethical rather than a political object. The whole piece is a moral *exhortation*, παραίνεσις, and this passage particularly seems to be a reproof to man, who while with his domestic animals he is curious to improve the race, by employing always the finest male, pays no attention to the improvement of his own race, but intermarries with the vicious, the ugly, or the old, for considerations of wealth or ambition. It is in conformity with the principle adopted afterwards by the Pythagoreans, and expressed by Ocellus in another form; περὶ δὲ τῆς ἐκ τῶν ἄλληλων ἀνθρώπων γενέσεως &c. – οὐχ ἡδονῆς ἕνεκα ἡ μίξις: which, as literally as intelligibility will admit, may be thus translated: "concerning the inter-procreation of men, how, and of whom it shall be, in a perfect manner, and according to the laws of modesty and sanctity, conjointly, this is what I think right. First to lay it down that we do not commix for the sake of pleasure, but of the procreation of children. For the powers, the organs and desires for coition have not been given by God to man for the sake of pleasure, but for the procreation of the race. For as it were incongruous, for a mortal born to partake of divine life, the immortality of the race being taken away, God fulfilled the purpose by making the generations uninterrupted and continuous. This, therefore, we are especially to lay down as a principle, that coition is not for the sake of pleasure." But nature, not trusting to this moral and abstract motive, seems to have provided more securely for the perpetuation of the species, by making it the effect of the *oestrum* implanted in the constitution of both sexes. And not only has the commerce of love been indulged on this unhallowed impulse, but made subservient also to wealth and ambition by marriage, without regard to the beauty, the healthiness, the understanding, or virtue of the subject from which we are to breed. The selecting the best male for a Harem of well chosen females also, which Theognis seems to recommend from the example of our sheep and asses, would doubtless improve the human, as it does the brute animal, and produce a race of veritable ἄριστοι. For experience proves, that the moral and physical qualities of man, whether good or evil, are transmissible in a certain degree from father to son. But I suspect that the equal rights of men will rise up against this privileged Solomon and his Harem, and oblige us to continue acquiescence under the "Ἀμαύρωσις γένεος ἀστῶν" which Theognis complains of, and to content ourselves with the accidental aristoi produced by the fortuitous concourse of breeders. For I agree with you that there is a natural aristocracy among men. The grounds of this are virtue and talents. Formerly, bodily powers gave place among the aristoi. But since the invention of gunpowder has armed the weak as well as the strong with missile death, bodily strength, like beauty, good humor, politeness and other accomplishments, has become but an auxiliary ground for distinction. There is also an artificial aristocracy, founded on wealth and birth, without either virtue or talents; for with these it would belong to the first class. The natural aristocracy I consider as the most precious gift of nature, for the instruction, the trusts, and government of society. And indeed, it would have been inconsistent in creation to have formed man for the social state, and not to have provided virtue and wisdom enough to manage the concerns of the society. May we not even say, that that form of government is the best, which provides the most effectually for a pure selection of these natural aristoi into the offices of government? The artificial aristocracy is a mischievous ingredient in government, and provision should be made to prevent its ascendency. On the question, what is the best provision, you and I differ; but we differ as rational friends, using the free exercise of our own reason, and mutually indulging its errors. You think it best to put the pseudo-aristoi into a separate chamber of legislation, where they may be hindered from doing mischief by their co-ordinate branches, and where, also, they may be a protection to wealth against the Agrarian and plundering enterprises of the majority of the people. I think that to give them power in order to prevent them from doing mischief, is arming them for it, and increasing instead of remedying the evil. For if the co-ordinate branches can arrest their action, so may they that of the co-ordinates. Mischief may be done negatively as well as positively. Of this, a cabal in the Senate of the United States has furnished many proofs. Nor do I believe them necessary to protect the wealthy; because enough of these will find their way into every branch of the legislation, to protect themselves. From fifteen to twenty legislatures of our own, in action for thirty years past, have proved that no fears of an equalization of property are to be apprehended from them. I think the best remedy is exactly that provided by all our constitutions, to leave to the citizens the free election and separation of the *aristoi* from the pseudo-*aristoi*, of the wheat from the chaff. In general they will elect the really good and wise. In some instances, wealth may corrupt, and birth blind them; but not in sufficient degree to endanger the society.

It is probable that our difference of opinion may, in some measure, be produced by a difference of character in those among whom we live. From what I have seen of Massachusetts and Connecticut myself, and still more from what I have heard, and the character given of the former by yourself, who know them so much better, there seems to be in those two States a traditionary reverence for certain families, which has rendered the offices of the government nearly hereditary in those families. I presume that from an early period of your history, members of those families happening to possess virtue and talents, have honestly exercised them for the good of the people, and by their services have endeared their names to them. In coupling Connecticut with you, I mean it politically only, not morally. For having made the Bible the common law of their land, they seemed to have modeled their morality on the story of Jacob and Laban. But although this hereditary succession to office with you, may, in some degree, be founded in real family merit, yet in a much higher degree, it has proceeded from your strict alliance of Church and State. These families are canonised in the eyes of the people on common principles, "you tickle me, and I will tickle you." In Virginia we have nothing of this. Our clergy, before the revolution, having been secured against rivalship by fixed salaries, did not give themselves the trouble of acquiring influence over the people. Of wealth, there were great accumulations in particular families, handed down from generation to generation, under the English law of entails. But the only object of ambition for the wealthy was a seat in the King's Council. All their court then was paid to the crown and its creatures; and they Philipised in all collisions between the King and the people. Hence they were unpopular; and that unpopularity continues attached to their names. A Randolph, a Carter, or a Burwell must have great personal superiority over a common competitor to be elected by the people even at this day. At the first session of our legislature after the Declaration of Independence, we passed a law abolishing entails. And this was followed by one abolishing the privilege of primogeniture, and dividing the lands of intestates equally among all their children, or other representatives. These laws, drawn by myself, laid the ax to the foot of pseudo-aristocracy. And had another which I prepared been adopted by the legislature, our work would have been complete. It was a bill for the more general diffusion of learning. This proposed to divide every county into wards of five or six miles square, like your townships; to establish in each ward a free school for reading, writing and common arithmetic; to provide for the annual selection of the best subjects from these schools, who might receive, at the public expense, a higher degree of education at a district school; and from these district schools to select a certain number of the most promising subjects, to be completed at an University, where all the useful sciences should be taught. Worth and genius would thus have been sought out from every condition of life, and completely prepared by education for defeating the competition of wealth and birth for public trusts. My proposition had, for a further object, to impart to these wards those portions of self-government for which they are best qualified, by confiding to them the care of their poor, their roads, police, elections, the nomination of jurors, administration of justice in small cases, elementary exercises of militia; in short, to have made them little republics, with a warden at the head of each, for all those concerns which, being under their eye, they would better manage than the larger republics of the county or State. A general call of ward meetings by their wardens on the same day through the State, would at any time produce the genuine sense of the people on any required point, and would enable the State to act in mass, as your people have so often done, and with so much effect by their town meetings. The law for religious freedom, which made a part of this system, having put down the aristocracy of the clergy, and restored to the citizen the freedom of the mind, and those of entails and descents nurturing an equality of condition among them, this on education would have raised the mass of the people to the high ground of moral respectability necessary to their own safety, and to orderly government; and would have completed the great object of qualifying them to select the veritable *aristoi*, for the trusts of government, to the exclusion of the pseudalists; and the same Theognis who has furnished the epigraphs of your two letters, assures us that "Οὐδεμίαν πώ, Κυρν', ἀγαθοὶ πόλιν ὤλεσαν ἄνδρες." Although this law has not yet been acted on but in a small and inefficient degree, it is still considered as before the legislature, with other bills of the revised code, not yet taken up, and I have great hope that some patriotic spirit will, at a favorable moment, call it up, and make it the key-stone of the arch of our government.

With respect to aristocracy, we should further consider, that before the establishment of the American States, nothing was known to history but the man of the old world, crowded within limits either small or overcharged, and steeped in the vices which that situation generates. A government adapted to such men would be one thing; but a very different one, that for the man of these States. Here every one may have land to labor for himself, if he chooses; or, preferring the exercise of any other industry, may exact for it such compensation as not only to afford a comfortable subsistence, but wherewith to provide for a cessation from labor in old age. Every one, by his property, or by his satisfactory situation, is interested in the support of law and order. And such men may safely and advantageously reserve to themselves a wholesome control over their public affairs, and a degree of freedom, which, in the hands of the *canaille* of the cities of Europe, would be instantly perverted to the demolition and destruction of everything public and private. The history of the last twenty-five years of France, and of the last forty years in America, nay of its last two hundred years, proves the truth of both parts of this observation.

But even in Europe a change has sensibly taken place in the mind of man. Science has liberated the ideas of those who read and reflect, and the American example had kindled feelings of right in the people. An insurrection has consequently begun, of science, talents, and courage, against rank and birth, which have fallen into contempt. It has failed in its first effort, because the mobs of the cities, the instrument used for its accomplishment, debased by ignorance, poverty and vice, could not be restrained to rational action. But the world will recover from the panic of this first catastrophe. Science is progressive, and talents and enterprise on the alert. Resort may be had to the people of the country, a more governable power from their principles and subordination; and rank, and birth, and tinsel-aristocracy will finally shrink into insignificance, even there. This, however, we have no right to meddle with. It suffices for us, if the moral and physical condition of our own citizens qualifies them to select the able and good for the direction of their government, with a recurrence of elections at such short periods as will enable them to displace an unfaithful servant, before the mischief he meditates may be irremediable.

I have thus stated my opinion on a point on which we differ, not with a view to controversy, for we are both too old to change opinions which are the result of a long life of inquiry and reflection; but on the suggestions of a former letter of yours, that we ought not to die before we have explained ourselves to each other. We acted in perfect harmony, through a long and perilous contest for our liberty and independence. A constitution has been acquired, which, though neither of us thinks perfect, yet both consider as competent to render our fellow citizens the happiest and the securest on whom the sun has ever shone. If we do not think exactly alike as to its imperfections, it matters little to our country, which, after devoting to it long lives of disinterested labor, we have delivered over to our successors in life, who will be able to take care of it and of themselves.

Of the pamphlet on aristocracy which has been sent to you, or who may be its author, I have heard nothing but through your letter. If the person you suspect, it may be known from the quaint, mystical, and hyperbolical ideas, involved in affected, new-fangled and pedantic terms which stamp his writings. Whatever it be, I hope your quiet is not to be affected at this day by the rudeness or intemperance of scribblers; but that you may continue in tranquillity to live and to rejoice in the prosperity of our country, until it shall be your own wish to take your seat among the *aristoi* who have gone before you. Ever and affectionately yours.

Ford IX: 424–30

## III.17 To the Marquis de Lafayette

November 30, 1813

My Dear Friend – The last letters I received from you are of Apr. 22, May 20, July 4 of the preceding year. They gave me information of your health, always welcome to the feelings of antient and constant friendship. I hope this continues & will continue until you tire of that and life together ... I join you sincerely, my friend, in wishes for the emancipation of South America. That they will be liberated from foreign subjection I have little doubt. But the result of my enquiries does not authorize me to hope they are capable of maintaining a free government. Their people are immersed in the darkest ignorance, and brutalised by bigotry & superstition. Their priests make of them what they please, and tho' they may have some capable leaders, yet nothing but intelligence in the people themselves can keep these faithful to their charge. Their efforts I fear therefore will end in establishing military despotisms in the several provinces. Among these there can be no confederacy. A republic of kings is impossible. But their future wars and quarrels among themselves will oblige them to bring the people into action, & into the exertion of their understandings. Light will at length beam in on their minds and the standing example we shall hold up, serving as an excitement as well as a model for their direction may in the long run qualify them for self government. This is the most I am able to hope for them. For I lay it down as one of the impossibilities of nature that ignorance should maintain itself free against cunning, where any government has been once admitted . . . I write to Mde de Tesse, M. de Tracy &c. and conclude with the assurance of my affectionate and unalterable friendship and respect.

Ford IX: 434–6

## III.18 To Baron von Humboldt

December 6, 1813

My Dear Friend and Baron, – I have to acknowledge your two letters of December 20 and 26, 1811, by Mr. Correa, and am first to thank you for making me acquainted with that most excellent character. He was so kind as to visit me at Monticello, and I found him one of the most learned and amiable of men. It was a subject of deep regret to separate from so much worth in the moment of its becoming known to us.

The *livraison* of your astronomical observations, and the 6th and 7th on the subject of New Spain, with the corresponding atlasses, are duly received, as had been the preceding *cahiers*. For these treasures of a learning so interesting to us, accept my sincere thanks. I

think it most fortunate that your travels in those countries were so
timed as to make them known to the world in the moment they
were about to become actors on its stage. That they will throw off
their European dependence I have no doubt; but in what kind of
government their revolution will end I am not so certain. History,
I believe, furnishes no example of a priest-ridden people maintaining a free civil government. This marks the lowest grade of
ignorance, of which their civil as well as religious leaders will always
avail themselves for their own purposes. The vicinity of New Spain
to the United States, and their consequent intercourse, may furnish
schools for the higher, and example for the lower classes of their
citizens. And Mexico, where we learn from you that men of science
are not wanting, may revolutionize itself under better auspices than
the Southern provinces. These last, I fear, must end in military
despotisms. The different casts of their inhabitants, their mutual
hatreds and jealousies, their profound ignorance and bigotry, will
be played off by cunning leaders, and each be made the instrument
of enslaving others. But of all this you can best judge, for in truth
we have little knowledge of them to be depended on, but through
you. But in whatever governments they end they will be *American*
governments, no longer to be involved in the never-ceasing broils
of Europe. The European nations constitute a separate division of
the globe; their localities make them part of a distinct system; they
have a set of interests of their own in which it is our business never
to engage ourselves. America has a hemisphere to itself. It must
have its separate system of interests, which must not be subordi-
nated to those of Europe. The insulated state in which nature has
placed the American continent, should so far avail it that no spark
of war kindled in the other quarters of the globe should be wafted
across the wide oceans which separate us from them. And it will be
so. In fifty years more the United States alone will contain fifty
millions of inhabitants, and fifty years are soon gone over. The
peace of 1763 is within that period. I was then twenty years old, and
of course remember well all the transactions of the war preceding it.
And you will live to see the epoch now equally ahead of us; and the
numbers which will then be spread over the other parts of the
American hemisphere, catching long before that the principles of
our portion of it, and concurring with us in the maintenance of the
same system. You see how readily we run into ages beyond the

grave; and even those of us to whom that grave is already opening its quiet bosom. I am anticipating events of which you will be the bearer to me in the Elsyian fields fifty years hence.

You know, my friend, the benevolent plan we were pursuing here for the happiness of the aboriginal inhabitants in our vicinities. We spared nothing to keep them at peace with one another. To teach them agriculture and the rudiments of the most necessary arts, and to encourage industry by establishing among them separate property. In this way they would have been enabled to subsist and multiply on a moderate scale of landed possession. They would have mixed their blood with ours, and been amalgamated and identified with us within no distant period of time. On the commencement of our present war, we pressed on them the observance of peace and neutrality, but the interested and unprincipled policy of England has defeated all our labors for the salvation of these unfortunate people. They have seduced the greater part of the tribes within our neighborhood, to take up the hatchet against us, and the cruel massacres they have committed on the women and children of our frontiers taken by surprise, will oblige us now to pursue them to extermination, or drive them to new seats beyond our reach. Already we have driven their patrons and seducers into Montreal, and the opening season will force them to their last refuge, the walls of Quebec. We have cut off all possibility of intercourse and of mutual aid, and may pursue at our leisure whatever plan we find necessary to secure ourselves against the future effects of their savage and ruthless warfare. The confirmed brutalization, if not the extermination of this race in our America, is therefore to form an additional chapter in the English history of the same colored man in Asia, and of the brethren of their own color in Ireland, and wherever else Anglo-mercantile cupidity can find a two-penny interest in deluging the earth with human blood. But let us turn from the loathsome contemplation of the degrading effects of commercial avarice.

That their Arrowsmith should have stolen your Map of Mexico, was in the piratical spirit of his country. But I should be sincerely sorry if our Pike[1] has made an ungenerous use of your candid communications here; and the more so as he died in the arms of victory

---

[1] Zebulon Pike (1779–1813), American army officer and explorer of the southwestern territories then under Spanish rule. He was killed in action in the War of 1812. – *Eds.*

gained over the enemies of his country. Whatever he did was on a principle of enlarging knowledge, and not for filthy shillings and pence of which he made none from that work. If what he has borrowed has any effect it will be to excite an appeal in his readers from his defective information to the copious volumes of it with which you have enriched the world. I am sorry he omitted even to acknowledge the source of his information. It has been an oversight, and not at all in the spirit of his generous nature. Let me solicit your forgiveness then of a deceased hero, of an honest and zealous patriot, who lived and died for his country.

You will find it inconceivable that Lewis's journey to the Pacific should not yet have appeared; nor is it in my power to tell you the reason. The measures taken by his surviving companion, Clarke, for the publication, have not answered our wishes in point of despatch. I think, however, from what I have heard, that the mere journal will be out within a few weeks in two volumes 8vo. These I will take care to send you with the tobacco seed you desired, if it be possible for them to escape the thousand ships of our enemies spread over the ocean. The botanical and zoological discoveries of Lewis will probably experience greater delay, and become known to the world through other channels before that volume will be ready. The Atlas, I believe, waits on the leisure of the engraver.

Although I do not know whether you are now at Paris or ranging the regions of Asia to acquire more knowledge for the use of men, I cannot deny myself the gratification of an endeavor to recall myself to your recollection, and of assuring you of my constant attachment, and of renewing to you the just tribute of my affectionate esteem and high respect and consideration.

Ford IX: 430–3

## III.19 To Joseph C. Cabell

Monticello, January 31, 1814

Dear Sir, – Your favor of the 23d is received. Say[1] had come to hand safely. But I regretted having asked the return of him; for I

---

[1] Jean-Baptiste Say (1767–1832), French economist famous for formulating Say's Law, which states that the supply of some goods creates its own demand. The fullest account of his views is to be found in his *Traité d'économique politique* (Paris, 1806). – *Eds.*

did not find in him one new idea upon the subject I had been contemplating; nothing more than a succinct, judicious digest of the tedious pages of Smith.[2]

You ask my opinion on the question, whether the States can add any qualifications to those which the constitution has prescribed for their members of Congress? It is a question I had never before reflected on; yet had taken up an off-hand opinion, agreeing with your first, that they could not; that to add new qualifications to those of the constitution, would be as much an alteration as to detract from them. And so I think the House of Representatives of Congress decided in some case; I believe that of a member from Baltimore. But your letter having induced me to look into the constitution, and to consider the question a little, I am again in your predicament, of doubting the correctness of my first opinion. Had the constitution been silent, nobody can doubt but that the right to prescribe all the qualifications and disqualifications of those they would send to represent them, would have belonged to the State. So also the constitution might have prescribed the whole, and excluded all others. It seems to have preferred the middle way. It has exercised the power in part, by declaring some disqualifications, to wit, those of not being twenty-five years of age, of not having been a citizen seven years, and of not being an inhabitant of the State at the time of election. But it does not declare, itself, that the member shall not be a lunatic, a pauper, a convict of treason, of murder, of felony, or other infamous crime, or a non-resident of his district; nor does it prohibit to the State the power of declaring these, or any other disqualifications which its particular circumstances may call for; and these may be different in different States. Of course, then, by the tenth amendment, the power is reserved to the State. If, wherever the constitution assumes a single power out of many which belong to the same subject, we should consider it as assuming the whole, it would vest the General Government with a mass of powers never contemplated. On the contrary, the assumption of particular powers seems an exclusion of all not assumed. This reasoning appears to me to be sound; but, on so recent a change of view, caution requires us not to be too confident, and

---

[2] Adam Smith (1723–90), Scottish moral philosopher, economist, and author of *The Wealth of Nations* (Glasgow, 1776). – *Eds.*

that we admit this to be one of the doubtful questions on which honest men may differ with the purest motives; and the more readily, as we find we have differed from ourselves on it.

I have always thought where the line of demarcation between the powers of the General and the State governments was doubtfully or indistinctly drawn, it would be prudent and praiseworthy in both parties, never to approach it but under the most urgent necessity. Is the necessity now urgent, to declare that no non-resident of his district shall be eligible as a member of Congress? It seems to me that, in practice, the partialities of the people are a sufficient security against such an election; and that if, in any instance, they should ever choose a non-resident, it must be one of such eminent merit and qualifications, as would make it a good, rather than an evil; and that, in any event, the examples will be so rare, as never to amount to a serious evil. If the case then be neither clear nor urgent, would it not be better to let it lie undisturbed? Perhaps its decision may never be called for. But if it be indispensable to establish this disqualification now, would it not look better to declare such others, at the same time, as may be proper? I frankly confide to yourself these opinions, or rather no-opinions, of mine; but would not wish to have them go any farther. I want to be quiet; and although some circumstances, now and then, excite me to notice them, I feel safe, and happier in leaving events to those whose turn it is to take care of them; and, in general, to let it be understood, that I meddle little or not at all with public affairs. There are two subjects, indeed, which I shall claim a right to further as long as I breathe, the public education, and the sub-division of counties into wards. I consider the continuance of republican government as absolutely hanging on these two hooks. Of the first, you will, I am sure, be an advocate, as having already reflected on it, and of the last, when you shall have reflected. Ever affectionately yours.

Ford IX: 451–3

## III.20 To the Marquis de Lafayette

Monticello, February 14, 1815

My Dear Friend, – Your letter of August the 14th has been received and read again, and again, with extraordinary pleasure. It is the first glimpse which has been furnished me of the interior workings of the late unexpected but fortunate revolution of your country. The newspapers told us only that the great beast [Napoleon Bonaparte] was fallen; but what part in this the patriots acted, and what the egotists, whether the former slept while the latter were awake to their own interests only, the hireling scribblers of the English press said little and knew less. I see now the mortifying alternative under which the patriot there is placed, of being either silent, or disgraced by an association in opposition with the remains of Bonapartism. A full measure of liberty is not now perhaps to be expected by your nation, nor am I confident they are prepared to preserve it. More than a generation will be requisite, under the administration of reasonable laws favoring the progress of knowledge in the general mass of the people, and their habituation to an independent security of person and property, before they will be capable of estimating the value of freedom, and the necessity of a sacred adherence to the principles on which it rests for preservation. Instead of that liberty which takes root and growth in the progress of reason, if recovered by mere force or accident, it becomes, with an unprepared people, a tyranny still, of the many, the few, or the one. Possibly you may remember, at the date of the *jeu de paume*, how earnestly I urged yourself and the patriots of my acquaintance, to enter then into a compact with the king, securing freedom of religion, freedom of the press, trial by jury, *habeas corpus*, and a national legislature, all of which it was known he would then yield, to go home, and let these work on the amelioration of the condition of the people, until they should have rendered them capable of more, when occasions would not fail to arise for communicating to them more. This was as much as I then thought them able to bear, soberly and usefully for themselves. You thought otherwise, and that the dose might still be larger. And I found you were right; for subsequent events proved they were equal to the constitution of 1791. Unfortunately, some of the most honest and enlightened of our patriotic friends (but closet politicians merely, unpractised in the knowledge of man), thought more could still be obtained and borne. They did not weigh the hazards of a transition from one form of government to another, the value of what they had already rescued from those hazards, and might hold in security if they pleased, nor the imprudence of giving up the certainty of such a degree of liberty, under a limited mon-

arch, for the uncertainty of a little more under the form of a republic. You differed from them. You were for stopping there, and for
securing the constitution which the National Assembly had
obtained. Here, too, you were right; and from this fatal error of the
republicans, from their separation from yourself and the consti-
tutionalists, in their councils, flowed all the subsequent sufferings
and crimes of the French nation. The hazards of a second change
fell upon them by the way. The foreigner gained time to anarchise
by gold the government he could not overthrow by arms, to crush
in their own councils the genuine republicans, by the fraternal
embraces of exaggerated and hired pretenders, and to turn the
machine of Jacobinism from the change to the destruction of order;
and, in the end, the limited monarchy they had secured was
exchanged for the unprincipled and bloody tyranny of Robespierre,
and the equally unprincipled and maniac tyranny of Bonaparte. You
are now rid of him, and I sincerely wish you may continue so. But
this may depend on the wisdom and moderation of the restored
dynasty. It is for them now to read a lesson in the fatal errors of
the republicans; to be contented with a certain portion of power,
secured by formal compact with the nation, rather than, grasping
at more, hazard all upon uncertainty, and risk meeting the fate of
their predecessor, or a renewal of their own exile. We are just
informed, too, of an example which merits, if true, their most profound contemplation. The gazettes say that Ferdinand of Spain is
dethroned, and his father re-established on the basis of their new
constitution. This order of magistrates must, therefore, see, that
although the attempts at reformation have not succeeded in their
whole length, and some secession from the ultimate point has taken
place, yet that men have by no means fallen back to their former
passiveness, but on the contrary, that a sense of their rights, and a
restlessness to obtain them, remain deeply impressed on every
mind, and, if not quieted by reasonable relaxations of power, will
break out like a volcano on the first occasion, and overwhelm everything again in its way. I always thought the present king an honest
and moderate man; and having no issue, he is under a motive the
less for yielding to personal considerations. I cannot, therefore, but
hope, that the patriots in and out of your legislature, acting in phalanx, but temperately and wisely, pressing unremittingly the principles omitted in the late capitulation of the king, and watching

the occasions which the course of events will create, may get those principles engrafted into it, and sanctioned by the solemnity of a national act . . .

[Our New England Federalists'] fears of republican France being now done away, they are directed to republican America, and they are playing the same game for disorganization here, which they played in your country. The Marats, the Dantons and Robespierres of Massachusetts are in the same pay, under the same orders, and making the same efforts to anarchise us, that their prototypes in France did there.

I do not say that all who met at Hartford[1] were under the same motives of money, nor were those of France. Some of them are Outs, and wish to be Inns; some the mere dupes of the agitators, or of their own party passions, while the Maratists alone are in the real secret; but they have very different materials to work on. The yeomanry of the United States are not the *canaille* of Paris. We might safely give them leave to go through the United States recruiting their ranks, and I am satisfied they could not raise one single regiment (gambling merchants and silk-stocking clerks excepted) who would support them in any effort to separate from the Union. The cement of this Union is in the heart-blood of every American. I do not believe there is on earth a government established on so immovable a basis. Let them, in any State, even in Massachusetts itself, raise the standard of separation, and its citizens will rise in mass, and do justice themselves on their own incendiaries. If they could have induced the government to some effort of suppression, or even to enter into discussion with them, it would have given them some importance, have brought them into some notice. But they have not been able to make themselves even a subject of conversation, either of public or private societies. A silent contempt has been the sole notice they excite; consoled, indeed, some of them, by the *palpable* favors of Philip. Have then no fears for us, my friend. The grounds of these exist only in English newspapers, edited or endowed by the Castlereaghs or the Cannings, or some other such models of pure and uncorrupted virtue. Their military heroes, by land and sea, may sink our oyster boats, rob our hen

---

[1] The Hartford [Connecticut] Convention of Dec. 1814–Jan. 1815 was convened by Federalists unhappy with the economic ill-effects of the Madison Administration's conduct of the War of 1812. – *Eds.*

roosts, burn our negro huts, and run off. But a campaign or two more will relieve them from further trouble or expense in defending their American possessions.

You once gave me a copy of the journal of your campaign in Virginia, in 1781, which I must have lent to some one of the under-takers to write the history of the revolutionary war, and forgot to reclaim. I conclude this, because it is no longer among my papers, which I have very diligently searched for it, but in vain. An author of real ability is now writing that part of the history of Virginia. He does it in my neighborhood, and I lay open to him all my papers. But I possess none, nor has he any, which can enable him to do justice to your faithful and able services in that campaign. If you could be so good as to send me another copy, by the very first vessel bound to any port in the United States, it might be here in time; for although he expects to begin to print within a month or two, yet you know the delays of these undertakings. At any rate it might be got in as a supplement. The old Count Rochambeau gave me also his *mémoire* of the operations at York, which is gone in the same way, and I have no means of applying to his family for it. Perhaps you could render them as well as us, the service of procuring another copy.

I learn, with real sorrow, the deaths of Monsieur and Madame de Tessé. They made an interesting part in the idle reveries in which I have sometimes indulged myself, of seeing all my friends of Paris once more, for a month or two; a thing impossible, which, however, I never permitted myself to despair of. The regrets, how-ever, of seventy-three at the loss of friends, may be the less, as the time is shorter within which we are to meet again, according to the creed of our education.

This letter will be handed you by Mr. Ticknor, a young gentle-man of Boston, of great erudition, indefatigable industry, and prep-aration for a life of distinction in his own country. He passed a few days with me here, brought high recommendations from Mr. Adams and others, and appeared in every respect to merit them. He is well worthy of those attentions which you so kindly bestow on our countrymen, and for those he may receive I shall join him in acknowledging personal obligations.

I salute you with assurances of my constant and affectionate friendship and respect.

P.S. February 26th. My letter had not yet been sealed, when I received news of our peace. I am glad of it, and especially that we closed our war with the *éclat* of the action at New Orleans. But I consider it as an armistice only, because no security is provided against the impressment of our seamen. While this is unsettled we are in hostility of mind with England, although actual deeds of arms may be suspended by a truce. If she thinks the exercise of this outrage is worth eternal war, eternal war it must be, or extermination of the one or the other party. The first act of impressment she commits on an American, will be answered by reprisal, or by a declaration of war here; and the interval must be merely a state of preparation for it. In this we have much to do, in further fortifying our seaport towns, providing military stores, classing and disciplining our militia, arranging our financial system, and above all, pushing our domestic manufactures, which have taken such root as never again can be shaken. Once more, God bless you.

Ford IX: 504–11

## III.21 To Joseph C. Cabell

Monticello, February 2, 1816

Dear Sir, – Your favors of the 23d and 24th *ultimo*, were a week coming to us. I instantly enclosed to you the deeds of Captain Miller, but I understand that the postmaster, having locked his mail before they got to the office, would not unlock it to give them a passage.

Having been prevented from retaining my collection of the acts and journals of our legislature by the lumping manner in which the Committee of Congress chose to take my library,[1] it may be useful to our public bodies to know what acts and journals I had, and where they can now have access to them. I therefore enclose you a copy of my catalogue, which I pray you to deposit in the Council office for public use. It is in the eighteenth and twenty-fourth chapters they will find what is interesting to them. The form of the catalogue has been much injured in the publication; for although

---

[1] Early in 1815 TJ had to sell his 6,700-volume library to pay off debts. The U.S. Congress bought it and made it the basis of the Library of Congress. – *Eds.*

they have preserved my division into chapters, they have reduced the books in each chapter to alphabetical order, instead of the chronological or analytical arrangements I had given them. You will see sketches of what were my arrangements at the heads of some of the chapters.[2]

The bill on the obstructions in our navigable waters appears to me proper; as do also the amendments proposed. I think the State should reserve a right to the use of the waters for navigation, and that where an individual landholder impedes that use, he shall remove that impediment, and leave the subject in as good a state as nature formed it. This I hold to be the true principle; and to this Colonel Green's amendments go. All I ask in my own case is, that the legislature will not take from me *my own works*. I am ready to cut my dam in any place, and at any moment requisite, so as to remove that impediment, if it be thought one, and to leave those interested to make the most of the natural circumstances of the place. But I hope they will never take from me my canal, made through the body of my own lands, at an expense of twenty thousand dollars, and which is no impediment to the navigation of the river. I have permitted the riparian proprietors above (and they not more than a dozen or twenty) to use it *gratis*, and shall not withdraw the permission unless they so use it as to obstruct too much the operations of my mills, of which there is some likelihood.

Doctor Smith, you say, asks what is the best elementary book on the principles of government? None in the world equal to the Review of Montesquieu,[3] printed at Philadelphia a few years ago. It has the advantage, too, of being equally sound and corrective of the principles of political economy; and all within the compass of a thin 8vo. Chipman's and Priestley's Principles of Government, and the Federalists, are excellent in many respects, but for fundamental principles not comparable to the Review. I have no objections to the printing my letter to Mr. Carr, if it will promote the interests of science; although it was not written with a view to its publication.

My letter of the 24th *ultimo* conveyed to you the grounds of the two articles objected to in the College bill. Your last presents one of them in a new point of view, that of the commencement of the

---

[2] For TJ's classification scheme, see *supra*, I. 18. – *Eds.*
[3] By Destutt de Tracy. – *Eds.*

ward schools as likely to render the law unpopular to the country. It must be a very inconsiderate and rough process of execution that would do this. My idea of the mode of carrying it into execution would be this: Declare the county *ipso facto* divided into wards for the present, by the boundaries of the militia captaincies; somebody attend the ordinary muster of each company, having first desired the captain to call together a full one. There explain the object of the law to the people of the company, put to their vote whether they will have a school established, and the most central and convenient place for it; get them to meet and build a log school-house; have a roll taken of the children who would attend it, and of those of them able to pay. These would probably be sufficient to support a common teacher, instructing *gratis* the few unable to pay. If there should be a deficiency, it would require too trifling a contribution from the county to be complained of; and especially as the whole county would participate, where necessary, in the same resource. Should the company, by its vote, decide that it would have no school, let them remain without one. The advantages of this proceeding would be that it would become the duty of the alderman elected by the county, to take an active part in pressing the introduction of schools, and to look out for tutors. If, however, it is intended that the State government shall take this business into its own hands, and provide schools for every county, then by all means strike out this provision of our bill. I would never wish that it should be placed on a worse footing than the rest of the State. But if it is believed that these elementary schools will be better managed by the Governor and Council, the commissioners of the literary fund, or any other general authority of the government, than by the parents within each ward, it is a belief against all experience. Try the principle one step further, and amend the bill so as to commit to the Governor and Council the management of all our farms, our mills, and merchants' stores. No, my friend, the way to have good and safe government, is not to trust it all to one, but to divide it among the many, distributing to every one exactly the functions he is competent to. Let the national government be entrusted with the defence of the nation, and its foreign and federal relations; the State governments with the civil rights, laws, police, and administration of what concerns the State generally; the counties with the local concerns of the counties, and each ward direct the interests within itself. It is by dividing and subdividing these republics from the great national one down through all its subordinations, until it ends in the administration of every man's farm by himself; by placing under every one what his own eye may superintend, that all will be done for the best. What has destroyed liberty and the rights of man in every government which has ever existed under the sun? The generalizing and concentrating all cares and powers into one body, no matter whether of the autocrats of Russia or France, or of the aristocrats of a Venetian senate. And I do believe that if the Almighty has not decreed that man shall never be free (and it is a blasphemy to believe it), that the secret will be found to be in the making himself the depository of the powers respecting himself, so far as he is competent to them, and delegating only what is beyond his competence by a synthetical process, to higher and higher orders of functionaries, so as to trust fewer and fewer powers in proportion as the trustees become more and more oligarchical. The elementary republics of the wards, the county republics, the State republics, and the republic of the Union, would form a gradation of authorities, standing each on the basis of law, holding every one its delegated share of powers, and constituting truly a system of fundamental balances and checks for the government. Where every man is a sharer in the direction of his ward-republic, or of some of the higher ones, and feels that he is a participator in the government of affairs, not merely at an election one day in the year, but every day; when there shall not be a man in the State who will not be a member of some one of its councils, great or small, he will let the heart be torn out of his body sooner than his power be wrested from him by a Cæsar or a Bonaparte. How powerfully did we feel the energy of this organization in the case of embargo? I felt the foundations of the government shaken under my feet by the New England townships. There was not an individual in their States whose body was not thrown with all its momentum into action; and although the whole of the other States were known to be in favor of the measure, yet the organization of this little selfish minority enabled it to overrule the Union. What would the unwieldy counties of the Middle, the South, and the West do? Call a county meeting, and the drunken loungers at and about the court-houses would have collected, the distances being too great for the good people and the industrious generally to attend. The character of those who really met would have been the measure of the weight they would have had in the scale of public opinion. As Cato, then, concluded every speech with the words, "*Carthago delenda est,*" so do I every opinion, with the injunction, "divide the counties into wards." Begin them only for a single purpose; they will soon show for what others they are the best instruments. God bless you, and all our rulers, and give them the wisdom, as I am sure they have the will, to fortify us against the degeneracy of our government, and the concentration of all its powers in the hands of the one, the few, the well-born or the many.

L & B XIV: 417–23

## III.22 To John Taylor

Monticello, May 28, 1816

Dear Sir, – On my return from a long journey and considerable absence from home, I found here the copy of your "Enquiry into the Principles of our Government," which you had been so kind as to send me; and for which I pray you to accept my thanks. The difficulties of getting new works in our situation, inland and without a single bookstore, are such as had prevented my obtaining a copy before; and letters which had accumulated during my absence, and were calling for answers, have not yet permitted me to give to the whole a thorough reading; yet certain that you and I could not think differently on the fundamentals of rightful government, I was impatient, and availed myself of the intervals of repose from the writing-table, to obtain a cursory idea of the body of the work.

I see in it much matter for profound reflection; much which should confirm our adhesion, in practice, to the good principles of our Constitution, and fix our attention on what is yet to be made good. The sixth section on the good moral principles of our government, I found so interesting and replete with sound principles, as to postpone my letter-writing to its thorough perusal and consideration. Besides much other good matter, it settles unanswerably the right of instructing representatives, and their duty to obey. The system of banking we have both equally and ever reprobated. I contemplate it as a blot left in all our Constitutions, which, if not covered, will end in their destruction, which is already hit by the gamblers in corruption, and is sweeping away in its progress the fortunes and morals of our citizens. Funding I consider as limited, rightfully, to a redemption of the debt within the lives of a majority of the generation contracting it; every generation coming equally, by the laws of the Creator of the world, to the free possession of the earth He made for their subsistence, unincumbered by their predecessors, who, like them, were but tenants for life. You have successfully and completely pulverized Mr. Adams' system of orders, and his opening the mantle of republicanism to every government of laws, whether consistent or not with natural right. Indeed, it must be acknowledged, that the term *republic* is of very vague application in every language. Witness the self-styled republics of Holland, Switzerland, Genoa, Venice, Poland. Were I to assign to this term a precise and definite idea, I would say, purely and simply, it means a government by its citizens in mass, acting directly and personally, according to rules established by the majority; and that every other government is more or less republican, in proportion as it has in its composition more or less of this ingredient of the direct action of the citizens. Such a government is evidently restrained to very narrow limits of space and population. I doubt if it would be practicable beyond the extent of a New England township. The first shade from this pure element, which, like that of pure vital air, cannot sustain life of itself, would be where the powers of the government, being divided, should be exercised each by representatives chosen either *pro hac vice*, or for such short terms as should render secure the duty of expressing the will of their constituents. This I should consider as the nearest approach to a pure republic, which is practicable on a large scale of country or population. And we have examples of it in some of our State Constitutions, which, if not poisoned by priest-craft, would prove its excellence over all mixtures with other elements; and, with only equal doses of poison, would still be the best. Other shades of republicanism may be found in other forms of government, where the executive, judiciary and legislative functions, and the different branches of the latter, are chosen by the people more or less directly, for longer terms of years, or for life, or made hereditary; or where there are mixtures of authorities, some dependent on, and others independent of the people. The further the departure from direct and constant control by the citizens, the less has the government of the ingredient of republicanism; evidently none where the authorities are hereditary, as in France, Venice, etc., or self-chosen, as in Holland; and little, where for life, in proportion as the life continues in being after the act of election.

The purest republican feature in the government of our own State, is the House of Representatives. The Senate is equally so the first year, less the second, and so on. The Executive still less, because not chosen by the people directly. The Judiciary seriously anti-republican, because for life; and the national arm wielded, as you observe, by military leaders, irresponsible but to themselves. Add to this the vicious constitution of our county courts (to whom the justice, the executive administration, the taxation, police, the military appointments of the county, and nearly all our daily concerns are confided), self-appointed, self-continued, holding their authorities for life, and with an impossibility of breaking in on the perpetual succession of any faction once possessed of the bench. They are in truth, the executive, the judiciary, and the military of their respective counties, and the sum of the counties makes the State. And add, also, that one-half of our brethren who fight and pay taxes, are excluded, like Helots, from the rights of representation, as if society were instituted for the soil, and not for the men inhabiting it; or one-half of these could dispose of the rights and the will of the other half, without their consent.

> "What constitutes a State?
> Not high-raised battlements, or labor'd mound,
>     Thick wall, or moated gate;
> Not cities proud, with spires and turrets crown'd;
>     No: men, high-minded men;
>     Men, who their duties know;
> But know their rights; and knowing, dare maintain.
>     These constitute a State."

In the General Government, the House of Representatives is mainly republican; the Senate scarcely so at all, as not elected by the people directly, and so long secured even against those who do elect them; the Executive more republican than the Senate, from its shorter term, its election by the people, in *practice* (for they vote for A only on an assurance that he will vote for B), and because, *in practice also*, a principle of rotation seems to be in a course of establishment; the judiciary independent of the nation, their coercion by impeachment being found nugatory.

If, then, the control of the people over the organs of their government be the measure of its republicanism, and I confess I know no other measure, it must be agreed that our governments have much less of republicanism than ought to have been expected; in other words, that the people have less regular control over their agents, than their rights and their interests require. And this I ascribe, not to any want of republican dispositions in those who formed these Constitutions, but to a submission of true principle to European authorities, to speculators on government, whose fears of the people have been inspired by the populace of their own great cities, and were unjustly entertained against the independent, the happy, and therefore orderly citizens of the United States. Much I apprehend that the golden moment is past for reforming these heresies. The functionaries of public power rarely strengthen in their dispositions to abridge it, and an unorganized call for timely amendment is not likely to prevail against an organized opposition to it. We are always told that things are going on well; why change them? "*Chi sta bene, non si muove*," said the Italian, "let him who stands well, stand still." This is true; and I verily believe they would go on well with us under an absolute monarch, while our present character remains, of order, industry and love of peace, and restrained, as he would be, by the proper spirit of the people. But it is while it remains such, we should provide against the consequences of its deterioration. And let us rest in the hope that it will yet be done, and spare ourselves the pain of evils which may never happen.

On this view of the import of the term *republic*, instead of saying, as has been said, "that it may mean anything or nothing," we may say with truth and meaning, that governments are more or less republican, as they have more or less of the element of popular election and control in their composition; and believing, as I do, that the mass of the citizens is the safest depository of their own rights and especially, that the evils flowing from the duperies of the people, are less injurious than those from the egoism of their agents, I am a friend to that composition of government which has in it the most of this ingredient. And I sincerely believe, with you, that banking establishments are more dangerous than standing armies; and that the principle of spending money to be paid by posterity, under the name of funding, is but swindling futurity on a large scale.

I salute you with constant friendship and respect.

L & B XV: 17–23

## III.23 To Samuel Kercheval

Monticello, July 12, 1816

Sir, – I duly received your favor of June the 13th, with the copy of the letters on the calling a convention, on which you are pleased to ask my opinion. I have not been in the habit of mysterious reserve on any subject, nor of buttoning up my opinions within my own doublet. On the contrary, while in public service especially, I thought the public entitled to frankness, and intimately to know whom they employed. But I am now retired: I resign myself, as a passenger, with confidence to those at present at the helm, and ask but for rest, peace and good will. The question you propose, on equal representation, has become a party one, in which I wish to take no public share. Yet, if it be asked for your own satisfaction only, and not to be quoted before the public, I have no motive to withhold it, and the less from you, as it coincides with your own. At the birth of our republic, I committed that opinion to the world, in the draught of a constitution annexed to the "Notes on Virginia," in which a provision was inserted for a representation permanently equal. The infancy of the subject at that moment, and our inexperience of self-government, occasioned gross departures in that draught from genuine republican canons. In truth, the abuses of monarchy had so much filled all the space of political contemplation, that we imagined everything republican which was not monarchy. We had not yet penetrated to the mother principle, that "governments are republican only in proportion as they embody the will of their people, and execute it." Hence, our first constitutions had really no leading principles in them. But experience and reflection have but more and more confirmed me in the particular importance of the equal representation then proposed. On that point, then, I am entirely in sentiment with your letters; and only lament that a copy-right of your pamphlet prevents their appearance in the newspapers, where alone they would be generally read, and produce general effect. The present vacancy too, of other matter, would give them place in every paper, and bring the question home to every man's conscience.

But inequality of representation in both Houses of our legislature, is not the only republican heresy in this first essay of our revolutionary patriots at forming a constitution. For let it be agreed that a government is republican in proportion as every member composing it has his equal voice in the direction of its concerns (not indeed in person, which would be impracticable beyond the limits of a city, or small township, but) by representatives chosen by himself, and responsible to him at short periods, and let us bring to the test of this canon every branch of our constitution.

In the legislature, the House of Representatives is chosen by less than half the people, and not at all in proportion to those who do choose. The Senate are still more disproportionate, and for long terms of irresponsibility. In the Executive, the Governor is entirely independent of the choice of the people, and of their control; his Council equally so, and at best but a fifth wheel to a wagon. In the Judiciary, the judges of the highest courts are dependent on none but themselves. In England, where judges were named and removable at the will of an hereditary executive, from which branch most misrule was feared, and has flowed, it was a great point gained, by fixing them for life, to make them independent of that executive. But in a government founded on the public will, this principle operates in an opposite direction, and against that will. There, too, they were still removable on a concurrence of the executive and legislative branches. But we have made them independent of the nation itself. They are irremovable, but by their own body, for any depravities of conduct, and even by their own body for the imbecilities of dotage. The justices of the inferior courts are self-chosen, are for life, and perpetuate their own body in succession forever, so that a faction once possessing themselves of the bench of a county, can never be broken up, but hold their county in chains, forever indissoluble. Yet these justices are the real executive as well as judiciary, in all our minor and most ordinary concerns. They tax us at will; fill the office of sheriff, the most important of all the executive officers of the county; name nearly all our military leaders, which leaders, once named, are removable but by themselves. The juries, our judges of all fact, and of law when they choose it, are not selected by the people, nor amenable to them. They are chosen by an officer named by the court and executive. Chosen, did I say? Picked up by the sheriff from the loungings of the court yard, after everything respectable has retired from it. Where then is our republicanism to be found? Not in our constitution certainly, but merely in the spirit of our people. That would oblige even a despot to govern us republicanly. Owing to this spirit, and to nothing in the form of our constitution, all things have gone well. But this fact, so triumphantly misquoted by the enemies of reformation, is not the fruit of our constitution, but has prevailed in spite of it. Our functionaries have done well, because generally honest men. If any were not so, they feared to show it.

But it will be said, it is easier to find faults than to amend them. I do not think their amendment so difficult as is pretended. Only lay down true principles, and adhere to them inflexibly. Do not be frightened into their surrender by the alarms of the timid, or the croakings of wealth against the ascendency of the people. If experience be called for, appeal to that of our fifteen or twenty governments for forty years, and show me where the people have done half the mischief in these forty years, that a single despot would have done in a single year; or show half the riots and rebellions, the crimes and the punishments, which have taken place in any single nation, under kingly government, during the same period. The true foundation of republican government is the equal right of every citizen, in his person and property, and in their management. Try by this, as a tally, every provision of our constitution, and see if it hangs directly on the will of the people. Reduce your legislature to a convenient number for full, but orderly discussion. Let every man who fights or pays, exercise his just and equal right in their election. Submit them to approbation or rejection at short intervals. Let the executive be chosen in the same way, and for the same term, by those whose agent he is to be; and leave no screen of a council behind which to skulk from responsibility. It has been thought that the people are not competent electors of judges *learned in the law*. But I do not know that this is true, and, if doubtful, we should follow principle. In this, as in many other elections, they would be guided by reputation, which would not err oftener, perhaps, than the present mode of appointment. In one State of the Union, at least, it has long been tried, and with the most satisfactory success. The judges of Connecticut have been chosen by the people every six months, for nearly two centuries, and I believe there has hardly ever been an instance of change; so powerful is the curb of incessant responsibility. If prejudice, however, derived from a monarchichal institution, is still to prevail against the vital elective principle of our own, and if the existing example among ourselves of periodical election of judges by the people be still mistrusted, let us at least not adopt the evil, and reject the good, of the English precedent; let us retain amovability on the concurrence of the executive and legislative branches, and nomination by the executive alone. Nomination to office is an executive function. To give it to the legislature, as we do, is a violation of the principle of the separation of powers. It swerves the members from correctness, by temptations to intrigue for office themselves, and to a corrupt barter of votes; and destroys responsibility by dividing it among a multitude. By leaving nomination in its proper place, among executive functions, the principle of the distribution of power is preserved, and responsibility weighs with its heaviest force on a single head.

The organization of our county administrations may be thought more difficult. But follow principle, and the knot unties itself. Divide the counties into wards of such size as that every citizen can attend, when called on, and act in person. Ascribe to them the government of their wards in all things relating to themselves exclusively. A justice, chosen by themselves, in each, a constable, a military company, a patrol, a school, the care of their own poor, their own portion of the public roads, the choice of one or more jurors to serve in some court, and the delivery, within their own wards, of their own votes for all elective officers of higher sphere, will relieve the county administration of nearly all its business, will have it better done, and by making every citizen an acting member of the government, and in the offices nearest and most interesting to him, will attach him by his strongest feelings to the independence of his country, and its republican constitution. The justices thus chosen by every ward, would constitute the county court, would do its judiciary business, direct roads and bridges, levy county and poor rates, and administer all the matters of common interest to the whole country. These wards, called townships in New England, are the vital principle of their governments, and have proved themselves the wisest invention ever devised by the wit of man for the perfect exercise of self-government, and for its preservation. We should thus marshal our government into, 1, the general federal republic, for all concerns foreign and federal: 2, that of the State, for what relates to our own citizens exclusively; 3, the county republics, for the duties and concerns of the county; and 4, the ward republics, for the small, and yet numerous and interesting concerns of the neighborhood; and in government, as well as in every other business of life, it is by division and subdivision of duties alone, that all matters, great and small, can be managed to perfection. And the whole is cemented by giving to every citizen, personally, a part in the administration of the public affairs.

The sum of these amendments is, 1. General Suffrage. 2. Equal representation in the legislature. 3. An executive chosen by the people. 4. Judges elective or amovable. 5. Justices, jurors, and sheriffs elective. 6. Ward divisions. And 7. Periodical amendments of the constitution.

I have thrown out these as loose heads of amendment, for consideration and correction; and their object is to secure self-government by the republicanism of our constitution, as well as by the spirit of the people; and to nourish and perpetuate that spirit. I am not among those who fear the people. They, and not the rich, are our dependence for continued freedom. And to preserve their independence, we must not let our rulers load us with perpetual debt. We must make our election between *economy and liberty*, or *profusion and servitude*. If we run into such debts, as that we must be taxed in our meat and in our drink, in our necessaries and our comforts, in our labors and our amusements, for our callings and our creeds, as the people of England are, our people, like them, must come to labor sixteen hours in the twenty-four, give the earnings of fifteen of these to the government for their debts and daily expenses; and the sixteenth being insufficient to afford us bread, we must live, as they now do, on oatmeal and potatoes; have no time to think, no means of calling the mismanagers to account; but be glad to obtain subsistence by hiring ourselves to rivet their chains on the necks of our fellow-sufferers. Our landholders, too, like theirs, retaining indeed the title and stewardship of estates called theirs, but held really in trust for the treasury, must wander, like theirs, in foreign countries, and be contented with penury, obscurity, exile, and the glory of the nation. This example reads to us the salutary lesson, that private fortunes are destroyed by public as well as by private extravagance. And this is the tendency of all human governments. A departure from principle in one instance becomes a precedent for a second; that second for a third; and so on, till the bulk of the society is reduced to be mere automatons of misery, and to have no sensibilities left but for sinning and suffering. Then begins, indeed, the *bellum omnium in omnia*, which some philosophers observing to be so general in this world, have mistaken it for the natural, instead of the abusive state of man. And the fore horse of this frightful team is public debt. Taxation follows that, and in its train wretchedness and oppression.

Some men look at constitutions with sanctimonious reverence, and deem them like the arc of the covenant, too sacred to be touched. They ascribe to the men of the preceding age a wisdom more than human, and suppose what they did to be beyond amendment. I knew that age well; I belonged to it, and labored with it. It deserved well of its country. It was very like the present, but without the experience of the present; and forty years of experience in government is worth a century of book-reading; and this they would say themselves, were they to rise from the dead. I am certainly not an advocate for frequent and untried changes in laws and constitutions. I think moderate imperfections had better be borne with; because, when once known, we accommodate ourselves to them, and find practical means of correcting their ill effects. But I know also, that laws and institutions must go hand in hand with the progress of the human mind. As that becomes more developed, more enlightened, as new discoveries are made, new truths disclosed, and manners and opinions change with the change of circumstances, institutions must advance also, and keep pace with the times. We might as well require a man to wear still the coat which fitted him when a boy, as civilized society to remain ever under the regimen of their barbarous ancestors. It is this preposterous idea which has lately deluged Europe in blood. Their monarchs, instead of wisely yielding to the gradual change of circumstances, of favoring progressive accommodation to progressive improvement, have clung to old abuses, entrenched themselves behind steady habits, and obliged their subjects to seek through blood and violence rash and ruinous innovations, which, had they been referred to the peaceful deliberations and collected wisdom of the nation, would have been put into acceptable and salutary forms. Let us follow no such examples, nor weakly believe that one generation is not as capable as another of taking care of itself, and of ordering its own affairs. Let us, as our sister States have done, avail ourselves of our reason and experience, to correct the crude essays of our first and unexperienced, although wise, virtuous, and well-meaning councils. And lastly, let us provide in our constitution for its revision at stated periods. What these periods should be, nature herself indicates. By the European tables of mortality, of the adults living at any one moment of time, a majority will be dead in about nineteen years. At the end of that period, then, a new majority is come into place; or, in other words, a new generation. Each generation is as independent as the one preceding, as that was of all which had gone before. It has then, like them, a right to choose for itself the form of government it believes most promotive of its own happiness; consequently, to accommodate to the circumstances in which it finds itself, that received from its predecessors; and it is for the peace and good of mankind, that a solemn opportunity of doing this every nineteen or twenty years, should be provided by the constitution; so that it may be handed on, with periodical repairs, from generation to generation, to the end of time, if anything human can so long endure. It is now forty years since the constitution of Virginia was formed. The same tables inform us, that, within that period, two-thirds of the adults then living are now dead. Have then the remaining third, even if they had the wish, the right to hold in obedience to their will, and to laws heretofore made by them, the other two-thirds, who, with themselves, compose the present mass of adults? If they have not, who has? The dead? But the dead have no rights. They are nothing; and nothing cannot own something. Where there is no substance, there can be no accident. This corporeal globe, and everything upon it, belong to its present corporeal inhabitants, during their generation. They alone have a right to direct what is the concern of themselves alone, and to declare the law of that direction; and this declaration can only be made by their majority. That majority, then, has a right to depute representatives to a convention, and to make the constitution what they think will be the best for themselves. But how collect their voice? This is the real difficulty. If invited by private authority, or county or district meetings, these divisions are so large that few will attend; and their voice will be imperfectly, or falsely pronounced. Here, then, would be one of the advantages of the ward divisions I have proposed. The mayor of every ward, on a question like the present, would call his ward together, take the simple yea or nay of its members, convey these to the county court, who would hand on those of all its wards to the proper general authority; and the voice of the whole people would be thus fairly, fully, and peaceably expressed, discussed, and decided by the common reason of the society. If this avenue be shut to the call of sufferance, it will make itself heard through that of force, and we shall go on, as other nations are doing, in the endless circle of oppression, rebellion, reformation; and oppression, rebellion, reformation, again; and so on forever.

These, Sir, are my opinions of the governments we see among men, and of the principles by which alone we may prevent our own from falling into the same dreadful track. I have given them at greater length than your letter called for. But I cannot say things by halves; and I confide them to your honor, so to use them as to preserve me from the gridiron of the public papers. If you shall approve and enforce them, as you have done that of equal representation, they may do some good. If not, keep them to yourself as the effusions of withered age and useless time. I shall, with not the less truth, assure you of my great respect and consideration.

Ford x: 37–45

## III.24 To Isaac H. Tiffany

Monticello, August 26, 1816

Sir, – In answer to your inquiry as to the merits of Gillies' translation of the Politics of Aristotle, I can only say that it has the reputation of being preferable to Ellis', the only rival translation into English. I have never seen it myself, and therefore do not speak of it from my own knowledge. But so different was the style of society then, and with these people, from what it is now and with us, that I think little edification can be obtained from their writings on the subject of government. They had just ideas of the value of personal liberty, but none at all of the structure of government best calculated to preserve it. They knew no medium between a democracy (the only pure republic, but impracticable beyond the limits of a town) and an abandonment of themselves to an aristocracy, or a tyranny independent of the people. It seems not to have occurred that where the citizens cannot meet to transact their business in person, they alone have the right to choose the agents who shall transact it; and that in this way a republican, or popular government, of the second grade of purity, may be exercised over any extent of country. The full experiment of a government democratical, but representative, was and is still reserved for us. The idea (taken, indeed, from the little specimen formerly existing in the English constitution, but now lost) has been carried by us, more or less, into all our legislative and executive departments; but it has not yet, by any of us, been pushed into all the ramifications of the system, so far as to leave no authority existing not responsible to the people; whose rights, however, to the exercise and fruits of their own industry, can never be protected against the selfishness of rulers not subject to their control at short periods. The introduction of this new principle of representative democracy has rendered useless almost everything written before on the structure of government; and, in a great measure, relieves our regret, if the political writings of Aristotle, or of any other ancient, have been lost, or are unfaithfully rendered or explained to us. My most earnest wish is to see the republican element of popular control pushed to the maximum of its practicable exercise. I shall then believe that our government may be pure and perpetual. Accept my respectful salutations.

Washington VII: 31–2

## III.25 To Samuel Kercheval

Monticello, September 5, 1816

Sir, – Your letter of August the 16th is just received. That which I wrote to you under the address of H. Tompkinson, was intended for the author of the pamphlet you were so kind as to send me, and therefore, in your hands, found its true destination. But I must beseech you, Sir, not to admit a possibility of its being published.

Many good people will revolt from its doctrines, and my wish is to offend nobody; to leave to those who are to live under it, the settlement of their own constitution, and to pass in peace the remainder of my time. If those opinions are sound, they will occur to others, and will prevail by their own weight, without the aid of names. I am glad to see that the Staunton meeting has rejected the idea of a limited convention. The article, however, nearest my heart, is the division of counties into wards. These will be pure and elementary republics, the sum of all which, taken together, composes the State, and will make of the whole a true democracy as to the business of the wards, which is that of nearest and daily concern. The affairs of the larger sections, of counties, of States, and of the Union, not admitting personal transactions by the people, will be delegated to agents elected by themselves; and representation will thus be substituted, where personal action becomes impracticable. Yet, even over these representative organs, should they become corrupt and perverted, the division into wards constituting the people, in their wards, a regularly organized power, enables them by that organization to crush, regularly and peaceably, the usurpations of their unfaithful agents, and rescues them from the dreadful necessity of doing it insurrectionally. In this way we shall be as republican as a large society can be; and secure the continuance of purity in our government, by the salutary, peaceable, and regular control of the people. No other depositories of power have ever yet been found, which did not end in converting to their own profit the earnings of those committed to their charge. George the III. in execution of the trust confided to him, has, within his own day, loaded the inhabitants of Great Britain with debts equal to the whole fee-simple value of their island, and under pretext of governing it, has alienated its whole soil to creditors who could lend money to be lavished on priests, pensions, plunder and perpetual war. This would not have been so, had the people retained organized means of acting on their agents. In this example then, let us read a lesson for ourselves, and not "go and do likewise."

Since writing my letter of July the 12th, I have been told, that on the question of equal representation, our fellow citizens in some sections of the State claim peremptorily a right of representation for their slaves. Principle will, in this, as in most other cases, open the way for us to correct conclusion. Were our State a pure democracy, in which all its inhabitants should meet together to transact all their business, there would yet be excluded from their deliberations, 1, infants, until arrived at years of discretion. 2. Women, who, to prevent depravation of morals and ambiguity of issue, could not mix promiscuously in the public meetings of men. 3. Slaves, from whom the unfortunate state of things with us takes away the rights of will and of property. Those then who have no will could be permitted to exercise none in the popular assembly; and of course, could delegate none to an agent in a representative assembly. The business, in the first case, would be done by qualified citizens only. It is true, that in the general Constitution, our State is allowed a larger representation on account of its slaves. But every one knows, that that Constitution was a matter of compromise; a capitulation between conflicting interests and opinions. In truth, the condition of different descriptions of inhabitants in any country is a matter of municipal arrangement, of which no foreign country has a right to take notice. All its inhabitants are men as to them. Thus, in the New England States, have the powers of citizens but those whom they call *freemen*; and none are *freemen* until admitted by a vote of the freemen of the town. Yet, in the General Government, these non-freemen are counted in their quantum of representation and of taxation. So, slaves with us have no powers as citizens; yet, in representation in the General Government, they count in the proportion of three to five; and so also in taxation. Whether this is equal, is not here the question. It is a capitulation of discordant sentiments and circumstances, and is obligatory on that ground. But this view shows there is no inconsistency in claiming representation for them for the other States, and refusing it within our own. Accept the renewal of assurances of my respect.

L & B, xv: 70–3

## III.26 To Baron von Humboldt

Monticello, June 13, 1817

Dear Sir, – The receipt of your *Distributio Geographica Plantarum*, with the duty of thanking you for a work which sheds so much new and valuable light on botanical science, excites the desire, also, of presenting myself to your recollection, and of expressing to you those sentiments of high admiration and esteem, which, although long silent, have never slept. The physical information you have given us of a country hitherto so shamefully unknown [Mexico], has come exactly in time to guide our understandings in the great political revolution now bringing it into prominence on the stage of the world.[1] The issue of its struggles, as they respect Spain, is no longer matter of doubt. As it respects their own liberty, peace and happiness, we cannot be quite so certain. Whether the blinds of bigotry, the shackles of the priesthood, and the fascinating glare of rank and wealth, give fair play to the common sense of the mass of their people, so far as to qualify them for self-government, is what we do not know. Perhaps our wishes may be stronger than our hopes. The first principle of republicanism is, that the *lex majoris partis* is the fundamental law of every society of individuals of equal rights; to consider the will of the society enounced by the majority of a single vote, as sacred as if unanimous, is the first of all lessons in importance, yet the last which is thoroughly learnt. This law once disregarded, no other remains but that of force, which ends necessarily in military despotism. This has been the history of the French revolution, and I wish the understanding of our Southern brethren may be sufficiently enlarged and firm to see that their fate depends on its sacred observance.

In our America we are turning to public improvements. Schools, roads, and canals, are everywhere either in operation or contemplation. The most gigantic undertaking yet proposed, is that of New York, for drawing the waters of Lake Erie into the Hudson. The distance is 353 miles, and the height to be surmounted 661 feet. The expense will be great, but its effect incalculably powerful in favor of the Atlantic States. Internal navigation by steamboats is rapidly spreading through all our States, and that by sails and oars will ere long be looked back to as among the curiosities of antiquity. We count much, too, on its efficacy for harbor defence; and it will soon be tried for navigation by sea. We consider the employment of the contributions which our citizens can spare, after feeding, and

---

[1] Mexico secured its independence from Spain in 1821. – *Eds.*

clothing, and lodging themselves comfortably, as more useful, more moral, and even more splendid, than that preferred by Europe, of destroying human life, labor and happiness.

I write this letter without knowing where it will find you. But wherever that may be, I am sure it will find you engaged in something instructive for man. If at Paris, you are of course in habits of society with Mr. Gallatin, our worthy, our able, and excellent minister, who will give you, from time to time, the details of the progress of a country in whose prosperity you are so good as to feel an interest, and in which your name is revered among those of the great worthies of the world. God bless you, and preserve you long to enjoy the gratitude of your fellow men, and to be blessed with honors, health and happiness.

Washington VII: 74–6

## III.27 To John Adams

Monticello, May 17, 1818

Dear Sir, – I was so unfortunate as not to receive from Mr. Holly's own hand your favor of January the 28th, being then at my other home. He dined only with my family, and left them with an impression which has filled me with regret that I did not partake of the pleasure his visit gave them. I am glad he is gone to Kentucky. Rational Christianity will thrive more rapidly there than here. They are freer from prejudices than we are, and bolder in grasping at truth. The time is not distant, though neither you nor I shall see it, when we shall be but a secondary people to them. Our greediness for wealth, and fantastical expense, have degraded, and will degrade, the minds of our maritime citizens. These are the peculiar vices of commerce.

I had been long without hearing *from* you, but I had heard *of* you through a letter from Doctor Waterhouse. He wrote to reclaim against an expression of Mr. Wirt's, as to the commencement of motion in the revolutionary ball. The lawyers say that words are always to be expounded *secundum subjectam materiem*, which, in Mr. Wirt's case, was Virginia. It would, moreover, be as difficult to say at what moment the Revolution began, and what incident set it in motion, as to fix the moment that the embryo becomes an animal, or the act which gives him a beginning. But the most agreeable part of his letter was that which informed me of your health, your activity, and strength of memory; and the most wonderful, that which assured me that you retained your industry and promptness in epistolary correspondence. Here you have entire advantage over me. My repugnance to the writing-table becomes daily and hourly more deadly and insurmountable. In place of this has come on a canine appetite for reading. And I indulge it, because I see in it a relief against the *tædium senectutis*; a lamp to lighten my path through the dreary wilderness of time before me, whose bourne I see not. Losing daily all interest in the things around us, something else is necessary to fill the void. With me it is reading, which occupies the mind without the labor of producing ideas from my own stock.

I enter into all your doubts as to the event of the revolution of South America. They will succeed against Spain. But the dangerous enemy is within their own breasts. Ignorance and superstition will chain their minds and bodies under religious and military despotism. I do believe it would be better for them to obtain freedom by degrees only; because that would by degrees bring on light and information, and qualify them to take charge of themselves understandingly; with more certainty, if in the meantime, under so much control as may keep them at peace with one another. Surely, it is our duty to wish them independence and self-government, because they wish it themselves, and they have the right, and we none, to choose for themselves; and I wish, moreover, that our ideas may be erroneous, and theirs prove well founded. But these are speculations, my friend, which we may as well deliver over to those who are to see their development. We shall only be lookers on, from the clouds above, as now we look down on the labors, the hurry and bustle of the ants and bees. Perhaps in that supermundane region, we may be amused with seeing the fallacy of our own guesses, and even the nothingness of those labors which have filled and agitated our own time here.

*En attendant*, with sincere affections to Mrs. Adams and yourself, I salute you both cordially.

L & B xv: 168–71

## III.28 To Isaac H. Tiffany

Monticello, April 4, 1819

Sir, – After thanking you for your comprehensive tabular chart of the governments of the U.S., I must give you the answer which I am obliged to give to all who propose to me to replunge myself into political speculations. "*Senex sum, et laecrissimis [sic ?] curis impar.*" I abandon politics, and accomodate myself chearfully to things as they go, confident in the wisdom of those who direct them, and that they will be better and better directed in the progressive course of knolege and experience. Our successors start on our shoulders. They know all that we know, and will add to that stock the discoveries of the next 50 years; and what will be their amount we may estimate from what the last 50 years have added to the science of human concerns. The thoughts of others, as I find them on paper, are my amusement and delight; but the labors of the mind in abstruse investigations are irksome, and writing itself is become a slow and painful operation, occasioned by a stiffened wrist, the consequence of a former dislocation. I will however essay the two definitions which you say are more particularly interesting at present. I mean those of the terms Liberty and Republic, aware however that they have been so multifariously applied as to convey no precise idea to the mind. Of Liberty then I would say that, in the whole plenitude of its extent, it is unobstructed action according to our will. But rightful liberty is unobstructed action according to our will, within the limits drawn around us by the equal rights of others. I do not add "within the limits of the law," because law is often but the tyrant's will and always so when it violates the right of an individual. I will add [secon]dly that a pure republic is a state of society in which every member, of mature and sound mind, has an equal right of participation, personally in the direction of the affairs of the society. Such a regimen is obviously impractical beyond the limits of an encampment, or of a very small village. When numbers, distance, or force oblige them to act by deputy, then their government continues republican in proportion only as the functions they still exercise in person are more or fewer, and as in those exercised by deputy the right of appointing their deputy is *pro hâc vice* only, or for more or fewer purposes, or for shorter or longer terms. If by the word *government*, you mean a classification of it's forms, I must refer you, for the soundest which has ever been given, to Tracy's Review of Montesquieu, the ablest political work which the last century of years has given us. It was translated from the original M.S., and published by Duane a few years ago; and is since published in the original French at Paris. With my thanks for your chart[,] accept the assurance of my great respect.

Jefferson MSS, Library of Congress

## III.29 To John Adams

Monticello, December 10, 1819

Dear Sir, – I have to acknolege the reciept of your favor of Nov. 23. The banks, bankrupt law, manufactures, Spanish treaty are nothing. These are occurences which like waves in a storm will pass under the ship. But the Missouri question [i.e. whether to admit Missouri as a free or a slave-owning state] is a breaker on which we lose the Missouri country by revolt, and what more, God only knows. From the battle of Bunker's hill to the treaty of Paris we never had so ominous a question. It even damps the joy with which I hear of your high health, and welcomes to me the consequences of my want of it. I thank god that I shall not live to witness it's issue. *Sed haec hactenus.*

I have been amusing myself latterly with reading the voluminous letters of Cicero. They certainly breathe the purest effusions of an exalted patriot, while the parricide Caesar is left in odious contrast. When the enthusiasm however kindled by Cicero's pen and principles, subsides into cool reflection, I ask myself What was that government which the virtues of Cicero were so zealous to restore, and the ambition of Caesar to subvert? And if Caesar had been as virtuous as he was daring and sagacious, what could he, even in the plenitude of his usurped power, have done to lead his fellow citizens into good government? I do not say to *restore it*, because they never had it, from the rape of the Sabines to the ravages of the Caesars. If their people indeed had been, like ours, enlightened, peaceable, and really free, the answer would be obvious. "Restore independence to all your foreign conquests, relieve Italy from the government of the rabble of Rome, consult it as a nation entitled to self government, and do it's will." But steeped in corruption, vice and venality as the whole nation was (and nobody had done more than Caesar to corrupt it), what could even Cicero, Cato, Brutus have done, had it been referred to them to establish a good government for their country? They had no ideas of government themselves but of their degenerate Senate, nor the people of liberty, but of the factious opposition of their tribunes. They had afterwards their Titusses, their Trajans and Antoninuses, who had the will to make them happy, and the power to mould their government into a good and permanent form. But it would seem as if they could not see their way clearly to do it. No government can continue good but under the controul of the people: and their people were so demoralised and depraved as to be incapable of exercising a wholsome controul. Their reformation then was to be taken up *ab incunabulis.* Their minds were to be informed, by education, what is right and what wrong, to be encoraged in habits of virtue, and deterred from those of vice by the dread of punishments, proportioned indeed, but irremissible; in all cases, to follow truth as the only safe guide, and to eschew error which bewilders us in one false consequence after another in endless succession. These are the inculcations necessary to render the people a sure basis for the structure of order and good government. But this would have been an operation of a generation or two at least, within which period would have succeeded many Neros and Commoduses, who would have quashed the whole process. I confess then I can neither see what Cicero, Cato and Brutus, united and uncontrouled, could have devised to lead their people into good government, nor how this ænigma can be solved, nor how further shewn why it has been the fate of that delightful country never to have known to this day, and through a course of five and twenty hundred years, the history of which we possess, one single day of free and rational government. Your intimacy with their history, antient, middle and modern, your familiarity with the improvements in the science of government at this time, will enable you, if any body, to go back with our principles and opinions to the times of Cicero, Cato, and Brutus, and tell us by what process these great and virtuous men could have led so unenlightened and vitiated a people into freedom and good government, *et eris mihi magnus Apollo. Cura ut valeas, et tibi persuade carissimum te mihi esse.*

L & B xv: 232–4

# III.30 To John Adams

Monticello, January 22, 1821

I was quite rejoiced, dear Sir, to see that you had health and spirits enough to take part in the late convention of your State, for revising its Constitution, and to bear your share in its debates and labors. The amendments of which we have as yet heard, prove the advance of liberalism in the intervening period; and encourage a hope that the human mind will some day get back to the freedom it enjoyed two thousand years ago. This country, which has given to the world the example of physical liberty, owes to it that of moral emancipation also, for as yet it is but nominal with us. The inquisition of public opinion overwhelms in practice, the freedom asserted by the laws in theory.

Our anxieties in this quarter are all concentrated in the question, what does the Holy Alliance in and out of Congress mean to do with us on the Missouri question? And this, by-the-bye, is but the name of the case, it is only the John Doe or Richard Roe of the ejectment. The real question, as seen in the States afflicted with this unfortunate population, is, are our slaves to be presented with freedom and a dagger? For if Congress has the power to regulate the conditions of the inhabitants of the States, within the States, it will be but another exercise of that power, to declare that all shall be free. Are we then to see again Athenian and Lacedemonian confederacies? To wage another Peloponnesian war to settle the ascendency between them? Or is this the tocsin of merely a servile war? That remains to be seen; but not, I hope, by you or me. Surely, they will parley awhile, and give us time to get out of the way. What a Bedlamite is man! But let us turn from our own uneasiness to the miseries of our southern friends. Bolivar and Morillo, it seems, have come to the parley, with dispositions at length to stop the useless effusion of human blood in that quarter. I feared from the beginning, that these people were not yet sufficiently enlightened for self-government; and that after wading through blood and slaughter, they would end in military tyrannies, more or less numerous. Yet as they wished to try the experiment, I wished them success in it; they have now tried it, and will possibly find that their safest road will be an accommodation with the Mother country, which shall hold them together by the single link of the same chief magistrate, leaving to him power enough to keep them in peace with one another, and to themselves the essential power of self-government and self-improvement, until they shall be sufficiently trained by education and habits of freedom to walk safely by themselves. Representative government, native functionaries, a qualified negative on their laws, with a previous security by compact for freedom of commerce, freedom of the press, *habeas corpus* and trial by jury, would make a good beginning. This last would be the school in which their people might begin to learn the exercise of civic duties as well as rights. For freedom of religion they are not yet prepared. The scales of bigotry have not sufficiently fallen from their eyes, to accept it for themselves individually, much less to trust others with it. But that will come in time, as well as a general ripeness to break entirely from the parent stem. You see, my dear Sir, how easily we prescribe for others a cure for their difficulties, while we cannot cure our own. We must leave both, I believe, to heaven, and wrap ourselves up in the mantle of resignation, and of that friendship of which I tender to you the most sincere assurances.

L & B XV: 308–10

## III.31 To Edward Livingston

Monticello, April 4, 1824

Dear Sir, – It was with great pleasure I learned that the good people of New Orleans had restored you again to the councils of our country. I did not doubt the aid it would bring to the remains of our old school in Congress, in which your early labors had been so useful. You will find, I suppose, on revisiting our maritime States, the names of things more changed than the things themselves; that though our old opponents have given up their appellation, they have not, in assuming ours, abandoned their views, and that they are as strong nearly as they ever were. These cares, however, are no longer mine. I resign myself cheerfully to the managers of the ship, and the more contentedly as I am near the end of my voyage. I have learned to be less confident in the conclusions of human reason, and give more credit to the honesty of contrary opinions. The radical idea of the character of the constitution of our government, which I have adopted as a key in cases of doubtful construction, is, that the whole field of government is divided into two departments, domestic and foreign (the States in their mutual relations being of the latter); that the former department is reserved exclusively to the respective States within their own limits, and the latter assigned to a separate set of functionaries, constituting what may be called the foreign branch, which, instead of a federal basis, is established as a distinct government *quoad hoc*, acting as the domestic branch does on the citizens directly and coercively; that these departments have distinct directories, co-ordinate, and equally independent and supreme, each within its own sphere of action. Whenever a doubt arises to which of these branches a power belongs, I try it by this test. I recollect no case where a question simply between citizens of the same State, has been transferred to the foreign department, except that of inhibiting tenders but of metallic money, and *ex post facto* legislation. The causes of these singularities are well remembered.

I thank you for the copy of your speech on the question of national improvement, which I have read with great pleasure, and recognize in it those powers of reasoning and persuasion of which I had formerly seen from you so many proofs. Yet, in candor, I must say it has not removed, in my mind, all the difficulties of the question. And I should really be alarmed at a difference of opinion with you, and suspicious of my own, were it not that I have, as companions in sentiments, the Madisons, the Monroes, the Randolphs, the Macons, all good men and true, of primitive principles. In one sentiment of the speech I particularly concur. "If we have a doubt relative to any power, we ought not to exercise it." When we consider the extensive and deep-seated opposition to this assumption, the conviction entertained by so many, that this deduction of powers by elaborate construction prostrates the rights reserved to the States, the difficulties with which it will rub along in the course of its exercise; that changes of majorities will be changing the system backwards and forwards, so that no undertaking under it will be safe; that there is not a State in the Union which would not give the power willingly, by way of amendment, with some little guard, perhaps, against abuse; I cannot but think it would be the wisest course to ask an express grant of the power. A government held together by the bands of reason only, requires much compromise of opinion; that things even salutary should not be crammed down the throats of dissenting brethren, especially when they may be put into a form to be willingly swallowed, and that a great deal of indulgence is necessary to strengthen habits of harmony and fraternity. In such a case, it seems to me it would be safer and wiser to ask an express grant of the power. This would render its exercise smooth and acceptable to all, and insure to it all the facilities which the States could contribute, to prevent that kind of abuse which all will fear, because all know it is so much practised in public bodies, I mean the bartering of votes. It would reconcile every one, if limited by the proviso, that the federal proportion of each State should be expended within the State. With this single security against partiality and corrupt bargaining, I suppose there is not a State, perhaps not a man in the Union, who would not consent to add this to the powers of the General Government. But age has weaned me from questions of this kind. My delight is now in the passive occupation of reading; and it is with great reluctance I permit my mind ever to encounter subjects of difficult investigation. You have many years yet to come of vigorous activity, and I confidently trust they will be employed in cherishing every measure which may foster our brotherly union, and perpetuate a constitution of government destined to be the primitive and precious model of what is to change the condition of man over the globe. With this confidence, equally strong in your powers and purposes, I pray you to accept the assurance of my cordial esteem and respect.

L & B xvi: 22–6

# IV  Moral Sense, Civic Education, and Freedom of the Press

## IV.1 To Robert Skipwith

Monticello, August 3, 1771

I sat down with a design of executing your request to form a catalogue of books to the amount of about 50 lib. sterl. But could by no means satisfy myself with any partial choice I could make. Thinking therefore it might be as agreeable to you I have framed such a general collection as I think you would wish and might in time find convenient to procure. Out of this you will chuse for yourself to the amount you mentioned for the present year and may hereafter as shall be convenient proceed in completing the whole. A view of the second column in this catalogue would I suppose extort a smile from the face of gravity. Peace to its wisdom! Let me not awaken it. A little attention however to the nature of the human mind evinces that the entertainments of fiction are useful as well as pleasant. That they are pleasant when well written every person feels who reads. But wherein is its utility, asks the reverend sage, big with the notion that nothing can be useful but the learned lumber of Greek and Roman reading with which his head is stored?

I answer, everything is useful which contributes to fix in the principles and practices of virtue. When any original act of charity or of gratitude, for instance, is presented either to our sight or imagination, we are deeply impressed with its beauty and feel a strong desire in ourselves of doing charitable and grateful acts also. On the contrary when we see or read of any atrocious deed, we are disgusted with it's deformity, and conceive an abhorence of vice. Now every emotion of this kind is an exercise of our virtuous dispositions, and dispositions of the mind, like limbs of the body, acquire strength by exercise. But exercise produces habit, and in the instance of which we speak the exercise being of the moral feelings produces a habit of thinking and acting virtuously. We never reflect whether the story we read be truth or fiction. If the painting be lively, and a tolerable picture of nature, we are thrown into a reverie, from which if we awaken it is the fault of the writer. I appeal to every reader of feeling and sentiment whether the fictitious murther of Duncan by Macbeth in Shakespeare does not excite in him as great a horror of villany, as the real one of Henry IV. by Ravaillac as related by Davila? And whether the fidelity of Nelson and generosity of Blandford in Marmontel do not dilate his breast and elevate his sentiments as much as any similar incident which real history can furnish? Does he not in fact feel himself a better man while reading them, and privately covenant to copy the fair example? We neither know nor care whether Lawrence Sterne really went to France, whether he was there accosted by the Franciscan, at first rebuked him unkindly, and then gave him a peace offering: or whether the whole be not fiction. In either case we equally are sorrowful at the rebuke, and secretly resolve *we* will never do so: we are pleased with the subsequent atonement, and view with emulation a soul candidly acknowleging it's fault and making a just reparation. Considering history as a moral exercise, her lessons would be too infrequent if confined to real life. Of those recorded by historians few incidents have been attended with such circumstances as to excite in any high degree this sympathetic emotion of virtue. We are therefore wisely framed to be as warmly interested for a fictitious as for a real personage. The field of imagination is thus laid open to our use and lessons may be formed to illustrate and carry home to the heart every moral rule of life. Thus a lively and lasting sense of filial duty is more effectually impressed on the mind of a son or daughter by reading King Lear, than by all the dry volumes of ethics, and divinity that ever were written. This is my idea of well written Romance, of Tragedy, Comedy and Epic poetry. – If you are fond of speculation the books under the head of Criticism will afford you much pleasure. Of Politics and Trade I have given you a few only of the best books, as you would probably chuse to be not unacquainted with those commercial principles which bring wealth into our country, and the constitutional security we have for the enjoiment of that wealth. In Law I mention a few systematical books, as a knowledge of the minutiae of that science is not necessary for a private gentleman. In Religion, History, Natural philosophy, I have followed the same plan in general. – But whence the necessity of this collection? Come to the new Rowanty,[1] from which you may reach your hand to a library formed on a more extensive plan. Separated from each other but a few paces the possessions of each would be open to the other. A spring centrically

---

[1] Probably Rowandiz, the Arcadian Olympus, the center around which the heavens revolved. TJ likens Monticello to this mythical point. – *Eds.*

situated might be the scene of every evening's joy. There we should talk over the lessons of the day, or lose them in music, chess or the merriments of our family companions. The heart thus lightened our pillows would be soft, and health and long life would attend the happy scene. Come then and bring our dear Tibby with you, the first in your affections, and second in mine. Offer prayers for me too at that shrine to which tho' absent I pray continual devotions. In every scheme of happiness she is placed in the foreground of the picture, as the principal figure. Take that away, and it is no picture for me. Bear my affections to Wintipock[2] clothed in the warmest expressions of sincerity; and to yourself be every human felicity. Adieu.

Ford I: 396–9

## IV.2 A Bill for the More General Diffusion of Knowledge

[1779]

Section I. Whereas it appeareth that however certain forms of government are better calculated than others to protect individuals in the free exercise of their natural rights, and are at the same time themselves better guarded against degeneracy, yet experience hath shewn, that even under the best forms, those entrusted with power have, in time, and by slow operations, perverted it into tyranny; and it is believed that the most effectual means of preventing this would be, to illuminate, as far as practicable, the minds of the people at large, and more especially to give them knowledge of those facts, which history exhibiteth, that, possessed thereby of the experience of other ages and countries, they may be enabled to know ambition under all its shapes, and prompt to exert their natural powers to defeat its purposes; And whereas it is generally true that that people will be happiest whose laws are best, and are best administered, and that laws will be wisely formed, and honestly administered, in proportion as those who form and administer them are wise and honest; whence it becomes expedient for promoting

---

[2] Also spelled Winterpock: the Eppes family plantation in Chesterfield County, Virginia. – *Eds.*

the publick happiness that those persons, whom nature hath endowed with genius and virtue, should be rendered by liberal education worthy to receive, and able to guard the sacred deposit of the rights and liberties of their fellow citizens, and that they should be called to that charge without regard to wealth, birth or other accidental condition or circumstance; but the indigence of the greater number disabling them from so educating, at their own expence, those of their children whom nature hath fitly formed and disposed to become useful instruments for the public, it is better that such should be sought for and educated at the common expence of all, than that the happiness of all should be confined to the weak or wicked:

Sect. II. Be it therefore enacted by the General Assembly, that in every county within this commonwealth, there shall be chosen annually, by the electors qualified to vote for Delegates, three of the most honest and able men of their county, to be called the Aldermen of the county; and that the election of the said Aldermen shall be held at the same time and place, before the same persons, and notified and conducted in the same manner as by law is directed, for the annual election of Delegates for the county.

Sect. III. The person before whom such election is holden shall certify to the court of the said county the names of the Aldermen chosen, in order that the same may be entered of record, and shall give notice of their election to the said Aldermen within a fortnight after such election.

Section IV. The said Aldermen on the first Monday in October, if it be fair, and if not, then on the next fair day, excluding Sunday, shall meet at the court-house of their county, and proceed to divide their said county into hundreds, bounding the same by water courses, mountains, or limits, to be run and marked, if they think necessary, by the county surveyor, and at the county expence, regulating the size of the said hundreds, according to the best of their discretion, so as that they may contain a convenient number of children to make up a school, and be of such convenient size that all the children within each hundred may daily attend the school to be established therein, and distinguishing each hundred by a particular name; which division, with the names of the several hundreds, shall be returned to the court of the county and be entered of record, and shall remain unaltered until the increase or decrease of inhabitants shall render an alteration necessary, in the opinion of any succeeding Alderman, and also in the opinion of the court of the county.

Section v. The electors aforesaid residing within every hundred shall meet on the third Monday in October after the first election of Aldermen, at such place, within their hundred, as the said Aldermen shall direct, notice thereof being previously given to them by such person residing within the hundred as the said Aldermen shall require who is hereby enjoined to obey such requisition, on pain of being punished by amercement [fines] and imprisonment. The electors being so assembled shall choose the most convenient place within their hundred for building a school-house. If two or more places, having a greater number of votes than any others, shall yet be equal between themselves, the Aldermen, or such of them as are not of the same hundred, on information thereof, shall decide between them. The said Aldermen shall forthwith proceed to have a school-house built at the said place, and shall see that the same shall be kept in repair, and, when necessary, that it be rebuilt; but whenever they shall think necessary that it be rebuilt, they shall give notice as before directed, to the electors of the hundred to meet at the said school-house, on such a day as they shall appoint, to determine by vote, in the manner before directed, whether it shall be rebuilt at the same, or what other place in the hundred.

Section vi. At every of those schools shall be taught reading, writing, and common arithmetick, and the books which shall be used therein for instructing the children to read shall be such as will at the same time make them acquainted with Græcian, Roman, English, and American history. At these schools all the free children, male and female, resident within the respective hundred, shall be intitled to receive tuition gratis, for the term of three years, and as much longer, at their private expence, as their parents, guardians, or friends shall think proper.

Section vii. Over every ten of these schools (or such other number nearest thereto, as the number of hundreds in the county will admit, without fractional divisions) an overseer shall be appointed annually by the aldermen at their first meeting, eminent for his learning, integrity, and fidelity to the commonwealth, whose business and duty it shall be, from time to time, to appoint a teacher to each school, who shall give assurance of fidelity to the commonwealth, and to remove him as he shall see cause; to visit every school once in every half year at the least; to examine the scholars; see that any general plan of reading and instruction recommended by the visiters of William and Mary College shall be observed; and to superintend the conduct of the teacher in everything relative to his school.

Section VIII. Every teacher shall receive a salary of — by the year, which, with the expenses of building and repairing the schoolhouses, shall be provided in such manner as other county expences are by law directed to be provided and shall also have his diet, lodging, and washing found him, to be levied in like manner, save only that such levy shall be on the inhabitants of each hundred for the board of their own teacher only.

Section IX. And in order that grammer schools may be rendered convenient to the youth in every part of the commonwealth, be it therefore enacted, that on the first Monday in November, after the first appointment of overseers for the hundred schools, if fair, and if not, then on the next fair day, excluding Sunday, after the hour of one in the afternoon, the said overseer appointed for the schools in the counties of Princess Ann, Norfolk, Nansemond and Isle-of-Wight, shall meet at Nansemond court-house; those for the counties of Southampton, Sussex, Surry and Prince George, shall meet at Sussex court-house; those for the counties of Brunswick, Mecklenburg and Lunenburg, shall meet at Lunenburg court-house; those for the counties of Dinwiddie, Amelia and Chesterfield, shall meet at Chesterfield court-house; those for the counties of Powhatan, Cumberland, Goochland, Henrico and Hanover, shall meet at Henrico court-house; those for the counties of Prince Edward, Charlotte and Halifax, shall meet at Charlotte court-house; those for the counties of Henry, Pittsylvania and Bedford, shall meet at Pittsylvania court-house; those for the counties of Buckingham, Amherst, Albemarle and Fluvanna, shall meet at Albemarle court-house; those for the counties of Botetourt, Rockbridge, Montgomery, Washington and Kentucky, shall meet at Botetourt court-house; those for the counties of Augusta, Rockingham and Greenbriar, shall meet at Augusta court-house; those for the counties of Accomack and Northampton, shall meet at Accomack court-house; those for the counties of Elizabeth City, Warwick, York, Gloucester, James City, Charles City and New-Kent, shall meet at James City court-house; those for the counties of Middlesex, Essex, King and Queen, King William and Caroline, shall meet at King and Queen court-house; those for the counties of Lancaster, Northumberland, Richmond and Westmoreland, shall meet at Richmond court-house; those for the counties of King George, Stafford, Spotsylvania, Prince William and Fairfax, shall meet at Spotsylvania court-house; those for the counties of Loudoun and Fauquier, shall meet at Loudoun court-house; those for the counties of Culpeper, Orange and Louisa, shall meet at Orange court-house; those for the county of Shenandoah and Frederick, shall meet at Frederick court-house; those for the counties of Hampshire and Berkeley, shall meet at Berkeley courthouse; and those for the counties of Yohogania, Monongalia, and Ohio, shall meet at the Monongalia court-house; and shall fix on such place in some one of the counties in their district as shall be most proper for situating a grammer school-house, endeavoring that the situation be as central as may be to the inhabitants of the said counties, that it be furnished with good water, convenient to plentiful supplies of provision and fuel, and more than all things that it be healthy. And if a majority of the overseers present should not concur in their choice of any one place proposed, the method of determining shall be as follows: If two places only were proposed, and the votes be divided, they shall decide between them by fair and equal lot; if more than two places were proposed, the question shall be put on those two which on the first division had the greater number of votes; or if no two places had a greater number of votes than the others, then it shall be decided by fair and equal lot (unless it can be agreed by a majority of votes) which of the places having equal numbers shall be thrown out of the competition, so that the question shall be put on the remaining two, and if on this ultimate question the votes shall be equally divided, it shall then be decided finally by lot.

Section x. The said overseers having determined the place at which the grammer school for their district shall be built, shall forthwith (unless they can otherwise agree with the proprietors of the circumjacent lands as to location and price) make application to the clerk of the county in which the said house is to be situated, who shall thereupon issue a writ, in the nature of a writ of *ad quod damnum*, directed to the sheriff of the said county commanding him to summon and impannel twelve fit persons to meet at the place, so destined for the grammer school-house, on a certain day, to be named in the said writ, not less than five, nor more than ten, days from the date thereof; and also to give notice of the same to the proprietors and tenants of the lands to be viewed if they be found within the county, and if not, then to their agents therein if any they have. Which freeholders shall be charged by the said sheriff impartially, and to the best of their skill and judgment to view the lands round about the said place, and to locate and circumscribe, by certain meets and bounds, one hundred acres thereof, having regard therein principally to the benefit and convenience of the said school, but respecting in some measure also the convenience of the said proprietors, and to value and appraise the same in so many several and distinct parcels as shall be owned or held by several and distinct owners or tenants, and according to their respective interests and estates therein. And after such location and appraisement so made, the said sheriff shall forthwith return the same under the hands and seals of the said jurors, together with the writ, to the clerk's office of the said county and the right and property of the said proprietors and tenants in the said lands so circumscribed shall be immediately devested and be transferred to the commonwealth for the use of the said grammer school, in full and absolute dominion, any want of consent or disability to consent in the said owners or tenants notwithstanding. But it shall not be lawful for the said overseers so to situate the grammer school-house, nor to the said jurors so to locate the said lands, as to include the mansion-house of the proprietor of the lands, nor the offices, curtilage, or garden, thereunto immediately belonging.

Sect. XI. The said overseers shall forthwith proceed to have a house of brick or stone, for the said grammer school, with necessary offices, built on the said lands, which grammer school-house shall contain a room for the school, a hall to dine in, four rooms for a master and usher, and ten or twelve lodging rooms for the scholars.

Sect. XII. To each of the said grammer schools shall be allowed out of the public treasury, the sum of _____ pounds, out of which shall be paid by the Treasurer, on warrant from the Auditors, to the proprietors or tenants of the lands located, the value of their several interests as fixed by the jury, and the balance thereof shall be delivered to the said overseers to defray the expense of the said buildings.

Sect. XIII. In either of these grammer schools shall be taught the Latin and Greek languages, English Grammer, geography, and the higher part of numerical arithmetick, to wit, vulgar and decimal fractions, and the extrication of the square and cube roots.

Sect. XIV. A visiter from each county constituting the district shall be appointed, by the overseers, for the county, in the month of October annually, either from their own body or from their county at large, which visiters, or the greater part of them, meeting together at the said grammer school on the first Monday in November, if fair, and if not, then on the next fair day, excluding Sunday, shall have power to choose their own Rector, who shall call and preside at future meetings, to employ from time to time a master, and if necessary, an usher, for the said school, to remove them at their will, and to settle the price of tuition to be paid by the scholars. They shall also visit the school twice in every year at the least, either together or separately at their discretion, examine the scholars, and see that any general plan of instruction recommended by the visiters of William and Mary College shall be observed. The said masters and ushers, before they enter on the execution of their office, shall give assurance of fidelity to the commonwealth.

Sect. XV. A steward shall be employed, and removed at will by the master, on such wages as the visiters shall direct; which steward shall see to the procuring provisions, fuel, servants for cooking, waiting, house cleaning, washing, mending, and gardening on the most reasonable terms; the expence of which, together with the steward's wages, shall be divided equally among all the scholars boarding either on the public or private expence. And the part of those who are on private expence, and also the price of their tuitions due to the master or usher, shall be paid quarterly by the respective scholars, their parents, or guardians, and shall be recoverable, if withheld, together with costs, on motion in any Court of Record, ten days notice thereof being previously given to the party, and a jury impannelled to try the issue joined, or enquire of the damages. The said steward shall also, under the direction of the visiters, see that the houses be kept in repair, and necessary enclosures be made and repaired, the accounts for which, shall, from time to time, be submitted to the Auditors, and on their warrant paid by the Treasurer.

Sect. XVI. Every overseer of the hundred schools shall, in the month of September annually, after the most diligent and impartial examination and inquiry, appoint from among the boys who shall have been two years at the least at some one of the schools under his superintendance, and whose parents are too poor to give them farther education, some one of the best and most promising genius and disposition, to proceed to the grammer school of his district; which appointment shall be made in the court-house of the county, and on the court day for that month if fair, and if not, then on the next fair day, excluding Sunday, in the presence of the Aldermen, or two of them at the least, assembled on the bench for that purpose, the said overseer being previously sworn by them to make such appointment, without favor or affection, according to the best of his skill and judgment, and being interrogated by the said Aldermen, either on their own motion, or on suggestions from the parents, guardians, friends, or teachers of the children, competitors for such appointment; which teachers the parents shall attend for the information of the Aldermen. On which interrogatories the said Aldermen, if they be not satisfied with the appointment proposed, shall have right to negative it; whereupon the said visiter may proceed to make a new appointment, and the said Aldermen again to interrogate and negative, and so *toties quoties* until an appointment be approved.

Sect. XVII. Every boy so appointed shall be authorized to proceed to the grammer school of his district, there to be educated and boarded during such time as is hereafter limited; and his quota of the expences of the house together with a compensation to the master or usher for his tuition, at the rate of twenty dollars by the year, shall be paid by the Treasurer quarterly on warrant from the Auditors.

Sect. XVIII. A visitation shall be held, for the purpose of probation, annually at the said grammer school on the last Monday in September, if fair, and if not, then on the next fair day, excluding Sunday, at which one third of the boys sent thither by appointment of the said overseers, and who shall have been there one year only, shall be discontinued as public foundationers, being those who, on the most diligent examination and inquiry, shall be thought to be the least promising genius and disposition; and of those who shall have been there two years, all shall be discontinued save one only the best in genius and disposition, who shall be at liberty to continue there four years longer on the public foundation, and shall thence forward be deemed a senior.

Sect. XIX. The visiters for the districts which, or any part of which, be southward and westward of James river, as known by that name, or by the names of Fluvanna and Jackson's river, in every other year, to wit, at the probation meetings held in the years, distinguished in the Christian computation by odd numbers, and the visiters for all the other districts at their said meetings to be held in those years, distinguished by even numbers, after diligent examination and inquiry as before directed, shall chuse one among the said seniors, of the best learning and most hopeful genius and disposition, who shall be authorized by them to proceed to William and Mary College; there to be educated, boarded, and clothed, three years; the expence of which annually shall be paid by the Treasurer on warrant from the Auditors.

Ford II: 220–9

## IV.3 To Peter Carr[1]

Paris, August 19, 1785

Dear Peter, – I received, by Mr. Mazzei, your letter of April the 20th. I am much mortified to hear that you have lost so much time; and that, when you arrived in Williamsburg, you were not at all advanced from what you were when you left Monticello. Time now begins to be precious to you. Every day you lose will retard a day your entrance on that public stage whereon you may begin to be useful to yourself. However, the way to repair the loss is to improve the future time. I trust, that with your dispositions, even the acquisition of science is a pleasing employment. I can assure you, that the possession of it is, what (next to an honest heart) will above all things render you dear to your friends, and give you fame and promotion in your own country. When your mind shall be well improved with science, nothing will be necessary to place you in the highest points of view, but to pursue the interests of your country, the interests of your friends, and your own interests also,

[1] TJ's nephew. – *Eds.*

with the purest integrity, the most chaste honor. The defect of these virtues can never be made up by all the other acquirements of body and mind. Make these, then, your first object. Give up money, give up fame, give up science, give the earth itself and all it contains, rather than do an immoral act. And never suppose, that in any possible situation, or under any circumstances, it is best for you to do a dishonorable thing, however slightly so it may appear to you. Whenever you are to do a thing, though it can never be known but to yourself, ask yourself how you would act were all the world looking at you, and act accordingly. Encourage all your virtuous dispositions, and exercise them whenever an opportunity arises; being assured that they will gain strength by exercise, as a limb of the body does, and that exercise will make them habitual. From the practice of the purest virtue, you may be assured you will derive the most sublime comforts in every moment of life, and in the moment of death. If ever you find yourself environed with difficulties and perplexing circumstances, out of which you are at a loss how to extricate yourself, do what is right, and be assured that that will extricate you the best out of the worst situations. Though you cannot see, when you take one step, what will be the next, yet follow truth, justice, and plain dealing, and never fear their leading you out of the labyrinth, in the easiest manner possible. The knot which you thought a Gordian one, will untie itself before you. Nothing is so mistaken as the supposition, that a person is to extricate himself from a difficulty, by intrigue, by chicanery, by dissimulation, by trimming, by an untruth, by an injustice. This increases the difficulties tenfold; and those, who pursue these methods, get themselves so involved at length, that they can turn no way but their infamy becomes more exposed. It is of great importance to set a resolution, not to be shaken, never to tell an untruth. There is no vice so mean, so pitiful, so contemptible; and he who permits himself to tell a lie once, finds it much easier to do it a second and third time, till at length it becomes habitual; he tells lies without attending to it, and truths without the world's believing him. This falsehood of the tongue leads to that of the heart, and in time depraves all its good dispositions.

An honest heart being the first blessing, a knowing head is the second. It is time for you now to begin to be choice in your reading; to begin to pursue a regular course in it; and not to suffer yourself to be turned to the right or left by reading anything out of that course. I have long ago digested a plan for you, suited to the circumstances in which you will be placed. This I will detail to you, from time to time, as you advance. For the present, I advise you to begin a course of ancient history, reading everything in the original and not in translations. First read Goldsmith's history of Greece. This will give you a digested view of that field. Then take up ancient history in the detail, reading the following books, in the following order: Herodotus, Thucydides, Xenophontis Anabasis, Arrian, Quintus Curtius, Diodorus Siculus, Justin. This shall form the first stage of your historical reading, and is all I need mention to you now. The next will be of Roman history (Livy, Sallust, Cæsar, Cicero's epistles, Suetonius, Tacitus, Gibbon). From that, we will come down to modern history. In Greek and Latin poetry, you have read or will read at school, Virgil, Terence, Horace, Anacreon, Theocritus, Homer, Euripides, Sophocles. Read also Milton's "Paradise Lost," Shakspeare, Ossian, Pope's and Swift's works, in order to form your style in your own language. In morality, read Epictetus, Xenophontis Memorabilia, Plato's Socratic dialogues, Cicero's philosophies, Antoninus, and Seneca. In order to assure a certain progress in this reading, consider what hours you have free from the school and the exercises of the school. Give about two of them, every day, to exercise; for health must not be sacrificed to learning. A strong body makes the mind strong. As to the species of exercise, I advise the gun. While this gives a moderate exercise to the body, it gives boldness, enterprise, and independence to the mind. Games played with the ball, and others of that nature, are too violent for the body, and stamp no character on the mind. Let your gun, therefore, be the constant companion of your walks. Never think of taking a book with you. The object of walking is to relax the mind. You should therefore not permit yourself even to think while you walk; but divert yourself by the objects surrounding you. Walking is the best possible exercise. Habituate yourself to walk very far. The Europeans value themselves on having subdued the horse to the uses of man; but I doubt whether we have not lost more than we have gained, by the use of this animal. No one has occasioned so much the degeneracy of the human body. An Indian goes on foot nearly as far in a day, for a long journey, as an enfeebled white does on his horse; and he will tire the best horses.

There is no habit you will value so much as that of walking far without fatigue. I would advise you to take your exercise in the afternoon: not because it is the best time for exercise, for certainly it is not; but because it is the best time to spare from your studies; and habit will soon reconcile it to health, and render it nearly as useful as if you gave to that the more precious hours of the day. A little walk of half an hour, in the morning, when you first rise, is advisable also. It shakes off sleep, and produces other good effects in the animal economy. Rise at a fixed and an early hour, and go to bed at a fixed and early hour also. Sitting up late at night is injurious to the health, and not useful to the mind. Having ascribed proper hours to exercise, divide what remain (I mean of your vacant hours) into three portions. Give the principal to History, the other two, which should be shorter, to Philosophy and Poetry. Write to me once every month or two, and let me know the progress you make. Tell me in what manner you employ every hour in the day. The plan I have proposed for you is adapted to your present situation only. When that is changed, I shall propose a corresponding change of plan. I have ordered the following books to be sent to you from London, to the care of Mr. Madison: Herodotus, Thucydides, Xenophon's Hellenics, Anabasis and Memorabilia, Cicero's works, Baretti's Spanish and English Dictionary, Martin's Philosophical Grammar, and Martin's Philosophia Britannica. I will send you the following from hence: Bezout's Mathematics, De la Lande's Astronomy, Muschenbrock's Physics, Quintus Curtius, Justin, a Spanish Grammar, and some Spanish books. You will observe that Martin, Bezout, De la Lande, and Muschenbrock, are not in the preceding plan. They are not to be opened till you go to the University. You are now, I expect, learning French. You must push this; because the books which will be put into your hands when you advance into Mathematics, Natural philosophy, Natural history, &c., will be mostly French, these sciences being better treated by the French than the English writers. Our future connection with Spain renders that the most necessary of the modern languages, after the French. When you become a public man, you may have occasion for it, and the circumstance of your possessing that language, may give you a preference over other candidates. I have nothing further to add for the present, but husband well your time, cherish your instructors,

strive to make everybody your friend; and be assured that nothing
will be so pleasing as your success to, Dear Peter,
>Yours affectionately.

>L & B v: 82–7

## iv.4 To John Banister, Junior

Paris, October 15, 1785

Dear Sir, – I should sooner have answered the paragraph in your
letter, of September the 19th, respecting the best seminary for the
education of youth in Europe, but that it was necessary for me to
make inquiries on the subject. The result of these has been, to
consider the competition as resting between Geneva and Rome.
They are equally cheap, and probably are equal in the course of
education pursued. The advantage of Geneva is, that students
acquire there the habit of speaking French. The advantages of Rome
are, the acquiring a local knowledge of a spot so classical and so
celebrated; the acquiring the true pronunciation of the Latin language; a just taste in the fine arts, more particularly those of painting, sculpture, architecture, and music; a familiarity with those
objects and processes of agriculture which experience has shown
best adapted to a climate like ours; and lastly, the advantage of a
fine climate for health. It is probable, too, that by being boarded in
a French family, the habit of speaking that language may be
obtained. I do not count on any advantage to be derived, in Geneva,
from a familiar acquaintance with the principles of that government.
The late revolution has rendered it a tyrannical aristocracy, more
likely to give ill than good ideas to an American. I think the balance
in favor of Rome. Pisa is sometimes spoken of as a place of education. But it does not offer the first and third of the advantages of
Rome. But why send an American youth to Europe for education?
What are the objects of an useful American education? Classical
knowledge, modern languages, chiefly French, Spanish, and Italian;
Mathematics, Natural philosophy, Natural history, Civil history,
and Ethics. In Natural philosophy, I mean to include Chemistry
and Agriculture, and in Natural history, to include Botany, as well

as the other branches of those departments. It is true that the habit of speaking the modern languages cannot be so well acquired in America; but every other article can be as well acquired at William and Mary college, as at any place in Europe. When college education is done with, and a young man is to prepare himself for public life, he must cast his eyes (for America) either on Law or Physics. For the former, where can he apply so advantageously as to Mr. Wythe? For the latter, he must come to Europe: the medical class of students, therefore, is the only one which need come to Europe. Let us view the disadvantages of sending a youth to Europe. To enumerate them all, would require a volume. I will select a few. If he goes to England, he learns drinking, horse racing, and boxing. These are the peculiarities of English education. The following circumstances are common to education in that, and the other countries of Europe. He acquires a fondness for European luxury and dissipation, and a contempt for the simplicity of his own country; he is fascinated with the privileges of the European aristocrats, and sees, with abhorrence, the lovely equality which the poor enjoy with the rich, in his own country; he contracts a partiality for aristocracy or monarchy; he forms foreign friendships which will never be useful to him, and loses the seasons of life for forming, in his own country, those friendships which, of all others, are the most faithful and permanent; he is led, by the strongest of all the human passions, into a spirit for female intrigue, destructive of his own and others' happiness, or a passion for whores, destructive of his health, and, in both cases, learns to consider fidelity to the marriage bed as an ungentlemanly practice, and inconsistent with happiness; he recollects the voluptuary dress and arts of the European women, and pities and despises the chaste affections and simplicity of those of his own country; he retains, through life, a fond recollection, and a hankering after those places, which were the scenes of his first pleasures and of his first connections; he returns to his own country, a foreigner, unacquainted with the practices of domestic economy, necessary to preserve him from ruin, speaking and writing his native tongue as a foreigner, and therefore unqualified to obtain those distinctions, which eloquence of the pen and tongue ensures in a free country; for I would observe to you, that what is called style in writing or speaking is formed very early in life, while the imagination is warm, and impressions are permanent. I am of opinion, that there never was an instance of a man's writing or speaking his native tongue with elegance, who passed from fifteen to twenty years of age out of the country where it was spoken. Thus, no instance exists of a person's writing two languages perfectly. That will always appear to be his native language, which was most familiar to him in his youth. It appears to me, then, that an American, coming to Europe for education, loses in his knowledge, in his morals, in his health, in his habits, and in his happiness. I had entertained only doubts on this head before I came to Europe: what I see and hear, since I came here, proves more than I had even suspected. Cast your eye over America: who are the men of most learning, of most eloquence, most beloved by their countrymen and most trusted and promoted by them? They are those who have been educated among them, and whose manners, morals, and habits, are perfectly homogeneous with those of the country.

Did you expect by so short a question, to draw such a sermon on yourself? I dare say you did not. But the consequences of foreign education are alarming to me, as an American. I sin, therefore, through zeal, whenever I enter on the subject. You are sufficiently American to pardon me for it. Let me hear of your health, and be assured of the esteem with which I am, dear Sir, your friend and servant.

L & B v: 185–8

## IV.5 To George Wythe

Paris, August 13, 1786

Dear Sir, – Your favors of Jan. 10 & Feb. 10, came to hand on the 20th & 2d of May. I availed myself of the first opportunity which occurred, by a gentleman going to England, of sending to Mr. Joddrel a copy of the Notes on our country, with a line informing him that it was you who had emboldened me to take that liberty. Madison, no doubt, informed you of the reason why I had sent only a single copy to Virginia. Being assured by him that they will not do the harm I had apprehended, but on the contrary may do some good, I propose to send thither the copies remaining on hand, which are fewer than I had intended. But of the numerous corrections they need, there are one or two so essential that I must have them made, by printing a few new leaves & substituting them for the old. This will be done while they are engraving a map which I have constructed of the country from Albemarle sound to Lake Erie, & which will be inserted in the book. A bad French translation which is getting out here, will probably oblige me to publish the original more freely, which it neither deserved nor was ever intended. Your wishes, which are laws to me, will justify my destining a copy for you, otherwise I should as soon have thought of sending you a horn-book [primer or elementary textbook]; for there is no truth there that is not familiar to you, and it's errors I should hardly have proposed to treat you with.

Immediately on the receipt of your letter, I wrote to a correspondent at Florence to inquire after the family of Tagliaferro as you desired. I received his answer two days ago, a copy of which I now inclose. The original shall be sent by some other occasion. I will have the copper-plate immediately engraved. This may be ready within a few days, but the probability is that I shall be long getting an opportunity of sending it to you, as these rarely occur. You do not mention the size of the plate but, presuming it is intended for labels for the inside of books, I shall have it made of a proper size for that. I shall omit the word *agisos*, according to the license you allow me, because I think the beauty of a motto is to condense much matter in as few words as possible. The word omitted will be supplied by every reader. The European papers have announced that the assembly of Virginia were occupied on the revisal of their code of laws. This, with some other similar intelligence, has contributed much to convince the people of Europe, that what the English papers are constantly publishing of our anarchy, is false; as they are sensible that such a work is that of a people only who are in perfect tranquillity. Our act for freedom of religion is extremely applauded.[1] The ambassadors & ministers of the several nations of Europe resident at this court have asked of me copies of it to send to their sovereigns, and it is inserted at full length in several books now in the press; among others, in the new *Encyclopédie*. I think it will produce considerable good even in these countries where ignorance, superstition, poverty, & oppression of body & mind in every

---

[1] A Bill for Establishing Religious Freedom, repr. *infra*, VII.1. – *Eds.*

form, are so firmly settled on the mass of the people, that their redemption from them can never be hoped. If the Almighty had begotten a thousand sons, instead of one, they would not have sufficed for this task. If all the sovereigns of Europe were to set themselves to work to emancipate the minds of their subjects from their present ignorance & prejudices, & that as zealously as they now endeavor the contrary, a thousand years would not place them on that high ground on which our common people are now setting out. Ours could not have been so fairly put into the hands of their own common sense had they not been separated from their parent stock & kept from contamination, either from them, or the other people of the old world, by the intervention of so wide an ocean. To know the worth of this, one must see the want of it here. I think by far the most important bill in our whole code is that for the diffusion of knowlege among the people.[2] No other sure foundation can be devised, for the preservation of freedom and happiness. If anybody thinks that kings, nobles, or priests are good conservators of the public happiness send them here. It is the best school in the universe to cure them of that folly. They will see here with their own eyes that these descriptions of men are an abandoned confederacy against the happiness of the mass of the people. The omnipotence of their effect cannot be better proved than in this country particularly, where notwithstanding the finest soil upon earth, the finest climate under heaven, and a people of the most benevolent, the most gay and amiable character of which the human form is susceptible, where such a people I say, surrounded by so many blessings from nature, are yet loaded with misery by kings, nobles and priests, and by them alone. Preach, my dear Sir, a crusade against ignorance; establish & improve the law for educating the common people. Let our countrymen know that the people alone can protect us against these evils, and that the tax which will be paid for this purpose is not more than the thousandth part of what will be paid to kings, priests & nobles who will rise up among us if we leave the people in ignorance. The people of England, I think, are less oppressed than here [i.e., France]. But it needs but half an eye to see, when among them, that the foundation is laid in their dispositions for the establishment of a despotism. Nobility, wealth &

[2] A Bill for the More General Diffusion of Knowledge, repr. *supra*, IV.2. – *Eds.*

pomp are the objects of their adoration. They are by no means the free-minded people we suppose them in America. Their learned men too are few in number, and are less learned and infinitely less emancipated from prejudice than those of this country. An event too seems to be preparing, in the order of things, which will probably decide the fate of that country. It is no longer doubtful that the harbour of Cherburg will be complete, that it will be a most excellent one, & capacious enough to hold the whole navy of France. Nothing has ever been wanting to enable this country to invade that, but a naval force conveniently stationed to protect the transports. This change of situation must oblige the English to keep up a great standing army, and there is no King, who, with sufficient force, is not always ready to make himself absolute. My paper warns me it is time to recommend myself to the friendly recollection of Mrs. Wythe, of Colo. Tagliaferro & his family & particularly of Mr. R. T.; and to assure you of the affectionate esteem with which I am Dear Sir your friend and servt.

Ford IV: 266–70

## IV.6 To Peter Carr

Paris, August 10, 1787

Dear Peter, – I have received your two letters of Decemb. 30 and April 18, and am very happy to find by them, as well as by letters from Mr. Wythe, that you have been so fortunate as to attract his notice & good will; I am sure you will find this to have been one of the most fortunate events of your life, as I have ever been sensible it was of mine. I inclose you a sketch of the sciences to which I would wish you to apply in such order as Mr. Wythe shall advise; I mention also the books in them worth your reading, which submit to his correction. Many of these are among your father's books, which you should have brought to you. As I do not recollect those of them not in his library, you must write to me for them, making out a catalogue of such as you think you shall have occasion for in 18 months from the date of your letter, & consulting Mr. Wythe on the subject. To this sketch I will add a few particular observations.

1. Italian. I fear the learning this language will confound your French and Spanish. Being all of them degenerated dialects of the

Latin, they are apt to mix in conversation. I have never seen a person speaking the three languages who did not mix them. It is a delightful language, but late events having rendered the Spanish more useful, lay it aside to prosecute that.

2. Spanish. Bestow great attention on this, & endeavor to acquire an accurate knowlege of it. Our future connections with Spain & Spanish America will render that language a valuable acquisition. The antient history of a great part of America, too, is written in that language. I send you a dictionary.

3. Moral philosophy. I think it lost time to attend lectures in this branch. He who made us would have been a pitiful bungler if he had made the rules of our moral conduct a matter of science. For one man of science, there are thousands who are not. What would have become of them? Man was destined for society. His morality therefore was to be formed to this object. He was endowed with a sense of right & wrong merely relative to this. This sense is as much a part of his nature as the sense of hearing, seeing, feeling; it is the true foundation of morality, & not the τὸ καλόν, truth, &c. as fanciful writers have imagined. The moral sense, or conscience, is as much a part of man as his leg or arm. It is given to all human beings in a stronger or weaker degree, as force of members is given them in a greater or less degree. It may be strengthened by exercise, as may any particular limb of the body. This sense is submitted indeed in some degree to the guidance of reason; but it is a small stock which is required for this: even a less one than what we call common sense. State a moral case to a ploughman & a professor. The former will decide it as well, & often better than the latter, because he has not been led astray by artificial rules. In this branch therefore read good books because they will encourage as well as direct your feelings. The writings of Sterne particularly form the best course of morality that ever was written. Besides these read the books mentioned in the enclosed paper; and above all things lose no occasion of exercising your dispositions to be grateful, to be generous, to be charitable, to be humane, to be true, just, firm, orderly, courageous &c. Consider every act of this kind as an exercise which will strengthen your moral faculties, & increase your worth.

4. Religion. Your reason is now mature enough to examine this object. In the first place divest yourself of all bias in favour of

novelty & singularity of opinion. Indulge them in any other subject rather than that of religion. It is too important, & the consequences of error may be too serious. On the other hand shake off all the fears & servile prejudices under which weak minds are servilely crouched. Fix reason firmly in her seat, and call to her tribunal every fact, every opinion. Question with boldness even the existence of a god; because, if there be one, he must more approve of the homage of reason, than that of blindfolded fear. You will naturally examine first the religion of your own country. Read the bible then, as you would read Livy or Tacitus. The facts which are within the ordinary course of nature you will believe on the authority of the writer, as you do those of the same kind in Livy & Tacitus. The testimony of the writer weighs in their favor in one scale, and their not being against the laws of nature does not weigh against them. But those facts in the bible which contradict the laws of nature, must be examined with more care, and under a variety of faces. Here you must recur to the pretensions of the writer to inspiration from god. Examine upon what evidence his pretensions are founded, and whether that evidence is so strong as that its falsehood would be more improbable than a change in the laws of nature in the case he relates. For example in the book of Joshua we are told the sun stood still several hours. Were we to read that fact in Livy or Tacitus we should class it with their showers of blood, speaking of statues, beasts, &c. But it is said that the writer of that book was inspired. Examine therefore candidly what evidence there is of his having been inspired. The pretension is entitled to your inquiry, because millions believe it. On the other hand you are astronomer enough to know how contrary it is to the law of nature that a body revolving on its axis as the earth does, should have stopped, should not by that sudden stoppage have prostrated animals, trees, buildings, and should after a certain time have resumed its revolution, & that without a second general prostration. Is this arrest of the earth's motion, or the evidence which affirms it, most within the law of probabilities? You will next read the new testament. It is the history of a personage called Jesus. Keep in your eye the opposite pretensions 1. of those who say he was begotten by god, born of a virgin, suspended & reversed the laws of nature at will, & ascended bodily into heaven: and 2. of those who say he was a man of illegitimate birth, of a benevolent heart, enthusiastic mind, who set out without pretensions to divinity, ended in believing them, & was punished capitally for sedition by being gibbeted according to the Roman law which punished the first commission of that offence by whipping, & the second by exile or death *in furcâ*. See this law in the *Digest Lib.* 48. tit. 19. § 28. 3. & *Lipsius Lib.* 2. *de cruce.* cap. 2. These questions are examined in the books I have mentioned under the head of religion, & several others. They will assist you in your inquiries, but keep your reason firmly on the watch in reading them all. Do not be frightened from this inquiry by any fear of it's consequences. If it ends in a belief that there is no god, you will find incitements to virtue in the comfort & pleasantness you feel in it's exercise, and the love of others which it will procure you. If you find reason to believe there is a god, a consciousness that you are acting under his eye, & that he approves you, will be a vast additional incitement; if that there be a future state, the hope of a happy existence in that increases the appetite to deserve it; if that Jesus was also a god, you will be comforted by a belief of his aid and love. *In fine*, I repeat that you must lay aside all prejudice on both sides, & neither believe nor reject anything because any other persons, or description of persons have rejected or believed it. Your own reason is the only oracle given you by heaven, and you are answerable not for the rightness but uprightness of the decision. I forgot to observe when speaking of the new testament that you should read all the histories of Christ, as well of those whom a council of ecclesiastics have decided for us to be Pseudo-evangelists, as those they named Evangelists. Because these Pseudo-evangelists pretended to inspiration as much as the others, and you are to judge their pretensions by your own reason, & not by the reason of those ecclesiastics. Most of these are lost. There are some however still extant, collected by Fabricius which I will endeavor to get & send you.

5. Travelling. This makes men wiser, but less happy. When men of sober age travel, they gather knolege which they may apply usefully for their country, but they are subject ever after to recollections mixed with regret, their affections are weakened by being extended over more objects, & they learn new habits which cannot be gratified when they return home. Young men who travel are exposed to all these inconveniences in a higher degree, to others still more serious, and do not acquire that wisdom for which a previous foundation is requisite by repeated & just observations at home.

The glare of pomp & pleasure is analogous to the motion of their blood, it absorbs all their affection & attention, they are torn from it as from the only good in this world, and return to their home as to a place of exile & condemnation. Their eyes are for ever turned back to the object they have lost, & it's recollection poisons the residue of their lives. Their first & most delicate passions are hackneyed on unworthy objects here, & they carry home only the dregs, insufficient to make themselves or anybody else happy. Add to this that a habit of idleness, an inability to apply themselves to business is acquired & renders them useless to themselves & their country. These observations are founded in experience. There is no place where your pursuit of knolege will be so little obstructed by foreign objects as in your own country, nor any wherein the virtues of the heart will be less exposed to be weakened. Be good, be learned, & be industrious, & you will not want the aid of travelling to render you precious to your country, dear to your friends, happy within yourself. I repeat my advice to take a great deal of exercise, & on foot. Health is the first requisite after morality. Write to me often & be assured of the interest I take in your success, as well as of the warmth of those sentiments of attachment with which I am, dear Peter, your affectionate friend.

P.S. Let me know your age in your next letter. Your cousins here are well & desire to be remembered to you.

Ford IV: 427–34

## IV.7 *Notes on Virginia:* Query XIV

... Another object of the revisal [of the laws of Virginia] is, to diffuse knowledge more generally through the mass of the people. This bill[1] proposes to lay off every country into small districts of five or six miles square, called hundreds and in each of them to establish a school for teaching, reading, writing, and arithmetic. The tutor to be supported by the hundred, and every person in it entitled to send their children three years gratis, and as much longer as they please, paying for it. These schools to be under

---

[1] See *supra*, IV.2. – *Eds.*

a visitor who is annually to chuse the boy of best genius in the school, of those whose parents are too poor to give them further education, and to send him forward to one of the grammar schools, of which twenty are proposed to be erected in different parts of the country, for teaching Greek, Latin, geography, and the higher branches of numerical arithmetic. Of the boys thus sent in any one year, trial is to be made at the grammar schools one or two years, and the best genius of the whole selected, and continued six years, and the residue dismissed. By this means twenty of the best geniuses will be raked from the rubbish annually, and be instructed, at the public expence, so far as the grammar schools go. At the end of six years instruction, one half are to be discontinued (from among whom the grammar schools will probably be supplied with future masters); and the other half, who are to be chosen for the superiority of their parts and disposition, are to be sent and continued three years in the study of such sciences as they shall chuse, at William and Mary college, the plan of which is proposed to be enlarged, as will be hereafter explained, and extended to all the useful sciences. The ultimate result of the whole scheme of education would be the teaching all the children of the State reading, writing, and common arithmetic; turning out ten annually, of superior genius, well taught in Greek, Latin, geography, and the higher branches of arithmetic; turning out ten others annually, of still superior parts, who, to those branches of learning, shall have added such of the sciences as their genius shall have led them to; the furnishing to the wealthier part of the people convenient schools at which their children may be educated at their own expence. – The general objects of this law are to provide an education adapted to the years, to the capacity, and the condition of every one, and directed to their freedom and happiness. Specific details were not proper for the law. These must be the business of the visitors entrusted with its execution. The first stage of this education being the schools of the hundreds, wherein the great mass of the people will receive their instruction, the principal foundations of future order will be laid here. Instead, therefore, of putting the Bible and Testament into the hands of the children at an age when their judgments are not sufficiently matured for religious inquiries, their memories may here be stored with the most useful facts from Grecian, Roman, European, and American history. The first elements of morality too may be instilled into their minds; such as, when further developed as their judgments advance in strength, may teach them how to work out their own greatest happiness, by shewing them that it does not depend on the condition of life in which chance has placed them, but is always the result of a good conscience, good health, occupation, and freedom in all just pursuits. – Those whom either the wealth of their parents or the adoption of the state shall destine to higher degrees of learning, will go on to the grammar schools, which constitute the next stage, there to be instructed in the languages. The learning Greek and Latin, I am told, is going into disuse in Europe. I know not what their manners and occupations may call for: but it would be very ill-judged in us to follow their example in this instance. There is a certain period of life, say from eight to fifteen or sixteen years of age, when the mind like the body is not yet firm enough for laborious and close operations. If applied to such, it falls an early victim to premature exertion; exhibiting, indeed, at first, in these young and tender subjects, the flattering appearance of their being men while they are yet children, but ending in reducing them to be children when they should be men. The memory is then most susceptible and tenacious of impressions; and the learning of languages being chiefly a work of memory, it seems precisely fitted to the powers of this period, which is long enough too for acquiring the most useful languages, antient and modern. I do not pretend that language is science. It is only an instrument for the attainment of science. But that time is not lost which is employed in providing tools for future operation: more especially as in this case the books put into the hands of the youth for this purpose may be such as will at the same time impress their minds with useful facts and good principles. If this period be suffered to pass in idleness, the mind becomes lethargic and impotent, as would the body it inhabits if unexercised during the same time. The sympathy between body and mind during their rise, progress and decline, is too strict and obvious to endanger our being misled while we reason from the one to the other. As soon as they are of sufficient age, it is supposed they will be sent on from the grammar schools to the university, which constitutes our third and last stage, there to study those sciences which may be adapted to their views. – By that part of our plan which prescribes the selection of the youths of genius from among the classes of the poor, we hope to avail the state of those talents which nature has sown as liberally among the poor as the rich, but which perish without use, if not sought for and cultivated. – But of all the views of this law none is more important, none more legitimate, than that of rendering the people the safe, as they are the ultimate, guardians of their own liberty. For this purpose the reading in the first stage, where *they* will receive their whole education, is proposed, as has been said, to be chiefly historical. History, by apprising them of the past, will enable them to judge of the future; it will avail them of the experience of other times and other nations; it will qualify them as judges of the actions and designs of men; it will enable them to know ambition under every disguise it may assume; and knowing it, to defeat its views. In every government on earth is some trace of human weakness, some germ of corruption and degeneracy, which cunning will discover, and wickedness insensibly open, cultivate and improve. Every government degenerates when trusted to the rulers of the people alone. The people themselves therefore are its only safe depositories. And to render even them safe, their minds must be improved to a certain degree. This indeed is not all that is necessary, though it be essentially necessary. An amendment of our constitution must here come in aid of the public education. The influence over government must be shared among all the people. If every individual which composes their mass participates of the ultimate authority, the government will be safe; because the corrupting the whole mass will exceed any private resources of wealth; and public ones cannot be provided but by levies on the people. In this case every man would have to pay his own price. The government of Great Britain has been corrupted, because but one man in ten has a right to vote for members of parliament. The sellers of the government, therefore, get nine-tenths of their price clear. It has been thought that corruption is restrained by confining the right of suffrage to a few of the wealthier of the people: but it would be more effectually restrained by an extension of that right to such numbers as would bid defiance to the means of corruption.

Lastly, it is proposed, by a bill in this revisal, to begin a public library and gallery, by laying out a certain sum annually in books, paintings, and statues.

Ford III: 251–5

## IV.8 To Thomas Mann Randolph

New York, May 30, 1790

Dear Sir, – I at length find myself, tho not quite well, yet sufficiently so to resume business in a moderate degree. I have therefore to answer your two favors of Apr 23 & May 3, and in the first place to thank you for your attention to the Paccan [pecan], Gloucester & European walnuts which will be great acquisitions at Monticello. I will still ask your attention to Mr. Foster's boring machine, lest he should go away suddenly, & so the opportunity of getting it be lost. – I enquired of Mr. Hamilton the quantity of coal imported; but he tells me there are not returns as yet sufficient to ascertain it; but as soon as there shall be I shall be informed. I am told there is a considerable prejudice against our coal in these Northern states. I do not know whence it proceeds: perhaps from the want of attention to the different species, and an ignorant application of them to cross-purposes. I have not begun my meteorological diary; because I have not yet removed to the house I have taken. I remove tomorrow: but as far as I can judge from it's aspects there will not be one position to be had for the thermometer free from the influence of the sun both morning & evening. However, as I go into it, only till I can get a better, I shall hope ere long to find a less objectionable situation. You know that during my short stay at Monticello I kept a diary of the weather. Mr. Madison has just received one, comprehending the same period, kept at his father's in Orange. The hours of observation were the same, and he has the fullest confidence in the accuracy of the observer. All the morning observations in Orange are lower than those of Monticello, from one to, I believe, 15 or 16 degrees: the afternoon observations are near as much higher than those of Monticello. Nor will the variations permit us to ascribe them to any supposed irregularities in either tube, because, in that case, at the same point the variations would always be the same, which it is not. You have often been sensible that in the afternoon, or rather evening, the air has become warmer in ascending the mountain. The same is true in the morning. This might account for a higher station of the mercury in the morning observations at Monticello. Again when the air is equally dry in the lower & higher situations, which may be supposed the case in the warmest part of the day, the mercury should be lower on the latter, because, all other circumstances the same, the nearer the common surface the warmer the air. So that on a mountain it ought really to be warmer in the morning & cooler in the heat of the day than on the common plain; but not in so great a degree as these observations indicate. As soon as I am well enough I intend to examine them more accurately. – Your resolution to apply to the study of the law is wise in my opinion, & at the same time to mix with it a good degree of attention to the farm. The one will relieve the other. The study of the law is useful in a variety of points of view. It qualifies a man to be useful to himself, to his neighbors, & to the public. It is the most certain stepping stone to preferment in the political line. In political economy I think [Adam] Smith's wealth of nations the best book extant, in the science of government Montesquieu's spirit of laws is generally recommended. It contains indeed a great number of political truths; but also an equal number of heresies: so that the reader must be constantly on his guard. There has been lately published a letter of Helvetius who was the intimate friend of Montesquieu & whom he consulted before the publication of his book. Helvetius advised him not to publish it: & in this letter to a friend he gives us a solution for the mixture of truth & error found in this book. He says Montesquieu was a man of immense reading, that he had commonplaced[1] all his reading, & that his object was to throw the whole contents of his commonplace book into systematical order, & to shew his ingenuity by reconciling the contradictory facts it presented. Locke's little book on government is perfect as far as it goes. Descending from theory to practice there is no

---

[1] I.e. Montesquieu had copied extracts from his extensive reading into his commonplace book. – *Eds.*

better book than the Federalist. Burgh's Political disquisitions are good also, especially after reading De Lolme. Several of Hume's political essays are good. There are some excellent books of Theory written by Turgot & the economists of France. For parliamentary knowlege, the *Lex parliamentaria* is the best book. – On my return to Virginia in the fall, I cannot help hoping some practicable plan may be devised for your settling in Albemarle, should your inclination lead you to it. Nothing could contribute so much to my happiness were it at the same time consistent with yours. You might get into the assembly for that county as soon as you should please. A motion has been made in the Senate to remove the federal government to Philadelphia. There was a trial of strength on a question for a week's postponement. On that it was found there would be 11 for the removal & 13 against it. The motion was therefore withdrawn & made in the other house where it is still depending, & of very incertain event. – The question of the assumption is again brought on.[2] The parties were so nearly equal on the former trial that it is very possible that with some modifications it may yet prevail. The tonnage bill will probably pass, and must, I believe, produce salutary effects. It is a mark of energy in our government, in a case where I believe it cannot be parried. The French revolution still goes on well, tho the danger of a suspension of paiment [payment] is very imminent. Their appeal to the inhabitants of their colonies to say on what footing they wish to be placed, will end, I hope, in our free admission into their islands with our produce. This precedent must have consequences. It is impossible the world should continue long insensible to so evident a truth as that the right to have commerce & intercourse with our neighbors is a natural right. To suppress this neighborly intercourse is an exercise of force, which we shall have a just right to remove when [we are] the superior force.

Present my warm affections to the girls. I am afraid they do not follow my injunctions of answering by the first post the weekly letter I address to them. I inclose some letters for Patsy from Paris,

---

[2] TJ refers to Treasury Secretary Alexander Hamilton's proposal (January 14, 1790) that the federal government assume responsibility for funding (i.e. paying off) the Revolutionary-era war debts of the several states. TJ vehemently but unsuccessfully opposed this scheme for the reasons given in VIII.14 – *Eds.*

and the newspapers for yourself with assurances of the sincere & cordial esteem of Dear Sir Your Affectionate friend.

P.S. I must refer the description of the Mould board[3] to another occasion. The President is well enough to do business. Colo. Bland dangerously ill.

Ford v: 171–5

## IV.9 To Dr. Joseph Priestley

Philadelphia, January 27, 1800

Dear Sir, – In my letter of the 18th, I omitted to say any thing of the languages as part of our proposed university. It was not that I think, as some do, that they are useless. I am of a very different opinion. I do not think them essential to the obtaining eminent degrees of science; but I think them very useful towards it. I suppose there is a portion of life during which our faculties are ripe enough for this, & for nothing more useful. I think the Greeks & Romans have left us the present models which exist of fine composition, whether we examine them as works of reason, or of style & fancy; and to them we probably owe these characteristics of modern composition. I know of no composition of any other antient people, which merits the least regard as a model for it's matter or style. To all this I add, that to read the Latin & Greek authors in their original, is a sublime luxury; and I deem luxury in science to be at least as justifiable as in architecture, painting, gardening, or the other arts. I enjoy Homer in his own language infinitely beyond Pope's translation of him, & both beyond the dull narrative of the same events by Dares Phrygius; & it is an innocent enjoyment. I thank on my knees, him who directed my early education, for having put into my possession this rich source of delight; and I would not exchange it for anything which I could then have acquired, & have not since acquired. With this regard for those languages, you will acquit me of meaning to omit them. About 20 years ago, I drew a bill for our legislature,[1] which proposed to lay off every county

[3] A curved metal plough blade that TJ invented. – *Eds.*
[1] See *supra*, IV.2. – *Eds.*

into hundreds or townships of 5 or 6 miles square, in the centre of each of which was to be a free English school; the whole state was further laid off into 10 districts, in each of which was to be a college for teaching the languages, geography, surveying, and other useful things of that grade; and then a single University for the sciences. It was received with enthusiasm; but as I had proposed that Wm & Mary, under an improved form, should be the University, & that was at that time pretty highly Episcopal, the dissenters after a while began to apprehend some secret design of a preference to that sect and nothing could then be done. About 3 years ago they enacted that part of my bill which related to English schools, except that instead of obliging, they left it optional in the court of every county to carry it into execution or not. I think it probable the part of the plan for the middle grade of education, may also be brought forward in due time. In the meanwhile, we are not without a sufficient number of good country schools, where the languages, geography, & the first elements of Mathematics, are taught. Having omitted this information in my former letter, I thought it necessary now to supply it, that you might know on what base your superstructure was to be reared. I have a letter from M. Dupont [de Nemours], since his arrival at N. York, dated the 20th, in which he says he will be in Philadelphia within about a fortnight from that time; but only on a visit. How much would it delight me if a visit from you at the same time, were to shew us two such illustrious foreigners embracing each other in my country, as the asylum for whatever is great & good. Pardon, I pray you, the temporary delirium which has been excited here, but which is fast passing away. The Gothic idea that we are to look backwards instead of forwards for the improvement of the human mind, and to recur to the annals of our ancestors for what is most perfect in government, in religion & in learning, is worthy of those bigots in religion & government, by whom it has been recommended, & whose purposes it would answer. But it is not an idea which this country will endure; and the moment of their showing it is fast ripening; and the signs of it will be their respect for you, & growing detestation of those who have dishonored our country by endeavors to disturb our tranquility in it. No one has felt this with more sensibility than, my dear Sir, your respectful & affectionate friend & servant.

Ford VII: 413–16

## IV.10 To Dr. Joseph Priestley

Washington, April 9, 1803

Dear Sir, – While on a short visit lately to Monticello, I received from you a copy of your comparative view of Socrates and Jesus, and I avail myself of the first moment of leisure after my return to acknowledge the pleasure I had in the perusal of it, and the desire it excited to see you take up the subject on a more extended scale. In consequence of some conversation with Dr. Rush, in the year 1798–99, I had promised some day to write him a letter giving him my view of the Christian system. I have reflected often on it since, and even sketched the outlines in my own mind. I should first take a general view of the moral doctrines of the most remarkable of the ancient philosophers, of whose ethics we have sufficient information to make an estimate, say Pythagoras, Epicurus, Epictetus, Socrates, Cicero, Seneca, Antoninus. I should do justice to the branches of morality they have treated well; but point out the importance of those in which they are deficient. I should then take a view of the deism and ethics of the Jews, and show in what a degraded state they were, and the necessity they presented of a reformation. I should proceed to a view of the life, character, and doctrines of Jesus who, sensible of incorrectness of their ideas of the Deity, and of morality, endeavored to bring them to the principles of a pure deism, and juster notions of the attributes of God, to reform their moral doctrines to the standard of reason, justice and philanthropy, and to inculcate the belief of a future state. This view would purposely omit the question of his divinity, and even his inspiration. To do him justice, it would be necessary to remark the disadvantages his doctrines had to encounter, not having been committed to writing by himself, but by the most unlettered of men, by memory, long after they had heard them from him; when much was forgotten, much misunderstood, and presented in every paradoxical shape. Yet such are the fragments remaining as to show a master workman, and that his system of morality was the most benevolent and sublime probably that has been ever taught, and consequently more perfect than those of any of the ancient philosophers. His character and doctrines have received still greater injury from those who pretend to be his special disciples, and who have disfigured and sophisticated his actions and precepts, from views of personal interest, so as to induce the unthinking part of mankind to throw off the whole system in disgust, and to pass sentence as an impostor on the most innocent, the most benevolent, the most eloquent and sublime character that ever has been exhibited to man. This is the outline; but I have not the time, and still less the information which the subject needs. It will, therefore, rest with me in contemplation only. You are the person of all others would do it best, and most promptly. You have all the materials at hand, and you put together with ease. I wish you could be induced to extend your late work to the whole subject. I have not heard particularly what is the state of your health; but as it has been equal to the journey to Philadelphia, perhaps it might encourage the curiosity you must feel to see for once this place, which nature has formed on a beautiful scale, and circumstances destine for a great one. As yet we are but a cluster of villages; we cannot offer you the learned society of Philadelphia; but you will have that of a few characters whom you esteem, and a bed and hearty welcome with one who will rejoice in every opportunity of testifying to you his high veneration and affectionate attachment.

Ford VIII: 224–5

## IV.11 To Dr. Benjamin Rush

Washington, April 21, 1803

Dear Sir, – In some of the delightful conversations with you, in the evenings of 1798–99, and which served as an anodyne to the afflictions of the crisis through which our country was then laboring, the Christian religion was sometimes our topic; and I then promised you, that one day or other, I would give you my views of it. They are the result of a life of inquiry and reflection, and very different from that anti-

Christian system imputed to me by those who know nothing of my opinions. To the corruptions of Christianity I am, indeed, opposed; but not to the genuine precepts of Jesus himself. I am a Christian, in the only sense in which he wished any one to be; sincerely attached to his doctrines, in preference to all others; ascribing to himself every *human* excellence; and believing he never claimed any other. At the short interval since these conversations, when I could justifiably abstract my mind from public affairs, the subject has been under my contemplation. But the more I considered it, the more it expanded beyond the measure of either my time or information. In the moment of my late departure from Monticello, I received from Dr. Priestley, his little treatise of "Socrates and Jesus Compared." This being a section of the general view I had taken of the field, it became a subject of reflection while on the road, and unoccupied otherwise. The result was, to arrange in my mind a syllabus, or outline of such an estimate of the comparative merits of Christianity, as I wished to see executed by some one of more leisure and information for the task, than myself. This I now send you, as the only discharge of my promise I can probably ever execute. And in confiding it to you, I know it will not be exposed to the malignant perversions of those who make every word from me a text for new misrepresentations and calumnies. I am moreover averse to the communication of my religious tenets to the public; because it would countenance the presumption of those who have endeavored to draw them before that tribunal, and to seduce public opinion to erect itself into that inquisition over the rights of conscience, which the laws have so justly proscribed. It behooves every man who values liberty of conscience for himself, to resist invasions of it in the case of others; or their case may, by change of circumstances, become his own. It behooves him, too, in his own case, to give no example of concession, betraying the common right of independent opinion, by answering questions of faith, which the laws have left between God and himself. Accept my affectionate salutations.

*Syllabus of an estimate of the merit of the doctrines of Jesus, compared with those of others*

In a comparative view of the Ethics of the enlightened nations of antiquity, of the Jews and of Jesus, no notice should be taken of the corruptions of reason among the ancients, to wit, the idolatry and superstition of the vulgar, nor of the corruptions of Christianity by the learned among its professors.

Let a just view be taken of the moral principles inculcated by the most esteemed of the sects of ancient philosophy, or of their individuals; particularly Pythagoras, Socrates, Epicurus, Cicero, Epictetus, Seneca, Antoninus.

I. Philosophers. 1. Their precepts related chiefly to ourselves, and the government of those passions which, unrestrained, would disturb our tranquillity of mind.[1] In this branch of philosophy they were really great.

2. In developing our duties to others, they were short and defective. They embraced, indeed, the circles of kindred and friends, and inculcated patriotism, or the love of our country in the aggregate, as a primary obligation: towards our neighbors and countrymen they taught justice, but scarcely viewed them as within the circle of benevolence. Still less have they inculcated peace, charity and love to our fellow men, or embraced with benevolence the whole family of mankind.

II. Jews. 1. Their system was Deism; that is, the belief in one only God. But their ideas of him and of his attributes were degrading and injurious.

2. Their Ethics were not only imperfect, but often irreconcilable with the sound dictates of reason and morality, as they respect intercourse with those around us; and repulsive and anti-social, as respecting other nations. They needed reformation, therefore, in an eminent degree.

III. Jesus. In this state of things among the Jews, Jesus appeared. His parentage was obscure; his condition poor; his education null; his natural endowments great; his life correct and innocent: he was meek, benevolent, patient, firm, disinterested, and of the sublimest eloquence.

---

[1] To explain, I will exhibit the heads of Seneca's and Cicero's philosophical works, the most extensive of any we have received from the ancients. Of ten heads in Seneca, seven relate to ourselves, viz. *de ira, consolatio, de tranquilitate, de constantia sapientis, de otio sapientis, de vita beata, de brevitate vitae*; two relate to others, *de clementia, de beneficiis*; and one relates to the government of the world, *de providentia*. Of eleven tracts of Cicero, five respect ourselves, viz. *de finibus, Tusculana, academica, paradoxa, de Senectute*; one, *de officiis*, relates partly to ourselves, partly to others; one, *de amicitia*, relates to others; and four are on different subjects, to wit, *de natura deorum, de divinatione, de fato*, and *somnium Scipionis*.

The disadvantages under which his doctrines appear are remarkable.

1. Like Socrates and Epictetus, he wrote nothing himself.

2. But he had not, like them, a Xenophon or an Arrian to write for him. I name not Plato, who only used the name of Socrates to cover the whimsies of his own brain. On the contrary, all the learned of his country, entrenched in its power and riches, were opposed to him, lest his labors should undermine their advantages; and the committing to writing his life and doctrines fell on unlettered and ignorant men; who wrote, too, from memory, and not till long after the transactions had passed.

3. According to the ordinary fate of those who attempt to enlighten and reform mankind, he fell an early victim to the jealousy and combination of the altar and the throne, at about thirty-three years of age, his reason having not yet attained the *maximum* of its energy, nor the course of his preaching, which was but of three years at most, presented occasions for developing a complete system of morals.

4. Hence the doctrines which he really delivered were defective as a whole, and fragments only of what he did deliver have come to us mutilated, misstated, and often unintelligible.

5. They have been still more disfigured by the corruptions of schismatizing followers, who have found an interest in sophisticating and perverting the simple doctrines he taught, by engrafting on them the mysticisms of a Grecian sophist, frittering them into subtleties, and obscuring them with jargon, until they have caused good men to reject the whole in disgust, and to view Jesus himself as an impostor.

Notwithstanding these disadvantages, a system of morals is presented to us, which, if filled up in the style and spirit of the rich fragments he left us, would be the most perfect and sublime that has ever been taught by man.

The question of his being a member of the Godhead, or in direct communication with it, claimed for him by some of his followers, and denied by others, is foreign to the present view, which is merely an estimate of the intrinsic merits of his doctrines.

1. He corrected the Deism of the Jews, confirming them in their belief of one only God, and giving them juster notions of his attributes and government.

2. His moral doctrines, relating to kindred and friends, were more pure and perfect than those of the most correct of the philosophers, and greatly more so than those of the Jews; and they went far beyond both in inculcating universal philanthropy, not only to kindred and friends, to neighbors and countrymen, but to all mankind, gathering all into one family, under the bonds of love, charity, peace, common wants and common aids. A development of this head will evince the peculiar superiority of the system of Jesus over all others.

3. The precepts of philosophy, and of the Hebrew code, laid hold of actions only. He pushed his scrutinies into the heart of man; erected his tribunal in the region of his thoughts, and purified the waters at the fountain head.

4. He taught, emphatically, the doctrines of a future state, which was either doubted, or disbelieved by the Jews; and wielded it with efficacy, as an important incentive, supplementary to the other motives to moral conduct.

L & B x: 379–85

## IV.12 To Judge John Tyler

Washington, June 28, 1804

Dear Sir, – Your favor of the 10th instant has been duly received. Amidst the direct falsehoods, the misrepresentations of truth, the calumnies and the insults resorted to by a faction to mislead the public mind, and to overwhelm those entrusted with its interests, our support is to be found in the approving voice of our conscience and country, in the testimony of our fellow citizens, that their confidence is not shaken by these artifices. When to the plaudits of the honest multitude, the sober approbation of the sage in his closet is added, it becomes a gratification of an higher order. It is the sanction of wisdom superadded to the voice of affection. The terms, therefore, in which you are so good as to express your satisfaction with the course of the present administration cannot but give me great pleasure. I may err in my measures, but never shall deflect from the intention to fortify the public liberty by every possible means, and to put it out of the power of the few to riot on the labors of the many. No experiment can be more interesting than that we are now trying, and which we trust will end in establishing the fact, that man may be governed by reason and truth. Our first object should therefore be, to leave open to him all the avenues to truth. The most effectual hitherto found, is the freedom of the press. It is therefore, the first shut up by those who fear the investigation of their actions. The firmness with which the people have withstood the late abuses of the press, the discernment they have manifested between truth and falsehood, show that they may safely be trusted to hear everything true and false, and to form a correct judgment between them. As little is it necessary to impose on their senses, or dazzle their minds by pomp, splendor, or forms. Instead of this artificial, how much surer is that real respect, which results from the use of their reason, and the habit of bringing everything to the test of common sense.

I hold it, therefore, certain, that to open the doors of truth, and to fortify the habit of testing everything by reason, are the most effectual manacles we can rivet on the hands of our successors to prevent their manacling the people with their own consent. The panic into which they were artfully thrown in 1798, the frenzy which was excited in them by their enemies against their apparent readiness to abandon all the principles established for their own protection, seemed for awhile to countenance the opinions of those who say they cannot be trusted with their own government. But I never doubted their rallying; and they did rally much sooner than I expected. On the whole, that experiment on their credulity has confirmed my confidence in their ultimate good sense and virtue.

I lament to learn that a like misfortune has enabled you to estimate the afflictions of a father on the loss of a beloved child. However terrible the possibility of such another accident, it is still a blessing for you of inestimable value that you would not even then descend childless to the grave. Three sons, and hopeful ones too, are a rich treasure. I rejoice when I hear of young men of virtue and talents, worthy to receive, and likely to preserve the splendid inheritance of self-government, which we have acquired and shaped for them.

The complement of midshipmen for the Tripoline squadron, is full; and I hope the frigates have left the Capes by this time. I have, however, this day, signed warrants of midshipmen for the two young gentlemen you recommended. These will be forwarded by the Secretary of the Navy. He tells me that their first services [are] to be performed on board the gun boats.

Accept my friendly salutations, and assurances of great esteem and respect.

Washington IV: 548–50

## IV.13 To Thomas Seymour

Washington, February 11, 1807

Sir, – The mass of business which occurs during a session of the Legislature, renders me necessarily unpunctual in acknowledging the receipt of letters, and in answering those which will admit of delay. This must be my apology for being so late in noticing the receipt of the letter of December 20th, addressed to me by yourself, and several other republican characters of your State of high respectability. I have seen with deep concern the afflicting oppression under which the republican citizens of Connecticut suffer from an unjust majority. The truths expressed in your letter have been long exposed to the nation through the channel of the public papers, and are the more readily believed because most of the States during the momentary ascendancy of kindred majorities, in them have seen the same spirit of opposition prevail.

With respect to the countervailing prosecutions now instituted in the Court of the United States in Connecticut, I had heard but little, and certainly, I believe, never expressed a sentiment on them. That a spirit of indignation and retaliation should arise when an opportunity should present itself, was too much within the human constitution to excite either surprise or censure, and confined to an appeal to truth only, it cannot lessen the useful freedom of the press.

As to myself, conscious that there was not a *truth* on earth which I feared should be known, I have lent myself willingly as the subject of a great experiment, which was to prove that an administration, conducting itself with integrity and common understanding, cannot be battered down, even by the falsehoods of a licentious press, and consequently still less by the press, as restrained within the legal and wholesome limits of truth. This experiment was wanting for the world to demonstrate the falsehood of the pretext that freedom of the press is incompatible with orderly government. I have never therefore even contradicted the thousands of calumnies so industriously propagated against myself. But the fact being once established, that the press is impotent when it abandons itself to falsehood, I leave to others to restore it to its strength, by recalling it within the pale of truth. Within that it is a noble institution, equally the friend of science and of civil liberty. If this can once be effected in your State, I trust we shall soon see its citizens rally to the republican principles of our Constitution, which unite their sister-States into one family. It would seem impossible that an intelligent people, with the faculty of reading and right of thinking, should continue much longer to slumber under the pupilage of an interested aristocracy of priests and lawyers, persuading them to distrust themselves, and to let them think for them. I sincerely wish that your efforts may awaken them from this voluntary degradation of mind, restore them to a due estimate of themselves and their fellow citizens, and a just abhorrence of the falsehoods and artifices which have seduced them. Experience of the use made by federalism of whatever comes from me, obliges me to suggest the caution of considering my letter as private. I pray you to present me respectfully to the other gentlemen who joined in the letter to me, and to whom this is equally addressed, and to accept yourself my salutations, and assurances of great esteem and consideration.

L & B XI: 154–6


## IV.14 To John Norvell

Washington, June 14, 1807

Sir, – Your letter of May 9 has been duly received. The subject it proposes would require time & space for even moderate development. My occupations limit me to a very short notice of them. I think there does not exist a good elementary work on the organization of society into civil government: I mean a work which presents in one full & comprehensive view the system of principles on which such an organization should be founded, according to the rights of

nature. For want of a single work of that character, I should recommend Locke on Government, Sidney, Priestley's Essay on the
first Principles of Government, Chipman's Principles of Government, & the Federalist. Adding, perhaps, Beccaria on crimes & punishments, because of the demonstrative manner in which he has
treated that branch of the subject. If your views of political inquiry
go further, to the subjects of money & commerce, Smith's Wealth
of Nations is the best book to be read, unless Say's Political Economy can be had, which treats the same subject on the same principles, but in a shorter compass & more lucid manner. But I believe
this work has not been translated into our language.

History, in general, only informs us what bad government is.
But as we have employed some of the best materials of the British
constitution in the construction of our own government, a knolege
of British history becomes useful to the American politician. There
is, however, no general history of that country which can be recommended. The elegant one of Hume[1] seems intended to disguise &
discredit the good principles of the government, and is so plausible & pleasing in it's style & manner, as to instil it's errors &
heresies insensibly into the minds of unwary readers. Baxter has
performed a good operation on it.[2] He has taken the text of Hume
as his ground work, abridging it by the omission of some details of
little interest, and wherever he has found him endeavoring to mislead, by either the suppression of a truth or by giving it a false
coloring, he has changed the text to what it should be, so that we
may properly call it Hume's history republicanised. He has moreover continued the history (but indifferently) from where Hume left
it, to the year 1800. The work is not popular in England, because
it is republican; and but a few copies have ever reached America. It
is a single 4to. volume. Adding to this Ludlow's Memoirs, Mrs.
M'Cauley's & Belknap's histories, a sufficient view will be presented
of the free principles of the English constitution.

To your request of my opinion of the manner in which a newspaper should be conducted, so as to be most useful, I should answer,
"by restraining it to true facts & sound principles only." Yet I fear
such a paper would find few subscribers. It is a melancholy truth,

---

[1] David Hume, *History of England* (London, 1762). – *Eds.*
[2] See also *infra*, IV.18 – *Eds.*

that a suppression of the press could not more compleatly deprive the nation of it's benefits, than is done by it's abandoned prostitution to falsehood. Nothing can now be believed which is seen in a newspaper. Truth itself becomes suspicious by being put into that polluted vehicle. The real extent of this state of misinformation is known only to those who are in situations to confront facts within their knolege with the lies of the day. I really look with commiseration over the great body of my fellow citizens, who, reading newspapers, live & die in the belief, that they have known something of what has been passing in the world in their time; whereas the accounts they have read in newspapers are just as true a history of any other period of the world as of the present, except that the real names of the day are affixed to their fables. General facts may indeed be collected from them, such as that Europe is now at war, that Bonaparte has been a successful warrior, that he has subjected a great portion of Europe to his will, &c., &c.; but no details can be relied on. I will add, that the man who never looks into a newspaper is better informed than he who reads them; inasmuch as he who knows nothing is nearer to truth than he whose mind is filled with falsehoods & errors. He who reads nothing will still learn the great facts, and the details are all false.

Perhaps an editor might begin a reformation in some such way as this. Divide his paper into 4 chapters, heading the 1st, Truths. 2d, Probabilities. 3d, Possibillities. 4th, Lies. The first chapter would be very short, as it would contain little more than authentic papers, and information from such sources, as the editor would be willing to risk his own reputation for their truth. The 2d would contain what, from a mature consideration of all circumstances, his judgment should conclude to be probably true. This, however, should rather contain too little than too much. The 3d & 4th should be professedly for those readers who would rather have lies for their money than the blank paper they would occupy.

Such an editor too, would have to set his face against the demoralising practice of feeding the public mind habitually on slander, & the depravity of taste which this nauseous aliment induces. Defamation is becoming a necessary of life; insomuch, that a dish of tea in the morning or evening cannot be digested without this stimulant. Even those who do not believe these abominations, still read them with complaisance to their auditors, and instead of the abhorrence & indignation which should fill a virtuous mind, betray a secret pleasure in the possibility that some may believe them, tho they do not themselves. It seems to escape them, that it is not he who prints, but he who pays for printing a slander, who is it's real author.

These thoughts on the subjects of your letter are hazarded at your request. Repeated instances of the publication of what has not been intended for the public eye, and the malignity with which political enemies torture every sentence from me into meanings imagined by their own wickedness only, justify my expressing a solicitude, that this hasty communication may in nowise be permitted to find it's way into the public papers. Not fearing these political bull-dogs, I yet avoid putting myself in the way of being baited by them, and do not wish to volunteer away that portion of tranquillity, which a firm execution of my duties will permit me to enjoy.

I tender you my salutations, and best wishes for your success.

Ford IX: 71–5

## IV.15 To William Short

Monticello, September 6, 1808

Dear Sir, – I avail myself of the last moment allowed by the departure of the post to acknowledge the receipt of your letters of the 27th and 31st *ultimo*, and to say in answer to the last, that any one of the three persons you there propose would be approved as to their politics, for in appointments to office the government refuses to know any differences between descriptions of republicans, all of whom are in principle, and co-operate, with the government. Biddle we know, and have formed an excellent opinion of him. His travelling and exercise in business must have given him advantages. I am much pleased with the account you give of the sentiments of the federalists of Philadelphia as to the embargo, and that they are not in sentiment with the insurgents of the north. The papers have lately advanced in boldness and flagitiousness beyond even themselves. Such daring and atrocious lies as fill the third and fourth columns of the third page of the *United States Gazette* of August 31st, were never before, I believe, published with impunity in any country. However, I have from the beginning determined to submit myself as the subject on whom may be proved the impotency of a free press in a country like ours, against those who conduct themselves honestly and enter into no intrigue. I admit at the same time that restraining the press *to truth*, as the present laws do, is the only way of making it useful. But I have thought necessary first to prove it can never be dangerous. Not knowing whether I shall have another occasion to address you here, be assured that my sincere affections and wishes for your success and happiness accompany you everywhere.

L & B XII: 159–60

## IV.16 To Thomas Jefferson Randolph[1]

Washington, November 24, 1808

My Dear Jefferson, – I have just recieved the inclosed letter under cover from Mr. Bankhead which I presume is from Anne and will inform you she is well. Mr. Bankhead has consented to go and pursue his studies at Monticello, and live with us till his pursuits or circumstances may require a separate establishment. Your situation, thrown at such a distance from us and alone, cannot but give us all, great anxieties for you. As much has been secured for you, by your particular position and the acquaintance to which you have been recommended, as could be done towards shielding you from the dangers which surround you. But thrown on a wide world, among entire strangers without a friend or guardian to advise so young too and with so little experience of mankind, your dangers are great, and still your safety must rest on yourself. A determination never to do what is wrong, prudence, and good humor, will go far towards securing to you the estimation of the world. When I recollect that at 14 years of age, the whole care and direction of my self was thrown on my self entirely, without a relation or friend qualified to advise or guide me, and recollect the various sorts of bad company with which I associated from time to time, I am astonished I did not turn off with some of them, and become as worthless to society

[1] TJ's grandson. – *Eds.*

as they were. I had the good fortune to become acquainted very early with some characters of very high standing, and to feel the incessant wish that I could even become what they were. Under temptations and difficulties, I could ask myself what would Dr. Small, Mr. Wythe, Peyton Randolph do in this situation? What course in it will ensure me their approbation? I am certain that this mode of deciding on my conduct tended more to it's correctness than any reasoning powers I possessed. Knowing the even and dignified line they pursued, I could never doubt for a moment which of two courses would be in character for them. Whereas seeking the same object through a process of moral reasoning, and with the jaundiced eye of youth, I should often have erred. From the circumstances of my position I was often thrown into the society of horse-racers, cardplayers, Foxhunters, scientific and professional men, and of dignified men; and many a time have I asked myself, in the enthusiastic moment of the death of a fox, the victory of a favorite horse, the issue of a question eloquently argued at the bar or in the great Council of the nation, well, which of these kinds of reputation should I prefer? That of a horse jockey? A foxhunter? An Orator? Or the honest advocate of my country's rights? Be assured my dear Jefferson, that these little returns into ourselves, this self-cathechising habit, is not trifling, nor useless, but leads to the prudent selection and steady pursuits of what is right. I have mentioned good humor as one of the preservatives of our peace and tranquillity. It is among the most effectual, and it's effect is so well imitated and aided artificially by politeness, that this also becomes an acquisition of first rate value. In truth, politeness is artificial good humor, it covers the natural want of it, and ends by rendering habitual a substitute nearly equivalent to the real virtue. It is the practice of sacrificing to those whom we meet in society all the little conveniences and preferences which will gratify them, and deprive us of nothing worth a moment's consideration; it is the giving a pleasing and flattering turn to our expressions which will conciliate others, and make them pleased with us as well as themselves. How cheap a price for the good will of another! When this is in return for a rude thing said by another, it brings him to his senses, it mortifies and corrects him in the most salutary way, and places him at the feet of your good nature in the eyes of the company. But in stating prudential rules for our government in society I must not omit the important one of never entering into dispute or argument with another. I never yet saw an instance of one of two disputants convincing the other by argument. I have seen many on their getting warm, becoming rude, and shooting one another. Conviction is the effect of our own dispassionate reasoning, either in solitude, or weighing within ourselves dispassionately what we hear from others standing uncommitted in argument ourselves. It was one of the rules which above all others made Doctr. Franklin the most amiable of men in society, "never to contradict any body." If he was urged to anounce an opinion, he did it rather by asking questions, as if for information, or by suggesting doubts. When I hear another express an opinion, which is not mine, I say to myself, He has a right to his opinion, as I to mine; why should I question it. His error does me no injury, and shall I become a Don Quixot to bring all men by force of argument, to one opinion? If a fact be misstated, it is probable he is gratified by a belief of it, and I have no right to deprive him of the gratification. If he wants information he will ask it, and then I will give it in measured terms; but if he still believes his own story, and shows a desire to dispute the fact with me, I hear him and say nothing. It is his affair, not mine, if he prefers error. There are two classes of disputants most frequently to be met with among us. The first is of young students just entered the threshold of science, with a first view of it's outlines, not yet filled up with the details and modifications which a further progress would bring to their knowledge. The other consists of the ill-tempered and rude men in society who have taken up a passion for politics. (Good humor and politeness never introduce into mixed society a question on which they foresee there will be a difference of opinion.) From both of these classes of disputants, my dear Jefferson, keep aloof, as you would from the infected subjects of yellow fever or pestilence. Consider yourself, when with them, as among the patients of Bedlam needing medical more than moral counsel. Be a listener only, keep within yourself, and endeavor to establish with yourself the habit of silence, especially in politics. In the fevered state of our country, no good can ever result from any attempt to set one of these fiery zealots to rights either in fact or principle. They are determined as to the facts they will believe, and the opinions on which they will act. Get by them, therefore as you would by an angry bull: it is not for a man of sense to dispute the road with such an animal. You will be more exposed than others to have these animals shaking their horns at you, because of the relation in which you stand with me and to hate me as a chief in the antagonist party your presence will be to them what the vomit-grass is to the sick dog, a nostrum for producing an ejaculation. Look upon them exactly with that eye, and pity them as objects to whom you can administer only occasional ease. My character is not within their power. It is in the hands of my fellow citizens at large, and will be consigned to honor or infamy by the verdict of the republican mass of our country, according to what themselves will have seen, not what their enemies and mine shall have said. Never therefore consider these puppies in politics as requiring any notice from you, and always shew that you are not afraid to leave my character to the umpirage of public opinion. Look steadily to the pursuits which have carried you to Philadelphia, be very select in the society you attach yourself to; avoid taverns, drinkers, smoakers, and idlers and dissipated persons generally; for it is with such that broils and contentions arise, and you will find your path more easy and tranquil. The limits of my paper warn me that it is time for me to close with my affectionate Adieux.

P.S. Present me affectionately to Mr. Ogilvie, and in doing the same to Mr. Peale tell him I am writing with his polygraph[1] and shall send him mine the first moment I have leisure enough to pack it.

Ford IX: 230–4

## IV.17 To James Fishback

Monticello, September 27, 1809

Sir, – Your favor of June 5th came to hand in due time, and I have to acknowledge my gratification at the friendly sentiments it breathes towards myself. We have been thrown into times of a peculiar character, and to work our way through them has required services and sacrifices from our countrymen generally, and to their

---

[1] TJ's copying-machine. – *Eds.*

great honor, these have been generally exhibited, by every one in his sphere, and according to the opportunities afforded. With them I have been a fellow laborer, endeavoring to do faithfully the part allotted to me, as they did theirs; and it is a subject of mutual congratulation that, in a state of things such as the world had never before seen, we have gotten on so far well; and my confidence in our present high functionaries, as well as in my countrymen generally, leaves me without much fear for the future.

I thank you for the pamphlet you were so kind as to send me. At an earlier period of life I pursued inquiries of that kind with industry and care. Reading, reflection and time have convinced me that the interests of society require the observation of those moral precepts only in which all religions agree (for all forbid us to murder, steal, plunder, or bear false witness), and that we should not intermeddle with the particular dogmas in which all religions differ, and which are totally unconnected with morality. In all of them we see good men, and as many in one as another. The varieties in the structure and action of the human mind as in those of the body, are the work of our Creator, against which it cannot be a religious duty to erect the standard of uniformity. The practice of morality being necessary for the well-being of society, he has taken care to impress its precepts so indelibly on our hearts that they shall not be effaced by the subtleties of our brain. We all agree in the obligation of the moral precepts of Jesus, and nowhere will they be found delivered in greater purity than in his discourses. It is, then, a matter of principle with me to avoid disturbing the tranquillity of others by the expression of any opinion on the innocent questions on which we schismatize. On the subject of your pamphlet, and the mode of treating it, I permit myself only to observe the candor, moderation and ingenuity with which you appear to have sought truth. This is of good example, and worthy of commendation. If all the writers and preachers on religious questions had been of the same temper, the history of the world would have been of much more pleasing aspect.

I thank you for the kindness towards myself which breathes through your letter. The first of all our consolations is that of having faithfully fulfilled our duties; the next, the approbation and good will of those who have witnessed it; and I pray you to accept my best wishes for your happiness and the assurances of my respect.

L & B XII: 314–16

## IV.18 To William Duane

Monticello, August 12, 1810

Sir, – Your letter of July 16th has been duly received, with the paper it enclosed, for which accept my thanks, and especially for the kind sentiments expressed towards myself. These testimonies of approbation, and friendly remembrance, are the highest gratifications I can receive from any, and especially from those in whose principles and zeal for the public good I have confidence. Of that confidence in yourself the military appointment to which you allude was sufficient proof, as it was made, not on the recommendations of others, but on our own knowledge of your principles and qualifications. While I cherish with feeling the recollections of my friends, I banish from my mind all political animosities which might disturb its tranquillity, or the happiness I derive from my present pursuits. I have thought it among the most fortunate circumstances of my late administration that, during its eight years continuance, it was conducted with a cordiality and harmony among all the members, which never were ruffled on any, the greatest or smallest occasion. I left my brethren with sentiments of sincere affection and friendship, so rooted in the uniform tenor of a long and intimate intercourse, that the evidence of my own senses alone ought to be permitted to shake them. Anxious, in my retirement, to enjoy undisturbed repose, my knowledge of my successor and late coadjutors, and my entire confidence in their wisdom and integrity, were assurances to me that I might sleep in security with such watchmen at the helm, and that whatever difficulties and dangers should assail our course, they would do what could be done to avoid or surmount them. In this confidence I envelope myself, and hope to slumber on to my last sleep. And should difficulties occur which they cannot avert, if we follow them in phalanx, we shall surmount them without danger.

I have been long intending to write to you as one of the associated company for printing useful works.

Our laws, language, religion, politics and manners are so deeply laid in English foundations, that we shall never cease to consider their history as a part of ours, and to study ours in that as its origin. Every one knows that judicious matter and charms of style have rendered Hume's history the manual of every student. I remember well the enthusiasm with which I devoured it when young, and the length of time, the research and reflection which were necessary to eradicate the poison it had instilled into my mind. It was unfortunate that he first took up the history of the Stuarts, became their apologist, and advocated all their enormities. To support his work, when done, he went back to the Tudors, and so selected and arranged the materials of their history as to present their arbitrary acts only, as the genuine samples of the constitutional power of the crown, and, still writing backwards, he then reverted to the early history, and wrote the Saxon and Norman periods with the same perverted view. Although all this is known, he still continues to be put into the hands of all our young people, and to infect them with the poison of his own principles of government. It is this book which has undermined the free principles of the English government, has persuaded readers of all classes that these were usurpations on the legitimate and salutary rights of the crown, and has spread universal toryism over the land. And the book will still continue to be read here as well as there. Baxter, one of Horne Tooke's associates in persecution, has hit on the only remedy the evil admits. He has taken Hume's work, corrected in the text his misrepresentations, supplied the truths which he suppressed, and yet has given the mass of the work in Hume's own words. And it is wonderful how little interpolation has been necessary to make it a sound history, and to justify what should have been its title, to wit, "Hume's history of England abridged and rendered faithful to fact and principle." I cannot say that his amendments are either in matter or manner in the fine style of Hume. Yet they are often unperceived, and occupy so little of the whole work as not to depreciate it. Unfortunately he has *abridged* Hume, by leaving out all the less important details. It is thus reduced to about one half its original size. He has also continued the history, but very summarily, to 1801. The whole work is of 834 quarto pages, printed close, of which the continuation occupies 283. I have read but little of this part. As far as I can judge from that little, it is a mere chronicle, offering nothing profound.

This work is so unpopular, so distasteful to the present Tory palates and principles of England, that I believe it has never reached a second edition. I have often inquired for it in our book shops, but never could find a copy in them, and I think it possible the one I imported may be the only one in America. Can we not have it reprinted here? It would be about four volumes 8vo.

I have another enterprise to propose for some good printer. I have in my possession a MS work in French, confided to me by a friend,[1] whose name alone would give it celebrity were it permitted to be mentioned. But considerations insuperable forbid that. It is a Commentary and Review of Montesquieu's Spirit of Laws. The history of that work is well known. He had been a great reader, and had commonplaced[2] everything he read. At length he wished to undertake some work into which he could bring his whole common-place book in a digested form. He fixed on the subject of his Spirit of Laws, and wrote the book. He consulted his friend Helvetius about publishing it, who strongly dissuaded it. He published it, however, and the work did not confirm Helvetius' opinion. Still, every man who reflects as he reads, has considered it as a book of paradoxes; having, indeed, much of truth and sound principle, but abounding also with inconsistencies, apochryphal facts and false inferences. It is a correction of these which has been executed in the work I mention, by way of commentary and review; not by criticising words or sentences, but by taking a book at a time, considering its general scope, and proceeding to confirm or confute it. And much of confutation there is, and of substitution of true for false principle, and the true principle is ever that of republicanism. I will not venture to say that every sentiment in the book will be approved, because, being in manuscript, and the French characters, I have not read the whole, but so much only as might enable me to estimate the soundness of the author's way of viewing his subject; and, judging from that which I have read, I infer with confidence that we shall find the work generally worthy of our high approbation, and that it everywhere maintains the preëminence of representative government, by showing that its foundations are laid in reason, in right, and in general good. I had expected this from my

---

[1] Destutt de Tracy. See *infra*, IV.22. – *Eds.*

[2] I.e. Montesquieu had copied extracts from his extensive reading into his commonplace book. – *Eds.*

knowledge of the other writings of the author, which have always a precision rarely to be met with. But to give you an idea of the manner of its execution, I translate and enclose his commentary on Montesquieu's eleventh book, which contains the division of the work. I wish I could have added his review at the close of the twelve first books, as this would give a more complete idea of the extraordinary merit of the work. But it is too long to be copied. I add from it, however, a few extracts of his reviews of some of the books, as specimens of his plan and principles. If printed in French, it would be of about 180 pages 8vo, or 23 sheets. If any one will undertake to have it translated and printed on their own account, I will send on the MS. by post, and they can take the copyright as of an original work, which it ought to be understood to be. I am anxious it should be ably translated by some one who possesses style as well as capacity to do justice to abstruse conceptions. I would even undertake to revise the translation if required. The original sheets must be returned to me, and I should wish the work to be executed with as little delay as possible.

I close this long letter with assurances of my great esteem and respect.

Washington v: 532–6

## IV.19 To Thomas Law

Poplar Forest, June 13, 1814

Dear Sir, – The copy of your Second Thoughts on Instinctive Impulses, with the letter accompanying it, was received just as I was setting out on a journey to this place, two or three days distant from Monticello. I brought it with me and read it with great satisfaction, and with the more as it contained exactly my own creed on the foundation of morality in man. It is really curious that on a question so fundamental, such a variety of opinions should have prevailed among men, and those, too, of the most exemplary virtue and first order of understanding. It shows how necessary was the care of the Creator in making the moral principle so much a part of our constitution as that no errors of reasoning or of speculation might lead us astray from its observance in practice. Of all the theories on this question, the most whimsical seems to have been that of Wollaston,[1] who considers *truth* as the foundation of morality. The thief who steals your guinea does wrong only inasmuch as he acts a lie in using your guinea as if it were his own. Truth is certainly a branch of morality, and a very important one to society. But presented as its foundation, it is as if a tree taken up by the roots, had its stem reversed in the air, and one of its branches planted in the ground. Some have made the *love of God* the foundation of morality. This, too, is but a branch of our moral duties, which are generally divided into duties to God and duties to man. If we did a good act merely from the love of God and a belief that it is pleasing to Him, whence arises the morality of the Atheist? It is idle to say, as some do, that no such being exists. We have the same evidence of the fact as of most of those we act on, to wit: their own affirmations, and their reasonings in support of them. I have observed, indeed, generally, that while in Protestant countries the defections from the Platonic Christianity of the priests is to Deism, in Catholic countries they are to Atheism. Diderot, D'Alembert, D'Holbach, Condorcet, are known to have been among the most virtuous of men. Their virtue, then, must have had some other foundation than the love of God.

The τό καλόν of others is founded in a different faculty, that of taste, which is not even a branch of morality. We have indeed an innate sense of what we call beautiful, but that is exercised chiefly on subjects addressed to the fancy, whether through the eye in visible forms, as landscape, animal figure, dress, drapery, architecture, the composition of colors, etc., or to the imagination directly, as imagery, style, or measure in prose or poetry, or whatever else constitutes the domain of criticism or taste, a faculty entirely distinct from the moral one. Self-interest, or rather self-love, or *egoism*, has been more plausibly substituted as the basis of morality. But I consider our relations with others as constituting the boundaries of morality. With ourselves we stand on the ground of identity, not of relation, which last, requiring two subjects, excludes self-love confined to a single one. To ourselves, in strict language, we can owe no duties, obligation requiring also two parties. Self-love, therefore,

---

[1] William Wollaston (1660–1724), author of *The Religion of Nature Delineated* (London, 1725) and other works. – *Eds.*

is no part of morality. Indeed it is exactly its counterpart. It is the sole antagonist of virtue, leading us constantly by our propensities to self-gratification in violation of our moral duties to others. Accordingly, it is against this enemy that are erected the batteries of moralists and religionists, as the only obstacle to the practice of morality. Take from man his selfish propensities, and he can have nothing to seduce him from the practice of virtue. Or subdue those propensities by education, instruction or restraint, and virtue remains without a competitor. Egoism, in a broader sense, has been thus presented as the source of moral action. It has been said that we feed the hungry, clothe the naked, bind up the wounds of the man beaten by thieves, pour oil and wine into them, set him on our own beast and bring him to the inn, because we receive ourselves pleasure from these acts. So Helvetius, one of the best men on earth, and the most ingenious advocate of this principle, after defining "interest" to mean not merely that which is pecuniary, but whatever may procure us pleasure or withdraw us from pain (*de l'esprit* 2, 1), says (*ib.* 2, 2), "the humane man is he to whom the sight of misfortune is insupportable, and who to rescue himself from this spectacle, is forced to succor the unfortunate object." This indeed is true. But it is one step short of the ultimate question. These good acts give us pleasure, but how happens it that they give us pleasure? Because nature hath implanted in our breasts a love of others, a sense of duty to them, a moral instinct, in short, which prompts us irresistibly to feel and to succor their distresses, and protests against the language of Helvetius (*ib.* 2, 5,), "what other motive than self-interest could determine a man to generous actions? It is as impossible for him to love what is good for the sake of good, as to love evil for the sake of evil." The Creator would indeed have been a bungling artist, had he intended man for a social animal, without planting in him social dispositions. It is true they are not planted in every man, because there is no rule without exceptions; but it is false reasoning which converts exceptions into the general rule. Some men are born without the organs of sight, or of hearing, or without hands. Yet it would be wrong to say that man is born without these faculties, and sight, hearing, and hands may with truth enter into the general definition of man.

The want or imperfection of the moral sense in some men, like the want or imperfection of the senses of sight and hearing in others, is no proof that it is a general characteristic of the species. When it is wanting, we endeavor to supply the defect by education, by appeals to reason and calculation, by presenting to the being so unhappily conformed, other motives to do good and to eschew evil, such as the love, or the hatred, or rejection of those among whom he lives, and whose society is necessary to his happiness and even existence; demonstrations by sound calculation that honesty promotes interest in the long run; the rewards and penalties established by the laws; and ultimately the prospects of a future state of retribution for the evil as well as the good done while here. These are the correctives which are supplied by education, and which exercise the functions of the moralist, the preacher, and legislator; and they lead into a course of correct action all those whose disparity is not too profound to be eradicated. Some have argued against the existence of a moral sense, by saying that if nature had given us such a sense, impelling us to virtuous actions, and warning us against those which are vicious, then nature would also have designated, by some particular ear-marks, the two sets of actions which are, in themselves, the one virtuous and the other vicious. Whereas, we find, in fact, that the same actions are deemed virtuous in one country and vicious in another. The answer is, that nature has constituted *utility* to man, the standard and test of virtue. Men living in different countries, under different circumstances, different habits and regimens, may have different utilities; the same act, therefore, may be useful, and consequently virtuous in one country which is injurious and vicious in another differently circumstanced. I sincerely, then, believe with you in the general existence of a moral instinct. I think it the brightest gem with which the human character is studded, and the want of it as more degrading than the most hideous of the bodily deformities. I am happy in reviewing the roll of associates in this principle which you present in your second letter, some of which I had not before met with. To these might be added Lord Kaims, one of the ablest of our advocates, who goes so far as to say, in his *Principles of Natural Religion*, that a man owes no duty to which he is not urged by some impulsive feeling. This is correct, if referred to the standard of general feeling in the given case, and not to the feeling of a single individual. Perhaps I may misquote him, it being fifty years since I read his book.

The leisure and solitude of my situation here has led me to the indiscretion of taxing you with a long letter on a subject whereon nothing new can be offered you. I will indulge myself no farther than to repeat the assurances of my continued esteem and respect.

L & B xiv: 138–44

## IV.20 To Dr. Thomas Cooper

Monticello, October 7, 1814

Dear Sir, – Your several favors of September 15th, 21st, 22d, came all together by our last mail. I have given to that of the 15th a single reading only, because the handwriting (not your own) is microscopic and difficult, and because I shall have an opportunity of studying it in the Portfolio in print. According to your request I return it for that publication, where it will do a great deal of good. It will give our young men some idea of what constitutes a well-educated man; that Cæsar and Virgil, and a few books of Euclid, do not really contain the sum of all human knowledge, nor give to a man figure in the ranks of science. Your letter will be a valuable source of consultation for us in our collegiate courses, when, and if ever, we advance to that stage of our establishment.

I agree with yours of the 22d, that a professorship of Theology should have no place in our institution. But we cannot always do what is absolutely best. Those with whom we act, entertaining different views, have the power and the right of carrying them into practice. Truth advances, and error recedes step by step only; and to do to our fellow men the most good in our power, we must lead where we can, follow where we cannot, and still go with them, watching always the favourable moment for helping them to another step. Perhaps I should concur with you also in excluding the *theory* (not the *practice*) of medicine. This is the charlatanerie of the body, as the other is of the mind. For classical learning I have ever been a zealous advocate; and in this, as in his theory of bleeding and mercury, I was ever opposed to my friend [Dr. Benjamin] Rush, whom I greatly loved; but who has done much harm, in the sincerest persuasion that he was preserving life and happiness to all around him. I have not, however, carried so far as you do my ideas of the importance of a hypercritical knowledge of the Latin and Greek languages. I have believed it sufficient to possess a substantial understanding of their authors.

In the exclusion of Anatomy and Botany from the eleventh grade of education, which is that of the man of independent fortune, we separate in opinion. In my view, no knowledge can be more satisfactory to a man than that of his own frame, its parts, their functions and actions. And Botany I rank with the most valuable sciences, whether we consider its subjects as furnishing the principal subsistence of life to man and beast, delicious varieties for our tables, refreshments from our orchards, the adornments of our flowerborders, shade and perfume of our groves, materials for our buildings, or medicaments for our bodies. To the gentleman it is certainly more interesting than Mineralogy (which I by no means, however, undervalue), and is more at hand for his amusement; and to a country family it constitutes a great portion of their social entertainment. No country gentleman should be without what amuses every step he takes into his fields.

I am sorry to learn the fate of your Emporium.[1] It was adding fast to our useful knowledge. Our artists particularly, and our statesmen, will have cause to regret it. But my hope is that its suspension will be temporary only; and that as soon as we get over the crisis of our disordered circulation, your publishers will resume it among their first enterprises. Accept my thanks for the benefit of your ideas to our scheme of education, and the assurance of my constant esteem and respect.

L & B XIV: 199–202

## IV.21 To P.-S. DuPont de Nemours

Poplar Forest, April 24, 1816

I received, my dear friend, your letter covering the constitution for your Equinoctial republics, just as I was setting out for this place. I brought it with me, and have read it with great satisfaction. I

---

[1] Cooper edited the *Emporium of Arts and Sciences*, a periodical devoted to the practical uses of scientific knowledge. – *Eds.*

suppose it well formed for those for whom it was intended, and the excellence of every government is its adaptation to the state of those to be governed by it. For us it would not do. Distinguishing between the structure of the government and the moral principles on which you prescribe its administration, with the latter we concur cordially, with the former we should not. We of the United States, you know, are constitutionally and conscientiously democrats. We consider society as one of the natural wants with which man has been created; that he has been endowed with faculties and qualities to effect its satisfaction by concurrence of others having the same want; that when, by the exercise of these faculties, he has procured a state of society, it is one of his acquisitions which he has a right to regulate and control, jointly indeed with all those who have concurred in the procurement, whom he cannot exclude from its use or direction more than they him. We think experience has proved it safer, for the mass of individuals composing the society, to reserve to themselves personally the exercise of all rightful powers to which they are competent, and to delegate those to which they are not competent to deputies named, and removable for unfaithful conduct, by themselves immediately. Hence, with us, the people (by which is meant the mass of individuals composing the society) being competent to judge of the facts occurring in ordinary life, they have retained the functions of judges of facts, under the name of jurors; but being unqualified for the management of affairs requiring intelligence above the common level, yet competent judges of human character, they chose, for their management, representatives, some by themselves immediately, others by electors chosen by themselves. Thus our President is chosen by ourselves, directly in *practice*, for we vote for A as elector only on the condition he will vote for B, our representatives by ourselves immediately, our Senate and judges of laws through electors chosen by ourselves. And we believe that this proximate choice and power of removal is the best security which experience has sanctioned for ensuring an honest conduct in the functionaries of society. Your three or four alembications have indeed a seducing appearance. We should conceive, *primâ facie*, that the last extract would be the pure alcohol of the substance, three or four times rectified. But in proportion as they are more and more sublimated, they are also farther and farther removed from the control of the society; and the human character, we believe, requires in general constant and immediate control, to prevent its being biased from right by the seductions of self-love. Your process produces therefore a structure of government from which the fundamental principle of ours is excluded. You first set down as zeros all individuals not having lands, which are the greater number in every society of long standing. Those holding lands are permitted to manage in person the small affairs of their commune or corporation, and to elect a deputy for the canton; in which election, too, every one's vote is to be an unit, a plurality, or a fraction, in proportion to his landed possessions. The assemblies of cantons, then, elect for the districts; those of districts for circles; and those of circles for the national assemblies. Some of these highest councils, too, are in a considerable degree self-elected, the regency partially, the judiciary entirely, and some are for life. Whenever, therefore, an *esprit de corps*, or of party, gets possession of them, which experience shows to be inevitable, there are no means of breaking it up, for they will never elect but those of their own spirit. Juries are allowed in criminal cases only. I acknowledge myself strong in affection to our own form, yet both of us act and think from the same motive, we both consider the people as our children, and love them with parental affection. But you love them as infants whom you are afraid to trust without nurses; and I as adults whom I freely leave to self-government. And you are right in the case referred to you; my criticism being built on a state of society not under your contemplation. It is, in fact, like a critic on Homer by the laws of the Drama.

But when we come to the moral principles on which the government is to be administered, we come to what is proper for all conditions of society. I meet you there in all the benevolence and rectitude of your native character; and I love myself always most where I concur most with you. Liberty, truth, probity, honor, are declared to be the four cardinal principles of your society. I believe with you that morality, compassion, generosity, are innate elements of the human constitution; that there exists a right independent of force; that a right to property is founded in our natural wants, in the means with which we are endowed to satisfy these wants, and the right to what we acquire by those means without violating the similar rights of other sensible beings; that no one has a right to obstruct another, exercising his faculties innocently for the relief of sensibilities made a part of his nature; that justice is the fundamental law of society; that the majority, oppressing an individual, is guilty of a crime, abuses its strength, and by acting on the law of the strongest breaks up the foundations of society; that action by the citizens in person, in affairs within their reach and competence, and in all others by representatives, chosen immediately, and removable by themselves, constitutes the essence of a republic; that all governments are more or less republican in proportion as this principle enters more or less into their composition; and that a government by representation is capable of extension over a greater surface of country than one of any other form. These, my friend, are the essentials in which you and I agree; however, in our zeal for their maintenance, we may be perplexed and divaricate, as to the structure of society most likely to secure them.

In the constitution of Spain, as proposed by the late Cortes [Spanish parliament], there was a principle entirely new to me, and not noticed in yours, that no person, born after that day, should ever acquire the rights of citizenship until he could read and write. It is impossible sufficiently to estimate the wisdom of this provision. Of all those which have been thought of for securing fidelity in the administration of the government, constant ralliance to the principles of the constitution, and progressive amendments with the progressive advances of the human mind, or changes in human affairs, it is the most effectual. Enlighten the people generally, and tyranny and oppressions of body and mind will vanish like evil spirits at the dawn of day. Although I do not, with some enthusiasts, believe that the human condition will ever advance to such a state of perfection as that there shall no longer be pain or vice in the world, yet I believe it susceptible of much improvement, and most of all, in matters of government and religion; and that the diffusion of knowledge among the people is to be the instrument by which it is to be effected. The constitution of the Cortes had defects enough; but when I saw in it this amendatory provision, I was satisfied all would come right in time, under its salutary operation. No people have more need of a similar provision than those for whom you have felt so much interest. No mortal wishes them more success than I do. But if what I have heard of the ignorance and bigotry of the mass be true, I doubt their capacity to understand and to support a free government; and fear that their emancipation from the foreign tyranny of Spain, will result in a military despotism at home. Palacios may be great; others may be great; but it is the multitude which possesses force; and wisdom must yield to that. For such a condition of society, the constitution you have devised is probably the best imaginable. It is certainly calculated to elicit the best talents; although perhaps not well guarded against the egoism of its functionaries. But that egoism will be light in comparison with the pressure of a military despot, and his army of Janissaries. Like Solon to the Athenians, you have given to your Columbians, not the best possible government, but the best they can bear. By-the-bye, I wish you had called them the Columbian republics, to distinguish them from our American republics. Theirs would be the most honorable name, and they best entitled to it; for Columbus discovered their continent, but never saw ours.

To them liberty and happiness; to you the meed of wisdom and goodness in teaching them how to attain them, with the affectionate respect and friendship of, [T. J.]

Washington VI: 589–93

## IV.22 To John Adams

Monticello, October 14, 1816

Your letter, dear Sir, of May 6. had already well explained the Uses of grief, that of Sep. 3. with equal truth adduces instances of it's abuse; and when we put into the same scale these abuses, with the afflictions of soul which even the Uses of grief cost us, we may consider it's value in the economy of the human being, as equivocal at least. Those afflictions cloud too great a portion of life to find a counterpoise in any benefits derived from it's uses. For setting aside it's paroxysms on the occasions of special bereavements, all the latter years of aged men are overshadowed with it's gloom. Whither, for instance, can you and I look without seeing the graves of those we have known? And whom can we call up, of our early companions, who has not left us to regret his loss? This indeed may be one of the salutary effects of grief; inasmuch as it prepares us to lose ourselves also without repugnance. Dr. Freeman's instances of female levity cured by grief are certainly to the point, and constitute an item of credit in the account we examine . . .

Your undertaking the 12 volumes of Dupuis is a degree of heroism to which I could not have aspired even in my younger days. I have been contented with the humble atchievement of reading the Analysis of his work by Destutt-Tracy in 200 pages 8vo. I believe I should have ventured on his own abridgment of the work in one 8vo. volume, had it ever come to my hands; but the marrow of it in Tracy has satisfied my appetite: and, even in that, the preliminary discourse of the Analyzer himself, and his Conclusion, are worth more in my eye than the body of the work. For the object of that seems to be to smother all history under the mantle of allegory. If histories so unlike as those of Hercules and Jesus, can, by a fertile imagination, and Allegorical interpretations, be brought to the same tally, no line of distinction remains between fact and fancy. As this pithy morsel will not overburthen the mail in passing and repassing between Quincy and Monticello, I send it for your perusal. Perhaps it will satisfy you, as it has me; and may save you the labor of reading 24 times it's volume. I have said to you that it was written by Tracy; and I had so entered it on the title-page, as I usually do on Anonymous works whose authors are known to me. But Tracy had requested me not to betray his anonyme, for reasons which may not yet perhaps have ceased to weigh. I am bound then to make the same reserve with you. Destutt-Tracy is, in my judgment, the ablest writer living on intellectual subjects, or the operations of the understanding. His three 8vo. volumes on Ideology, which constitute the foundation of what he has since written, I have not entirely read; because I am not fond of reading what is merely abstract, and unapplied immediately to some useful science. Bonaparte, with his repeated derisions of Ideologists (squinting at this author),[1] has by this time felt that true wisdom does not lie in mere practice without principle. The next work Tracy wrote was the Commentary on Montesquieu, never published in the original, because not safe; but translated and published in Philadelphia, yet without the author's name. He has since permitted his name to be mentioned. Although called a Commentary, it is in truth an elementary work on the principles of government, comprised in about 300 pages 8vo. He has

---

[1] Napoleon was hostile to Destutt de Tracy (at whom he is here "squinting") and other champions of *idéologie*, the "science" that purported to explain how and where ideas originate. It was indeed Napoleon who first gave the term "ideology" its negative connotation as something fanciful or false. – *Eds.*

lately published a third work on Political economy, comprising the whole subject within about the same compass; in which all it's principles are demonstrated with the severity of Euclid, and, like him, without ever using a superfluous word. I have procured this to be translated, and have been 4 years endeavoring to get it printed. But, as yet, without success. In the mean time the author has published the original in France, which he thought unsafe while Bonaparte was in power. No printed copy, I believe, has yet reached this country. He has his 4th. and last work now in the press at Paris, closing, as he concieves, the circle of metaphysical sciences. This work which is on Ethics, I have not seen, but suspect I shall differ from it in it's foundation, altho not in it's deductions. I gather from his other works that he adopts the principle of Hobbes, that justice is founded in contract solely, and does not result from the construction of man. I believe, on the contrary, that it is instinct, and innate, that the moral sense is as much a part of our constitution as that of feeling, seeing, or hearing; as a wise creator must have seen to be necessary in an animal destined to live in society: that every human mind feels pleasure in doing good to another; that the non-existence of justice is not to be inferred from the fact that the same act is deemed virtuous and right in one society, which is held vicious and wrong in another; because as the circumstances and opinions of different societies vary, so the acts which may do them right or wrong must vary also: for virtue does not consist in the act we do, but in the end it is to effect. If it is to effect the happiness of him to whom it is directed, it is virtuous, while in a society under different circumstances and opinions the same act might produce pain, and would be vicious. The essence of virtue is in doing good to others, while what is good may be one thing in one society, and it's contrary in another. Yet, however we may differ as to the foundation of morals (and as many foundations have been assumed as there are writers on the subject nearly), so correct a thinker as Tracy will give us a sound system of morals. And indeed it is remarkable that so many writers, setting out from so many different premises, yet meet, all, in the same conclusions. This looks as if they were guided, unconsciously, by the unerring hand of instinct . . .

I salute Mrs. Adams and yourself with every sentiment of affectionate cordiality and respect.

L & B xv: 73–8

## IV.23 Report of the Commissioners for the University of Virginia

August 4, 1818

The Commissioners for the University of Virginia, having met, as by law required, at the tavern, in Rockfish Gap, on the Blue Ridge, on the first day of August, of this present year, 1818; and having formed a board, proceeded on that day to the discharge of the duties assigned to them by the act of the Legislature, entitled "An act, appropriating part of the revenue of the literary fund, and for other purposes"; and having continued their proceedings by adjournment, from day to day, to Tuesday, the 4th day of August, have agreed to a report on the several matters with which they were charged, which report they now respectfully address and submit to the Legislature of the State.

The first duty enjoined on them, was to enquire and report a site, in some convenient and proper part of the State, for an university, to be called the "University of Virginia." In this inquiry, they supposed that the governing considerations should be the healthiness of the site, the fertility of the neighboring country, and its centrality to the white population of the whole State. For, although the act authorized and required them to receive any voluntary contributions, whether conditional or absolute, which might be offered through them to the President and Directors of the Literary Fund, for the benefit of the University, yet they did not consider this as establishing an auction, or as pledging the location to the highest bidder.

Three places were proposed, to wit: Lexington, in the county of Rockbridge, Staunton, in the county of Augusta, and the Central College, in the county of Albemarle. Each of these was unexceptionable as to healthiness and fertility. It was the degree of centrality to the white population of the State which alone then constituted the important point of comparison between these places; and the Board, after full inquiry, and impartial and mature consideration, are of opinion, that the central point of the white population of the State is nearer to the Central College than to either Lexington or Staunton, by great and important differences; and all other circumstances of the place in general being favourable to it, as a position for an

297

university, they do report the Central College, in Albemarle, to be a convenient and proper part of the State for the University of Virginia.

2. The Board having thus agreed on a proper site for the University, to be reported to the Legislature, proceed to the second of the duties assigned to them – that of proposing a plan for its buildings – and they are of opinion that it should consist of distinct houses or pavilions, arranged at proper distances on each side of a lawn of a proper breadth, and of indefinite extent, in one direction, at least; in each of which should be a lecturing room, with from two to four apartments, for the accommodation of a professor and his family; that these pavilions should be united by a range of dormitories, sufficient each for the accommodation of two students only, this provision being deemed advantageous to morals, to order, and to uninterrupted study; and that a passage of some kind, under cover from the weather, should give a communication along the whole range. It is supposed that such pavilions, on an average of the larger and smaller, will cost each about $5,000; each dormitory about $350, and hotels of a single room, for a refectory, and two rooms for the tenant, necessary for dieting the students, will cost about $3,500 each. The number of these pavilions will depend on the number on professors, and that of the dormitories and hotels on the number of students to be lodged and dieted. The advantages of this plan are: greater security against fire and infection; tranquillity and comfort to the professors and their families thus insulated; retirement to the students; and the admission of enlargement to any degree to which the institution may extend in future times. It is supposed probable, that a building of somewhat more size in the middle of the grounds may be called for in time, in which may be rooms for religious worship, under such impartial regulations as the Visitors shall prescribe, for public examinations, for a library, for the schools of music, drawing, and other associated purposes.

3, 4. In proceeding to the third and fourth duties prescribed by the Legislature, of reporting "the branches of learning, which should be taught in the University, and the number and description of the professorships they will require," the Commissioners were first to consider at what point it was understood that university education should commence? Certainly not with the alphabet, for reasons of expediency and impracticability, as well from the obvious sense of the Legislature, who, in the same act, make other provision for the primary instruction of the poor children, expecting, doubtless, that in other cases it would be provided by the parent, or become, perhaps, subject of future and further attention of the Legislature. The objects of this primary education determine its character and limits. These objects would be,

To give to every citizen the information he needs for the transaction of his own business;

To enable him to calculate for himself, and to express and preserve his ideas, his contracts and accounts, in writing;

To improve, by reading, his morals and faculties;

To understand his duties to his neighbours and country, and to discharge with competence the functions confided to him by either;

To know his rights; to exercise with order and justice those he retains; to choose with discretion the fiduciary of those he delegates; and to notice their conduct with diligence, with candor, and judgment;

And, in general, to observe with intelligence and faithfulness all the social relations under which he shall be placed.

To instruct the mass of our citizens in these, their rights, interests and duties, as men and citizens, being then the objects of education in the primary schools, whether private or public, in them should be taught reading, writing and numerical arithmetic, the elements of mensuration (useful in so many callings), and the outlines of geography and history. And this brings us to the point at which are to commence the higher branches of education, of which the Legislature require the development; those, for example, which are,

To form the statesman, legislators and judges, on whom public prosperity and individual happiness are so much to depend;

To expound the principles and structure of government, the laws which regulate the intercourse of nations, those formed municipally for our own government, and a sound spirit of legislation, which, banishing all arbitrary and unnecessary restraint on individual action, shall leave us free to do whatever does not violate the equal rights of another;

To harmonize and promote the interests of agriculture, manufactures and commerce, and by well informed views of political economy to give a free scope to the public industry;

To develop the reasoning faculties of our youth, enlarge their minds, cultivate their morals, and instill into them the precepts of virtue and order;

To enlighten them with mathematical and physical sciences, which advance the arts, and administer to the health, the subsistence, and comforts of human life;

And, generally, to form them to habits of reflection and correct action, rendering them examples of virtue to others, and of happiness within themselves.

These are the objects of that higher grade of education, the benefits and blessings of which the Legislature now propose to provide for the good and ornament of their country, the gratification and happiness of their fellow-citizens, of the parent especially, and his progeny, on which all his affections are concentrated.

In entering on this field, the Commissioners are aware that they have to encounter much difference of opinion as to the extent which it is expedient that this institution should occupy. Some good men, and even of respectable information, consider the learned sciences as useless acquirements; some think that they do not better the condition of man; and others that education, like private and individual concerns, should be left to private individual effort; not reflecting that an establishment embracing all the sciences which may be useful and even necessary in the various vocations of life, with the buildings and apparatus belonging to each, are far beyond the reach of individual means, and must either derive existence from public patronage, or not exist at all. This would leave us, then, without those callings which depend on education, or send us to other countries to seek the instruction they require. But the Commissioners are happy in considering the statute under which they are assembled as proof that the Legislature is far from the abandonment of objects so interesting. They are sensible that the advantages of well-directed education, moral, political and economical, are truly above all estimate. Education generates habits of application, of order, and the love of virtue; and controls, by the force of habit, any innate obliquities in our moral organization. We should be far, too, from the discouraging persuasion that man is fixed, by the law of his nature, at a given point; that his improvement is a chimera, and the hope delusive of rendering ourselves wiser, happier or better than our forefathers were. As well might it be urged that the wild and uncultivated tree, hitherto yielding sour and bitter fruit only, can never be made to yield better; yet we know that the grafting art implants a new tree on the savage stock, producing what is most estimable both in kind and degree. Education, in like manner, engrafts a new man on the native stock, and improves what in his nature was vicious and perverse into qualities of virtue and social worth. And it cannot be but that each generation succeeding to the knowledge acquired by all those who preceded it, adding to it their own acquisitions and discoveries, and handing the mass down for successive and constant accumulation, must advance the knowledge and well-being of mankind, not *infinitely*, as some have said, but *indefinitely*, and to a term which no one can fix and foresee. Indeed, we need look back half a century, to times which many now living remember well, and see the wonderful advances in the sciences and arts which have been made within that period. Some of these have rendered the elements themselves subservient to the purposes of man, have harnessed them to the yoke of his labors, and effected the great blessings of moderating his own, of accomplishing what was beyond his feeble force, and extending the comforts of life to a much enlarged circle, to those who had before known its necessaries only. That these are not the vain dreams of sanguine hope, we have before our eyes real and living examples. What, but education, has advanced us beyond the condition of our indigenous neighbors? And what chains them to their present state of barbarism and wretchedness, but a bigotted veneration for the supposed superlative wisdom of their fathers, and the preposterous idea that they are to look backward for better things, and not forward, longing, as it should seem, to return to the days of eating acorns and roots, rather than indulge in the degeneracies of civilisation? And how much more encouraging to the achievements of science and improvement is this, than the desponding view that the condition of man cannot be ameliorated, that what has been must ever be, and that to secure ourselves where we are, we must tread with awful reverence in the footsteps of our fathers. This doctrine is the genuine fruit of the alliance between Church and State; the tenants of which, finding themselves but too well in their present condition, oppose all advances which might unmask their usurpations, and monopolies of honors, wealth, and power, and fear every change, as endangering the comforts they now hold. Nor must we omit to mention, among the benefits of education, the incalculable advantage of training up able counsellors to administer the affairs of our country in all its departments, legislative, executive and judiciary, and to bear their proper share in the councils of our national government; nothing more than education advancing the prosperity, the power, and the happiness of a nation.

Encouraged, therefore, by the sentiments of the Legislature, manifested in this statute, we present the following tabular statement of the branches of learning which we think should be taught in the University, forming them into groups, each of which are within the powers of a single professor:

I. Languages, ancient:
  Latin,
  Greek,
  Hebrew.
II. Languages, modern:
  French,
  Spanish,
  Italian,
  German,
  Anglo-Saxon.
III. Mathematics, pure:
  Algebra,
  Fluxions,
  Geometry, Elementary,
    Transcendental.
  Architecture, Military,
    Naval.
IV. Physico-Mathematics:
  Mechanics,
  Statics,
  Dynamics,
  Pneumatics,
  Acoustics,
  Optics,
  Astronomy,
  Geography.
V. Physics, or Natural
    Philosophy:
  Chemistry,
  Mineralogy.
VI. Botany, Zoology.
VII. Anatomy, Medicine.
VIII. Government,
  Political Economy,
  Law of Nature and Nations,
  History, being interwoven
    with Politics and Law.
IX. Law, municipal.
X. Ideology,
  General Grammar,
  Ethics, Rhetoric,
  *Belles Lettres*, and the fine
    arts.

Some of the terms used in this table being subject to a difference of acceptation, it is proper to define the meaning and comprehension intended to be given them here:

Geometry, Elementary, is that of straight lines and of the circle.

Transcendental, is that of all other curves; it includes, of course, *Projectiles*, a leading branch of the military art.

Military Architecture includes Fortification, another branch of that art.

Statics respect matter generally, in a state of rest, and include Hydrostatics, or the laws of fluids particularly, at rest or in equilibrio.

Dynamics, used as a general term, include

Dynamics proper, or the laws of *solids* in motion; and

Hydrodynamics, or Hydraulics, those of *fluids* in motion.

Pneumatics teach the theory of air, its weight, motion, condensation, rarefaction, &c.

Acoustics, or Phonics, the theory of sound.

Optics, the laws of light and vision.

Physics, or Physiology, in a general sense, mean the doctrine of the physical objects of our senses.

Chemistry is meant, with its other usual branches, to comprehend the theory of agriculture.

Mineralogy, in addition to its peculiar subjects, is here understood to embrace what is real in geology.

Ideology is the doctrine of thought.

General Grammar explains the construction of language.

Some articles in this distribution of sciences will need observation. A professor is proposed for ancient languages, the Latin, Greek, and Hebrew, particularly; but these languages being the foundation common to all the sciences, it is difficult to foresee what may be the extent of this school. At the same time, no greater obstruction to industrious study could be proposed than the presence, the intrusions and the noisy turbulence of a multitude of small boys; and if they are to be placed here for the rudiments of the languages, they may be so numerous that its character and value as an University will be merged in those of a Grammar school. It is, therefore, greatly to be wished, that preliminary schools, either on private or public establishment, could be distributed in districts through the State, as preparatory to the entrance of students into the University. The tender age at which this part of education commences, generally about the tenth year, would weigh heavily with parents in sending their sons to a school so distant as the central establishment would be from most of them. Districts of such extent as that every parent should be within a day's journey of his son at school, would be desirable in cases of sickness, and convenient for supplying their ordinary wants, and might be made to lessen sensibly the expense of this part of their education. And where a sparse population would not, within such a compass, furnish subjects sufficient to maintain a school, a competent enlargement of district must, of necessity, there be submitted to. At these district schools or colleges, boys should be rendered able to read the easier authors, Latin and Greek. This would be useful and sufficient for many not intended for an University education. At these, too, might be taught English grammar, the higher branches of numerical arithmetic, the geometry of straight lines and of the circle, the elements of navigation, and geography to a sufficient degree, and thus afford to greater numbers the means of being qualified for the various vocations of life, needing more instruction than merely menial or prædial [agricultural] labor, and the same advantages to youths whose education may have been neglected until too late to lay a foundation in the learned languages. These institutions, intermediate between the primary schools and University, might then be the passage of entrance for youths into the University, where their classical learning might be critically completed, by a study of the authors of highest degree; and it is at this stage only that they should be received at the University. Giving then a portion of their time to a finished knowledge of the Latin and Greek, the rest might be appropriated to the modern languages, or to the commencement of the course of science for which they should be destined. This would generally be about the fifteenth year of their age, when they might go with more safety and contentment to that distance from their parents. Until this preparatory provision shall be made, either the University will be overwhelmed with the grammar school, or a separate establishment, under one or more ushers, for its lower classes, will be advisable, at a mile or two distant from the general one; where, too, may be exercised the stricter government necessary for young boys, but unsuitable for youths arrived at years of discretion.

The considerations which have governed the specification of languages to be taught by the professor of modern languages were, that the French is the language of general intercourse among nations, and as a depository of human science, is unsurpassed by any other language, living or dead; that the Spanish is highly interesting to us, as the language spoken by so great a portion of the inhabitants of our continents, with whom we shall probably have great intercourse ere long, and is that also in which is written the greater part of the earlier history of America. The Italian abounds with works of very superior order, valuable for their matter, and still more distinguished as models of the finest taste in style and composition. And the German now stands in a line with that of the most learned nations in richness of erudition and advance in the sciences. It is too of common descent with the language of our own country, a branch of the same original Gothic stock, and furnishes valuable illustrations for us. But in this point of view, the Anglo-Saxon is of peculiar value. We have placed it among the modern languages, because it is in fact that which we speak, in the earliest form in which we have knowledge of it. It has been undergoing, with time, those gradual changes which all languages, ancient and modern, have experienced; and even now needs only to be printed in the modern character and orthography to be intelligible, in a considerable degree, to an English reader. It has this value, too, above the Greek and Latin, that while it gives the radix [root] of the mass of our language, they explain its innovations only. Obvious proofs of this have been presented to the modern reader in the disquisitions of Horn Tooke; and Fortescue Aland has well explained the great instruction which may be derived from it to a full understanding of our ancient common law, on which, as a stock, our whole system of law is engrafted. It will form the first link in the chain of an historical review of our language through all its successive changes to the present day, will constitute the foundation of that critical instruction in it which ought to be found in a seminary of general learning, and thus reward amply the few weeks of attention which would alone be requisite for its attainment; a language already fraught with all the eminent science of our parent country, the future vehicle of whatever we may ourselves achieve, and destined to occupy so much space on the globe, claims distinguished attention in American education.

Medicine, where fully taught, is usually subdivided into several professorships, but this cannot well be without the accessory of an hospital, where the student can have the benefit of attending clinical lectures, and of assisting at operations of surgery. With this accessory, the seat of our University is not yet prepared, either by its population or by the numbers of poor who would leave their own houses, and accept of the charities of an hospital. For the present, therefore, we propose but a single professor for both medicine and anatomy. By him the medical science may be taught, with a history and explanations of all its successive theories from Hippocrates to the present day; and anatomy may be fully treated. Vegetable pharmacy will make a part of the botanical course, and mineral and chemical pharmacy of those of mineralogy and chemistry. This degree of medical information is such as the mass of scientific students would wish to possess, as enabling them in their course through life, to estimate with satisfaction the extent and limits of the aid to human life and health, which they may understandingly expect from that art; and it constitutes such a foundation for those intended for the profession, that the finishing course of practice at the bed-sides of the sick, and at the operations of surgery in a hospital, can neither be long nor expensive. To seek this finishing elsewhere, must therefore be submitted to for a while.

In conformity with the principles of our Constitution, which places all sects of religion on an equal footing, with the jealousies of the different sects in guarding that equality from encroachment and surprise, and with the sentiments of the Legislature in favor of freedom of religion, manifested on former occasions, we have proposed no professor of divinity; and the rather as the proofs of the being of a God, the creator, preserver, and supreme ruler of the universe, the author of all the relations of morality, and of the laws and obligations these infer, will be within the province of the professor of ethics; to which adding the developments of these moral obligations, of those in which all sects agree, with a knowledge of the languages, Hebrew, Greek, and Latin, a basis will be formed common to all sects. Proceeding thus far without offence to the Constitution, we have thought it proper at this point to leave every sect to provide, as they think fittest, the means of further instruction in their own peculiar tenets.

We are further of opinion, that after declaring by law that certain sciences shall be taught in the University, fixing the number of professors they require, which we think should, at present, be ten, limiting (except as to the professors who shall be first engaged in each branch) a maximum for their salaries (which should be a certain but moderate subsistence, to be made up by liberal tuition fees, as an excitement to assiduity), it will be best to leave to the discretion of the Visitors, the grouping of these sciences together, according to the accidental qualifications of the professors; and the introduction also of other branches of science, when enabled by private donations, or by public provision, and called for by the increase of population, or other change of circumstances; to establish beginnings, in short, to be developed by time, as those who come after us shall find expedient. They will be more advanced than we are in science and in useful arts, and will know best what will suit the circumstances of their day.

We have proposed no formal provision for the gymnastics of the school, although a proper object of attention for every institution of youth. These exercises with ancient nations, constituted the principal part of the education of their youth. Their arms and mode of warfare rendered them severe in the extreme; ours, on the same correct principle, should be adapted to our arms and warfare; and the manual exercise, military manœuvres, and tactics generally, should be the frequent exercises of the students, in their hours of recreation. It is at that age of aptness, docility, and emulation of the practices of manhood, that such things are soonest learnt and longest remembered. The use of tools too in the manual arts is worthy of encouragement, by facilitating to such as choose it, an admission into the neighboring workshops. To these should be added the arts which embellish life, dancing, music, and drawing; the last more especially, as an important part of military education. These innocent arts furnish amusement and happiness to those who, having time on their hands, might less inoffensively employ it. Needing, at the same time, no regular incorporation with the institution, they may be left to accessory teachers, who will be paid by the individuals employing them, the University only providing proper apartments for their exercise.

The fifth duty prescribed to the Commissioners, is to propose such general provisions as may be properly enacted by the Legislature, for the better organizing and governing the University.

In the education of youth, provision is to be made for, 1, tuition; 2, diet; 3, lodging; 4, government; and 5, honorary excitements. The first of these constitutes the proper functions of the professors;

2, the dieting of the students should be left to private boarding houses of their own choice, and at their own expense; to be regulated by the Visitors from time to time, the house only being provided by the University within its own precincts, and thereby of course subjected to the general regimen, moral or sumptuary, which they shall prescribe. 3. They should be lodged in dormitories, making a part of the general system of buildings. 4. The best mode of government for youth, in large collections, is certainly a desideratum not yet attained with us. It may be well questioned whether *fear* after a certain age, is a motive to which we should have ordinary recourse. The human character is susceptible of other incitements to correct conduct, more worthy of employ, and of better effect. Pride of character, laudable ambition, and moral dispositions are innate correctives of the indiscretions of that lively age; and when strengthened by habitual appeal and exercise, have a happier effect on future character than the degrading motive of fear. Hardening them to disgrace, to corporal punishments, and servile humiliations cannot be the best process for producing erect character. The affectionate deportment between father and son, offers in truth the best example for that of tutor and pupil; and the experience and practice of other[1] countries, in this respect, may be worthy of inquiry and consideration with us. It will then be for the wisdom and discretion of the Visitors to devise and perfect a proper system of government, which, if it be founded in reason and comity, will be more likely to nourish in the minds of our youth the combined spirit of order and self-respect, so congenial with our political institutions, and so important to be woven into the American character. 5. What qualifications shall be required to entitle to entrance into the University, the arrangement of the days and hours of lecturing for the different schools, so as to facilitate to the students the circle of attendance on them; the establishment of periodical and public examinations, the premiums to be given for distinguished merit; whether honorary degrees shall be conferred, and by what appellations; whether the title to these shall depend on the time the candidate has been at the University, or, where nature has given a greater share of understanding, attention, and application; whether

[1] A police exercised by the students themselves, under proper discretion, has been tried with success in some countries, and then rather as forming them for initiation into the duties and practices of civil life.

he shall not be allowed the advantages resulting from these endowments, with other minor items of government, we are of opinion should be entrusted to the Visitors; and the statute under which we act having provided for the appointment of these, we think they should moreover be charged with

The erection, preservation, and repair of the buildings, the care of the grounds and appurtenances, and of the interest of the University generally.

That they should have power to appoint a bursar, employ a proctor, and all other necessary agents.

To appoint and remove professors, two-thirds of the whole number of Visitors voting for the removal.

To prescribe their duties and the course of education, in conformity with the law.

To establish rules for the government and discipline of the students, not contrary to the laws of the land.

To regulate the tuition fees, and the rent of the dormitories they occupy.

To prescribe and control the duties and proceedings of all officers, servants, and others, with respect to the buildings, lands, appurtenances, and other property and interests of the University.

To draw from the literary fund such moneys as are by law charged on it for this institution; and in general

To direct and do all matters and things which, not being inconsistent with the laws of the land, as to them shall seem most expedient for promoting the purposes of the said institution; which several functions they should be free to exercise in the form of by-laws, rules, resolutions, orders, instructions, or otherwise, as they should deem proper.

That they should have two stated meetings in the year, and occasional meetings at such times as they should appoint, or on a special call with such notice as themselves shall prescribe by a general rule; which meetings should be at the University, a majority of them constituting a quorum for business; and that on the death or resignation of a member, or on his removal by the President and Directors of the Literary Fund, or the Executive, or such other authority as the Legislature shall think best, such President and Directors, or the Executive, or other authority, shall appoint a successor.

That the said Visitors should appoint one of their own body to be Rector, and with him be a body corporate, under the style and title of the Rector and Visitors of the University of Virginia, with the right, as such, to use a common seal; that they should have capacity to plead and be impleaded in all courts of justice, and in all cases interesting to the University, which may be the subjects of legal cognizance and jurisdiction; which pleas should not abate by the determination of their office, but should stand revived in the name of their successors, and they should be capable in law and in trust for the University, of receiving subscriptions and donations, real and personal, as well from bodies corporate, or persons associated, as from private individuals.

And that the said Rector and Visitors should, at all times, conform to such laws as the Legislature may, from time to time, think proper to enact for their government; and the said University should, in all things, and at all times, be subject to the control of the Legislature . . .

> Nathaniel F. Cabell (ed.), *Early History of the University of Virginia* (Richmond, 1856), 432–44

## IV.24 To John Brazier

Poplar Forest, August 24, 1819

Sir, – The acknowledgment of your favor of July 15th, and thanks for the Review which it covered of Mr. Pickering's Memoir on the Modern Greek, have been delayed by a visit to an occasional but distant residence from Monticello, and to an attack here of rheumatism which is just now moderating. I had been much pleased with the memoir, and was much also with your review of it. I have little hope indeed of the recovery of the ancient pronunciation of that finest of human languages, but still I rejoice at the attention the subject seems to excite with you, because it is an evidence that our country begins to have a taste for something more than merely as much Greek as will pass a candidate for clerical ordination.

You ask my opinion on the extent to which classical learning should be carried in our country. A sickly condition permits me to think, and a rheumatic hand to write too briefly on this litigated question. The utilities we derive from the remains of the Greek and Latin languages are, first, as models of pure taste in writing. To these we are certainly indebted for the national and chaste style of modern composition which so much distinguishes the nations to whom these languages are familiar. Without these models we should probably have continued the inflated style of our northern ancestors, or the hyperbolical and vague one of the east. Second. Among the values of classical learning, I estimate the luxury of reading the Greek and Roman authors in all the beauties of their originals. And why should not this innocent and elegant luxury take its preëminent stand ahead of all those addressed merely to the senses? I think myself more indebted to my father for this than for all the other luxuries his cares and affections have placed within my reach; and more now than when younger, and more susceptible of delights from other sources. When the decays of age have enfeebled the useful energies of the mind, the classic pages fill up the vacuum of *ennui*, and become sweet composers to that rest of the grave into which we are all sooner or later to descend. Third. A third value is in the stores of real science deposited and transmitted us in these languages, to-wit: in history, ethics, arithmetic, geometry, astronomy, natural history, &c.

But to whom are these things useful? Certainly not to all men. There are conditions of life to which they must be forever estranged, and there are epochs of life too, after which the endeavor to attain them would be a great misemployment of time. Their acquisition should be the occupation of our early years only, when the memory is susceptible of deep and lasting impressions, and reason and judgment not yet strong enough for abstract speculations. To the moralist they are valuable, because they furnish ethical writings highly and justly esteemed: although in my own opinion, the moderns are far advanced beyond them in this line of science, the divine finds in the Greek language a translation of his primary code, of more importance to him than the original because better understood; and, in the same language, the newer code, with the doctrines of the earliest fathers, who lived and wrote before the simple precepts of the founder of this most benign and pure of all systems of morality became frittered into subtleties and mysteries, and hidden under jargons incomprehensible to the human mind.

To these original sources he must now, therefore, return, to recover the virgin purity of his religion. The lawyer finds in the Latin language the system of civil law most conformable with the principles of justice of any which has ever yet been established among men, and from which much has been incorporated into our own. The physician as good a code of his art as has been given us to this day. Theories and systems of medicine, indeed, have been in perpetual change from the days of the good Hippocrates to the days of good [Dr. Benjamin] Rush, but which of them is the true one? the present, to be sure, as long as it is the present, but to yield its place in turn to the next novelty, which is then to become the true system, and is to mark the vast advance of medicine since the days of Hippocrates. Our situation is certainly benefited by the discovery of some new and very valuable medicines; and substituting those for some of his with the treasure of facts, and of sound observations recorded by him (mixed to be sure with anilities [folk or home remedies] of his day) and we shall have nearly the present sum of the healing art. The statesman will find in these languages history, politics, mathematics, ethics, eloquence, love of country, to which he must add the sciences of his own day, for which of them should be unknown to him? And all the sciences must recur to the classical languages for the etymon [real or original meaning], and sound understanding of their fundamental terms. For the merchant I should not say that the languages are a necessary. Ethics, mathematics, geography, political economy, history, seem to constitute the immediate foundations of his calling. The agriculturist needs ethics, mathematics, chemistry and natural philosophy. The mechanic the same. To them the languages are but ornament and comfort. I know it is often said there have been shining examples of men of great abilities in all the businesses of life, without any other science than what they had gathered from conversations and intercourse with the world. But who can say what these men would not have been had they started in the science on the shoulders of a Demosthenes or Cicero, of a Locke or Bacon, or a Newton? To sum the whole, therefore, it may truly be said that the classical languages are a solid basis for most, and an ornament to all the sciences.

I am warned by my aching fingers to close this hasty sketch, and to place here my last and fondest wishes for the advancement of our country in the useful sciences and arts, and my assurances of respect and esteem for the Reviewer of the Memoir on modern Greek.

Washington VII: 130–3

## IV.25 To William Short

Monticello, October 31, 1819

Dear Sir, – Your favor of the 21st is received. My late illness, in which you are so kind as to feel an interest, was produced by a spasmodic stricture of the ileum, which came upon me on the 7th inst. The crisis was short, passed over favorably on the fourth day, and I should soon have been well but that a dose of calomel and jalap, in which were only eight or nine grains of the former, brought on a salivation. Of this, however, nothing now remains but a little soreness of the mouth. I have been able to get on horseback for three or four days past.

As you say of yourself, I too am an Epicurian. I consider the genuine (not the imputed) doctrines of Epicurus as containing everything rational in moral philosophy which Greece and Rome have left us. Epictetus indeed, has given us what was good of the Stoics; all beyond, of their dogmas, being hypocrisy and grimace. Their great crime was in their calumnies of Epicurus and misrepresentations of his doctrines; in which we lament to see the candid character of Cicero engaging as an accomplice. Diffuse, vapid, rhetorical, but enchanting. His prototype Plato, eloquent as himself, dealing out mysticisms incomprehensible to the human mind, has been deified by certain sects usurping the name of Christians; because, in his foggy conceptions, they found a basis of impenetrable darkness whereon to rear fabrications as delirious, of their own invention. These they fathered blasphemously on Him whom they claimed as their Founder, but who would disclaim them with the indignation which their caricatures of His religion so justly excite. Of Socrates we have nothing genuine but in the *Memorabilia* of Xenophon; for Plato makes him one of his Collocutors merely to cover his own whimsies under the mantle of his name; a liberty of which we are told Socrates himself complained. Seneca is indeed a fine moralist, disfiguring his work at times with some Stoicisms, and affecting too much of antithesis and point, yet giving us on the whole a great deal of sound and practical morality. But the greatest of all the reformers of the depraved religion of His own country, was Jesus of Nazareth. Abstracting what is really His from the rubbish in which it is buried, easily distinguished by its lustre from the dross of His biographers, and as separable from that as the diamond from the dunghill, we have the outlines of a system of the most sublime morality which has ever fallen from the lips of man; outlines which it is lamentable He did not live to fill up. Epictetus and Epicurus give laws for governing ourselves, Jesus a supplement of the duties and charities we owe to others. The establishment of the innocent and genuine character of this benevolent Moralist, and the rescuing it from the imputation of imposture, which has resulted from artificial Systems,[1] invented by ultra-Christian sects, unauthorized by a single word ever uttered by Him, is a most desirable object, and one to which Priestley[2] has successfully devoted his labors and learning. It would in time, it is to be hoped, effect a quiet euthanasia of the heresies of bigotry and fanaticism which have so long triumphed over human reason, and so generally and deeply afflicted mankind; but this work is to be begun by winnowing the grain from the chaff of the historians of His life. I have sometimes thought of translating Epictetus (for he has never been tolerably translated into English) by adding the genuine doctrines of Epicurus from the *Syntagma* of Gassendi, and an abstract from the Evangelists of whatever has the stamp of the eloquence and fine imagination of Jesus. The last I attempted too hastily some twelve or fifteen years ago. It was the work of two or three nights only, at Washington, after getting through the evening task of reading the letters and papers of the day. But with one foot in the grave, these are now idle projects for me. My business is to beguile the wearisomeness of declining life, as I endeavour to do, by the delights of classical reading and of mathematical truths, and by the consolations of a sound philosophy, equally indifferent to hope and fear.

---

[1] *E.g.* The immaculate conception of Jesus, His deification, the creation of the world by Him. His miraculous powers, His resurrection and visible ascension. His corporeal presence in the Eucharist, the Trinity, original sin, atonement, regeneration, election, orders of Hierarchy, etc.

[2] See *supra*, IV.10. – *Eds.*

I take the liberty of observing that you are not a true disciple of our master Epicurus, in indulging the indolence to which you say you are yielding. One of his canons, you know, was that "that indulgence which presents a greater pleasure, or produces a greater pain, is to be avoided." Your love of repose will lead, in its progress, to a suspension of healthy exercise, a relaxation of mind, an indifference to everything around you, and finally to a debility of body, and hebetude of mind, the farthest of all things from the happiness which the well-regulated indulgences of Epicurus ensure; fortitude, you know, is one of his four cardinal virtues. That teaches us to meet and surmount difficulties; not to fly from them, like cowards; and to fly, too, in vain, for they will meet and arrest us at every turn of our road. Weigh this matter well; brace yourself up; take a seat with Corrèa [da Serra], and come and see the finest portion of your country, which, if you have not forgotten, you still do not know, because it is no longer the same as when you knew it. It will add much to the happiness of my recovery to be able to receive Correa and yourself, and prove the estimation in which I hold you both. Come, too, and see our incipient University [of Virginia], which has advanced with great activity this year. By the end of the next, we shall have elegant accommodations for seven professors, and the year following the professors themselves. No secondary character will be received among them. Either the ablest which America or Europe can furnish, or none at all. They will give us the selected society of a great city separated from the dissipations and levities of its ephemeral insects.

I am glad the bust of Condorcet has been saved and so well placed. His genius should be before us; while the lamentable, but singular act of ingratitude which tarnished his latter days, may be thrown behind us.

I will place under this a syllabus of the doctrines of Epicurus, somewhat in the lapidary style, which I wrote some twenty years ago; a like one of the philosophy of Jesus, of nearly the same age, is too long to be copied. *Vale, et tibi persuade carissimum te esse mihi.*

### *Syllabus of the doctrines of Epicurus.*

*Physical.* – The Universe eternal.
Its parts, great and small, interchangeable.

Matter and Void alone.

Motion inherent in matter which is weighty and declining.

Eternal circulation of the elements of bodies.

Gods, an order of beings next superior to man, enjoying in their sphere, their own felicities; but not meddling with the concerns of the scale of beings below them.

*Moral.* – Happiness the aim of life.

Virtue the foundation of happiness.

Utility the test of virtue.

Pleasure active and In-do-lent.

In-do-lence is the absence of pain, the true felicity.

Active, consists in agreeable motion; it is not happiness, but the means to produce it.

Thus the absence of hunger is an article of felicity; eating the means to obtain it.

The *summum bonum* is to be not pained in body, nor troubled in mind.

*i.e.* In-do-lence of body, tranquillity of mind.

To procure tranquillity of mind we must avoid desire and fear, the two principal diseases of the mind.

Man is a free agent.

Virtue consists in 1. Prudence. 2. Temperance. 3. Fortitude. 4. Justice.

To which are opposed, 1. Folly. 2. Desire. 3. Fear. 4. Deceit.

L & B xv: 219–24


## IV.26 To —[1]

Monticello, February 3, 1825

Dear Sir, – Although our professors were, on the 5th of December, still in an English port, that they were safe raises me from the dead, for I was almost ready to give up the ship. That was eight weeks ago; they may therefore be daily expected.

In most public seminaries text-books are prescribed to each of the several schools, as the *norma docendi* in that school; and this

---

[1] Addressee unknown. – *Eds.*

is generally done by authority of the trustees. I should not propose this generally in our University, because I believe none of us are so much at the heights of science in the several branches, as to undertake this, and therefore that it will be better left to the professors until occasion of interference shall be given. But there is one branch in which we are the best judges, in which heresies may be taught, of so interesting a character to our own State and to the United States, as to make it a duty in us to lay down the principles which are to be taught. It is that of government. Mr. Gilmer being withdrawn, we know not who his successor may be. He may be a Richmond lawyer, or one of that school of quondam federalism, now consolidation. It is our duty to guard against such principles being disseminated among our youth, and the diffusion of that poison, by a previous prescription of the texts to be followed in their discourses. I therefore enclose you a resolution which I think of proposing at our next meeting, strictly confiding it to your own knowledge alone, and to that of Mr. Loyall, to whom you may communicate it, as I am sure it will harmonize with his principles. I wish it kept to ourselves, because I have always found that the less such things are spoken of beforehand, the less obstruction is contrived to be thrown in their way. I have communicated it to Mr. Madison.

Should the bill for district colleges pass in the end, our scheme of education will be complete. But the branch of primary schools may need attention, and should be brought, like the rest, to the forum of the legislature. The Governor, in his annual message, gives a favorable account of them in the lump. But this is not sufficient. We should know the operation of the law establishing these schools more in detail. We should know how much money is furnished to each county every year, and how much education it distributes every year, and such a statement should be laid before the legislature every year. The sum of education rendered in each county in each year should be estimated by adding together the number of months which each scholar attended, and stating the sum total of the months which all of them together attended, *e.g.*, if in any county one scholar attended two months, three others four months each, eight others six months each, then the sum of these added together will make sixty-two months of schooling afforded in the county that year; and the number of sixty-two months entered in a table opposite to the name of the county, gives a satisfactory idea of the sum or quantum of education it rendered in that year. This will enable us to take many interesting and important views of the sufficiency of the plan established, and of the amendments necessary to produce the greatest effect. I enclose a form of the table which would be required, in which you will of course be sensible that the numbers entered are at hap-hazard, and *exempli gratia*, as I know nothing of the sums furnished or quantum of education rendered in each or any county. I send also the form of such a resolution as should be passed by the one or the other House, perhaps better in the lower one, and moved by some member nowise connected with us, for the less we appear before the House, the less we shall excite dissatisfaction.

I mentioned to you formerly our want of an anatomical hall for dissection. But if we get the fifty thousand dollars from Congress, we can charge to that, as the library fund, the six thousand dollars of the building fund which we have advanced for it in books and apparatus, and repaying from the former the six thousand dollars due to the latter, apply so much of it as is necessary for the anatomical building. No application on the subject need therefore be made to our legislature. But I hear nothing of our prospects before Congress. Yours affectionately.

*Resolved*, That the Governor be requested to have prepared and laid before the legislature, at their next session, a statement in detail of the sum of education which, under the law establishing primary schools, has been rendered in the schools of each county respectively; that it be stated in a tabular form, in the first column of which table shall be the names of the counties alphabetically arranged, and then, for every year, two other columns, in the first of which shall be entered, opposite to the name of each county, the sum of money furnished it in that year, and in the second shall be stated the sum of education rendered in the same county and year; which sum is to be estimated by adding together the number of months of schooling which the several individuals attending received. And that hence forward a similar statement be prepared and laid before the legislature every year for that year.

| | | | |
|---|---|---|---|
| Accomac............... | $400 | 216 | months schooling. |
| Albemarle............... | 500 | 234 | months schooling. |
| Amelia.................... | 250 | 183 | months schooling. |
| Amherst ................. | 400 | 210 | months schooling. |
| Augusta.................. | 800 | 461 | months schooling. |

etc.

L & B XVI: 103–7

# v    The Constitutions of Virginia and France

## v.1 From the *Autobiography*

In giving this account of the laws of which I was myself the mover & draughtsman, I by no means mean to claim to myself the merit of obtaining their passage. I had many occasional and strenuous coadjutors in debate, and one most steadfast, able, and zealous; who was himself a host. This was George Mason, a man of the first order of wisdom among those who acted on the theatre of the revolution, of expansive mind, profound judgment, cogent in argument, learned in the lore of our former constitution, and earnest for the republican change on democratic principles. His elocution was neither flowing nor smooth, but his language was strong, his manner most impressive, and strengthened by a dash of biting cynicism when provocation made it seasonable.

Mr. [George] Wythe, while speaker in the two sessions of 1777 between his return from Congress and his appointment to the Chancery, was an able and constant associate in whatever was before a committee of the whole. His pure integrity, judgment and reasoning powers gave him great weight. Of him see more in some notes inclosed in my letter of August 31. 1821, to Mr. John Saunderson.

Mr. [James] Madison came into the House in 1776 a new member and young; which circumstances, concurring with his extreme modesty, prevented his venturing himself in debate before his removal to the Council of State in Nov. 77. From thence he went to Congress, then consisting of few members. Trained in these successive schools, he acquired a habit of self-possession which placed at ready command the rich resources of his luminous and discriminating mind, & of his extensive information, and rendered him the first of every assembly afterwards of which he became a member. Never wandering from his subject into vain declamation, but pursuing it closely in language pure, classical, and copious, soothing always the feelings of his adversaries by civilities and softness of expression, he rose to the eminent station which he held in the great National convention of 1787 and in that of Virginia which followed, he sustained the new constitution in all its parts, bearing off the palm against the logic of George Mason, and the fervid declamation of Mr. [Patrick] Henry. With these consummate powers were united a pure and spotless virtue which no calumny has ever attempted to sully. Of the powers and polish of his pen, and of the wisdom of his administration in the highest office of the nation, I need say nothing. They have spoken, and will forever speak for themselves.

So far we were proceeding in the details of reformation only; selecting points of legislation prominent in character & principle, urgent, and indicative of the strength of the general pulse of reformation. When I left Congress, in 76, it was in the persuasion that our whole [Virginia] code must be reviewed, adapted to our republican form of government, and, now that we had no negatives of Councils, Governors & Kings to restrain us from doing right, that it should be corrected, in all it's parts, with a single eye to reason, & the good of those for whose government it was framed. Early therefore in the session of 76 to which I returned, I moved and presented a bill for the revision of the laws; which was passed on the 24th of October, and on the 5th of November Mr. [Edmund] Pendleton, Mr. Wythe, George Mason, Thomas L. Lee and myself were appointed a committee to execute the work. We agreed to meet at Fredericksburg to settle the plan of operation and to distribute the work. We met there accordingly, on the 13th of January 1777. The first question was whether we should propose to abolish the whole existing system of laws, and prepare a new and complete *Institute*, or preserve the general system, and only modify it to the present state of things. Mr. Pendleton, contrary to his usual disposition in favor of antient things, was for the former proposition, in which he was joined by Mr. Lee. To this it was objected that to abrogate our whole system would be a bold measure, and probably far beyond the views of the legislature; that they had been in the practice of revising from time to time the laws of the colony, omitting the expired, the repealed and the obsolete, amending only those retained, and probably meant we should now do the same, only including the British statutes as well as our own: that to compose a new *Institute* like those of Justinian and Bracton, or that of Blackstone, which was the model proposed by Mr. Pendleton, would be an arduous undertaking, of vast research, of great consideration & judgment; and when reduced to a text, every word of that text, from the imperfection of human language, and it's incompetence to express distinctly every shade of idea, would become a subject of question & chicanery until settled by repeated adjudications; that this would involve us for ages in litigation, and render property uncertain until, like the statutes of old, every word had been tried, and settled by numerous decisions, and by new volumes of reports & commentaries; and that no one of us probably would undertake such a work, which, to be systematical, must be the work of one hand. This last was the opinion of Mr. Wythe, Mr. Mason & myself. When we proceeded to the distribution of the work, Mr. Mason excused himself as, being no lawyer, he felt himself unqualified for the work, and he resigned soon after. Mr. Lee excused himself on the same ground, and died indeed in a short time. The other two gentlemen therefore and myself divided the work among us. The common law and statutes to the 4 James I (when our separate legislature was established) were assigned to me; the British statutes from that period to the present day to Mr. Wythe, and the Virginia laws to Mr. Pendleton. As the law of Descents, & the criminal law fell of course within my portion, I wished the comm[itt]ee to settle the leading principles of these, as a guide for me in framing them. And with respect to the first, I proposed to abolish the law of primogeniture, and to make real estate descendible in parcenary [joint heirship] to the next of kin, as personal property is by the statute of distribution. Mr. Pendleton wished to preserve the right of primogeniture, but seeing at once that that could not prevail, he proposed we should adopt the Hebrew principle, and give a double portion to the elder son. I observed that if the eldest son could eat twice as much, or do double work, it might be a natural evidence of his right to a double portion; but being on a par in his powers & wants, with his brothers and sisters, he should be on a par also in the partition of the patrimony, and such was the decision of the other members.

On the subject of the Criminal law, all were agreed that the punishment of death should be abolished, except for treason and murder; and that, for other felonies should be substituted hard labor in the public works, and in some cases, the *Lex talionis.* How this last revolting principle came to obtain our approbation, I do not remember. There remained indeed in our laws a vestige of it in a single case of a slave. It was the English law in the time of the Anglo-Saxons, copied probably from the Hebrew law of "an eye for an eye, a tooth for a tooth," and it was the law of several antient people. But the modern mind had left it far in the rear of it's advances. These points however being settled, we repaired to our respective homes for the preparation of the work.

Feb. 6. In the execution of my part I thought it material not to vary the diction of the antient statutes by modernizing it, nor to give rise to new questions by new expressions. The text of these statutes had been so fully explained and defined by numerous adjudications, as scarcely ever now to produce a question in our courts. I thought it would be useful also, in all new draughts, to reform the style of the later British statutes, and of our own acts of assembly, which from their verbosity, their endless tautologies, their involutions of case within case, and parenthesis within parenthesis, and their multiplied efforts at certainty by *saids* and *aforesaids*, by *ors* and by *ands*, to make them more plain, do really render them more perplexed and incomprehensible, not only to common readers, but to the lawyers themselves.

Ford I: 56–61

## v.2 *Notes on Virginia*: Query XIII

[Defects of the Virginia State Constitution]

This constitution was formed when we were new and unexperienced in the science of government. It was the first, too, which was formed in the whole United States. No wonder then that time and trial have discovered very capital defects in it.

1. The majority of the men in the state, who pay and fight for its support, are unrepresented in the legislature, the roll of free-holders entitled to vote, not including generally the half of those on the roll of the militia, or of the tax-gatherers.

2. Among those who share the representation, the shares are very unequal. Thus the county of Warwick, with only one hundred fighting men, has an equal representation with the county of Loudon, which has 1,746. So that every man in Warwick has as much influence in the government as 17 men in Loudon. But lest it should be thought that an equal interspersion of small among large counties, through the whole state, may prevent any danger of injury to particular parts of it, we will divide it into districts, and shew the proportions of land, of fighting men, and of representation in each.

| | Square miles | Fighting men | Delegates | Senators |
|---|---|---|---|---|
| Between the sea-coast and falls of the rivers............................ | [1]11,205 | 19,012 | 71 | 12 |
| Between the falls of the rivers and Blue Ridge of mountains | 18,759 | 18,828 | 46 | 8 |
| Between the Blue Ridge and the Alleghany........................ | 11,911 | 7,673 | 16 | 2 |
| Between the Alleghany and Ohio...................................... | [2]79,650 | 4,458 | 16 | 2 |
| Total.......................................... | 121,525 | 49,971 | 149 | 24 |

[1] Of these, 542 are on the eastern shore.
[2] Of these, 22,616 are Eastward of the meridian of the mouth of the Great Kanhaway.

An inspection of this table will supply the place of commentaries on it. It will appear at once that nineteen thousand men, living below the falls of the rivers, possess half of the senate, and want four members only of possessing a majority of the house of delegates; a want more than supplied by the vicinity of their situation to the seat of government, and of course the greater degree of convenience and punctuality with which their members may and will attend in the legislature. These nineteen thousand, therefore, living in one part of the country, give law to upwards of thirty thousand living in another, and appoint all their chief officers executive and judiciary. From the difference of their situation and circumstances, their interests will often be very different.

3. The senate is, by its constitution, too homogenous with the house of delegates. Being chosen by the same electors, at the same time, and out of the same subjects, the choice falls of course on men of the same description. The purpose of establishing different houses of legislation is to introduce the influence of different interests or different principles. Thus in Great Britain it is said their constitution relies on the house of commons for honesty, and the lords for wisdom; which would be a rational reliance, if honesty were to be bought with money, and if wisdom were hereditary. In some of the American States, the delegates and senators are so chosen, as that the first represent the persons, and the second the

property of the State. But with us, wealth and wisdom have equal chance for admission into both houses. We do not, therefore, derive from the separation of our legislature into two houses, those benefits which a proper complication of principles is capable of producing, and those which alone can compensate the evils which may be produced by their dissensions.

4. All the powers of government, legislative, executive, and judiciary, result to the legislative body. The concentrating these in the same hands is precisely the definition of despotic government. It will be no alleviation that these powers will be exercised by a plurality of hands, and not by a single one. 173 despots would surely be as oppressive as one. Let those who doubt it turn their eyes on the republic of Venice. As little will it avail us that they are chosen by ourselves. An *elective despotism* was not the government we fought for, but one which should not only be founded on free principles, but in which the powers of government should be so divided and balanced among several bodies of magistracy, as that no one could transcend their legal limits, without being effectually checked and restrained by the others. For this reason that convention, which passed the ordinance of government, laid its foundation on this basis, that the legislative, executive and judiciary departments should be separate and distinct, so that no person should exercise the powers of more than one of them at the same time. But no barrier was provided between these several powers. The judiciary and executive members were left dependent on the legislative, for their subsistence in office, and some of them for their continuance in it. If therefore the legislature assumes executive and judiciary powers, no opposition is likely to be made; nor, if made, can it be effectual; because in that case they may put their proceedings into the form of an act of assembly, which will render them obligatory on the other branches. They have accordingly in many instances, decided rights which should have been left to judiciary controversy: and the direction of the executive, during the whole time of their session, is becoming habitual and familiar. And this is done with no ill intention. The views of the present members are perfectly upright. When they are led out of their regular province, it is by art in others, and inadvertence in themselves. And this will probably be the case for some time to come. But it will not be a very long time. Mankind soon learn to make interested uses of every right

and power which they possess, or may assume. The public money and public liberty, intended to have been deposited with three branches of magistracy, but found inadvertently to be in the hands of one only, will soon be discovered to be sources of wealth and dominion to those who hold them; distinguished, too, by this tempting circumstance, that they are the instrument, as well as the object, of acquisition. With money we will get men, said Cæsar, and with men we will get money. Nor should our assembly be deluded by the integrity of their own purposes, and conclude that these unlimited powers will never be abused, because themselves are not disposed to abuse them. They should look forward to a time, and that not a distant one, when a corruption in this, as in the country from which we derive our origin, will have seized the heads of government, and be spread by them through the body of the people; when they will purchase the voices of the people, and make them pay the price. Human nature is the same on every side of the Atlantic, and will be alike influenced by the same causes. The time to guard against corruption and tyranny, is before they shall have gotten hold of us. It is better to keep the wolf out of the fold, than to trust to drawing his teeth and talons after he shall have entered. To render these considerations the more cogent, we must observe in addition:

5. That the ordinary legislature may alter the constitution itself. On the discontinuance of assemblies, it became necessary to substitute in their place some other body, competent to the ordinary business of government, and to the calling forth the powers of the State for the maintenance of our opposition to Great Britain. Conventions were therefore introduced, consisting of two delegates from each county, meeting together and forming one house, on the plan of the former house of Burgesses, to whose places they succeeded. These were at first chosen anew for every particular session. But in March 1775, they recommended to the people to choose a convention, which should continue in office a year. This was done, accordingly, in April 1775, and in the July following that convention passed an ordinance for the election of delegates in the month of April annually. It is well known, that in July 1775, a separation from Great Britain and establishment of republican government, had never yet entered into any person's mind. A convention, therefore, chosen under that ordinance, cannot be said to have been chosen for the

purposes which certainly did not exist in the minds of those who passed it. Under this ordinance, at the annual election in April 1776, a convention for the year was chosen. Independance, and the establishment of a new form of government, were not even yet the objects of the people at large. One extract from the pamphlet called Common sense[3] had appeared in the Virginia papers in February, and copies of the pamphlet itself had got in a few hands. But the idea had not been opened to the mass of the people in April, much less can it be said that they had made up their minds in its favor. So that the electors of April 1776, no more than the legislators of July 1775, not thinking of independance and a permanent republic, could not mean to vest in these delegates powers of establishing them, or any authorities other than those of the ordinary legislature. So far as a temporary organization of government was necessary to render our opposition energetic, so far their organization was valid. But they received in their creation no powers but what were given to every legislature before and since. They could not, therefore, pass an act transcendent to the powers of other legislatures. If the present assembly pass an act, and declare it shall be irrevocable by subsequent assemblies, the declaration is merely void, and the act repealable, as other acts are. So far, and no farther authorized, they organized the government by the ordinance entituled a Constitution or Form of government. It pretends to no higher authority than the other ordinance of the same session; it does not say that it shall be perpetual; that it shall be unalterable by other legislatures; that it shall be transcendent above the powers of those who they knew would have equal power with themselves. Not only the silence of the instrument is a proof they thought it would be alterable, but their own practice also; for this very convention, meeting as a House of Delegates in General assembly with the Senate in the autumn of that year, passed acts of assembly in contradiction to their ordinance of government; and every assembly from that time to this has done the same. I am safe therefore in the position that the constitution itself is alterable by the ordinary legislature. Though this opinion seems founded on the first elements of common sense, yet is the contrary maintained by some persons. 1. Because, say they, the conventions were vested with every power necessary to make effectual

---

[3] Thomas Paine, *Common Sense* (Philadelphia, 1775; 2nd edn. 1776). – *Eds.*

opposition to Great Britain. But to complete this argument, they must go on, and say further, that effectual opposition could not be made to Great Britain without establishing a form of government perpetual and unalterable by the legislature; which is not true. An opposition which at some time or other was to come to an end, could not need a perpetual institution to carry it on: and a government amendable as its defects should be discovered, was as likely to make effectual resistance, as one that should be unalterably wrong. Besides, the assemblies were as much vested with all powers requisite for resistance as the Conventions were. If therefore these powers included that of modelling the form of government in the one case, they did so in the other. The assemblies then as well as the conventions may model the government; that is, they may alter the ordinance of government. 2. They urge that if the convention had meant that this instrument should be alterable, as their other ordinances were, they would have called it an ordinance; but they have called it a *constitution*, which, *ex vi termini*, means "an act above the power of the ordinary legislature." I answer that *constitutio, constitutum, statutum, lex*, are convertible terms. "*Constitutio* dicitur jus quod a principe conditur." "*Constitutum*, quod ab imperatoribus rescriptum statutumve est." "*Statutum*, idem quod lex." *Calvini Lexicon juridicum. Constitution* and *statute* were originally terms of the[4] civil law, and from thence introduced by Ecclesiastics into the English law. Thus in the statute 25 Hen. VIII. c. 19, § 1, "*Constitutions* and *ordinances*" are used as synonimous. The term *constitution* has many other significations in physics and politics; but in Jurisprudence, whenever it is applied to any act of the legislature, it invariably means a statute, law, or ordinance, which is the present case. No inference then of a different meaning can be drawn from the adoption of this title: on the contrary, we might conclude that, by their affixing to it a term synonimous with ordinance or statute, they meant it to be an ordinance or statute. But of what consequence is their meaning, where their power is denied? If they meant to do more than they had power to do, did this give them power? It is not the name, but the authority which renders an act obligatory. Lord Coke[5] says, "an article of the statute, 11. R. II. c. 5. that no

---

[4] To bid, to set, was the ancient legislative word of the English. Ll. Hlotharri and Eadrici. Ll. Inæ. Ll. Eadwerdi. Ll. Æathelstani.

[5] See *supra*, III.14, note 2. – *Eds.*

person should attempt to revoke any ordinance then made, is repealed, for that such restraint is against the jurisdiction and power
of the parliament." 4. inst. 42. and again, "though divers parliaments have attempted to restrain subsequent parliaments, yet could
they never effect it; for the latter parliament hath ever power to
abrogate, suspend, qualify, explain, or make void the former in the
whole or in any part thereof, notwithstanding any words of
restraint, prohibition, or penalty, in the former; for it is a maxim in
the laws of the parliament, 'quo leges posteriores priores contrarias
abrogant.'" 4. inst. 43. – To get rid of the magic supposed to be in
the word *constitution*, let us translate it into its definition as given
by those who think it above the power of the law; and let us suppose
the convention, instead of saying, "We the ordinary legislature,
establish a *constitution*," had said, "We the ordinary legislature,
establish an act *above the power of the ordinary legislature*." Does not
this expose the absurdity of the attempt? 3. But, say they, the people
have acquiesced, and this has given it an authority superior to the
laws. It is true that the people did not rebel against it: and was
that a time for the people to rise in rebellion? Should a prudent
acquiescence, at a critical time, be construed into a confirmation of
every illegal thing done during that period? Besides, why should
they rebel? At an annual election they had chosen delegates for the
year, to exercise the ordinary powers of legislation, and to manage
the great contest in which they were engaged. These delegates
thought the contest would be best managed by an organized government. They therefore, among others, passed an ordinance of
government. They did not presume to call it perpetual and unalterable. They well knew they had no power to make it so; that our
choice of them had been for no such purpose, and at a time when
we could have no such purpose in contemplation. Had an unalterable form of government been meditated, perhaps we should have
chosen a different set of people. There was no cause then for the
people to rise in rebellion. But to what dangerous lengths will this
argument lead? Did the acquiescence of the colonies under the various acts of power exercised by Great Britain in our infant state,
confirm these acts, and so far invest them with the authority of the
people as to render them unalterable, and our present resistance
wrong? On every unauthoritative exercise of power by the legislature must the people rise in rebellion, or their silence be construed

into a surrender of that power to them? If so, how many rebellions should we have had already? One certainly for every session of assembly. The other states in the union have been of opinion that to render a form of government unalterable by ordinary acts of assembly, the people must delegate persons with special powers. They have accordingly chosen special conventions to form and fix their governments. The individuals then who maintain the contrary opinion in this country, should have the modesty to suppose it possible that they may be wrong, and the rest of America right. But if there be only a possibility of their being wrong, if only a plausible doubt remains of the validity of the ordinance of government, is it not better to remove that doubt by placing it on a bottom which none will dispute? If they be right we shall only have the unnecessary trouble of meeting once in convention. If they be wrong, they expose us to the hazard of having no fundamental rights at all. True it is, this is no time for deliberating on forms of government. While an enemy is within our bowels, the first object is to expel him. But when this shall be done, when peace shall be established, and leisure given us for intrenching within good forms, the rights for which we have bled, let no man be found indolent enough to decline a little more trouble for placing them beyond the reach of question. If anything more be requisite to produce a conviction of the expediency of calling a convention at a proper season to fix our form of government, let it be the reflection:

6. That the assembly exercises a power of determining the quorum of their own body which may legislate for us. After the establishment of the new form they adhered to the *Lex majoris partis,* founded in[6] common law as well as common right. It is the[7] natural law of every assembly of men, whose numbers are not fixed by any other law. They continued for some time to require the presence of a majority of their whole number, to pass an act. But the British parliament fixes its own quorum; our former assemblies fixed their own quorum; and one precedent in favor of power is stronger than an hundred against it. The house of delegates, therefore, have[8] lately voted that, during the present dangerous invasion, forty members shall be a house to proceed to business. They have

[6] Bro. Abr. Corporations, 31, 34. Hakewell, 93.
[7] Puff. Off. hom. L. 2, c. 6, § 12.
[8] June 4, 1781.

been moved to this by the fear of not being able to collect a house. But this danger could not authorize them to call that a house which was none; and if they may fix it at one number, they may at another, till it loses its fundamental character of being a representative body. As this vote expires with the present invasion, it is probable the former rule will be permitted to revive; because at present no ill is meant. The power, however, of fixing their own quorum has been avowed, and a precedent set. From forty it may be reduced to four, and from four to one; from a house to a committee, from a committee to a chairman or speaker, and thus an oligarchy or monarchy be substituted under forms supposed to be regular. "Omnia mala exempla ex bonis orta sunt; sed ubi imperium ad ignaros aut minus bonos pervenit, novum illud exemplum ab dignis et idoneis ad indignos et non idoneos fertur." When, therefore, it is considered, that there is no legal obstacle to the assumption by the assembly of all the powers legislative, executive, and judiciary, and that these may come to the hands of the smallest rag of delegation, surely the people will say, and their representatives, while yet they have honest representatives, will advise them to say, that they will not acknowledge as laws any acts not considered and assented to by the major part of their delegates.

In enumerating the defects of the constitution, it would be wrong to count among them what is only the error of particular persons. In December 1776, our circumstances being much distressed, it was proposed in the house of delegates to create a *dictator*, invested with every power legislative, executive, and judiciary, civil and military, of life and of death, over our persons and over our properties: and in June 1781, again under calamity, the same proposition was repeated, and wanted a few votes only of being passed. – One who entered into this contest from a pure love of liberty, and a sense of injured rights, who determined to make every sacrifice, and to meet every danger, for the re-establishment of those rights on a firm basis, who did not mean to expend his blood and substance for the wretched purpose of changing this master for that, but to place the powers of governing him in a plurality of hands of his own choice, so that the corrupt will of no one man might in future oppress him, must stand confounded and dismayed when he is told, that a considerable portion of that plurality had meditated the surrender of them into a single hand, and, in lieu of a limited monarch, to deliver him over to a despotic one! How must we find his efforts and sacrifices abused and baffled, if he may still, by a single vote, be laid prostrate at the feet of one man! In God's name, from whence have they derived this power? Is it from our ancient laws? None such can be produced. Is it from any principle in our new constitution expressed or implied? Every lineament of that expressed or implied, is in full opposition to it. Its fundamental principle is, that the state shall be governed as a commonwealth. It provides a republican organization, proscribes under the name of *prerogative* the exercise of all powers undefined by the laws; places on this basis the whole system of our laws; and by consolidating them together, chooses that they shall be left to stand or fall together, never providing for any circumstances, nor admitting that such could arise, wherein either should be suspended; no, not for a moment. Our antient laws expressly declare, that those who are but delegates themselves shall not delegate to others powers which require judgment and integrity in their exercise. – Or was this proposition moved on a supposed right in the movers, of abandoning their posts in a moment of distress? The same laws forbid the abandonment of that post, even on ordinary occasions; and much more a transfer of their powers into other hands and other forms, without consulting the people. They never admit the idea that these, like sheep or cattle, may be given from hand to hand without an appeal to their own will. – Was it from the necessity of the case? Necessities which dissolve a government, do not convey its authority to an oligarchy or a monarchy. They throw back, into the hands of the people, the powers they had delegated, and leave them as individuals to shift for themselves. A leader may offer, but not impose himself, nor be imposed on them. Much less can their necks be submitted to his sword, their breath be held at his will or caprice. The necessity which should operate these tremendous effects should at least be palpable and irresistible. Yet in both instances, where it was feared, or pretended with us, it was belied by the event. It was belied, too, by the preceding experience of our sister states, several of whom had grappled through greater difficulties without abandoning their forms of government. When the proposition was first made, Massachusetts had found even the government of committees sufficient to carry them through an invasion. But we at the time of that proposition, were under no invasion. When the second was made, there had been added to this example those of Rhode-Island, New-York, New-Jersey, and Pennsylvania, in all of which the republican form had been found equal to the task of carrying them through the severest trials. In this state alone did there exist so little virtue, that fear was to be fixed in the hearts of the people, and to become the motive of their exertions, and the principle of their government? The very thought alone was treason against the people; was treason against mankind in general; as riveting forever the chains which bow down their necks, by giving to their oppressors a proof, which they would have trumpeted through the universe, of the imbecility of republican government, in times of pressing danger, to shield them from harm. Those who assume the right of giving away the reins of government in any case, must be sure that the herd, whom they hand on to the rods and hatchet of the dictator, will lay their necks on the block when he shall nod to them. But if our assemblies supposed such a resignation in the people, I hope they mistook their character. I am of opinion, that the government, instead of being braced and invigorated for greater exertions under their difficulties, would have been thrown back upon the bungling machinery of county committees for administration, till a convention could have been called, and its wheels again set into regular motion. What a cruel moment was this for creating such an embarrassment, for putting to the proof the attachment of our countrymen to republican government! Those who meant well, of the advocates for this measure (and most of them meant well, for I know them personally, had been their fellow-labourers in the common cause, and had often proved the purity of their principles), had been seduced in their judgment by the example of an antient republic, whose constitution and circumstances were fundamentally different. They had sought this precedent in the history of Rome, where alone it was to be found, and where at length, too, it had proved fatal. They had taken it from a republic rent by the most bitter factions and tumults, where the government was of a heavy-handed unfeeling aristocracy, over a people ferocious, and rendered desperate by poverty and wretchedness; tumults which could not be allayed under the most trying circumstances, but by the omnipotent hand of a single despot. Their constitution, therefore, allowed a temporary tyrant to be erected, under the name of a Dictator; and that temporary tyrant, after a few examples, became perpetual. They misapplied this precedent to a people mild in their dispositions, patient under their trial, united for the public liberty, and affectionate to their leaders. But if from the constitution of the Roman government there resulted to their Senate a power of submitting all their rights to the will of one man, does it follow that the assembly of Virginia have the same authority? What clause in our constitution has substituted that of Rome, by way of residuary provision, for all cases not otherwise provided for? Or if they may step *ad libitum* into any other form of government for precedents to rule us by, for what oppression may not a precedent be found in this world of the *bellum omnium in omnia*? Searching for the foundations of this proposition, I can find none which may pretend a colour of right or reason, but the defect before developed, that there being no barrier between the legislative, executive, and judiciary departments, the legislature may seize the whole: that having seized it, and possessing a right to fix their own quorum, they may reduce that quorum to one, whom they may call a chairman, speaker, dictator, or by any other name they please. – Our situation is indeed perilous, and I hope my countrymen will be sensible of it, and will apply, at a proper season, the proper remedy; which is a convention to fix the constitution, to amend its defects, to bind up the several branches of government by certain laws, which, when they transgress, their acts shall become nullities; to render unnecessary an appeal to the people, or in other words a rebellion, on every infraction of their rights, on the peril that their acquiescence shall be construed into an intention to surrender those rights.

Ford III: 222–35

## v.3 To Edmund Pendleton

Philadelphia, August 26, 1776

Dear Sir, – Your's of the 10th. inst. came to hand about three days ago, the post having brought no mail with him the last week. You seem to have misapprehended my proposition for the choice of a Senate. I had two things in view: to get the wisest men chosen, and to make them perfectly independent when chosen. I have ever observed that a choice by the people themselves is not generally distinguished for it's wisdom. This first secretion from them is usually crude and heterogeneous. But give to those so chosen by the people a second choice themselves, and they generally will chuse wise men. For this reason it was that I proposed the representatives (and not the people) should chuse the Senate, and thought I had notwithstanding that made the Senators (when chosen) perfectly independent of their electors. However I should have no objection to the mode of election proposed in the printed plan of your committee, to wit, that the people of each county should chuse twelve electors, who should meet those of the other counties in the same district and chuse a senator. I should prefer this too for another reason, that the upper as well as lower house should have an opportunity of superintending and judging of the situation of the whole state and be not all of one neighborhood as our upper house used to be. So much for the wisdom of the Senate. To make them independent, I had proposed that they should hold their places for nine years, and then go out (one third every three years) and be incapable for ever of being re-elected to that house. My idea was that if they might be re-elected, they would be casting their eyes forward to the period of election (however distant) and be currying favor with the electors, and consequently dependent on them. My reason for fixing them in office for a term of years rather than for life, was that they might have in idea that they were at a certain period to return into the mass of the people and become the governed instead of the governors which might still keep alive that regard to the public good that otherwise they might perhaps be induced by their independance to forget. Yet I could submit, tho' not so willingly to an appointment for life, or to any thing rather than a mere creation by and dependance on the people. I think the present mode of election objectionable because the larger county will be able to send and will always send a man (less fit perhaps) of their own county to the exclusion of a fitter who may chance to live in a smaller county. I wish experience may contradict my fears. That the Senate as well as lower (or shall I speak truth and call it upper) house should hold no office of profit I am clear; but not that they should of necessity possess distinguished property. You have lived longer than I have and perhaps may have formed a different judgment on better grounds; but my observations do not enable me to say I think integrity the characteristic of wealth. In general I beleive the decisions of the people, in a body, will be more honest and more disinterested than those of wealthy men: and I can never doubt an attachment to his country in any man who has his family and peculium [fortune] in it. – Now as to the representative house which ought to be so constructed as to answer that character truly. I was for extending the right of suffrage (or in other words the rights of a citizen) to all who had a permanent intention of living in the country. Take what circumstances you please as evidence of this, either the having resided a certain time, or having a family, or having property, any or all of them. Whoever intends to live in a country must wish that country well, and has a natural right of assisting in the preservation of it. I think you cannot distinguish between such a person residing in the country and having no fixed property, and one residing in a township whom you say you would admit to a vote. – The other point of equal representation I think capital and fundamental. I am glad you think an alteration may be attempted in that matter. – The fantastical idea of virtue and the public good being a sufficient security to the state against the commission of crimes, which you say you have heard insisted on by some, I assure you was never mine. It is only the sanguinary hue of our penal laws which I meant to object to. Punishments I know are necessary, and I would provide them, strict and inflexible, but proportioned to the crime. Death might be inflicted for murther and perhaps for treason if you would take out of the description of treason all crimes which are not such in their nature. Rape, buggery &c. punish by castration. All other crimes by working on high roads, rivers, gallies &c. a certain time proportioned to the offence. But as this would be no punishment or change of condition to slaves (*me miserum!*) let them be sent to other countries. By these means we should be freed from the wickedness of the latter, and the former would be living monuments of public vengeance. Laws thus proportionate and mild should never be dispensed with. Let mercy be the character of the law-giver, but let the judge be a mere machine. The mercies of the law will be

dispensed equally and impartially to every description of men; those
of the judge, or of the executive power, will be the eccentric
impulses of whimsical, capricious designing man . . .

MS, Massachussetts Historical Society

## v.4 Proposed Constitution for Virginia[1]

[June, 1783]

To the citizens of the commonwealth of Virginia, and all others
whom it may concern, the delegates for the said commonwealth in
Convention assembled, send greeting:

It is known to you and to the world, that the government of
Great Britain, with which the American States were not long since
connected, assumed over them an authority unwarrantable and
oppressive; that they endeavoured to enforce this authority by arms,
and that the States of New Hampshire, Massachusetts, Rhode
Island, Connecticut, New York, New Jersey, Pennsylvania, Delaware, Maryland, Virginia, North Carolina, South Carolina, and
Georgia, considering resistance, with all its train of horrors, as a
lesser evil than abject submission, closed in the appeal to arms. It
hath pleased the Sovereign Disposer of all human events to give to
this appeal an issue favorable to the rights of the States; to enable
them to reject forever all dependence on a government which had
shown itself so capable of abusing the trusts reposed in it; and to
obtain from that government a solemn and explicit acknowledgment
that they are free, sovereign, and independent States. During the
progress of that war, through which we had to labor for the establishment of our rights, the legislature of the commonwealth of Virginia found it necessary to make a temporary organization of
government for preventing anarchy, and pointing our efforts to the
two important objects of war against our invaders, and peace and
happiness among ourselves. But this, like all other acts of legislation,
being subject to change by subsequent legislatures, possessing equal
powers with themselves; it has been thought expedient, that it
should receive those amendments which time and trial have sug-

---

[1] Jefferson deeply disliked the Virginia Constitution of 1776 and hoped to replace it
with this one. He was, however, unsuccessful. – *Eds.*

gested, and be rendered permanent by a power superior to that of the ordinary legislature. The general assembly therefore of this State recommended it to the good people thereof, to choose delegates to meet in general convention, with powers to form a constitution of government for them, and to declare those fundamentals to which all our laws present and future shall be subordinate; and, in compliance with this recommendation, they have thought proper to make choice of us, and to vest us with powers for this purpose.

We, therefore, the delegates, chosen by the said good people of this State for the purpose aforesaid, and now assembled in general convention, do, in execution of the authority with which we are invested, establish the following constitution and fundamentals of government for the said State of Virginia:

The said State shall forever hereafter be governed as a commonwealth.

The powers of government shall be divided into three distinct departments, each of them to be confided to a separate body of magistracy; to wit, those which are legislative to one, those which are judiciary to another, and those which are executive to another. No person, or collection of persons, being of one of these departments, shall exercise any power properly belonging to either of the others, except in the instances hereinafter expressly permitted.

The legislature shall consist of two branches, the one to be called the House of Delegates, the other the Senate, and both together the General Assembly. The concurrence of both of these, expressed on three several readings, shall be necessary to the passage of a law.

Delegates for the general assembly shall be chosen on the last Monday of November in every year. But if an election cannot be concluded on that day, it may be adjourned from day to day till it can be concluded.

The number of delegates which each county may send shall be in proportion to the number of its qualified electors; and the whole number of delegates for the State shall be so proportioned to the whole number of qualified electors in it, that they shall never exceed three hundred, nor be fewer than one hundred. Whenever such excess or deficiency shall take place, the House of Delegates so deficient or excessive shall, notwithstanding this, continue in being during its legal term; but they shall, during that term, re-adjust the proportion, so as to bring their number within the limits before mentioned at the ensuing election. If any county be reduced in its qualified electors below the number authorized to send one delegate, let it be annexed to some adjoining county.

For the election of senators, let the several counties be allotted by the senate from time to time, into such and so many districts as they shall find best; and let each county at the time of electing its delegates, choose senatorial electors, qualified as themselves are, and four in number for each delegate their county is entitled to send, who shall convene, and conduct themselves, in such manner as the legislature shall direct, with the senatorial electors from the other counties of their district, and then choose, by ballot, one senator for every six delegates which their district is entitled to choose. Let the senatorial districts be divided into two classes, and let the members elected for one of them be dissolved at the first ensuing general election of delegates, the other at the next, and so on alternately forever.

All free male citizens, of full age, and sane mind, who for one year before shall have been resident in the county, or shall through the whole of that time have possessed therein real property of the value of—; or shall for the same time have been enrolled in the militia, and no others, shall have a right to vote for delegates for the said county, and for senatorial electors for the district. They shall give their votes personally, and *viva voce*.

The general assembly shall meet at the place to which the last adjournment was, on the forty-second day after the day of election of delegates, and thenceforward at any other time or place on their own adjournment, till their office expires, which shall be on the day preceding that appointed for the meeting of the next general assembly. But if they shall at any time adjourn for more than one year, it shall be as if they had adjourned for one year precisely. Neither house, without the concurrence of the other, shall adjourn for more than one week, nor to any other place than the one at which they are sitting. The governor shall also have power, with the advice of the council of State, to call them at any other time to the same place, or to a different one, if that shall have become, since the last adjournment, dangerous from an enemy, or from infection

A majority of either house shall be a quorum, and shall be requisite for doing business; but any smaller proportion which from time to time shall be thought expedient by the respective houses, shall be sufficient to call for, and to punish, their non-attending members, and to adjourn themselves for any time not exceeding one week.

The members, during their attendance on the general assembly, and for so long a time before and after as shall be necessary for travelling to and from the same, shall be privileged from all personal restraint and assault, and shall have no other privilege whatsoever. They shall receive, during the same time, daily wages in gold or silver, equal to the value of two bushels of wheat. This value shall be deemed one dollar by the bushel till the year 1790, in which and in every tenth year thereafter, the general court, at their first sessions in the year, shall cause a special jury, of the most respectable merchants and farmers, to be summoned, to declare what shall have been the averaged value of wheat during the last ten years; which averaged value shall be the measure of wages for the ten subsequent years.

Of this general assembly, the treasurer, attorney general, register, ministers of the gospel, officers of the regular armies of this State, or of the United States, persons receiving salaries or emoluments from any power foreign to our confederacy, those who are not resident in the county for which they are chosen delegates, or districts for which they are chosen senators, those who are not qualified as electors, persons who shall have committed treason, felony, or such other crime as would subject them to infamous punishment, or who shall have been convicted by due course of law of bribery or corruption, in endeavoring to procure an election to the said assembly, shall be incapable of being members. All others, not herein elsewhere excluded, who may elect, shall be capable of being elected thereto.

Any member of the said assembly accepting any office of profit under this State, or the United States, or any of them, shall thereby vacate his seat, but shall be capable of being re-elected.

Vacancies occasioned by such disqualifications, by death, or otherwise, shall be supplied by the electors, on a writ from the speaker of the respective house.

The general assembly shall not have power to infringe this constitution; to abridge the civil rights of any person on account of his religious belief; to restrain him from professing and supporting that belief, or to compel him to contributions, other than those he shall have personally stipulated for the support of that or any other; to ordain death for any crime but treason or murder, or military offences; to pardon, or give a power of pardoning, persons duly convicted of treason or felony, but instead thereof they may substitute one or two new trials, and no more; to pass laws for punishing actions done before the existence of such laws; to pass any bill of attainder of treason or felony; to prescribe torture in any case whatever; nor to permit the introduction of any more slaves to reside in this State, or the continuance of slavery beyond the generation which shall be living on the thirty-first day of December, one thousand eight hundred; all persons born after that day being hereby declared free.

The general assembly shall have power to sever from this State all or any parts of its territory westward of the Ohio, or of the meridian of the mouth of the Great Kanhaway, and to cede to Congress one hundred square miles of territory in any other part of this State, so long as Congress shall hold their sessions therein, or in any territory adjacent thereto, which may be tendered to them by any other State.

They shall have power to appoint the speakers of their respective houses, treasurer, auditors, attorney general, register, all general officers of the military, their own clerks and serjeants, and no other officers, except where, in other parts of this constitution, such appointment is expressly given them.

The executive powers shall be exercised by a *Governor*, who shall be chosen by joint ballot of both houses of assembly, and when chosen shall remain in office five years, and be ineligible a second time. During his term he shall hold no other office or emolument under this State, or any other State or power whatsoever. By executive powers, we mean no reference to those powers exercised under our former government by the crown as of its prerogative, nor that these shall be the standard of what may or may not be deemed the rightful powers of the governor. We give them those powers only, which are necessary to execute the laws (and administer the government), and which are not in their nature either legislative or judiciary. The application of this idea must be left to reason. We do however expressly deny him the prerogative powers of erecting courts, offices, boroughs, corporations, fairs, markets, ports, beacons, light-houses, and sea-marks; of laying embargoes, of establishing precedence, of retaining within the State, or recalling to it any citizen thereof, and of making denizens, except so far as he may be authorized from time to time by the legislature to exercise any of those powers. The power of declaring war and concluding peace, of contracting alliances, of issuing letters of marque and reprisal, of raising and introducing armed forces, of building armed vessels, forts, or strongholds, of coining money or regulating its value, of regulating weights and measures, we leave to be exercised under the authority of the confederation; but in all cases respecting them which are out of the said confederation, they shall be exercised by the governor, under the regulation of such laws as the legislature may think it expedient to pass.

The whole military of the State, whether regular, or of militia, shall be subject to his directions; but he shall leave the execution of those directions to the general officers appointed by the legislature.

His salary shall be fixed by the legislature at the session of the assembly in which he shall be appointed, and before such appointment be made; or if it be not then fixed, it shall be the same which his next predecessor in office was entitled to. In either case he may demand it quarterly out of any money which shall be in the public treasury; and it shall not be in the power of the legislature to give him less or more, either during his continuance in office, or after he shall have gone out of it. The lands, houses, and other things appropriated to the use of the governor, shall remain to his use during his continuance in office.

A *Council of State* shall be chosen by joint ballot of both houses of assembly, who shall hold their offices seven years, and be ineligible a second time, and who, while they shall be of the said council, shall hold no other office or emolument under this State, or any other state or power whatsoever. Their duty shall be to attend and advise the governor when called on by him, and their advice in any case shall be a sanction to him. They shall also have power, and it shall be their duty, to meet at their own will, and to give their advice, though not required by the governor, in cases where they shall think the public good calls for it. Their advice and proceedings shall be entered in books to be kept for that purpose, and shall be signed as approved or disapproved by the members present. These books shall be laid before either house of assembly when called for by them. The said council shall consist of eight members for the present; but their numbers may be increased or reduced by the legislature, whenever they shall think it necessary; provided such reduction be made only as the appointments become vacant by death, resignation, disqualification, or regular deprivation. A majority of their actual number, and not fewer, shall be a quorum. They shall be allowed for the present — each by the year, payable quarterly out of any money which shall be in the public treasury. Their salary, however, may be increased or abated from time to time at the discretion of the legislature; provided such increase or abatement shall not, by any ways or means, be made to affect either then, or at any future time, anyone of those then actually in office. At the end of each quarter their salary shall be divided into equal portions by the number of days on which, during that quarter, a council has been held, or required by the governor, or by their own adjournment, and one of those portions shall be withheld from each member for every of the said days which, without cause allowed good by the board, he failed to attend, or departed before adjournment without their leave. If no board should have been held during that quarter, there shall be no deduction.

They shall annually choose a *President*, who shall preside in council in the absence of the governor, and who, in case of his office becoming vacant by death or otherwise, shall have authority to exercise all his functions, till a new appointment be made, as he shall also in any interval during which the governor shall declare himself unable to attend to the duties of his office.

The *Judiciary* powers shall be exercised by county courts and such other inferior courts as the legislature shall think proper to continue or to erect, by three superior courts, to wit, a Court of Admiralty, a general Court of Common Law, and a High Court of Chancery; and by one Supreme Court, to be called the Court of Appeals.

The judges of the high court of chancery, general court, and court of admiralty, shall be four in number each, to be appointed by joint ballot of both houses of assembly, and to hold their offices during good behavior. While they continue judges, they shall hold no other office or emolument, under this State, or any other State or power whatsoever, except that they may be delegated to Congress, receiving no additional allowance.

These judges, assembled together, shall constitute the Court of Appeals, whose business shall be to receive and determine appeals from the three superior courts, but to receive no original causes, except in the cases expressly permitted herein.

A majority of the members of either of these courts, and not fewer, shall be a quorum. But in the Court of Appeals nine members shall be necessary to do business. Any smaller numbers however may be authorized by the legislature to adjourn their respective courts.

They shall be allowed for the present — each by the year, payable quarterly out of any money which shall be in the public treasury. Their salaries, however, may be increased or abated, from time to time, at the discretion of the legislature, provided such increase or abatement shall not by any ways or means, be made to affect, either then, or at any future time, any one of those then actually in office. At the end of each quarter their salary shall be divided into equal portions by the number of days on which, during that quarter, their respective courts sat or should have sat, and one of these portions shall be withheld from each member for every of the said days which, without cause allowed good by his court, he failed to attend, or departed before adjournment without their leave. If no court should have been held during the quarter, there shall be no deduction.

There shall, moreover, be a *Court of Impeachments*, to consist of three members of the Council of State, one of each of the superior courts of Chancery, Common Law, and Admiralty, two members of the house of delegates and one of the Senate, to be chosen by the body respectively of which they are. Before this court any member of the three branches of government, that is to say, the governor, any member of the council, of the two houses of legislature, or of the superior courts, may be impeached by the governor, the council, or either of the said houses or courts, and by no other, for such misbehavior in office as would be sufficient to remove him therefrom; and the only sentence they shall have authority to pass shall be that of deprivation and future incapacity of office. Seven members shall be requisite to make a court, and two-thirds of those present must concur in the sentence. The offences cognizable by this court shall be cognizable by no other, and they shall be triers of the fact as well as judges of the law.

The justices or judges of the inferior courts already erected, or hereafter to be erected, shall be appointed by the governor, on advice of the council of State, and shall hold their offices during good behavior, or the existence of their courts. For breach of the good behavior, they shall be tried according to the laws of the land, before the Court of Appeals, who shall be judges of the fact as well as of the law. The only sentence they shall have authority to pass shall be that of deprivation and future incapacity of office, and two-thirds of the members present must concur in this sentence.

All courts shall appoint their own clerks, who shall hold their offices during good behavior, or the existence of their court; they shall also appoint all other attending officers to continue during their pleasure. Clerks appointed by the supreme or superior courts shall be removable by their respective courts. Those to be appointed by other courts shall have been previously examined, and certified to be duly qualified, by some two members of the general court, and shall be removable for breach of the good behavior by the Court of Appeals only, who shall be judges of the fact as well as of the law. Two-thirds of the members present must concur in the sentence.

The justices or judges of the inferior courts may be members of the legislature.

The judgment of no inferior court shall be final, in any civil case, of greater value than fifty bushels of wheat, as last rated in the general court for setting the allowance to the members of the general assembly, nor in any case of treason, felony, or other crime which should subject the party to infamous punishment.

In all causes depending before any court, other than those of impeachments, of appeals, and military courts, facts put in issue shall be tried by jury, and in all courts whatever witnesses shall give testimony *viva voce* in open court, wherever their attendance can be procured; and all parties shall be allowed counsel and compulsory process for their witnesses.

Fines, amercements, and terms of imprisonment left indefinite by the law, other than for contempts, shall be fixed by the jury, triers of the offence.

The governor, two councillors of State, and a judge from each of the superior Courts of Chancery, Common Law, and Admiralty, shall be a council to revise all bills which shall have passed both houses of assembly, in which council the governor, when present, shall preside. Every bill, before it becomes a law, shall be represented to this council, who shall have a right to advise its rejection, returning the bill, with their advice and reasons in writing, to the house in which it originated, who shall proceed to reconsider the said bill. But if after such reconsideration, two-thirds of the house shall be of opinion that the bill should pass finally, they shall pass and send it, with the advice and written reasons of the said Council of Revision, to the other house, wherein if two-thirds also shall be of opinion it should pass finally, it shall thereupon become law; otherwise it shall not.

If any bill, presented to the said council, be not, within one week (exclusive of the day of presenting it) returned by them, with their advice of rejection and reasons, to the house wherein it originated, or to the clerk of the said house, in case of its adjournment over the expiration of the week, it shall be law from the expiration of the week, and shall then be demandable by the clerk of the House of Delegates, to be filed of record in his office.

The bills which they approve shall become law from the time of such approbation, and shall then be returned to, or demandable by, the clerk of the House of Delegates, to be filed of record in his office.

A bill rejected on advice of the Council of Revision may again be proposed, during the same session of assembly, with such alterations as will render it conformable to their advice.

The members of the said Council of Revision shall be appointed from time to time by the board or court of which they respectively are. Two of the executive and two of the judiciary members shall be requisite to do business; and to prevent the evils of non-attendance, the board and courts may at any time name all, or so many as they will, of their members, in the particular order in which they would choose the duty of attendance to devolve from preceding to subsequent members, the preceding failing to attend. They shall have additionally for their services in this council the same allowance as members of assembly have.

The confederation is made a part of this constitution, subject to such future alterations as shall be agreed to by the legislature of this State, and by all the other confederating States.

The delegates to Congress shall be five in number; any three of whom, and no fewer, may be a representation. They shall be appointed by joint ballot of both houses of assembly for any term not exceeding one year, subject to be recalled, within the term, by joint vote of both the said houses. They may at the same time be members of the legislative or judiciary departments, but not of the executive.

The benefits of the writ of *habeas corpus* shall be extended, by the legislature, to every person within this State, and without fee, and shall be so facilitated that no person may be detained in prison more than ten days after he shall have demanded and been refused such writ by the judge appointed by law, or if none be appointed, then by any judge of a superior court, nor more than ten days after such writ shall have been served on the person detaining him, and no order given, on due examination, for his remandment or discharge.

The military shall be subordinate to the civil power.

Printing presses shall be subject to no other restraint than liableness to legal prosecution for false facts printed and published.

Any two of the three branches of government concurring in opinion, each by the voice of two-thirds of their whole existing number, that a convention is necessary for altering this constitution, or correcting breaches of it, they shall be authorized to issue writs to every county for the election of so many delegates as they are authorized to send to the general assembly, which elections shall be held, and writs returned, as the laws shall have provided in the case of elections of delegates of assembly, *mutatis mutandis*, and the said delegates shall meet at the usual place of holding assemblies, three months after date of such writs, and shall be acknowledged to have equal powers with this present convention. The said writs shall be signed by all the members approving the same.

*To introduce this government*, the following special and temporary provision is made.

This convention being authorized only to amend those laws which constituted the form of government, no general dissolution of the whole system of laws can be supposed to have taken place; but all laws in force at the meeting of this convention, and not inconsistent with this constitution, remain in full force, subject to alterations by the ordinary legislature.

The present general assembly shall continue till the forty-second day after the last Monday of November in this present year. On the said last Monday of November in this present year, the several counties shall, by their electors qualified as provided by this constitution, elect delegates, which for the present shall be, in number, one for every — militia of the said county, according to the latest returns in possession of the governor, and shall also choose senatorial electors in proportion thereto, which senatorial electors shall meet on the fourteenth day after the day of their election, at the court house of that county of their present district which would stand first in an alphabetical arrangement of their counties, and shall choose senators in the proportion fixed by this constitution. The elections and returns shall be conducted, in all circumstances not hereby particularly prescribed, by the same persons and under the same forms as prescribed by the present laws in elections of senators and delegates of assembly. The said senators and delegates shall constitute the first general assembly of the new government, and shall specially apply themselves to the procuring an exact return from every county of the number of its qualified electors, and to the settlement of the number of delegates to be elected for the ensuing general assembly.

The present governor shall continue in office to the end of the term for which he was elected.

All other officers of every kind shall continue in office as they would have done had their appointment been under this constitution, and new ones, where new are hereby called for, shall be appointed by the authority to which such appointment is referred. One of the present judges of the general court, he consenting thereto, shall by joint ballot of both houses of assembly, at their first meeting, be transferred to the High Court of Chancery.

Ford III: 320–33

## v.5 To Rabaut de St. Etienne

Paris, June 3, 1789

Sir, – After you quitted us yesterday evening, we continued our conversation (Monsr. de la Fayette, Mr. Short & myself) on the subject of the difficulties which environ you. The desirable object being to secure the good which the King has offered & to avoid the ill which seems to threaten, an idea was suggested, which appearing to make an impression on Monsr. de la Fayette, I was encouraged to pursue it on my return to Paris, to put it into form, & now to send it to you & him. It is this, that the King, in a *séance royale*, should come forward with a Charter of Rights in his hand, to be signed by himself & by every member of the three orders. This charter to contain the five great points which the *Résultat* of December offered on the part of the King, the abolition of pecuniary privileges offered by the privileged orders, & the adoption of the National debt and a grant of the sum of money asked from the nation. This last will be a cheap price for the preceding articles, and let the same act declare your immediate separation till the next anniversary meeting. You will carry back to your constituents more good than ever was effected before without violence, and you will stop exactly at the point where violence would otherwise begin. Time will be gained, the public mind will continue to ripen & to be informed, a basis of support may be prepared with the people themselves, and expedients occur for gaining still something further at your next meeting, & for stopping again at the point of force. I have ventured to send to yourself & Monsieur de la Fayette a sketch of my ideas of what this act might contain without endangering any dispute. But it is offered merely as a canvas for you to work on, if it be fit to work on at all. I know too little of the subject, & you know too much of it to justify me in offering anything but a hint. I have done it too in a hurry: insomuch that since committing it to writing it occurs to me that the 5th article may give alarm, that it is in a good degree included in the 4th, and is therefore useless. But after all what excuse can I make, Sir, for this presumption. I have none but an unmeasureable love for your nation and a painful anxiety lest Despotism, after an unaccepted offer to bind it's own hands, should seize you again with tenfold fury. Permit me to add to these very sincere assurances of the sentiments of esteem & respect with which I have the honor to be, Sir, Your most obedt. & most humble servt.

### Proposed Charter for France

June 3, 1789

*A Charter of Rights, solemnly established by the King and Nation;*

1. The States General shall assemble, uncalled, on the first day of November, annually, and shall remain together so long as they shall

see cause. They shall regulate their own elections and proceedings, and until they shall ordain otherwise, their elections shall be in the forms observed in the present year, and shall be triennial.

2. The States General alone shall levy money on the nation, and shall appropriate it.

3. Laws shall be made by the States General only, with the consent of the King.

4. No person shall be restrained of his liberty, but by regular process from a court of justice, authorized by a general law. (Except that a Noble may be imprisoned by order of a court of justice, on the prayer of twelve of his nearest relations.) On complaint of an unlawful imprisonment, to any judge whatever, he shall have the prisoner immediately brought before him, and shall discharge him, if his imprisonment be unlawful. The officer in whose custody the prisoner is, shall obey the orders of the judge; and both judge and officer shall be responsible, civilly and criminally, for a failure of duty herein.

5. The military shall be subordinate to the civil authority.

6. Printers shall be liable to legal prosecution for printing and publishing false facts, injurious to the party prosecuting; but they shall be under no other restraint.

7. All pecuniary privileges and exemptions, enjoyed by any description of persons, are abolished.

8. All debts already contracted by the King, are hereby made the debts of the nation; and the faith thereof is pledged for their payment in due time.

9. Eighty millions of *livres* are now granted to the King, to be raised by loan, and reimbursed by the nation; and the taxes heretofore paid, shall continue to be paid to the end of the present year, and no longer.

10. The States General shall now separate, and meet again on the 1st day of November next.

Done, on behalf of the whole nation, by the King and their representatives in the States General, at Versailles, this — day of June, 1789.

Signed by the King, and by every member individually, and in his presence.

Ford v: 99–102

351

# VI   The U.S. Constitution

*of the highest duties of a good citizen, but it is not* the highest.
*The laws of necessity, of self-preservation, of saving our country
when in danger, are of higher obligation."*

VI.12 To Judge Spencer Roane, Sept. 6, 1819
*On the dangers of judicial activism by independent and unelected
judges and Supreme Court Justices who view "the Constitution
. . . [as] a mere thing of wax in the hands of the judiciary,
which they may twist and shape into any form they please . . .
Independence can be trusted nowhere but with the people in
mass. They are inherently independent of all but moral law."*

VI.13 To William Charles Jarvis, Sept. 28, 1820
VI.14 To Major John Cartwright, June 5, 1824
*Even the most fundamental laws should be open to amendment
or abolition by those now living: "A generation . . . may change
their laws and institutions to suit themselves. Nothing then is
unchangeable but the inherent and unalienable rights of man."*

## VI.1 From the *Autobiography*

Our first essay in America to establish a federative government had fallen, on trial, very short of it's object.[1] During the war of Independance, while the pressure of an external enemy hooped us together, and their enterprises kept us necessarily on the alert, the spirit of the people, excited by danger, was a supplement to the Confederation, and urged them to zealous exertions, whether claimed by that instrument, or not. But when peace and safety were restored, and every man became engaged in useful and profitable occupation, less attention was paid to the calls of Congress. The fundamental defect of the Confederation was that Congress was not authorized to act immediately on the people, & by it's own officers. Their power was only requisitory, and these requisitions were addressed to the several legislatures, to be by them carried into execution, without other coercion than the moral principle of duty. This allowed in fact a negative to every legislature, on every measure proposed by Congress; a negative so frequently exercised in practice as to benumb the action of the federal government, and to render it inefficient in it's general objects, & more especially in pecuniary and foreign concerns. The want too of a separation of the legislative, executive, & judiciary functions worked disadvantageously in practice. Yet this state of things afforded a happy augury of the future march of our confederacy, when it was seen that the good sense and good dispositions of the people, as soon as they perceived the incompetence of their first compact, instead of leaving it's correction to insurrection and civil war, agreed with one voice to elect deputies to a general convention, who should peaceably meet and agree on such a constitution as "would ensure peace, justice, liberty, the common defence & general welfare."

This Convention met at Philadelphia on the 25th. of May '87. It sate with closed doors, and kept all it's proceedings secret, until it's dissolution on the 17th. of September, when the results of their labors were published all together. I received a copy early in November, and read and contemplated it's provisions with great satisfaction. As not a member of the Convention however, nor probably a single citizen of the Union, had approved it in all it's parts, so I

---

[1] TJ refers here to the Articles of Confederation (1781). – *Eds.*

too found articles which I thought objectionable. The absence of express declarations ensuring freedom of religion, freedom of the press, freedom of the person under the uninterrupted protection of the *habeas corpus*, & trial by jury in civil as well as in criminal cases excited my jealousy; and the re-eligibility of the President for life, I quite disapproved. I expressed freely in letters to my friends, and most particularly to Mr. Madison & General Washington, my approbations and objections. How the good should be secured, and the ill brought to rights was the difficulty. To refer it back to a new Convention might endanger the loss of the whole. My first idea was that the 9 states first acting should accept it unconditionally, and thus secure what in it was good, and that the 4 last should accept on the previous condition that certain amendments should be agreed to, but a better course was devised of accepting the whole and trusting that the good sense & honest intentions of our citizens would make the alterations which should be deemed necessary. Accordingly all accepted, 6 without objection, and 7 with recommendations of specified amendments. Those respecting the press, religion, & juries, with several others, of great value, were accordingly made; but the *habeas corpus* was left to the discretion of Congress, and the amendment against the reeligibility of the President was not proposed by that body. My fears of that feature were founded on the importance of the office, on the fierce contentions it might excite among ourselves, if continuable for life, and the dangers of interference either with money or arms, by foreign nations, to whom the choice of an American President might become interesting. Examples of this abounded in history; in the case of the Roman emperors for instance, of the Popes while of any significance, of the German emperors, the Kings of Poland, & the Deys of Barbary. I had observed too in the feudal History, and in the recent instance particularly of the Stadtholder of Holland, how easily offices or tenures for life slide into inheritances. My wish therefore was that the President should be elected for 7 years & be ineligible afterwards. This term I thought sufficient to enable him, with the concurrence of the legislature, to carry thro' & establish any system of improvement he should propose for the general good. But the practice adopted I think is better allowing his continuance for 8 years with a liability to be dropped at half way of the term, making that a period of probation. That his continuance should be restrained to

7 years was the opinion of the Convention at an early stage of it's session, when it voted that term by a majority of 8 against 2 and by a simple majority that he should be ineligible a second time. This opinion &c. was confirmed by the house so late as July 26, referred to the committee of detail, reported favorably by them, and changed to the present form by final vote on the last day but one only of their session. Of this change three states expressed their disapprobation, N. York by recommending an amendment that the President should not be eligible a third time, and Virginia and N. Carolina that he should not be capable of serving more than 8 in any term of 16 years. And altho' this amendment has not been made in form, yet practice seems to have established it. The example of 4 Presidents voluntarily retiring at the end of their 8th year, & the progress of public opinion that the principle is salutary, have given it in practice the force of precedent & usage; insomuch that should a President consent to be a candidate for a 3d. election, I trust he would be rejected on this demonstration of ambitious views.

But there was another amendment of which none of us thought at the time and in the omission of which lurks the germ that is to destroy this happy combination of National powers in the General government for matters of National concern, and independent powers in the states for what concerns the states severally. In England it was a great point gained at the Revolution, that the commissions of the judges, which had hitherto been during pleasure, should thenceforth be made during good behavior. A Judiciary dependent on the will of the King had proved itself the most oppressive of all tools in the hands of that Magistrate. Nothing then could be more salutary than a change there to the tenure of good behavior; and the question of good behavior left to the vote of a simple majority in the two houses of parliament. Before the revolution we were all good English Whigs, cordial in their free principles, and in their jealousies of their executive Magistrate. These jealousies are very apparent in all our state constitutions; and, in the general government in this instance, we have gone even beyond the English caution, by requiring a vote of two thirds in one of the Houses for removing a judge; a vote so impossible where[2] any

---

[2] In the impeachment of judge Pickering of New Hampshire, a habitual & maniac drunkard, no defence was made. Had there been, the party vote of more than one third of the Senate would have acquitted him.

defence is made, before men of ordinary prejudices & passions, that our judges are effectually independent of the nation. But this ought not to be. I would not indeed make them dependant on the Executive authority, as they formerly were in England; but I deem it indispensable to the continuance of this government that they should be submitted to some practical & impartial controul: and that this, to be imparted, must be compounded of a mixture of state and federal authorities. It is not enough that honest men are appointed judges. All know the influence of interest on the mind of man, and how unconsciously his judgment is warped by that influence. To this bias add that of the *esprit de corps*, of their peculiar maxim and creed that "it is the office of a good judge to enlarge his jurisdiction," and the absence of responsibility, and how can we expect impartial decision between the General government, of which they are themselves so eminent a part, and an individual state from which they have nothing to hope or fear. We have seen too that, contrary to all correct example, they are in the habit of going out of the question before them, to throw an anchor ahead and grapple further hold for future advances of power. They are then in fact the corps of sappers & miners, steadily working to undermine the independant rights of the States, & to consolidate all power in the hands of that government in which they have so important a freehold estate. But it is not by the consolidation, or concentration of powers, but by their distribution, that good government is effected. Were not this great country already divided into states, that division must be made, that each might do for itself what concerns itself directly, and what it can so much better do than a distant authority. Every state again is divided into counties, each to take care of what lies within it's local bounds; each county again into townships or wards, to manage minuter details; and every ward into farms, to be governed each by it's individual proprietor. Were we directed from Washington when to sow, & when to reap, we should soon want bread. It is by this partition of cares, descending in gradation from general to particular, that the mass of human affairs may be best managed for the good and prosperity of all. I repeat that I do not charge the judges with wilful and ill-intentioned error; but honest error must be arrested where it's toleration leads to public ruin. As, for the safety of society, we commit honest maniacs to Bedlam, so judges should be withdrawn from their bench, whose erroneous biases are leading us to dissolution. It may indeed injure them in fame or in fortune; but it saves the republic, which is the first and supreme law.

Ford I: 107–14

## VI.2 To Dr. Richard Price

Paris, February 1, 1785

Sir, – The copy of your Observations on the American Revolution which you were so kind as to direct to me came duly to hand, and I should sooner have acknowledged the receipt of it but that I awaited a private coveiance [conveyance] for my letter, having experienced much delay and uncertainty in the posts between this place and London. I have read it with very great pleasure, as have done many others to whom I have communicated it. The spirit which it breathes is as affectionate as the observations themselves are wise and just. I have no doubt it will be reprinted in America and produce much good there. The want of power in the federal head was early perceived, and foreseen to be the flaw in our constitution which might endanger its destruction. I have the pleasure to inform you that when I left America in July the people were becoming universally sensible of this, and a spirit to enlarge the powers of Congress was becoming general. Letters and other information recently received shew that this has continued to increase, and that they are likely to remedy this evil effectually. The happiness of governments like ours, wherein the people are truly the mainspring, is that they are never to be despaired of. When an evil becomes so glaring as to strike them generally, they arrouse themselves, and it is redressed. He only is then the popular man and can get into office who shews the best dispositions to reform the evil. This truth was obvious on several occasions during the late war, and this character in our governments saved us. Calamity was our best physician. Since the peace it was observed that some nations of Europe, counting on the weakness of Congress and the little probability of a union in measure among the States, were proposing to grasp at unequal advantages in our commerce. The people are become sensible of this, and you may be assured that this evil will be immediately redressed, and redressed radically. I doubt still whether in this moment they will enlarge those powers in Congress which are necessary to keep the peace among the States. I think it possible that this may be suffered to lie till some two States commit hostilities on each other, but in that moment the hand of the union will be lifted up and interposed, and the people will themselves demand a general concession to Congress of means to prevent similar mischeifs. Our motto is truly "nil desperandum." The apprehensions you express of danger from the want of powers in Congress, led me to note to you this character in our governments, which, since the retreat behind the Delaware, and the capture of Charlestown, has kept my mind in perfect quiet as to the ultimate fate of our union; and I am sure, from the spirit which breathes thro your book, that whatever promises permanence to that will be a comfort to your mind. I have the honour to be, with very sincere esteem and respect, Sir, Your most obedient and most humble servt.

*Massachusetts Historical Society Proceedings*, 2nd Series 17 (1903): 325–6

## VI.3 To John Adams

Paris, November 13, 1787

Dear Sir, – . . . How do you like our new constitution? I confess there are things in it which stagger all my dispositions to subscribe to what such an Assembly has proposed. The house of federal representatives will not be adequate to the management of affairs, either foreign or federal. Their President seems a bad edition of a Polish King. He may be elected from four years to four years, for life. Reason and experience prove to us, that a chief magistrate, so continuable, is an office for life. When one or two generations shall have proved that this is an office for life, it becomes, on every occasion, worthy of intrigue, of bribery, of force, and even of foreign interference. It will be of great consequence to France and England, to have America governed by a Galloman or Angloman. Once in office, and possessing the military force of the Union, without the aid or check of a council, he would not be easily dethroned, even if the people could be induced to withdraw their votes from him. I wish that at the end of the four years, they had made him forever ineligible a second time. Indeed, I think all the good of this new constitution might have been couched in three or four new articles, to be added to the good, old and venerable fabric, which should have been preserved even as a religious relique. Present me and my daughters affectionately to Mrs. Adams. The younger one continues to speak of her warmly. Accept yourself, assurances of the sincere esteem and respect with which I have the honor to be, dear Sir, your friend and servant.

L & B VI: 370–1

## VI.4 To James Madison

Paris, December 20, 1787

Dear Sir, – ... The season admitting only of operations in the Cabinet, and these being in a great measure secret, I have little to fill a letter. I will therefore make up the deficiency by adding a few words on the Constitution proposed by our Convention. I like much the general idea of framing a government which should go on of itself peaceably, without needing continual recurrence to the state legislatures. I like the organization of the government into Legislative, Judiciary & Executive. I like the power given the Legislature to levy taxes, and for that reason solely approve of the greater house being chosen by the people directly. For tho' I think a house chosen by them will be very illy qualified to legislate for the Union, for foreign nations &c. yet this evil does not weigh against the good of preserving inviolate the fundamental principle that the people are not to be taxed but by representatives chosen immediately by themselves. I am captivated by the compromise of the opposite claims of the great & little states, of the latter to equal, and the former to proportional influence. I am much pleased too with the substitution of the method of voting by persons, instead of that of voting by states: and I like the negative given to the Executive with a third of either house, though I should have liked it better had the Judiciary been associated for that purpose, or invested with a similar and separate power. There are other good things of less moment. I will now add what I do not like. First the omission of a bill of rights providing clearly & without the aid of sophisms for freedom of religion, freedom of the press, protection against standing armies, restriction against monopolies, the eternal & unremitting force of the *habeas corpus* laws, and trials by jury in all matters of fact triable by the laws of the land & not by the law of nations. To say, as Mr. [James] Wilson does, that a bill of rights was not necessary because all is reserved in the case of the general government which is not given, while in the particular ones all is given which is not reserved, might do for the audience to whom it was addressed, but is surely a *gratis dictum*, opposed by strong inferences from the body of the instrument, as well as from the omission of the clause of our present confederation which had declared that in express terms. It was a hard conclusion to say because there has been no uniformity among the states as to the cases triable by jury, because some have been so incautious as to abandon this mode of trial, therefore the more prudent states shall be reduced to the same level of calamity. It would have been much more just & wise to have concluded the other way that as most of the states had judiciously preserved this palladium, those who had wandered should be brought back to it, and to have established general right instead of general wrong. Let me add that a bill of rights is what the people are entitled to against every government on earth, general or particular, & what no just government should refuse, or rest on inferences. The second feature I dislike, and greatly dislike, is the abandonment in every instance of the necessity of rotation in office, and most particularly in the case of the President. Experience concurs with reason in concluding that the first magistrate will always be re-elected if the Constitution permits it. He is then an officer for life. This once observed, it becomes of so much consequence to certain nations to have a friend or a foe at the head of our affairs that they will interfere with money & with arms. A Galloman or an Angloman will be supported by the nation he befriends. If once elected, and at a second or third election out voted by one or two votes, he will pretend false votes, foul play, hold possession of the reins of government, be supported by the States voting for him, especially if they are the central ones lying in a compact body themselves & separating their opponents: and they will be aided by one nation of Europe, while the majority are aided by another. The election of a President of America some years hence will be much more interesting to certain nations of Europe than ever the election of a king of Poland was. Reflect on all the instances in history antient & modern, of elective monarchies, and say if they do not give foundation for my fears. The Roman emperors, the popes, while they were of any importance, the German emperors till they became hereditary in practice, the kings of Poland, the Deys of the Ottoman dependances. It may be said that if elections are to be attended with these disorders, the seldomer they are renewed the better. But experience shews that the only way to prevent disorder is to render them uninteresting by frequent changes. An incapacity to be elected a second time would have been the only effectual preventative. The power of removing him every fourth year by the vote of the people is a power which will not be exercised. The king of Poland is removeable every day by the Diet, yet he is never removed. – Smaller objections are the Appeal in fact as well as law, and the binding all persons Legislative Executive & Judiciary by oath to maintain that constitution. I do not pretend to decide what would be the best method of procuring the establishment of the manifold good things in this constitution, and of getting rid of the bad. Whether by adopting it in hopes of future amendment, or, after it has been duly weighed & canvassed by the people, after seeing the parts they generally dislike, & those they generally approve, to say to them "We see now what you wish. Send together your deputies again, let them frame a constitution for you omitting what you have condemned, & establishing the powers you approve. Even these will be a great addition to the energy of your government." – At all events I hope you will not be discouraged from other trials, if the present one should fail of its full effect. – I have thus told you freely what I like & dislike: merely as a matter of curiosity, for I know your own judgment has been formed on all these points after having heard everything which could be urged on them. I own I am not a friend to a very energetic government. It is always oppressive. The late rebellion in Massachusetts[1] has given more alarm than I think it should have done. Calculate that one rebellion in 13 states in the course of 11 years, is but one for each state in a century & a half. No country should be so long without one. Nor will any degree of power in the hands of government prevent insurrections. France, with all it's despotism, and two or three hundred thousand men always in arms, has

---

[1] Shays's Rebellion – *Eds.*

had three insurrections in the three years I have been here in every one of which greater numbers were engaged than in Massachusetts & a great deal more blood was split. In Turkey, which Montesquieu supposes more despotic, insurrections are the events of every day. In England, where the hand of power is lighter than here, but heavier than with us, they happen every half dozen years. Compare again the ferocious depredations of their insurgents with the order, the moderation & the almost self extinguishment of ours. – After all, it is my principle that the will of the majority should always prevail. If they approve the proposed Convention in all it's parts, I shall concur in it chearfully, in hopes that they will amend it whenever they shall find it work wrong. I think our governments will remain virtuous for many centuries; as long as they are chiefly agricultural; and this will be as long as there shall be vacant lands in any part of America. When they get piled upon one another in large cities, as in Europe, they will become corrupt as in Europe. Above all things I hope the education of the common people will be attended to; convinced that on their good sense we may rely with the most security for the preservation of a due degree of liberty. I have tired you by this time with my disquisitions & will therefore only add assurances of the sincerity of those sentiments of esteem & attachment with which I am Dear Sir your affectionate friend & servant

P.S. The instability of our laws is really an immense evil. I think it would be well to provide in our constitutions that there shall always be a twelve-month between the ingrossing a bill & passing it: that it should then be offered to it's passage without changing a word: and that if circumstances should be thought to require a speedier passage, it should take two thirds of both houses instead of a bare majority.

Ford IV: 475–80

## VI.5 To Edward Carrington

Paris, May 27, 1788

Dear Sir, – I have received with great pleasure your friendly letter of Apr. 24. It has come to hand after I had written my letters for

the present conveiance, and just in time to add this to them. I learn
with great pleasure the progress of the new Constitution. Indeed I
have presumed it would gain on the public mind, as I confess it has
on my own. At first, tho' I saw that the great mass & ground work
was good, I disliked many appendages. Reflection and discussion
have cleared off most of these. You have satisfied me as to the query
I had put to you about the right of direct taxation. My first wish
was that 9 States would adopt it in order to ensure what was good
in it, & that the others might, by holding off, produce the necessary
amendments. But the plan of Massachusetts is far preferable, and
will I hope be followed by those who are yet to decide. There are
two amendments only which I am anxious for. 1. A bill of rights,
which it is so much the interest of all to have, that I conceive it
must be yielded. The 1st amendment proposed by Massachusetts
will in some degree answer this end, but not so well. It will do too
much in some instances & too little in others. It will cripple the
federal government in some cases where it ought to be free, and not
restrain it in some others where restraint would be right. The 2d
amendment which appears to me essential is the restoring the principle of necessary rotation, particularly to the Senate & Presidency:
but most of all to the last. Re-eligibility makes him an officer for
life, and the disastors inseparable from an elective monarchy, render
it preferable, if we cannot tread back that step, that we should go
forward & take refuge in an hereditary one. Of the correction of
this Article however I entertain no present hope, because I find it
has scarcely excited an objection in America. And if it does not take
place ere long, it assuredly never will. The natural progress of
things is for liberty to yield, & government to gain ground. As yet
our spirits are free. Our jealousy is only put to sleep by the unlimited confidence we all repose in the person to whom we all look as
our president. After him inferior characters may perhaps succeed
and awaken us to the danger which his merit has led us into. For
the present, however, the general adoption is to be prayed for; and
I wait with great anxiety for the news from Maryland & S. Carolina
which have decided [to ratify the new constitution] before this, and
with that Virginia, now in session, may give the 9th vote of approbation. There could then be no doubt of N. Carolina, N. York, &
New Hampshire, but what do you propose to do with Rhode island?
As long as there is hope, we should give her time. I cannot conceive

but that she will come to rights in the long run. Force, in whatever form, would be a dangerous precedent . . .

Ford x: 19–21

## VI.6 To James Madison

Paris, July 31, 1788

Dear Sir, – . . . I send you a book of Dupont's on the subject of the commercial treaty with England. Tho it's general matter may not be interesting, yet you will pick up in various parts of it such excellent principles and observations as will richly repay the trouble of reading it. I send you also two little pamphlets of the Marquis de Condorcet, wherein is the most judicious statement I have seen of the great questions which agitate this nation at present. The new regulations present a preponderance of good over their evil but they suppose that the King can model the constitution at will, or in other words that his government is a pure despotism. The question then arising is whether a pure despotism in a single head, or one which is divided among a king, nobles, priesthood, & numerous magistracy is the least bad. I should be puzzled to decide: but I hope they will have neither, and that they are advancing to a limited, moderate government, in which the people will have a good share.

I sincerely rejoice at the acceptance of our new constitution by nine states. It is a good canvass, on which some strokes only want retouching. What these are, I think are sufficiently manifested by the general voice from North to South, which calls for a bill of rights. It seems pretty generally understood that this should go to Juries, *habeas corpus*, Standing armies, Printing, Religion & Monopolies. I conceive there may be difficulty in finding general modifications of these, suited to the habits of all the states. But if such cannot be found then it is better to establish trials by Jury, the right of *habeas corpus*, freedom of press & freedom of religion, in all cases, and to abolish standing armies in time of peace, and Monopolies in all cases, than not do it in any. The few cases wherein these things may do evil, cannot be weighed against the multitude wherein the want of them will do evil. In disputes between a foreigner & a native, a trial by jury may be improper. But if this exception cannot

365

be agreed to, the remedy will be to model the jury by giving the *mediatas linguæ* in civil as well as criminal cases. Why suspend the *Hab. Corp.* in insurrections & rebellions? The parties who may be arrested may be charged instantly with a well defined crime, of course the judge will remand them. If publick safety requires that the government should have a man imprisoned on less probable testimony in those than in other emergencies; let him be taken & tried, retaken & retried, while the necessity continues, only giving him redress against the government for damages. Examine the history of England. See how few of the cases of the suspension of the *Habeas corpus* law have been worthy of that suspension. They have been either real treasons wherein the parties might as well have been charged at once, or sham plots where it was shameful they should ever have been suspected. Yet for the few cases wherein the suspension of the *hab. corp.* has done real good, that operation is now become habitual, & the minds of the nation almost prepared to live under its constant suspension. A declaration that the federal government will never restrain the presses from printing anything they please, will not take away the liability of the printers for false facts printed. The declaration that religious faith shall be unpunished, does not give impunity to criminal acts dictated by religious error. The saying there shall be no monopolies lessens the incitements to ingenuity, which spurred on by the hope of a monopoly for a limited time, as of 14 years; but the benefit even of limited monopolies is too doubtful to be opposed to that of their general suppression. If no check can be found to keep the number of standing troops within safe bounds, while they are tolerated as far as necessary, abandon them altogether, discipline well the militia, & guard the magazines with them. More than magazine guards will be useless if few, & dangerous if many. No European nation can ever send against us such a regular army as we need fear, & it is hard if our militia are not equal to those of Canada or Florida. My idea then is, that tho' proper exceptions to these general rules are desirable, & probably practicable, yet if the exceptions cannot be agreed on, the establishment of the rules in all cases will do ill in very few. I hope therefore a bill of rights will be formed to guard the people against the federal government, as they are already guarded against their state governments in most instances. The abandoning the principle of necessary rotation in the Senate, has I see been disapproved by many; in the case of the President, by none. I readily therefore suppose my opinion wrong, when opposed by the majority as in the former instance, & the totality as in the latter. In this however I should have done it with more complete satisfaction, had we all judged from the same position . . .

Ford v: 45–8

## VI.7 To James Madison

Paris, March 15, 1789

Dear Sir, – . . . your thoughts on the subject of the Declaration of rights in the letter of Oct 17. I have weighed with great satisfaction. Some of them had not occurred to me before, but were acknoleged just in the moment they were presented to my mind. In the arguments in favor of a declaration of rights, you omit one which has great weight with me, the legal check which it puts into the hands of the judiciary. This is a body, which if rendered independent & kept strictly to their own department, merits great confidence for their learning & integrity. In fact what degree of confidence would be too much for a body composed of such men as Wythe, Blair & Pendleton? On characters like these the "*civium ardor prava jubentium*" would make no impression. I am happy to find that on the whole you are a friend to this amendment. The Declaration of rights is like all other human blessings alloyed with some inconveniences, and not accomplishing fully it's object. But the good in this instance vastly overweighs the evil. I cannot refrain from making short answers to the objections which your letter states to have been raised. 1. That the rights in question are reserved by the manner in which the federal powers are granted. Answer. A constitutive act may certainly be so formed as to need no declaration of rights. The act itself has the force of a declaration as far as it goes; and if it goes to all material points nothing more is wanting. In the draught of a constitution which I had once a thought of proposing in Virginia,[1] & printed afterwards, I endeavored to reach all the great objects of public liberty, and did not mean to add a declaration

[1] See *supra*, v.4. – *Eds.*

of rights. Probably the object was imperfectly executed; but the
deficiencies would have been supplied by others, in the course of
discussion. But in a constitutive act which leaves some precious
articles unnoticed, and raises implications against others, a declaration of rights becomes necessary by way of supplement. This is
the case of our new federal constitution. This instrument forms us
into one state as to certain objects, and gives us a legislative &
executive body for these objects. It should therefore guard us
against their abuses of power within the field submitted to them. 2.
A positive declaration of some essential rights could not be obtained
in the requisite latitude. Answer. Half a loaf is better than no bread.
If we cannot secure all our rights, let us secure what we can. 3.
The limited powers of the federal government & jealousy of the
subordinate governments afford a security which exists in no other
instance. Answer. The first member of this seems resolvable into
the first objection before stated. The jealousy of the subordinate
governments is a precious reliance. But observe that those governments are only agents. They must have principles furnished them
whereon to found their opposition. The declaration of rights will
be the text whereby they will try all the acts of the federal government. In this view it is necessary to the federal government also; as
by the same text they may try the opposition of the subordinate
governments. 4. Experience proves the inefficacy of a bill of rights.
True. But tho it is not absolutely efficacious under all circumstances, it is of great potency always, and rarely inefficacious. A
brace the more will often keep up the building which would have
fallen with that brace the less. There is a remarkable difference
between the characters of the Inconveniences which attend a Declaration of rights, & those which attend the want of it. The inconveniences of the Declaration are that it may cramp government in
it's useful exertions. But the evil of this is short-lived, trivial &
reparable. The inconveniences of the want of a Declaration are permanent, afflicting & irreparable. They are in constant progression
from bad to worse. The executive in our governments is not the
sole, it is scarcely the principal object of my jealousy. The tyranny
of the legislatures is the most formidable dread at present, and will
be for long years. That of the executive will come in it's turn, but
it will be at a remote period. I know there are some among us who
would now establish a monarchy. But they are inconsiderable in

number and weight of character. The rising race are all republicans. We were educated in royalism; no wonder if some of us retain that idolatry still. Our young people are educated in republicanism, an apostasy from that to royalism is unprecedented & impossible. I am much pleased with the prospect that a declaration of rights will be added; and hope it will be done in that way which will not endanger the whole frame of the government, or any essential part of it . . .

Ford v: 80-3

## VI.8 To John Taylor

Monticello, November 26, 1798

Dear Sir, – We formerly had a debtor and creditor account of letters on farming; but the high price of tobacco, which is likely to continue for some short time, has tempted me to go entirely into that culture, and in the meantime, my farming schemes are in abeyance, and my farming fields at nurse against the time of my resuming them. But I owe you a political letter. Yet the infidelities of the post office and the circumstances of the times are against my writing fully and freely, whilst my own dispositions are as much against mysteries, innuendoes and half-confidences. I know not which mortifies me most, that I should fear to write what I think, or my country bear such a state of things. Yet Lyon's judges, and a jury of all nations, are objects of national fear. We agree in all the essential ideas of your letter. We agree particularly in the necessity of some reform, and of some better security for civil liberty. But perhaps we do not see the existing circumstances in the same point of view. There are many consideration *dehors* of the State, which will occur to you without enumeration. I should not apprehend them, if all was sound within. But there is a most respectable part of our State who have been enveloped in the X. Y. Z. delusion,[1] and who destroy our unanimity for the present moment. This disease of the imagination will pass over, because the patients are essentially republicans. Indeed, the Doctor is now on his way to cure it, in the guise of a tax gatherer. But give time for the medicine to work, and for the

[1] See *supra*, I.9, note I. – *Eds.*

369

repetition of stronger doses, which must be administered. The principle of the present majority is *excessive expense*, money enough to fill all their maws, or it will not be worth the risk of their supporting. They cannot borrow a dollar in Europe, or above two or three millions in America. This is not the fourth of the expenses of this year, unprovided for. Paper money would be perilous even to the paper men. Nothing then but excessive taxation can get us along; and this will carry reason and reflection to every man's door, and particularly in the hour of election.

I wish it were possible to obtain a single amendment to our Constitution. I would be willing to depend on that alone for the reduction of the administration of our government to the genuine principles of its Constitution; I mean an additional article, taking from the federal government the power of borrowing. I now deny their power of making paper money or anything else a legal tender. I know that to pay all proper expenses within the year, would, in case of war, be hard on us. But not so hard as ten wars instead of one. For wars would be reduced in that proportion; besides that the State governments would be free to lend *their credit* in borrowing quotas. For the present, I should be for resolving the alien and sedition laws to be against the Constitution and merely void, and for addressing the other States to obtain similar declarations; and I would not do anything at this moment which should commit us further, but reserve ourselves to shape our future measures or no measures, by the events which may happen. It is a singular phenomenon, that while our State governments are the very *best in the world*, without exception or comparison, our General Government has, in the rapid course of nine or ten years, become more arbitrary, and has swallowed more of the public liberty than even that of England. I enclose you a column, cut out of a London paper, to show you that the English, though charmed with our making their enemies our enemies, yet blush and weep over our sedition law. But I enclose you something more important. It is a petition for a reformation in the manner of appointing our juries, and a remedy against the *jury of all nations*, which is handing about here for signature, and will be presented to your House. I know it will require but little ingenuity to make objections to the details of its execution; but do not be discouraged by small difficulties; make it as perfect as you can at a first essay, and depend on amending its defects as they develop themselves in practice. I hope it will meet with your approbation and patronage. It is the only thing which can yield us a little present protection against the dominion of a faction, while circumstances are maturing for bringing and keeping the government in real unison with the spirit of their constituents. I am aware that the act of Congress has directed that juries shall be appointed by lot or otherwise, as the laws *now* (at the date of the act) in force in the several States provide. The New England States have always had them elected by their select men, who are elected by the people. Several or most of the other States have a large number appointed (I do not know how) to attend, out of whom twelve for each cause are taken by lot. This provision of Congress will render it necessary for our Senators or Delegates to apply for an amendatory law, accommodated to that prayed for in the petition. In the meantime, I would pass the law as if the amendatory one existed, in reliance that our select jurors attending, the federal judge will, under a sense of right, direct the juries to be taken from among them. If he does not, or if Congress refuses to pass the amendatory law, it will serve as eye-water for their constituents. Health, happiness, *safety* and esteem to yourself and my ever-honored and ancient friend, Mr. Pendleton. Adieu.

L & B x: 63–7

## VI.9 To Dr. Joseph Priestley

Washington, June 19, 1802

Dear Sir, – Your favor of the 12th has been duly received, and with that pleasure which the approbation of the good and the wise must ever give. The sentiments it impresses are far beyond my merits or pretensions; they are precious testimonies to me, however, that my sincere desire to do what is right and just is viewed with candor. That it should be handed to the world under the authority of your name is securing its credit with posterity. In the great work which has been effected in America, no individual has a right to take any great share to himself. Our people in a body are wise, because they are under the unrestrained and unperverted operation of their own understanding. Those whom they have assigned to the direction of

371

their affairs, have stood with a pretty even front. If any one of them
was withdrawn, many others entirely equal have been ready to fill
his place with as good abilities. A nation, composed of such materials, and free in all its members from distressing wants, furnishes
hopeful implements for the interesting experiment of self-
government; and we feel that we are acting under obligations not
confined to the limits of our own society. It is impossible not to be
sensible that we are acting for all mankind; that circumstances
denied to others, but indulged to us, have imposed on us the duty
of proving what is the degree of freedom and self-government in
which a society may venture to leave its individual members. One
passage, in the paper you enclosed me, must be corrected. It is the
following, "and all say it was yourself more than any other individual, that planned and established it," *i.e.*, the Constitution. I was in
Europe when the Constitution was planned, and never saw it till
after it was established. On receiving it I wrote strongly to Mr.
Madison,[1] urging the want of provision for the freedom of religion,
freedom of the press, trial by jury, *habeas corpus*, the substitution of
militia for a standing army, and an express reservation to the States
of all rights not specifically granted to the Union. He accordingly
moved in the first session of Congress for these amendments, which
were agreed to and ratified by the States as they now stand. This is
all the hand I had in what related to the Constitution. Our predecessors made it doubtful how far even these were of any value; for
the very law which endangered your personal safety, as well as that
which restrained the freedom of the press, were gross violations of
them. However, it is still certain that though written constitutions
may be violated in moments of passion or delusion, yet they furnish
a text to which those who are watchful may again rally and recall
the people; they fix too for the people the principles of their political
creed. We shall all absent ourselves from this place during the sickly
season; say from about the 22d of July to the last of September.
Should your curiosity lead you hither either before or after that
interval, I shall be very happy to receive you, and shall claim you
as my guest. I wish the advantages of a mild over a winter climate
had been tried for you before you were located where you are. I
have ever considered this as a public as well as personal misfortune.

---

[1] See *supra*, VI. 4 and VI.6 – *Eds.*

The choice you made of our country for your asylum was honorable to it; and I lament that for the sake of your happiness and health its most benign climates were not selected. Certainly it is a truth that climate is one of the sources of the greatest sensual enjoyment. I received in due time the letter of April 10th referred to in your last, with the pamphlet it enclosed, which I read with the pleasure I do everything from you. Accept assurances of my highest veneration and respect.

L & B x: 324–6

## VI.10 To Wilson C. Nicholas

Monticello, September 7, 1803

Dear Sir, – Your favor of the 3d was delivered me at court; but we were much disappointed at not seeing you here, Mr. Madison and the Governor being here at the time. I enclose you a letter from Monroe on the subject of the late treaty. You will observe a hint in it, to do without delay what we are bound to do. There is reason, in the opinion of our ministers, to believe, that if the thing were to do over again, it could not be obtained, and that if we give the least opening, they will declare the treaty void. A warning amounting to that has been given to them, and an unusual kind of letter written by their minister to our Secretary of State, direct. Whatever Congress shall think it necessary to do, should be done with as little debate as possible, and particularly so far as respects the constitutional difficulty. I am aware of the force of the observations you make on the power given by the Constitution to Congress, to admit new States into the Union, without restraining the subject to the territory then constituting the United States. But when I consider that the limits of the United States are precisely fixed by the treaty of 1783, that the Constitution expressly declares itself to be made for the United States, I cannot help believing the intention was not to permit Congress to admit into the Union new States, which should be formed out of the territory for which, and under whose authority alone, they were then acting. I do not believe it was meant that they might receive England, Ireland, Holland, &c. into it, which would be the case on your construction [i.e., interpretation].

373

When an instrument admits two constructions, the one safe, the other dangerous, the one precise, the other indefinite, I prefer that which is safe and precise. I had rather ask an enlargement of power from the nation, where it is found necessary, than to assume it by a construction which would make our powers boundless. Our peculiar security is in the possession of a written Constitution. Let us not make it a blank paper by construction. I say the same as to the opinion of those who consider the grant of the treaty making power as boundless. If it is, then we have no Constitution. If it has bounds, they can be no others than the definitions of the powers which that instrument gives. It specifies and delineates the operations permitted to the federal government, and gives all the powers necessary to carry these into execution. Whatever of these enumerated objects is proper for a law, Congress may make the law; whatever is proper to be executed by way of a treaty, the President and Senate may enter into the treaty; whatever is to be done by a judicial sentence, the judges may pass the sentence. Nothing is more likely than that their enumeration of powers is defective. This is the ordinary case of all human works. Let us go on then perfecting it, by adding, by way of amendment to the Constitution, those powers which time and trial show are still wanting. But it has been taken too much for granted, that by this rigorous construction the treaty power would be reduced to nothing. I had occasion once to examine its effect on the French treaty, made by the old Congress, and found that out of thirty odd articles which that contained, there were one, two, or three only which could not now be stipulated under our present Constitution. I confess then, I think it important, in the present case, to set an example against broad construction, by appealing for new power to the people. If, however, our friends shall think differently, certainly I shall acquiesce with satisfaction; confiding, that the good sense of our country will correct the evil of construction when it shall produce ill effects.

No apologies for writing or speaking to me freely are necessary. On the contrary, nothing my friends can do is so dear to me, and proves to me their friendship so clearly, as the information they give me of their sentiments and those of others on interesting points where I am to act, and where information and warning is so essential to excite in me that due reflection which ought to precede action. I leave this about the 21st, and shall hope the District Court will give me an opportunity of seeing you.

Accept my affectionate salutations, and assurances of cordial esteem and respect.

Washington IV: 505–7

## VI.11 To John B. Colvin[1]

Monticello, September 20, 1810

Sir, – Your favor of the 14th has been duly received, and I have to thank you for the many obliging things respecting myself which are said in it. If I have left in the breasts of my fellow citizens a sentiment of satisfaction with my conduct in the transaction of their business, it will soften the pillow of my repose through the residue of life.

The question you propose, whether circumstances do not sometimes occur, which make it a duty in officers of high trust, to assume authorities beyond the law, is easy of solution in principle, but sometimes embarrassing in practice. A strict observance of the written laws is doubtless *one* of the high duties of a good citizen, but it is not *the highest*. The laws of necessity, of self-preservation, of saving our country when in danger, are of higher obligation. To lose our country by a scrupulous adherence to written law, would be to lose the law itself, with life, liberty, property and all those who are enjoying them with us; thus absurdly sacrificing the end to the means. When, in the battle of Germantown, General Washington's army was annoyed from Chew's house, he did not hesitate to plant his cannon against it, although the property of a citizen. When he besieged Yorktown, he leveled the suburbs, feeling that the laws of property must be postponed to the safety of the nation. While the army was before York, the Governor of Virginia took horses, carriages, provisions and even men by force, to enable that army to stay together till it could master the public enemy; and he was justified. A ship at sea in distress for provisions, meets another

---

[1] John Colvin was editor of *The Republican Advocate* in Fredericktown, Maryland. – *Eds.*

having abundance, yet refusing a supply; the law of self-preservation authorizes the distressed to take a supply by force. In all these cases, the unwritten laws of necessity, of self-preservation, and of the public safety, control the written laws of *meum* and *tuum*. Further to exemplify the principle, I will state an hypothetical case. Suppose it had been made known to the Executive of the Union in the autumn of 1805, that we might have the Floridas for a reasonable sum, that that sum had not indeed been so appropriated by law, but that Congress were to meet within three weeks, and might appropriate it on the first or second day of their session. Ought he, for so great an advantage to his country, to have risked himself by transcending the law and making the purchase? The public advantage offered, in this supposed case, was indeed immense; but a reverence for law, and the probability that the advantage might still be *legally* accomplished by a delay of only three weeks, were powerful reasons against hazarding the act. But suppose it foreseen that a John Randolph would find means to protract the proceeding on it by Congress, until the ensuing spring, by which time new circumstances would change the mind of the other party. Ought the Executive, in that case, and with that foreknowledge, to have secured the good to his country, and to have trusted to their justice for the transgression of the law? I think he ought, and that the act would have been approved. After the affair of the Chesapeake, we thought war a very possible result. Our magazines were illy provided with some necessary articles, nor had any appropriations been made for their purchase. We ventured, however, to provide them, and to place our country in safety; and stating the case to Congress, they sanctioned the act.

To proceed to the conspiracy of [Aaron] Burr, and particularly to General Wilkinson's situation in New Orleans. In judging this case, we are bound to consider the state of the information, correct and incorrect, which he then possessed. He expected Burr and his band from above, a British fleet from below, and he knew there was a formidable conspiracy within the city. Under these circumstances, was he justifiable, 1st, in seizing notorious conspirators? On this there can be but two opinions; one, of the guilty and their accomplices; the other, that of all honest men. 2d. In sending them to the seat of government, when the written law gave them a right to trial in the territory? The danger of their rescue, of their continuing their machinations, the tardiness and weakness of the law, apathy of the judges, active patronage of the whole tribe of lawyers, unknown disposition of the juries, an hourly expectation of the enemy, salvation of the city, and of the Union itself, which would have been convulsed to its centre, had that conspiracy succeeded; all these constituted a law of necessity and self-preservation, and rendered the *salus populi* supreme over the written law. The officer who is called to act on this superior ground, does indeed risk himself on the justice of the controlling powers of the constitution, and his station makes it his duty to incur that risk. But those controlling powers, and his fellow citizens generally, are bound to judge according to the circumstances under which he acted. They are not to transfer the information of this place or moment to the time and place of his action; but to put themselves into his situation. We knew here that there never was danger of a British fleet from below, and that Burr's band was crushed before it reached the Mississippi. But General Wilkinson's information was very different, and he could act on no other.

From these examples and principles you may see what I think on the question proposed. They do not go to the case of persons charged with petty duties, where consequences are trifling, and time allowed for a legal course, nor to authorize them to take such cases out of the written law. In these, the example of over-leaping the law is of greater evil than a strict adherence to its imperfect provisions. It is incumbent on those only who accept of great charges, to risk themselves on great occasions, when the safety of the nation, or some of its very high interests are at stake. An officer is bound to obey orders; yet he would be a bad one who should do it in cases for which they were not intended, and which involved the most important consequences. The line of discrimination between cases may be difficult; but the good officer is bound to draw it at his own peril, and throw himself on the justice of his country and the rectitude of his motives.

I have indulged freer views on this question, on your assurances that they are for your own eye only, and that they will not get into the hands of newswriters. I met their scurrilities without concern, while in pursuit of the great interests with which I was charged. But in my present retirement, no duty forbids my wish for quiet.

Accept the assurances of my esteem and respect.

Ford IX: 279–82

VI.12 To Judge Spencer Roane

Poplar Forest, September 6, 1819

Dear Sir, – I had read in the Enquirer, and with great approbation, the pieces signed Hampden, and have read them again with redoubled approbation, in the copies you have been so kind as to send me. I subscribe to every tittle of them. They contain the true principles of the revolution of 1800, for that was as real a revolution in the principles of our government as that of 1776 was in its form; not effected indeed by the sword, as that, but by the rational and peaceable instrument of reform, the suffrage of the people. The nation declared its will by dismissing functionaries of one principle, and electing those of another, in the two branches, executive and legislature, submitted to their election. Over the judiciary department, the Constitution had deprived them of their control. That, therefore, has continued the reprobated system, and although new matter has been occasionally incorporated into the old, yet the leaven of the old mass seems to assimilate to itself the new, and after twenty years' confirmation of the federated system by the voice of the nation, declared through the medium of elections, we find the judiciary on every occasion, still driving us into consolidation.

In denying the right they usurp of exclusively explaining the Constitution, I go further than you do, if I understand rightly your quotation from the Federalist,[1] of an opinion that "the judiciary is the last resort in relation *to the other departments* of the government, but not in relation to the rights of the parties to the compact under which the judiciary is derived." If this opinion be sound, then indeed is our Constitution a complete *felo de se*. For intending to establish three departments, co-ordinate and independent, that they might check and balance one another, it has given, according to this opinion, to one of them alone, the right to prescribe rules for the government of the others, and to that one too, which is unelected by, and independent of the nation. For experience has already shown that the impeachment it has provided is not even a scarecrow; that such opinions as the one you combat sent cautiously out, as you observe also, by detachment, not belonging to the case often,

---

[1] James Madison, Alexander Hamilton, and John Jay, *The Federalist Papers.* – *Eds.*

378

but sought for out of it, as if to rally the public opinion beforehand to their views, and to indicate the line they are to walk in, have been so quietly passed over as never to have excited animadversion, even in a speech of any one of the body entrusted with impeachment. The Constitution, on this hypothesis, is a mere thing of wax in the hands of the judiciary, which they may twist and shape into any form they please. It should be remembered, as an axiom of eternal truth in politics, that whatever power in any government is independent, is absolute also; in theory only, at first, while the spirit of the people is up, but in practice, as fast as that relaxes. Independence can be trusted nowhere but with the people in mass. They are inherently independent of all but moral law. My construction [i.e. interpretation] of the Constitution is very different from that you quote. It is that each department is truly independent of the others, and has an equal right to decide for itself what is the meaning of the Constitution in the cases submitted to its action; and especially, where it is to act ultimately and without appeal. I will explain myself by examples, which, having occurred while I was in office, are better known to me, and the principles which governed them.

A legislature had passed the sedition law.[2] The federal courts had subjected certain individuals to its penalties of fine and imprisonment. On coming into office, I released these individuals by the power of pardon committed to executive discretion, which could never be more properly exercised than where citizens were suffering without the authority of law, or, which was equivalent, under a law unauthorized by the Constitution, and therefore null. In the case of Marbury and Madison,[3] the federal judges declared that commissions, signed and sealed by the President, were valid, although not delivered. I deemed delivery essential to complete a deed, which, as long as it remains in the hands of the party, is as yet no deed; it is *in posse* only, but not *in esse*, and I withheld delivery of the commissions. They cannot issue a *mandamus* to the President or legislature, or to any of their officers. When the British treaty of — arrived, without any provision against the impressment of our seamen, I determined not to ratify it. The Senate thought I should

---

[2] The Sedition Act of 1798 was used by Federalists to silence their Republican critics, who were convicted and imprisoned for treason. – *Eds.*

[3] *Marbury* v. *Madison* (1803). – *Eds.*

ask their advice. I thought that would be a mockery of them, when I was predetermined against following it, should they advise its ratification. The Constitution had made their advice necessary to confirm a treaty, but not to reject it. This has been blamed by some; but I have never doubted its soundness. In the cases of two persons, *antenati*, under exactly similar circumstances, the federal court had determined that one of them (Duane) was not a citizen; the House of Representatives nevertheless determined that the other (Smith, of South Carolina) was a citizen, and admitted him to his seat in their body. Duane was a republican, and Smith a federalist, and these decisions were made during the federal ascendency.

These are examples of my position, that each of the three departments has equally the right to decide for itself what is its duty under the Constitution, without any regard to what the others may have decided for themselves under a similar question. But you intimate a wish that my opinion should be known on this subject. No, dear Sir, I withdraw from all contests of opinion, and resign everything cheerfully to the generation now in place. They are wiser than we were, and their successors will be wiser than they, from the progressive advance of science. Tranquillity is the *summum bonum* of age. I wish, therefore, to offend no man's opinion, nor to draw disquieting animadversions on my own. While duty required it, I met opposition with a firm and fearless step. But loving mankind in my individual relations with them, I pray to be permitted to depart in their peace; and like the superannuated soldier, *"quadragenis stipendiis emeritis,"* to hang my arms [weapons] on the post. I have unwisely, I fear, embarked in an enterprise of great public concern, but not to be accomplished within my term, without their liberal and prompt support. A severe illness the last year, and another from which I am just emerged, admonish me that repetitions may be expected, against which a declining frame cannot long bear up. I am anxious, therefore, to get our University [of Virginia] so far advanced as may encourage the public to persevere to its final accomplishment. That secured, I shall sing my *nunc dimittis*. I hope your labors will be long continued in the spirit in which they have always been exercised, in maintenance of those principles on which I verily believe the future happiness of our country essentially depends. I salute you with affectionate and great respect.

L & B XV: 212–16

## VI.13 To William Charles Jarvis

Monticello, September 28, 1820

I thank you, Sir, for the copy of your *Republican* which you have been so kind as to send me, and I should have acknowledged it sooner but that I am just returned home after a long absence. I have not yet had time to read it seriously, but in looking over it cursorily I see much in it to approve, and shall be glad if it shall lead our youth to the practice of thinking on such subjects and for themselves. That it will have this tendency may be expected, and for that reason I feel an urgency to note what I deem an error in it, the more requiring notice as your opinion is strengthened by that of many others. You seem, in pages 84 and 148, to consider the judges as the ultimate arbiters of all constitutional questions; a very dangerous doctrine indeed, and one which would place us under the despotism of an oligarchy. Our judges are as honest as other men, and not more so. They have, with others, the same passions for party, for power, and the privilege of their corps. Their maxim is "*boni judicis est ampliare jurisdictionem*," and their power the more dangerous as they are in office for life, and not responsible, as the other functionaries are, to the elective control. The Constitution has erected no such single tribunal, knowing that to whatever hands confided, with the corruptions of time and party, its members would become despots. It has more wisely made all the departments co-equal and co-sovereign within themselves. If the legislature fails to pass laws for a census, for paying the judges and other officers of government, for establishing a militia, for naturalization as prescribed by the Constitution, or if they fail to meet in congress, the judges cannot issue their *mandamus* to them; if the President fails to supply the place of judge, to appoint other civil or military officers, to issue requisite commissions, the judges cannot force him. They can issue their *mandamus* or *distringas* to no executive or legislative officer to enforce the fulfilment of their official duties, any more than the President or legislature may issue orders to the judges or their officers. Betrayed by English example, and unaware, as it should seem, of the control of our Constitution in this particular, they have at times overstepped their limit by undertaking to command executive officers in the discharge of their executive duties; but the Constitution, in keeping three departments distinct and independent, restrains the authority of the judges to judiciary organs, as it does the executive and legislative to executive and legislative organs. The judges certainly have more frequent occasion to act on constitutional questions, because the laws of *meum* and *tuum* and of criminal action, forming the great mass of the system of law, constitute their particular department. When the legislative or executive functionaries act unconstitutionally, they are responsible to the people in their elective capacity. The exemption of the judges from that is quite dangerous enough. I know no safe depository of the ultimate powers of the society but the people themselves; and if we think them not enlightened enough to exercise their control with a wholesome discretion, the remedy is not to take it from them, but to inform their discretion by education. This is the true corrective of abuses of constitutional power. Pardon me, Sir, for this difference of opinion. My personal interest in such questions is entirely extinct, but not my wishes for the longest possible continuance of our government on its pure principles; if the three powers maintain their mutual independence on each other it may last long, but not so if either can assume the authorities of the other. I ask your candid re-consideration of this subject, and am sufficiently sure you will form a candid conclusion. Accept the assurance of my great respect.

L & B xv: 276–7

## VI.14 To Major John Cartwright

Monticello, June 5, 1824

Dear and Venerable Sir, – I am much indebted for your kind letter of February the 29th, and for your valuable volume on the English Constitution. I have read this with pleasure and much approbation, and think it has deduced the Constitution of the English nation from its rightful root, the Anglo-Saxon. It is really wonderful, that so many able and learned men should have failed in their attempts to define it with correctness. No wonder then, that Paine, who thought more than he read, should have credited the great authorities who have declared, that the will of Parliament is the Constitution of England. So Marbois, before the French Revolution, observed to me that the Almanac Royal was the Constitution of France. Your derivation of it from the Anglo-Saxons, seems to be made on legitimate principles. Having driven out the former inhabitants of that part of the island called England, they became aborigines as to you, and your lineal ancestors. They doubtless had a constitution; and although they have not left it in a written formula, to the precise text of which you may always appeal, yet they have left fragments of their history and laws, from which it may be inferred with considerable certainty. Whatever their history and laws show to have been practised with approbation, we may presume was permitted by their constitution; whatever was not so practiced, was not permitted. And although this constitution was violated and set at naught by Norman force, yet force cannot change right. A perpetual claim was kept up by the nation, by their perpetual demand of a restoration of their Saxon laws; which shows they were never relinquished by the will of the nation. In the pullings and haulings for these ancient rights, between the nation, and its kings of the races of Plantagenets, Tudors and Stuarts, there was sometimes gain, and sometimes loss, until the final reconquest of their rights from the Stuarts. The destruction and expulsion of this race broke the thread of pretended inheritance, extinguished all regal usurpations, and the nation re-entered into all its rights; and although in their bill of rights they specifically reclaimed some only, yet the omission of the others was no renunciation of the right to assume their exercise also, whenever occasion should occur. The new King received no rights or powers, but those expressly granted to him. It has ever appeared to me, that the difference between the Whig and the Tory of England is, that the Whig deduces his rights from the Anglo-Saxon source, and the Tory from the Norman. And Hume, the great apostle of Toryism, says, in so many words, note AA to chapter 42, that, in the reign of the Stuarts, "it was the people who encroached upon the sovereign, not the sovereign who attempted, as is pretended, to usurp upon the people." This supposes the Norman usurpations to be rights in his successors. And again, C, 159, "the commons established a principle, which is noble in itself, and seems specious, but is belied by all history and experience, *that the people are the origin of all just power.*"[1] And where else will this degenerate son of science, this traitor to his fellow men, find the origin of *just* powers, if not in the majority of the society? Will it be in the minority? Or in an individual of that minority?

Our Revolution commenced on more favorable ground. It presented us an album on which we were free to write what we pleased. We had no occasion to search into musty records, to hunt up royal parchments, or to investigate the laws and institutions of a semi-barbarous ancestry. We appealed to those of nature, and found them engraved on our hearts. Yet we did not avail ourselves of all the advantages of our position. We had never been permitted to exercise self-government. When forced to assume it, we were novices in its science. Its principles and forms had entered little into our former education. We established, however, some, although not all its important principles. The constitutions of most of our States assert, that all power is inherent in the people; that they may exercise it by themselves, in all cases to which they think themselves competent (as in electing their functionaries executive and legislative, and deciding by a jury of themselves, in all judiciary cases in which any fact is involved), or they may act by representatives, freely and equally chosen; that it is their right and duty to be at all times armed; that they are entitled to freedom of person, freedom of religion, freedom of property, and freedom of the press. In the structure of our legislatures, we think experience has proved the benefit of subjecting questions to two separate bodies of deliberants; but in constituting these, natural right has been mistaken, some making one of these bodies, and some both, the representatives of property instead of persons; whereas the double deliberation might be as well obtained without any violation of true principle, either by requiring a greater age in one of the bodies, or by electing a proper number of representatives of persons, dividing them by lots into two chambers, and renewing the division at frequent intervals, in order to break up all cabals. Virginia, of which I am myself a native and resident, was not

---

[1] David Hume, *History of England* (1762). – *Eds.*

only the first of the States, but, I believe I may say, the first of the nations of the earth, which assembled its wise men peaceably together to form a fundamental constitution, to commit it to writing, and place it among their archives, where every one should be free to appeal to its text. But this act was very imperfect. The other States, as they proceeded successively to the same work, made successive improvements; and several of them, still further corrected by experience, have, by conventions, still further amended their first forms. My own State has gone on so far with its *première ébauche*; but it is now proposing to call a convention for amendment. Among other improvements, I hope they will adopt the subdivision of our counties into wards. The former may be estimated at an average of twenty-four miles square; the latter should be about six miles square each, and would answer to the hundreds of your Saxon Alfred. In each of these might be, 1st, an elementary school; 2d, a company of militia, with its officers; 3d, a justice of the peace and constable; 4th, each ward should take care of their own poor; 5th, their own roads; 6th, their own police; 7th, elect within themselves one or more jurors to attend the courts of justice; and 8th, give in at their folk-house, their votes for all functionaries reserved to their election. Each ward would thus be a small republic within itself, and every man in the State would thus become an acting member of the common government, transacting in person a great portion of its rights and duties, subordinate indeed, yet important, and entirely within his competence. The wit of man cannot devise a more solid basis for a free, durable and well-administered republic.

With respect to our State and federal governments, I do not think their relations correctly understood by foreigners. They generally suppose the former subordinate to the latter. But this is not the case. They are co-ordinate departments of one simple and integral whole. To the State governments are reserved all legislation and administration, in affairs which concern their own citizens only, and to the federal government is given whatever concerns foreigners, or the citizens of other States; these functions alone being made federal. The one is the domestic, the other the foreign branch of the same government; neither having control over the other, but within its own department. There are one or two exceptions only to this partition of power. But, you may ask, if the two departments should claim each the same subject of power, where is the common umpire to decide ultimately between them? In cases of little importance or urgency, the prudence of both parties will keep them aloof from the questionable ground; but if it can neither be avoided nor compromised, a convention of the States must be called, to ascribe the doubtful power to that department which they may think best. You will perceive by these details, that we have not yet so far perfected our constitutions as to venture to make them unchangeable. But still, in their present state, we consider them not otherwise changeable than by the authority of the people, on a special election of representatives for that purpose expressly: they are until then the *lex legum.*

But can they be made unchangeable? Can one generation bind another, and all others, in succession forever? I think not. The Creator has made the earth for the living, not the dead. Rights and powers can only belong to persons, not to things, not to mere matter, unendowed with will. The dead are not even things. The particles of matter which composed their bodies, make part now of the bodies of other animals, vegetables, or minerals, of a thousand forms. To what then are attached the rights and powers they held while in the form of men? A generation may bind itself as long as its majority continues in life; when that has disappeared, another majority is in place, holds all the rights and powers their predecessors once held, and may change their laws and institutions to suit themselves. Nothing then is unchangeable but the inherent and unalienable rights of man.

I was glad to find in your book a formal contradiction, at length, of the judiciary usurpation of legislative powers; for such the judges have usurped in their repeated decisions, that Christianity is a part of the common law. The proof of the contrary, which you have adduced, is incontrovertible; to wit, that the common law existed while the Anglo-Saxons were yet pagans, at a time when they had never yet heard the name of Christ pronounced, or knew that such a character had ever existed. But it may amuse you, to show when, and by what means, they stole this law in upon us. In a case of *quare impedit* in the Year-book 34, H. 6, folio 38 (anno 1458), a question was made, how far the ecclesiastical law was to be respected in a common law court? And Prisot, Chief Justice, gives his opinion in these words: "A tiel leis qu'ils de seint eglise ont en *ancien scripture*, covient à nous à donner credence; car ceo common ley sur quels touts manners leis sont fondés. Et auxy, Monsieur, nous sumus oblègés de conustre lour ley de saint eglise; et semblablement ils sont obligé de consustre nostre ley. Et, Monsieur, si poit apperer or à nous que l'evesque ad fait come un ordinary fera en tiel cas, adong nous devons cee adjuger bon, ou auterment nemy," etc. See S. C. Fitzh. Abr. Qu. imp. 89, Bro. Abr. Qu. imp. 12. Finch in his first book, c. 3, is the first afterwards who quotes this case and mistakes it thus: "To such laws of the church as have warrant in *holy scripture*, our law giveth credence." And cites Prisot; mistranslating *"ancien scripture,"* into *"holy scripture."* Whereas Prisot palpably says, "to such laws as those of holy church have in *ancient writing*, it is proper for us to give credence," to wit, to their *ancient written* laws. This was in 1613, a century and a half after the dictum of Prisot. Wingate, in 1658, erects this false translation into a maxim of the common law, copying the words of Finch, but citing Prisot, Wing. Max. 3. And Sheppard, title, "Religion," in 1675, copies the same mistranslation, quoting the Y. B. Finch and Wingate. Hale expresses it in these words: "Christianity is parcel of the laws of England." 1 Ventr. 293, 3 Keb. 607. But he quotes no authority. By these echoings and re-echoings from one to another, it had become so established in 1728, that in the case of the King *vs.* Woolston, 2 Stra. 834, the court would not suffer it to be debated, whether to write against Christianity was punishable in the temporal court at common law? Wood, therefore, 409, ventures still to vary the phrase, and say, that all blasphemy and profaneness are offences by the common law; and cites 2 Stra. Then Blackstone, in 1763, IV. 59, repeats the words of Hale, that "Christianity is part of the laws of England," citing Ventris and Strange. And finally, Lord Mansfield, with a little qualification, in Evans' case, in 1767, says that "the essential principles of revealed religion are part of the common law." Thus ingulfing Bible, Testament and all into the common law, without citing any authority. And thus we find this chain of authorities hanging link by link, one upon another, and all ultimately on one and the same hook, and that a mistranslation of the words *"ancien scripture,"* used by Prisot. Finch quotes Prisot; Wingate does the same. Sheppard quotes Prisot, Finch and Wingate. Hale cites nobody. The court in Woolston's case, cites Hale.

Wood cites Woolston's case. Blackstone quotes Woolston's case and Hale. And Lord Mansfield, like Hale, ventures it on his own authority. Here I might defy the best-read lawyer to produce another scrip of authority for this judiciary forgery; and I might go on further to show, how some of the Anglo-Saxon priests interpolated into the text of Alfred's laws, the 20th, 21st, 22d, and 23d chapters of Exodus, and the 15th of the Acts of the Apostles, from the 23d to the 29th verses. But this would lead my pen and your patience too far. What a conspiracy this, between Church and State! Sing Tantarara, rogues all, rogues all, Sing Tantarara, rogues all!

I must still add to this long and rambling letter, my acknowledgments for your good wishes to the University we are now establishing in this State. There are some novelties in it. Of that of a professorship of the principles of government, you express your approbation. They will be founded in the rights of man. That of agriculture, I am sure, you will approve; and that also of Anglo-Saxon. As the histories and laws left us in that type and dialect, must be the text-books of the reading of the learners, they will imbibe with the language their free principles of government. The volumes you have been so kind as to send, shall be placed in the library of the University. Having at this time in England a person sent for the purpose of selecting some professors, a Mr. [Francis W.] Gilmer of my neighborhood, I cannot but recommend him to your patronage, counsel and guardianship, against imposition, misinformation, and the deceptions of partial and false recommendations, in the selection of characters. He is a gentleman of great worth and correctness, my particular friend, well educated in various branches of science, and worthy of entire confidence.

Your age of eighty-four and mine of eighty-one years, insure us a speedy meeting. We may then commune at leisure, and more fully, on the good and evil which, in the course of our long lives, we have both witnessed; and in the meantime, I pray you to accept assurances of my high veneration and esteem for your person and character.

L & B xvi: 42–52

# VII Religious Liberty and Toleration

## VII.1 A Bill for Establishing Religious Freedom
## (1777)[1]

Section 1. Well aware that the opinions and belief of men depend
not on their own will, but follow involuntarily the evidence
proposed to their minds; that Almighty God hath created the
mind free, and manifested his supreme will that free it shall
remain by making it altogether insusceptible of restraint; that all
attempts to influence it by temporal punishments, or burthens,
or by civil incapacitations, tend only to beget habits of hypocrisy
and meanness, and are a departure from the plan of the holy
author of our religion, who being lord both of body and mind,
yet choose not to propagate it by coercions on either, as was in
his Almighty power to do, but to exalt it by its influence on
reason alone; that the impious presumption of legislature and
ruler, civil as well as ecclesiastical, who, being themselves but
fallible and uninspired men, have assumed dominion over the
faith of others, setting up their own opinions and modes of
thinking as the only true and infallible, and as such endeavoring
to impose them on others, hath established and maintained false
religions over the greatest part of the world and through all time:
That to compel a man to furnish contributions of money for the
propagation of opinions which he disbelieves and abhors, is sinful
and tyrannical; that even the forcing him to support this or that
teacher of his own religious persuasion, is depriving him of the
comfortable liberty of giving his contributions to the particular
pastor whose morals he would make his pattern, and whose
powers he feels most persuasive to righteousness; and is withdrawing from the ministry those temporary rewards, which proceeding from an approbation of their personal conduct, are an
additional incitement to earnest and unremitting labours for the
instruction of mankind; that our civil rights have no dependance
on our religious opinions, any more than our opinions in physics
or geometry; and therefore the proscribing any citizen as
unworthy the public confidence by laying upon him an incapacity
of being called to offices of trust or emolument, unless he profess
or renounce this or that religious opinion, is depriving him

---

[1] Drafted in 1777 but not amended and passed by the Virginia legislature until 1786,
this bill was regarded by Jefferson as one of his three greatest achievements. – *Eds.*

injudiciously of those privileges and advantages to which, in common with his fellow-citizens, he has a natural right; that it tends also to corrupt the principles of that very religion it is meant to encourage, by bribing with a monopoly of worldly honours and emoluments, those who will externally profess and conform to it; that though indeed these are criminals who do not withstand such temptation, yet neither are those innocent who lay the bait in their way; that the opinions of men are not the object of civil government, nor under its jurisdiction; that to suffer the civil magistrate to intrude his powers into the field of opinion and to restrain the profession or propagation of principles on supposition of their ill tendency is a dangerous falacy, which at once destroys all religious liberty, because he being of course judge of that tendency will make his opinions the rule of judgment, and approve or condemn the sentiments of others only as they shall square with or suffer from his own; that it is time enough for the rightful purposes of civil government for its officers to interfere when principles break out into overt acts against peace and good order; and finally, that truth is great and will prevail if left to herself; that she is the proper and sufficient antagonist to error, and has nothing to fear from the conflict unless by human interposition disarmed of her natural weapons, free argument and debate; errors ceasing to be dangerous when it is permitted freely to contradict them.

Sect. II. We the General Assembly of Virginia do enact that no man shall be compelled to frequent or support any religious worship, place, or ministry whatsoever, nor shall be enforced, restrained, molested, or burthened in his body or goods; or shall otherwise suffer, on account of his religious opinions or belief; but that all men shall be free to profess, and by argument to maintain, their opinions in matters of religion, and that the same shall in no wise diminish, enlarge, or affect their civil capacities.

Sect. III. And though we well know that this Assembly, elected by the people for their ordinary purposes of legislation only, have no power to restrain the acts of succeeding Assemblies, constituted with powers equal to our own, and that therefore to declare this act to be irrevocable would be of no effect in law; yet we are free to declare, and do declare, that the rights hereby asserted are of the natural rights of mankind, and that if any act shall be hereafter passed to repeal the present or to narrow its operations, such act will be an infringement of natural right.

Ford II: 237–9

## VII.2 *Notes on Virginia*: Query XVII

*The different religions received into that state?*

The first settlers in this country were emigrants from England, of the English church, just at a point of time when it was flushed with complete victory over the religious of all other persuasions. Possessed, as they became, of the powers of making, administering and executing the laws, they shewed equal intolerance in this country with their Presbyterian brethren, who had emigrated to the northern government. The poor Quakers were flying from persecution in England. They cast their eyes on these new countries as asylums of civil and religious freedom; but they found them free only for the reigning sect. Several acts of the Virginia assembly of 1659, 1662, and 1693, had made it penal in parents to refuse to have their children baptized; had prohibited the unlawful assembling of Quakers; had made it penal for any master of a vessel to bring a Quaker into the state; had ordered those already here, and such as should come thereafter, to be imprisoned till they should abjure the country; provided a milder punishment for their first and second return, but death for their third; had inhibited all persons from suffering their meetings in or near their houses, entertaining them individually, or disposing of books which supported their tenets. If no capital execution took place here, as did in New-England, it was not owing to the moderation of the church, or spirit of the legislature, as may be inferred from the law itself; but to historical circumstances which have not been handed down to us. The Anglicans retained full possession of the country about a century. Other opinions began then to creep in, and the great care of the government to support their own church, having begotten an equal degree of indolence in its clergy, two thirds of the people had become dissenters at the commencement of the present revolution. The laws indeed were still oppressive on them, but the spirit of the one party had subsided into moderation, and of the other had risen to a degree of determination which commanded respect.

The present state of our laws on the subject of religion is this. The convention of May 1776, in their declaration of rights, declared it to be a truth, and a natural right, that the exercise of religion should be free; but when they proceeded to form on that declaration the ordinance of government, instead of taking up every principle declared in the bill of rights, and guarding it by legislative sanction, they passed over that which asserted our religious rights, leaving them as they found them. The same convention, however, when they met as a member of the general assembly in October 1776, repealed all *acts of parliament* which had rendered criminal the maintaining any opinions in matters of religion, the forbearing to repair to church, and the exercising any mode of worship; and suspended the laws giving salaries to the clergy, which suspension was made perpetual in October 1779. Statutory oppressions in religion being thus wiped away, we remain at present under those only imposed by the common law, or by our own acts of assembly. At the common law, *heresy* was a capital offence, punishable by burning. Its definition was left to the ecclesiastical judges, before whom the conviction was, till the statute of the 1 El. c. 1. circumscribed it, by declaring that nothing should be deemed heresy but what had been so determined by authority of the canonical scriptures, or by one of the four first general councils, or by some other council having for the grounds of their declaration the express and plain words of the scriptures. Heresy, thus circumscribed, being an offence at the common law, our act of assembly of October 1777, c. 17 gives cognizance of it to the general court, by declaring that the jurisdiction of that court shall be general in all matters at the common law. The execution is by the writ *De hæretico comburendo.* By our own act of assembly of 1705, c. 30, if a person brought up in the christian religion denies the being of a God, or the trinity, or asserts there are more Gods that one, or denies the christian religion to be true, or the scriptures to be of divine authority, he is punishable on the first offence by incapacity to hold any office or employment ecclesiastical, civil, or military; on the second by disability to sue, to take any gift or legacy, to be guardian, executor or administrator, and by three years imprisonment, without bail. A father's right to the custody of his own children being founded in law on his right of guardianship, this being taken away, they may of course be severed from him and put, by the authority of a court, into more orthodox hands. This is a summary view of that religious slavery under which a people have been willing to remain who have lavished their lives and fortunes for the establishment of their civil freedom. The error seems not sufficiently eradicated, that the operations of the mind, as well as the acts of the body, are subject to the coercion of the laws.[1] But our rulers can have authority over such natural rights, only as we have submitted to them. The rights of conscience we never submitted, we could not submit. We are answerable for them to our God. The legitimate powers of government extend to such acts only as are injurious to others. But it does me no injury for my neighbor to say there are twenty gods, or no god. It neither picks my pocket nor breaks my leg. If it be said his testimony in a court of justice cannot be relied on, reject it then, and be the stigma on him. Constraint may make him worse by making him a hypocrite, but it will never make him a truer man. It may fix him obstinately in his errors, but will not cure them. Reason and free inquiry are the only effectual agents against error. Give a loose to them, they will support the true religion by bringing every false one to their tribunal, to the test of their investigation. They are the natural enemies of error, and of error only. Had not the Roman government permitted free inquiry, christianity could never have been introduced. Had not free inquiry been indulged, at the æra of the reformation, the corruptions of christianity could not have been purged away. If it be restrained now, the present corruptions will be protected, and new ones encouraged. Was the government to prescribe to us our medicine and diet, our bodies would be in such keeping as our souls are now. Thus in France the emetic was once forbidden as a medicine, and the potatoe as an article of food. Government is just as infallible, too, when it fixes systems in physics. Galileo was sent to the inquisition for affirming that the earth was a sphere; the government had declared it to be as flat as a trencher, and Galileo was obliged to abjure his error. This error however at length prevailed, the earth became a globe, and Descartes declared it was whirled round its axis by a vortex. The government in which he lived was wise enough to see that this was no question of civil jurisdiction, or we should all have been involved

---

[1] Furneaux *passim.* [Philip Furneaux, *The Palladium of Conscience; or, The Foundations of Religious Liberty* . . . (Philadelphia, 1773). – *Eds.*]

by authority in vortices. In fact the vortices have been exploded, and the Newtonian principle of gravitation is now more firmly established, on the basis of reason, than it would be were the government to step in and to make it an article of necessary faith. Reason and experiment have been indulged, and error has fled before them. It is error alone which needs the support of government. Truth can stand by itself. Subject opinion to coercion: whom will you make your inquisitors? Fallible men; men governed by bad passions, by private as well as public reasons. And why subject it to coercion? To produce uniformity. But is uniformity of opinion desireable? No more than of face and stature. Introduce the bed of Procrustes then, and as there is danger that the large men may beat the small, make us all of a size, by lopping the former and stretching the latter. Difference of opinion is advantageous in religion. The several sects perform the office of a *Censor morum* over each other. Is uniformity attainable? Millions of innocent men, women and children, since the introduction of Christianity, have been burnt, tortured, fined, imprisoned: yet we have not advanced one inch towards uniformity. What has been the effect of coercion? To make one half the world fools, and the other half hypocrites. To support roguery and error all over the earth. Let us reflect that it is inhabited by a thousand millions of people. That these profess probably a thousand different systems of religion. That ours is but one of that thousand. That if there be but one right, and ours that one, we should wish to see the 999 wandering sects gathered into the fold of truth. But against such a majority we cannot effect this by force. Reason and persuasion are the only practicable instruments. To make way for these, free inquiry must be indulged; and how can we wish others to indulge it while we refuse it ourselves. But every state, says an inquisitor, has established some religion. "No two, say I, have established the same." Is this a proof of the infallibility of establishments? Our sister states of Pennsylvania and New York, however, have long subsisted without any establishment at all. The experiment was new and doubtful when they made it. It has answered beyond conception. They flourish infinitely. Religion is well supported; of various kinds indeed, but all good enough; all sufficient to preserve peace and order: or if a sect arises whose tenets would subvert morals, good sense has fair play, and reasons and laughs it out of doors, without suffering the state to be troubled with it. They do not hang more malefactors than we do. They are not more disturbed with religious dissentions. On the contrary, their harmony is unparalleled, and can be ascribed to nothing but their unbounded tolerance, because there is no other circumstance in which they differ from every nation on earth. They have made the happy discovery, that the way to silence religious disputes, is to take no notice of them. Let us too give this experiment fair play, and get rid, while we may, of those tyrannical laws. It is true we are as yet secured against them by the spirit of the times. I doubt whether the people of this country would suffer an execution for heresy, or a three years imprisonment for not comprehending the mysteries of the trinity. But is the spirit of the people an infallible, a permanent reliance? Is it government? Is this the kind of protection we receive in return for the rights we give up? Besides, the spirit of the times may alter, will alter. Our rulers will become corrupt, our people careless. A single zealot may commence persecuter, and better men be his victims. It can never be too often repeated, that the time for fixing every essential right on a legal basis is while our rulers are honest, and ourselves united. From the conclusion of this war[2] we shall be going down hill. It will not then be necessary to resort every moment to the people for support. They will be forgotten therefore, and their rights disregarded. They will forget themselves, but in the sole faculty of making money, and will never think of uniting to effect a due respect for their rights. The shackles, therefore, which shall not be knocked off at the conclusion of this war, will remain on us long, will be made heavier and heavier, till our rights shall revive or expire in a convulsion.

Ford III: 261–6

## VII.3 To Messrs. Nehemiah Dodge, Ephram Robbins, and Stephen S. Nelson, a Committee of the Danbury Baptist Association, in the State of Connecticut

January 1, 1802

Gentlemen, – The affectionate sentiments of esteem and approbation which you are so good as to express towards me, on behalf of the Dan-

---

[2] I.e., the American Revolution which ended in 1783, a year after Jefferson completed a full first draft of his *Notes on Virginia*. – Eds.

bury Baptist Association, give me the highest satisfaction. My duties dictate a faithful and zealous pursuit of the interests of my constituents, and in proportion as they are persuaded of my fidelity to those duties, the discharge of them becomes more and more pleasing.

Believing with you that religion is a matter which lies solely between man and his God, that he owes account to none other for his faith or his worship, that the legislative powers of government reach actions only, and not opinions, I contemplate with sovereign reverence that act of the whole American people which declared that their legislature should "make no law respecting an establishment of religion, or prohibiting the free exercise thereof," thus building a wall of separation between church and State. Adhering to this expression of the supreme will of the nation in behalf of the rights of conscience, I shall see with sincere satisfaction the progress of those sentiments which tend to restore to man all his natural rights, convinced he has no natural right in opposition to his social duties.

I reciprocate your kind prayers for the protection and blessing of the common Father and Creator of man, and tender you for yourselves and your religious association, assurances of my high respect and esteem.

Washington VIII: 113–14

## VII.4 To Rev. Samuel Miller

Washington, January 23, 1808

Sir, – I have duly received your favor of the 18th and am thankful to you for having written it, because it is more agreeable to prevent than to refuse what I do not think myself authorized to comply with. I consider the government of the U.S. as interdicted by the Constitution from intermeddling with religious institutions, their doctrines, discipline, or exercises. This results not only from the provision that no law shall be made respecting the establishment, or free exercise, of religion, but from that also which reserves to the states the powers not delegated to the U.S. Certainly no power to prescribe any religious exercise, or to assume authority in religious discipline, has been delegated to the general government. It must then rest with the states, as far as it can be in any human authority. But it is only proposed that I should *recommend*, not prescribe a day of fasting & prayer. That is, that I should *indirectly* assume to the U.S. an authority over religious exercises which the Constitution has directly precluded them from. It must be meant too that this recommendation is to carry some authority, and to be sanctioned by some penalty on those who disregard it; not indeed of fine and imprisonment, but of some degree of proscription perhaps in public opinion. And does the change in the nature of the penalty make the recommendation the less *a law* of conduct for those to whom it is directed? I do not believe it is for the interest of religion to invite the civil magistrate to direct it's exercises, it's discipline, or it's doctrines; nor of the religious societies that the general government should be invested with the power of effecting any uniformity of time or matter among them. Fasting & prayer are religious exercises. The enjoining them an act of discipline. Every religious society has a right to determine for itself the times for these exercises, & the objects proper for them, according to their own particular tenets; and this right can never be safer than in their own hands, where the constitution has deposited it.

I am aware that the practice of my predecessors may be quoted. But I have ever believed that the example of state executives led to the assumption of that authority by the general government, without due examination, which would have discovered that what might be a right in a state government, was a violation of that right when assumed by another. Be this as it may, every one must act according to the dictates of his own reason, & mine tells me that civil powers alone have been given to the President of the U.S. and no authority to direct the religious exercises of his constituents.

I again express my satisfaction that you have been so good as to give me an opportunity of explaining myself in a private letter, in which I could give my reasons more in detail than might have been done in a public answer: and I pray you to accept the assurances of my high esteem & respect.

Ford IX: 174–6

## VII.5 To Mrs. Samuel H. Smith

Monticello, August 6, 1816

I have received, dear Madam, your very friendly letter of July 21st, and assure you that I feel with deep sensibility its kind expressions towards myself, and the more as from a person than whom no others could be more in sympathy with my own affections. I often call to mind the occasions of knowing your worth, which the societies of Washington furnished; and none more than those derived from your much valued visit to Monticello. I recognize the same motives of goodness in the solicitude you express on the rumor supposed to proceed from a letter of mine to Charles Thomson,[1] on the subject of the Christian religion. It is true that, in writing to the translator of the Bible and Testament, that subject was mentioned; but equally so that no adherence to any particular mode of Christianity was there expressed, nor any change of opinions suggested. A change from what? the priests indeed have heretofore thought proper to ascribe to me religious, or rather anti-religious sentiments, of their own fabric, but such as soothed their resentments against the act of Virginia for establishing religious freedom. They wished him to be thought atheist, deist, or devil, who could advocate freedom from their religious dictations. But I have ever thought religion a concern purely between our God and our consciences, for which we were accountable to him, and not to the priests. I never told my own religion, nor scrutinized that of another. I never attempted to make a convert, nor wished to change another's creed. I have ever judged of the religion of others by their lives, and by this test, my dear Madam, I have been satisfied yours must be an excellent one, to have produced a life of such exemplary virtue and correctness. For it is in our lives, and not from our words, that our religion must be read. By the same test the world must judge me. But this does not satisfy the priesthood. They must have a positive, a declared assent to all their interested absurdities. My opinion is that there would never have been an infidel, if there had never been a priest. The artificial structures they have built on the purest of all moral systems, for the purpose of deriving from it pence and power, revolts those who think for themselves, and who read in that system only what is really there. These, therefore, they brand with such nicknames as their enmity chooses gratuitously to impute. I have left the world, in silence, to judge of causes from their effects; and I am consoled in this course, my dear friend, when I perceive the candor with which I am judged by your justice and discernment; and that,

[1] TJ to Charles Thompson, Jan. 9, 1816 in Ford x: 5–7. – *Eds.*

notwithstanding the slanders of the saints, my fellow citizens have thought me worthy of trusts. The imputations of irreligion having spent their force; they think an imputation of change might now be turned to account as a holster for their duperies. I shall leave them, as heretofore, to grope on in the dark.

Our family at Monticello is all in good health; Ellen speaking of you with affection, and Mrs. Randolph always regretting the accident which so far deprived her of the happiness of your former visit. She still cherishes the hope of some future renewal of that kindness; in which we all join her, as in the assurances of affectionate attachment and respect.

Washington VII: 27–9

## VII.6 To Mathew Carey

### Poplar Forest near Lynchburg, November 11, 1816

Dear Sir, – I received here (where I pass a good deal of my time) your favor of Oct. 22. covering a Prospectus of a new edition of your Olive branch. I subscribe to it with pleasure, because I believe it has done and will do much good, in holding up the mirror to both parties, and exhibiting to both their political errors. That I have had my share of them, I am not vain enough to doubt, and some indeed I have recognized. There is one however which I do not, altho' charged to my account, in your book, and as that is the subject of this letter, & I have my pen in my hand, I will say a very few words on it. It is my rejection of a British treaty without laying it before the Senate. It has never, I believe, been denied that the President may reject a treaty after it's ratification has been advised by the Senate, then certainly he may before that advice: and if he has made up his mind to reject it, it is more respectful to the Senate to do it without, than against their advice. It must not be said that their advice may cast new light on it. Their advice is a bald resolution of yea or nay, without assigning a single reason or motive.

You ask if I mean to publish anything on the subject of a letter of mine to my friend Charles Thompson?[1] Certainly not. I write

---

[1] TJ to Charles Thompson, Jan. 9, 1816 in Ford X: 5–7. – *Eds.*

nothing for publication, and last of all things should it be on the subject of religion. On the dogmas of religion as distinguished from moral principles, all mankind, from the beginning of the world to this day, have been quarrelling, fighting, burning and torturing one another, for abstractions unintelligible to themselves and to all others, and absolutely beyond the comprehension of the human mind. Were I to enter on that arena, I should only add an unit to the number of Bedlamites. Accept the assurance of my great esteem and respect.

Ford x: 67–8

## VII.7 To William Short

Monticello, August 4, 1820

Dear Sir, – I owe you a letter for your favour of June the 29th, which was received in due time; and there being no subject of the day, of particular interest, I will make this a supplement to mine of April the 13th. My aim in that was to justify the character of Jesus against the fictions of His pseudo-followers, which have exposed Him to the inference of being an impostor. For if we could believe that He really countenanced the follies, the falsehoods, and the charlatanism which His biographers father on Him, and admit the misconstructions, interpolations, and theorizations of the fathers of the early, and fanatics of the latter ages, the conclusion would be irresistible by every sound mind, that He was an impostor. I give no credit to their falsifications of His actions and doctrines, and to rescue His character, the postulate in my letter asked only what is granted in reading every other historian. When Livy and Siculus, for example, tell us things which coincide with our experience of the order of nature, we credit them on their word, and place their narrations among the records of credible history. But when they tell us of calves speaking, of statues sweating blood, and other things against the course of nature, we reject these as fables not belonging to history. In like manner, when an historian, speaking of a character well known and established on satisfactory testimony, imputes to it things incompatible with that character, we reject them without hesitation, and assent to that only of which we have better evidence.

Had Plutarch informed us that Cæsar and Cicero passed their whole lives in religious exercises, and abstinence from the affairs of the world, we should reject what was so inconsistent with their established characters, still crediting what he relates in conformity with our ideas of them. So again, the superlative wisdom of Socrates is testified by all antiquity, and placed on ground not to be questioned. When, therefore, Plato puts into his mouth such paralogisms, such quibbles on words, and sophisms as a schoolboy would be ashamed of, we conclude they were the whimsies of Plato's own foggy brain, and acquit Socrates of puerilities so unlike his character. (Speaking of Plato, I will add, that no writer, ancient or modern, has bewildered the world with more *ignes fatui*, than this renowned philosopher, in Ethics, in Politics, and Physics. In the latter, to specify a single example, compare his views of the animal economy, in his Timæus, with those of Mrs. Bryan in her Conversations on Chemistry, and weigh the science of the canonized philosopher against the good sense of the unassuming lady. But Plato's visions have furnished a basis for endless systems of mystical theology, and he is therefore all but adopted as a Christian saint. It is surely time for men to think for themselves, and to throw off the authority of names so artificially magnified. But to return from this parenthesis.) I say, that this free exercise of reason is all I ask for the vindication of the character of Jesus. We find in the writings of His biographers matter of two distinct descriptions. First, a groundwork of vulgar ignorance, of things impossible, of superstitions, fanaticisms, and fabrications. Inter-mixed with these, again, are sublime ideas of the Supreme Being, aphorisms, and precepts of the purest morality and benevolence, sanctioned by a life of humility, innocence, and simplicity of manners, neglect of riches, absence of worldly ambition and honors, with an eloquence and persuasiveness which have not been surpassed. These could not be inventions of the grovelling authors who relate them. They are far beyond the powers of their feeble minds. They show that there was a character, the subject of their history, whose splendid conceptions were above all suspicion of being interpolations from their hands. Can we be at a loss in separating such materials, and ascribing each to its genuine author? The difference is obvious to the eye and to the understanding, and we may read as we run to each his part; and I will venture to affirm, that he who, as I have done, will undertake to winnow this grain from the chaff, will find it not to require a moment's consideration. The parts fall asunder of themselves, as would those of an image of metal and clay.

There are, I acknowledge, passages not free from objection, which we may, with probability, ascribe to Jesus Himself; but claiming indulgence from the circumstances under which He acted. His object was the reformation of some articles in the religion of the Jews, as taught by Moses. That sect had presented for the object of their worship, a Being of terrific character, cruel, vindictive, capricious, and unjust. Jesus, taking for His type the best qualities of the human head and heart, wisdom, justice, goodness, and adding to them power, ascribed all of these, but in infinite perfection, to the Supreme Being, and formed Him really worthy of their adoration. Moses had either not believed in a future state of existence, or had not thought it essential to be explicitly taught to his people. Jesus inculcated that doctrine with emphasis and precision. Moses had bound the Jews to many idle ceremonies, mummeries, and observances, of no effect towards producing the social utilities which constitute the essence of virtue; Jesus exposed their futility and insignificance. The one instilled into his people the most anti-social spirit towards other nations; the other preached philanthropy and universal charity and benevolence. The office of reformer of the superstitions of a nation, is ever dangerous. Jesus had to walk on the perilous confines of reason and religion; and a step to right or left might place Him within the grasp of the priests of the superstition, a bloodthirsty race, as cruel and remorseless as the Being whom they represented as the family God of Abraham, of Isaac and of Jacob, and the local God of Israel. They were constantly laying snares, too, to entangle Him in the web of the law. He was justifiable, therefore, in avoiding these by evasions, by sophisms, by misconstructions and misapplications of scraps of the prophets, and in defending Himself with these their own weapons, as sufficient, *ad homines*, at least. That Jesus did not mean to impose Himself on mankind as the Son of God, physically speaking, I have been convinced by the writings of men more learned than myself in that lore. But that He might conscientiously believe Himself inspired from above, is very possible. The whole religion of the Jew, inculcated on him from his infancy, was founded in the belief of divine inspiration. The fumes of the most disordered imaginations were recorded in their religious code, as special communications of the Deity; and as it could not but happen that, in the course of ages, events would now and then turn up to which some of these vague rhapsodies might be accommodated by the aid of allegories, figures, types, and other tricks upon words, they have not only preserved their credit with the Jews of all subsequent times, but are the foundation of much of the religions of those who have schismatised from them. Elevated by the enthusiasm of a warm and pure heart, conscious of the high strains of an eloquence which had not been taught Him, he might readily mistake the coruscations of His own fine genius for inspirations of an higher order. This belief carried, therefore, no more personal imputation, than the belief of Socrates, that himself was under the care and admonitions of a guardian Dæmon. And how many of our wisest men still believe in the reality of these inspirations, while perfectly sane on all other subjects. Excusing, therefore, on these considerations, those passages in the Gospels which seem to bear marks of weakness in Jesus, ascribing to Him what alone is consistent with the great and pure character of which the same writings furnish proofs, and to their proper authors their own trivialities and imbecilities, I think myself authorized to conclude the purity and distinction of His character, in opposition to the impostures which those authors would fix upon Him; and that the postulate of my former letter is no more than is granted in all other historical works.

Mr. Corrèa [da Serra] is here, on his farewell visit to us. He has been much pleased with the plan and progress of our University,[1] and has given some valuable hints to its botanical branch. He goes to do, I hope, much good in his new country; the public instruction there, as I understand, being within the department destined for him. He is not without dissatisfaction, and reasonable dissatisfaction too, with the piracies of Baltimore;[2] but his justice and friendly dispositions will, I am sure, distinguish between the iniquities of a few plunderers, and the sound principles of our country at large, and of our government especially. From many conversations with him, I hope he sees, and will promote in his new situation, the advantages of a cordial fraternization among all the American

[1] The University of Virginia. – *Eds.*

[2] Apparently a reference to Lord Baltimore's receipt of large tracts of land from Charles II. See II.1, note 1. – *Eds.*

nations, and the importance of their coalescing in an American system of policy, totally independent of and unconnected with that of Europe. The day is not distant, when we may formally require a meridian of partition through the ocean which separates the two hemispheres, on the hither side of which no European gun shall ever be heard, nor an American on the other; and when, during the rage of the eternal wars of Europe, the lion and the lamb, within our regions, shall lie down together in peace. The excess of population in Europe, and want of room, render war, in their opinion, necessary to keep down that excess of numbers. Here, room is abundant, population scanty, and peace the necessary means for producing men, to whom the redundant soil is offering the means of life and happiness. The principles of society there and here, then, are radically different, and I hope no American patriot will ever lose sight of the essential policy of interdicting in the seas and territories of both Americas, the ferocious and sanguinary contests of Europe. I wish to see this coalition begun. I am earnest for an agreement with the maritime powers of Europe, assigning them the task of keeping down the piracies of their seas and the cannibalisms of the African coasts, and to us, the suppression of the same enormities within our seas; and for this purpose, I should rejoice to see the fleets of Brazil and the United States riding together as brethren of the same family, and pursuing the same object. And indeed it would be of happy augury to begin at once this concert of action here, on the invitation of either to the other government, while the way might be preparing for withdrawing our cruisers from Europe, and preventing naval collisions there which daily endanger our peace.

Accept assurances of the sincerity of my friendship and respect for you.

L & B xv: 257–64

## VII.8 To Dr. Thomas Cooper

Monticello, November 2, 1822

Dear Sir, – Your favor of October the 18th came to hand yesterday. The atmosphere of our country is unquestionably charged with a threatening cloud of fanaticism, lighter in some parts, denser in others, but too heavy in all. I had no idea, however, that in Pennsylvania, the cradle of toleration and freedom of religion, it could have arisen to the height you describe. This must be owing to the growth of Presbyterianism. The blasphemy and absurdity of the five points of Calvin, and the impossibility of defending them, render their advocates impatient of reasoning, irritable, and prone to denunciation. In Boston, however, and its neighborhood, Unitarianism has advanced to so great strength, as now to humble this haughtiest of all religious sects; insomuch, that they condescend to interchange with them and the other sects, the civilities of preaching freely and frequently in each others' meeting-houses. In Rhode Island, on the other hand, no sectarian preacher will permit an Unitarian to pollute his desk. In our Richmond there is much fanaticism, but chiefly among the women. They have their night meetings and praying parties, where, attended by their priests, and sometimes by a henpecked husband, they pour forth the effusions of their love to Jesus, in terms as amatory and carnal, as their modesty would permit them to use to a mere earthly lover. In our village of Charlottesville, there is a good degree of religion, with a small spice only of fanaticism. We have four sects, but without either church or meeting-house. The court-house is the common temple, one Sunday in the month to each. Here, Episcopalian and Presbyterian, Methodist and Baptist, meet together, join in hymning their Maker, listen with attention and devotion to each others' preachers, and all mix in society with perfect harmony. It is not so in the districts where Presbyterianism prevails undividedly. Their ambition and tyranny would tolerate no rival if they had power. Systematical in grasping at an ascendency over all other sects, they aim, like the Jesuits, at engrossing the education of the country, are hostile to every institution which they do not direct, and jealous at seeing others begin to attend at all to that object. The diffusion of instruction, to which there is now so growing an attention, will be the remote remedy to this fever of fanaticism; while the more proximate one will be the progress of Unitarianism. That this will, ere long, be the religion of the majority from North to South, I have no doubt.

In our university[1] you know there is no Professorship of Divinity. A handle has been made of this, to disseminate an idea that this is

---

[1] The University of Virginia. – *Eds.*

an institution, not merely of no religion, but against all religion. Occasion was taken at the last meeting of the Visitors, to bring forward an idea that might silence this calumny, which weighed on the minds of some honest friends to the institution. In our annual report to the legislature, after stating the constitutional reasons against a public establishment of any religious instruction, we suggest the expediency of encouraging the different religious sects to establish, each for itself, a professorship of their own tenets, on the confines of the university, so near as that their students may attend the lectures there, and have the free use of our library, and every other accommodation we can give them; preserving, however, their independence of us and of each other. This fills the chasm objected to ours, as a defect in an institution professing to give instruction in *all* useful sciences. I think the invitation will be accepted, by some sects from candid intentions, and by others from jealousy and rivalship. And by bringing the sects together, and mixing them with the mass of other students, we shall soften their asperities, liberalize and neutralize their prejudices, and make the general religion a religion of peace, reason, and morality.

The time of opening our university is still as uncertain as ever. All the pavilions, boarding-houses, and dormitories are done. Nothing is now wanting but the central building for a library and other general purposes. For this we have no funds, and the last legislature refused all aid. We have better hopes of the next. But all is uncertain. I have heard with regret of disturbances on the part of the students in your seminary. The article of discipline is the most difficult in American education. Premature ideas of independence, too little repressed by parents, beget a spirit of insubordination, which is the great obstacle to science with us, and a principal cause of its decay since the Revolution. I look to it with dismay in our institution, as a breaker ahead, which I am far from being confident we shall be able to weather. The advance of age, and tardy pace of the public patronage, may probably spare me the pain of witnessing consequences.

I salute you with constant friendship and respect.

Ford x: 242–4

# VIII  Political Parties

## VIII.1 To Francis Hopkinson

Paris, March 13, 1789

Dear Sir, – You say that I have been dished up to you as an antifederalist, and ask me if it be just. My opinion was never worthy enough of notice to merit citing; but since you ask it I will tell it you. I am not a Federalist, because I never submitted the whole system of my opinions to the creed of any party of men whatever in religion, in philosophy, in politics, or in anything else where I was capable of thinking for myself. Such an addiction is the last degradation of a free and moral agent. If I could not go to heaven but with a party, I would not go there at all. Therefore I protest to you I am not of the party of federalists. But I am much farther from that of the Antifederalists. I approved, from the first moment, of the great mass of what is in the new constitution, the consolidation of the government, the organization into Executive, legislative & judiciary, the subdivision of the legislative, the happy compromise of interests between the great & little states by the different manner of voting in the different houses, the voting by persons instead of states, the qualified negative on laws given to the Executive which however I should have liked better if associated with the judiciary also as in New York, and the power of taxation. I thought at first that the latter might have been limited. A little reflection soon convinced me it ought not to be. What I disapproved from the first moment also was the want of a bill of rights to guard liberty against the legislative as well as executive branches of the government, that is to say to secure freedom in religion, freedom of the press, freedom from monopolies, freedom from unlawful imprisonment, freedom from a permanent military, and a trial by jury in all cases determinable by the laws of the land. I disapproved also the perpetual reeligibility of the President. To these points of disapprobation I adhere. My first wish was that the 9 first conventions might accept the constitution, as the means of securing to us the great mass of good it contained, and that the 4 last might reject it, as the means of obtaining amendments. But I was corrected in this wish the moment I saw the much better plan of Massachusetts[1] and which had never occurred to me. With respect to the declaration of rights I suppose the majority of the United states are of my opinion: for I apprehend all the antifederalists, and a very respectable proportion of the federalists, think that such a declaration should now be annexed. The enlightened part of Europe have given us the greatest credit for inventing this instrument of security for the rights of the people, and have been not a little surprised to see us so soon give it up. With respect to the re-eligibility of the president, I find myself differing from the majority of my countrymen, for I think there are but three states out of the 11 which have desired an alteration of this. And indeed, since the thing is established, I would wish it not to be altered during the life of our great leader, whose executive talents are superior to those I believe of any man in the world, and who alone by the authority of his name and the confidence reposed in his perfect integrity, is fully qualified to put the new government so under way as to secure it against the efforts of opposition. But having derived from our error all the good there was in it I hope we shall correct it the moment we can no longer have the same name at the helm. These, my dear friend, are my sentiments, by which you will see I was right in saying I am neither federalist nor antifederalist; that I am of neither party, nor yet a trimmer between parties. These my opinions I wrote within a few hours after I had read the constitution, to one or two friends in America. I had not then read one single word printed on the subject. I never had an opinion in politics or religion which I was afraid to own. A costive reserve on these subjects might have procured me more esteem from some people, but less from myself. My great wish is to go on in a strict but silent performance of my duty; to avoid attracting notice & to keep my name out of newspapers, because I find the pain of a little censure, even when it is unfounded, is more acute than the pleasure of much praise. The attaching circumstance of my present office is that I can do it's duties unseen by those for whom they are done. – You did not think, by so short a phrase

---

[1] The Massachusetts ratification convention (Jan. 14 – Feb. 6, 1788) ratified the new Constitution on condition that it be amended to include a Bill of Rights and other safeguards. – *Eds.*

in your letter, to have drawn on yourself such an egotistical dissertation.

*Ford* v: 75–8

## VIII.2 To James Madison

Philadelphia, June 29, 1792

Dear Sir, – I wrote you last on the 21st. The present will cover Fenno['s *Gazette*][1] of the 23d & 27th. In the last you will discover Hamilton's pen in defence of the bank, and daring to call the republican party *a faction*. I learn that he has expressed the strongest desire that [John] Marshall should come into Congress from Richmond, declaring that there is no man in Virginia whom he wishes so much to see there; and I am told that Marshall has expressed half a mind to come. Hence I conclude that Hamilton has plyed him well with flattery & sollicitation, and I think nothing better could be done than to make him a judge. I have reason to believe that a regular attack, in phalanx, is to be made on the Residence act at the next session, with a determination to repeal it if the further assumption is not agreed to. I think this also comes from Hamilton tho' it is thro' two hands, if not more, before it comes to me.

Brandt went off yesterday, apparently in the best dispositions, & with some hopes of effecting peace. A letter received yesterday from Mr. Short gives the most flattering result of conversations he had had with Claviere & Dumourier. Claviere declared he had nothing so much at heart as to encourage our navigation, & the present system of commerce with us. Agreed they ought immediately to repeal their late proceedings with respect to tob[acc]o. & ships, and receive our salted provisions favorably, and to proceed to treat with us on broad ground. Dumourier expressed the same sentiments. Mr. Short had then received notice that G[ouverneur] M[orris] would be there in a few days, and therefore told the ministers that this was only a preliminary conversation on what Mr. Morris would undertake regularly. This ministry, which is of the Jacobin party, cannot but be favorable to us, as that whole party must be. Indeed

---

[1] See *supra*, I.7, note 2. – *Eds.*

notwithstanding the very general abuse of the Jacobins, I begin to consider them as representing the true revolution-spirit of the whole nation, and as carrying the nation with them. The only things wanting with them is more experience in business, and a little more conformity to the established style of communication with foreign powers. The latter want will I fear bring enemies into the field, who would have remained at home; the former leads them to domineer over their executive so as to render it unequal to it's proper objects. I sincerely wish our new minister may not spoil our chance of extracting good from the present situation of things. The President leaves this about the middle of July. I shall set out some days later, & have the pleasure of seeing you in Orange. Adieu, my dear Sir.

Ford VI: 95–7

## VIII.3 To William Branch Giles

Monticello, December 31, 1795

Dear Sir, – Your favors of Dec. 15. & 20, came to hand by the last post. I am well pleased with the manner in which your house has testified their sense of the treaty. While their refusal to pass the original clause of the reported answer proved their condemnation of it, the contrivance to let it disappear silently respected appearances in favor of the President, who errs as other men do, but errs with integrity. [Edmund] Randolph seems to have hit upon the true theory of our constitution, that when a treaty is made, involving matters confided by the constitution to the three branches of the legislature conjointly, the representatives are as free as the President & Senate were to consider whether the national interest requires or forbids their giving the forms & force of law to the articles over which they have a power. – I thank you much for the pamphlet[1] – his narrative is so straight & plain, that even those who did not know him will acquit him of the charge of bribery; those who knew him had done it from

---

[1] Edmund Randolph, *A Vindication of Mr. Randolph's Resignation* (Philadelphia, 1795), a defense of his actions as Secretary of State and subsequent resignation from that post. – *Eds.*

the first. Tho' he mistakes his own political character in the aggregate, yet he gives it to you in the detail. Thus he supposes himself a man of no party (page 97), that his opinions not containing any systematic adherence to party, fall sometimes on one side and sometimes on the other (pa. 58). Yet he gives you these facts, which shew that they fall generally on both sides, & are complete inconsistencies – 1. He never gave an opinion in the Cabinet against the rights of the people (pa. 97) yet he advised the denunciation of the popular societies (67). 2. He would not neglect the overtures of a commercial treaty with France (79) yet he always opposed it while att[orne]y-general, and never seems to have proposed it while Secretary of State. 3. He concurs in resorting to the militia to quell the pretended insurrection in the west (81) and proposes an augmentation from 12,500 to 15,000 to march against men at their ploughs (pa. 80), yet on the 5th of Aug. he is against their marching (83, 101) and on the 25th of Aug. he is for it (84). 4. He concurs in the measure of a mission extraordinary to London (as inferred from pa. 58) but objects to the men, to wit Hamilton & Jay (58). 5. He was against granting commercial powers to Mr. Jay (58) yet he besieged the doors of the Senate to procure their advice to ratify. – 6. He advises the President to a ratification on the merits of the treaty (– 7) but to a suspension till the provision order is repealed (98). The fact is that he has generally given his principles to the one party & his practice to the other; the oyster to one, the shell to the other. Unfortunately the shell was generally the lot of his friends the French and republicans, & the oyster of their antagonists. Had he been firm to the principles he professes in the year 1793 the President would have been kept from a habitual concert with the British & Antirepublican party, but at that time I do not know which R[andolph] feared most, a British fleet, or French disorganisers. Whether his conduct is to be ascribed to a superior view of things, an adherence to right without regard to party, as he pretends, or to an anxiety to trim between both, those who know his character and capacity will decide. Were parties here divided merely by a greediness for office, as in England, to take a part with either would be unworthy of a reasonable or moral man, but where the principle of difference is as substantial and as strongly pronounced as between the republicans & the Monocrats[2] of our country, I hold it as honorable to take a firm & decided part, and as immoral to pursue a middle line, as between the parties of Honest men, & Rogues, into which every country is divided.

A copy of the pamphlet came by this post to Charlottesville. I suppose we shall be able to judge soon what kind of impression it is likely to make. It has been a great treat to me, as it is a continuation of that Cabinet history with the former part of which I was intimate. I remark in the reply of the President a small travestie of the sentiment contained in the answer of the Representatives. They acknowledge that he has *contributed* a great share to the national happiness by his services. He thanks them for ascribing to his *agency* a great share of those benefits. The former keeps in view the co-operation of others towards the public good, the latter presents to view his sole agency. At a time when there would have been less anxiety to publish to the people a strong approbation from your house, this strengthening of your expression would not have been noticed. Our attentions have been so absorbed by the first manifestations of the sentiments of your house, that we have lost sight of our own legislature: insomuch that I do not know whether they are sitting or not.

The rejection of Mr. [Edward] Rutledge by the Senate is a bold thing, because they cannot pretend any objection to him but his disapprobation of the treaty. It is of course a declaration that they will receive none but tories hereafter into any department of the government. I should not wonder if [James] Monroe were to be recalled under the idea of his being of the partisans of France, whom the President considers as the partisans of *war & confusion* in his letter of July 31, and as disposed to excite them to hostile measures, or at least to unfriendly sentiments. A most infatuated blindness to the true character of the sentiments entertained in favor of France. The bottom of my page warns me that it is time to end my commentaries on the facts you have furnished me. You would of course however wish to know the sensations here on those facts.

---

[2] Monocrats: advocates of monarchy, i.e. Hamilton and his fellow Federalists, whom TJ deeply mistrusted. – *Eds.*

My friendly respects to Mrs. Madison, to whom the next week's
dose will be directed. Adieu affectionately.

Ford VII: 41–4

## VIII.4 To Philip Mazzei

Monticello, April 24, 1796

My Dear Friend, – The aspect of our politics has wonderfully
changed since you left us. In place of that noble love of liberty, &
republican government which carried us triumphantly thro' the
war, an Anglican monarchical, & aristocratical party has sprung up,
whose avowed object is to draw over us the substance, as they have
already done the forms, of the British government. The main body
of our citizens, however, remain true to their republican principles;
the whole landed interest is republican, and so is a great mass of
talents. Against us are the Executive, the Judiciary, two out of three
branches of the legislature, all the officers of the government, all
who want to be officers, all timid men who prefer the calm of despotism to the boisterous sea of liberty, British merchants & Americans trading on British capitals, speculators & holders in the
banks & public funds, a contrivance invented for the purposes of
corruption, & for assimilating us in all things to the rotten as well
as the sound parts of the British model. It would give you a fever
were I to name to you the apostates who have gone over to these
heresies, men who were Samsons in the field & Solomons in the
council, but who have had their heads shorn by the harlot England.
In short, we are likely to preserve the liberty we have obtained only
by unremitting labors & perils. But we shall preserve them; and our
mass of weight & wealth on the good side is so great, as to leave no
danger that force will ever be attempted against us. We have only
to awake and snap the Lilliputian cords with which they have been
entangling us during the first sleep which succeeded our labors . . .
I begin to feel the effects of age. My health has suddenly broke
down, with symptoms which give me to believe I shall not have
much to encounter of the *tedium vitæ*. While it remains, however,
my heart will be warm in it's friendships, and among these, will

416

always foster the affection with which I am, dear Sir, your friend and servant.

Ford VII: 75–8

## VIII.5 To James Sullivan

Monticello, February 9, *1797*

Dear Sir, – I have many acknolegements to make for the friendly anxiety you are pleased to express in your letter of Jan 12, for my undertaking the office to which I have been elected.[1] The idea that I would accept the office of President, but not that of Vice-President of the U.S., had not its origin with me. I never thought of questioning the free exercise of the right of my fellow citizens, to marshal those whom they call into their service according to their fitness, nor ever presumed that they were not the best judges of these. Had I indulged a wish in what manner they should dispose of me, it would precisely have coincided with what they have done. Neither the splendor, nor the power, nor the difficulties, nor the fame or defamation, as may happen, attached to the first magistracy, have any attractions for me. The helm of a free government is always arduous, & never was ours more so, than at a moment when two friendly people are like to be committed in war by the ill temper of their administrations. I am so much attached to my domestic situation, that I would not have wished to leave it at all. However, if I am to be called from it, the shortest absences & most tranquil station suit me best. I value highly, indeed, the part my fellow citizens gave me in their late vote, as an evidence of their esteem, & I am happy in the information you are so kind as to give, that many in the Eastern quarter entertain the same sentiment.

Where a constitution, like ours, wears a mixed aspect of monarchy & republicanism, its citizens will naturally divide into two classes of sentiment, according as their tone of body or mind, their habits, connections & callings, induce them to wish to strengthen either the monarchial or the republican features of the constitution. Some will consider it as an elective monarchy, which had better be

---

[1] The U.S. Vice-Presidency. – *Eds.*

made hereditary, & therefore endeavor to lead towards that all the forms and principles of its administration. Others will view it as an energetic republic, turning in all its points on the pivot of free and frequent elections. The great body of our native citizens are unquestionably of the republican sentiment. Foreign education, & foreign connections of interest, have produced some exceptions in every part of the Union, North and South, & perhaps other circumstances in your quarter, better known to you, may have thrown into the scale of exceptions a greater number of the rich. Still there, I believe, and here, I am sure, the great mass is republican. Nor do any of the forms in which the public disposition has been pronounced in the last half dozen years, evince the contrary. All of them, when traced to their true source, have only been evidences of the preponderant popularity of a particularly great character. That influence once withdrawn, & our countrymen left to the operation of their own unbiassed good sense, I have no doubt we shall see a pretty rapid return of general harmony, & our citizens moving in phalanx in the paths of regular liberty, order, and a sacrosanct adherence to the constitution. Thus I think it will be, if war with France can be avoided. But if that untoward event comes athwart us in our present point of deviation, nobody, I believe, can foresee into what port it will drive us.

I am always glad of an opportunity of inquiring after my most antient & respected friend mr. Samuel Adams. His principles, founded on the immovable basis of equal right & reason, have continued pure & unchanged. Permit me to place here my sincere veneration for him, & wishes for his health & happiness; & to assure yourself of the sentiments of esteem & respect with which I am, Dear Sir, your most obedient & most humble servant.

Ford VII: 116–18

## VIII.6 To John Taylor

Philadelphia, June 1, 1798

Mr. New showed me your letter on the subject of the patent, which gave me an opportunity of observing what you said as to the effect, with you, of public proceedings, and that it was not usual now to estimate the separate mass of Virginia and North Carolina, with a view to their separate existence. It is true that we are completely under the saddle of Massachusetts and Connecticut, and that they ride us very hard, cruelly insulting our feelings, as well as exhausting our strength and subsistence. Their natural friends, the three other eastern States, join them from a sort of family pride, and they have the art to divide certain other parts of the Union, so as to make use of them to govern the whole. This is not new, it is the old practice of despots; to use a part of the people to keep the rest in order. And those who have once got an ascendancy, and possessed themselves of all the resources of the nation, their revenues and offices, have immense means for retaining their advantage. But our present situation is not a natural one. The republicans, through every part of the Union, say, that it was the irresistible influence and popularity of General Washington played off by the cunning of Hamilton, which turned the government over to anti-republican hands, or turned the republicans chosen by the people into anti-republicans. He delivered it over to his successor in this state, and very untoward events since, improved with great artifice, have produced on the public mind the impressions we see. But still I repeat it, this is not the natural state. Time alone would bring round an order of things more correspondent to the sentiments of our constituents. But are there no events impending, which will do it within a few months? The crisis with England, the public and authentic avowal of sentiments hostile to the leading principles of our Constitution, the prospect of a war, in which we shall stand alone, land tax, stamp tax, increase of public debt, &c. Be this as it may, in every free and deliberating society, there must, from the nature of man, be opposite parties, and violent dissensions and discords; and one of these, for the most part, must prevail over the other for a longer or shorter time. Perhaps this party division is necessary to induce each to watch and delate to the people the proceedings of the other. But if on a temporary superiority of the one party, the other is to resort to a scission of the Union, no federal government can ever exist. If to rid ourselves of the present rule of Massachusetts and Connecticut, we break the Union, will the evil stop there? Suppose the New England States alone cut off, will our nature be changed? Are we not men still to the south of that, and with all the passions of men? Immediately, we shall see a Pennsylvania and a

Virginia party arise in the residuary confederacy, and the public mind will be distracted with the same party spirit. What a game too will the one party have in their hands, by eternally threatening the other that unless they do so and so, they will join their northern neighbors. If we reduce our Union to Virginia and North Carolina, immediately the conflict will be established between the representatives of these two States, and they will end by breaking into their simple units. Seeing, therefore, that an association of men who will not quarrel with one another is a thing which never yet existed, from the greatest confederacy of nations down to a town meeting or a vestry; seeing that we must have somebody to quarrel with, I had rather keep our New England associates for that purpose, than to see our bickerings transferred to others. They are circumscribed within such narrow limits, and their population so full, that their numbers will ever be the minority, and they are marked, like the Jews, with such a perversity of character, as to constitute, from that circumstance, the natural division of our parties.

A little patience, and we shall see the reign of witches pass over, their spells dissolved, and the people recovering their true sight, restoring their government to its true principles. It is true, that in the meantime, we are suffering deeply in spirit, and incurring the horrors of a war, and long oppressions of enormous public debt. But who can say what would be the evils of a scission, and when and where they would end? Better keep together as we are, haul off from Europe as soon as we can, and from all attachments to any portions of it; and if they show their power just sufficiently to hoop us together, it will be the happiest situation in which we can exist. If the game runs sometimes against us at home, we must have patience till luck turns, and then we shall have an opportunity of winning back the *principles* we have lost. For this is a game where principles are the stake. Better luck, therefore, to us all, and health, happiness and friendly salutations to yourself. Adieu.

P.S. It is hardly necessary to caution you to let nothing of mine get before the public; a single sentence got hold of by the Porcupines,[1] will suffice to abuse and persecute me in their papers for months.

Ford VII: 263–6

---

[1] The prickly and ardently anti-Jeffersonian Federalists whose spokesman, William Cobbett (1763–1835), wrote under the pen-name "Peter Porcupine." – *Eds.*

## VIII.7 Notes for the First Inaugural Address

[1801]

Wherever there are men there will be parties & wherever there are free men they will make themselves heard. Those of firm health & spirits are unwilling to cede more of their liberty than is necessary to preserve order, those of feeble const[itutio]ns will wish to see one strong arm able to protect them from the many. These are the whigs and tories of nature. These mutual jealousies produce mutual security: and while the laws shall be obeyed all will be safe. He alone is your enemy who disobeys them. In all cases of danger or commotion learn to consider the laws as the standard to which you are to rally. If you find there your officers civil and military, go with them to the establishm[en]t of order. If you find them not there, they are out of their place and must be bro[ugh]t back to the laws. Let this then be the distinctive mark of an American that in cases of commotion he enlists himself under no man's banner, enquires for no man's name but repairs to the standard of the laws. Do this & you need never fear anarchy or tyranny. Your gov[ern]-m[en]t will be perpetual.

Ford IX: 193

## VIII.8 To Joel Barlow

Washington, May 3, 1802

Dear Sir, – I have doubted whether to write to you, because yours of Aug. 25, received only March 27, gives me reason to expect you are now on the ocean. However, as I know voyages so important are often delayed, I shall venture a line with Mr. Dupont de Nemours. The Legislature rises this day. They have carried into execution steadily almost all the propositions submitted to them in my message at the opening of the session. Some few are laid over for want of time. The most material of which is the militia, the plan of which they cannot easily modify to the general approbation. Our majority in the House of Representatives has been about two to one – in the Senate, eighteen to fourteen. After another election it will be two to one in the Senate, and it would not be for the public good to have it greater, a respectable minority is useful as censors.

The present one is not respectable; being the bitterest cup of the remains of Federalism rendered desperate and furious by despair. A small check in the tide of republicanism in Massachusetts, which has showed itself very unexpectedly at the late election, is not accounted for. Everywhere else we are becoming one. In Rhode Island the late election gave us two to one through the whole state. Vermont is decidedly with us. It is said and believed that New Hampshire has got a majority of republicans now in its Legislature; and wanted a few hundreds only of turning out their federal governor. He goes assuredly the next trial. Connecticut is supposed to have gained for us about fifteen or twenty percent, since her last election; but the exact issue is not yet known here. Nor is it certainly known how we shall stand in the House of Representatives of Massachusetts. In the Senate there, we have lost ground. The candid federalists acknowledged that their party can never more raise its head. The operations of this session of Congress, when known among the people at large, will consolidate them. We shall now be so strong that we shall certainly split again; for freemen thinking differently and speaking and acting as they think, will form into classes of sentiment, but it must be under another name, that of federalism is to become so scouted that no party can rise under it. As the division between whig and tory is founded in the nature of men, the weakly and nerveless, the rich and the corrupt seeing more safety and accessibility in a strong executive; the healthy, firm and virtuous feeling confidence in their physical and moral resources, and willing to part with only so much power as is necessary for their good government, and therefore to retain the rest in the hands of the many, the division will substantially be into whig and tory, as in England, formerly. As yet no symptoms show themselves, nor will till after election.

I am extremely happy to learn that you are so much at your ease that you can devote the rest of your life to the information of others. The choice of a place of residence is material. I do not think you can do better than to fix here for a while, until you become Americanized and understand the map of the country. This may be considered as a pleasant country-residence, with a number of neat little villages scattered around within the distance of a mile and a half, and furnishing a plain and substantially good society. They have begun their buildings in about four or five different points, at each of which there are buildings enough to be considered as a village. The whole population is about six thousand. Mr. Madison and myself have cut out a piece of work for you, which is to write the history of the United States, from the close of the War downwards. We are rich ourselves in materials, and can open all the public archives to you; but your residence here is essential, because a great deal of the knowledge of things is not on paper, but only within ourselves for verbal communication. [Chief Justice] John Marshall is writing the life of Gen. Washington from his papers. It is intended to come out just in time to influence the next presidential election. It is written therefore principally with a view to election-eering purposes; but it will consequently be out in time to aid you with information as well as to point out the perversions of truth necessary to be rectified. Think of this, and agree to it, and be assured of my high esteem and attachment.

Ford VIII: 148–51

## VIII.9 To Abigail Adams

Monticello, September 11, 1804

Your letter, Madam, of the 18th. of Aug. has been some days re-cieved, but a press of business has prevented the acknolegement of it. Perhaps indeed I may have already trespassed too far on your attention. With those who wish to think amiss of me, I have learnt to be perfectly indifferent: but where I know a mind to be ingenu-ous, and to need only truth to set it to rights, I cannot be as passive . . .

. . . I tolerate with the utmost latitude the right of others to differ from me in opinion without imputing to them criminality. I know too well the weakness and uncertainty of human reason to wonder at it's different results. Both of our political parties, at least the honest portion of them, agree conscientiously in the same object, the public good: but they differ essentially in what they deem the means of promoting that good. One side believes it best done by one composition of the governing powers, the other by a different one. One fears most the ignorance of the people: the other the selfishness of rulers independant of them. Which is right, time and experience will prove. We think that one side of this experiment has been long enough tried, and proved not to promote the good of the many; and that the other has not been fairly and sufficiently tried. Our opponents think the reverse. With whichever opinion the body of the nation concurs, that must prevail. My anxieties on the subject will never carry me beyond the use of fair and honorable means, of truth and reason: nor have they ever lessened my esteem for moral worth; nor alienated my affections from a single friend who did not first withdraw himself. Wherever this has happened I confess I have not been insensible to it: yet have ever kept myself open to a return of their justice.

I conclude with sincere prayers for your health and happiness that yourself and Mr. Adams may long enjoy the tranquility you desire and merit, and see, in the prosperity of your family, what is the consummation of the last and warmest of human wishes.

L & B XI: 49–55

## VIII.10 To Thomas Cooper

Washington, July 9, 1807

Dear Sir, – Your favor of June 23d is received. I had not before learned that a life of Dr. Priestley had been published, or I should certainly have procured it, for no man living had a more affectionate respect for him. In religion, in politics, in physics, no man has rendered more service.

I had always expected that when the republicans should have put down all things under their feet, they would schismatize among themselves. I always expected, too, that whatever names the parties might bear, the real division would be into moderate and ardent republicanism. In this division there is no great evil, – not even if the minority obtain the ascendency by the accession of federal votes to their candidate; because this gives us one shade only, instead of another, of republicanism. It is to be considered as apostasy only when they purchase the votes of federalists, with a participation in honor and power. The gross insult lately received from the English has forced the latter into a momentary coalition with the mass of republicans; but the moment we begin to act in the very line they have joined in approving, all will be wrong, and every act the reverse of what it should have been. Still, it is better to admit their coalescence, and leave to themselves their short-lived existence. Both reason and the usage of nations required we should give Great Britain an opportunity of disavowing and repairing the insult of their officers. It gives us at the same time an opportunity of getting home our vessels, our property, and our seamen, – the only means of carrying on the kind of war we should attempt. The only difference, I believe, between your opinion and mine, as to the protection of commerce, is the forcing the nation to take the best road, and the letting them take the worse, if such is their will. I salute you with great esteem and respect.

L & B XI: 265–6

## VIII. 11 To Dr. Benjamin Rush

Monticello, January 16, 1811

Dear Sir, – I had been considering for some days, whether it was not time by a letter, to bring myself to your recollection, when I received your welcome favour of the 2d instant. I had before heard of the heart-rending calamity you mention, and had sincerely sympathized with your afflictions. But I had not made it the subject of a letter, because I knew that condolences were but renewals of grief. Yet I thought, and still think, this is one of the cases wherein we should "not sorrow, even as others who have no hope." I have myself known so many cases of recovery from confirmed insanity, as to reckon it ever among the recoverable diseases. One of them was that of a near relative and namesake of mine, who, after many years of madness of the first degree, became entirely sane, and amused himself to a good old age in keeping school; was an excellent teacher and much valued citizen.

You ask if I have read Hartley?[1] I have not. My present course of life admits less reading than I wish. From breakfast, or noon at latest, to dinner, I am mostly on horseback, attending to my farm or other concerns, which I find healthful to my body, mind and

---

[1] David Hartley (1705–57), English philosopher and author of *Observations on Man, his Frame, his Duty and his Expectations* (London, 1749). – Eds.

affairs; and the few hours I can pass in my cabinet, are devoured by correspondences; not those with my intimate friends, with whom I delight to interchange sentiments, but with others, who, writing to me on concerns of their own in which I have had an agency, or from motives of mere respect and approbation, are entitled to be answered with respect and a return of good will. My hope is that this obstacle to the delights of retirement, will wear away with the oblivion which follows that, and that I may at length be indulged in those studious pursuits, from which nothing but revolutionary duties would ever have called me.

I shall receive your proposed publication and read it with the pleasure which everything gives me from your pen. Although much of a sceptic in the practice of medicine, I read with pleasure its ingenious theories.

I receive with sensibility your observations on the discontinuance of friendly correspondence between Mr. Adams and myself, and the concern you take in its restoration. This discontinuance has not proceeded from me, nor from the want of sincere desire and of effort on my part, to renew our intercourse. You know the perfect coincidence of principle and of action, in the early part of the Revolution, which produced a high degree of mutual respect and esteem between Mr. Adams and myself. Certainly no man was ever truer than he was, in that day, to those principles of rational republicanism which, after the necessity of throwing off our monarchy, dictated all our efforts in the establishment of a new government. And although he swerved, afterwards, towards the principles of the English constitution, our friendship did not abate on that account. While he was Vice-President, and I Secretary of State, I received a letter from President Washington, then at Mount Vernon, desiring me to call together the Heads of departments, and to invite Mr. Adams to join us (which, by-the-bye, was the only instance of that being done) in order to determine on some measure which required despatch; and he desired me to act on it, as decided, without again recurring to him. I invited them to dine with me, and after dinner, sitting at our wine, having settled our question, other conversation came on, in which a collision of opinion arose between Mr. Adams and Colonel Hamilton, on the merits of the British constitution, Mr. Adams giving it as his opinion, that, if some of its defects and abuses were corrected, it would be the most perfect constitution of government ever devised by man. Hamilton, on the contrary, asserted, that with its existing vices, it was the most perfect model of government that could be formed; and that the correction of its vices would render it an impracticable government. And this you may be assured was the real line of difference between the political principles of these two gentlemen. Another incident took place on the same occasion, which will further delineate Mr. Hamilton's political principles. The room being hung around with a collection of the portraits of remarkable men, among them those of Bacon, Newton and Locke, Hamilton asked me who they were. I told him they were my trinity of the three greatest men the world had ever produced, naming them. He paused for some time: "the greatest man," said he, "that ever lived, was Julius Cæsar." Mr. Adams was honest as a politician, as well as a man; Hamilton honest as a man, but, as a politician, believing in the necessity of either force or corruption to govern men.

You remember the machinery which the federalists played off, about that time, to beat down the friends to the real principles of our constitution, to silence by terror every expression in their favor, to bring us into war with France and alliance with England, and finally to homologize our constitution with that of England. Mr. Adams, you know, was overwhelmed with feverish addresses, dictated by the fear, and often by the pen, of the *bloody buoy*, and was seduced by them into some open indications of his new principles of government, and in fact, was so elated as to mix with his kindness a little superciliousness towards me. Even Mrs. Adams, with all her good sense and prudence, was sensibly [visibly] flushed. And you recollect the short suspension of our intercourse, and the circumstance which gave rise to it, which you were so good as to bring to an early explanation, and have set to rights, to the cordial satisfaction of us all. The nation at length passed condemnation on the political principles of the federalists, by refusing to continue Mr. Adams in the Presidency. On the day on which we learned in Philadelphia the vote of the city of New York, which it was well known would decide the vote of the State, and that, again, the vote of the Union, I called on Mr. Adams on some official business. He was very sensibly affected, and accosted me with these words: "Well, I understand that you are to beat me in this contest, and I will only say that I will be as faithful a subject as any you will have." "Mr.

Adams," said I, "this is no personal contest between you and me. Two systems of principles on the subject of government divide our fellow citizens into two parties. With one of these you concur, and I with the other. As we have been longer on the public stage than most of those now living, our names happen to be more generally known. One of these parties, therefore, has put your name at its head, the other mine. Were we both to die to-day, to-morrow two other names would be in the place of ours, without any change in the motion of the machinery. Its motion is from its principle, not from you or myself." "I believe you are right," said he, "that we are but passive instruments, and should not suffer this matter to affect our personal dispositions." But he did not long retain this just view of the subject. I have always believed that the thousand calumnies which the federalists, in bitterness of heart, and mortification at their ejection, daily invented against me, were carried to him by their busy intriguers, and made some impression. When the election between [Aaron] Burr and myself was kept in suspense by the federalists, and they were mediating to place the President of the Senate at the head of the government, I called on Mr. Adams with a view to have this desperate measure prevented by his negative. He grew warm in an instant, and said with a vehemence he had not used towards me before, "Sir, the event of the election is within your own power. You have only to say you will do justice to the public creditors, maintain the navy, and not disturb those holding offices, and the government will instantly be put into your hands. We know it is the wish of the people it should be so." "Mr. Adams," said I, "I know not what part of my conduct, in either public or private life, can have authorized a doubt of my fidelity to the public engagements. I say, however, I will not come into the government by capitulation. I will not enter on it, but in perfect freedom to follow the dictates of my own judgment." I had before given the same answer to the same intimation from Gouverneur Morris. "Then," said he, "things must take their course." I turned the conversation to something else, and soon took my leave. It was the first time in our lives we had ever parted with anything like dissatisfaction. And then followed those scenes of midnight appointment, which have been condemned by all men. The last day of his political power, the last hours, and even beyond the midnight, were employed in filling all offices, and especially permanent ones, with the bitterest federalists, and providing for me the alternative, either to execute the government by my enemies, whose study it would be to thwart and defeat all my measures, or to incur the odium of such numerous removals from office, as might bear me down. A little time and reflection effaced in my mind this temporary dissatisfaction with Mr. Adams, and restored me to that just estimate of his virtues and passions, which a long acquaintance had enabled me to fix. And my first wish became that of making his retirement easy by any means in my power; for it was understood he was not rich. I suggested to some republican members of the delegation from his State, the giving him, either directly or indirectly, an office, the most lucrative in that State, and then offered to be resigned, if they thought he would not deem it affrontive. They were of opinion he would take great offence at the offer; and moreover, that the body of republicans would consider such a step in the outset as arguing very ill of the course I meant to pursue. I dropped the idea, therefore, but did not cease to wish for some opportunity of renewing our friendly understanding.

Two or three years after, having had the misfortune to lose a daughter, between whom and Mrs. Adams there had been a considerable attachment, she made it the occasion of writing me a letter, in which, with the tenderest expressions of concern at this event, she carefully avoided a single one of friendship towards myself, and even concluded it with the wishes "of her who *once* took pleasure in subscribing herself your friend, Abigail Adams." Unpromising as was the complexion of this letter, I determined to make an effort towards removing the cloud from between us. This brought on a correspondence which I now enclose for your perusal, after which be so good as to return it to me, as I have never communicated it to any mortal breathing, before. I send it to you, to convince you I have not been wanting either in the desire, or the endeavor to remove this misunderstanding. Indeed, I thought it highly disgraceful to us both, as indicating minds not sufficiently elevated to prevent a public competition from affecting our personal friendship. I soon found from the correspondence that conciliation was desperate [i.e. hopeless], and yielding to an intimation in her last letter, I ceased from further explanation. I have the same good opinion of Mr. Adams which I ever had. I know him to be an honest man, an able one with his pen, and he was a powerful advocate on the floor of Congress. He has been alienated from me, by belief in the lying suggestions contrived for electioneering purposes, that I perhaps mixed in the activity and intrigues of the occasion. My most intimate friends can testify that I was perfectly passive. They would sometimes, indeed, tell me what was going on; but no man ever heard me take part in such conversations; and none ever misrepresented Mr. Adams in my presence, without my asserting his just character. With very confidential persons I have doubtless disapproved of the principles and practices of his administration. This was unavoidable. But never with those with whom it could do him any injury. Decency would have required this conduct from me, if disposition had not; and I am satisfied Mr. Adams' conduct was equally honorable towards me. But I think it part of his character to suspect foul play in those of whom he is jealous, and not easily to relinquish his suspicions.

I have gone, my dear friend, into these details, that you might know everything which had passed between us, might be fully possessed of the state of facts and dispositions, and judge for yourself whether they admit a revival of that friendly intercourse for which you are so kindly solicitous. I shall certainly not be wanting in anything on my part which may second your efforts, which will be the easier with me, inasmuch as I do not entertain a sentiment of Mr. Adams, the expression of which could give him reasonable offence. And I submit the whole to yourself, with the assurance, that whatever be the issue, my friendship and respect for yourself will remain unaltered and unalterable.

Ford IX: 294–9

## VIII.12 To John Melish

Monticello, January 13, 1813

Dear Sir, – I received duly your favor of December the 15th, and with it the copies of your map and travels, for which be pleased to accept my thanks. The book I have read with extreme satisfaction and information. As to the western States, particularly, it has greatly edified me; for of the actual condition of that interesting portion of our country, I had not an adequate idea. I feel myself now as familiar with it as with the condition of the maritime States. I had no conception that manufactures had made such progress there, and particularly of the number of carding and spinning machines dispersed through the whole country. We are but beginning here to have them in our private families. Small spinning jennies of from half a dozen to twenty spindles, will soon, however, make their way into the humblest cottages, as well as the richest houses; and nothing is more certain, than that the coarse and middling clothing for our families, will forever hereafter continue to be made within ourselves. I have hitherto myself depended entirely on foreign manufactures; but I have now thirty-five spindles agoing, a hand carding machine, and looms with the flying shuttle, for the supply of my own farms, which will never be relinquished in my time. The continuance of the war will fix the habit generally, and out of the evils of impressment and of the orders of council, a great blessing for us will grow. I have not formerly been an advocate for great manufactories. I doubted whether our labor, employed in agriculture, and aided by the spontaneous energies of the earth, would not procure us more than we could make ourselves of other necessaries. But other considerations entering into the question, have settled my doubts.

The candor with which you have viewed the manners and condition of our citizens, is so unlike the narrow prejudices of the French and English travellers preceding you, who, considering each the manners and habits of their own people as the only orthodox, have viewed everything differing from that test as boorish and barbarous, that your work will be read here extensively, and operate great good.

Amidst this mass of approbation which is given to every other part of the work, there is a single sentiment which I cannot help wishing to bring to what I think the correct one; and, on a point so interesting, I value your opinion too highly not to ambition its concurrence with my own. Stating in volume one, page sixty-three, the principle of difference between the two great political parties here, you conclude it to be, "whether the controlling power shall be vested in this or that set of men." That each party endeavours to get into the administration of the government, and exclude the other from power, is true, and may be stated as a motive of action: but this is only secondary; the primary motive being a real and radical difference of political principle. I sincerely wish our differences were but personally who should govern, and that the principles of our constitution were those of both parties. Unfortunately, it is otherwise; and the question of preference between monarchy and republicanism, which has so long divided mankind elsewhere, threatens a permanent division here.

Among that section of our citizens called federalists, there are three shades of opinion. Distinguishing between the *leaders* and *people* who compose it, the *leaders* consider the English constitution as a model of perfection, some, with a correction of its vices, others, with all its corruptions and abuses. This last was Alexander Hamilton's opinion, which others, as well as myself, have often heard him declare, and that a correction of what are called its vices, would render the English an impracticable government. This government they wished to have established here, and only accepted and held fast, *at first*, to the present constitution, as a stepping-stone to the final establishment of their favorite model. This party has therefore always clung to England as their prototype, and great auxiliary in promoting and effecting this change. A weighty MINORITY, however, of these *leaders*, considering the voluntary conversion of our government into a monarchy as too distant, if not desperate [i.e. hopeless], wish to break off from our Union its eastern fragment, as being, in truth, the hot-bed of American monarchism, with a view to a commencement of their favorite government, from whence the other States may gangrene by degrees, and the whole be thus brought finally to the desired point. For Massachusetts, the prime mover in this enterprise, is the last State in the Union to mean a *final* separation, as being of all the most dependent on the others. Not raising bread for the sustenance of her own inhabitants, not having a stick of timber for the construction of vessels, her principal occupation, nor an article to export in them, where would she be, excluded from the ports of the other States, and thrown into dependence on England, her direct and natural, but now insidious rival? At the head of this MINORITY is what is called the Essex Junto of Massachusetts. But the MAJORITY of these *leaders* do not aim at separation. In this, they adhere to the known principle of General [Alexander] Hamilton, never, under any views, to break the Union. Anglomany, monarchy, and separation, then, are the principles of the Essex federalists. Anglomany and monarchy, those of the Ham-

iltonians, and Anglomany alone, that of the portion among the
*people* who call themselves federalists. These last are as good republicans as the brethren whom they oppose, and differ from them only
in their devotion to England and hatred of France which they have
imbibed from their leaders. The moment that these leaders should
avowedly propose a separation of the Union, or the establishment
of regal government, their popular adherents would quit them to a
man, and join the republican standard; and the partisans of this
change, even in Massachusetts, would thus find themselves an army
of officers without a soldier.

The party called republican is steadily for the support of the
present constitution. They obtained at its commencement, all the
amendments to it they desired. These reconciled them to it perfectly, and if they have any ulterior view, it is only, perhaps, to
popularize it further, by shortening the Senatorial term, and devising a process for the responsibility of judges, more practical than
that of impeachment. They esteem the people of England and
France equally, and equally detest the governing powers of both.

This I verily believe, after an intimacy of forty years with the
public councils and characters, is a true statement of the grounds
on which they are at present divided, and that it is not merely an
ambition for power. An honest man can feel no pleasure in the
exercise of power over his fellow citizens. And considering as the
only offices of power those conferred by the people directly, that is
to say, the executive and legislative functions of the General and
State governments, the common refusal of these and multiplied res-
ignations, are proofs sufficient that power is not alluring to pure
minds, and is not, with them, the primary principle of contest. This
is my belief of it; it is that on which I have acted; and had it been
a mere contest who should be permitted to administer the government according to its genuine republican principles, there has never
been a moment of my life in which I should have relinquished for
it the enjoyments of my family, my farm, my friends and books.

You expected to discover the difference of our party principles in
General Washington's valedictory, and my inaugural address. Not at
all. General Washington did not harbor one principle of federalism.
He was neither an Angloman, a monarchist, nor a separatist. He sincerely wished the people to have as much self-government as they
were competent to exercise themselves. The only point on which he

and I ever differed in opinion, was, that I had more confidence than he had in the natural integrity and discretion of the people, and in the safety and extent to which they might trust themselves with a control over their government. He has asseverated to me a thousand times his determination that the existing government should have a fair trial, and that in support of it he would spend the last drop of his blood. He did this the more repeatedly, because he knew General Hamilton's political bias, and my apprehensions from it. It is a mere calumny, therefore, in the monarchists, to associate General Washington with their principles. But that may have happened in this case which has been often seen in ordinary cases, that, by oft repeating an untruth, men come to believe it themselves. It is a mere artifice in this party to bolster themselves up on the revered name of that first of our worthies. If I have dwelt longer on this subject than was necessary, it proves the estimation in which I hold your ultimate opinions, and my desire of placing the subject truly before them. In so doing, I am certain I risk no use of the communication which may draw me into contention before the public. Tranquillity is the *summum bonum* of a Septagenaire.

To return to the merits of your work: I consider it as so lively a picture of the real state of our country, that if I can possibly obtain opportunities of conveyance, I propose to send a copy to a friend in France, and another to one in Italy, who, I know, will translate and circulate it as an antidote to the misrepresentations of former travellers. But whatever effect my profession of political faith may have on your general opinion, a part of my object will be obtained, if it satisfies you as to the principles of my own action, and of the high respect and consideration with which I tender you my salutations.

Ford IX: 373–7

## VIII.13 To John Adams

Monticello, June 27, 1813

Ἴδαν ἐς πολύδενδρον ἀνὴρ ὑλητόμος ἐλθὼν
Παπταίνει, παρεόντος ἅδην, πόθεν ἄρξεται ἔργου,
Τί πρᾶτον καταλέξω; ἐπεὶ πάρα μυρία εἰπεῖν.

And I too, my dear Sir, like the wood-cutter of Ida, should doubt where to begin, were I to enter the forest of opinions, discussions, and contentions which have occurred in our day. I should say with Theocritus, Τί πρᾶτον καταλέξω; ἐπεὶ πάρα μυρία εἰπεῖν. But I shall not do it. The *summum bonum* with me is now truly epicurian, ease of body and tranquillity of mind; and to these I wish to consign my remaining days. Men have differed in opinion, and been divided into parties by these opinions, from the first origin of societies, and in all governments where they have been permitted freely to think and to speak. The same political parties which now agitate the United States, have existed through all time. Whether the power of the people or that of the ἄριστοι should prevail, were questions which kept the States of Greece and Rome in eternal convulsions, as they now schismatize every people whose minds and mouths are not shut up by the gag of a despot. And in fact, the terms of whig and tory belong to natural as well as to civil history. They denote the temper and constitution of mind of different individuals. To come to our own country, and to the times when you and I became first acquainted, we well remember the violent parties which agitated the old Congress, and their bitter contests. There you and I were together, and the Jays, and the Dickinsons, and other anti-independents, were arrayed against us. They cherished the monarchy of England, and we the rights of our countrymen. When our present government was in the mew [i.e. in transition], passing from Confederation to Union, how bitter was the schism between the Feds and Antis! Here you and I were together again. For although, for a moment, separated by the Atlantic from the scene of action, I favored the opinion that nine states should confirm the constitution, in order to secure it, and the others hold off until certain amendments, deemed favorable to freedom, should be made. I rallied in the first instant to the wiser proposition of Massachusetts, that all should confirm, and then all instruct their delegates to urge those amendments. The amendments were made, and all were reconciled to the government. But as soon as it was put into motion, the line of division was again drawn. We broke into two parties, each wishing to give the government a different direction; the one to strengthen the most popular branch, the other the more permanent branches, and to extend their permanence. Here you and I separated for the first time, and as we had been longer than most others on the public theatre, and our names therefore were more familiar to our countrymen, the party which considered you as thinking with them, placed your name at their head; the other, for the same reason, selected mine. But neither decency nor inclination permitted us to become the advocates of ourselves, or to take part personally in the violent contests which followed. We suffered ourselves, as you so well expressed it, to be passive subjects of public discussion. And these discussions, whether relating to men, measures or opinions, were conducted by the parties with an animosity, a bitterness and an indecency which had never been exceeded. All the resources of reason and of wrath were exhausted by each party in support of its own, and to prostrate the adversary opinions; one was upbraided with receiving the anti-federalists, the other the old tories and refugees, into their bosom. Of this acrimony, the public papers of the day exhibit ample testimony, in the debates of Congress, of State Legislatures, of stump-orators, in addresses, answers, and newspaper essays; and to these, without question, may be added the private correspondences of individuals; and the less guarded in these, because not meant for the public eye, not restrained by the respect due to that, but poured forth from the overflowings of the heart into the bosom of a friend, as a momentary easement of our feelings. In this way, and in answers to addresses, you and I could indulge ourselves. We have probably done it, sometimes with warmth, often with prejudice, but always, as we believed, adhering to truth. I have not examined my letters of that day. I have no stomach to revive the memory of its feelings. But one of these letters, it seems, has got before the public, by accident and infidelity, by the death of one friend to whom it was written, and of his friend to whom it had been communicated, and by the malice and treachery of a third person, of whom I had never before heard, merely to make mischief, and in the same satanic spirit in which the same enemy had intercepted and published, in 1776, your letter animadverting on [John] Dickinson's character. How it happened that I quoted you in my letter to Doctor [Joseph] Priestley, and for whom, and not for yourself, the strictures were meant, has been explained to you in my letter of the 15th, which had been committed to the post eight days before I received yours of the 10th, 11th, and 14th. That gave you the reference which these asked to the particular answer alluded to in the one to Priestley. The renewal of these old discussions, my friend, would be equally useless and irksome. To the volumes then written on these subjects, human ingenuity can add nothing new, and the rather, as lapse of time has obliterated many of the facts. And shall you and I, my dear Sir, at our age, like Priam of old, gird on the "*arma, diu desueta, trementibus ævo humeris?*" Shall we, at our age, become the Athletæ of party, and exhibit ourselves as gladiators in the arena of the newspapers? Nothing in the universe could induce me to it. My mind has been long fixed to bow to the judgment of the world, who will judge by my acts, and will never take counsel from me as to what that judgment shall be. If your objects and opinions have been misunderstood, if the measures and principles of others have been wrongfully imputed to you, as I believe they have been, that you should leave an explanation of them, would be an act of justice to yourself. I will add, that it has been hoped that you would leave such explanations as would place every saddle on its right horse, and replace on the shoulders of others the burdens they shifted on yours.

But all this, my friend, is offered, merely for your consideration and judgment, without presuming to anticipate what you alone are qualified to decide for yourself. I mean to express my own purpose only, and the reflections which have led to it. To me, then, it appears, that there have been differences of opinion and party differences, from the first establishment of governments to the present day, and on the same question which now divides our own country; that these will continue through all future time; that every one takes his side in favor of the many, or of the few, according to his constitution, and the circumstances in which he is placed; that opinions, which are equally honest on both sides, should not affect personal esteem or social intercourse; that as we judge between the Claudii and the Gracchi, the Wentworths and the Hampdens of past ages, so of those among us whose names may happen to be remembered for awhile, the next generations will judge, favorably or unfavorably, according to the complexion of individual minds, and the side they shall themselves have taken; that nothing new can be added by you or me to what has been said by others, and will be said in every age in support of the conflicting opinions on government; and that wisdom and duty dictate an humble resignation to the verdict of our future peers. In doing this myself, I shall certainly not suffer moot questions to affect the sentiments of sincere friendship and respect, consecrated to you by so long a course of time, and of which I now repeat sincere assurances.

L & B XIII: 279–84

## VIII.14 From the *Anas*

[Preface, February 4, 1818]

*Explanation of the three volumes bound in marbled paper*

In these three volumes will be found copies of the official opinions given in writing by me to General Washington, while I was Secretary of State, with sometimes the documents belonging to the case. Some of these are the rough draughts, some press copies, some fair ones. In the earlier part of my acting in that office, I took no other note of the passing transactions; but after awhile, I saw the importance of doing it in aid of my memory. Very often, therefore, I made memorandums on loose scraps of paper, taken out of my pocket in the moment, and laid by to be copied fair at leisure, which, however, they hardly ever were. These scraps, therefore, ragged, rubbed, and scribbled as they were, I had bound with the others by a binder who came into my cabinet, did it under my own eye, and without the opportunity of reading a single paper. At this day, after the lapse of twenty-five years, or more, from their dates, I have given to the whole a calm revisal, when the passions of the time are passed away, and the reasons of the transactions act alone on the judgment. Some of the informations I had recorded, are now cut out from the rest, because I have seen that they were incorrect, or doubtful, or merely personal or private, with which we have nothing to do. I should perhaps have thought the rest not worth preserving, but for their testimony against the only history of that period, which pretends to have been compiled from authentic and unpublished documents.

But a short review of facts will show, that the contests of that day[1] were contests of principle, between the advocates of republican, and those of kingly government, and that had not the former made the efforts they did, our government would have been, even at this

---

[1] The 1790s. – *Eds.*

early day, a very different thing from what the successful issue of those efforts have made it.

The alliance between the States under the old Articles of Confederation, for the purpose of joint defence against the aggression of Great Britain, was found insufficient, as treaties of alliance generally are, to enforce compliance with their mutual stipulations; and these, once fulfilled, that bond was to expire of itself, and each State to become sovereign and independent in all things. Yet it could not but occur to every one, that these separate independencies, like the petty States of Greece, would be eternally at war with each other, and would become at length the mere partisans and satellites of the leading powers of Europe. All then must have looked forward to some further bond of union, which would insure eternal peace, and a political system of our own, independent of that of Europe. Whether all should be consolidated into a single government, or each remain independent as to internal matters, and the whole form a single nation as to what was foreign only, and whether that national government should be a monarchy or republic, would of course divide opinions, according to the constitutions, the habits, and the circumstances of each individual. Some officers of the army, as it has always been said and believed (and Steuben and Knox[2] have ever been named as the leading agents), trained to monarchy by military habits, are understood to have proposed to General Washington to decide this great question by the army before its disbandment, and to assume himself the crown on the assurance of their support. The indignation with which he is said to have scouted this parricide proposition was equally worthy of his virtue and wisdom. The next effort was (on suggestion of the same individuals, in the moment of their separation), the establishment of an hereditary order under the name of the Cincinnati, ready prepared by that distinction to be ingrafted into the future frame of government, and placing General Washington still at their head. The General wrote to me on this subject, while I was in Congress at Annapolis, and an extract from my letter is inserted in 5th Marshall's history,[3] page

---

[2] Baron Friedrich Wilhelm von Steuben and Henry Knox were key figures in the Order of Cincinnati which favored royal rule with "Cincinnatus" (George Washington) as king. – *Eds.*

[3] John Marshall, *The Life of George Washington* (Philadelphia, 1804–7), vol. v. – *Eds.*

28. He afterwards called on me at that place on his way to a meeting of the society [i.e. the Order of Cincinnati], and after a whole evening of consultation, he left that place fully determined to use all his endeavors for its total suppression. But he found it so firmly riveted in the affections of the members, that, strengthened as they happened to be by an adventitious occurrence of the moment, he could effect no more than the abolition of its hereditary principle. He called again on his return, and explained to me fully the opposition which had been made, the effect of the occurrence from France, and the difficulty with which its duration had been limited to the lives of the present members. Further details will be found among my papers, in his and my letters, and some in the *Encyclopédie Méthodique et Dictionnaire d'Economie Politique*, communicated by myself to M. Meusnier, its author, who had made the establishment of this society the ground, in that work, of a libel on our country.

The want of some authority which should procure justice to the public creditors, and an observance of treaties with foreign nations, produced, some time after, the call of a convention of the States at Annapolis. Although, at this meeting, a difference of opinion was evident on the question of a republican or kingly government, yet so general through the States was the sentiment in favor of the former, that the friends of the latter confined themselves to a course of obstruction only, and delay, to everything proposed; they hoped, that nothing being done, and all things going from bad to worse, a kingly government might be usurped, and submitted to by the people, as better than anarchy and wars internal and external, the certain consequences of the present want of a general government. The effect of their manœuvres, with the defective attendance of Deputies from the States, resulted in the measure of calling a more general convention, to be held at Philadelphia. At this, the same party exhibited the same practices, and with the same views of preventing a government of concord, which they foresaw would be republican, and of forcing through anarchy their way to monarchy. But the mass of that convention was too honest, too wise, and too steady, to be baffled and misled by their manœuvres. One of these was a form of government proposed by Colonel Hamilton, which would have been in fact a compromise between the two parties of royalism and republicanism. According to this, the executive and one branch of the legislature were to be during good behavior, *i.e.* for life, and the governors of the States were to be named by these two permanent organs. This, however, was rejected; on which Hamilton left the convention, as desperate, and never returned again until near its final conclusion. These opinions and efforts, secret or avowed, of the advocates for monarchy, had begotten great jealousy through the States generally; and this jealousy it was which excited the strong opposition to the conventional constitution; a jealousy which yielded at last only to a general determination to establish certain amendments as barriers against a government either monarchical or consolidated. In what passed through the whole period of these conventions, I have gone on the information of those who were members of them, being absent myself on my mission to France.

I returned from that mission in the first year of the new government, having landed in Virginia in December, 1789, and proceeded to New York in March, 1790, to enter on the office of Secretary of State. Here, certainly, I found a state of things which, of all I had ever contemplated, I the least expected. I had left France in the first year of her revolution, in the fervor of natural rights, and zeal for reformation. My conscientious devotion to these rights could not be heightened, but it had been aroused and excited by daily exercise. The President received me cordially, and my colleagues and the circle of principal citizens apparently with welcome. The courtesies of dinner parties given me, as a stranger newly arrived among them, placed me at once in their familiar society. But I cannot describe the wonder and mortification with which the table conversations filled me. Politics were the chief topic, and a preference of kingly over republican government was evidently the favorite sentiment. An apostate I could not be, nor yet a hypocrite; and I found myself, for the most part, the only advocate on the republican side of the question, unless among the guests there chanced to be some member of that party from the legislative Houses. Hamilton's financial system had then passed. It had two objects; 1st, as a puzzle, to exclude popular understanding and inquiry; 2d, as a machine for the corruption of the legislature; for he avowed the opinion, that man could be governed by one of two motives only, force or interest; force, he observed, in this country was out of the question, and the interests, therefore, of the members must be laid hold of, to keep the legislative in unison with the executive. And with grief and shame it must be acknowledged that his machine was not without effect; that even in this, the birth of our government, some members were found sordid enough to bend their duty to their interests, and to look after personal rather than public good.

It is well known that during the war the greatest difficulty we encountered was the want of money or means to pay our soldiers who fought, or our farmers, manufacturers and merchants, who furnished the necessary supplies of food and clothing for them. After the expedient of paper money had exhausted itself, certificates of debt were given to the individual creditors, with assurance of payment so soon as the United States should be able. But the distresses of these people often obliged them to part with these for the half, the fifth, and even a tenth of their value; and speculators had made a trade of cozening them from the holders by the most fraudulent practices, and persuasions that they would never be paid. In the bill for funding and paying these, Hamilton made no difference between the original holders and the fraudulent purchasers of this paper. Great and just repugnance arose at putting these two classes of creditors on the same footing, and great exertions were used to pay the former the full value, and to the latter, the price only which they had paid, with interest, But this would have prevented the game which was to be played, and for which the minds of greedy members were already tutored and prepared. When the trial of strength on these several efforts had indicated the form in which the bill would finally pass, this being known within doors sooner than without, and especially, than to those who were in distant parts of the Union, the base scramble began. Couriers and relay horses by land, and swift sailing pilot boats by sea, were flying in all directions. Active partners and agents were associated and employed in every State, town, and country neighborhood, and this paper was bought up at five shillings, and even as low as two shillings in the pound, before the holder knew that Congress had already provided for its redemption at par. Immense sums were thus filched from the poor and ignorant, and fortunes accumulated by those who had themselves been poor enough before. Men thus enriched by the dexterity of a leader, would follow of course the chief who was leading them to fortune, and become the zealous instruments of all his enterprises.

This game was over, and another was on the carpet at the moment of my arrival; and to this I was most ignorantly and innocently made to hold the candle. This fiscal maneuvre is well known by the name of the Assumption. Independently of the debts of Congress, the States had during the war contracted separate and heavy debts; and Massachusetts particularly, in an absurd attempt, absurdly conducted, on the British post of Penobscott: and the more debt Hamilton could rake up, the more plunder for his mercenaries. This money, whether wisely or foolishly spent, was pretended to have been spent for general purposes, and ought, therefore, to be paid from the general purse. But it was objected, that nobody knew what these debts were, what their amount, or what their proofs. No matter; we will guess them to be twenty millions. But of these twenty millions, we do not know how much should be reimbursed to one State, or how much to another. No matter; we will guess. And so another scramble was set on foot among the several States, and some got much, some little, some nothing. But the main object was obtained, the phalanx of the Treasury was reinforced by additional recruits. This measure produced the most bitter and angry contest ever known in Congress, before or since the Union of the States. I arrived in the midst of it. But a stranger to the ground, a stranger to the actors on it, so long absent as to have lost all familiarity with the subject, and as yet unaware of its object, I took no concern in it. The great and trying question, however, was lost in the House of Representatives. So high were the feuds excited by this subject, that on its rejection business was suspended. Congress met and adjourned from day to day without doing any thing, the parties being too much out of temper to do business together. The eastern members particularly, who, with Smith from South Carolina, were the principal gamblers in these scenes, threatened a secession and dissolution. Hamilton was in despair. As I was going to the President's one day, I met him in the street. He walked me backwards and forwards before the President's door for half an hour. He painted pathetically the temper into which the legislature had been wrought; the disgust of those who were called the creditor States; the danger of the *secession* of their members, and the separation of the States. He observed that the members of the administration ought to act in concert; that though this question was not of my department, yet a common duty should make it a common concern; that the President was the centre on which all administrative questions ultimately rested, and that all of us should rally around him, and support, with joint efforts, measures approved by him; and that the question having been lost by a small majority only, it was probable that an appeal from me to the judgment and discretion of some of my friends, might effect a change in the vote, and the machine of government, now suspended, might be again set into motion. I told him that I was really a stranger to the whole subject; that not having yet informed myself of the system of finances adopted, I knew not how far this was a necessary sequence; that undoubtedly, if its rejection endangered a dissolution of our Union at this incipient stage, I should deem that the most unfortunate of all consequences, to avert which all partial and temporary evils should be yielded. I proposed to him, however, to dine with me the next day, and I would invite another friend or two, bring them into conference together, and I thought it impossible that reasonable men, consulting together coolly, could fail, by some mutual sacrifices of opinion, to form a compromise which was to save the Union. The discussion took place. I could take no part in it but an exhortatory one, because I was a stranger to the circumstances which should govern it. But it was finally agreed, that whatever importance had been attached to the rejection of this proposition, the preservation of the Union and of concord among the States was more important, and that therefore it would be better that the vote of rejection should be rescinded, to erect which, some members should change their votes. But it was observed that this pill would be peculiarly bitter to the southern States, and that some concomitant measure should be adopted, to sweeten it a little to them. There had before been propositions to fix the seat of government either at Philadelphia, or at Georgetown on the Potomac; and it was thought that by giving it to Philadelphia for ten years, and to Georgetown permanently afterwards, this might, as an anodyne, calm in some degree the ferment which might be excited by the other measure alone. So two of the Potomac members (White and Lee, but White with a revulsion of stomach almost convulsive), agreed to change their votes, and Hamilton undertook to carry the other point. In doing this, the influence he had established over the eastern members, with the agency of Robert Morris with those of the middle States, effected his side of the engagement; and so the Assumption was passed, and twenty millions of stock divided among favored States, and thrown in as a pabulum to the stock-jobbing herd. This added to the number of votaries to the Treasury, and made its chief the master of every vote in the legislature, which might give to the government the direction suited to his political views.

I know well, and so must be understood, that nothing like a majority in Congress had yielded to this corruption. Far from it. But a division, not very unequal, had already taken place in the honest part of that body, between the parties styled republican and federal. The latter being monarchists in principle, adhered to Hamilton of course, as their leader in that principle, and this mercenary phalanx added to them, insured him always a majority in both Houses: so that the whole action of legislature was now under the direction of the Treasury. Still the machine was not complete. The effect of the funding system, and of the Assumption, would be temporary; it would be lost with the loss of the individual members whom it has enriched, and some engine of influence more permanent must be contrived, while these myrmidons were yet in place to carry it through all opposition. This engine was the Bank of the United States. All that history is known, so I shall say nothing about it. While the government remained at Philadelphia, a selection of members of both Houses were constantly kept as directors who, on every question interesting to that institution, or to the views of the federal head, voted at the will of that head; and, together with the stock-holding members, could always make the federal vote that of the majority. By this combination, legislative expositions were given to the constitution, and all the administrative laws were shaped on the model of England, and so passed. And from this influence we were not relieved, until the removal from the precincts of the bank, to Washington.

Here then was the real ground of the opposition which was made to the course of administration. Its object was to preserve the legislature pure and independent of the executive, to restrain the administration to republican forms and principles, and not permit the constitution to be construed into a monarchy, and to be warped, in practice, into all the principles and pollutions of their favorite English model. Nor was this an opposition to General Washington. He was true to the republican charge confided to him; and has solemnly and repeatedly protested to me, in our conversations, that he would lose the last drop of his blood in support of it; and he did this the oftener and with the more earnestness, because he knew my suspicions of Hamilton's designs against it, and wished to quiet them. For he was not aware of the drift, or of the effect of Hamilton's schemes. Unversed in financial projects and calculations and budgets, his approbation of them was bottomed on his confidence in the man.

But Hamilton was not only a monarchist, but for a monarchy bottomed on corruption. In proof of this, I will relate an anecdote, for the truth of which I attest the God who made me. Before the President set out on his southern tour in April, 1791, he addressed a letter of the fourth of that month, from Mount Vernon, to the Secretaries of State, Treasury and War, desiring that if any serious and important cases should arise during his absence, they would consult and act on them. And he requested that the Vice-President should also be consulted. This was the only occasion on which that officer was ever requested to take part in a cabinet question. Some occasion for consultation arising, I invited those gentlemen (and the Attorney General, as well as I remember), to dine with me, in order to confer on the subject. After the cloth was removed, and our question agreed and dismissed, conversation began on other matters, and by some circumstance, was led to the British constitution, on which Mr. Adams observed, "purge that constitution of its corruption, and give to its popular branch equality of representation, and it would be the most perfect constitution ever devised by the wit of man." Hamilton paused and said, "purge it of its corruption, and give to its popular branch equality of representation, and it would become an *impracticable* government: as it stands at present, with all its supposed defects, it is the most perfect government which ever existed." And this was assuredly the exact line which separated the political creeds of these two gentlemen. The one was for two hereditary branches and an honest elective one: the other, for an hereditary King, with a House of Lords and Commons corrupted to his will, and standing between him and the people. Hamilton was, indeed, a singular character. Of acute understanding, disinterested, honest, and honorable in all private transactions, amiable in society, and duly valuing virtue in private life, yet so bewitched and perverted by the British example, as to be under thorough conviction that corruption was essential to the government of a nation.

Mr. Adams had originally been a republican. The glare of royalty and nobility, during his mission to England, had made him believe their fascination a necessary ingredient in government; and Shays's rebellion, not sufficiently understood where he then was, seemed to prove that the absence of want and oppression, was not a sufficient guarantee of order. His book on the American constitutions[4] having made known his political bias, he was taken up by the monarchical federalists in his absence, and on his return to the United States, he was by them made to believe that the general disposition of our citizens was favorable to monarchy. He here wrote his Davila, as a supplement to a former work, and his election to the Presidency confirmed him in his errors. Innumerable addresses too, artfully and industriously poured in upon him, deceived him into a confidence that he was on the pinnacle of popularity, when the gulf was yawning at his feet, which was to swallow up him and his deceivers. For when General Washington was withdrawn, these *energumeni* of royalism, kept in check hitherto by the dread of his honesty, his firmness, his patriotism, and the authority of his name, now mounted on the car of State and free from control, like Phaeton on that of the sun, drove headlong and wild, looking neither to right nor left, nor regarding anything but the objects they were driving at; until, displaying these fully, the eyes of the nation were opened, and a general disbandment of them from the public councils took place.

Mr. Adams, I am sure, has been long since convinced of the treacheries with which he was surrounded during his administration. He has since thoroughly seen, that his constituents were devoted to republican government, and whether his judgment is re-settled on its ancient basis, or not, he is conformed as a good citizen to the will of the majority, and would now, I am persuaded, maintain its republican structure with the zeal and fidelity belonging to his character. For even an enemy has said, "he is always an honest man, and often a great one." But in the fervor of the fury and follies of those who made him their stalking horse, no man who did not witness it can form an idea of their unbridled madness, and the terrorism with which they surrounded themselves. The horrors of the French revolution, then raging, aided them mainly, and using

---

[4] John Adams, *A Defence of the Constitutions of Government of the United States of America* (London, 1787). – *Eds.*

that as a raw head and bloody bones, they were enabled by their stratagems of X. Y. Z.[5] in which ******** was a leading mountebank, their tales of tub-plots,[6] ocean massacres, bloody buoys and pulpit lyings and slanderings, and maniacal ravings of their Gardeners, their Osgoods and Parishes, to spread alarm into all but the firmest breasts. Their Attorney General had the impudence to say to a republican member, that deportation must be resorted to, of which, said he, "you republicans have set the example"; thus daring to identify us with the murderous Jacobins of France. These transactions, now recollected but as dreams of the night, were then sad realities; and nothing rescued us from their liberticide effect, but the unyielding opposition of those firm spirits who sternly maintained their post in defiance of terror, until their fellow citizens could be aroused to their own danger, and rally and rescue the standard of the constitution. This has been happily done. Federalism and monarchism have languished from that moment, until their treasonable combinations with the enemies of their country during the late war, their plots of dismembering the Union, and their Hartford convention, have consigned them to the tomb of the dead; and I fondly hope, "we may now truly say, we are all republicans, all federalists," and that the motto of the standard to which our country will forever rally, will be, "federal union, and republican government"; and sure I am we may say, that we are indebted for the preservation of this point of ralliance, to that opposition of which so injurious an idea is so artfully insinuated and excited in this history.

Much of this relation is notorious to the world; and many intimate proofs of it will be found in these notes. From the moment where they end, of my retiring from the administration, the federalists[7] got unchecked hold of General Washington. His memory was already sensibly impaired by age, the firm tone of mind for which he had been remarkable, was beginning to relax, its energy was abated, a listlessness of labor, a desire for tranquillity had crept on him, and a willingness to let others act, and even think for him. Like the rest of mankind, he was disgusted with atrocities of the

---

[5] See *supra*, 1.9, note 1. – *Eds.*

[6] Presumably tales with plots as absurd and far-fetched as Jonathan Swift's *A Tale of a Tub* (London, 1704). – *Eds.*

[7] I.e. the Federalist party. – *Eds.*

French revolution, and was not sufficiently aware of the difference between the rabble who were used as instruments of their perpetration, and the steady and rational character of the American people, in which he had not sufficient confidence. The opposition too of the republicans to the British treaty, and the zealous support of the federalists in that unpopular but favorite measure of theirs, had made him all their own. Understanding, moreover, that I disapproved of that treaty, and copiously nourished with falsehoods by a malignant neighbor of mine, who ambitioned to be his correspondent, he had become alienated from myself personally, as from the republican body generally of his fellow-citizens; and he wrote the letters to Mr. Adams and Mr. [Charles] Carroll, over which, in devotion to his imperishable fame, we must forever weep as monuments of mortal decay.

Washington IX: 87–99

## VIII.15 To William Johnson

Monticello, October 27, 1822

Dear Sir, – . . . What do you think of the state of parties at this time? An opinion prevails that there is no longer any distinction, that the republicans & Federalists are compleatly amalgamated but it is not so. The amalgamation is of name only, not of principle. All indeed call themselves by the name of Republicans, because that of Federalists was extinguished in the battle of New Orleans.[1] But the truth is that finding that monarchy is a desperate wish in this country, they rally to the point which they think next best, a consolidated government. Their aim is now therefore to break down the rights reserved by the constitution to the states as a bulwark against that consolidation, the fear of which produced the whole of the opposition to the constitution at it's birth. Hence new Republicans in Congress, preaching the doctrines of the old Federalists, and the new nick-names of Ultras and Radicals. But I trust they will fail under the new, as the old name, and that the friends of the real constitution and union will prevail against consolidation, as they

---

[1] I.e. the victory of American forces (under the command of General Andrew Jackson) over British troops at New Orleans in 1815. – *Eds.*

have done against monarchism. I scarcely know myself which is most to be deprecated, a consolidation, or dissolution of the states. The horrors of both are beyond the reach of human foresight.

Ford x: 225–6

## VIII.16 To William Johnson

Monticello, June 12, 1823

Dear Sir, – Our correspondence is of that accommodating character, which admits of suspension at the convenience of either party, without inconvenience to the other. Hence this tardy acknowledgment of your favor of April the 11th. I learn from that with great pleasure, that you have resolved on continuing your history of parties. Our opponents are far ahead of us in preparations for placing their cause favorably before posterity. Yet I hope even from some of them the escape of precious truths, in angry explosions or effusions of vanity, which will betray the genuine monarchism of their principles. They do not themselves believe what they endeavor to inculcate, that we were an opposition party, not on principle, but merely seeking for office. The fact is, that at the formation of our government, many had formed their political opinions on European writings and practices, believing the experience of old countries, and especially of England, abusive as it was, to be a safer guide than mere theory. The doctrines of Europe were, that men in numerous associations cannot be restrained within the limits of order and justice, but by forces physical and moral, wielded over them by authorities independent of their will. Hence their organization of kings, hereditary nobles, and priests. Still further to constrain the brute force of the people, they deem it necessary to keep them down by hard labor, poverty and ignorance, and to take from them, as from bees, so much of their earnings, as that unremitting labor shall be necessary to obtain a sufficient surplus barely to sustain a scanty and miserable life. And these earnings they apply to maintain their privileged orders in splendor and idleness, to fascinate the eyes of the people, and excite in them an humble adoration and submission, as to an order of superior beings. Although few among us had gone all these lengths of opinion, yet many had advanced, some more, some less, on the way. And in the convention which formed our government, they endeavored to draw the cords of power as tight as they could obtain them, to lessen the dependence of the general functionaries on their constituents, to subject to them those of the States, and to weaken their means of maintaining the steady equilibrium which the majority of the convention had deemed salutary for both branches, general and local. To recover, therefore, in practice the powers which the nation had refused, and to warp to their own wishes those actually given, was the steady object of the federal party. Ours, on the contrary, was to maintain the will of the majority of the convention, and of the people themselves. We believed, with them, that man was a rational animal, endowed by nature with rights, and with an innate sense of justice; and that he could be restrained from wrong and protected in right by moderate powers, confided to persons of his own choice, and held to their duties by dependence on his own will. We believed that the complicated organization of kings, nobles, and priests, was not the wisest nor best to effect the happiness of associated man; that wisdom and virtue were not hereditary, that the trappings of such a machinery, consumed by their expense, those earnings of industry, they were meant to protect, and, by the inequalities they produced, exposed liberty to sufferance. We believed that men, enjoying in ease and security the full fruits of their own industry, enlisted by all their interests on the side of law and order, habituated to think for themselves, and to follow their reason as their guide, would be more easily and safely governed, than with minds nourished in error, and vitiated and debased, as in Europe, by ignorance, indigence and oppression. The cherishment of the people then was our principle, the fear and distrust of them, that of the other party. Composed, as we were, of the landed and laboring interests of the country, we could not be less anxious for a government of law and order than were the inhabitants of the cities, the strongholds of federalism. And whether our efforts to save the principles and form of our constitution have not been salutary, let the present republican freedom, order and prosperity of our country determine. History may distort truth, and will distort it for a time, by the superior efforts at justification of those who are conscious of needing it most. Nor will the opening scenes of our present government be seen in their true aspect, until the letters of the day, now held in private hoards, shall be broken up and laid open to public view. What a treasure will be found in General Washington's cabinet, when it shall pass into the hands of as candid a friend to truth as he was himself! When no longer, like Cæsar's notes and memorandums in the hands of Anthony, it shall be open to the high priests of federalism only, and garbled to say so much, and no more, as suits their views!

With respect to his farewell address, to the authorship of which, it seems, there are conflicting claims, I can state to you some facts. He had determined to decline re-election at the end of his first term, and so far determined, that he had requested Mr. Madison to prepare for him something valedictory, to be addressed to his constituents on his retirement. This was done, but he was finally persuaded to acquiesce in a second election, to which no one more strenuously pressed him than myself, from a conviction of the importance of strengthening, by longer habit, the respect necessary for that office, which the weight of his character only could effect. When, at the end of his second term, his Valedictory came out, Mr. Madison recognized in it several passages of his draught, several others, we were both satisfied, were from the pen of Hamilton, and others from that of the President himself. These he probably put into the hands of Hamilton to form into a whole, and hence it may all appear in Hamilton's hand-writing, as if it were all of his composition.

I have stated above, that the original objects of the federalists were, 1st, to warp our government more to the form and principles of monarchy, and; 2d, to weaken the barriers of the State governments as coördinate powers. In the first they have been so completely foiled by the universal spirit of the nation, that they have abandoned the enterprise, shrunk from the odium of their old appellation, taken to themselves a participation of ours, and under the pseudo-republican mask, are now aiming at their second object, and strengthened by unsuspecting or apostate recruits from our ranks, are advancing fast towards an ascendancy. I have been blamed for saying, that a prevalence of the doctrine of consolidation would one day call for reformation or *revolution*. I answer by asking if a single State of the Union would have agreed to the constitution, had it given all powers to the General Government? If the whole opposition to it did not proceed from the jealousy and fear of every State, of being subjected to the other States in matters merely its own? And if there is any reason to believe the States more disposed now than then, to acquiesce in this general surrender of all their rights and powers to a consolidated government, one and undivided?

You request me confidentially, to examine the question, whether the Supreme Court has advanced beyond its constitutional limits, and trespassed on those of the State authorities? I do not undertake it, my dear Sir, because I am unable. Age and the wane of mind consequent on it, have disqualified me from investigations so severe, and researches so laborious. And it is the less necessary in this case, as having been already done by others with a logic and learning to which I could add nothing. On the decision of the case of Cohens *vs.* The State of Virginia, in the Supreme Court of the United States, in March, 1821, Judge Roane, under the signature of Algernon Sidney, wrote for the Enquirer a series of papers on the law of that case. I considered these papers maturely as they came out, and confess that they appeared to me to pulverize every word which had been delivered by Judge John Marshall, of the extra-judicial part of his opinion; and all was extra-judicial, except the decision that the act of Congress had not purported to give to the corporation of Washington the authority claimed by their lottery law, of controlling the laws of the States within the States themselves. But unable to claim that case, he could not let it go entirely, but went on gratuitously to prove, that notwithstanding the eleventh amendment of the constitution, a State *could* be brought as a defendant, to the bar of his court; and again, that Congress might authorize a corporation of its territory to exercise legislation within a State, and paramount to the laws of that State. I cite the sum and result only of his doctrines, according to the impression made on my mind at the time, and still remaining. If not strictly accurate in circumstance, it is so in substance. This doctrine was so completely refuted by Roane, that if he can be answered, I surrender human reason as a vain and useless faculty, given to bewilder, and not to guide us. And I mention this particular case as one only of several, because it gave occasion to that thorough examination of the constitutional limits between the General and State jurisdictions, which you have asked for. There were two other writers in the same paper, under the signatures of Fletcher of Saltoun, and Somers, who, in a few essays, presented some very luminous and striking views of the question. And there was a particular paper which recapitulated all the cases in which it was thought the federal court had usurped on the State jurisdictions. These essays will be found in the Enquirers of 1821, from May the 10th to July the 13th. It is not in my present power to send them to you, but if Thomas Ritchie can furnish them, I will procure and forward them. If they had been read in the other States, as they were here, I think they would have left, there as here, no dissentients from their doctrine. The subject was taken up by our legislature of 1821–'22, and two draughts of remonstrances were prepared and discussed. As well as I remember, there was no difference of opinion as to the matter of right; but there was as to the expediency of a remonstrance at that time, the general mind of the States being then under extraordinary excitement by the Missouri question;[1] and it was dropped on that consideration. But this case is not dead, it only sleepeth. The Indian Chief said he did not go to war for every petty injury by itself, but put it into his pouch, and when that was full, he then made war. Thank Heaven, we have provided a more peaceable and rational mode of redress.

This practice of Judge Marshall, of travelling out of his case to prescribe what the law would be in a moot case not before the court, is very irregular and very censurable. I recollect another instance, and the more particularly, perhaps, because it in some measure bore on myself. Among the midnight appointments of Mr. Adams, were commissions to some federal justices of the peace for Alexandria. These were signed and sealed by him, but not delivered. I found them on the table of the department of State, on my entrance into office, and I forbade their delivery. Marbury, named in one of them, applied to the Supreme Court for a *mandamus* to the Secretary of State, (Mr. Madison) to deliver the commission intended for him. The court determined at once, that being an original process, they had no cognizance of it; and therefore the question before them was ended. But the Chief Justice went on to lay down what the law would be, had they jurisdiction of the case, to wit: that they should command the delivery. The object was clearly to instruct any other court having the jurisdiction, what they should do if Marbury should apply to them. Besides the impropriety of this gratuitous

---

[1] In 1818, when Missouri petitioned for statehood, the question arose as to whether it should be admitted as a free or a slave state. The furore lasted for three years and resulted in the Missouri Compromise of 1821. – *Eds.*

interference, could anything exceed the perversion of law? For if there is any principle of law never yet contradicted, it is that delivery is one of the essentials to the validity of the deed. Although signed and sealed, yet as long as it remains in the hands of the party himself, it is in *fieri* only, it is not a deed, and can be made so only by its delivery. In the hands of a third person it may be made an escrow. But whatever is in the executive offices is certainly deemed to be in the hands of the President; and in this case, was actually in my hands, because, when I countermanded them, there was as yet no Secretary of State. Yet this case of Marbury and Madison is continually cited by bench and bar, as if it were settled law, without any animadversion on its being merely an *obiter* dissertation of the Chief Justice.

It may be impracticable to lay down any general formula of words which shall decide at once, and with precision, in every case, this limit of jurisdiction. But there are two canons which will guide us safely in most of the cases. 1st. The capital and leading object of the constitution was to leave with the States all authorities which respected their own citizens only, and to transfer to the United States those which respected citizens of foreign or other States: to make us several as to ourselves, but one as to all others. In the latter case, then, constructions should lean to the general jurisdiction, if the words will bear it; and in favor of the States in the former, if possible to be so construed. And indeed, between citizens and citizens of the same State, and under their own laws, I know but a single case in which a jurisdiction is given to the General Government. That is, where anything but gold or silver is made a lawful tender, or the obligation of contracts is any otherwise impaired. The separate legislatures had so often abused that power, that the citizens themselves chose to trust it to the general, rather than to their own special authorities. 2d. On every question of construction, carry ourselves back to the time when the constitution was adopted, recollect the spirit manifested in the debates, and instead of trying what meaning may be squeezed out of the text, or invented against it, conform to the probable one in which it was passed. Let us try Cohen's [*sic*] case[2] by these canons only, referring always, however, for all argument, to the essays before cited.

---

[2] The Supreme Court case *Cohens* v. *Virginia* (1821). – *Eds.*

1. It was between a citizen and his own State, and under a law of his State. It was a domestic case, therefore, and not a foreign one.

2. Can it be believed, that under the jealousies prevailing against the General Government, at the adoption of the constitution, the States meant to surrender the authority of preserving order, of enforcing moral duties and restraining vice, within their own territory? And this is the present case, that of Cohen being under the ancient and general law of gaming. Can any good be effected by taking from the States the moral rule of their citizens, and subordinating it to the general authority, or to one of their corporations, which may justify forcing the meaning of words, hunting after possible constructions, and hanging inference on inference, from heaven to earth, like Jacob's ladder? Such an intention was impossible, and such a licentiousness of construction and inference, if exercised by both governments, as may be done with equal right, would equally authorize both to claim all power, general and particular, and break up the foundations of the Union. Laws are made for men of ordinary understanding, and should, therefore, be construed by the ordinary rules of common sense. Their meaning is not to be sought for in metaphysical subtleties, which may make anything mean everything or nothing, at pleasure. It should be left to the sophisms of advocates, whose trade it is, to prove that a defendant is a plaintiff, though dragged into court, *torto collo*, like Bonaparte's volunteers, into the field in chains, or that a power has been given, because it ought to have been given, *et alia talia*. The States supposed that by their tenth amendment, they had secured themselves against constructive powers. They were not lessoned [made aware] yet by Cohen's case, nor aware of the slipperiness of the eels of the law. I ask for no straining of words against the General Government, nor yet against the States. I believe the States can best govern our home concerns, and the General Government our foreign ones. I wish, therefore, to see maintained that wholesome distribution of powers established by the constitution for the limitation of both; and never to see all offices transferred to Washington, where, further withdrawn from the eyes of the people, they may more secretly be bought and sold as at market.

But the Chief Justice says, "there must be an ultimate arbiter somewhere." True, there must; but does that prove it is either party? The ultimate arbiter is the people of the Union, assembled by their deputies in convention, at the call of Congress, or of two-thirds of the States. Let them decide to which they mean to give an authority claimed by two of their organs. And it has been the peculiar wisdom and felicity of our constitution, to have provided this peaceable appeal, where that of other nations is at once to force.

I rejoice in the example you set of *seriatim* opinions. I have heard it often noticed, and always with high approbation. Some of your brethren will be encouraged to follow it occasionally, and in time, it may be felt by all as a duty, and the sound practice of the primitive court be again restored. Why should not every judge be asked his opinion, and give it from the bench, if only by yea or nay? Besides ascertaining the fact of his opinion, which the public have a right to know, in order to judge whether it is impeachable or not, it would show whether the opinions were unanimous or not, and thus settle more exactly the weight of their authority.

The close of my second sheet warns me that it is time now to relieve you from this letter of unmerciful length. Indeed, I wonder how I have accomplished it, with two crippled wrists, the one scarcely able to move my pen, the other to hold my paper. But I am hurried sometimes beyond the sense of pain, when unbosoming myself to friends who harmonize with me in principle. You and I may differ occasionally in details of minor consequence, as no two minds, more than two faces, are the same in every feature. But our general objects are the same, to preserve the republican form and principles of our constitution and cleave to the salutary distribution of powers which that has established. These are the two sheet anchors of our Union. If driven from either, we shall be in danger of foundering. To my prayers for its safety and perpetuity, I add those for the continuation of your health, happiness, and usefulness to your country.

Ford x: 226–32

## VIII.17 To the Marquis de Lafayette

Monticello, November 4, 1823

My Dear Friend, – Two dislocated wrists and crippled fingers have rendered writing so slow and laborious, as to oblige me to withdraw from nearly all correspondence; not, however, from yours, while I can make a stroke with a pen. We have gone through too many trying scenes together, to forget the sympathies and affections they nourished.

Your trials have indeed been long and severe. When they will end, is yet unknown, but where they will end, cannot be doubted. Alliances, Holy or Hellish, may be formed, and retard the epoch of deliverance, may swell the rivers of blood which are yet to flow, but their own will close the scene, and leave to mankind the right of self-government. I trust that Spain will prove, that a nation cannot be conquered which determines not to be so, and that her success will be the turning of the tide of liberty, no more to be arrested by human efforts. Whether the state of society in Europe can bear a republican government, I doubted, you know, when with you, and I do now. An hereditary chief, strictly limited, the right of war vested in the legislative body, a rigid economy of the public contributions, and absolute interdiction of all useless expenses, will go far towards keeping the government honest and unoppressive. But the only security of all, is in a free press. The force of public opinion cannot be resisted, when permitted freely to be expressed. The agitation it produces must be submitted to. It is necessary, to keep the waters pure.

We are all, for example, in agitation even in our peaceful country. For in peace as well as in war, the mind must be kept in motion. Who is to be the next President, is the topic here of every conversation. My opinion on that subject is what I expressed to you in my last letter. The question will be ultimately reduced to the northernmost and southernmost candidate. The former will get every federal vote in the Union, and many republicans; the latter, all of those denominated *of the old school*; for you are not to believe that these two parties are amalgamated, that the lion and the lamb are lying down together. The Hartford Convention, the victory of [New] Orleans,[1] the peace of Ghent, prostrated the name of federalism. Its votaries abandoned it through shame and mortification; and now call themselves republicans. But the name alone is changed, the principles are the same. For in truth, the parties of Whig and Tory, are those of nature. They exist in all countries, whether called by

---

[1] See *supra*, VIII.15, note 1. – *Eds.*

these names, or by those of Aristocrats and Democrats, *Côté Droite* and *Côté Gauche*, Ultras and Radicals, Serviles, and Liberals. The sickly, weakly, timid man, fears the people, and is a Tory by nature. The healthy, strong and bold, cherishes them, and is formed a Whig by nature. On the eclipse of federalism with us, although not its extinction, its leaders got up the Missouri question,[2] under the false front of lessening the measure of slavery, but with the real view of producing a geographical division of parties, which might insure them the next President. The people of the North went blindfold into the snare, followed their leaders for awhile with a zeal truly moral and laudable, until they became sensible [aware] that they were injuring instead of aiding the real interests of the slaves, that they had been used merely as tools for electioneering purposes; and that trick of hypocrisy then fell as quickly as it had been got up. To that is now succeeding a distinction, which, like that of Republican and Federal, or Whig and Tory, being equally intermixed through every State, threatens none of those geographical schisms which go immediately to a separation. The line of division now, is the preservation of State rights, as reserved in the Constitution, or by strained constructions of that instrument, to merge all into a consolidated government. The Tories are for strengthening the Executive and General Government; the Whigs cherish the representative branch, and the rights reserved by the States, as the bulwark against consolidation, which must immediately generate monarchy. And although this division excites, as yet, no warmth, yet it exists, is well understood, and will be a principle of voting at the ensuing election, with the reflecting men of both parties.

I thank you much for the two books you were so kind as to send me by Mr. [Albert] Gallatin. Miss Wright had before favored me with the first edition of her American work; but her "Few Days in Athens," was entirely new, and has been a treat to me of the highest order. The matter and manner of the dialogue is strictly ancient; and the principles of the sects are beautifully and candidly explained and contrasted; and the scenery and portraiture of the interlocutors are of higher finish than anything in that line left us by the ancients; and like [the poet] Ossian, if not ancient, it is equal to the best morsels of antiquity. I augur, from this instance, that Herculaneum

---

[2] See *supra*, VIII.16, note 1. – *Eds.*

is likely to furnish better specimens of modern than of ancient genius; and may we not hope more from the same pen?

After much sickness, and the accident of a broken and disabled arm, I am again in tolerable health, but extremely debilitated, so as to be scarcely able to walk into my garden. The hebetude of age, too, and extinguishment of interest in the things around me, are weaning me from them, and dispose me with cheerfulness to resign them to the existing generation, satisfied that the daily advance of science will enable them to administer the commonwealth with increased wisdom. You have still many valuable years to give to your country, and with my prayers that they may be years of health and happiness, and especially that they may see the establishment of the principles of government which you have cherished through life, accept the assurance of my affectionate and constant friendship and respect.

L & B xv: 490–4

## VIII.18 To Henry Lee

Monticello, August 10, 1824

Sir, – I have duly received your favor of the 14th and with it the prospectus of a newspaper which it covered. If the style and spirit of that should be maintained in the paper itself it will be truly worthy of the public patronage. As to myself it is many years since I have ceased to read but a single paper. I am no longer therefore a general subscriber for any other. Yet to encourage the hopeful in the outset I have sometimes subscribed for the 1st year on the condition of being discontinued at the end of it, without further warning. I do the same now with pleasure for yours, and unwilling to have outstanding accounts which I am liable to forget, I now inclose the price of the tri-weekly paper. I am no believer in the amalgamation of parties, nor do I consider it as either desirable or useful for the politics should never be permitted to enter into social intercourse, or to disturb it's friendships, its charities or justice. In that form they are censors of the conduct of each other, and useful watchmen for the public. Men by their constitutions are naturally divided into two parties. 1. Those who fear and distrust the people, and wish to draw all powers from them into the hands of the higher classes. 2ndly those who identify themselves with the people, have confidence in them, cherish and consider them as the most honest & safe, altho' not the most wise depository of the public interests. In every country these two parties exist, and in every one where they are free to think, speak, and write, they will declare themselves. Call them therefore liberals and serviles, Jacobins and Ultras, whigs and tories, republicans and federalists, aristocrats and democrats or by whatever name you please, they are the same parties still and pursue the same object. The last appellation of aristocrats and democrats is the true one expressing the essence of all. A paper which shall be governed by the spirit of Mr. Madison's celebrated report, of which you express in your prospectus so just and high an approbation, cannot be false to the rights of all classes. The grandfathers of the present generation of your family I knew well. They were friends and fellow-laborers with me in the same cause and principle. Their descendants cannot follow better guides. Accept the assurance of my best wishes & respectful consideration.

Ford x: 317–18

## VIII.19 To William Short

Monticello, January 8, 1825

Dear Sir, – I returned the first volume of Hall by a mail of a week ago, and by this, shall return the second. We have kept them long, but every member of the family wished to read his book, in which case, you know, it had a long gauntlet to run. It is impossible to read thoroughly such writings as those of Harper and Otis, who take a page to say what requires but a sentence, or rather, who give you whole pages of what is nothing to the purpose. A cursory race over the ground is as much as they can claim. It is easy for them, at this day, to endeavor to whitewash their party, when the greater part are dead of those who witnessed what passed, others old and become indifferent to the subject, and others indisposed to take the trouble of answering them. As to Otis, his attempt is to prove that the sun does not shine at mid-day; that that is not a fact which everyone saw. He merits no notice. It is well known that Harper had little scruple about facts where detection was not obvious. By placing in false lights whatever admits it, and passing over in silence what does not, a plausible aspect may be presented of anything. He takes great pains to prove, for instance, that Hamilton was no monarchist, by exaggerating his own intimacy with him, and the impossibility, if he was so, that he should not, at some time, have betrayed it to him. This may pass with uninformed readers, but not with those who have had it from Hamilton's own mouth. I am one of those, and but one of many. At my own table, in presence of Mr. Adams, Knox,[1] Randolph, and myself, in a dispute between Mr. Adams and himself, he avowed his preference of monarchy over every other government, and his opinion that the English was the most perfect model of government ever devised by the wit of man, Mr. Adams agreeing "if its corruptions were done away." While Hamilton insisted that "with these corruptions it was perfect, and without them it would be an impracticable government." Can any one read Mr. Adam's defence of the American constitutions[2] without seeing that he was a monarchist? And J. Q. Adams, the son, was more explicit than the father, in his answer to Pain[e]'s *Rights of Man.* So much for leaders. Their followers were divided. Some went the same lengths, others, and I believe the greater part, only wished a stronger Executive. When I arrived at New York in 1790, to take a part in the administration, being fresh from the French revolution, while in its first and pure stage, and consequently somewhat whetted up in my own republican principles, I found a state of things, in the general society of the place, which I could not have supposed possible. Being a stranger there, I was feasted from table to table, at large set dinners, the parties generally from twenty to thirty. The revolution I had left, and that we had just gone through in the recent change of our own government, being the common topics of conversation, I was astonished to find the general prevalence of monarchical sentiments, insomuch that in maintaining those of republicanism, I had always the whole company on my hands, never scarcely finding among them a single co-advocate in that argument, unless some old member of Congress happened to be present. The furthest that any one would go, in support of the

---

[1] See *supra*, VIII.14, note 2. – *Eds.*
[2] John Adams, *A Defense of the Constitutions of Government of the United States of America* (Philadelphia, 1787). – *Eds.*

republican features of our new government, would be to say, "the present constitution is well as a beginning, and may be allowed a fair trial; but it is, in fact, only a stepping stone to something better." Among their writers, Denny, the editor of the Portfolio, who was a kind of oracle with them, and styled the Addison of America, openly avowed his preference of monarchy over all other forms of government, prided himself on the avowal, and maintained it by argument freely and without reserve, in his publications. I do not, myself, know that the Essex junto[3] of Boston were monarchists, but I have always heard it so said, and never doubted.

These, my dear Sir, are but detached items from a great mass of proofs then fully before the public. They are unknown to you, because you were absent in Europe, and they are now disavowed by the party. But, had it not been for the firm and determined stand then made by a counter-party, no man can say what our government would have been at this day. Monarchy, to be sure, is now defeated, and they wish it should be forgotten that it was ever advocated. They see that it is desperate [i.e. hopeless], and treat its imputation to them as a calumny; and I verily believe that none of them have it now in direct aim. Yet the spirit is not done away. The same party takes now what they deem the next best ground, the consolidation of the government; the giving to the federal member of the government, by unlimited constructions [interpretations] of the constitution, a control over all the functions of the States, and the concentration of all power ultimately at Washington.

The true history of that conflict of parties will never be in possession of the public, until, by the death of the actors in it, the hoards of their letters shall be broken up and given to the world. I should not fear to appeal to those of Harper himself, if he has kept copies of them, for abundant proof that he was himself a monarchist. I shall not live to see these unrevealed proofs, nor probably you; for time will be requisite. But time will, in the end, produce the truth. And, after all, it is but a truth which exists in every country, where not suppressed by the rod of despotism. Men, according to their constitutions, and the circumstances in which they are placed, differ honestly in opinion. Some are whigs, liberals, democrats, call them what you please. Others are tories, serviles,

[3] See *supra*, I.19, note I. – *Eds.*

aristocrats, &c. The latter fear the people, and wish to transfer all power to the higher classes of society; the former consider the people as the safest depository of power in the last resort; they cherish them therefore, and wish to leave in them all the powers to the exercise of which they are competent. This is the division of sentiment now existing in the United States. It is the common division of whig and tory, or according to our denominations of republican and federal; and is the most salutary of all divisions, and ought, therefore, to be fostered, instead of being amalgamated. For, take away this, and some more dangerous principle of division will take its place. But there is really no amalgamation. The parties exist now as heretofore. The one, indeed, has thrown off its old name, and has not yet assumed a new one, although obviously consolidationists. And among those in the offices of every denomination I believe it to be a bare minority.

I have gone into these facts to show how one-sided a view of this case Harper has presented. I do not recall these recollections with pleasure, but rather wish to forget them, nor did I ever permit them to affect social intercourse. And now, least of all, am disposed to do so. Peace and good will with all mankind is my sincere wish. I willingly leave to the present generation to conduct their affairs as they please. And in my general affection to the whole human family, and my particular devotion to my friends, be assured of the high and special estimation in which yourself is cordially held.

Ford x: 328–35

# IX  Race and Slavery

*whom he much admired, and whom he had appointed official surveyor of the District of Columbia – "No body wishes more than I do to see such proofs as you exhibit, that nature has given to our black brethren, talents equal to those of the other colors of men, and that the appearance of a want of them is owing merely to the degraded condition of their existence, both in Africa & America."*

## IX.I Report of Government for the Western Territory

[March 22, 1784]

The Committee to whom was recommitted the report of a plan for a temporary government of the Western territory have agreed to the following resolutions.

Resolved, that so much of the territory ceded or to be ceded by individual states to the United States as is already purchased or shall be purchased of the Indian inhabitants & offered for sale by Congress, shall be divided into distinct states, in the following manner, as nearly as such cessions will admit; that is to say, by parallels of latitude, so that each state shall comprehend from South to North two degrees of latitude beginning to count from the completion of thirty-one degrees North of the Equator; and by meridians of longitude, one of which shall pass thro' the lowest point of the rapids of Ohio, and the other through the Western Cape of the mouth of the Great Kanhaway, but the territory Eastward of this last meridian, between the Ohio, Lake Erie, & Pennsylvania shall be one state, whatsoever may be its comprehension of latitude. That which may lie beyond the completion of the 45th degree between the s[ai]d. meridians shall make part of the state adjoining it on the South, and that part of the Ohio which is between the same meridians coinciding nearly with the parallel of 39° shall be substituted so far in lieu of that parallel as a boundary line.

That the settlers on any territory so purchased & offered for sale shall, either on their own petition, or on the order of Congress, receive authority from them with appointments of time & place for their free males of full age, within the limits of their state, to meet together for the purpose of establishing a temporary government, to adopt the constitution and laws of any one of the original states, so that such laws nevertheless shall be subject to alteration by their ordinary legislature; & to erect, subject to a like alteration, counties or townships for the election of members for their legislature.

That such temporary government shall only continue in force in any state until it shall have acquired 20,000 free inhabitants, when giving due proof thereof to Congress, they shall receive from them authority with appointment of time & place to call a convention of representatives to establish a permanent Constitution & Government for themselves. Provided that both the temporary & permanent governments be established on these principles as their basis. 1. That they shall forever remain a part of this confederacy of the United States of America. 2. That in their persons, property & territory they shall be subject to the Government of the United States in Congress assembled, & to the articles of Confederation in all those cases in which the original states shall be so subject. 3. That they shall be subject to pay a part of the federal debts contracted or to be contracted, to be apportioned on them by Congress, according to the same common rule & measure, by which apportionments thereof shall be made on the other states. 4. That their respective Governments shall be in republican forms and shall admit no person to be a citizen who holds any hereditary title. 5. That after the year 1800 of the Christian æra, there shall be neither slavery nor involuntary servitude in any of the s[ai]d states, otherwise than in punishment of crimes whereof the party shall have been convicted to have been personally guilty.

That whensoever any of the s[ai]d states shall have, of free inhabitants, as many as shall then be in any one the least numerous, of the thirteen original states, such state shall be admitted by it's delegates into the Congress of the United States on an equal footing with the said original states: provided nine States agree to such admission according to the reservation of the 11th of the articles of Confederation, and in order to adopt the s[ai]d articles of confederation to the state of Congress when it's numbers shall be thus increased, it shall be proposed to the legislatures of the states originally parties thereto, to require the assent of two thirds of the United States in Congress assembled in all those cases wherein by the said articles the assent of nine states is now required; which being agreed to by them shall be binding on the new states. Until such admission by their delegates into Congress, any of the said states after the establishment of their temporary government shall have authority to keep a sitting member in Congress, with a right of debating, but not of voting.

That the preceding articles shall be formed into a charter of compact, shall be duly executed by the president of the United States in Congress assembled, under his hand & the seal of the United States, shall be promulgated & shall stand as fundamental constitutions between the thirteen original states and each of the several states now newly described unalterable but by the joint consent of the United States in Congress assembled, & of the particular state within which such alteration is proposed to be made.

That measures not inconsistent with the principles of the Confedn. & necessary for the preservation of peace & good order among the settlers in any of the said new states until they shall assume a temporary Government as aforesaid, may from time to time be taken by the U.S. in Congress assembled.

Ford III: 429–32

## IX.2 To Dr. Richard Price

Paris, August 7, 1785

Sir, – Your favor of July 2. came duly to hand. The concern you therein express as to the effect of your pamphlet[1] in America, induces me to trouble you with some observations on that subject. From my acquaintance with that country I think I am able to judge with some degree of certainty of the manner in which it will have been received. Southward of the Chesapeak it will find but few readers concurring with it in sentiment on the subject of slavery. From the mouth to the head of the Chesapeak, the bulk of the people will approve it in theory, and it will find a respectable minority ready to adopt it in practice, a minority which for weight & worth of character preponderates against the greater number, who have not the courage to divest their families of a property which however keeps their conscience inquiet. Northward of the Chesapeak you may find here & there an opponent to your doctrine as you may find here & there a robber & a murderer, but in no greater number. In that part of America, there being but few slaves, they can easily disencumber themselves of them, and emancipation is put into such a train that in a few years there will be no slaves northward of Maryland. In Maryland I do not find such a disposition to begin the redress of this enormity as in Virginia. This is the next state to which we may turn our eyes for the interesting spectacle of

[1] Richard Price, *Observations on the American War* (Philadelphia, 1785). – *Eds.*

justice in conflict with avarice & oppression: a conflict wherein the sacred side is gaining daily recruits, from the influx into office of young men grown & growing up. These have sucked in the principles of liberty as it were with their mother's milk; and it is to them I look with anxiety to turn the fate of this question. Be not therefore discouraged. What you have written will do a great deal of good: and could you still trouble yourself with our welfare, no man is more able to give aid to the labouring side. The college of William & Mary in Williamsburg, since the remodelling of it's plan, is the place where are collected together all the young men (of Virginia) under preparation for public life. They are there under the direction (most of them) of a Mr. [George] Wythe one of the most virtuous of characters, and whose sentiments on the subject of slavery are unequivocal. I am satisfied if you could resolve to address an exhortation to those young men, with all that eloquence of which you are master, that it's influence on the future decision of this important question would be great, perhaps decisive. Thus you see that, so far from thinking you have cause to repent of what you have done, I wish you to do more, and wish it on an assurance of it's effect. The information I have received from America of the reception of your pamphlet in the different states agrees with the expectations I had formed. Our country is getting into a ferment against yours, or rather has caught it from yours. God knows how this will end; but assuredly in one extreme or the other. There can be no medium between those who have loved so much. I think the decision is in your power as yet, but will not be so long. I pray you to be assured of the sincerity of the esteem & respect with which I have the honour to be Sir your most obed[ien]t humble serv[an]t.

Ford IV: 82–4

## IX.3 A Bill Concerning Slaves

[October 1785]

Section I. Be it enacted by the General Assembly, that no person shall, henceforth, be slaves within this commonwealth, except such as were so on the first day of this present session of Assembly, and the descendants of the females of them.

Sect. II. Negroes and mulattoes which shall hereafter be brought into this commonwealth and kept therein one whole year, together, or so long at different times as shall amount to one year, shall be free. But if they shall not depart the commonwealth within one year thereafter they shall be out of the protection of the laws.

Sect. III. Those which shall come into this commonwealth of their own accord shall be out of the protection of the laws; save only such as being seafaring persons and navigating vessels hither, shall not leave the same while here more than twenty four hours together.

Sect. IV. It shall not be lawful for any person to emancipate a slave but by deed executed, proved and recorded as is required by law in the case of a conveyance of goods and chattels, on consideration not deemed valuable in law, or by last will and testament, and with the free consent of such slave, expressed in presence of the court of the county wherein he resides. And if such slave, so emancipated, shall not within one year thereafter, depart the commonwealth, he shall be out of the protection of the laws. All conditions, restrictions and limitations annexed to any act of emancipation shall be void from the time such emancipation is to take place.

Sect. V. If any white woman shall have a child by a negro or mulatto, she and her child shall depart the commonwealth within one year thereafter. If they shall fail so to do, the woman shall be out of the protection of the laws, and the child shall be bound out by the Aldermen of the county, in like manner as poor orphans are by law directed to be, and within one year after its term of service expired shall depart the commonwealth, or on failure so to do, shall be out of the protection of the laws.

Sect. VI. Where any of the persons before described shall be disabled from departing the commonwealth by grievous sickness, the protection of the law shall be continued to him until such disability be removed: And if the county shall in the meantime, incur any expense in taking care of him, as of other county poor, the Aldermen shall be intitled to recover the same from his master, if he had one, his heirs, executors and administrators.

Sect. VII. No negro or mulatto shall be a witness except in pleas of the commonwealth against negroes or mulattoes, or in civil pleas wherein negroes or mulattoes alone shall be parties.

Sect. VIII. No slave shall go from the tenements of his master, or other person with whom he lives, without a pass, or some letter or token whereby it may appear that he is proceeding by authority from his master, employer, or overseer: If he does, it shall be lawful for any person to apprehend and carry him before a Justice of the Peace to be by his order punished with stripes, or not, in his discretion.

Sect. IX. No slaves shall keep any arms whatever, nor pass, unless with written orders from his master or employer, or in his company, with arms from one place to another. Arms in possession of a slave contrary to this prohibition shall be forfeited to him who will seize them.

Sect. X. Riots, routs, unlawful assemblies, trespasses and seditious speeches by a negro or mulatto shall be punished with stripes at the discretion of a Justice of the Peace; and he who will may apprehend and carry him before such Justice.

Ford II: 201–3

## IX.4 To Jean Nicholas Démeunier[1]

[June 26, 1786]

... M. de Meusnier [Démeunier], where he mentions that the slave-law has been passed in Virginia, without the clause of emancipation, is pleased to mention that neither Mr. Wythe nor Mr. Jefferson were present to make the proposition they had meditated; from which people, who do not give themselves the trouble to reflect or enquire, might conclude hastily that their absence was the cause why the proposition was not made; and of course that there were not in the assembly persons of virtue and firmness enough to propose the clause for emancipation. This supposition would not be true. There were persons there who wanted neither the virtue to propose, nor talents to enforce the proposition had they seen that the disposition of the legislature was ripe for it. These worthy characters would feel themselves wounded, degraded, and discouraged by this idea. Mr. Jefferson would therefore be obliged to M. de Meusnier to mention it in some such manner as this. "Of the

---

[1] Jean Nicholas Démeunier was editor of the *Encyclopédie Méthodique*. He asked TJ to comment on his article "Etats Unis" and to answer a series of queries about American law, government, and sundry subjects. – *Eds.*

two commissioners who had concerted the amendatory clause for the gradual emancipation of slaves Mr. Wythe could not be present as being a member of the judiciary department, and Mr. Jefferson was absent on the legation to France. But there wanted not in that assembly men of virtue enough to propose, and talents to vindicate this clause. But they saw that the moment of doing it with success was not yet arrived, and that an unsuccesful effort, as too often happens, would only rivet still closer the chains of bondage, and retard the moment of delivery to this oppressed description of men. What a stupendous, what an incomprehensible machine is man! Who can endure toil, famine, stripes, imprisonment or death itself in vindication of his own liberty, and the next moment be deaf to all those motives whose power supported him thro' his trial, and inflict on his fellow men a bondage, one hour of which is fraught with more misery than ages of that which he rose in rebellion to oppose. But we must await with patience the workings of an over-ruling providence, and hope that that is preparing the deliverance of these our suffering brethren. When the measure of their tears shall be full, when their groans shall have involved heaven itself in darkness, doubtless a god of justice will awaken to their distress, and by diffusing light and liberality among their oppressors, or at length by his exterminating thunder, manifest his attention to the things of this world, and that they are not left to the guidance of a blind fatality."

Ford IV: 184–5

## IX.5 To Jean Pierre Brissot de Warville

Paris, February 11, 1788

Sir, – I am very sensible [aware] of the honour you propose to me of becoming a member of the society for the abolition of the slave trade. You know that nobody wishes more ardently to see an abolition not only of the trade but of the condition of slavery: and certainly nobody will be more willing to encounter every sacrifice for that object. But the influence & information of the friends to this proposition in France will be far above the need of my association. I am here as a public servant; and those whom I serve having never yet been able to give their voice against this practice, it is decent for me to avoid too public a demonstration of my wishes to see it abolished. Without serving the cause here, it might render me less able to serve it beyond the water. I trust you will be sensible of the prudence of those motives therefore which govern my conduct on this occasion, & be assured of my wishes for the success of your undertaking, and the sentiments of esteem & respect with which I have the honour to be Sir your most obed[ien]t. humble serv[an]t.

Ford v: 6–7

## IX.6 *Notes on Virginia*: Query XIV

### Laws

To emancipate all slaves born after passing the act. The bill reported by the revisers[1] does not itself contain this proposition; but an amendment containing it was prepared, to be offered to the legislature whenever the bill should be taken up and further directing, that they should continue with their parents to a certain age, then be brought up, at the public expence, to tillage, arts, or sciences, according to their geniusses, till the females should be eighteen, and the males twenty-one years of age, when they should be colonized to such place as the circumstances of the time should render most proper, sending them out with arms, implements of houshold and of the handicraft arts, seeds, pairs of the useful domestic animals, &c. to declare them a free and independant people, and extend to them our alliance and protection, till they shall have acquired strength; and to send vessels at the same time to other parts of the world for an equal number of white inhabitants; to induce whom to migrate hither, proper encouragements were to be proposed. It will probably be asked, Why not retain and incorporate the blacks into the state, and thus save the expence of supplying by importation of white settlers, the vacancies they will leave? Deep rooted prejudices entertained by the whites; ten thousand recollections, by the blacks, of the injuries they have sustained; new provocations; the real distinctions which nature has made; and many other

---

[1] *The Report of the Revisors* was prepared by Jefferson, Wythe, and Pendleton, and reported to the legislature on June 18, 1779. – *Eds.*

circumstances will divide us into parties, and produce convulsions, which will probably never end but in the extermination of the one or the other race. – To these objections, which are political, may be added others, which are physical and moral. The first difference which strikes us is that of colour. Whether the black of the negro resides in the reticular membrane between the skin and scarfskin, or in the scarfskin itself; whether it proceeds from the colour of the blood, the colour of the bile, or from that of some other secretion, the difference is fixed in nature, and is as real as if its seat and cause were better known to us. And is this difference of no importance? Is it not the foundation of a greater or less share of beauty in the two races? Are not the fine mixtures of red and white, the expressions of every passion by greater or less suffusions of colour in the one, preferable to that eternal monotony, which reigns in the countenances, that immovable veil of black which covers all the emotions of the other race? Add to these, flowing hair, a more elegant symmetry of form, their own judgment in favour of the whites, declared by their preference of them as uniformly as is the preference of the Oran ootan [orangutan] for the black woman over those of his own species. The circumstance of superior beauty, is thought worthy attention in the propagation of our horses, dogs, and other domestic animals; why not in that of man? Besides those of colour, figure, and hair, there are other physical distinctions proving a difference of race. They have less hair on the face and body. They secrete less by the kidnies, and more by the glands of the skin, which gives them a very strong and disagreeable odour. This greater degree of transpiration, renders them more tolerant of heat, and less so of cold than the whites. Perhaps too a difference of structure in the pulmonary apparatus, which a late ingenious[2] experimentalist has discovered to be the principal regulator of animal heat, may have disabled them from extricating, in the act of inspiration, so much of that fluid from the outer air, or obliged them in expiration, to part with more of it. They seem to require less sleep. A black after hard labour through the day, will be induced by the slightest amusements to sit up till midnight or later, though knowing he must be out with the first dawn of the morning. They are at least as brave,

---

[2] Crawford. [Adair Crawford, *Experiments & Observations on Animal Heat* (London, 1779). – *Eds.*]

and more adventuresome. But this may perhaps proceed from a want of forethought, which prevents their seeing a danger till it be present. When present, they do not go through it with more coolness or steadiness than the whites. They are more ardent after their female; but love seems with them to be more an eager desire, than a tender delicate mixture of sentiment and sensation. Their griefs are transient. Those numberless afflictions, which render it doubtful whether heaven has given life to us in mercy or in wrath, are less felt, and sooner forgotten with them. In general, their existence appears to participate more of sensation than reflection. To this must be ascribed their disposition to sleep when abstracted from their diversions, and unemployed in labour. An animal whose body is at rest, and who does not reflect, must be disposed to sleep of course. Comparing them by their faculties of memory, reason, and imagination, it appears to me that in memory they are equal to the whites; in reason much inferior, as I think one could scarcely be found capable of tracing and comprehending the investigations of Euclid: and that in imagination they are dull, tasteless, and anomalous. It would be unfair to follow them to Africa for this investigation. We will consider them here, on the same stage with the whites, and where the facts are not apochryphal on which a judgment is to be formed. It will be right to make great allowances for the difference of condition, of education, of conversation, of the sphere in which they move. Many millions of them have been brought to, and born in America. Most of them, indeed, have been confined to tillage, to their own homes, and their own society: yet many have been so situated, that they might have availed themselves of the conversation of their masters; many have been brought up to the handicraft arts, and from that circumstance have always been associated with the whites. Some have been liberally educated, and all have lived in countries where the arts and sciences are cultivated to a considerable degree, and have had before their eyes samples of the best works from abroad. The Indians, with no advantages of this kind, will often carve figures on their pipes not destitute of design and merit. They will crayon out an animal, a plant, or a country, so as to prove the existence of a germ in their minds which only wants cultivation. They astonish you with strokes of the most sublime oratory; such as prove their reason and sentiment strong, their imagination glowing and elevated. But never yet could I find that a black had uttered a thought above the level of plain narration; never seen even an elementary trait of painting or sculpture. In music they are more generally gifted than the whites, with accurate ears for tune and time, and they have been found capable of imagining a small catch.[3] Whether they will be equal to the composition of a more extensive run of melody, or of complicated harmony, is yet to be proved. Misery is often the parent of the most affecting touches in poetry. – Among the blacks is misery enough, God knows, but no poetry. Love is the peculiar œstrum of the poet. Their love is ardent, but it kindles the senses only, not the imagination. Religion, indeed, has produced a Phyllis Whately;[4] but it could not produce a poet. The compositions published under her name are below the dignity of criticism. The heroes of the Dunciad are to her, as Hercules to the author of that poem. Ignatius Sancho[5] has approached nearer to merit in composition; yet his letters do more honour to the heart than the head. They breathe the purest effusions of friendship and general philanthropy, and show how great a degree of the latter may be compounded with strong religious zeal. He is often happy in the turn of his compliments, and his style is easy and familiar, except when he affects a Shandean fabrication of words.[6] But his imagination is wild and extravagant, escapes incessantly from every restraint of reason and taste, and, in the course of its vagaries, leaves a tract of thought as incoherent and eccentric, as is the course of a meteor through the sky. His subjects should often have led him to a process of sober reasoning; yet we find him always substituting sentiment for demonstration. Upon the whole, though we admit him to the first place among those of his own color who have presented themselves to the public judgment, yet when we compare him with the writers of the race among whom he lived and particularly with the epistolary class in which he has taken his own stand, we are compelled to enrol him at the bottom of the column. This criticism supposes the letters published under his name to be genuine, and to have received

---

[3] The instrument proper to them is the Banjar [banjo], which they brought hither from Africa, and which is the original of the guitar, its chords being precisely the four lower chords of the guitar.

[4] Phyllis Wheatley, *Poems on Various Subjects* . . . (London, 1773). – *Eds.*

[5] Ex-slave and author of *Letters, with Memoirs of his Life* (London, 1782). – *Eds.*

[6] TJ refers to Laurence Sterne's *Tristram Shandy*, one of his favorite novels, and its author's penchant for freely associating words and ideas. – *Eds.*

amendment from no other hand; points which would not be of easy investigation. The improvement of the blacks in body and mind, in the first instance of their mixture with the whites, has been observed by every one, and proves that their inferiority is not the effect merely of their condition of life. We know that among the Romans, about the Augustan age especially, the condition of their slaves was much more deplorable than that of the blacks on the continent of America. The two sexes were confined in separate apartments, because to raise a child cost the master more than to buy one. Cato, for a very restricted indulgence to his slaves in this particular,[7] took from them a certain price. But in this country the slaves multiply as fast as the free inhabitants. Their situation and manners place the commerce between the two sexes almost without restraint. – The same Cato, on a principle of economy, always sold his sick and superannuated slaves. He gives it as a standing precept to a master visiting his farm, to sell his old oxen, old waggons, old tools, old and diseased servants, and everything else become useless. "Vendat boves vetulos, plaustrum vetus, feramenta vetera, servum senem, servum morbosum, si quid aliud supersit vendat." Cato de re rusticâ, c. 2. The American slaves cannot enumerate this among the injuries and insults they receive. It was the common practice to expose in the island Æsculapius, in the Tyber, diseased slaves whose cure was like to become tedious.[8] The Emperor Claudius, by an edict, gave freedom to such of them as should recover, and first declared that if any person chose to kill rather than to expose them, it should be deemed homicide. The exposing them is a crime of which no instance has existed with us; and were it to be followed by death, it would be punished capitally. We are told of a certain Vedius Pollio, who, in the presence of Augustus, would have given a slave as food to his fish, for having broken a glass. With the Romans, the regular method of taking the evidence of their slaves was under torture. Here it has been thought better never to resort to their evidence. When a master was murdered, all his slaves, in the same house, or within hearing, were condemned to death. Here punishment falls on the guilty only, and as precise proof is required against him as against a freeman. Yet notwithstanding these and

---

[7] Τοὺς δούλους ἔταξεν ὡρισμένου νομίσματος ὁμιλεῖν ταῖς θεραπαινίσιν. – Plutarch. Cato.

[8] Suet. Claud. 25.

other discouraging circumstances among the Romans, their slaves were often their rarest artists. They excelled too in science, insomuch as to be usually employed as tutors to their master's children. Epictetus, Terence, and Phædrus, were slaves. But they were of the race of whites. It is not their condition then, but nature, which has produced the distinction. – Whether further observation will or will not verify the conjecture, that nature has been less bountiful to them in the endowments of the head, I believe that in those of the heart she will be found to have done them justice. That disposition to theft with which they have been branded, must be ascribed to their situation, and not to any depravity of the moral sense. The man in whose favour no laws of property exist, probably feels himself less bound to respect those made in favour of others. When arguing for ourselves, we lay it down as a fundamental, that laws, to be just, must give a reciprocation of right: that, without this, they are mere arbitrary rules of conduct, founded in force, and not in conscience; and it is a problem which I give to the master to solve, whether the religious precepts against the violation of property were not framed for him as well as his slave? And whether the slave may not as justifiably take a little from one who has taken all from him, as he may slay one who would slay him? That a change in the relations in which a man is placed should change his ideas of moral right and wrong, is neither new, nor peculiar to the colour of the blacks. Homer tells us it was so 2600 years ago.

Ἥμισυ, γὰρ τ᾽ ἀρετῆς ἀποαίνυται εὐρύοπα Ζεὺς
Ἀνέρος, εὖτ᾽ ἄν μιν κατὰ δούλιον ἦμαρ ἕλῃσιν.

*Od. 17. 323.*

Jove fix'd it certain, that whatever day
Makes man a slave, takes half his worth away.

But the slaves of which Homer speaks were whites. Notwithstanding these considerations which must weaken their respect for the laws of property, we find among them numerous instances of the most rigid integrity, and as many as among their better instructed masters, of benevolence, gratitude, and unshaken fidelity. The opinion that they are inferior in the faculties of reason and imagination, must be hazarded with great diffidence. To justify a general conclusion, requires many observations, even where the subject may be submitted to the Anatomical knife, to Optical glasses, to analysis by fire or by solvents. How much more then where it is a faculty, not a substance, we are examining; where it eludes the research of all the senses; where the conditions of its existence are various and variously combined; where the effects of those which are present or absent bid defiance to calculation; let me add too, as a circumstance of great tenderness, where our conclusion would degrade a whole race of men from the rank in the scale of beings which their Creator may perhaps have given them. To our reproach it must be said, that though for a century and a half we have had under our eyes the races of black and of red men, they have never yet been viewed by us as subjects of natural history. I advance it, therefore, as a suspicion only, that the blacks, whether originally a distinct race, or made distinct by time and circumstances, are inferior to the whites in the endowments both of body and mind. It is not against experience to suppose that different species of the same genus, or varieties of the same species, may possess different qualifications. Will not a lover of natural history then, one who views the gradations in all the races of animals with the eye of philosophy, excuse an effort to keep those in the department of man as distinct as nature has formed them? This unfortunate difference of colour, and perhaps of faculty, is a powerful obstacle to the emancipation of these people. Many of their advocates, while they wish to vindicate the liberty of human nature, are anxious also to preserve its dignity and beauty. Some of these, embarrassed by the question, "What further is to be done with them?" join themselves in opposition with those who are actuated by sordid avarice only. Among the Romans emancipation required but one effort. The slave, when made free, might mix with, without staining the blood of his master. But with us a second is necessary, unknown to history. When freed, he is to be removed beyond the reach of mixture.

Ford III: 243–50

## IX.7 *Notes on Virginia*: Query XVIII

*The particular customs and manners that may happen to be received in that State?*

It is difficult to determine on the standard by which the manners of a nation may be tried, whether *catholic* or *particular*. It is more difficult for a native to bring to that standard the manners of his own nation, familiarized to him by habit. There must doubtless be an unhappy influence on the manners of our people produced by the existence of slavery among us. The whole commerce between master and slave is a perpetual exercise of the most boisterous passions, the most unremitting despotism on the one part, and degrading submissions on the other. Our children see this, and learn to imitate it; for man is an imitative animal. This quality is the germ of all education in him. From his cradle to his grave he is learning to do what he sees others do. If a parent could find no motive either in his philanthropy or his self-love, for restraining the intemperance of passion towards his slave, it should always be a sufficient one that his child is present. But generally it is not sufficient. The parent storms, the child looks on, catches the lineaments of wrath, puts on the same airs in the circle of smaller slaves, gives a loose to the worst of passions, and thus nursed, educated, and daily exercised in tyranny, cannot but be stamped by it with odious peculiarities. The man must be a prodigy who can retain his manners and morals undepraved by such circumstances. And with what execrations should the statesman be loaded, who permitting one half the citizens thus to trample on the rights of the other, transforms those into despots, and these into enemies, destroys the morals of the one part, and the *amor patriæ* of the other. For if a slave can have a country in this world, it must be any other in preference to that in which he is born to live and labour for another: in which he must lock up the faculties of his nature, contribute as far as depends on his individual endeavours to the evanishment of the human race, or entail his own miserable condition on the endless generations proceeding from him. With the morals of the people, their industry also is destroyed. For in a warm climate, no man will labour for himself who can make another labour for him. This is so true, that of the proprietors of slaves a very small proportion indeed are ever seen to labour. And can the liberties of a nation be thought secure when we have removed their only firm basis, a conviction in the minds of the people that these liberties are of the gift of God? That they are not to be violated but with his wrath? Indeed I tremble for my country when I reflect that God is just: that his justice cannot sleep forever: that considering numbers, nature and natural means only, a revolution of the wheel of fortune, an exchange of situation, is among possible events: that it may become probable by super-natural interference! The Almighty has no attribute which can take side with us in such a contest. – But it is impossible to be temperate and to pursue this subject through the various considerations of policy, of morals, of history natural and civil. We must be contented to hope they will force their way into every one's mind. I think a change already perceptible, since the origin of the present revol-ution. The spirit of the master is abating, that of the slave rising from the dust, his condition mollifying, the way I hope preparing, under the auspices of heaven, for a total emancipation, and that this is disposed, in the order of events, to be with the consent of the masters, rather than by their extirpation.

Ford III: 266–8

## IX.8 To Dr. Edward Bancroft

Paris, January 26, 1789

Dear Sir, – I have deferred answering your letter on the subject of slaves because you permitted me to do it till a moment of leisure, and that moment rarely comes, and because too I could not answer you with such a degree of certainty as to merit any notice. I do not recollect the conversation at Vincennes to which you allude but can repeat still on the same ground, on which I must have done then, that as far as I can judge from the experiments which have been made to give liberty to, or rather, to abandon persons whose habits have been formed in slavery is like abandoning children. Many quakers in Virginia seated their slaves on their lands as tenants. They were distant from me, and therefore I cannot be particular in the details, because I never had very particular information. I cannot say whether they were to pay a rent in money, or a share of the produce: but I remember that the landlord was obliged to plan their crops for them, to direct all their operations during every season & accord-ing to the weather. But what is more afflicting, he was obliged to watch them daily & almost constantly to make them work, & even to whip them. A man's moral sense must be unusually strong, if slavery does not make him a thief. He who is permitted by law to have no property of his own, can with difficulty conceive that property is founded in anything but force. These slaves chose to steal from their neighbors rather than work; they became public nuisances and in most instances were reduced to slavery again. But I will beg of you to make no use of this imperfect information (unless in common conversation). I shall go to America in the Spring & return in the fall. During my stay in Virginia I shall be in the neighborhood where many of these trials were made. I will inform myself very particularly of them, & communicate the information to you. Besides these there is an instance since I came away of a young man (Mr. Mayo) who died and gave freedom to all his slaves, about 200. This is about 4 years ago. I shall know how they have turned out. Notwithstanding the discouraging result of these experiments, I am decided on my final return to America to try this one. I shall endeavor to import as many Germans as I have grown slaves. I will settle them and my slaves, on farms of 50 acres each, intermingled, and place all on the footing of the Metayers (Medietani) of Europe. Their children shall be brought up, as others are, in habits of property and foresight, & I have no doubt but that they will be good citizens. Some of their fathers will be so: others I suppose will need government. With these, all that can be done is to oblige them to labour as the labouring poor of Europe do, and to apply to their comfortable subsistence the produce of their labour, retaining such a moderate portion of it as may be a just equivalent for the use of the lands they labour and the stocks & other necessary advances . . .

Ford v: 66–8

## IX.9 To Benjamin Banneker

Philadelphia, August 30, 1791

Sir, – I thank you sincerely for your letter of the 19th instant and for the Almanac it contained. No body wishes more than I do to see such proofs as you exhibit, that nature has given to our black brethren, talents equal to those of the other colors of men, and that the appearance of a want of them is owing merely to the degraded condition of their existence, both in Africa & America. I can add with truth, that no body wishes more ardently to see a good system commenced for raising the condition both of their body & mind to what it ought to be, as fast as the imbecility of their present existence, and other circumstances which cannot be neglected, will admit. I have taken the liberty of sending your Almanac to Monsieur de Condorcet, Secretary of the Academy of Sciences at Paris, and member of the Philanthropic society, because I considered it as a document to which your whole colour had a right for their justification against the doubts which have been entertained of them. I am with great esteem, Sir Your most obed[ien]t humble serv[an]t.

Ford v: 377–8

## IX.10 To the Marquis de Condorcet[1]

Philadelphia, August 30, 1791

Dear Sir, – I am to acknowledge the receipt of your favor on the subject of the element of measure adopted by France. Candor obliges me to confess that it is not what I would have approved. It is liable to the inexactitude of mensuration as to that part of the quadrant of the earth which is to be measured, that is to say as to one tenth of the quadrant, and as to the remaining nine tenths they are to be calculated on conjectural data, presuming the figure of the earth which has not yet been proved. It is liable too to the objection that no nation but your own can come at it; because yours is the only nation within which a meridian can be found of such extent crossing the 45th degree & terminating at both ends in a level. We may certainly say then that this measure is uncatholic, and I would rather have seen you depart from Catholicism in your religion than in your Philosophy.

I am happy to be able to inform you that we have now in the United States a negro, the son of a black man born in Africa, and of a black woman born in the United States, who is a very

---

[1] Jean Antoine Nicolas de Caritat, Marquis de Condorcet (1743–94), French scientist and mathematician and author of many books, including *Réflections sur l'esclavage des Nègres* (Neuchâtel, 1781). – *Eds.*

respectable mathematician. I procured him to be employed under one of our chief directors in laying out the new federal city on the Potowmac,[2] & in the intervals of his leisure, while on that work, he made an Almanac for the next year, which he sent me in his own hand writing, & which I inclose to you. I have seen very elegant solutions of Geometrical problems by him. Add to this that he is a very worthy & respectable member of society. He is a free man. I shall be delighted to see these instances of moral eminence so multiplied as to prove that the want of talents observed in them is merely the effect of their degraded condition, and not proceeding from any difference in the structure of the parts on which intellect depends.

I am looking ardently to the completion of the glorious work in which your country is engaged.[3] I view the general condition of Europe as hanging on the success or failure of France. Having set such an example of philosophical arrangement within, I hope it will be extended without your limits also, to your dependants and to your friends in every part of the earth.

Present my affectionate respects to Madame de Condorcet, and accept yourself assurances of the sentiments of esteem & attachment with which I have the honour to be Dear Sir your most obed[ien]t & most humble serv[an]t.

Ford v: 378–9

## IX.11 To St. George Tucker

Monticello, August 28, 1797

Dear Sir, – I have to acknowledge the receipt of your two favors of the 2d & 22d inst. and to thank you for the pamphlet covered by the former.[1] You know my subscription to it's doctrines; and to the mode of emancipation, I am satisfied that that must be a matter of compromise between the passions, the prejudices, & the real difficulties which will each have their weight in that operation. Perhaps the first chapter of this history, which has

[2] Washington, D.C. – *Eds.*
[3] The French Revolution. – *Eds.*
[1] St. George Tucker, *Dissertation on Slavery* (Philadelphia, 1796). – *Eds.*

begun in St. Domingo, & the next succeeding ones, which will recount how all the whites were driven from all the other islands, may prepare our minds for a peaceable accommodation between justice, policy & necessity; & furnish an answer to the difficult question, whither shall the colored emigrants go? and the sooner we put some plan underway, the greater hope there is that it may be permitted to proceed peaceably to it's ultimate effect. But if something is not done, & soon done, we shall be the murderers of our own children. The "murmura venturos nautis prodentia ventos" has already reached us; the revolutionary storm, now sweeping the globe, will be upon us, and happy if we make timely provision to give it an easy passage over our land. From the present state of things in Europe & America, the day which begins our combustion must be near at hand; and only a single spark is wanting to make that day to-morrow. If we had begun sooner, we might probably have been allowed a lengthier operation to clear ourselves, but every day's delay lessens the time we may take for emancipation. Some people derive hope from the aid of the confederated States. But this is a delusion. There is but one state in the Union which will aid us sincerely, if an insurrection begins, and that one may, perhaps, have it's own fire to quench at the same time. The facts stated in yours of the 22d, were not identically known to me, but others like them were. From the general government no interference need be expected. Even the merchant and navigator, the immediate sufferers, are prevented by various motives from wishing to be redressed. I see nothing but a State procedure which can vindicate us from the insult. It is in the power of any single magistrate, or of the Attorney for the Commonwealth, to lay hold of the commanding officer, whenever he comes ashore, for the breach of the peace, and to proceed against him by indictment. This is so plain an operation, that no power can prevent it's being carried through with effect, but the want of will in the officers of the State. I think that the matter of finances, which has set the people of Europe to thinking, is now advanced to that point with us, that the next step, & it is an unavoidable one, a land tax, will awaken our constituents, and call for inspection into past proceedings. I am, with great esteem, dear Sir, your friend and servant.

Ford VII: 167–9

## IX.12 To the Governor of Virginia (James Monroe)

Washington, November 24, 1801

Dear Sir, – I had not been unmindful of your letter of June 15, covering a resolution[1] of the House of Representatives of Virginia, and referred to in yours of the 17th inst. The importance of the subject, and the belief that it gave us time for consideration till the next meeting of the Legislature, have induced me to defer the answer to this date. You will perceive that some circumstances connected with the subject, & necessarily presenting themselves to view, would be improper but for yours' & the legislative ear. Their publication might have an ill effect in more than one quarter. In confidence of attention to this, I shall indulge greater freedom in writing.

Common malefactors, I presume, make no part of the object of that resolution. Neither their numbers, nor the nature of their offences, seem to require any provisions beyond those practised heretofore, & found adequate to the repression of ordinary crimes. Conspiracy, insurgency, treason, rebellion, among that description of persons who brought on us the alarm, and on themselves the tragedy, of 1800, were doubtless within the view of every one; but many perhaps contemplated, and one expression of the resolution might comprehend, a much larger scope. Respect to both opinions makes it my duty to understand the resolution in all the extent of which it is susceptible.

The idea seems to be to provide for these people by a purchase of lands; and it is asked whether such a purchase can be made of the U.S. in their western territory? A very great extent of country, north of the Ohio, has been laid off into townships, and is now at market, according to the provisions of the acts of Congress, with which you are acquainted. There is nothing which would restrain the State of Virginia either in the purchase or the application of these lands; but a purchase, by the acre, might perhaps be a more expensive provision than the H. of Representatives contemplated. Questions would also arise whether the establishment of such a colony within our limits, and to become a part of our union, would

---

[1] Fearing slave conspiracies and revolts, the Virginia legislature resolved to explore the possibility, desirability and legality of relocating slaves deemed dangerous to the western territories. – *Eds.*

be desirable to the State of Virginia itself, or to the other States – especially those who would be in its vicinity?

Could we procure lands beyond the limits of the U.S. to form a receptacle for these people? On our northern boundary, the country not occupied by British subjects, is the property of Indian nations, whose title would be to be extinguished, with the consent of Great Britain; & the new settlers would be British subjects. It is hardly to be believed that either Great Britain or the Indian proprietors have so disinterested a regard for us, as to be willing to relieve us, by receiving such a colony themselves; and as much to be doubted whether that race of men could long exist in so rigorous a climate. On our western & southern frontiers, Spain holds an immense country, the occupancy of which, however, is in the Indian natives, except a few insulated spots possessed by Spanish subjects. It is very questionable, indeed, whether the Indians would sell? whether Spain would be willing to receive these people? and nearly certain that she would not alienate the sovereignty. The same question to ourselves would recur here also, as did in the first case: should we be willing to have such a colony in contact with us? However our present interests may restrain us within our own limits, it is impossible not to look forward to distant times, when our rapid multiplication will expand itself beyond those limits, & cover the whole northern, if not the southern continent, with a people speaking the same language, governed in similar forms, & by similar laws; nor can we contemplate with satisfaction either blot or mixture on that surface. Spain, France, and Portugal hold possessions on the southern continent, as to which I am not well enough informed to say how far they might meet our views. But either there or in the northern continent, should the constituted authorities of Virginia fix their attention, of preference, I will have the dispositions of those powers sounded in the first instance.

The West Indies offer a more probable & practicable retreat for them. Inhabited already by a people of their own race & color; climates congenial with their natural constitution; insulated from the other descriptions of men; nature seems to have formed these islands to become the receptacle of the blacks transplanted into this hemisphere. Whether we could obtain from the European sovereigns of those islands leave to send thither the persons under consideration, I cannot say; but I think it more probable than the former propositions, because of their being already inhabited more or less by the same race. The most promising portion of them is the island of St. Domingo, where the blacks are established into a sovereignty *de facto*, & have organized themselves under regular laws & government. I should conjecture that their present ruler might be willing, on many considerations, to receive even that description which would be exiled for acts deemed criminal by us, but meritorious, perhaps, by him. The possibility that these exiles might stimulate & conduct vindicative or predatory descents on our coasts, & facilitate concert with their brethren remaining here, looks to a state of things between that island & us not probable on a contemplation of our relative strength, and of the disproportion daily growing; and it is overweighed by the humanity of the measures proposed, & the advantages of disembarrassing ourselves of such dangerous characters. Africa would offer a last & undoubted resort, if all others more desirable should fail us. Whenever the Legislature of Virginia shall have brought it's mind to a point, so that I may know exactly what to propose to foreign authorities, I will execute their wishes with fidelity & zeal. I hope, however, they will pardon me for suggesting a single question for their own consideration. When we contemplate the variety of countries & of sovereigns towards which we may direct our views, the vast revolutions & changes of circumstances which are now in a course of progression, the possibilities that arrangements now to be made, with a view to any particular plan, may, at no great distance of time, be totally deranged by a change of sovereignty, of government, or of other circumstances, it will be for the Legislature to consider whether, after they shall have made all those general provisions which may be fixed by legislative authority, it would be reposing too much confidence in their Executive to leave the place of relegation to be decided on by *them*. They could accommodate their arrangements to the actual state of things, in which countries or powers may be found to exist at the day; and may prevent the effect of the law from being defeated by intervening changes. This, however, is for them to decide. Our duty will be to respect their decision.

Ford VIII: 101–2

## IX.13 To Christopher Ellery

Washington, May 19, 1803

Dear Sir, – I have lately received a letter from Ingraham, who is in prison under a ca. sa. on a judgment of 14000 dollars & costs, one moiety (I presume) to the U.S. for having been the master of a vessel which brought from Africa a cargo of the natives of that country to be sold in slavery. He petitions for a pardon, as does his wife on behalf of herself, her children & his mother. His situation, as far as respects himself, merits no commiseration: that of his wife, children & mother, suffering for want of his aid, does: so also does the condition of the unhappy human beings whom he forcibly brought away from their native country, & whose wives, children & parents are now suffering for want of their aid & comfort. Between these two sets of suffering beings whom his crimes have placed in that condition, we are to apportion our commiseration. I presume his conviction was under the act of 1794, c. 11 – which inflicts pecuniary punishment only, without imprisonment, as that punishment was sometimes evaded by the insolvency of the offenders, the legislature in 1800, added for subsequent cases, imprisonment not exceeding 2 years. Ingraham's case is exactly such an one as the law of 1800 intended to meet; and tho' it could not be retrospective, yet if its measure be just now, it would have been just then, and consequently we shall act according to the views of the legislature, by restricting his imprisonment to their maximum of 2 years, instead of letting it be perpetual as the law of '94, under which he was convicted, would make it, in his case of insolvency. He must remain therefore the 2 years in prison: and at the end of that term I would wish a statement by the Judges & District attorney, who acted in the cause, of such facts as are material, & of their judgment on them, recommending him, or not, at their discretion, to pardon at the end of 2 years or any other term they think will be sufficient to operate as a terror to others meditating the same crime, without losing a just attention to the sufferings of his family. This of course can only respect the moiety of the U.S. The interest you took in this case during the last Congress has encouraged me to hope you would lend your instrumentality to the bringing it to a close, which would gratify me, so far as it could be done without abusing the power of pardon, confided to the discretion of the Executive to be used in cases, which tho' within the words, are not within the intention of the law. The law certainly did not intend perpetual imprisonment. Accept my friendly salutations and high respect.

Ford VIII: 231–2

## IX.14 To William A. Burwell

Washington, January 28, 1805

Dear Sir, – Your letter of the 18th has been duly received and Mr. Coles consents to remain here till the 4th of March, when I shall leave this place for Monticello and pass a month there. Consequently if you can join me here the second week in April it will be as early as your absence could effect my convenience. I have long since given up the expectation of any early provision for the extinguishment of slavery among us. There are many virtuous men who would make any sacrifices to affect it, many equally virtuous who persuade themselves either that the thing is not wrong, or that it cannot be remedied, and very many with whom interest is morality. The older we grow, the larger we are disposed to believe the last party to be. But interest is really going over to the side of morality. The value of the slave is every day lessening; his burden on his master dayly increasing. Interest is therefore preparing the disposition to be just; and this will be goaded from time to time by the insurrectionary spirit of the slaves. This is easily quelled in it's first efforts; but from being local it will become general, and whenever it does it will rise more formidable after every defeat, until we shall be forced, after dreadful scenes & sufferings, to release them in their own way, which, without such sufferings, we might now model after our own convenience. Accept my affectionate salutations.

Ford VIII: 340–1

## IX.15 To Henri Grégoire

Washington, February 25, 1809

Sir, – I have received the favor of your letter of August 17th, and with it the volume you were so kind as to send me on the "Literature of Negroes."[1] Be assured that no person living wishes more sincerely than I do, to see a complete refutation of the doubts I have myself entertained and expressed on the grade of understanding allotted to them by nature, and to find that in this respect they are on a par with ourselves. My doubts [in *Notes on Virginia*][2] were the result of personal observation on the limited sphere of my own State, where the opportunities for the development of their genius were not favorable, and those of exercising it still less so. I expressed them therefore with great hesitation; but whatever be their degree of talent it is no measure of their rights. Because Sir Isaac Newton was superior to others in understanding, he was not therefore lord of the person or property of others. On this subject they are gaining daily in the opinions of nations, and hopeful advances are making towards their re-establishment on an equal footing with the other colors of the human family. I pray you therefore to accept my thanks for the many instances you have enabled me to observe of respectable intelligence in that race of men, which cannot fail to have effect in hastening the day of their relief; and to be assured of the sentiments of high and just esteem and consideration which I tender to yourself with all sincerity.

Ford IX: 246–7

## IX.16 To Edward Coles

Monticello, August 25, 1814

Dear Sir, – Your favour of July 31, was duly received, and was read with peculiar pleasure. The sentiments breathed through the whole do honor to both the head and heart of the writer. Mine on the subject of slavery of negroes have long since been in possession of the public, and time has only served to give them stronger root. The love of justice and the love of country plead equally the cause of these people, and it is a moral reproach to us that they should have pleaded it so long in vain, and should have produced not a single effort, nay I fear not much serious willingness to relieve

[1] *De la littérature des Nègres* (Paris, 1808). – *Eds.*
[2] See *supra*, IX.6. – *Eds.*

them & ourselves from our present condition of moral & political reprobation. From those of the former generation who were in the fulness of age when I came into public life, which was while our controversy with England was on paper only, I soon saw that nothing was to be hoped. Nursed and educated in the daily habit of seeing the degraded condition, both bodily and mental, of those unfortunate beings, not reflecting that that degradation was very much the work of themselves & their fathers, few minds have yet doubted but that they were as legitimate subjects of property as their horses and cattle. The quiet and monotonous course of colonial life has been disturbed by no alarm, and little reflection on the value of liberty. And when alarm was taken at an enterprize on their own, it was not easy to carry them to the whole length of the principles which they invoked for themselves. In the first or second session of the Legislature after I became a member, I drew to this subject the attention of Col. Bland, one of the oldest, ablest, & most respected members, and he undertook to move for certain moderate extensions of the protection of the laws to these people. I seconded his motion, and, as a younger member, was more spared in the debate; but he was denounced as an enemy of his country, & was treated with the grossest indecorum. From an early stage of our revolution other & more distant duties were assigned to me, so that from that time till my return from Europe in 1789, and I may say till I returned to reside at home in 1809, I had little opportunity of knowing the progress of public sentiment here on this subject. I had always hoped that the younger generation receiving their early impressions after the flame of liberty had been kindled in every breast, & had become as it were the vital spirit of every American, that the generous temperament of youth, analogous to the motion of their blood, and above the suggestions of avarice, would have sympathized with oppression wherever found, and proved their love of liberty beyond their own share of it. But my intercourse with them, since my return, has not been sufficient to ascertain that they had made towards this point the progress I had hoped. Your solitary but welcome voice is the first which has brought this sound to my ear; and I have considered the general silence which prevails on this subject as indicating an apathy unfavorable to every hope. Yet the hour of emancipation is advancing, in the march of time. It will come; and whether brought on by the generous energy of our own minds; or by the bloody process of St. Domingo,[1] excited and conducted by the power of our present enemy,[2] if once stationed permanently within our Country, and offering asylum & arms to the oppressed, is a leaf of our history not yet turned over. As to the method by which this difficult work is to be effected, if permitted to be done by ourselves, I have seen no proposition so expedient on the whole, as that [of] emancipation of those born after a given day, and of their education and expatriation after a given age. This would give time for a gradual extinction of that species of labour & substitution of another, and lessen the severity of the shock which an operation so fundamental cannot fail to produce. For men probably of any color, but of this color we know, brought from their infancy without necessity for thought or forecast, are by their habits rendered as incapable as children of taking care of themselves, and are extinguished promptly wherever industry is necessary for raising young. In the mean time they are pests in society by their idleness, and the depredations to which this leads them. Their amalgamation with the other color produces a degradation to which no lover of his country, no lover of excellence in the human character can innocently consent. I am sensible [aware] of the partialities with which you have looked towards me as the person who should undertake this salutary but arduous work. But this, my dear sir, is like bidding old Priam to buckle the armour of Hector "trementibus æquo humeris et inutile ferruncingi." No, I have overlived the generation with which mutual labors & perils begat mutual confidence and influence. This enterprise is for the young; for those who can follow it up, and bear it through to its consummation. It shall have all my prayers, & these are the only weapons of an old man. But in the mean time are you right in abandoning this property, and your country with it? I think not. My opinion has ever been that, until more can be done for them, we should endeavor, with those whom fortune has thrown on our hands, to feed and clothe them well, protect them from all ill usage, require such reasonable labor only as is performed voluntarily by freemen, & be led by no repugnancies

[1] TJ refers to the unsuccessful slave revolt led by Toussaint l'Ouverture in St.-Domingue (Haiti) in 1791 and put down with great ferocity by French forces in 1802. – *Eds.*
[2] I.e. Great Britain. The War of 1812 was still being waged. – *Eds.*

to abdicate them, and our duties to them. The laws do not permit us to turn them loose, if that were for their good: and to commute them for other property is to commit them to those whose usage of them we cannot control. I hope then, my dear sir, you will reconcile yourself to your country [i.e. Virginia] and its unfortunate condition; that you will not lessen its stock of sound disposition by withdrawing your portion from the mass. That, on the contrary you will come forward in the public councils, become the missionary of this doctrine truly christian; insinuate & inculcate it softly but steadily, through the medium of writing and conversation; associate others in your labors, and when the phalanx is formed, bring on and press the proposition perseveringly until its accomplishment. It is an encouraging observation that no good measure was ever proposed, which, if duly pursued, failed to prevail in the end. We have proof of this in the history of the endeavors in the English parliament to suppress that very trade which brought this evil on us. And you will be supported by the religious precept, "be not weary in well-doing." That your success may be as speedy & complete, as it will be of honorable & immortal consolation to yourself, I shall as fervently and sincerely pray as I assure you of my great friendship and respect.

Ford XI: 477–9

## IX.17 To Dr. Thomas Humphreys

Monticello, February 8, 1817

Dear Sir, – Your favor of January 2d did not come to my hands until the 5th instant. I concur entirely in your leading principles of gradual emancipation, of establishment on the coast of Africa, and the patronage of our nation until the emigrants shall be able to protect themselves. The subordinate details might be easily arranged. But the bare proposition of purchase by the United States generally, would excite infinite indignation in all the States north of Maryland. The sacrifice must fall on the States alone which hold them; and the difficult question will be how to lessen this so as to reconcile our fellow citizens to it. Personally I am ready and desirous to make any sacrifice which shall ensure their gradual but complete retirement from the State, and effectually, at the same time, establish them elsewhere in freedom and safety. But I have not perceived the growth of this disposition in the rising generation, of which I once had sanguine hopes. No symptoms inform me that it will take place in my day. I leave it, therefore, to time, and not at all without hope that the day will come, equally desirable and welcome to us as to them. Perhaps the proposition now on the carpet at Washington to provide an establishment on the coast of Africa for voluntary emigrations of people of color, may be the corner stone of this future edifice. Praying for its completion as early as may most promote the good of all, I salute you with great esteem and respect.

Ford x: 76–7

## IX.18 To John Holmes

Monticello, April 22, 1820

I thank you, dear Sir, for the copy you have been so kind as to send me of the letter to your constituents on the Missouri question.[1] It is a perfect justification to them. I had for a long time ceased to read newspapers, or pay any attention to public affairs, confident they were in good hands, and content to be a passenger in our bark to the shore from which I am not distant. But this momentous question, like a fire bell in the night, awakened and filled me with terror. I considered it at once as the knell of the Union. It is hushed, indeed, for the moment. But this is a reprieve only, not a final sentence. A geographical line, coinciding with a marked principle, moral and political, once conceived and held up to the angry passions of men, will never be obliterated; and every new irritation will mark it deeper and deeper. I can say, with conscious truth, that there is not a man on earth who would sacrifice more than I would to relieve us from this heavy reproach, in any *practicable* way. The cession of that kind of property, for so it is misnamed, is a bagatelle which would not cost me a second thought, if, in that way, a general emancipation and *expatriation* could be effected; and gradually, and

[1] See *Supra*, VIII.16, note 1.

with due sacrifices, I think it might be. But as it is, we have the wolf by the ears, and we can neither hold him, nor safely let him go. Justice is in one scale, and self-preservation in the other. Of one thing I am certain, that as the passage of slaves from one State to another, would not make a slave of a single human being who would not be so without it, so their diffusion over a greater surface would make them individually happier, and proportionally facilitate the accomplishment of their emancipation, by dividing the burthen on a greater number of coadjutors. An abstinence too, from this act of power, would remove the jealousy excited by the undertaking of Congress to regulate the condition of the different descriptions of men composing a State. This certainly is the exclusive right of every State, which nothing in the constitution has taken from them and given to the General Government. Could Congress, for example, say, that the non-freemen of Connecticut shall be freemen, or that they shall not emigrate into any other State?

I regret that I am now to die in the belief, that the useless sacrifice of themselves by the generation of 1776, to acquire self-government and happiness to their country, is to be thrown away by the unwise and unworthy passions of their sons, and that my only consolation is to be, that I live not to weep over it. If they would but dispassionately weigh the blessings they will throw away, against an abstract principle more likely to be effected by union than by scission, they would pause before they would perpetrate this act of suicide on themselves, and of treason against the hopes of the world. To yourself, as the faithful advocate of the Union, I tender the offering of my high esteem and respect.

Ford x: 157–8

## ix.19 To James Heaton

Monticello, May 20, 1826

Dear Sir, – The subject of your letter of April 20, is one on which I do not permit myself to express an opinion, but when time, place, and occasion may give it some favorable effect. A good cause is often injured more by ill-timed efforts of its friends than by the arguments of its enemies. Persuasion, perseverance, and patience are the best advocates on questions depending on the will of others. The revolution in public opinion which this cause[1] requires, is not to be expected in a day, or perhaps in an age; but time, which outlives all things, will outlive this evil also. My sentiments have been forty years before the public. Had I repeated them forty times, they would only have become the more stale and threadbare. Although I shall not live to see them consummated, they will not die with me; but living or dying, they will ever be in my most fervent prayer. This is written for yourself and not for the public, in compliance with your request of two lines of sentiment on the subject. Accept the assurance of my good will and respect.

H. S. Randall, *Life of Thomas Jefferson* (New York, 1857), III: 539

---

[1] The abolition of slavery. – *Eds.*

# x  Native Americans

## x.1 *Notes on Virginia*: Query VI

... Of the Indian of South America I know nothing; for I would not honor with the appellation of knowledge, what I derive from the fables published of them. These I believe to be just as true as the fables of Æsop. This belief is founded on what I have seen of man, white, red, and black, and what has been written of him by authors, enlightened themselves, and writing among an enlightened people. The Indian of North America being more within our reach, I can speak of him somewhat from my own knowledge, but more from the information of others better acquainted with him, and on whose truth and judgment I can rely. From these sources I am able to say, in contradiction to this representation, that he is neither more defective in ardor, nor more impotent with his female, than the white reduced to the same diet and exercise; that he is brave, when an enterprise depends on bravery; education with him making the point of honor consist in the destruction of an enemy by strategem, and in the preservation of his own person free from injury; or, perhaps, this is nature, while it is education which teaches us to[1] honor force more than that he will defend himself against a host of enemies, always choosing to be killed, rather than to surrender,[2]

---

[1] *Sol Rodomonte sprezza di venire*
*Se non, dove la via meno è ficura.* – Ariosto, 14, 117.

[2] In so judicious an author as Don Ulloa [Jorge Juan y Antonio de Ulloa (1716–95), author of *Viage a la América Meridional* ("Voyage to South America") (Madrid, 1748) and other works. – *Eds.*], and one to whom we are indebted for the most precise information we have of South America, I did not expect to find such assertions as the following: "Los Indios vencidos son los mas cobardes y pusilanimes que se pueden vér: – se hacen inòcentes, se humillan hasta el desprecio, disculpan su inconsiderado arrojo, y con las suplicas y los ruegos dán seguras pruebas de su pusilanimidad. – ó lo que resieren las historias de la Conquista, sobre sus grandes acciones, es en un sendito figurado, ó el caracter de estas gentes no es ahora segun era entonces; pero lo que no tiene duda es, que las Naciones de la parte Septentrional subsisten en la misma libertad que siempre han tenido, sin haber sido sojuzgados por algun Principe extraño, y que viven segun su régimen y costumbres de toda la vida, sin que haya habido motivo para que muden de caracter; y en estos se vé lo mismo, que sucede en los del Peru, y de toda la América Meridional, reducidos, y que nunca lo han estado." *Noticias Americanas, Entretenimiento,* xviii, § 1. Don Ulloa here admits, that the authors who have described the Indians of South America, before they were enslaved, had represented them as a brave people, and therefore seems to have suspected that the cowardice which he had observed in those of the present race might be the effect of subjugation. But, supposing the Indians of North America to be cowards also, he concludes the ancestors of those of South America to have been so too, and,

though it be to the whites, who he knows will treat him well; that in other situations, also, he meets death with more deliberation, and endures tortures, with a firmness unknown almost to religious enthusiasm with us; that he is affectionate to his children, careful of them, and indulgent in the extreme; that his affections comprehend his other connections, weakening, as with us, from circle to circle, as they recede from the centre; that his friendships are strong and faithful to the uttermost[3] extremity; that his sensibility is keen, even the warriors weeping most bitterly on the loss of their children, though in general they endeavor to appear superior to human events; that his vivacity and activity of mind is equal to ours in the same situation; hence his eagerness for hunting, and for games of chance. The women are submitted to unjust drudgery. This I believe is the case with every barbarous people. With such, force is law. The stronger sex therefore imposes on the weaker. It is civilization alone which replaces women in the enjoyment of their natural equality. That first teaches us to subdue the selfish passions, and to respect those rights in others which we value in ourselves. Were we

therefore, that those authors have given fictions for truth. He was probably not acquainted himself with the Indians of North America, and had formed his opinion from hear-say. Great numbers of French, of English, and of Americans, are perfectly acquainted with these people. Had he had an opportunity of inquiring of any of these, they would have told him, that there never was an instance known of an Indian begging his life when in the power of his enemies; on the contrary, that he courts death by every possible insult and provocation. His reasoning, then, would have been reversed thus: "Since the present Indian of North America is brave, and authors tell us that the ancestors of those of South America were brave also, it must follow that the cowardice of their descendants is the effect of subjugation and ill treatment." For he observes, *ib.*, §. 27, that "los obrages los aniquillan por la inhumanidad con que se les trata."

[3] A remarkable instance of this appeared in the case of the late Colonel Byrd, who was sent to the Cherokee nation to transact some business with them. It happened that some of our disorderly people had just killed one or two of that nation. It was therefore proposed in the council of the Cherokees that Colonel Byrd should be put to death, in revenge for the loss of their countrymen. Among them was a chief named Silòuee, who, on some former occasion, had contracted an acquaintance and friendship with Colonel Byrd. He came to him every night in his tent, and told him not to be afraid, they should not kill him. After many days' deliberation, however, the determination was, contrary to Silòuee's expectation, that Byrd should be put to death, and some warriors were despatched as executioners. Silòuee attended them, and when they entered the tent, he threw himself between them and Byrd, and said to the warriors, "This man is my friend; before you get at him, you must kill me." On which they returned, and the council respected the principle so much as to recede from their determination.

in equal barbarism, our females would be equal drudges. The man with them is less strong than with us, but their woman stronger than ours; and both for the same obvious reason; because our man and their woman is habituated to labor, and formed by it. With both races the sex which is indulged with ease is the least athletic. An Indian man is small in the hand and wrist, for the same reason for which a sailor is large and strong in the arms and shoulders, and a porter in the legs and thighs. They raise fewer children than we do. The causes of this are to be found, not in a difference of nature, but of circumstance. The women very frequently attending the men in their parties of war and of hunting, child-bearing becomes extremely inconvenient to them. It is said, therefore, that they have learned the practice of procuring abortion by the use of some vegetable; and that it even extends to prevent conception for a considerable time after. During these parties they are exposed to numerous hazards, to excessive exertions, to the greatest extremities of hunger. Even at their homes the nation depends for food, through a certain part of every year, on the gleanings of the forest; that is, they experience a famine once in every year. With all animals, if the female be illy fed, or not fed at all, her young perish; and if both male and female be reduced to like want, generation becomes less active, less productive. To the obstacles, then, of want and hazard, which nature has opposed to the multiplication of wild animals, for the purpose of restraining their numbers within certain bounds, those of labour and of voluntary abortion are added with the Indian. No wonder, then, if they multiply less than we do. Where food is regularly supplied, a single farm will show more of cattle, than a whole country of forests can of buffalos. The same Indian women, when married to white traders, who feed them and their children plentifully and regularly, who exempt them from excessive drudgery, who keep them stationary and unexposed to accident, produce and raise as many children as the white women. Instances are known, under these circumstances, of their rearing a dozen children. An inhuman practice once prevailed in this country, of making slaves of the Indians. It is a fact well known with us, that the Indian women so enslaved produced and raised as numerous families as either the whites or blacks among whom they lived. It has been said that Indians have less hair than the whites, except on the head. But this is a fact of which fair proof can scarcely be had.

With them it is disgraceful to be hairy on the body. They say it likens them to hogs. They therefore pluck the hair as fast as it appears. But the traders who marry their women, and prevail on them to discontinue this practice, say, that nature is the same with them as with the whites. Nor, if the fact be true, is the consequence necessary which has been drawn from it. Negroes have notoriously less hair than the whites; yet they are more ardent. But if cold and moisture be the agents of nature for diminishing the races of animals, how comes she all at once to suspend their operation as to the physical man of the new world, whom the Count[4] acknowledges to be "à peu près de même stature que l'homme de notre monde," and to let loose their influence on his moral faculties? How has this "combination of the elements and other physical causes, so contrary to the enlargement of animal nature in this new world, these obstacles to the development and formation of great germs,"[5] been arrested and suspended, so as to permit the human body to acquire its just dimensions, and by what inconceivable process has their action been directed on his mind alone? To judge of the truth of this, to form a just estimate of their genius and mental powers, more facts are wanting, and great allowance to be made for those circumstances of their situation which call for a display of particular talents only. This done, we shall probably find that they are formed in mind as well as body, on the same module with the[6] "Homo sapiens Europæus." The principles of their society forbidding all compulsion, they are to be led to duty and to enterprise by personal influence and persuasion. Hence eloquence in council, bravery and address in war, become the foundations of all consequence with them. To these acquirements all their faculties are directed. Of their bravery and address in war we have multiplied proofs, because we have been the subjects on which they were exercised. Of their eminence in oratory we have fewer examples, because it is displayed chiefly in their own councils. Some, however, we have, of very superior lustre. I may challenge the whole orations of Demosthenes and Cicero, and of any more eminent orator, if Europe has furnished any more eminent, to produce a single passage, superior to the speech of Logan, a Mingo chief, to Lord Dunmore, when

[4] I.e. Buffon, the French naturalist (see *supra*, I.3, note 2). – *Eds.*
[5] XVIII.146.
[6] Linn. Syst. Definition of a Man.

governor of this state. And as a testimony of their talents in this line, I beg leave to introduce it, first stating the incidents necessary for understanding it. In the spring of the year 1774, a robbery and murder were committed on an inhabitant of the frontier of Virginia, by two Indians of the Shawanee tribe. The neighbouring whites, according to their custom, undertook to punish this outrage in a summary way. Col. Cresap, a man infamous for the many murders he had committed on those much injured people, collected a party and proceeded down the Kanhaway in quest of vengeance. Unfortunately a canoe of women and children, with one man only, was seen coming from the opposite shore, unarmed, and unsuspecting an hostile attack from the whites. Cresap and his party concealed themselves on the bank of the river, and the moment the canoe reached the shore, singled out their objects, and at one fire, killed every person in it. This happened to be the family of Logan, who had long been distinguished as a friend of the whites. This unworthy return provoked his vengeance. He accordingly signalized himself in the war which ensued. In the autumn of the same year a decisive battle was fought at the mouth of the Great Kanhaway, between the collected forces of the Shawanese, Mingoes and Delawares, and a detachment of the Virginia militia. The Indians were defeated and sued for peace. Logan, however, disdained to be seen among the suppliants. But lest the sincerity of a treaty should be distrusted, from which so distinguished a chief absented himself, he sent, by a messenger, the following speech, to be delivered to Lord Dunmore.

> I appeal to any white man to say, if ever he entered Logan's cabin hungry, and he gave him not meat; if ever he came cold and naked, and he cloathed him not. During the course of the last long and bloody war Logan remained idle in his cabin an advocate for peace. Such was my love for the whites, that my countrymen pointed as they passed, and said, "Logan is the friend of white men." I had even thought to have lived with you, but for the injuries of one man. Colonel Cresap, the last spring, in cold blood, and unprovoked, murdered all the relations of Logan, not sparing even my women and children. There runs not a drop of my blood in the veins of any living creature. This called on me for revenge. I have sought it: I have killed many: I have fully glutted my vengeance: for my country I rejoice at the beams of peace. But do not harbour a thought that mine is the joy of fear. Logan never felt fear. He will not

turn on his heel to save his life. Who is there to mourn for
Logan? – Not one.

Before we condemn the Indians of this continent as wanting
genius, we must consider that letters have not yet been introduced
among them. Were we to compare them in their present state with
the Europeans North of the Alps, when the Roman arms and arts
first crossed those mountains, the comparison would be unequal,
because, at that time, those parts of Europe were swarming with
numbers; because numbers produce emulation and multiply the
chances of improvement, and one improvement begets another. Yet
I may safely ask, how many good poets, how many able mathema-
ticians, how many great inventors in arts or sciences, had Europe,
North of the Alps, then produced? And it was sixteen centuries
after this before a Newton could be formed. I do not mean to deny
that there are varieties in the race of man, distinguished by their
powers both of body and mind. I believe there are, as I see to be
the case in the races of other animals. I only mean to suggest a
doubt, whether the bulk and faculties of animals depend on the side
of the Atlantic on which their food happens to grow, or which
furnishes the elements of which they are compounded? Whether
nature has enlisted herself as a Cis- or Trans-Atlantic partisan? I
am induced to suspect there has been more eloquence than sound
reasoning displayed in support of this theory; that it is one of those
cases where the judgment has been seduced by a glowing pen; and
whilst I render every tribute of honor and esteem to the celebrated
Zoologist [Buffon], who has added, and is still adding, so many
precious things to the treasures of science, I must doubt whether in
this instance he has not cherished error also by lending her for a
moment his vivid imagination and bewitching language.

So far the Count de Buffon has carried this new theory of the tendency of nature to belittle her productions on this side of the Atlantic.
Its application to the race of whites, transplanted from Europe,
remained for the Abbé Raynal.[7] "*On doit être étonné que l'Amérique
n'ait pas encore produit un bon poète, un habile mathématicien, un homme
de génie dans un seul art, ou une seule science.*" 7. Hist. Philos. p. 92.

[7] Abbé Guillaume Thomas François Raynal (1713–96), *Histoire Philosophique et Politique des Establissements et du Commerce des Européens dans les deux Indes*
(Amsterdam, 1770). – *Eds.*

ed. Maestricht. 1774. "America has not yet produced one good poet."
When we shall have existed as a people as long as the Greeks did
before they produced a Homer, the Romans a Virgil, the French a
Racine and Voltaire, the English a Shakespeare and Milton, should
this reproach be still true, we will inquire from what unfriendly causes
it has proceeded, that the other countries of Europe and quarters of
the earth shall not have inscribed any name in the roll of poets.[8] But
neither has America produced "one able mathematician, one man of
genius in a single art or a single science." In war we have produced a
Washington, whose memory will be adored while liberty shall have
votaries, whose name will triumph over time, and will in future ages
assume its just station among the most celebrated worthies of the
world, when that wretched philosophy shall be forgotten which
would have arranged him among the degeneracies of nature. In physics we have produced a Franklin, than whom no one of the present
age has made more important discoveries, nor has enriched philosophy with more, or more ingenious solutions of the phænomena of
nature. We have supposed Mr. Rittenhouse second to no astronomer
living: that in genius he must be the first, because he is self-taught. As
an artist he has exhibited as great a proof of mechanical genius as the
world has ever produced. He has not indeed made a world; but he has
by imitation approached nearer its Maker than any man who has lived
from the creation to this day.[9] As in philosophy and war, so in government, in oratory, in painting, in the plastic art, we might shew that
America, though but a child of yesterday, has already given hopeful
proofs of genius, as well of the nobler kinds, which arouse the best
feelings of man, which call him into action, which substantiate his
freedom, and conduct him to happiness, as of the subordinate, which
serve to amuse him only. We therefore suppose, that this reproach is
as unjust as it is unkind; and that, of the geniuses which adorn the

[8] Has the world as yet produced more than two poets, acknowledged to be such by
all nations? An Englishman, only, reads Milton with delight, an Italian Tasso, a
Frenchman the Henriade, a Portuguese Camouens: but Homer and Virgil have
been the rapture of every age and nation: they are read with enthusiasm in their
originals by those who can read the originals, and in translations by those who
cannot.

[9] There are various ways of keeping truth out of sight. Mr. Rittenhouse's model of
the planetary system has the plagiary appellation of an orrery; and the quadrant
invented by Godfrey, an American also, and with the aid of which the European
nations traverse the globe, is called Hadley's quadrant.

present age, America contributes its full share. For comparing it with those countries, where genius is most cultivated, where are the most excellent models for art, and scaffoldings for the attainment of science, as France and England for instance, we calculate thus. The United States contain three millions of inhabitants; France twenty millions; and the British islands ten. We produce a Washington, a Franklin, a Rittenhouse. France then should have half a dozen in each of these lines, and Great-Britain half that number, equally eminent. It may be true, that France has: we are but just becoming acquainted with her, and our acquaintance so far gives us high ideas of the genius of her inhabitants. It would be injuring too many of them to name particularly a Voltaire, a Buffon, the constellation of Encyclopedists, the Abbé Raynal himself, &c. &c. We therefore have reason to believe she can produce her full quota of genius. The present war having so long cut off all communication with Great-Britain, we are not able to make a fair estimate of the state of science in that country. The spirit in which she wages war is the only sample before our eyes, and that does not seem the legitimate offspring either of science or of civilization. The sun of her glory is fast descending to the horizon. Her philosophy has crossed the channel, her freedom the Atlantic, and herself seems passing to that awful dissolution, whose issue is not given human foresight to scan.[10]

Ford III: 151–65

[10] In a later edition of the Abbé Raynal's work, he has withdrawn his censure from that part of the new world inhabited by the Federo-Americans; but has left it still on the other parts. North America has always been more accessible to strangers than South. If he was mistaken then as to the former, he may be so as to the latter. The glimmerings which reach us from South America enable us only to see that its inhabitants are held under the accumulated pressure of slavery, superstition, and ignorance. Whenever they shall be able to rise under this weight, and to shew themselves to the rest of the world, they will probably shew they are like the rest of the world. We have not yet sufficient evidence that there are more *lakes* and *fogs* in South America than in other parts of the earth. As little do we know what would be their operation on the mind of man. That country has been visited by Spaniards and Portuguese chiefly, and almost exclusively. These, going from a country of the old world remarkably dry in its soil and climate, fancied there were more lakes and fogs in South America than in Europe. An inhabitant of Ireland, Sweden, or Finland, would have formed the contrary opinion. Had South America then been discovered and seated by a people from a fenny country, it would probably have been represented as much drier than the old world. A patient pursuit of facts, and cautious combination and comparison of them, is the drudgery to which man is subjected by his Maker, if he wishes to attain sure knowledge.

## x.2 *Notes on Virginia*: Query XI

*A description of the Indians established in that State?*

When the first effectual settlement of our colony was made, which was in 1607, the country from the sea-coast to the mountains, and from the Patowmac to the most southern waters of James river, was occupied by upwards of forty different tribes of Indians. Of these the *Powhatans*, the *Mannahoacs*, and *Monacans*, were the most powerful. Those between the sea-coast and falls of the rivers, were in amity with one another, and attached to the *Powhatans* as their link of union. Those between the falls of the rivers and the mountains, were divided into two confederacies; the tribes inhabiting the head waters of Patowmac and Rappahannoc, being attached to the *Mannahoacs*; and those on the upper parts of James river to the *Monacans*. But the *Monacans* and their friends were in amity with the *Mannahoacs* and their friends, and waged joint and perpetual war against the *Powhatans*. We are told that the Powhatans, Mannahoacs, and Monacans, spoke languages so radically different, that interpreters were necessary when they transacted business. Hence we may conjecture, that this was not the case between all the tribes, and, probably, that each spoke the language of the nation to which it was attached; which we know to have been the case in many particular instances. Very possibly there may have been anciently three different stocks, each of which multiplying in a long course of time, had separated into so many little societies, [the principles of their government being so weak as to give this liberty to all its members].[1]

---

[1] In the 1787 and later editions the words in brackets are omitted, and the following paragraph inserted: "This practice results from the circumstance of their having never submitted themselves to any laws, any coercive power, any shadow of government. Their only controls are their manners, and that moral sense of right and wrong, which, like the sense of tasting and feeling in every man, makes a part of his nature. An offence against these is punished by contempt, by exclusion from society, or, where the case is serious, as that of murder, by the individuals whom it concerns. Imperfect as this species of coercion may seem, crimes are very rare among them, insomuch that were it made a question, whether no law, as among the savage Americans, or too much law, as among the civilized Europeans, submits man to the greatest evil, one who has seen both conditions of existence would pronounce it to be the last; and that the sheep are happier of themselves, than under care of the wolves. It will be said, that great societies cannot exist without government. The savages, therefore, break them into small ones." – *Eds.*

The territories of the *Powhatan* confederacy, south of the Patowmac, comprehended about 8,000 square miles, 30 tribes, and 2,400 warriors. Captain Smith tells us, that within 60 miles of James town were 5,000 people, of whom 1,500 were warriors. From this we find the proportion of their warriors to their whole inhabitants, was as 3 to 10. The *Powhatan* confederacy, then, would consist of about 8,000 inhabitants, which was one for every square mile; being about the twentieth part of our present population in the same territory, and the hundredth of that of the British islands.

Besides these were the *Nòttoways*, living on Nottoway river, the *Mehèrrins* and *Tùteloes* on Meherrin river, who were connected with the Indians of Carolina, probably with the Chòwanocs.

The preceding table[2] contains a state of these several tribes, according to their confederacies and geographical situations, with their numbers when we first became acquainted with them, where these numbers are known. The numbers of some of them are again stated as they were in the year 1669, when an attempt was made by the assembly to enumerate them. Probably the enumeration is imperfect, and in some measure conjectural, and that a farther search into the records would furnish many more particulars. What would be the melancholy sequel of their history, may, however, be argued from the census of 1669; by which we discover that the tribes therein enumerated were, in the space of 62 years, reduced to about one-third of their former numbers. Spirituous liquors, the small-pox, war, and an abridgement of territory to a people who lived principally on the spontaneous productions of nature, had committed terrible havoc among them, which generation, under the obstacles opposed to it among them, was not likely to make good. That the lands of this country were taken from them by conquest, is not so general a truth as is supposed. I find in our historians and records, repeated proofs of purchase, which cover a considerable part of the lower country; and many more would doubtless be found on further search. The upper country, we know, has been acquired altogether by purchases made in the most unexceptionable form.

Westward of all these tribes, beyond the mountains, and extending to the great lakes, were the *Massawòmecs*, a most powerful confederacy, who harrassed unremittingly the *Powhatàns* and

---

[2] Omitted. – *Eds.*

Manahoàcs. These were probably the ancestors of tribes known at present by the name of the *Six Nations*.

Very little can now be discovered of the subsequent history of these tribes severally. The *Chickahòminies* removed about the year 1661, to Mattapony river. Their chief, with one from each of the Pamùnkies and Màttaponies, attended the treaty of Albany in 1685. This seems to have been the last chapter in their history. They retained, however, their separate name so late as 1705, and were at length blended with the Pamùnkies and Màttaponies, and exist at present only under their names. There remain of the *Màttaponies* three or four men only, and they have more negro than Indian blood in them. They have lost their language, have reduced themselves, by voluntary sales, to about fifty acres of land, which lie on the river of their own name, and have from time to time, been joining the Pamùnkies, from whom they are distant but 10 miles. The *Pamùnkies* are reduced to about 10 or 12 men, tolerably pure from mixture with other colors. The older ones among them preserve their language in a small degree, which are the last vestiges on earth, as far as we know, of the Powhatan language. They have about 300 acres of very fertile land, on Pamunkey river, so encompassed by water that a gate shuts in the whole. Of the *Nottoways*, not a male is left. A few women constitute the remains of that tribe. They are seated on the Nottoway river, in Southampton country, on very fertile lands. At a very early period, certain lands were marked out and appropriated to these tribes, and were kept from encroachment by the authority of the laws. They have usually had trustees appointed, whose duty was to watch over their interests, and guard them from insult and injury.

The *Mònacans* and their friends, better known latterly by the name of *Tuscaròras*, were probably connected with the Massawòmecs, or Five nations. For though we are[3] told their languages were so different that the intervention of interpreters was necessary between them, yet do we also[4] learn that the Erigas, a nation formerly inhabiting on the Ohio, were of the same original stock with the Five Nations, and that they partook also of the Tuscaròra language. Their dialects might, by long separation, have become so

---

[3] Smith.
[4] Evans.

unlike as to be unintelligible to one another. We know that ir the Five nations received the Tuscaròras into their confe and made them the Sixth nation. They received the Mehèrrins ana Tùteloes also into their protection: and it is most probable, that the remains of many other of the tribes, of whom we find no particular account, retired westwardly in like manner, and were incorporated with one or the other of the western tribes.

I know of no such thing existing as an Indian monument; for I would not honor with that name arrow points, stone hatchets, stone pipes, and half shapen images. Of labor on the large scale, I think there is no remain as respectable as would be a common ditch for the draining of lands; unless indeed it would be the Barrows, of which many are to be found all over this country. These are of different sizes, some of them constructed of earth, and some of loose stones. That they were repositories of the dead, has been obvious to all; but on what particular occasion constructed, was a matter of doubt. Some have thought they covered the bones of those who have fallen in battles fought on the spot of interment. Some ascribed them to the custom, said to prevail among the Indians, of collecting, at certain periods, the bones of all their dead, wheresoever deposited at the time of death. Others again supposed them the general sepulchres for towns, conjectured to have been on or near these grounds; and this opinion was supported by the quality of the lands in which they are found (those constructed of earth being generally in the softest and most fertile meadow-grounds on river sides), and by a tradition, said to be handed down from the aboriginal Indians, that, when they settled in a town, the first person who died was placed erect, and earth put about him, so as to cover and support him; that when another died, a narrow passage was dug to the first, the second reclined against him, and the cover of earth replaced, and so on. There being one of these in my neighbourhood, I wished to satisfy myself whether any, and which of these opinions were just. For this purpose I determined to open and examine it thoroughly. It was situated on the low grounds of the Rivanna, about two miles above its principal fork, and opposite to some hills, on which had been an Indian town. It was of a spheroidical form, of about 40 feet diameter at the base, and had been of about twelve feet altitude, though now reduced by the plough to seven and a half, having been under cultivation about a dozen years. Before this it was covered with trees of twelve inches diameter, and round the base was an excavation of five feet depth and width, from whence the earth had been taken of which the hillock was formed. I first dug superficially in several parts of it, and came to collections of human bones, at different depths, from six inches to three feet below the surface. These were lying in the utmost confusion, some vertical, some oblique, some horizontal, and directed to every point of the compass, entangled and held together in clusters by the earth. Bones of the most distant parts were found together, as, for instance, the small bones of the foot in the hollow of a scull; many sculls would sometimes be in contact, lying on the face, on the side, on the back, top or bottom, so as, on the whole, to give the idea of bones emptied promiscuously from a bag or a basket, and covered over with earth, without any attention to their order. The bones of which the greatest numbers remained, were sculls, jaw bones, teeth, the bones of the arms, thighs, legs, feet and hands. A few ribs remained, some vertebræ of the neck and spine, without their processes, and one instance only of the[5] bone which serves as a base to the vertebral column. The sculls were so tender, that they generally fell to pieces on being touched. The other bones were stronger. There were some teeth which were judged to be smaller than those of an adult; a scull, which on a slight view, appeared to be that of an infant, but it fell to pieces on being taken out, so as to prevent satisfactory examination; a rib, and a fragment of the under jaw of a person about half grown; another rib of an infant; and a part of the jaw of a child, which had not cut its teeth. This last furnishing the most decisive proof of the burial of children here, I was particular in my attention to it. It was part of the right half of the under jaw. The processes, by which it was articulated to the temporal bones, were entire, and the bone itself firm to where it had been broken off, which, as nearly as I could judge, was about the place of the eye tooth. Its upper edge, wherein would have been the sockets of the teeth, was perfectly smooth. Measuring it with that of an adult, by placing their hinder processes together, its broken end extended to the penultimate grinder of the adult. This bone was white, all the others of a sand colour. The bones of infants being soft, they probably decay sooner, which might be the cause so few

---

[5] The *os sacrum*.

were found here. I proceeded then to make a perpendicular cut through the body of the barrow, that I might examine its internal structure. This passed about three feet from its centre, was opened to the former surface of the earth, and was wide enough for a man to walk through and examine its sides. At the bottom, that is, on the level of the circumjacent plain, I found bones; above these a few stones, brought from a cliff a quarter of a mile off, and from the river one eighth of a mile off; then a large interval of earth, then a stratum of bones, and so on. At one end of the section were four strata of bones plainly distinguishable; at the other, three; the strata in one part not ranging with those in another. The bones nearest the surface were least decayed. No holes were discovered in any of them, as if made with bullets, arrows, or other weapons. I conjectured that in this barrow might have been a thousand skeletons. Every one will readily seize the circumstances above related, which militate against the opinion, that it covered the bones only of persons fallen in battle; and against the tradition also, which would make it the common sepulchre of a town, in which the bodies were placed upright, and touching each other. Appearances certainly indicate that it has derived both origin and growth from the accustomary collection of bones, and deposition of them together; that the first collection had been deposited on the common surface of the earth, a few stones put over it, and then a covering of earth, that the second had been laid on this, had covered more or less of it in proportion to the number of bones, and was then also covered with earth; and so on. The following are the particular circumstances which give it this aspect. 1. The number of bones. 2. Their confused position. 3. Their being in different strata. 4. The strata in one part having no correspondence with those in another. 5. The different states of decay in these strata, which seem to indicate a difference in the time of inhumation. 6. The existence of infant bones among them.

But on whatever occasion they may have been made, they are of considerable notoriety among the Indians; for a party passing, about thirty years ago, through the part of the country where this barrow is, went through the woods directly to it, without any instructions or inquiry, and having staid about it for some time, with expressions which were construed to be those of sorrow, they returned to the high road, which they had left about half a dozen miles to pay this visit, and pursued their journey. There is another barrow much resembling this, in the low grounds of the South branch of Shenandoah, where it is crossed by the road leading from the Rock-fish gap to Staunton. Both of these have, within these dozen years, been cleared of their trees and put under cultivation, are much reduced in their height, and spread in width, by the plough, and will probably disappear in time. There is another on a hill in the Blue ridge of mountains, a few miles North of Wood's gap, which is made up of small stones thrown together. This has been opened and found to contain human bones, as the others do. There are also many others in other parts of the country.

Great question has arisen from whence came those aboriginals of America? Discoveries, long ago made, were sufficient to show that the passage from Europe to America was always practicable, even to the imperfect navigation of ancient times. In going from Norway to Iceland, from Iceland to Grœnland, from Grœnland to Labrador, the first traject is the widest; and this having been practised from the earliest times of which we have any account of that part of the earth, it is not difficult to suppose that the subsequent trajects may have been sometimes passed. Again, the late discoveries of Captain Cook, coasting from Kamschatka to California, have proved that if the two continents of Asia and America be separated at all, it is only by a narrow streight. So that from this side also, inhabitants may have passed into America; and the resemblance between the Indians of America and the eastern inhabitants of Asia, would induce us to conjecture, that the former are the descendants of the latter, or the latter of the former; excepting indeed the Esquimaux, who, from the same circumstance of resemblance, and from identity of language, must be derived from the Grœnlanders, and these probably from some of the northern parts of the old continent. A knowledge of their several languages would be the most certain evidence of their derivation which could be produced. In fact, it is the best proof of the affinity of nations which ever can be referred to. How many ages have elapsed since the English, the Dutch, the Germans, the Swiss, the Norwegians, Danes and Swedes have separated from their common stock? Yet how many more must elapse before the proofs of their common origin, which exists in their several languages, will disappear? It is to be lamented, then, very much to be lamented, that we have suffered so many of the Indian tribes already to extinguish, without our having previously collected and deposited in the records of literature, the general rudiments at least of the languages they spoke. Were vocabularies formed of all the languages spoken in North and South America, preserving their appellations of the most common objects in nature, of those which must be present to every nation barbarous or civilized, with the inflections of their nouns and verbs, their principles of regimen and concord, and these deposited in all the public libraries, it would furnish opportunities to those skilled in the languages of the old world to compare them with these, now, or at any future time, and hence to construct the best evidence of the derivation of this part of the human race.[6] . . .

Ford III: 194–207

## x.3 To General Chastellux

Paris, June 7, 1785

Dear Sir, – I have been honored with the receipt of your letter of the 2d instant, and am to thank you, as I do sincerely, for the partiality with which you receive the copy of the Notes on my country.[1] As I can answer for the facts, therein reported, on my own observation, and have admitted none on the report of others, which were not supported by evidence sufficient to command my own assent, I am not afraid that you should make any extracts you please for the *Journal de Physique*, which come within their plan of publication. The strictures on slavery and on the constitution of

---

[6] In the 1787 edition of the *Notes on Virginia*, the following paragraph is inserted: "But imperfect as is our knowledge of the tongues spoken in America, it suffices to discover the following remarkable fact: Arranging them under the radical ones to which they may be palpably traced, and doing the same by those of the red men of Asia, there will be found probably twenty in America, for one in Asia, of those radical languages, so called because if they were ever the same they have lost all resemblance to one another. A separation into dialects may be the work of a few ages only, but for two dialects to recede from one another till they have lost all vestiges of their common origin, must require an immense course of time; perhaps not less than many people give to the age of the earth. A greater number of those radical changes of language having taken place among the red men of America, proves them of greater antiquity than those of Asia." – *Eds.*

[1] I.e., Jefferson's *Notes on the State of Virginia*, first published in Paris in a limited edition in 1785. – *Eds.*

Virginia, are not of that kind, and they are the parts which I do not wish to have made public, at least till I know whether their publication would do most harm or good. It is possible, that in my own country, these strictures might produce an irritation, which would indispose the people towards the two great objects I have in view; that is, the emancipation of their slaves, and the settlement of their constitution on a firmer and more permanent basis. If I learn from thence, that they will not produce that effect, I have printed and reserved just copies enough to be able to give one to every young man at the College. It is to them I look, to the rising generation, and not to the one now in power, for these great reformations. The other copy, delivered at your hotel, was for Monsieur de Buffon.[2] I meant to ask the favor of you to have it sent to him, as I was ignorant how to do it. I have also one for Monsieur Daubenton, but being utterly unknown to him, I cannot take the liberty of presenting it, till I can do it through some common acquaintance.

I will beg leave to say here a few words on the general question of the degeneracy of animals in America. 1. As to the degeneracy of the man of Europe transplanted to America, it is no part of Monsieur de Buffon's system. He goes, indeed, within one step of it, but he stops there. The Abbé Raynal[3] alone has taken that step. Your knowledge of America enables you to judge this question, to say, whether the lower class of people in America are less informed and less susceptible of information, than the lower class in Europe; and whether those in America, who have received such an education as that country can give, are less improved by it than Europeans of the same degree of education. 2. As to the aboriginal man of America, I know of no respectable evidence on which the opinion of his inferiority of genius has been founded, but that of Don Ulloa.[4] As to Robertson,[5] he never was in America, he relates nothing on his own knowledge, he is a compiler only of the relations of others, and a mere translator of the opinions of Monsieur de Buffon. I should as soon, therefore, add the translators of Robertson to the witnesses

[2] The French naturalist (see *supra*, 1.3, note 2). – *Eds.*
[3] See *supra*, x.1, note 7. – *Eds.*
[4] See *supra*, x.1, note 2. – *Eds.*
[5] William Robertson (1721–93), Scottish historian and author of *History of America* (London, 1774). – *Eds.*

of this fact, as himself. Paw [*sic*]⁶, the beginner of this charge, was a compiler from the works of others; and of the most unlucky description; for he seems to have read the writings of travellers, only to collect and republish their lies. It is really remarkable, that in three volumes 12mo, of small print, it is scarcely possible to find one truth, and yet, that the author should be able to produce authority for every fact he states, as he says he can. Don Ulloa's testimony is the most respectable. He wrote of what he saw, but he saw the Indian of South America only, and that after he had passed through ten generations of slavery. It is very unfair, from this sample, to judge of the natural genius of this race of men; and, after supposing that Don Ulloa had not sufficiently calculated the allowance which should be made for this circumstance, we do him no injury in considering the picture he draws of the present Indians of South America, as no picture of what their ancestors were three hundred years ago. It is in North America we are to seek their original character. And I am safe in affirming, that the proofs of genius given by the Indians of North America place them on a level with whites in the same uncultivated state. The North of Europe furnishes subjects enough for comparison with them, and for a proof of their equality. I have seen some thousands myself, and conversed much with them, and have found in them a masculine, sound understanding. I have had much information from men who had lived among them, and whose veracity and good sense were so far known to me, as to establish a reliance on their information. They have all agreed in bearing witness in favor of the genius of this people. As to their bodily strength, their manners rendering it disgraceful to labor, those muscles employed in labor will be weaker with them, than with the European laborer; but those which are exerted in the chase, and those faculties which are employed in the tracing an enemy or a wild beast, in contriving ambuscades for him, and in carrying them through their execution, are much stronger than with us, because they are more exercised. I believe the Indian, then, to be, in body and mind, equal to the white man. I have supposed the black man, in his present state, might not be so; but it would be hazardous to affirm, that, equally cultivated for a few

---

⁶ Cornelius Pauw, *Recherches Philosophiques sur les Américains* (Berlin, 1770). – *Eds.*

generations, he would not become so. 3. As to the inferiority of the other animals of America, without more facts, I can add nothing to what I have said in my Notes.

As to the theory of Monsieur de Buffon, that heat is friendly, and moisture adverse to the production of large animals, I am lately furnished with a fact by Dr. [Benjamin] Franklin, which proves the air of London and of Paris to be more humid than that of Philadelphia, and so creates a suspicion that the opinion of the superior humidity of America may, perhaps, have been too hastily adopted. And, supposing that fact admitted, I think the physical reasonings urged to show, that in a moist country animals must be small, and that in a hot one they must be large, are not built on the basis of experiment. These questions, however, cannot be decided, ultimately, at this day. More facts must be collected, and more time flow off, before the world will be ripe for decision. In the meantime, doubt is wisdom.

I have been fully sensible [aware] of the anxieties of your situation, and that your attentions were wholly consecrated, where alone they were wholly due, to the succor of friendship and worth. However much I prize your society, I wait with patience the moment when I can have it without taking what is due to another. In the meantime, I am solaced with the hope of possessing your friendship, and that it is not ungrateful to you to receive assurances of that with which I have the honor to be, dear Sir,

Your most obedient, and most humble servant.

L & B, v: 3–7

## x.4 To Charles Carroll

Philadelphia, April 15, 1791

Dear Sir, – I received last night your favor of the 10th, with Mr. Brown's receipt, and thank you for the trouble you have been so kind as to take in this business.

Our news from the westward is disagreeable. Constant murders committing by the Indians, and their combination threatens to be more and more extensive. I hope we shall give them a thorough drubbing this summer, and then change our tomahawk into a golden chain of friendship. The most economical as well as most humane conduct towards them is to bribe them into peace, and to retain them in peace by eternal bribes. The expedition this year would have served for presents on the most liberal scale for one hundred years; nor shall we otherwise ever get rid of any army, or of our debt. The least rag of Indian depredation will be an excuse to raise troops for those who love to have troops, and for those who think that a public debt is a good thing. Adieu, my dear Sir. Yours affectionately.

Washington III: 246–7

## x.5 To Brother Handsome Lake

Washington, November 3, 1802

To Brother Handsome Lake: – I have received the message in writing which you sent me through Captain Irvine, our confidential agent, placed near you for the purpose of communicating and transacting between us, whatever may be useful for both nations. I am happy to learn you have been so far favored by the Divine spirit as to be made sensible [aware] of those things which are for your good and that of your people, and of those which are hurtful to you; and particularly that you and they see the ruinous effects which the abuse of spirituous liquors have produced upon them. It has weakened their bodies, enervated their minds, exposed them to hunger, cold, nakedness, and poverty, kept them in perpetual broils, and reduced their population. I do not wonder then, brother, at your censures, not only on your own people, who have voluntarily gone into these fatal habits, but on all the nations of white people who have supplied their calls for this article. But these nations have done to you only what they do among themselves. They have sold what individuals wish to buy, leaving to every one to be the guardian of his own health and happiness. Spirituous liquors are not in themselves bad, they are often found to be an excellent medicine for the sick; it is the improper and intemperate use of them, by those in health, which makes them injurious. But as you find that your people cannot refrain from an ill use of them, I greatly applaud your resolution not to use them at all. We have too affectionate a concern for your happiness to place the paltry gain on the sale of these articles in competition with the injury they do you. And as it is the desire of your nation, that no spirits should be sent among them, I am authorized by the great council of the United States to prohibit them. I will sincerely cöoperate with your wise men in any proper measures for this purpose, which shall be agreeable to them.

You remind me, brother, of what I said to you, when you visited me the last winter, that the lands you then held would remain yours, and shall never go from you but when you should be disposed to sell. This I now repeat, and will ever abide by. We, indeed, are always ready to buy land; but we will never ask but when you wish to sell; and our laws, in order to protect you against imposition, have forbidden individuals to purchase lands from you; and have rendered it necessary, when you desire to sell, even to a State, that an agent from the United States should attend the sale, see that your consent is freely given, a satisfactory price paid, and report to us what has been done, for our approbation. This was done in the late case of which you complain. The deputies of your nation came forward, in all the forms which we have been used to consider as evidence of the will of your nation. They proposed to sell to the State of New York certain parcels of land, of small extent, and detached from the body of your other lands; the State of New York was desirous to buy. I sent an agent, in whom we could trust, to see that your consent was free, and the sale fair. All was reported to be free and fair. The lands were your property. The right to sell is one of the rights of property. To forbid you the exercise of that right would be a wrong to your nation. Nor do I think, brother, that the sale of lands is, under all circumstances, injurious to your people. While they depended on hunting, the more extensive the forest around them, the more game they would yield. But going into a state of agriculture, it may be as advantageous to a society, as it is to an individual, who has more land than he can improve, to sell a part, and lay out the money in stocks and implements of agriculture, for the better improvement of the residue. A little land well stocked and improved, will yield more than a great deal without stock or improvement. I hope, therefore, that on further reflection, you will see this transaction in a more favorable light, both as it concerns the interest of your nation, and the exercise of that super-intending care which I am sincerely anxious to employ for their

subsistence and happiness. Go on then, brother, in the great reformation you have undertaken. Persuade our red brethren then to be
sober, and to cultivate their lands; and their women to spin and
weave for their families. You will soon see your women and children
well fed and clothed, your men living happily in peace and plenty,
and your numbers increasing from year to year. It will be a great
glory to you to have been the instrument of so happy a change, and
your children's children, from generation to generation, will repeat
your name with love and gratitude forever. In all your enterprises
for the good of your people, you may count with confidence on the
aid and protection of the United States, and on the sincerity and
zeal with which I am myself animated in the furthering of this
humane work. You are our brethren of the same land; we wish your
prosperity as brethren should do. Farewell.

L & B XVI: 393–6

## x.6 To Benjamin Hawkins

Washington, February 18, 1803

Dear Sir, – . . . Altho' you will receive, thro' the official channel of
the War Office, every communication necessary to develop to you
our views respecting the Indians, and to direct your conduct, yet,
supposing it will be satisfactory to you, and to those with whom
you are placed, to understand my personal dispositions and opinions
in this particular, I shall avail myself of this private letter to state
them generally. I consider the business of hunting as already
become insufficient to furnish clothing and subsistence to the Indians. The promotion of agriculture, therefore, and household manufacture, are essential in their preservation, and I am disposed to aid
and encourage it liberally. This will enable them to live on much
smaller portions of land, and indeed will render their vast forests
useless but for the range of cattle; for which purpose, also, as they
become better farmers, they will be found useless, and even disadvantageous. While they are learning to do better on less land, our
increasing numbers will be calling for more land, and thus a coincidence of interests will be produced between those who have lands
to spare, and want other necessaries, and those who have such

necessaries to spare, and want lands. This commerce, then, will be for the good of both, and those who are friends to both ought to encourage it. You are in the station peculiarly charged with this interchange, and who have it peculiarly in your power to promote among the Indians a sense of the superior value of a little land, well cultivated, over a great deal, unimproved, and to encourage them to make this estimate truly. The wisdom of the animal which amputates & abandons to the hunter the parts for which he is pursued should be theirs, with this difference, that the former sacrifices what is useful, the latter what is not. In truth, the ultimate point of rest & happiness for them is to let our settlements and theirs meet and blend together, to intermix, and become one people. Incorporating themselves with us as citizens of the U.S., this is what the natural progress of things will of course bring on, and it will be better to promote than to retard it. Surely it will be better for them to be identified with us, and preserved in the occupation of their lands, than be exposed to the many casualties which may endanger them while a separate people. I have little doubt but that your reflections must have led you to view the various ways in which their history may terminate, and to see that this is the one most for their happiness. And we have already had an application from a settlement of Indians to become citizens of the U.S. It is possible, perhaps probable, that this idea may be so novel as that it might shock the Indians, were it even hinted to them. Of course, you will keep it for your own reflection; but, convinced of its soundness, I feel it consistent with pure morality to lead them towards it, to familiarize them to the idea that it is for their interest to cede lands at times to the U.S., and for us thus to procure gratifications to our citizens, from time to time, by new acquisitions of land. From no quarter is there at present so strong a pressure on this subject as from Georgia for the residue of the fork of Oconee & Ockmulgee [rivers]; and indeed I believe it will be difficult to resist it. As it has been mentioned that the Creeks had at one time made up their minds to sell this, and were only checked in it by some indiscretions of an individual, I am in hopes you will be able to bring them to it again. I beseech you to use your most earnest endeavors; for it will relieve us here from a great pressure, and yourself from the unreasonable suspicions of the Georgians which you notice, that you are more attached to the interests of the Indians than of the U.S., and throw cold water on their willingness to part with lands. It is so easy to excite suspicion, that none are to be wondered at; but I am in hopes it will be in your power to quash them by effecting the object.

Mr. Madison enjoys better health since his removal to this place than he had done in Orange. Mr. Giles is in a state of health feared to be irrecoverable, although he may hold on for some time, and perhaps be re-established. Browze Trist is now in the Mississippi territory, forming an establishment for his family, which is still in Albemarle, and will remove to the Mississippi in the spring. Mrs. Trist, his mother, begins to yield a little to time. I retain myself very perfect health, having not had 20 hours of fever in 42 years past. I have sometimes had a troublesome headache, and some slight rheumatic pains; but now sixty years old nearly, I have had as little to complain of in point of health as most people. I learn you have the gout. I did not expect that Indian cookery or Indian fare would produce that; but it is considered as a security for good health otherwise. That it may be so with you, I sincerely pray, and tender you my friendly and respectful salutations.

Ford VIII: 213–16

## x.7 To Governor Wm. Henry Harrison[1]

Washington, February 27, 1803

Dear Sir, – While at Monticello in August last I received your favor of August 8th, and meant to have acknowledged it on my return to the seat of government at the close of the ensuing month, but on my return I found that you were expected to be on here in person, and this expectation continued till winter. I have since received your favor of December 30th.

In the former you mentioned the plan of the town which you had done me the honor to name after me, and to lay out according to an idea I had formerly expressed to you. I am thoroughly persuaded that it will be found handsome and pleasant, and I do believe it to be the best means of preserving the cities of America from the scourge of the yellow fever, which being peculiar to our country, must be derived

---

[1] Of the newly created Indiana Territory. He was appointed Governor by President-John Adams in 1800. – *Eds.*

from some peculiarity in it. That peculiarity I take to be our cloudless skies. In Europe, where the sun does not shine more than half the number of days in the year which it does in America, they can build their town in a solid block with impunity; but here a constant sun produces too great an accumulation of heat to admit that. Ventilation is indispensably necessary. Experience has taught us that in the open air of the country the yellow fever is not only not generated, but ceases to be infectious. I cannot decide from the drawing you sent me, whether you have laid off streets round the squares thus:

or only the diagonal streets therein marked. The former was my idea, and is, I imagine, most convenient.

You will receive herewith an answer to your letter as President of the Convention; and from the Secretary of War you receive from time to time information and instructions as to our Indian affairs. These communications being for the public records, are restrained always to particular objects and occasions; but this letter being unofficial and private, I may with safety give you a more extensive view of our policy respecting the Indians, that you may the better comprehend the parts dealt out to you in detail through the official channel, and observing the system of which they make a part, conduct yourself in unison with it in cases where you are obliged to act without instruction. Our system is to live in perpetual peace with the Indians, to cultivate an affectionate attachment from them, by everything just and liberal which we can do for them within the bounds of reason, and by giving them effectual protection against wrongs from our own people. The decrease of game rendering their subsistence by hunting insufficient, we wish to draw them to agriculture, to spinning and weaving. The latter branches they take up with great readiness, because they fall to the women, who gain by quitting the labors of the field for those which are exercised within doors. When they withdraw themselves to the culture of a small piece of land, they will perceive how useless to them are their extensive forests, and will be willing to pare them off from time to time in exchange for necessaries for their farms and families. To promote this disposition to exchange lands, which they have to spare and we want, for necessaries, which we have to spare and they want, we shall push our trading uses, and be glad to see the good and influential individuals among them run in debt, because we observe that when these debts get beyond what the individuals can pay, they become willing to lop them off by a cession of lands. At our trading houses, too, we mean to sell so low as merely to repay us cost and charges, so as neither to lessen or enlarge our capital. This is what private traders cannot do, for they must gain; they will consequently retire from the competition, and we shall thus get clear of this pest without giving offence or umbrage to the Indians. In this way our settlements will gradually circumscribe and approach the Indians, and they will in time either incorporate with us as citizens of the United States, or remove beyond the Mississippi. The former is certainly the termination of their history most happy for themselves; but, in the whole course of this, it is essential to cultivate their love. As to their fear, we presume that our strength and their weakness is now so visible that they must see we have only to shut our hand to crush them, and that all our liberalities to them proceed from motives of pure humanity only. Should any tribe be fool-hardy enough to take up the hatchet at any time, the seizing the whole country of that tribe, and driving them across the Mississippi, as the only condition of peace, would be an example to others, and a furtherance of our final consolidation.

Combined with these views, and to be prepared against the occupation of Louisiana by a powerful and enterprising people, it is important that, setting less value on interior extension of purchases from the Indians, we bend our whole views to the purchase and settlement of the country on the Mississippi, from its mouth to its northern regions, that we may be able to present as strong a front on our western as on our eastern border, and plant on the Mississippi itself the means of its own defence. We now own from 31 [i.e. 31°N. latitude] to the Yazoo, and hope this summer to purchase what belongs to the Choctaws from the Yazoo up to their boundary, supposed to be about opposite the mouth of Acanza. We wish at the same time to begin in your quarter, for which there is at present a favorable opening. The Cahokias extinct, we are entitled to their country by our paramount sovereignty. The Piorias, we understand, have all been driven off from their country, and we might claim it in the same way; but as we understand there is one chief remaining, who would, as the survivor of the tribe, sell the right, it is better to give him such terms as will make him easy for life, and take a conveyance from him. The Kaskaskias being reduced to a few families, I presume we may purchase their whole country for what would place every individual of them at his ease, and be a small price to us, – say by laying off for each family, whenever they would choose it, as much rich land as they could cultivate, adjacent to each other, enclosing the whole in a single fence, and giving them such an annuity in money or goods forever as would place them in happiness; and we might take them also under the protection of the United States. Thus possessed of the rights of these tribes, we should proceed to the settling their boundaries with the Poutewatamies and Kickapoos; claiming all doubtful territory, but paying them a price for the relinquishment of their concurrent claim, and even prevailing on them, if possible, to *cede*, for a price, such of their own unquestioned territory as would give us a convenient northern boundary. Before breaching this, and while we are bargaining with the Kaskaskies, the minds of the Poutewatamies and Kickapoos should be soothed and conciliated by liberalities and sincere assurances of friendship. Perhaps by sending a well-qualified character to stay some time in Decoigne's village, as if on other business, and to sound him and introduce the subject by degrees to his mind and that of the other heads of families, inculcating in the way of conversation, all those considerations which prove the advantages they would receive by a cession on these terms, the object might be more easily and effectually obtained than by abruptly proposing it to them at a formal treaty. Of the means, however, of obtaining what we wish, you will be the best judge; and I have given you this view of the system which we suppose will best promote the interests of the Indians and ourselves, and finally consolidate our whole country to one nation only; that you may be enabled the better to adapt your means to the object, for this purpose we have given you a general commission for treating. The crisis is pressing: whatever can now be obtained must be obtained quickly. The occupation of New Orleans, hourly expected, by the French, is already felt like a light breeze by the Indians. You know the sentiments they entertain of that nation; under the hope of their protection they will immediately stiffen against cessions of lands to us. We had better, therefore, do at once what can now be done.

I must repeat that this letter is to be considered as private and friendly, and is not to control any particular instructions which you may receive through official channel. You will also perceive how sacredly it must be kept within your own breast, and especially how improper to be understood by the Indians. For their interests and their tranquillity it is best they should see only the present age of their history. I pray you to accept assurances of my esteem and high consideration.

Washington IV: 471–5

## x.8 To the Brothers of the Choctaw Nation

December 17, 1803

Brothers of the Choctaw Nation: – We have long heard of your nation as a numerous, peaceable, and friendly people; but this is the first visit we have had from its great men at the seat of our government. I welcome you here; am glad to take you by the hand, and to assure you, for your nation, that we are their friends. Born in the same land, we ought to live as brothers, doing to each other all the good we can, and not listening to wicked men, who may endeavor to make us enemies. By living in peace, we can help and prosper one another; by waging war, we can kill and destroy many on both sides; but those who survive will not be the happier for that. Then, brothers, let it forever be peace and good neighborhood between us. Our seventeen States compose a great and growing nation. Their children are as the leaves of the trees, which the winds are spreading over the forest. But we are just also. We take from no nation what belongs to it. Our growing numbers make us always willing to buy lands from our red brethren, when they are willing to sell. But be assured we never mean to disturb them in their possessions. On the contrary, the lines established between us by mutual consent, shall be sacredly preserved, and will protect your lands from all encroachments by our own people or any others. We will give you a copy of the law, made by our great Council, for punishing our people, who may encroach on your lands, or injure you otherwise. Carry it with you to your homes, and preserve it, as the shield which we spread over you, to protect your land, your property and persons.

It is at the request which you sent me in September, signed by Puckshanublee and other chiefs, and which you now repeat, that I listen to your proposition to sell us lands. You say you owe a great debt to your merchants, that you have nothing to pay it with but lands, and you pray us to take lands, and pay your debt. The sum you have occasion for, brothers, is a very great one. We have never yet paid as much to any of our red brethren for the purchase of lands. You propose to us some on the Tombigbee, and some on the Mississippi. Those on the Mississippi suit us well. We wish to have establishments on that river, as resting places for our boats, to furnish them provisions, and to receive our people who fall sick on the way to or from New Orleans, which is now ours. In that quarter, therefore, we are willing to purchase as much as you will spare. But as to the manner in which the line shall be run, we are not judges of it here, nor qualified to make any bargain. But we will appoint persons hereafter to treat with you on the spot, who, knowing the country and quality of the lands, will be better able to agree with you on a line which will give us a just equivalent for the sum of money you want paid.

You have spoken, brothers, of the lands which your fathers formerly sold and marked off to the English, and which they ceded to us with the rest of the country they held here; and you say that, though you do not know whether your fathers were paid for them, you have marked the line over again for us, and do not ask repayment. It has always been the custom, brothers, when lands were bought of the red men, to pay for them immediately, and none of us have ever seen an example of such a debt remaining unpaid. It is to satisfy their immediate wants that the red men have usually sold lands; and in such a case, they would not let the debt be unpaid. The presumption from custom then is strong; so it is also from the great length of time since your fathers sold these lands. But we have, moreover, been informed by persons now living, and who assisted the English in making the purchase, that the price was paid at the time. Were it otherwise, as it was their contract, it would be their debt, not ours.

I rejoice, brothers, to hear you propose to become cultivators of the earth for the maintenance of your families. Be assured you will support them better and with less labor, by raising stock and bread, and by spinning and weaving clothes, than by hunting. A little land cultivated, and a little labor, will procure more provisions than the most successful hunt; and a woman will clothe more by spinning and weaving, than a man by hunting. Compared with you, we are but as of yesterday in this land. Yet see how much more we have multiplied by industry, and the exercise of that reason which you possess in common with us. Follow then our example, brethren, and we will aid you with great pleasure.

The clothes and other necessaries which we sent you the last year, were, as you supposed, a present from us. We never meant to ask land or any other payment for them; and the store which we sent on, was at your request also; and to accommodate you with necessaries at a reasonable price, you wished of course to have it on your land; but the land would continue yours, not ours.

As to the removal of the store, the interpreter, and the agent, and any other matters you may wish to speak about, the Secretary at War will enter into explanations with you, and whatever he says, you may consider as said by myself, and what he promises you will be faithfully performed.

I am glad, brothers, you are willing to go and visit some other parts of our country. Carriages shall be ready to convey you, and you shall be taken care of on your journey; and when you shall have returned here and rested yourselves to your own mind, you shall be sent home by land. We had provided for your coming by land, and were sorry for the mistake which carried you to Savannah instead of Augusta, and exposed you to the risks of a voyage by sea. Had any accident happened to you, though we could not help it, it would have been a cause of great mourning to us. But we thank the Great Spirit who took care of you on the ocean, and brought you safe and in good health to the seat of our great Council, and we hope His care will accompany and protect you, on your journey and return home; and that He will preserve and prosper your nation in all its just pursuits.

L & B XIX: 146–9

## x.9 Second Inaugural Address[1]

March 4, 1805

Proceeding, fellow citizens, to that qualification which the constitution requires, before my entrance on the charge again conferred upon me, it is my duty to express the deep sense I entertain of this new proof of confidence from my fellow citizens at large, and the zeal with which it inspires me, so to conduct myself as may best satisfy their just expectations.

On taking this station on a former occasion, I declared the principles on which I believed it my duty to administer the affairs of our commonwealth. My conscience tells me that I have, on every occasion, acted up to that declaration, according to its obvious import, and to the understanding of every candid mind.

In the transaction of your foreign affairs, we have endeavored to cultivate the friendship of all nations, and especially of those with

---

[1] From Jefferson's "Notes of a Draft for a Second Inaugural Address": "The former one [i.e., the First Inaugural Address] was an exposition of the principles on which I thought it my duty to administer the government. The second then should naturally be a *conte rendu*, or a statement of facts, shewing that I have conformed to those principles. The former was *promise:* this is *performance.* Yet the nature of the occasion requires that details should be avoided, that, the most prominent heads only should be selected and these placed in a strong light but in as few words as possible. These heads are Foreign affairs; Domestic do., viz. Taxes, Debts, Louisiana, Religion, Indians, The Press. None of these heads need any commentary but that of the Indians. This is a proper topic not only to promote the work of humanizing our citizens towards these people, but to conciliate to us the good opinion of Europe on the subject of the Indians. This, however, might have been done in half the compass it here occupies. But every respector of science, every friend to political reformation must have observed with indignation the hue & cry raised against philosophy & the rights of man; and it really seems as if they would be overborne & barbarism, bigotry & despotism would recover the ground they have lost by the advance of the public understanding. I have thought the occasion justified some discountenance of these anti-social doctrines, some testimony against them, but not to commit myself in direct warfare on them, I have thought it best to say what is directly applied to the Indians only, but admits by inference a more general extension." – *Eds.*

which we have the most important relations. We have done them justice on all occasions, favored where favor was lawful, and cherished mutual interests and intercourse on fair and equal terms. We are firmly convinced, and we act on that conviction, that with nations, as with individuals, our interests soundly calculated, will ever be found inseparable from our moral duties; and history bears witness to the fact, that a just nation is taken on its word, when recourse is had to armaments and wars to bridle others.

At home, fellow citizens, you best know whether we have done well or ill. The suppression of unnecessary offices, of useless establishments and expenses, enabled us to discontinue our internal taxes. These covering our land with officers, and opening our doors to their intrusions, had already begun that process of domiciliary vexation which, once entered, is scarcely to be restrained from reaching successively every article of produce and property. If among these taxes some minor ones fell which had not been inconvenient, it was because their amount would not have paid the officers who collected them, and because, if they had any merit, the state authorities might adopt them, instead of others less approved.

The remaining revenue on the consumption of foreign articles, is paid cheerfully by those who can afford to add foreign luxuries to domestic comforts, being collected on our seaboards and frontiers only, and incorporated with the transactions of our mercantile citizens, it may be the pleasure and pride of an American to ask, what farmer, what mechanic, what laborer, ever sees a tax-gatherer of the United States? These contributions enable us to support the current expenses of the government, to fulfil contracts with foreign nations, to extinguish the native right of soil within our limits, to extend those limits, and to apply such a surplus to our public debts, as places at a short day their final redemption, and that redemption once effected, the revenue thereby liberated may, by a just repartition among the states, and a corresponding amendment of the constitution, be applied, *in time of peace*, to rivers, canals, roads, arts, manufactures, education, and other great objects within each state. *In time of war*, if injustice, by ourselves or others, must sometimes produce war, increased as the same revenue will be increased by population and consumption, and aided by other resources reserved for that crisis, it may meet within the year all the expenses of the year, without encroaching on the rights of future generations, by burdening them with the debts of the past. War will then be but a suspension of useful works, and a return to a state of peace, a return to the progress of improvement.

I have said, fellow citizens, that the income reserved had enabled us to extend our limits; but that extension may possibly pay for itself before we are called on, and in the meantime, may keep down the accruing interest; in all events, it will repay the advances we have made. I know that the acquisition of Louisiana has been disapproved by some, from a candid apprehension that the enlargement of our territory would endanger its union. But who can limit the extent to which the federative principle may operate effectively? The larger our association, the less will it be shaken by local passions; and in any view, is it not better that the opposite bank of the Mississippi should be settled by our own brethren and children, than by strangers of another family? With which shall we be most likely to live in harmony and friendly intercourse?

In matters of religion, I have considered that its free exercise is placed by the constitution independent of the powers of the general government. I have therefore undertaken, on no occasion, to prescribe the religious exercises suited to it; but have left them, as the constitution found them, under the direction and discipline of state or church authorities acknowledged by the several religious societies.

The aboriginal inhabitants of these countries [i.e. states] I have regarded with the commiseration their history inspires. Endowed with the faculties and the rights of men, breathing an ardent love of liberty and independence, and occupying a country which left them no desire but to be undisturbed, the stream of overflowing population from other regions directed itself on these shores; without power to divert, or habits to contend against, they have been overwhelmed by the current, or driven before it; now reduced within limits too narrow for the hunter's state, humanity enjoins us to teach them agriculture and the domestic arts; to encourage them to that industry which alone can enable them to maintain their place in existence, and to prepare them in time for that state of society, which to bodily comforts adds the improvement of the mind and morals. We have therefore liberally furnished them with the implements of husbandry and household use; we have placed among them instructors in the arts of first necessity; and they are covered with the ægis of the law against aggressors from among ourselves.

But the endeavors to enlighten them on the fate which awaits their present course of life, to induce them to exercise their reason, follow its dictates, and change their pursuits with the change of circumstances, have powerful obstacles to encounter; they are combated by the habits of their bodies, prejudice of their minds, ignorance, pride, and the influence of interested and crafty individuals among them, who feel themselves something in the present order of things, and fear to become nothing in any other. These persons inculcate a sanctimonious reverence for the customs of their ancestors; that whatsoever they did, must be done through all time; that reason is a false guide, and to advance under its counsel, in their physical, moral, or political condition, is perilous innovation; that their duty is to remain as their Creator made them, ignorance being safety, and knowledge full of danger; in short, my friends, among them is seen the action and counteraction of good sense and bigotry; they, too, have their anti-philosophers, who find an interest in keeping things in their present state, who dread reformation, and exert all their faculties to maintain the ascendency of habit over the duty of improving our reason, and obeying its mandates.

In giving these outlines, I do not mean, fellow citizens, to arrogate to myself the merit of the measures; that is due, in the first place, to the reflecting character of our citizens at large, who, by the weight of public opinion, influence and strengthen the public measures; it is due to the sound discretion with which they select from among themselves those to whom they confide the legislative duties; it is due to the zeal and wisdom of the characters thus selected, who lay the foundations of public happiness in wholesome laws, the execution of which alone remains for others; and it is due to the able and faithful auxiliaries, whose patriotism has associated with me in the executive functions.

During this course of administration, and in order to disturb it, the artillery of the press has been levelled against us, charged with whatsoever its licentiousness could devise or dare. These abuses of an institution so important to freedom and science, are deeply to be regretted, inasmuch as they tend to lessen its usefulness, and to sap its safety; they might, indeed, have been corrected by the wholesome punishments reserved and provided by the laws of the several States against falsehood and defamation; but public duties more urgent press on the time of public servants, and the offenders have therefore been left to find their punishment in the public indignation.

Nor was it uninteresting to the world, that an experiment should be fairly and fully made, whether freedom of discussion, unaided by power, is not sufficient for the propagation and protection of truth – whether a government, conducting itself in the true spirit of its constitution, with zeal and purity, and doing no act which it would be unwilling the whole world should witness, can be written down by falsehood and defamation. The experiment has been tried; you have witnessed the scene; our fellow citizens have looked on, cool and collected; they saw the latent source from which these outrages proceeded; they gathered around their public functionaries, and when the constitution called them to the decision by suffrage, they pronounced their verdict, honorable to those who had served them, and consolatory to the friend of man, who believes he may be intrusted with his own affairs.

No inference is here intended, that the laws, provided by the State against false and defamatory publications, should not be enforced; he who has time, renders a service to public morals and public tranquillity, in reforming these abuses by the salutary coercions of the law; but the experiment is noted, to prove that, since truth and reason have maintained their ground against false opinions in league with false facts, the press, confined to truth, needs no other legal restraint; the public judgment will correct false reasonings and opinions, on a full hearing of all parties; and no other definite line can be drawn between the inestimable liberty of the press and its demoralizing licentiousness. If there be still improprieties which this rule would not restrain, its supplement must be sought in the censorship of public opinion.

Contemplating the union of sentiment now manifested so generally, as auguring harmony and happiness to our future course, I offer to our country sincere congratulations. With those, too, not yet rallied to the same point, the disposition to do so is gaining strength; facts are piercing through the veil drawn over them; and our doubting brethren will at length see, that the mass of their fellow citizens, with whom they cannot yet resolve to act, as to principles and measures, think as they think, and desire what they desire; that our wish, as well as theirs, is, that the public efforts may be directed honestly to the public good, that peace be culti-vated, civil and religious liberty unassailed, law and order preserved; equality of rights maintained, and that state of property, equal or unequal, which results to every man from his own industry, or that of his fathers. When satisfied of these views, it is not in human nature that they should not approve and support them; in the mean-time, let us cherish them with patient affection; let us do them justice, and more than justice, in all competitions of interest; and we need not doubt that truth, reason, and their own interests, will at length prevail, will gather them into the fold of their country, and will complete their entire union of opinion, which gives to a nation the blessing of harmony, and the benefit of all its strength.

I shall now enter on the duties to which my fellow citizens have again called me, and shall proceed in the spirit of those principles which they have approved. I fear not that any motives of interest may lead me astray; I am sensible [aware] of no passion which could seduce me knowingly from the path of justice; but the weakness of human nature, and the limits of my own understanding, will produce errors of judgment sometimes injurious to your interests. I shall need, there-fore, all the indulgence I have heretofore experienced – the want of it will certainly not lessen with increasing years. I shall need, too, the favor of that Being in whose hands we are, who led our forefathers, as Israel of old, from their native land, and planted them in a country flowing with all the necessaries and comforts of life; who has covered our infancy with his providence, and our riper years with his wisdom and power; and to whose goodness I ask you to join with me in suppli-cations, that he will so enlighten the minds of your servants, guide their councils, and prosper their measures, that whatsoever they do, shall result in your good, and shall secure to you the peace, friendship, and approbation of all nations.

Ford VIII: 341–8

## x.10 To the Secretary of War (Henry Dearborn)

Monticello, September 2, 1807

Dear Sir, – My letter of August 28th, on the dispositions of the Indians, was to go the rounds of all our brethren, and to be finally

sent to you with their separate opinions. I think it probable, therefore, that the enclosed extract of a letter from a priest at Detroit to
Bishop Carroll, may reach you as soon, or sooner, than that. I therefore forward it, because it throws rather a different light on the
dispositions of the Indians from that given by Hull and Dunham. I
do not think, however, that it ought to slacken our operations,
because those proposed are all precautionary. But it ought absolutely to stop our negotiations for land, otherwise the Indians will
think that these preparations are meant to intimidate them into a
sale of their lands, an idea which would be most pernicious, and
would poison all our professions of friendship to them. The
immediate acquisition of the land is of less consequence to us than
their friendship and a thorough confidence in our justice. We had
better let the purchase lie till they are in better temper. I salute you
with affection and respect.

L & B XI: 354–5

## X.11 To John Adams

Monticello, June 11, 1812

Dear Sir, – By our post preceding that which brought your letter
of May 21st, I had received one from Mr. Malcolm on the same
subject with yours, and by the return of the post had stated to the
President my recollections of him. But both your letters were probably too late; as the appointment had been already made, if we may
credit the newspapers.

You ask if there is any book that pretends to give any account of
the traditions of the Indians, or how one can acquire an idea of
them? Some scanty accounts of their traditions, but fuller of their
customs and characters, are given us by most of the early travellers
among them; these you know were mostly French. Lafitau, among
them, and Adair an Englishman, have written on this subject; the
former two volumes, the latter one, all in 4to. But unluckily Lafitau
had in his head a preconceived theory on the mythology, manners,
institutions and government of the ancient nations of Europe, Asia
and Africa, and seems to have entered on those of America only to
fit them into the same frame, and to draw from them a confirmation

of his general theory. He keeps up a perpetual parallel, in all those articles, between the Indians of America and the ancients of the other quarters of the globe. He selects, therefore, all the facts and adopts all the falsehoods which favor his theory, and very gravely retails such absurdities as zeal for a theory could alone swallow. He was a man of much classical and scriptural reading, and has rendered his book not unentertaining. He resided five years among the Northern Indians, as a Missionary, but collects his matter much more from the writings of others, than from his own observation.

Adair too had his kink. He believed all the Indians of America to be descended from the Jews; the same laws, usages, rites and ceremonies, the same sacrifices, priests, prophets, fasts and festivals, almost the same religion, and that they all spoke Hebrew. For, although he writes particularly of the Southern Indians only, the Catawbas, Creeks, Cherokees, Chickasaws and Chocktaws, with whom alone he was personally acquainted, yet he generalizes whatever he found among them, and brings himself to believe that the hundred languages of America, differing fundamentally every one from every other, as much as Greek from Gothic, yet have all one common prototype. He was a trader, a man of learning, a self-taught Hebraist, a strong religionist, and of as sound a mind as Don Quixotte in whatever did not touch his religious chivalry. His book contains a great deal of real instruction on its subject, only requiring the reader to be constantly on his guard against the wonderful obliquities of his theory.

The scope of your inquiry would scarcely, I suppose, take in the three folio volumes of Latin of De Bry. In these, facts and fable are mingled together, without regard to any favorite system. They are less suspicious, therefore, in their complexion, more original and authentic, than those of Lafitau and Adair. This is a work of great curiosity, extremely rare, so as never to be bought in Europe, but on the breaking up and selling some ancient library. On one of these occasions a bookseller procured me a copy, which, unless you have one, is probably the only one in America.

You ask further, if the Indians have any order of priesthood among them, like the Druids, Bards or Minstrels of the Celtic nations? Adair alone, determined to see what he wished to see in every object, metamorphoses their Conjurers into an order of priests, and describes their sorceries as if they were the great religious ceremonies of the nation. Lafitau called them by their proper names, Jongleurs, Devins, Sortileges; De Bry præstigiatores; Adair himself sometimes Magi, Archimagi, cunning men, Seers, rain makers; and the modern Indian interpreters call them conjurers and witches. They are persons pretending to have communications with the devil and other evil spirits, to foretell future events, bring down rain, find stolen goods, raise the dead, destroy some and heal others by enchantment, lay spells, &c. And Adair, without departing from his parallel of the Jews and Indians, might have found their counterpart much more aptly, among the soothsayers, sorcerers and wizards of the Jews, their Gannes and Gambres, their Simon Magus, Witch of Endor, and the young damsel whose sorceries disturbed Paul so much; instead of placing them in a line with their high-priest, their chief priests, and their magnificent hierarchy generally. In the solemn ceremonies of the Indians, the persons who direct or officiate, are their chiefs, elders and warriors, in civil ceremonies or in those of war; it is the head of the cabin in their private or particular feasts or ceremonies; and sometimes the matrons, as in their corn feasts. And even here, Adair might have kept up his parallel, with ennobling his conjurers. For the ancient patriarchs, the Noahs, the Abrahams, Isaacs and Jacobs, and even after the consecration of Aaron, the Samuels and Elijahs, and we may say further, every one for himself offered sacrifices on the altars. The true line of distinction seems to be, that solemn ceremonies, whether public or private, addressed to the Great Spirit, are conducted by the worthies of the nation, men or matrons, while conjurers are resorted to only for the invocation of evil spirits. The present state of the several Indian tribes, without any public order of priests, is proof sufficient that they never had such an order. Their steady habits permit no innovations, not even those which the progress of science offers to increase the comforts, enlarge the understanding, and improve the morality of mankind. Indeed, so little idea have they of a regular order of priests, that they mistake ours for their conjurers, and call them by that name.

So much in answer to your inquiries concerning Indians, a people with whom, in the early part of my life, I was very familiar, and acquired impressions of attachment and commiseration for them which have never been obliterated. Before the revolution, they were in the habit of coming often and in great numbers to the seat of government, where I was very much with them. I knew much the great Outassetè, the warrior and orator of the Cherokees; he was always the guest of my father, on his journeys to and from Williamsburg. I was in his camp when he made his great farewell oration to his people the evening before his departure for England. The moon was in full splendor, and to her he seemed to address himself in his prayers for his own safety on the voyage, and that of his people during his absence; his sounding voice, distinct articulation, animated action, and the solemn silence of his people at their several fires, filled me with awe and veneration, although I did not understand a word he uttered. That nation, consisting now of about 2,000 warriors, and the Creeks of about 3,000 are far advanced in civilization. They have good cabins, enclosed fields, large herds of cattle and hogs, spin and weave their own clothes of cotton, have smiths and other of the most necessary tradesmen, write and read, are on the increase in numbers, and a branch of Cherokees is now instituting a regular representative government. Some other tribes are advancing in the same line. On those who have made any progress, English seductions will have no effect. But the backward will yield, and be thrown further back. Those will relapse into barbarism and misery, lose numbers by war and want, and we shall be obliged to drive them with the beasts of the forest into the stony mountains. They will be conquered, however, in Canada. The possession of that country secures our women and children forever from the tomahawk and scalping knife, by removing those who excite them; and for this possession orders, I presume, are issued by this time; taking for granted that the doors of Congress will re-open with a declaration of war. That this may end in indemnity for the past, security for the future, and complete emancipation from Anglomany, Gallomany, and all the manias of demoralized Europe, and that you may live in health and happiness to see all this, is the sincere prayer of yours affectionately.

Ford ix: 355–9

# xi   Women (not) in Politics

## XI.1 To Anne Willing Bingham

Paris, February 7, 1787

I know, Madam, that the twelve month is not yet expired; but it will be, nearly, before this will have the honor of being put into your hands. You are then engaged to tell me, truly and honestly, whether you do not find the tranquil pleasures of America, preferable to the empty bustle of Paris. For, to what does that bustle tend? At eleven o'clock, it is day, *chez madame*. The curtains are drawn. Propped on bolsters and pillows, and her head scratched into a little order, the bulletins of the sick are read, and the billets of the well. She writes to some of her acquaintance, and receives the visits of others. If the morning is not very thronged, she is able to get out and hobble round the cage of the Palais Royal; but she must hobble quickly, for the *coiffeur's* turn is come; and a tremendous turn it is! Happy, if he does not make her arrive when dinner is half over! The torpitude of digestion a little passed, she flutters half an hour through the streets, by way of paying visits, and then to the spectacles. These finished, another half hour is devoted to dodging in and out of the doors of her very sincere friends, and away to supper. After supper, cards; and after cards, bed; to rise at noon the next day, and to tread, like a mill horse, the same trodden circle over again. Thus the days of life are consumed, one by one, without an object beyond the present moment; ever flying from the ennui of that, yet carrying it with us; eternally in pursuit of happiness, which keeps eternally before us. If death or bankruptcy happen to trip us out of the circle, it is matter for the buzz of the evening, and is completely forgotten by the next morning. In America, on the other hand, the society of your husband, the fond cares for the children, the arrangements of the house, the improvements of the grounds, fill every moment with a healthy and an useful activity. Every exertion is encouraging, because, to present amusement, it joins the promise of some future good. The intervals of leisure are filled by the society of real friends, whose affections are not thinned to cob-web, by being spread over a thousand objects. This is the picture, in the light it is presented to my mind; now let me have it in yours.

If we do not concur this year, we shall the next; or if not then, in a year or two more. You see I am determined not to suppose myself mistaken.

To let you see that Paris is not changed in its pursuits, since it was honored with your presence, I send you its monthly history. But this relating only to the embellishments of their persons, I must add, that those of the city go on well also. A new bridge, for example, is begun at the Place Louis Quinze; the old ones are clearing off the rubbish which encumbered them in the form of houses; new hospitals erecting; magnificent walls of inclosure, and Customhouses at their entrances, &c., &c., &c. I know of no interesting change among those whom you honored with your acquaintance, unless Monsieur de Saint James was of that number. His bankruptcy, and taking asylum in the Bastile, have furnished matter of astonishment. His garden, at the Pont de Neuilly, where, on seventeen acres of ground, he had laid out fifty thousand *louis*, will probably sell for somewhat less money. The workmen of Paris are making rapid strides towards English perfection. Would you believe, that in the course of the last two years, they have learned even to surpass their London rivals in some articles? Commission me to have you a phaeton made, and, if it is not as much handsomer than a London one, as that is than a *Fiacre* [small coach], send it back to me. Shall I fix the box with caps, bonnets, &c.? Not of my own choosing, but – I was going to say, of Mademoiselle Bertin's, forgetting, for the moment, that she too is a bankrupt. They shall be chosen then by whom you please; or, if you are altogether nonplused by her eclipse, we will call an *Assemblée des Notables* to help you out of the difficulty, as is now the fashion. In short, honor me with your commands of any kind, and they shall be faithfully executed. The packets now established from Havre to New York, furnish good opportunities of sending whatever you wish.

I shall end where I began, like a Paris day, reminding you of your engagement to write me a letter of respectable length, an engagement the more precious to me, as it has furnished the occasion, after presenting my respects to Mr. Bingham, of assuring you of the sincerity of those sentiments of esteem and respect with which I have the honor to be, dear Madam, your most obedient, and most humble servant.

L & B VI: 81–4

## XI.2 To Anne Willing Bingham

Paris, May 11, 1788

Dear Madam, – A gentleman going to Philadelphia furnishes me the occasion of sending you some numbers of the *Cabinet des Modes* & some new theatrical pieces. These last have had great success on the stage, where they have excited perpetual applause. We have now need of something to make us laugh, for the topics of the times are sad and eventful. The gay and thoughtless Paris is now become a furnace of Politics. All the world is now politically mad. Men, women, children talk nothing else, & you know that naturally they talk much, loud & warm. Society is spoilt by it, at least for those who, like myself, are but lookers on. – You too have had your political fever. But our good ladies, I trust, have been too wise to wrinkle their foreheads with politics. They are contented to soothe & calm the minds of their husbands returning ruffled from political debate. They have the good sense to value domestic happiness above all other, and the art to cultivate it beyond all others. There is no part of the earth where so much of this is enjoyed as in America. You agree with me in this; but you think that the pleasures of Paris more than supply its wants; in other words that a Parisian is happier than an American. You will change your opinion, my dear Madam, and come over to mine in the end. Recollect the women of this capital, some on foot, some on horses, & some in carriages hunting pleasure in the streets, in routs & assemblies, and forgetting that they have left it behind them in their nurseries; compare them with our own countrywomen occupied in the tender and tranquil amusements of domestic life, and confess that it is a comparison of Americans and Angels. – You will have known from the public papers that Monsieur de Buffon, the father, is dead & you have known long ago that the son and his wife are separated. They are pursuing pleasure in opposite directions. Madame de Rochambeau is well: so is Madame de la Fayette. I recollect no other *Nouvelles de société* interesting to you. And as for political news of battles & sieges, Turks & Russians, I will not detail them to you, because you would be less handsome after reading them. I have only to add then, what I take a pleasure in repeating, tho' it will be the thousandth time that I have the honour to be with sentiments of very sincere respect & attachment, dear Madam, your most obedient & most humble servant.

Ford V: 8–10

## XI.3 To General George Washington

Paris, December 4, 1788

Sir, – . . . The [French] nation has been awaked by our Revolution, they feel their strength, they are enlightened, their lights are spreading, and they will not retrograde. The first States General may establish three important points, without opposition from the court: 1, their own periodical convocation; 2, their exclusive right of taxation (which has been confessed by the King); 3, the right of registering laws, and of previously proposing amendments to them, as the parliaments have, by usurpation, been in the habit of doing. The court will consent to this, from its hatred to the parliaments, and from the desire of having to do with one, rather than many legislatures. If the States are prudent, they will not aim at more than this at first, lest they should shock the dispositions of the court, and even alarm the public mind, which must be left to open itself by degrees to successive improvements. These will follow, from the nature of things; how far they can proceed, in the end, towards a thorough reformation of abuse, cannot be foreseen. In my opinion, a kind of influence which none of their plans of reform take into account, will elude them all; I mean the influence of women, in the government. The manners of the nation allow them to visit, alone, all persons in office, to solicit the affairs of the husband, family, or friends, and their solicitations bid defiance to laws and regulations. This obstacle may seem less to those who, like our countrymen, are in the precious habit of considering right, as a barrier against all solicitation. Nor can such an one, without the evidence of his own eyes, believe in the desperate state to which things are reduced in this country from the omnipotence of an influence which, fortunately for the happiness of the sex itself, does not endeavor to extend itself in our country beyond the domestic line . . .

L & B VII: 227–8

## XI.4 To the Secretary of the Treasury (Albert Gallatin)

January 13, 1807

The appointment of a woman to office is an innovation for which the public is not prepared, nor am I. Shall we appoint Springs, or wait the further recommendations spoken of by Bloodworth? Briggs has resigned, and I wish to consult with you when convenient on his successor, as well as on an Attorney-General. Affectionate salutations.

Ford IX: 7

## XI.5 To Nathaniel Burwell

Monticello, March 14, 1818

Dear Sir, – Your letter of February 17th found me suffering under an attack of rheumatism, which has but now left me at sufficient ease to attend to the letters I have received. A plan of female education has never been a subject of systematic contemplation with me. It has occupied my attention so far only as the education of my own daughters occasionally required. Considering that they would be placed in a country situation, where little aid could be obtained from abroad, I thought it essential to give them a solid education, which might enable them, when become mothers, to educate their own daughters, and even to direct the course for sons, should their fathers be lost, or incapable, or inattentive. My surviving daughter accordingly, the mother of many daughters as well as sons, has made their education the object of her life, and being a better judge of the practical part than myself, it is with her aid and that of one of her *élèves*, that I shall subjoin a catalogue of the books for such a course of reading as we have practiced.

A great obstacle to good education is the inordinate passion prevalent for novels, and the time lost in that reading which should be instructively employed. When this poison infects the mind, it destroys its tone and revolts it against wholesome reading. Reason and fact, plain and unadorned, are rejected. Nothing can engage attention unless dressed in all the figments of fancy, and nothing so bedecked comes amiss. The result is a bloated imagination, sickly judgment, and disgust towards all the real businesses of life. This mass of trash, however, is not without some distinction; some few modelling their narratives, although fictitious, on the incidents of real life, have been able to make them interesting and useful vehicles of a sound morality. Such, I think, are Marmontel's new moral tales, but not his old ones, which are really immoral. Such are the writings of Miss Edgeworth, and some of those of Madame Genlis. For a like reason, too, much poetry should not be indulged. Some is useful for forming style and taste. Pope, Dryden, Thompson, Shakspeare, and of the French, Molière, Racine, the Corneilles, may be read with pleasure and improvement.

The French language, become that of the general intercourse of nations, and from their extraordinary advances, now the depository of all science, is an indispensable part of education for both sexes. In the subjoined catalogue, therefore, I have placed the books of both languages indifferently, according as the one or the other offers what is best.

The ornaments too, and the amusements of life, are entitled to their portion of attention. These, for a female, are dancing, drawing, and music. The first is a healthy exercise, elegant and very attractive for young people. Every affectionate parent would be pleased to see his daughter qualified to participate with her companions, and without awkwardness at least, in the circles of festivity, of which she occasionally becomes a part. It is a necessary accomplishment, therefore, although of short use; for the French rule is wise, that no lady dances after marriage. This is founded in solid physical reasons, gestation and nursing leaving little time to a married lady when this exercise can be either safe or innocent. Drawing is thought less of in this country than in Europe. It is an innocent and engaging amusement, often useful, and a qualification not to be neglected in one who is to become a mother and an instructor. Music is invaluable where a person has an ear. Where they have not, it should not be attempted. It furnishes a delightful recreation for the hours of respite from the cares of the day, and lasts us through life. The taste of this country, too, calls for this accomplishment more strongly than for either of the others.

I need say nothing of household economy, in which the mothers of our country are generally skilled, and generally careful to instruct their daughters. We all know its value, and that diligence and dexterity in all its processes are inestimable treasures. The order and economy of a house are as honorable to the mistress as those of the farm to the master, and if either be neglected, ruin follows, and children destitute of the means of living.

This, Sir, is offered as a summary sketch on a subject on which I have not thought much. It probably contains nothing but what has already occurred to yourself, and claims your acceptance on no other ground than as a testimony of my respect for your wishes, and of my great esteem and respect.

L & B xv: 165–8

# XII  Law of Nations

## XII.1 To John Jay

Paris, August 23, 1785

Dear Sir, – I shall sometimes ask your permission to write you letters, not official but private. The present is of this kind, and is occasioned by the question proposed in yours of June 14. "whether it would be useful to us to carry all our own productions, or none?" Were we perfectly free to decide this question, I should reason as follows. We have now lands enough to employ an infinite number of people in their cultivation. Cultivators of the earth are the most valuable citizens. They are the most vigorous, the most independant, the most virtuous, & they are tied to their country & wedded to it's liberty & interests by the most lasting bonds. As long therefore as they can find employment in this line, I would not convert them into mariners, artisans or anything else. But our citizens will find employment in this line till their numbers, & of course their productions, become too great for the demand both internal & foreign. This is not the case as yet, & probably will not be for a considerable time. As soon as it is, the surplus of hands must be turned to something else. I should then perhaps wish to turn them to the sea in preference to manufactures, because comparing the characters of the two classes I find the former the most valuable citizens. I consider the class of artificers as the panders of vice & the instruments by which the liberties of a country are generally overturned. However we are not free to decide this question on principles of theory only. Our people are decided in the opinion that it is necessary for us to take a share in the occupation of the ocean, & their established habits induce them to require that the sea be kept open to them, and that that line of policy be pursued which will render the use of that element as great as possible to them. I think it a duty in those entrusted with the administration of their affairs to conform themselves to the decided choice of their constituents: and that therefore we should in every instance preserve an equality of right to them in the transportation of commodities, in the right of fishing, & in the other uses of the sea. But what will be the consequence? Frequent wars without a doubt. Their property will be violated on the sea, & in foreign ports, their persons will be insulted, imprisoned &c. for pretended debts, contracts, crimes, contraband, &c., &c. These insults must be resented, even if we had no feelings, yet to prevent their eternal repetition, or in other words, our commerce on the ocean & in other countries must be paid for by frequent war. The justest dispositions possible in ourselves will not secure us against it. It would be necessary that all other nations were just also. Justice indeed on our part will save us from those wars which would have been produced by a contrary disposition. But to prevent those produced by the wrongs of other nations? By putting ourselves in a condition to punish them. Weakness provokes insult & injury, while a condition to punish it often prevents it. This reasoning leads to the necessity of some naval force, that being the only weapon with which we can reach an enemy. I think it to our interest to punish the first insult; because an insult unpunished is the parent of many others. We are not at this moment in a condition to do it, but we should put ourselves into it as soon as possible. If a war with England should take place, it seems to me that the first thing necessary would be a resolution to abandon the carrying trade because we cannot protect it. Foreign nations must in that case be invited to bring us what we want & to take our productions in their own [ship] bottoms. This alone could prevent the loss of those productions to us & the acquisition of them to our enemy. Our seamen might be employed in depredations on their trade. But how dreadfully we shall suffer on our coasts, if we have no force on the water, former experience has taught us. Indeed I look forward with horror to the very possible case of war with an European power, & think there is no protection against them but from the possession of some force on the sea. Our vicinity to their West India possessions & to the fisheries is a bridle which a small naval force on our part would hold in the mouths of the most powerful of these countries. I hope our land office will rid us of our debts, & that our first attention then will be to the beginning a naval force of some sort. This alone can countenance our people as carriers on the water, & I suppose them to be determined to continue such.

I wrote you two public letters on the 14th inst., since which I have received yours of July 13. I shall always be pleased to receive from you in a private way such communications as you might not chuse to put into a public letter.

Ford IV: 87–90

## XII.2 To Count Hogendorp

Paris, October 13, 1785

Dear Sir, – Having been much engaged lately, I have been unable sooner to acknowledge the receipt of your favor of September the 8th. What you are pleased to say on the subject of my Notes [on Virginia] is more than they deserve. The condition in which you first saw them would prove to you how hastily they had been originally written, as you may remember the numerous insertions I had made in them from time to time, when I could find a moment for turning to them from other occupations. I have never yet seen Monsieur de Buffon.[1] He has been in the country all the summer. I sent him a copy of the book, and have only heard his sentiments on one particular of it, that of the identity of the mammoth and elephant. As to this, he retains his opinion that they are the same. If you had formed any considerable expectations from our revised code of laws, you will be much disappointed. It contains not more than three or four laws which could strike the attention of a foreigner. Had it been a digest of all our laws, it would not have been comprehensible or instructive but to a native. But it is still less so, as it digests only the British statutes and our own acts of Assembly, which are but a supplementary part of our law. The great basis of it is anterior to the date of the Magna Charta, which is the oldest statute extant. The only merit of this work is, that it may remove from our book shelves about twenty folio volumes of our statutes, retaining all the parts of them which either their own merit or the established system of laws required.

You ask me what are those operations of the British nation which are likely to befriend us, and how they will produce this effect? The British government, as you may naturally suppose, have it much at heart to reconcile their nation to the loss of America. This is essential to the repose, perhaps even to the safety of the King and his

---

[1] The French naturalist. See *supra*, I.3, note 2. – *Eds.*

ministers. The most effectual engines for this purpose are the public papers. You know well that that government always kept a kind of standing army of newswriters, who, without any regard to truth, or to what should be like truth, invented and put into the papers whatever might serve the ministers. This suffices with the mass of the people, who have no means of distinguishing the false from the true paragraphs of a newspaper. When forced to acknowledge our independence, they were forced to redouble their efforts to keep the nation quiet. Instead of a few of the papers formerly engaged, they now engaged every one. No paper, therefore, comes out without a dose of paragraphs against America. These are calculated for a secondary purpose also, that of preventing the emigrations of their people to America. They dwell very much on American bankruptcies. To explain these would require a long detail, but would show you that nine-tenths of these bankruptcies are truly English bankruptcies, in no wise chargeable on America. However, they have produced effects the most desirable of all others for us. They have destroyed our credit, and thus checked our disposition to luxury; and, forcing our merchants to buy no more than they have ready money to pay for, they force them to go to those markets where that ready money will buy most. Thus you see, they check our luxury, they force us to connect ourselves with all the world, and they prevent foreign emigrations to our country, all of which I consider as advantageous to us. They are doing us another good turn. They attempt, without disguise, to possess themselves of the carriage of our produce, and to prohibit our own vessels from participating of it. This has raised a general indignation in America. The States see, however, that their constitutions have provided no means of counteracting it. They are, therefore, beginning to invest Congress with the absolute power of regulating their commerce, only reserving all revenue arising from it to the State in which it is levied. This will consolidate our federal building very much, and for this we shall be indebted to the British.

You ask what I think on the expediency of encouraging our States to be commercial? Were I to indulge my own theory, I should wish them to practise neither commerce nor navigation, but to stand, with respect to Europe, precisely on the footing of China. We should thus avoid wars, and all our citizens would be husbandmen. Whenever, indeed, our numbers should so increase as that our produce would overstock the markets of those nations who should come to seek it, the farmers must either employ the surplus of their time in manufactures, or the surplus of our hands must be employed in manufactures or in navigation. But that day would, I think, be distant, and we should long keep our workmen in Europe, while Europe should be drawing rough materials, and even subsistence from America. But this is theory only, and a theory which the servants of America are not at liberty to follow. Our people have a decided taste for navigation and commerce. They take this from their mother country; and their servants are in duty bound to calculate all their measures on this datum: we wish to do it by throwing open all the doors of commerce, and knocking off its shackles. But as this cannot be done for others, unless they will do it for us, and there is no great probability that Europe will do this, I suppose we shall be obliged to adopt a system which may shackle them in our ports, as they do us in theirs.

With respect to the sale of our lands, that cannot begin till a considerable portion shall have been surveyed. They cannot begin to survey till the fall of the leaf of this year, nor to sell probably till the ensuing spring. So that it will be yet a twelve-month before we shall be able to judge of the efficacy of our land office to sink our national debt. It is made a fundamental, that the proceeds shall be solely and sacredly applied as a sinking fund to discharge the capital only of the debt.

It is true that the tobaccos of Virginia go almost entirely to England. The reason is, the people of that State owe a great debt there, which they are paying as fast as they can. I think I have now answered your several queries, and shall be happy to receive your reflections on the same subjects, and at all times to hear of your welfare, and to give you assurances of the esteem, with which I have the honor to be, dear Sir, your most obedient, and most humble servant.

Ford IV: 102–6

## XII.3 Opinion on the French Treaties

April 28, 1793

I proceed, in compliance with the requisition of the President to give an opinion in writing on the general Question, Whether the

U.S. have a right to renounce their treaties with France, or to hold them suspended till the government of that country shall be established?

In the Consultation at the President's on the 19th inst. the Secretary of the Treasury took the following positions & consesequences. "France was a monarchy when we entered into treaties with it: but it has now declared itself a Republic, & is preparing a Republican form of government. As it may issue in a Republic, or a Military despotism, or in something else which may possibly render our alliance with it dangerous to ourselves, we have a right of election to renounce the treaty altogether, or to declare it suspended till their government shall be settled in the form it is ultimately to take; and then we may judge whether we will call the treaties into operation again, or declare them forever null. Having that right of election now, if we receive their minister without any qualifications, it will amount to an act of election to continue the treaties; & if the change they are undergoing should issue in a form which should bring danger on us, we shall not be then free to renounce them. To elect to continue them is equivalent to the making a new treaty at this time in the same form, that is to say, with a clause of guarantee; but to make a treaty with a clause of guarantee, during a war, is a departure from neutrality, and would make us associates in the war. To renounce or suspend the treaties therefore is a necessary act of neutrality."

If I do not subscribe to the soundness of this reasoning, I do most fully to its ingenuity. – I shall now lay down the principles which according to my understanding govern the case.

I consider the people who constitute a society or nation as the source of all authority in that nation, as free to transact their common concerns by any agents they think proper, to change these agents individually, or the organisation of them in form or function whenever they please: that all the acts done by those agents under the authority of the nation, are the acts of the nation, are obligatory on them, & enure to their use, & can in no wise be annulled or affected by any change in the form of the government, or of the persons administering it. Consequently the Treaties between the U.S. and France, were not treaties between the U.S. & Louis Capet [i.e. the king], but between the two nations of America & France, and the nations remaining in existance, tho' both of them have since

changed their forms of government, the treaties are not annulled by
these changes.

The Law of nations, by which this question is to be determined,
is composed of three branches. 1. The Moral law of our nature. 2.
The Usages of nations. 3. Their special Conventions. The first of
these only, concerns this question, that is to say the Moral law to
which Man has been subjected by his creator, & of which his feelings, or Conscience as it is sometimes called, are the evidence with
which his creator has furnished him. The Moral duties which exist
between individual and individual in a state of nature, accompany
them into a state of society & the aggregate of the duties of all the
individuals composing the society constitutes the duties of that
society towards any other; so that between society & society the
same moral duties exist as did between the individuals composing
them while in an unassociated state, their maker not having released
them from those duties on their forming themselves into a nation.
Compacts then between nation & nation are obligatory on them by
the same moral law which obliges individuals to observe their compacts. There are circumstances however which sometimes excuse
the non-performance of contracts between man & man: so are there
also between nation & nation. When performance, for instance,
becomes *impossible*, non-performance is not immoral. So if performance becomes *self-destructive* to the party, the law of self-
preservation overrules the laws of obligation to others. For the
reality of these principles I appeal to the true fountains of evidence,
the head & heart of every rational & honest man. It is there Nature
has written her moral laws, & where every man may read them for
himself. He will never read there the permission to annul his obligations for a time, or for ever, whenever they become "dangerous,
useless, or disagreeable." Certainly not when merely *useless* or *disagreeable*, as seems to be said in an authority which has been quoted,
Vattel. 2. 197,[1] and tho he may under certain degrees of *danger*, yet
the danger must be imminent, & the degree great. Of these, it is
true, that nations are to be judges for themselves, since no one
nation has a right to sit in judgment over another. But the tribunal

---

[1] Emmerich de Vattel, *Le Droit de Gens; ou Principes de la loi naturelle appliquée à
la conduite . . . des nations et des souverains* (London, 1758); Engl. trans. *The Law
of Nations or the Principles of Natural Law Applied to the Conduct . . . of Nations
and Sovereigns* (Philadelphia, 1817). – Eds.

of our consciences remains, & that also of the opinion of the world. These will revise the sentence we pass in our own case, & as we respect these, we must see that in judging ourselves we have honestly done the part of impartial & vigorous judges.

But Reason, which gives this right of self-liberation from a contract in certain cases, has subjected it to certain just limitations. 1. The danger which absolves us must be great, inevitable & imminent. Is such the character of that now apprehended from our treaties with France? What is that danger. 1. Is it that if their government issues in a military despotism, an alliance with them may taint us with despotic principles? But their government, when we allied ourselves to it, was a perfect despotism, civil & military, yet the treaties were made in that very state of things, & therefore that danger can furnish no just cause. 2. Is it that their government may issue in a republic, and too much strengthen our republican principles? But this is the hope of the great mass of our constituents, & not their dread. They do not look with longing to the happy mean of a limited monarchy. 3. But, says the doctrine I am combating, the change the French are undergoing may possibly end in something we know not what, and bring on us danger we know not whence. In short it may end in a Rawhead & bloody-bones in the dark. Very well. Let Rawhead & bloody bones come, & then we shall be justified in making our peace with him, by renouncing our antient friends & his enemies. For observe, it is not the *possibility of danger*, which absolves a party from his contract: for that possibility always exists, & in every case. It existed in the present one at the moment of making the contract. If *possibilities* would avoid contracts, there never could be a valid contract. For possibilities hang over everything. Obligation is not suspended, till the danger is become real, & the moment of it so imminent, that we can no longer avoid decision without forever losing the opportunity to do it. But can a danger which has not yet taken it's shape, which does not yet exist, & never may exist, which cannot therefore be defined, can such a danger I ask, be so imminent that if we fail to pronounce on it in this moment we can never have another opportunity of doing it?

4. The danger apprehended, is it that, the treaties remaining valid, the clause guarantying their West India islands will engage

us in the war? But Does the Guarantee engage us to enter into the war in any event?

Are we to enter into it before we are called on by our allies? Have we been called on by them? – shall we ever be called on? Is it their interest to call on us?

Can they call on us before their islands are invaded, or imminently threatened?

If they can save them themselves, have they a right to call on us?

Are we obliged to go to war at once, without trying peaceable negociations with their enemy?

If all these questions be against us, there are still others behind.

Are we in a condition to go to war?

Can we be expected to begin before we are in condition?

Will the islands be lost if we do not save them? Have we the means of saving them?

If we cannot save them are we bound to go to war for a desperate object?

Will not a 10 years forbearance in us to call them into the guarantee of our posts, entitle us to some indulgence?

Many, if not most of these questions offer grounds of doubt whether the clause of guarantee will draw us into the war. Consequently if this be the danger apprehended, it is not yet certain enough to authorize us in sound morality to declare, at this moment, the treaties null.

5. Is the danger apprehended from the 17th article of the treaty of Commerce, which admits French ships of war & privateers to come and go freely, with prizes made on their enemies, while their enemies are not to have the same privilege with prizes made on the French? But Holland & Prussia have approved of this article in our treaty with France, by subscribing to an express Salvo [exemption] of it in our treaties with them. [Dutch treaty 22. Convention 6. Prussian treaty 19.][2] And England in her last treaty with France [art. 40] has entered into the same stipulation verbatim, & placed us in her ports on the same footing on which she is in ours, in case of a war of either of us with France. If we are engaged in such a war, England must receive prizes made on us by the French, &

---

[2] Bracketed references are TJ's. – *Eds.*

exclude those made on the French by us. Nay further, in this very article of her treaty with France, is a salvo of any similar article in any anterior treaty of either party, and ours with France being anterior, this salvo confirms it expressly. Neither of these three powers then have a right to complain of this article in our treaty.

6. Is the danger apprehended from the 22d Art. of our treaty of commerce, which prohibits the enemies of France from fitting out privateers in our ports, or selling their prizes here. But we are free to refuse the same thing to France, there being no stipulation to the contrary, and we ought to refuse it on principles of fair neutrality.

7. But the reception of a Minister from the Republic of France, without qualifications, it is thought will bring us into danger: because this, it is said, will determine the continuance of the treaty, and take from us the right of self-liberation when at any time hereafter our safety would require us to use it. The reception of the Minister at all (in favor of which Colo. [Alexander] Hamilton has given his opinion, tho reluctantly as he confessed) is an acknolegement of the legitimacy of their government: and if the qualifications meditated are to deny that legitimacy, it will be a curious compound which is to admit & deny the same thing. But I deny that the reception of a Minister has any thing to do with the treaties. There is not a word, in either of them, about sending ministers. This has been done between us under the common usage of nations, & can have no effect either to continue or annul the treaties.

But how can any act of election have the effect to continue a treaty which is acknoleged to be going on still? For it was not pretended the treaty was void, but only voidable if we chuse to declare it so. To make it void would require an act of election, but to let it go on requires only that we should do nothing, and doing nothing can hardly be an infraction of peace or neutrality.

But I go further & deny that the most explicit declaration made at this moment that we acknolege the obligation of the treatys could take from us the right of non-compliance at any future time when compliance would involve us in great & inevitable danger.

I conclude then that few of these sources threaten any danger at all; and from none of them is it inevitable: & consequently none of them give us the right at this moment of releasing ourselves from our treaties.

II. A second limitation on our right of releasing ourselves is that we are to do it from so much of the treaties only as is bringing great & inevitable danger on us, & not from the residue, allowing to the other party a right at the same time to determine whether on our non-compliance with that part they will declare the whole void. This right they would have, but we should not. Vattel. 2. 202. The only part of the treaties which can really lead us into danger is the clause of guarantee. That clause is all then we could suspend in any case, and the residue will remain or not at the will of the other party.

III. A third limitation is that where a party from necessity or danger withholds compliance with part of a treaty, it is bound to make compensation where the nature of the case admits & does not dispense with it. 2. Vattel 324. Wolf [*sic*]. 270. 443.[3] If actual circumstances excuse us from entering into the war under the clause of guarantee, it will be a question whether they excuse us from compensation. Our weight in the war admits of an estimate; & that estimate would form the measure of compensation.

If in withholding a compliance with any part of the treaties, we do it without just cause or compensation, we give to France a cause of war, and so become associated in it on the other side. An injured friend is the bitterest of foes, & France had not discovered [disclosed or revealed] either timidity, or over-much forbearance on the late occasions. Is this the position we wish to take for our constituents? It is certainly not the one they would take for themselves.

I will proceed now to examine the principal authority which has been relied on for establishing the right of self liberation; because tho' just in part, it would lead us far beyond justice, if taken in all the latitude of which his expressions would admit. Questions of natural right are triable by their conformity with the moral sense & reason of man. Those who write treatises of natural law, can only declare what their own moral sense & reason dictate in the several cases they state. Such of them as happen to have feelings & a reason coincident with those of the wise & honest part of mankind, are respected & quoted as witnesses of what is morally right or wrong in particular cases.

---

[3] Christian Wolff, *Jus gentium methodo scientifico pertractum* (1764); Engl. trans. *The Law of Nations Treated According to Scientific Method* (Oxford, 1934). – Eds.

Grotius,[4] Puffendorf [*sic*][5], Wolf, & Vattel are of this number. Where they agree their authority is strong. But where they differ, & they often differ, we must appeal to our own feelings and reason to decide between them.

The passages in question shall be traced through all these writers, that we may see wherein they concur, & where that concurrence is wanting. It shall be quoted from them in the order in which they wrote, that is to say, from Grotius first, as being the earliest writer, Puffendorf next, then Wolf, & lastly Vattel as latest in time.

| Grotius.2.16.16. | Puffendorf.8.9.6. | Wolf.1146. | Vattel.2.197. |
|---|---|---|---|
| "Hither must be referred the common question, concerning personal & real treaties. If indeed it be with a free people, there can be no doubt but that the engagement is in it's nature real, because the subject is a permanent thing, and even tho the government of the state be changed into a Kingdom, the treaty remains, because the same body remains, tho' the head is changed, and, as we have before said, the government which is exercised by a King, does not | "It is certain that every alliance made with a republic, is real, & continues consequently to the term agreed on by the treaty, altho' the magistrates who concluded it be dead before, or that the form of government is changed, even from a democracy to a monarchy: for in this case the people does not cease to be the same, and the King, in the case supposed, being established by the consent of the people, who abolished the republican government, is understood to | "The alliance which is made with a free people, or with a popular government, is a real alliance; and as when the form of government changes, the people remains the same (for it is the association which forms the people, & not the manner of administering the government), this alliance subsists, tho' the form of government changes, *unless*, as is evident, the reason of the alliance was particular to the popular state." | "The same question presents itself in real alliances, & in general on every alliance made with a state, & not in particular with a King for the defense of his person. We ought without doubt to defend our ally against all invasion, against all foreign violence, & even against rebel subjects. We ought in like manner to defend a republic against the enterprises of an oppressor of the public liberty. But we ought to recollect that we are the ally of the state, or of the nation, & |

---

[4] Hugo Grotius, *De jure belli ac pacis* (1646); Engl. trans. *On the Law of War and Peace* (London, 1964). – Eds.

[5] Samuel Pufendorf, *De jure naturae et gentium* (1744): Engl. trans. *The Law of Nature and Nations* (Oxford, 1934). – Eds.

cease to be the government of the people. There is an *exception*, when the object seems peculiar to the government as if free cities contract a league for the defence of their freedom."

accept the crown with all the engagements which the people conferring it had contracted, as being free & governing themselves. There must nevertheless be an *Exception* of the alliances contracted with a view to preserve the present government. As if two Republics league for neutral defence against those who would undertake to invade their liberty: for if one of these two people consent afterwards voluntarily to change the form of their government, the alliance ends of itself, because the reason on which it was founded no longer subsists."

not it's judge. If the nation has deposed it's King in form, if the people of a republic has driven away it's magistrates, & have established themselves free, or if they have acknoleged the authority of an usurper, whether expressly or tacitly, to oppose these domestic arrangements, to contest their justice or validity, would be to meddle with the government of the nation, & to do it an injury. The ally remains the ally of the state, notwithstanding the change which has taken place. *But if this change renders the alliance useless, dangerous or disagreeable to it, it is free to renounce it. For it may say with truth, that it would not have allied itself with this nation, if it had been under the present form of it's government."*

The doctrine then of Grotius, Puffendorf & Wolf is that "treaties remain obligatory notwithstanding any change in the form of government, except in the single case where the preservation of that form was the object of the treaty." There the treaty extinguishes, not by the election or declaration of the party remaining in *statu quo*; but independantly of that, by the evanishment of the object. Vattel lays down, in fact, the same doctrine, that treaties continue obligatory, notwithstanding a change of government by the will of the other party, that to oppose that will would be a wrong, & that the ally remains an ally notwithstanding the change. So far he concurs with all the previous writers. But he then adds what they had not said, nor would say "but if this change renders the alliance *useless*, dangerous, or *disagreeable* to it, it is free to renounce it." It was unnecessary for him to have specified the exception of *danger* in this particular case, because that exception exists in all cases & it's extent has been considered. But when he adds that, because a contract is become merely *useless* or *disagreeable*, we are free to renounce it, he is in opposition to Grotius, Puffendorf, & Wolf, who admit no such licence against the obligation of treaties, & he is in opposition to the morality of every honest man, to whom we may safely appeal to decide whether he feels himself free to renounce a contract the moment it becomes merely *useless* or *disagreeable*, to him? We may appeal too to Vattel himself, in those parts of his book where he cannot be misunderstood, & to his known character, as one of the most zealous & constant advocates for the preservation of good faith in all our dealings. Let us hear him on other occasions; & first where he shews what degree of danger or injury will authorize self-liberation from a treaty. "If simple lezion" (lezion means the loss sustained by selling a thing for less than half value, which degree of loss rendered the sale void by the Roman law), "if simple lezion, says he, or some degree of disadvantage in a treaty does not suffice to render it invalid, it is not so as to inconveniences which would go to the *ruin* of the nation. As every treaty ought to be made by a sufficient power, a treaty pernicious to the state is null, & not at all obligatory; no governor of a nation having power to engage things capable of *destroying* the state, for the safety of which the empire is trusted to him. The nation itself, bound necessarily to whatever it's preservation & safety require, cannot enter into engagements contrary to it's indispensable obligations." Here then we find that the degree of injury or danger which he deems sufficient to liberate us from a treaty, is that which would go to the absolute *ruin* or *destruction* of the state; not simply the lezion of the Roman law, not merely the being disadvantageous, or dangerous. For as he says himself, § 158, "lezion cannot render a treaty invalid. It is his duty, who enters into engagements, to weigh well all things before he concludes. He may do with his property what he pleases, he may relinquish his rights, renounce his advantages, as he judges proper: the acceptant is not obliged to inform himself of his motives, nor to weigh their just value. If we could free ourselves from a compact because we find ourselves injured by it, there would be nothing firm in the contracts of nations. Civil laws may set limits to lezion, & determine the degree capable of producing a nullity of the contract. But sovereigns acknolege no judge. How establish lezion among them? Who will determine the degree sufficient to invalidate a treaty? The happiness & peace of nations require manifestly that their treaties should not depend on a means of nullity so vague & so dangerous."

Let us hear him again on the general subject of the observance of treaties, § 163. "It is demonstrated in natural law that he who promises another confers on him a perfect right to require the thing promised, & that, consequently, not to observe a perfect promise, is to violate the right of another; it is as manifest injustice as to plunder any one of their right. All the tranquillity, the happiness & security of mankind rest on justice, on the obligation to respect the rights of others. The respect of others for our rights of domain & property is the security of our actual possessions; the faith of promises is our security for the things which cannot be delivered or executed on the spot. No more security, no more commerce among men, if they think themselves not obliged to preserve faith, to keep their word. This obligation then is as necessary as it is natural & indubitable, among nations who live together in a state of nature, & who acknolege no superior on earth, to maintain order & peace in their society. Nations & their governors then ought to observe inviolably their promises & their treaties. This great truth, altho' too often neglected in practice, is generally acknoleged by all nations: the reproach of perfidy is a bitter affront among sovereigns: now he who does not observe a treaty is assuredly perfidious, since he violates his faith. On the contrary nothing is so glorious to a prince & his nation, as the reputation of inviolable fidelity to his word." Again § 219. "Who will doubt that treaties are of the things sacred among nations? They decide matters the most important. They impose rules on the pretensions of sovereigns: they cause the rights of nations to be acknoleged, they assure their most precious interests. Among political bodies, sovereigns, who acknolege no superior on earth, treaties are the only means of adjusting their different pretensions, of establishing a rule, to know on what to count, on what to depend. But treaties are but vain words if nations do not consider them as respectable engagements, as rules, inviolable for sovereigns, & sacred through the whole earth. § 220. The faith of treaties, that firm & sincere will, that invariable constancy in fulfilling engagements, of which a declaration is made in a treaty, is there holy & sacred, among nations, whose safety & repose it ensures; & if nations will not be wanting to themselves, they will load with infamy whoever violates his faith."

After evidence so copious & explicit of the respect of this author for the sanctity of treaties, we should hardly have expected that his authority would have been resorted to for a wanton invalidation of them whenever they should become merely *useless* or *disagreeable*. We should hardly have expected that, rejecting all the rest of his book, this scrap would have been culled, & made the hook whereon to hang such a chain of immoral consequences. Had the passage accidentally met our eye, we should have imagined it had fallen from the author's pen under some momentary view, not sufficiently developed to found a conjecture what he meant: and we may certainly affirm that a fragment like this cannot weigh against the authority of all other writers, against the uniform & systematic doctrine of every work from which it is torn, against the moral feelings & the reason of all honest men. If the terms of the fragment are not misunderstood, they are in full contradiction to all the written & unwritten evidences of morality: if they are misunderstood, they are no longer a foundation for the doctrines which have been built on them.

But even had this doctrine been as true as it is manifestly false, it would have been asked, to whom is it that the treaties with France have become *disagreeable?* How will it be proved that they are *useless?*

The conclusion of the sentence suggests a reflection too strong to be suppressed "for the party may say with truth that it would not have allied itself with this nation, if it had been under the present form of it's government." The Republic of the U.S. allied itself with France when under a despotic government. She changes her government, declares it shall be a Republic, prepares a form of

Republic extremely free, and in the mean time is governing herself as such, and it is proposed that America shall declare the treaties void because "it may say with truth that it would not have allied itself with that nation, if it had been under the present form of it's government!" Who is the American who can say with truth that he would not have allied himself to France if she had been a republic? or that a Republic of any form would be as *disagreeable* as her antient despotism?

Upon the whole I conclude

That the treaties are still binding, notwithstanding the change of government in France: that no part of them, but the clause of guarantee, holds up *danger*, even at a distance.

And consequently that a liberation from no other part could be proposed in any case: that if that clause may ever bring *danger*, it is neither extreme, nor imminent, nor even probable: that the authority for renouncing a treaty, when *useless* or *disagreeable*, is either misunderstood, or in opposition to itself, to all their writers, & to every moral feeling: that were it not so, these treaties are in fact neither useless nor disagreeable.

That the receiving a Minister from France at this time is an act of no significance with respect to the treaties, amounting neither to an admission nor a denial of them, forasmuch as he comes not under any stipulation in them:

That were it an explicit admission, or were an express declaration of this obligation now to be made, it would not take from us that right which exists at all times of liberating ourselves when an adherence to the treaties would be *ruinous* or *destructive* to the society: and that the not renouncing the treaties now is so far from being a breach of neutrality, that the doing it would be the breach, by giving just cause of war to France.

Ford VI: 218–31

## XII.4 To Benjamin Austin

Monticello, January 9, 1816

Dear Sir, – Your favor of December 21st has been received, and I am first to thank you for the pamphlet it covered. The same description of persons which is the subject of that is so much multiplied here too, as to be almost a grievance, and by their numbers in the public councils, have wrested from the public hand the direction of the pruning knife. But with us as a body, they are republican, and mostly moderate in their views; so far, therefore, less objects of jealousy than with you. Your opinions on the events which have taken place in France, are entirely just, so far as these events are yet developed. But they have not reached their ultimate termination. There is still an awful void between the present and what is to be the last chapter of that history; and I fear it is to be filled with abominations as frightful as those which have already disgraced it. That nation is too high-minded, has too much innate force, intelligence and elasticity, to remain under its present compression. Samson will arise in his strength, as of old, and as of old will burst asunder the withes and the cords, and the webs of the Philistines. But what are to be the scenes of havoc and horror, and how widely they may spread between brethren of the same house, our ignorance of the interior feuds and antipathies of the country places beyond our ken. It will end, nevertheless, in a representative government, in a government in which the will of the people will be an effective ingredient. This important element has taken root in the European mind, and will have its growth; their despots, sensible of this are already offering this modification of their governments, as if of their own accord. Instead of the parricide treason of Bonaparte, in perverting the means confided to him as a republican magistrate, to the subversion of that republic and erection of a military despotism for himself and his family, had he used it honestly for the establishment and support of a free government in his own country, France would now have been in freedom and rest; and her example operating in a contrary direction, every nation in Europe would have had a government over which the will of the people would have had some control. His atrocious egotism has checked the salutary progress of principle, and deluged it with rivers of blood which are not yet run out. To the vast sum of devastation and of human misery, of which he has been the guilty cause, much is still to be added. But the object is fixed in the eye of nations, and they will press on to its accomplishment and to the general amelioration of the condition of man. What a germ have we planted, and how faithfully should we cherish the parent tree at home!

You tell me I am quoted by those who wish to continue our dependence on England for manufactures. There was a time when I might have been so quoted with more candor, but within the thirty years which have since elapsed, how are circumstances changed! We were then in peace. Our independent place among nations was acknowledged. A commerce which offered the raw material in exchange for the same material after receiving the last touch of industry, was worthy of welcome to all nations. It was expected that those especially to whom manufacturing industry was important, would cherish the friendship of such customers by every favor, by every inducement, and particularly cultivate their peace by every act of justice and friendship. Under this prospect the question seemed legitimate, whether, with such an immensity of unimproved land, courting the hand of husbandry, the industry of agriculture, or that of manufactures, would add most to the national wealth? And the doubt was entertained on this consideration chiefly, that to the labor of the husbandman a vast addition is made by the spontaneous energies of the earth on which it is employed: for one grain of wheat committed to the earth, she renders twenty, thirty, and even fifty fold, whereas to the labor of the manufacturer nothing is added. Pounds of flax, in his hands, yield, on the contrary, but pennyweights of lace. This exchange, too, laborious as it might seem, what a field did it promise for the occupations of the ocean; what a nursery for that class of citizens who were to exercise and maintain our equal rights on that element? This was the state of things in 1785, when the "Notes on Virginia" were first printed; when, the ocean being open to all nations, and their common right in it acknowledged and exercised under regulations sanctioned by the assent and usage of all, it was thought that the doubt might claim some consideration. But who in 1785 could foresee the rapid depravity which was to render the close of that century the disgrace of the history of man? Who could have imagined that the two most distinguished in the rank of nations, for science and civilization, would have suddenly descended from that honourable eminence, and setting at defiance all those moral laws established by the Author of nature between nation and nation, as between man and man, would cover earth and sea with robberies and piracies, merely because strong enough to do it with temporal impunity; and that under this disbandment of nations from social order, we should have been despoiled of a thousand ships, and have thousands of our citizens reduced to Algerine slavery. Yet all this has taken place. One of these nations interdicted to our vessels all harbors of the globe without having first proceeded to some one of hers, there paid a tribute proportioned to the cargo, and obtained her license to proceed to the port of destination. The other declared them to be lawful prize if they had touched at the port, or been visited by a ship of the enemy nation. Thus were we completely excluded from the ocean. Compare this state of things with that of '85, and say whether an opinion founded in the circumstances of that day can be fairly applied to those of the present. We have experienced what we did not then believe, that there exists both profligacy and power enough to exclude us from the field of interchange with other nations: that to be independent for the comforts of life we must fabricate them ourselves. We must now place the manufacturer by the side of the agriculturist. The former question is suppressed, or rather assumes a new form. Shall we make our own comforts, or go without them, at the will of a foreign nation? He, therefore, who is now against domestic manufacture, must be for reducing us either to dependence on that foreign nation, or to be clothed in skins, and to live like wild beasts in dens and caverns. I am not one of these; experience has taught me that manufactures are now as necessary to our independence as to our comfort; and if those who quote me as of a different opinion, will keep pace with me in purchasing nothing foreign where an equivalent of domestic fabric can be obtained, without regard to difference of price, it will not be our fault if we do not soon have a supply at home equal to our demand, and wrest that weapon of distress from the hand which has wielded it. If it shall be proposed to go beyond our own supply, the question of '85 will then recur, will our *surplus* labor be then most beneficially employed in the culture of the earth, or in the fabrications of art? We have time yet for consideration, before that question will press upon us; and the maxim to be applied will depend on the circumstances which shall then exist; for in so complicated a science as political economy, no one axiom can be laid down as wise and expedient for all times and circumstances, and for their contraries. Inattention to this is what has called for this explanation, which reflection would have rendered unnecessary with the candid, while nothing will do it with those who use the former opinion only as a stalking horse, to cover their disloyal propensities to keep us in eternal vassalage to a foreign and unfriendly people.

I salute you with assurances of great respect and esteem.

Ford x: 7–11

# XIII    Innovation and Progress

## XIII.1 To Dr. Joseph Priestley

Washington, March 21, 1801

Dear Sir, – I learnt some time ago that you were in Philadelphia, but that it was only for a fortnight; & supposed you were gone. It was not till yesterday I received information that you were still there, had been very ill, but were on the recovery. I sincerely rejoice that you are so. Yours is one of the few lives precious to mankind, & for the continuance of which every thinking man is solicitous. Bigots may be an exception. What an effort, my dear Sir, of bigotry in Politics & Religion have we gone through! The barbarians really flattered themselves they should be able to bring back the times of Vandalism, when ignorance put everything into the hands of power & priestcraft. All advances in science were proscribed as innovations. They pretended to praise and encourage education, but it was to be the education of our ancestors. We were to look backwards, not forwards, for improvement; the President himself declaring, in one of his answers to addresses, that we were never to expect to go beyond them in real science. This was the real ground of all the attacks on you. Those who live by mystery & *charlatanerie*, fearing you would render them useless by simplifying the Christian philosophy, – the most sublime & benevolent, but most perverted system that ever shone on man, – endeavored to crush your well-earnt & well-deserved fame. But it was the Lilliputians upon Gulliver. Our countrymen have recovered from the alarm into which art & industry had thrown them; science & honesty are replaced on their high ground; and you, my dear Sir, as their great apostle, are on it's pinnacle. It is with heartfelt satisfaction that, in the first moments of my public action, I can hail you with welcome to our land, tender to you the homage of it's respect & esteem, cover you under the protection of those laws which were made for the wise and good like you, and disdain the legitimacy of that libel on legislation, which, under the form of a law[1] was for some time placed among them.

As the storm is now subsiding, and the horizon becoming serene, it is pleasant to consider the phenomenon with attention. We can

---

[1] TJ alludes to the Alien Act of 1798. – *Eds.*

no longer say there is nothing new under the sun. For this whole chapter in the history of man is new. The great extent of our Republic is new. Its sparse habitation is new. The mighty wave of public opinion which has rolled over it is new. But the most pleasing novelty is, it's so quickly subsiding over such an extent of surface to it's true level again. The order & good sense displayed in this recovery from delusion, and in the momentous crisis which lately arose, really bespeak a strength of character in our nation which augurs well for the duration of our Republic; & I am much better satisfied now of it's stability than I was before it was tried. I have been, above all things, solaced by the prospect which opened on us, in the event of a non-election of a President; in which case, the federal government would have been in the situation of a clock or watch run down. There was no idea of force, nor of any occasion for it. A convention, invited by the Republican members of Congress, with the virtual President & Vice-President, would have been on the ground in 8 weeks, would have repaired the Constitution where it was defective, & wound it up again. This peaceable & legitimate resource, to which we are in the habit of implicit obedience, superseding all appeal to force, and being always within our reach, shows a precious principle of self-preservation in our composition, till a change of circumstances shall take place, which is not within prospect at any definite period.

But I have got into a long disquisition on politics, when I only meant to express my sympathy in the state of your health, and to tender you all the affections of public & private hospitality. I should be very happy indeed to see you here. I leave this about the 30th inst., to return about the twenty-fifth of April. If you do not leave Philadelphia before that, a little excursion hither would help your health. I should be much gratified with the possession of a guest I so much esteem, and should claim a right to lodge you, should you make such an excursion.

Ford VIII: 21–3

## XIII.2 To John Adams

Monticello, June 15, 1813

Dear Sir, – I wrote you a letter on the 27th of May, which probably would reach you about the 3d instant, and on the 9th I received yours of the 29th of May. Of Lindsay's Memoirs I had never before heard, and scarcely indeed of himself. It could not, therefore, but be unexpected, that two letters of mine should have anything to do with his life. The name of his editor was new to me, and certainly presents itself for the first time under unfavorable circumstances. Religion, I suppose, is the scope of his book; and that a writer on that subject should usher himself to the world in the very act of the grossest abuse of confidence, by publishing private letters which passed between two friends, with no views to their ever being made public, is an instance of inconsistency as well as of infidelity, of which I would rather be the victim than the author.

By your kind quotation of the dates of my two letters, I have been enabled to turn to them. They had completely vanished from my memory. The last is on the subject of religion, and by its publication will gratify the priesthood with new occasion of repeating their comminations against me. They wish it to be believed that he can have no religion who advocates its freedom. This was not the doctrine of Dr. Joseph Priestley; and I honored him for the example of liberality he set to his order. The first letter is political. It recalls to our recollection the gloomy transactions of the times, the doctrines they witnessed, and the sensibilities they excited. It was a confidential communication of reflections on these from one friend to another, deposited in his bosom, and never meant to trouble the public mind. Whether the character of the times is justly portrayed or not, posterity will decide. But on one feature of them they can never decide, the sensations excited in free yet firm minds by the terrorism of the day. None can conceive who did not witness them, and they were felt by one party only. This letter exhibits their side of the medal. The federalists,[1] no doubt, have presented the other in their private correspondences as well as open action. If these correspondences should ever be laid open to the public eye, they will probably be found not models of comity towards their adversaries. The readers of my letter should be cautioned not to confine its view to this country alone. England and its alarmists were equally under consideration. Still less must they consider it as looking personally towards you. You happen, indeed, to be quoted, because you happened to express more pithily than had been done by themselves, one of the mottos of the party. This was in your answer to

---

[1] I.e. the Federalist Party. – *Eds.*

the address of the young men of Philadelphia. [See Selection of Patriotic Addresses, page 198.][2] One of the questions, you know, on which our parties took different sides, was on the improvability of the human mind in science, in ethics, in government, &c. Those who advocated reformation of institutions, *pari passu* with the progress of science, maintained that no definite limits could be assigned to that progress. The enemies of reform, on the other hand, denied improvement, and advocated steady adherence to the principles, practices and institutions of our fathers, which they represented as the consummation of wisdom, and acme of excellence, beyond which the human mind could never advance. Although in the passage of your answer alluded to, you expressly disclaim the wish to influence the freedom of inquiry, you predict that that will produce nothing more worthy of transmission to posterity than the principles, institutions and systems of education received from their ancestors. I do not consider this as your deliberate opinion. You possess, yourself, too much science, not to see how much is still ahead of you, unexplained and unexplored. Your own consciousness must place you as far before our ancestors as in the rear of our posterity. I consider it as an expression lent to the prejudices of your friends; and although I happened to cite it from you, the whole letter shows I had them only in view. In truth, my dear Sir, we [Republicans] were far from considering you as the author of all the measures we blamed. They were placed under the protection of your name, but we were satisfied they wanted much of your approbation. We ascribed them to their real authors, the Pickerings, the Wolcotts, the Tracys, the Sedgwicks, *et id genus omne*, with whom we supposed you in a state of duresse. I well remember a conversation with you in the morning of the day on which you nominated to the Senate a substitute for Pickering, in which you expressed a just impatience under "the legacy of secretaries which General Washington had left you," and whom you seemed, therefore, to consider as under public protection. Many other incidents showed how differently you would have acted with less impassioned advisers; and subsequent events have proved that your minds were not together. You would do me great injustice, therefore, by taking to yourself what was intended for men who were then your secret,

---

[2] TJ's bracketed note. – *Eds.*

as they are now your open enemies. Should you write on the subject, as you propose, I am sure we shall see you place yourself farther from them than from us.

As to myself, I shall take no part in any discussions. I leave others to judge of what I have done, and to give me exactly that place which they shall think I have occupied. [Chief Justice John] Marshall has written libels on one side; others, I suppose, will be written on the other side; and the world will sift both and separate the truth as well as they can. I should see with reluctance the passions of that day rekindled in this, while so many of the actors are living, and all are too near the scene not to participate in sympathies with them. About facts you and I cannot differ; because truth is our mutual guide. And if any opinions you may express should be different from mine, I shall receive them with the liberality and indulgence which I ask for my own, and still cherish with warmth the sentiments of affectionate respect, of which I can with so much truth tender you the assurance.

Washington VI: 125–7

## XIII.3  To Isaac McPherson

Monticello, August 13, 1813

Sir, – Your letter of August 3d asking information on the subject of Mr. Oliver Evans' exclusive right to the use of what he calls his Elevators, Conveyers, and Hopper-boys, has been duly received. My wish to see new inventions encouraged, and old ones brought again into useful notice, has made me regret the circumstances which have followed the expiration of his first patent. I did not expect the retrospection which has been given to the reviving law. For although the second proviso seemed not so clear as it ought to have been, yet it appeared susceptible of a just construction; and the retrospective one being contrary to natural right, it was understood to be a rule of law that where the words of a statute admit of two constructions, the one just and the other unjust, the former is to be given them. The first proviso takes care of those who had lawfully used Evans' improvements under the first patent; the second was meant for those who had lawfully erected and used them

575

after that patent expired, declaring they "should not be liable to damages therefor." These words may indeed be restrained to uses already past, but as there is parity of reason for those to come, there should be parity of law. Every man should be protected in his lawful acts, and be certain that no *ex post facto* law shall punish or endamage him for them. But he is endamaged, if forbidden to use a machine lawfully erected, at considerable expense, unless he will pay a new and unexpected price for it. The proviso says that he who erected and used lawfully should not be liable to pay damages. But if the proviso had been omitted, would not the law, construed by natural equity, have said the same thing? In truth both provisos are useless. And shall useless provisos, inserted *pro majori cautela* only, authorize inferences against justice? The sentiment that *ex post facto* laws are against natural right, is so strong in the United States, that few, if any, of the State constitutions have failed to proscribe them. The federal constitution indeed interdicts them in criminal cases only; but they are equally unjust in civil as in criminal cases, and the omission of a caution which would have been right, does not justify the doing what is wrong. Nor ought it to be presumed that the legislature meant to use a phrase in an unjustifiable sense, if by rules of construction it can be ever strained to what is just. The law books abound with similar instances of the care the judges take of the public integrity. Laws, moreover, abridging the natural right of the citizen, should be restrained by rigorous constructions within their narrowest limits.

Your letter, however, points to a much broader question, whether what have received from Mr. Evans the new and proper name of Elevators, are of his invention. Because, if they are not, his patent gives him no right to obstruct others in the use of what they possessed before. I assume it is a Lemma, that it is the invention of the machine itself, which is to give a patent right, and not the application of it to any particular purpose, of which it is susceptible. If one person invents a knife convenient for pointing our pens, another cannot have a patent right for the same knife to point our pencils. A compass was invented for navigating the sea; another could not have a patent right for using it to survey land. A machine for threshing *wheat* has been invented in Scotland; a second person cannot get a patent right for the same machine to thresh *oats*, a third *rye*, a fourth *peas*, a fifth *clover*, etc. A string of buckets is invented and used for raising water, ore, etc.; can a second have a patent right to the same machine for raising wheat, a third oats, a fourth rye, a fifth peas, etc.? The question then whether such a string of buckets was invented first by Oliver Evans, is a mere question of fact in mathematical history. Now, turning to such books only as I happen to possess, I find abundant proof that this simple machinery has been in use from time immemorial. Doctor Shaw, who visited Egypt and the Barbary coast in the years 1727–8–9, in the margin of his map of Egypt, gives us the figure of what he calls a Persian wheel, which is a string of round cups or buckets hanging on a pulley, over which they revolved, bringing up water from a well and delivering it into a trough above. He found this used at Cairo, in a well 264 feet deep, which the inhabitants believe to have been the work of the patriarch Joseph. Shaw's travels, 341, Oxford edition of 1738 in folio, and the Universal History, I. 416, speaking of the manner of watering the higher lands in Egypt, says, "formerly they made use of Archimedes' screw, thence named the Egyptian pump, but they now generally use wheels (wallowers) which carry a rope or chain of earthen pots holding about seven or eight quarts apiece, and draw the water from the canals. There are besides a vast number of wells in Egypt, from which the water is drawn in the same manner to water the gardens and fruit trees; so that it is no exaggeration to say, that there are in Egypt above 200,000 oxen daily employed in this labor." Shaw's name of Persian wheel has been since given more particularly to a wheel with buckets, either fixed or suspended on pins, at its periphery. Mortimer's husbandry, I. 18, Duhamel III. II., Ferguson's Mechanic's plate, XIII; but his figure, and the verbal description of the Universal History, prove that the string of buckets is meant under that name. His figure differs from Evans' construction in the circumstances of the buckets being round, and strung through their bottom on a chain. But it is the principle, to wit, a string of buckets, which constitutes the invention, not the form of the buckets, round, square, or hexagon; nor the manner of attaching them, nor the material of the connecting band, whether chain, rope, or leather. Vitruvius, L. X. c. 9, describes this machinery as a windlass, on which is a chain descending to the water, with vessels of copper attached to it; the windlass being turned, the chain moving on it will raise the vessel, which in passing over the windlass will empty the water they have brought up into a reservoir. And Perrault, in his edition of Vitruvius, Paris, 1684, folio plates 61, 62, gives us three forms of these water elevators, in one of which the buckets are square, as Mr. Evans' are. Bossuet, *Histoire des Mathématiques*, i. 86, says, "the drum wheel, the wheel with buckets and the *Chapelets*, are hydraulic machines which come to us from the ancients. But we are ignorant of the time when they began to be put into use." The *Chapelets* are the revolving bands of the buckets which Shaw calls the Persian wheel, the moderns a chain-pump, and Mr. Evans elevators. The next of my books in which I find these elevators is Wolf's *Cours de Mathématiques*, i. 370, and plate I, Paris, 1747, 8vo; here are two forms. In one of them the buckets are square, attached to two chains, passing over a cylinder or wallower at top, and under another at bottom, by which they are made to revolve. It is a nearly exact representation of Evans' Elevators. But a more exact one is to be seen in Desagulier's Experimental Philosophy, ii. plate 34; in the *Encyclopédie de Diderot et D'Alembert*, 8vo edition of Lausanne, first volume of plates in the four subscribed *Hydraulique. Norie*, is one where round eastern pots are tied by their collars between two endless ropes suspended on a revolving lantern or wallower. This is said to have been used for raising ore out of a mine. In a book which I do not possess, *L'Architecture Hidraulique de Belidor*, the second volume of which is said [De la Lande's continuation of Montuclas' *Histoire de Mathématiques*, iii. 711][1] to contain a detail of all the pumps, ancient and modern, hydraulic machines, fountains, wells, etc., I have no doubt this Persian wheel, chain pump, *chapelets*, elevators, by whichever name you choose to call it, will be found in various forms. The last book I have to quote for it is Prony's *Architecture Hydraulique* i., *Avertissement* vii., and § 648, 649, 650. In the latter of which passages he observes that the first idea which occurs for raising water is to lift it in a bucket by hand. When the water lies too deep to be reached by hand, the bucket is suspended by a chain and let down over a pulley or windlass. If it be desired to raise a continued stream of water, the simplest means which offers itself to the mind is to attach to an endless chain or cord a number of pots or buckets, so disposed that, the chain being suspended on a lanthorn or wallower above, and plunged in water

---

[1] TJ's bracketed note. – *Eds.*

below, the buckets may descend and ascend alternately, filling themselves at bottom and emptying at a certain height above, so as to give a constant stream. Some years before the date of Mr. Evans' patent, a Mr. Martin of Caroline county in this State, constructed a drill-plough, in which he used the band of buckets for elevating the grain from the box into the funnel, which let them down into the furrow. He had bands with different sets of buckets adapted to the size of peas, of turnip seed, etc. I have used this machine for sowing Benni seed also, and propose to have a band of buckets for drilling Indian corn, and another for wheat. Is it possible that in doing this I shall infringe Mr. Evans' patent? That I can be debarred of any use to which I might have applied my drill, when I bought it, by a patent issued after I bought it?

These verbal descriptions, applying so exactly to Mr. Evans' elevators, and the drawings exhibited to the eye, flash conviction both on reason and the senses that there is nothing new in these elevators but their being strung together on a strap of leather. If this strap of leather be an invention, entitling the inventor to a patent right, it can only extend to the strap, and the use of the string of buckets must remain free to be connected by chains, ropes, a strap of hempen girthing, or any other substance except leather. But, indeed, Mr. Martin had before used the strap of leather.

The screw of Archimedes is as ancient, at least, as the age of that mathematician, who died more than 2,000 years ago. Diodorus Siculus speaks of it, L. i., p. 21, and L. v., p. 217, of Stevens' edition of 1559, folio; and Vitruvius, xii. The cutting of its spiral worm into sections for conveying flour or grain, seems to have been an invention of Mr. Evans, and to be a fair subject of a patent right. But it cannot take away from others the use of Archimedes' screw with its perpetual spiral, for any purposes of which it is susceptible.

The hopper-boy is an useful machine, and so far as I know, original.

It has been pretended by some (and in England especially), that inventors have a natural and exclusive right to their inventions, and not merely for their own lives, but inheritable to their heirs. But while it is a moot question whether the origin of any kind of property is derived from nature at all, it would be singular to admit a natural and even an hereditary right to inventors. It is agreed by those who have seriously considered the subject, that no individual has, of natural right, a separate property in an acre of land, for instance. By an universal law, indeed, whatever, whether fixed or movable, belongs to all men equally and in common, is the property for the moment of him who occupies it, but when he relinquishes the occupation, the property goes with it. Stable ownership is the gift of social law, and is given late in the progress of society. It would be curious then, if an idea, the fugitive fermentation of an individual brain, could, of natural right, be claimed in exclusive and stable property. If nature has made any one thing less susceptible than all others of exclusive property, it is the action of the thinking power called an idea, which an individual may exclusively possess as long as he keeps it to himself; but the moment it is divulged, it forces itself into the possession of every one, and the receiver cannot dispossess himself of it. Its peculiar character, too, is that no one possesses the less, because every other possesses the whole of it. He who receives an idea from me, receives instruction himself without lessening mine; as he who lights his taper at mine, receives light without darkening me. That ideas should freely spread from one to another over the globe, for the moral and mutual instruction of man, and improvement of his condition, seems to have been peculiarly and benevolently designed by nature, when she made them, like fire, expansible over all space, without lessening their density in any point, and like the air in which we breathe, move, and have our physical being, incapable of confinement or exclusive appropriation. Inventions then cannot, in nature, be a subject of property. Society may give an exclusive right to the profits arising from them, as an encouragement to men to pursue ideas which may produce utility, but this may or may not be done, according to the will and convenience of the society, without claim or complaint from anybody. Accordingly, it is a fact, as far as I am informed, that England was, until we copied her, the only country on earth which ever, by a general law, gave a legal right to the exclusive use of an idea. In some other countries it is sometimes done, in a great case, and by a special and personal act, but, generally speaking, other nations have thought that these monopolies produce more embarrassment than advantage to society; and it may be observed that the nations which refuse monopolies of invention, are as fruitful as England in new and useful devices.

Considering the exclusive right to invention as given not of natural right, but for the benefit of society, I know well the difficulty of drawing a line between the things which are worth to the public the embarrassment of an exclusive patent, and those which are not. As a member of the patent board for several years, while the law authorized a board to grant or refuse patents, I saw with what slow progress a system of general rules could be matured. Some, however, were established by that board. One of these was, that a machine of which we were possessed, might be applied by every man to any use of which it is susceptible, and that this right ought not to be taken from him and given to a monopolist, because the first perhaps had occasion so to apply it. Thus a screw for crushing plaster might be employed for crushing corn-cobs. And a chain-pump for raising water might be used for raising wheat: this being merely a change of application. Another rule was that a change of material should not give title to a patent. As the making a plough-share of cast rather than of wrought iron; a comb of iron instead of horn or of ivory, or the connecting buckets by a band of leather rather than of hemp or iron. A third was that a mere change of form should give no right to a patent, as a high-quartered shoe instead of a low one; a round hat instead of a three-square; or a square bucket instead of a round one. But for this rule, all the changes of fashion in dress would have been under the tax of patentees. These were among the rules which the uniform decisions of the board had already established, and under each of them Mr. Evans' patent would have been refused. First, because it was a mere change of application of the chain-pump, from raising water to raise wheat. Secondly, because the using a leathern instead of a hempen band, was a mere change of material; and thirdly, square buckets instead of round, are only a change of form, and the ancient forms, too, appear to have been indifferently square or round. But there were still abundance of cases which could not be brought under rule, until they should have presented themselves under all their aspects; and these investigations occupying more time of the members of the board than they could spare from higher duties, the whole was turned over to the judiciary, to be matured into a system, under which every one might know when his actions were safe and lawful. Instead of refusing a patent in the first instance, as the board was authorized to do, the patent now issues of course, subject to be declared void on such principles as should be established by the courts of law. This business, however, is but little analogous to their course of reading, since we might in vain turn over all the lubberly [large and clumsy] volumes of the law to find a single ray which would lighten the path of the mechanic or the mathematician. It is more within the information of a board of academical professors, and a previous refusal of patent would better guard our citizens against harassment by lawsuits. But England had given it to her judges, and the usual predominancy of her examples carried it to ours.

It happened that I had myself a mill built in the interval between Mr. Evans' first and second patents. I was living in Washington, and left the construction to the millwright. I did not even know he had erected elevators, conveyers and hopper-boys, until I learnt it by an application from Mr. Evans' agent for the patent price. Although I had no idea he had a right to it by law (for no judicial decision had then been given), yet I did not hesitate to remit to Mr. Evans the old and moderate patent price, which was what he then asked, from a wish to encourage even the useful revival of ancient inventions. But I then expressed my opinion of the law in a letter, either to Mr. Evans or to his agent.

I have thus, Sir, at your request, given you the facts and ideas which occur to me on this subject. I have done it without reserve, although I have not the pleasure of knowing you personally. In thus frankly committing myself to you, I trust you will feel it as a point of honor and candor, to make no use of my letter which might bring disquietude on myself ...

L & B XIII: 326–37

## XIII.4 To John Waldo

Monticello, August 16, 1813

Sir, – Your favor of March 27th came during my absence on a journey of some length. It covered your "Rudiments of English Grammar," for which I pray you to accept my thanks. This acknowledgment of it has been delayed, until I could have time to give the work such a perusal as the avocations to which I am subject would permit. In the rare and short intervals which these have allotted me, I have gone over with pleasure a considerable part, although not yet the whole of it. But I am entirely unqualified to give that critical opinion of it which you do me the favor to ask. Mine has been a life of business, of that kind which appeals to a man's conscience, as well as his industry, not to let it suffer, and the few moments allowed me from labor have been devoted to more attractive studies, that of grammar having never been a favorite with me. The scanty foundation, laid in at school, has carried me through a life of much hasty writing, more indebted for style to reading and memory, than to rules of grammar. I have been pleased to see that in all cases you appeal to usage, as the arbiter of language; and justly consider that as giving law to grammar, and not grammar to usage. I concur entirely with you in opposition to Purists, who would destroy all strength and beauty of style, by subjecting it to a rigorous compliance with their rules. Fill up all the ellipses and syllepses of Tacitus, Sallust, Livy, &c., and the elegance and force of their sententious brevity are extinguished.

"Auferre, trucidare, rapere, falsis nominibus, imperium appellant." "Deorum injurias, diis curæ." "Allieni appetens, sui profusus; ardens in cupiditatibus; satis loquentiæ, sapientiæ parum." "Annibal peto pacem." "Per diem Sol non *uret* te, neque Luna per noctem." Wire-draw these expressions by filling up the whole syntax and sense, and they become dull paraphrases on rich sentiments. We may say then truly with Quinctilian, "Aliud est Grammaticé, aliud Latiné loqui." I am no friend, therefore, to what is called *Purism*, but a zealous one to the *Neology* which has introduced these two words without the authority of any dictionary. I consider the one as destroying the nerve and beauty of language, while the other improves both, and adds to its copiousness. I have been not a little disappointed, and made suspicious of my own judgment, on seeing the Edinburgh Reviews, the ablest critics of the age, set their faces against the introduction of new words into the English language; they are particularly apprehensive that the writers of the United States will adulterate it. Certainly so great growing a population, spread over such an extent of country, with such a variety of climates, of productions, of arts, must enlarge their language, to make it answer its purpose of expressing all ideas, the new as well as the old. The new circumstances under which we are placed, call for new words, new phrases, and for the transfer of old words to new objects. An American dialect will therefore be formed; so will a West-Indian and Asiatic, as a Scotch and an Irish are already formed. But whether will these adulterate, or enrich the English language? Has the beautiful poetry of Burns, or his Scottish dialect, disfigured it? Did the Athenians consider the Doric, the Ionian, the Æolic, and other dialects, as disfiguring or as beautifying their language? Did they fastidiously disavow Herodotus, Pindar, Theocritus, Sappho, Alcæus, or Grecian writers? On the contrary, they were sensible [aware] that the variety of dialects, still infinitely varied by poetical license, constituted the riches of their language, and made the Grecian Homer the first of poets, as he must ever remain, until a language equally ductile and copious shall again be spoken.

Every language has a set of terminations, which make a part of its peculiar idiom. Every root among the Greeks was permitted to vary its termination, so as to express its radical idea in the form of any one of the parts of speech; to wit, as a noun, an adjective, a verb, participle, or adverb; and each of these parts of speech again, by still varying the termination, could vary the shade of idea existing in the mind.

\* \* \* \* \*[1]

It was not, then, the number of Grecian roots (for some other languages may have as many) which made it the most copious of the ancient languages; but the infinite diversification which each of these admitted. Let the same license be allowed in English, the roots of which, native and adopted, are perhaps more numerous, and its idiomatic terminations more various than of the Greek, and see what the language would become. Its idiomatic terminations are: –

> *Subst.* Gener-ation–ator; degener-acy; gener-osity–ousness–
> alship–alissimo; king-dom–ling; joy-ance; enjoy-er–ment;
> herb-age–alist; sanct-uary–imony–itude; royal-ism; lamb-kin;

---

[1] The Greek here is omitted in all published collections of TJ's letters. – *Eds.*

child-hood; bishop-ric; proceed-ure; horseman-ship; worthi-ness.

*Adj.* Gener-ant–ative–ic–ical–able–ous–al; joy-ful–less–some; herb-y; accous-escent–ulent; child-ish; wheat-en.

*Verb.* Gener-ate–alize.

*Part.* Gener-ating–ated.

*Adv.* Gener-al–ly.

I do not pretend that this is a complete list of all the terminations of the two languages. It is as much so as a hasty recollection suggests, and the omissions are as likely to be to the disadvantage of the one as the other. If it be a full, or equally fair enumeration, the English are the double of the Greek terminations.

But there is still another source of copiousness more abundant than that of termination. It is the composition of the root, and of every member of its family, 1, with prepositions, and 2, with other words. The prepositions used in the composition of Greek words are: –

\* \* \* \* \*

Now multiply each termination of a family into every preposition, and how prolific does it make each root! But the English language, besides its own prepositions, about twenty in number, which it compounds with English roots, uses those of the Greek for adopted Greek roots, and of the Latin for Latin roots. The English prepositions, with examples of their use, are a, as in a-long, a-board, a-thirst, a-clock; be, as in be-lie; mis, as in mis-hap; these being inseparable. The separable, with examples, are above-cited, after-thought, gain-say, before-hand, fore-thought, behind-hand, by-law, for-give, fro-ward, in-born, on-set, over-go, out-go, thorough-go, under-take, up-lift, with-stand. Now let us see what copiousness this would produce, were it allowed to compound every root and its family with every preposition, where both sense and sound would be in its favor. Try it on an English root, the verb "to place," Anglo Saxon *plæce*,[2] for instance, and the Greek and Latin roots, of

---

[2] Johnson derives "place" from the French "place," an open square in a town. But its northern parentage is visible in its syno-nime *platz*, Teutonic, and *plattse*, Belgic, both of which signify *locus*, and the Anglo-Saxon *plæce*, [which signifies] *platea, vicus.*

kindred meaning, adopted in English, to wit, θεσις and *locatio*, with their prepositions.

| | | | |
|---|---|---|---|
| mis-place | amphi-thesis | a-location | inter-location |
| after-place | ana-thesis | ab-location | intro-location |
| gain-place | anti-thesis | abs-location | juxta-location |
| fore-place | apo-thesis | al-location | ob-location |
| hind-place | dia-thesis | anti-location | per-location |
| by-place | ek-thesis | circum-location | post-location |
| for-place | en-thesis | cis-location | pre-location |
| fro-place | epi-thesis | col-location | preter-location |
| in-place | cata-thesis | contra-location | pro-location |
| on-place | para-thesis | de-location | retro-location |
| over-place | peri-thesis | di-location | re-location |
| out-place | pro-thesis | dis-location | se-location |
| thorough-place | pros-thesis | e-location | sub-location |
| under-place | syn-thesis | ex-location | super-location |
| up-place | hyper-thesis | extra-location | trans-location |
| with-place | hypo-thesis | il-location | ultra-location |

Some of these compounds would be new; but all present distinct meanings, and the synonisms of the three languages offer a choice of sounds to express the same meaning; add to this, that in some instances, usage has authorized the compounding an English root with a Latin preposition, as in de-place, dis-place, re-place. This example may suffice to show what the language would become, in strength, beauty, variety, and every circumstance which gives perfection to language, were it permitted freely to draw from all its legitimate sources.

The second source of composition is of one family of roots with another. The Greek avails itself of this most abundantly, and beautifully. The English once did it freely, while in its Anglo-Saxon form, *e.g. boc-cræfi*, book-craft, learning, *riht-ʒeleaf-full*, right-belief-ful, orthodox. But it has lost by desuetude much of this branch of composition, which it is desirable however to resume.

If we wish to be assured from experiment of the effect of a judicious spirit of Neology, look at the French language. Even before the revolution, it was deemed much more copious than the English; at a time, too, when they had an academy which endeavored to arrest the progress of their language, by fixing it to a Dictionary, out of which no word was ever to be sought, used, or tolerated. The institution of parliamentary assemblies in 1789, for which their language had no opposite terms or phrases, as having never before needed them, first obliged them to adopt the Parliamentary vocabulary of England; and other new circumstances called for corresponding new words; until by the number of these adopted, and by the analogies for adoption which they have legitimated, I think we may say with truth that a *Dictionnaire Néologique* of these would be half as large as the dictionary of the academy; and that at this time it is the language in which every shade of idea, distinctly perceived by the mind, may be more exactly expressed, than in any language at this day spoken by man. Yet I have no hesitation in saying that the English language is founded on a broader base, native and adopted, and capable, with the like freedom of employing its materials, of becoming superior to that in copiousness and euphony. Not indeed by holding fast to Johnson's Dictionary; not by raising a hue and cry against every word he has not licensed; but by encouraging and welcoming new compositions of its elements. Learn from Lye and Benson[3] what the language would now have been if restrained to their vocabularies. Its enlargement must be the consequence, to a certain degree, of its transplantation from the latitude of London into every climate of the globe; and the greater the degree the more precious will it become as the organ of the development of the human mind.

These are my visions on the improvement of the English language by a free use of its faculties. To realize them would require a course of time. The example of good writers, the approbation of men of letters, the judgment of sound critics, and of none more than of the Edinburgh Reviewers, would give it a beginning, and once begun, its progress might be as rapid as it has been in France, where we see what a period of only twenty years has effected. Under the auspices of British science and example it might commence with hope. But the dread of innovation there, and especially of any example set by France, has, I fear, palsied the spirit of improvement. Here, where all is new, no innovation is feared which offers

---

[3] Edward Lye (1694–1767), English lexicographer and author of *Etymologicum anglicanum* (Oxford, 1743); Thomas Benson, *Vocabularium anglo-saxonicum* (Oxford, 1701). – *Eds.*

good. But we have no distinct class of *literati* in our country. Every man is engaged in some industrious pursuit, and science is but a secondary occupation, always subordinate to the main business of his life. Few therefore of those who are qualified, have leisure to write. In time it will be otherwise. In the meanwhile, necessity obliges us to neologize. And should the language of England continue stationary, we shall probably enlarge our employment of it, until its new character may separate it in name as well as in power, from the mother-tongue.

Although the copiousness of a language may not in strictness make a part of its grammar, yet it cannot be deemed foreign to a general course of lectures on its structure and character; and the subject having been presented to my mind by the occasion of your letter, I have indulged myself in its speculation, and hazarded to you what has occurred, with the assurance of my great respect.

Washington VI: 184–9

## XIII.5 To Joseph Milligan

Monticello, April 6, 1816

Sir, – Your favor of March 6th did not come to hand until the 15th. I then expected I should finish revising the translation of Tracy's book[1] within a week, and could send the whole together. I got through it, but, on further consideration, thought I ought to read it over again, lest any errors should have been left in it. It was fortunate I did so, for I found several little errors. The whole is now done and forwarded by this mail . . .

Although the work now offered is but a translation, it may be considered in some degree as the original, that having never been published in the country in which it was written. The author would there have been submitted to the unpleasant alternative either of mutilating his sentiments, where they were either free or doubtful, or of risking himself under the unsettled regimen of the press. A

---

[1] See *supra*, II.14, note 1. Milligan was Tracy's American publisher. – *Eds.*

manuscript copy communicated to a friend here has enabled him to give it to a country which is afraid to read nothing, and which may be trusted with anything, so long as its reason remains unfettered by law.

In the translation, fidelity has been chiefly consulted. A more correct style would sometimes have given a shade of sentiment which was not the author's, and which, in a work standing in the place of the original, would have been unjust towards him. Some Gallicisms have, therefore, been admitted, where a single word gives an idea which would require a whole phrase of dictionary English. Indeed, the horrors of Neologism, which startle the purist, have given no alarm to the translator. Where brevity, perspicuity, and even euphony can be promoted by the introduction of a new word, it is an improvement to the language. It is thus the English language has been brought to what it is; one-half of it having been innovations, made at different times, from the Greek, Latin, French, and other languages. And is it the worse for these? Had the preposterous idea of fixing the language been adopted by our Saxon ancestors, of Pierce Plowman, of Chaucer, of Spenser, the progress of ideas must have stopped with that of the language. On the contrary, nothing is more evident than that as we advance in the knowledge of new things, and of new combinations of old ones, we must have new words to express them. Were Van Helmont, Stane, Scheele, to rise from the dead at this time, they would scarcely understand one word of their own science. Would it have been better, then, to have abandoned the science of Chemistry, rather than admit innovations in its terms? What a wonderful accession of copiousness and force has the French language attained, by the innovations of the last thirty years! And what do we not owe to Shakespeare for the enrichment of the language, by his free and magical creation of words? In giving a loose to Neologism, indeed, uncouth words will sometimes be offered; but the public will judge them, and receive or reject, as sense or sound shall suggest, and authors will be approved or condemned according to the use they make of this license, as they now are from their use of the present vocabulary. The claim of the present translation, however, is limited to its duties of fidelity and justice to the sense of its original; adopting the author's own word only where no term of our own language would convey his meaning.

L & B XIV: 456–64

## XIII.6 To William Ludlow

Monticello, September 6, 1824

Sir, – The idea which you present in your letter of July 30th, of the progress of society from its rudest state to that it has now attained, seems comformable to what may be probably conjectured. Indeed, we have under our eyes tolerable proofs of it. Let a philosophic observer commence a journey from the savages of the Rocky Mountains, eastwardly towards our seacoast. These he would observe in the earliest stage of association living under no law but that of nature, subsisting and covering themselves with the flesh and skins of wild beasts. He would next find those on our frontiers in the pastoral state, raising domestic animals to supply the defects of hunting. Then succeed our own semi-barbarous citizens, the pioneers of the advance of civilization, and so in his progress he would meet the gradual shades of improving man until he would reach his, as yet, most improved state in our seaport towns. This, in fact, is equivalent to a survey, in time, of the progress of man from the infancy of creation to the present day. I am eighty-one years of age, born where I now live, in the first range of mountains in the interior of our country. And I have observed this march of civilization advancing from the sea-coast, passing over us like a cloud of light, increasing our knowledge and improving our condition, insomuch as that we are at this time more advanced in civilization here than the seaports were when I was a boy. And where this progress will stop no one can say. Barbarism has, in the meantime, been receding before the steady step of amelioration; and will in time, I trust, disappear from the earth. You seem to think that this advance has brought on too complicated a state of society, and that we should gain in happiness by treading back our steps a little way. I think, myself, that we have more machinery of government than is necessary, too many parasites living on the labor of the industrious. I believe it might be much simplified to the relief of those who maintain it. Your experiment seems to have this in view. A society of seventy families, the number you name, may very possibly be governed as a single family, subsisting on their common industry, and holding all things in common. Some regulators of the family you still must have, and it remains to be seen at what period of your increasing population your simple regulations will cease to be sufficient to preserve order, peace, and justice. The experiment is interesting; I shall not live to see its issue, but I wish it success equal to your hopes, and to yourself and society prosperity and happiness.

L & B XVI: 74–6

# XIV    Relations between Generations

## XIV.1 To James Madison

Paris, September 6, 1789

Dear Sir, – I sit down to write to you without knowing by what occasion I shall send my letter. I do it because a subject comes into my head which I would wish to develope a little more than is practicable in the hurry of the moment of making up general despatches.

The question Whether one generation of men has a right to bind another, seems never to have been started either on this or our side of the water. Yet it is a question of such consequences as not only to merit decision, but place also, among the fundamental principles of every government. The course of reflection in which we are immersed here on the elementary principles of society has presented this question to my mind; and that no such obligation can be transmitted I think very capable of proof. I set out on this ground which I suppose to be self evident, *"that the earth belongs in usufruct to the living"*; that the dead have neither powers nor rights over it. The portion occupied by any individual ceases to be his when himself ceases to be, and reverts to the society. If the society has formed no rules for the appropriation of its lands in severalty, it will be taken by the first occupants. These will generally be the wife and children of the decedent. If they have formed rules of appropriation, those rules may give it to the wife and children, or to some one of them, or to the legatee of the deceased. So they may give it to his creditor. But the child, the legatee or creditor takes it, not by any natural right, but by a law of the society of which they are members, and to which they are subject. Then no man can by *natural right* oblige the lands he occupied, or the persons who succeed him in that occupation, to the paiment of debts contracted by him. For if he could, he might during his own life, eat up the usufruct of the lands for several generations to come, and then the lands would belong to the dead, and not to the living, which would be reverse of our principle. What is true of every member of the society individually, is true of them all collectively, since the rights of the whole can be no more than the sum of the rights of individuals. To keep our ideas clear when applying them to a multitude, let us suppose a whole generation of men to be born on the same day, to attain mature age on the same day, and to die on the same day, leaving a succeeding generation in the moment of attaining their mature age all together. Let the ripe age be supposed of 21 years, and their period of life 34 years more, that being the average term given by the bills of mortality to persons who have already attained 21 years of age. Each successive generation would, in this way, come on and go off the stage at a fixed moment, as individuals do now. Then I say the earth belongs to each of these generations during it's course, fully, and in their own right. The 2d. generation receives it clear of the debts and incumbrances of the 1st., the 3d. of the 2d. and so on. For if the 1st. could charge it with a debt, then the earth would belong to the dead and not the living generation. Then no generation can contract debts greater than may be paid during the course of it's own existence. At 21 years of age they may bind themselves and their lands for 34 years to come: at 22 for 33: at 23 for 32 and at 54 for one year only; because these are the terms of life which remain to them at those respective epochs. But a material difference must be noted between the succession of an individual and that of a whole generation. Individuals are parts only of a society, subject to the laws of a whole. These laws may appropriate the portion of land occupied by a decedent to his creditor rather than to any other, or to his child, on condition he satisfies his creditor. But when a whole generation, that is, the whole society dies, as in the case we have supposed, and another generation or society succeeds, this forms a whole, and there is no superior who can give their territory to a third society, who may have lent money to their predecessors beyond their faculty of paying.

What is true of a generation all arriving to self-government on the same day, and dying all on the same day, is true of those on a constant course of decay and renewal, with this only difference. A generation coming in and going out entire, as in the first case, would have a right in the 1st year of their self dominion to contract a debt for 33 years, in the 10th. for 24, in the 20th. for 14, in the 30th. for 4, whereas generations changing daily, by daily deaths and births, have one constant term beginning at the date of their contract, and ending when a majority of those of full age at that date shall be dead. The length of that term may be estimated from the tables of mortality, corrected by the circumstances of climate, occupation &c. peculiar to the country of the contractors. Take, for instance, the table of M. de Buffon wherein he states that [*sic*] 23,994 deaths, and the ages at which they happened. Suppose a society in which 23,994 persons are born every year and live to the ages stated in this table. The conditions of that society will be as follows. 1st. it will consist constantly of 617,703 persons of all ages. 2dly. of those living at any one instant of time, one half will be dead in 24 years 8 months. 3dly. 10,675 will arrive every year at the age of 21 years complete. 4thly. it will constantly have 348,417 persons of all ages above 21 years. 5ly. and the half of those of 21 years and upwards living at any one instant of time will be dead in 18 years 8 months, or say 19 years as the nearest integral number. Then 19 years is the term beyond which neither the representatives of a nation, nor even the whole nation itself assembled, can validly extend a debt.

To render this conclusion palpable by example, suppose that Louis XIV and XV had contracted debts in the name of the French nation to the amount of 10,000 milliards of *livres* and that the whole had been contracted in Genoa. The interest of this sum would be 500 milliards, which is said to be the whole rent-roll, or nett proceeds of the territory of France. Must the present generation of men have retired from the territory in which nature produced them, and ceded it to the Genoese creditors? No. They have the same rights over the soil on which they were produced, as the preceding generations had. They derive these rights not from their predecessors, but from nature. They then and their soil are by nature clear of the debts of their predecessors. Again suppose Louis XV and his contemporary generation had said to the money lenders of Genoa, give us money that we may eat, drink, and be merry in our day; and on condition you will demand no interest till the end of 19 years, you shall then forever after receive an annual interest of[1] 12.5 percent. The money is lent on these conditions, is divided among the living, eaten, drank, and squandered. Would the present generation be obliged to apply the produce of the earth and of their labour to replace their dissipations? Not at all.

I suppose that the received opinion, that the public debts of one generation devolve on the next, has been suggested by our seeing habitually in private life that he who succeeds to lands is required to pay the debts of his ancestor or testator, without considering that

---

[1] 100£, at a compound interest of 5 percent, makes, at the end of 19 years, an aggregate of principal and interest of £252–14, the interest of which is 12£–12s–7d which is nearly 12⅝ percent on the first capital of 100£.

this requisition is municipal only, not moral, flowing from the will of the society which has found it convenient to appropriate the lands become vacant by the death of their occupant on the condition of a paiment of his debts; but that between society and society, or generation and generation there is no municipal obligation, no umpire but the law of nature. We seem not to have perceived that, by the law of nature, one generation is to another as one independant nation to another.

The interest of the national debt of France being in fact but a two thousandth part of it's rent-roll, the paiment of it is practicable enough; and so becomes a question merely of honor or expediency. But with respect to future debts; would it not be wise and just for that nation to declare in the constitution they are forming that neither the legislature, nor the nation itself can validly contract more debt, than they may pay within their own age, or within the term of 19 years? And that all future contracts shall be deemed void as to what shall remain unpaid at the end of 19 years from their date? This would put the lenders, and the borrowers also, on their guard. By reducing too the faculty of borrowing within its natural limits, it would bridle the spirit of war, to which too free a course has been procured by the inattention of money lenders to this law of nature, that succeeding generations are not responsible for the preceding.

On similar ground it may be proved that no society can make a perpetual constitution, or even a perpetual law. The earth belongs always to the living generation. They may manage it then, and what proceeds from it, as they please, during their usufruct. They are masters too of their own persons, and consequently may govern them as they please. But persons and property make the sum of the objects of government. The constitution and the laws of their predecessors extinguished them, in their natural course, with those whose will gave them being. This could preserve that being till it ceased to be itself, and no longer. Every constitution, then, and every law, naturally expires at the end of 19 years. If it be enforced longer, it is an act of force and not of right.

It may be said that the succeeding generation exercising in fact the power of repeal, this leaves them as free as if the constitution or law had been expressly limited to 19 years only. In the first place, this objection admits the right, in proposing an equivalent. But the power of repeal is not an equivalent. It might be indeed if every form of government were so perfectly contrived that the will of the majority could always be obtained fairly and without impediment. But this is true of no form. The people cannot assemble themselves; their representation is unequal and vicious. Various checks are opposed to every legislative proposition. Factions get possession of the public councils. Bribery corrupts them. Personal interests lead them astray from the general interests of their constituents; and other impediments arise so as to prove to every practical man that a law of limited duration is much more manageable than one which needs a repeal.

This principle that the earth belongs to the living and not to the dead is of very extensive application and consequences in every country, and most especially in France. It enters into the resolution of the questions Whether the nation may change the descent of lands holden in tail? Whether they may change the appropriation of lands given antiently to the church, to hospitals, colleges, orders of chivalry, and otherwise in perpetuity? Whether they may abolish the charges and privileges attached on lands, including the whole catalogue ecclesiastical and feudal? It goes to hereditary offices, authorities and jurisdictions; to hereditary orders, distinctions and appellations; to perpetual monopolies in commerce, the arts or sciences; with a long train of *et ceteras*: and it renders the question of reimbursement a question of generosity and not of right. In all these cases the legislature of the day could authorize such appropriations and establishments for their own time, but no longer; and the present holders, even where they or their ancestors have purchased, are in the case of *bona fide* purchasers of what the seller had no right [to] convey.

Turn this subject in your mind, my Dear Sir, and particularly as to the power of contracting debts, and develope it with that perspicuity and cogent logic which is so peculiarly yours.[2] Your station in the councils of our country gives you an opportunity of producing it to public consideration, of forcing it into discussion. At first blush it may be rallied as a theoretical speculation; but examination will prove it to be solid and salutary. It would furnish matter for a fine preamble to our first law for appropriating the public revenue; and

---

[2] For Madison's reply see *infra*, Appendix A. – *Eds.*

it will exclude, at the threshold of our new government, the contagious and ruinous errors of this quarter of the globe, which have armed despots with means not sanctioned by nature for binding in chains their fellow-men. We have already given, in example, one effectual check to the Dog of war, by transferring the power of letting him loose from the executive to the Legislative body, from those who are to spend to those who are to pay. I should be pleased to see this second obstacle held out by us also in the first instance. No nation can make a declaration against the validity of long-contracted debts so disinterestedly as we, since we do not owe a shilling which may not be paid with ease, principal and interest, within the time of our own lives. Establish the principle also in the new law to be passed for protecting copy rights and new inventions, by securing the exclusive right for 19 instead of 14 years. Besides familiarising us to this term, it will be an instance the more of our taking reason for our guide instead of English precedents, the habit of which fetters us, with all the political herecies of a nation, equally remarkable for it's encitement from some errors, as long slumbering under others. I write you no news, because when an occasion occurs I shall write a separate letter for that.

Ford V: 115–24

## XIV.2 To John Wayles Eppes

Monticello, June 24, 1813

Dear Sir, – This letter will be on politics only. For although I do not often permit myself to think on that subject, it sometimes obtrudes itself, and suggests ideas which I am tempted to pursue. Some of these relating to the business of finance, I will hazard to you, as being at the head of that committee, but intended for yourself individually, or such as you trust, but certainly not for a mixed committee.

It is a wise rule, and should be fundamental in a government disposed to cherish its credit, and at the same time to restrain the use of it within the limits of its faculties, "never to borrow a dollar without laying a tax in the same instant for paying the interest annually, and the principal within a given term; and to consider that tax as pledged to the creditors on the public faith." On such a pledge as this, sacredly observed, a government may always command, on a *reasonable interest*, all the lendable money of their citizens, while the necessity of an equivalent tax is a salutary warning to them and their constituents against oppressions, bankruptcy, and its inevitable consequence, revolution. But the term of redemption must be moderate, and at any rate within the limits of their rightful powers. But what limits, it will be asked, does this prescribe to their powers? What is to hinder them from creating a perpetual debt? The laws of nature, I answer. The earth belongs to the living, not to the dead. The will and the power of man expire with his life, by nature's law. Some societies give it an artificial continuance, for the encouragement of industry; some refuse it, as our aboriginal neighbors, whom we call barbarians. The generations of men may be considered as bodies or corporations. Each generation has the usufruct of the earth during the period of its continuance. When it ceases to exist, the usufruct passes on to the succeeding generation, free and unincumbered, and so on, successively, from one generation to another forever. We may consider each generation as a distinct nation, with a right, by the will of its majority, to bind themselves, but none to bind the succeeding generation, more than the inhabitants of another country. Or the case may be likened to the ordinary one of a tenant for life, who may hypothecate the land for his debts, during the continuance of his usufruct; but at his death, the reversioner (who is also for life only) receives it exonerated from all burthen. The period of a generation, or the term of its life, is determined by the laws of mortality, which, varying a little only in different climates, offer a general average, to be found by observation. I turn, for instance, to Buffon's tables, of twenty-three thousand nine hundred and ninety-four deaths, and the ages at which they happened, and I find that of the numbers of all ages living at one moment, half will be dead in twenty-four years and eight months. But (leaving out minors, who have not the power of self-government) of the adults (of twenty-one years of age) living at one moment, a majority of whom act for the society, one-half will be dead in eighteen years and eight months. At nineteen years then from the date of a contract, the majority of the contractors are dead, and their contract with them. Let this general theory be applied to a particular case. Suppose the annual births of the State of New

York to be twenty-three thousand nine hundred and ninety-four, the whole number of its inhabitants, according to Buffon, will be six hundred and seventeen thousand seven hundred and three, of all ages. Of these there would constantly be two hundred and sixty-nine thousand two hundred and eighty-six minors, and three hundred and forty-eight thousand four hundred and seventeen adults, of which last, one hundred and seventy-four thousand two hundred and nine will be a majority. Suppose that majority, on the first day of the year 1794, had borrowed a sum of money equal to the fee-simple value of the State, and to have consumed it in eating, drinking and making merry in their day; or, if you please, in quarrelling and fighting with their unoffending neighbors. Within eighteen years and eight months, one-half of the adult citizens were dead. Till then, being the majority, they might rightfully levy the interest of their debt annually on themselves and their fellow revellers, or fellow champions. But at that period, say at this moment, a new majority have come into place, in their own right, and not under the rights, the conditions, or laws of their predecessors. Are they bound to acknowledge the debt, to consider the preceding generation as having had a right to eat up the whole soil of their country, in the course of a life, to alienate it from them (for it would be an alienation to the creditors), and would they think themselves either legally or morally bound to give up their country and emigrate to another for subsistence? Every one will say no; that the soil is the gift of God to the living, as much as it had been to the deceased generation; and that the laws of nature impose no obligation on them to pay this debt. And although, like some other natural rights, this has not yet entered into any declaration of rights, it is no less a law, and ought to be acted on by honest governments. It is, at the same time, a salutary curb on the spirit of war and indebtment, which, since the modern theory of the perpetuation of debt, has drenched the earth with blood, and crushed its inhabitants under burdens ever accumulating. Had this principle been declared in the British bill of rights, England would have been placed under the happy disability of waging eternal war, and of contracting her thousand millions of public debt. In seeking, then, for an ultimate term for the redemption of our debts, let us rally to this principle, and provide for their payment within the term of nineteen years at the farthest. Our government has not, as yet, begun to act on the rule of loans and taxation going hand in hand. Had any loan taken place in my time, I should have strongly urged a redeeming tax. For the loan which has been made since the last session of Congress, we should now set the example of appropriating some particular tax, sufficient to pay the interest annually, and the principal within a fixed term, less than nineteen years. And I hope yourself and your [congressional] committee will render the immortal service of introducing this practice. Not that it is expected that Congress should formally declare such a principle. They wisely enough avoid deciding on abstract questions. But they may be induced to keep themselves within its limits.

I am sorry to see our loans begin at so exorbitant an interest. And yet, even at that you will soon be at the bottom of the loan-bag. We are an agricultural nation. Such an one employs its sparings in the purchase or improvement of land or stocks. The lendable money among them is chiefly that of orphans and wards in the hands of executors and guardians, and that which the farmer lays by till he has enough for the purchase in view. In such a nation there is one and one only resource for loans, sufficient to carry them through the expense of a war; and that will always be sufficient, and in the power of an honest government, punctual in the preservation of its faith. The fund I mean, is *the mass of circulating coin*. Every one knows, that although not literally, it is nearly true, that every paper dollar emitted banishes a silver one from the circulation. A nation, therefore, making its purchases and payments with bills fitted for circulation, thrusts an equal sum of coin out of circulation. This is equivalent to borrowing that sum, and yet the vendor receiving payment in a medium as effectual as coin for his purchases or payments, has no claim to interest. And so the nation may continue to issue its bills as far as its wants require, and the limits of the circulation will admit. Those limits are understood to extend with us at present, to two hundred millions of dollars, a greater sum than would be necessary for any war. But this, the only resource which the government could command with certainty, the States have unfortunately fooled away, nay corruptly alienated to swindlers and shavers, under the cover of private banks. Say, too, as an additional evil, that the disposal funds of individuals, to this great amount, have thus been withdrawn from improvement and useful enterprise, and employed in the useless, usurious and demoralizing practices of bank directors and their accomplices. In the war of 1755 [i.e. the French and Indian War], our State availed itself of this fund by issuing a paper money, bottomed on a specific tax for its redemption, and, to insure its credit, bearing an interest of five percent. Within a very short time, not a bill of this emission was to be found in circulation. It was locked up in the chests of executors, guardians, widows, farmers, etc. We then issued bills bottomed on a redeeming tax, but bearing no interest. These were readily received, and never depreciated a single farthing. In the Revolutionary war, the old Congress and the States issued bills without interest, and without tax. They occupied the channels of circulation very freely, till those channels were overflowed by an excess beyond all the calls of circulation. But although we have so improvidently suffered the field of circulating medium to be filched from us by private individuals, yet I think we may recover it in part, and even in the whole, if the States will co-operate with us. If treasury bills are emitted on a tax appropriated for their redemption in fifteen years, and (to insure preference in the first moments of competition) bearing an interest of six percent, there is no one who would not take them in preference to the bank paper now afloat, on a principle of patriotism as well as interest; and they would be withdrawn from circulation into private hoards to a considerable amount. Their credit once established, others might be emitted, bottomed also on a tax, but not bearing interest; and if ever their credit faltered, open public loans, on which these bills alone should be received as specie. These, operating as a sinking fund, would reduce the quantity in circulation, so as to maintain that in an equilibrium with specie. It is not easy to estimate the obstacles which, in the beginning, we should encounter in ousting the banks from their possession of the circulation; but a steady and judicious alternation of emissions and loans, would reduce them in time. But while this is going on, another measure should be pressed, to recover ultimately our right to the circulation. The States should be applied to, to transfer the right of issuing circulating paper to Congress exclusively, *in perpetuum*, if possible, but during the war at least, with a saving of charter rights. I believe that every State west and south of Connecticut river, except Delaware, would immediately do it; and the others would follow in time. Congress would, of course, begin by obliging unchartered banks to wind up their affairs within a short time, and

the others as their charters expired, forbidding the subsequent circulation of their paper. This they would supply with their own,
bottomed, every emission, on an adequate tax, and bearing or not
bearing interest, as the state of the public pulse [purse?] should
indicate. Even in the non-complying States, these bills would make
their way, and supplant the unfunded paper of their banks, by their
solidity, by the universality of their currency, and by their receiv-
ability for customs and taxes. It would be in their power, too, to
curtail those banks to the amount of their actual specie, by gathering
up their paper, and running it constantly on them. The national
paper might thus take place even in the non-complying States. In
this way, I am not without a hope, that this great, this sole resource
for loans in an agricultural country, might yet be recovered for the
use of the nation during war; and, if obtained *in perpetuum*, it would
always be sufficient to carry us through any war; provided, that in
the interval between war and war, all the outstanding paper should
be called in, coin be permitted to flow in again, and to hold the
field of circulation until another war should require its yielding
place again to the national medium.

But it will be asked, are we to have no banks? Are merchants and
others to be deprived of the resource of short accommodations,
found so convenient? I answer, let us have banks; but let them be
such as are alone to be found in any country on earth, except Great
Britain. There is not a bank of discount on the continent of Europe
(at least there was not one when I was there), which offers anything
but cash in exchange for discounted bills. No one has a natural right
to the trade of a money lender, but he who has the money to lend.
Let those then among us, who have a moneyed capital, and who
prefer employing it in loans rather than otherwise, set up banks,
and give cash or national bills for the notes they discount. Perhaps,
to encourage them, a larger interest than is legal in the other cases
might be allowed them, on the condition of their lending for short
periods only. It is from Great Britain we copy the idea of giving
paper in exchange for discounted bills; and while we have derived
from that country some good principles of government and legislation, we unfortunately run into the most servile imitation of all
her practices, ruinous as they prove to her, and with the gulf yawning before us into which these very practices are precipitating her.
The unlimited emission of bank paper has banished all her specie,

and is now, by a depreciation acknowledged by her own statesmen, carrying her rapidly to bankruptcy, as it did France, as it did us, and will do us again, and every country permitting paper to be circulated, other than that by public authority, rigorously limited to the just measure for circulation. Private fortunes, in the present state of our circulation, are at the mercy of those self-created money lenders, and are prostrated by the floods of nominal money with which their avarice deluges us. He who lent his money to the public or to an individual, before the institution of the United States Bank, twenty years ago, when wheat was well sold at a dollar the bushel, and receives now his nominal sum when it sells at two dollars, is cheated of half his fortune; and by whom? By the banks, which, since that, have thrown into circulation ten dollars of their nominal money where was one at that time.

Reflect, if you please, on these ideas, and use them or not as they appear to merit. They comfort me in the belief, that they point out a resource ample enough, without overwhelming war taxes, for the expense of the war, and possibly still recoverable; and that they hold up to all future time a resource within ourselves, ever at the command of government, and competent to any wars into which we may be forced. Nor is it a slight object to equalize taxes through peace and war.

Ever affectionately yours.

L & B xiii: 268–79

# Appendices

# Appendix A: James Madison to Jefferson

New York, February 4, 1790

Dear Sir, – Your favor of the 9th. of Jany. inclosing one of Sepr. last did not get to hand till a few days ago. The idea which the latter[1] evolves is a great one, and suggests many interesting reflections to legislators; particularly when contracting and providing for public debts. Whether it can be received in the extent your reasonings give it, is a question which I ought to turn more in my thoughts than I have yet been able to do, before I should be justified in making up a full opinion on it. My first thoughts, though coinciding with many of yours, lead me to view the doctrine as not in *all* respects compatible with the course of human affairs. I will endeavor to sketch the grounds of my skepticism.

"As the earth belongs to the living, not to the dead, a living generation can bind itself only: In every society the will of the majority binds the whole: According to the laws of mortality, a majority of those ripe at any moment for the exercise of their will do not live beyond nineteen years: To that term then is limited the validity of *every* act of the Society; Nor within that limitation, can any declaration of the public will be valid which is not *express*." This I understand to be the outline of the argument.

The acts of a political Society may be divided into three classes.

1. The fundamental Constitution of the Government.

2. Laws involving stipulations which render them irrevocable at the will of the Legislature.

3. Laws involving no such irrevocable quality.

However applicable in Theory the doctrine may be to a Constitution, it seems liable in practice to some very powerful objections. Would not a Government so often revised become too mutable to retain those prejudices in its favor which antiquity inspires, and which are perhaps a salutary aid to the most rational Government in the most enlightened age? Would not such a periodical revision engender pernicious factions that might not otherwise come into existence? Would not, *in fine*, a Government depending for its existence beyond a fixed date, on some positive and authentic inter-

---

[1] See TJ to Madison, Sept. 6, 1789; *supra*, XIV.1. – *Eds.*

vention of the Society itself, be too subject to the casualty and consequences of an actual interregnum?

In the 2d. class, exceptions at least to the doctrine seem to be *requisite* both in Theory and practice:

If the earth be the gift of nature to the living their title can extend to the earth in its natural State only. The *improvements* made by the dead form a charge against the living who take the benefit of them. This charge can no otherwise be satisfyed than by executing the will of the dead accompanying the improvements.

Debts may be incurred for purposes which interest the unborn, as well as the living: such are debts for repelling a conquest, the evils of which descend through many generations. Debts may even be incurred principally for the benefit of posterity: such perhaps is the present debt of the U. States, which far exceeds any burdens which the present generation could well apprehend for itself. The term of 19 years might not be sufficient for discharging the debts in either of these cases.

There seems then to be a foundation in the nature of things, in the relation which one generation bears to another, for the *descent* of obligations from one to another. Equity requires it. Mutual good is promoted by it. All that is indispensable in adjusting the account between the dead and the living is to see that the debits against the latter do not exceed the advances made by the former. Few of the incumbrances entailed on nations would bear a liquidation even on this principle.

The objections to the doctrine as applied to the 3d. class of acts may perhaps be merely practical. But in that view they appear to be of great force.

Unless such laws should be kept in force by new acts regularly anticipating the end of the term, all the rights depending on positive laws, that is, most of the rights of property, would become absolutely defunct; and the most violent struggles be generated between those interested in reviving and those interested in new-modelling the former state of property. Nor would events of this kind be improbable. The obstacles to the passage of laws which render a power to repeal inferior to an opportunity of rejecting, as a security against oppression, would here render an opportunity of rejecting an insecure provision against anarchy. Add, that the possibility of an event so hazardous to the rights of property could not fail to depreciate its value; that the approach of the crisis would increase this effect; that the frequent return of periods superseding all the obligations depending on antecedent laws and usages, must be weak[en]ing the reverence for those obligations, co-operate with motives to licentiousness already too powerful; and that the uncertainty incident to such a state of things would on one side discourage the steady exertions of industry produced by permanent laws, and on the other, give a disproportionate advantage to the more, over the less, sagacious and interprizing part of the Society.

I find no releif from those consequences, but in the received doctrine that a tacit assent may be given to established Constitutions and laws, and that this assent may be inferred, where no positive dissent appears. It seems less impracticable to remedy, by wise plans of Government, the dangerous operation of this doctrine, than to find a remedy for the difficulties inseparable from the other.

May it not be questioned whether it be possibly to exclude wholly the idea of tacit assent, without subverting the foundation of civil Society?

On what principle does the voice of the majority bind the minority? It does not result I conceive from the law of nature, but from compact founded on conveniency. A greater proportion might be required by the fundamental constitution of a Society if it were judged eligible. Prior then to the establishment of this principle, *unanimity* was necessary; and strict Theory at all times presupposes the assent of every member to the establishment of the rule itself. If this assent can not be given tacitly, or be not implied where no positive evidence forbids, persons born in Society would not on attaining ripe age be bound by acts of the Majority; and either a *unanimous* repetition of every law would be necessary on the accession of new members, or an express assent must be obtained from these to the rule by which the voice of the Majority is made the voice of the whole.

If the observations I have hazarded be not misapplied, it follows that a limitation of the validity of national acts to the computed life of a nation, is in some instances not required by Theory, and in others cannot be accomodated to practice. The observations are not meant however to impeach either the utility of the principle in some particular cases; or the general importance of it in the eye of the philosophical Legislator. On the contrary it would give me singular pleasure to see it first announced in the proceedings of the U. States, and always kept in their view, as a salutary curb on the living generation from imposing unjust or unnecessary burdens on their successors. But this is a pleasure which I have little hope of enjoying. The spirit of philosophical legislation has never reached some parts of the Union, and is by no means the fashion here, either within or without Congress. The evils suffered and feared from weakness in Government, and licentiousness in the people, have turned the attention more towards the means of strengthening the former than of narrowing its extent in the minds of the latter. Besides this, it is so much easier to espy the little difficulties immediately incident to every great plan, than to comprehend its general and remote benefits, that our hemisphere must be still more enlightened before many of the sublime truths which are seen thro' the medium of Philosophy, become visible to the naked eye of the ordinary Politician. I have nothing to add at present but that I remain always and most affect[ionate]ly yours.

Ford v: 437–41

## Appendix B: John Adams to Timothy Pickering

[August 22, 1822]

You inquire why so young a man as Mr. Jefferson was placed at the head of the Committee for preparing a Declaration of Independence? I answer: it was the Frankfort advice, to place Virginia at the head of every thing. Mr. Richard Henry Lee might be gone to Virginia, to his sick family, for aught I know, but that was not the reason of Mr. Jefferson's appointment. There were three committees appointed at the same time. One for the Declaration of Independence, another for preparing the articles of Confederation, another for preparing a treaty to be proposed to France. Mr. Lee was chosen for the committee of Confederation, and it was not thought convenient that the same person should be upon both. Mr. Jefferson came into Congress, in June, 1775, and brought with him a reputation for literature, science, and a happy talent of composition. Writings of his were handed about, remarkable for the peculiar felicity of expression. Though a silent member in Congress, he was so prompt, frank, explicit, and decisive upon committees and in conversation, not even Samuel Adams was more so, that he soon seized upon my heart and upon this occasion I gave him my vote, and did all in my power to procure the votes of others. I think he had one more vote than any other, and that placed him at the head of the committee. I had the next highest number, and that placed me the second. The committee met, discussed the subject, and then appointed Mr. Jefferson and me to make the draft, I suppose because we were the two first on the list.

The sub-committee met. Jefferson proposed to me to make the draft. I said: "I will not." "You should do it." "Oh! no." "Why will you not? You ought to do it." "I will not." "Why?" "Reasons enough." "What can be your reasons?" "Reason first – You are a Virginian, and a Virginian ought to appear at the head of this business. Reason second – I am obnoxious, suspected, and unpopular. You are very much otherwise. Reason third – You can write ten times better than I can." "Well," said Jefferson, "If you are decided, I will do as well as I can." "Very well. When you have drawn it up, we will have a meeting."

A meeting we accordingly had, and conned the paper over. I was delighted with its high tone and the flights of oratory with which it abounded, especially that concerning negro slavery, which, though I knew his Southern brethren would never suffer to pass in Congress, I certainly never would oppose. There were other expressions which I would not have inserted, if I had drawn it up, particularly that which called the King tyrant. I thought this too personal; for I never believed George to be a tyrant in disposition and in nature; I always believed him to be deceived by his courtiers on both sides of the Atlantic, and in his official capacity only, cruel. I thought the expression too passionate, and too much like scolding, for so grave and solemn a document; but as Franklin and Sherman were to inspect it afterwards, I thought it would not become me to strike it out. I consented to report it, and do not now remember that I made or suggested a single alteration.

We reported it to the committee of five. It was read, and I do not remember that Franklin or Sherman criticised any thing. We were all in haste. Congress was impatient, and the instrument was reported, as I believe, in Jefferson's handwriting, as he first drew it. Congress cut off about a quarter of it, as I expected they would;

but they obliterated some of the best of it, and left all that was exceptionable, if anything in it was. I have long wondered that the original draught has not been published. I suppose the reason is, the vehement philippic against negro slavery.

Ford I: 25–6

## Appendix C: Seneca Falls Declaration

[July 19, 1848]

When, in the course of human events, it becomes necessary for one portion of the family of man to assume among the people of the earth a position different from that which they have hitherto occupied, but one to which the laws of nature and of nature's God entitle them, a decent respect to the opinions of mankind requires that they should declare the causes that impel them to such a course.

We hold these truths to be self-evident: that all men and women are created equal; that they are endowed by their Creator with certain inalienable rights; that among these are life, liberty, and the pursuit of happiness; that to secure these rights governments are instituted, deriving their just powers from the consent of the governed. Whenever any form of government becomes destructive of these ends, it is the right of those who suffer from it to refuse allegiance to it, and to insist upon the institution of a new government, laying its foundation on such principles, and organizing its powers in such form, as to them shall seem most likely to effect their safety and happiness. Prudence, indeed, will dictate that governments long established should not be changed for light and transient causes; and accordingly all experience hath shown that mankind are more disposed to suffer, while evils are sufferable, than to right themselves by abolishing the forms to which they were accustomed. But when a long train of abuses and usurpations, pursuing invariably the same object, evinces a design to reduce them under absolute despotism, it is their duty to throw off such government, and to provide new guards for their future security. Such has been the patient sufferance of the women under this government, and such is now the necessity which constrains them to demand the equal station to which they are entitled.

The history of mankind is a history of repeated injuries and usurpations on the part of man toward woman, having in direct object the establishment of an absolute tyranny over her. To prove this, let facts be submitted to a candid world.

He has never permitted her to exercise her inalienable right to the elective franchise.

He has compelled her to submit to laws, in the formation of which she had no voice.

He has withheld from her rights which are given to the most ignorant and degraded men – both natives and foreigners.

Having deprived her of this first right of a citizen, the elective franchise, thereby leaving her without representation in the halls of legislation, he has oppressed her on all sides.

He has made her, if married, in the eye of the law, civilly dead.

He has taken from her all right in property, even to the wages she earns.

He has made her, morally, an irresponsible being, as she can commit many crimes with impunity, provided they be done in the presence of her husband. In the covenant of marriage, she is compelled to promise obedience to her husband, he becoming, to all intents and purposes, her master – the law giving him power to deprive her of her liberty, and to administer chastisement.

He has so framed the laws of divorce, as to what shall be the proper causes, and in case of separation, to whom the guardianship of the children shall be given, as to be wholly regardless of the happiness of women – the law, in all cases, going upon a false supposition of the supremacy of man, and giving all power into his hands.

After depriving her of all rights as a married woman, if single, and the owner of property, he has taxed her to support a government which recognizes her only when her property can be made profitable to it.

He has monopolized nearly all the profitable employments, and from those she is permitted to follow, she receives but a scanty remuneration. He closes against her all the avenues to wealth and distinction which he considers most honorable to himself. As a teacher of theology, medicine, or law, she is not known.

He has denied her the facilities for obtaining a thorough education, all colleges being closed against her.

He allows her in Church, as well as State, but a subordinate position, claiming Apostolic authority for her exclusion from the ministry, and, with some exceptions, from any public participation in the affairs of the Church.

He has created a false public sentiment by giving to the world a different code of morals for men and women, by which moral delinquencies which exclude women from society, are not only tolerated, but deemed of little account in man.

He has usurped the prerogative of Jehovah himself, claiming it as his right to assign for her a sphere of action, when that belongs to her conscience and to her God.

He has endeavored, in every way that he could, to destroy her confidence in her own powers, to lessen her self-respect, and to make her willing to lead a dependent and abject life.

Now, in view of this entire disfranchisement of one-half the people of this country, their social and religious degradation – in view of the unjust laws above mentioned, and because women do feel themselves aggrieved, oppressed, and fraudulently deprived of their most sacred rights, we insist that they have immediate admission to all the rights and privileges which belong to them as citizens of the United States.

In entering upon the great work before us, we anticipate no small amount of misconception, misrepresentation, and ridicule; but we shall use every instrumentality within our power to effect our object. We shall employ agents, circulate tracts, petition the State and National legislatures, and endeavor to enlist the pulpit and the press in our behalf. We hope this Convention will be followed by a series of Conventions embracing every part of the country.

> From: Elizabeth Cady Stanton, Susan B. Anthony, and Matilda Joslyn Gage (eds.), *History of Woman Suffrage*, 2 vols. (New York, 1881), I: 70–1

## Appendix D: The Gettysburg Address (Abraham Lincoln)

[November 19, 1863]

Fourscore and seven years ago[1] our fathers brought forth on this continent a new nation, conceived in liberty, and dedicated to the proposition that all men are created equal.

---

[1] I.e., in 1776 (1863 – 87 = 1776). – *Eds.*

Now we are engaged in a great civil war, testing whether that nation, or any nation so conceived and so dedicated, can long endure. We are met on a great battle-field of that war. We have come to dedicate a portion of that field as a final resting-place for those who here gave their lives that that nation might live. It is altogether fitting and proper that we should do this.

But, in a larger sense, we cannot dedicate – we cannot consecrate – we cannot hallow – this ground. The brave men, living and dead, who struggled here, have consecrated it far above our poor power to add or detract. The world will little note nor long remember what we say here, but it can never forget what they did here. It is for us, the living, rather, to be dedicated here to the unfinished work which they who fought here have thus far so nobly advanced. It is rather for us to be here dedicated to the great task remaining before us – that from these honored dead we take increased devotion to that cause for which they gave the last full measure of devotion; that we here highly resolve that these dead shall not have died in vain; that this nation, under God, shall have a new birth of freedom; and that government of the people, by the people, for the people, shall not perish from the earth.

*Complete Works of Abraham Lincoln*, ed. J. G. Nicolay and J. Hay
(New York, 1905), IX: 209–10

# Index

# Cambridge Texts in the History of Political Thought

*Titles published in the series thus far*

Aristotle *The Politics* and *The Constitution of Athens* (edited by Stephen Everson)
    0 521 48400 6 paperback
Arnold *Culture and Anarchy and other writings* (edited by Stefan Collini)
    0 521 37796 x paperback
Astell *Political Writings* (edited by Patricia Springborg)
    0 521 42845 9 paperback
Austin *The Province of Jurisprudence Determined* (edited by Wilfrid E. Rumble)
    0 521 44756 9 paperback
Bacon *The History of the Reign of King Henry VII* (edited by Brian Vickers)
    0 521 58663 1 paperback
Bakunin *Statism and Anarchy* (edited by Marshall Shatz)
    0 521 36973 8 paperback
Baxter *A Holy Commonwealth* (edited by William Lamont)
    0 521 40580 7 paperback
Beccaria *On Crimes and Punishments and other writings* (edited by Richard Bellamy)
    0 521 47982 7 paperback
Bentham *A Fragment on Government* (introduction by Ross Harrison)
    0 521 35929 5 paperback
Bernstein *The Preconditions of Socialism* (edited by Henry Tudor)
    0 521 39808 8 paperback
Bodin *On Sovereignty* (edited by Julian H. Franklin)
    0 521 34992 3 paperback
Bolingbroke *Political Writings* (edited by David Armitage)
    0 521 58697 6 paperback
Bossuet *Politics Drawn from the Very Words of Holy Scripture* (edited by Patrick Riley)
    0 521 36807 3 paperback
*The British Idealists* (edited by David Boucher)
    0 521 45951 6 paperback
Burke *Pre-Revolutionary Writings* (edited by Ian Harris)
    0 521 36800 6 paperback

Christine de Pizan *The Book of the Body Politic* (edited by Kate
  Langdon Forhan)
  0 521 42259 0 paperback
Cicero *On Duties* (edited by M. T. Griffin and E. M. Atkins)
  0 521 34835 8 paperback
*Conciliarism and Papalism* (edited by J. H. Burns and Thomas M.
  Izbicki)
  0 521 47674 7 paperback
Constant *Political Writings* (edited by Biancamaria Fontana)
  0 521 31632 4 paperback
Dante *Monarchy* (edited by Prue Shaw)
  0 521 56781 5 paperback
Diderot *Political Writings* (edited by John Hope Mason and Robert
  Wokler)
  0 521 36911 8 paperback
*The Dutch Revolt* (edited by Martin van Gelderen)
  0 521 39809 6 paperback
*The Early Political Writings of the German Romantics* (edited by Frederick
  C. Beiser)
  0 521 44951 0 paperback
*Early Greek Political Thought from Homer to the Sophists* (edited by
  Michael Gagarin and Paul Woodruff)
  0 521 43768 7 paperback
Erasmus *The Education of a Christian Prince* (edited by Lisa Jardine)
  0 521 58811 1 paperback
Ferguson *An Essay on the History of Civil Society* (edited by Fania
  Oz-Salzberger)
  0 521 44736 4 paperback
Filmer *Patriarcha and Other Writings* (edited by Johann P. Sommerville)
  0 521 39903 3 paperback
Fletcher *Political Works* (edited by John Robertson)
  0 521 43994 9 paperback
Sir John Fortescue *On the Laws and Governance of England* (edited by
  Shelley Lockwood)
  0 521 58996 7 paperback
Fourier *The Theory of the Four Movements* (edited by Gareth Stedman
  Jones and Ian Patterson)
  0 521 35693 8 paperback

Gramsci *Pre-Prison Writings* (edited by Richard Bellamy)
o 521 42307 4 paperback

Guicciardini *Dialogue on the Government of Florence* (edited by Alison Brown)
o 521 45623 1 paperback

Harrington *A Commonwealth of Oceana* and *A System of Politics* (edited by J. G. A. Pocock)
o 521 42329 5 paperback

Hegel *Elements of the Philosophy of Right* (edited by Allen W. Wood and H. B. Nisbet)
o 521 34888 9 paperback

Hobbes *Leviathan* (edited by Richard Tuck)
o 521 56797 1 paperback

Hobhouse *Liberalism and Other Writings* (edited by James Meadowcroft)
o 521 43726 1 paperback

Hooker *Of the Laws of Ecclesiastical Polity* (edited by A. S. McGrade)
o 521 37908 3 paperback

Hume *Political Essays* (edited by Knud Haakonssen)
o 521 46639 3 paperback

King James VI and I *Political Writings* (edited by Johann P. Sommerville)
o 521 44729 1 paperback

John of Salisbury *Policraticus* (edited by Cary Nederman)
o 521 36701 8 paperback

Kant *Political Writings* (edited by H. S. Reiss and H. B. Nisbet)
o 521 39837 1 paperback

Knox *On Rebellion* (edited by Roger A. Mason)
o 521 39988 2 paperback

Kropotkin *The Conquest of Bread and other writings* (edited by Marshall Shatz)
o 521 45990 7 paperback

Lawson *Politica sacra et civilis* (edited by Conal Condren)
o 521 39248 9 paperback

Leibniz *Political Writings* (edited by Patrick Riley)
o 521 35899 X paperback

*The Levellers* (edited by Andrew Sharp)
o 521 62511 4 paperback

Locke *Political Essays* (edited by Mark Goldie)
0 521 47861 8 paperback
Locke *Two Treatises of Government* (edited by Peter Laslett)
0 521 35730 6 paperback
Loyseau *A Treatise of Orders and Plain Dignities* (edited by Howell A.
Lloyd)
0 521 45624 X paperback
*Luther and Calvin on Secular Authority* (edited by Harro Höpfl)
0 521 34986 9 paperback
Machiavelli *The Prince* (edited by Quentin Skinner and Russell Price)
0 521 34993 1 paperback
de Maistre *Considerations on France* (edited by Isaiah Berlin and Richard
Lebrun)
0 521 46628 8 paperback
Malthus *An Essay on the Principle of Population* (edited by Donald
Winch)
0 521 42972 2 paperback
Marsiglio of Padua *Defensor minor* and *De translatione Imperii* (edited by
Cary Nederman)
0 521 40846 6 paperback
Marx *Early Political Writings* (edited by Joseph O'Malley)
0 521 34994 X paperback
Marx *Later Political Writings* (edited by Terrell Carver)
0 521 36739 5 paperback
James Mill *Political Writings* (edited by Terence Ball)
0 521 38748 5 paperback
J. S. Mill *On Liberty*, with *The Subjection of Women* and *Chapters on
Socialism* (edited by Stefan Collini)
0 521 37917 2 paperback
Milton *Political Writings* (edited by Martin Dzelzainis)
0 521 34866 8 paperback
Montesquieu *The Spirit of the Laws* (edited by Anne M. Cohler,
Basia Carolyn Miller and Harold Samuel Stone)
0 521 36974 6 paperback
More *Utopia* (edited by George M. Logan and Robert M. Adams)
0 521 40318 9 paperback
Morris *News from Nowhere* (edited by Krishan Kumar)
0 521 42233 7 paperback
Nicholas of Cusa *The Catholic Concordance* (edited by Paul E. Sigmund)
0 521 56773 4 paperback

CPSIA information can be obtained at www.ICGtesting.com
Printed in the USA
LVOW05s0957061213

364163LV00001B/1/A